# AutoCAD® Architecture 2008
## A Comprehensive Tutorial

## H. Edward Goldberg, AIA, NCARB

### *Registered Architect*

**PEARSON**

Prentice
Hall

Upper Saddle River, New Jersey
Columbus, Ohio

Library of Congress Control Number: 2007922123

**Editor in Chief:** Vernon Anthony
**Acquisitions Editor:** Jill Jones-Renger
**Editorial Assistant:** Doug Greive
**Development Editor:** Lisa S. Garboski, bookworks publishing services
**Production Editor:** Louise N. Sette
**Production Supervision:** Lisa S. Garboski, bookworks publishing services
**Design Coordinator:** Diane Ernsberger
**Cover Designer:** Jason Moore
**Art Coordinator:** Janet Portisch
**Production Manager:** Deidra M. Schwartz
**Director of Marketing:** David Gesell
**Marketing Manager:** Jimmy Stephens
**Marketing Coordinator:** Alicia Dysert

This book was set by Aptara, Inc. It was printed and bound by Bind-Rite Graphics. The cover was printed by Coral Graphic Services, Inc.

Certain images and material contained in this text were reproduced with the permission of Autodesk, Inc. © 2007. All rights reserved. Autodesk and AutoCAD are registered trademarks of Autodesk, Inc., in the U.S.A. and certain other countries.

---

**Disclaimer:**

The publication is designed to provide tutorial information about AutoCAD® and/or other Autodesk computer programs. Every effort has been made to make this publication complete and as accurate as possible. The reader is expressly cautioned to use any and all precautions necessary, and to take appropriate steps to avoid hazards, when engaging in the activities described herein.

Neither the author nor the publisher makes any representations or warranties of any kind, with respect to the materials set forth in this publication, express or implied, including without limitation any warranties of fitness for a particular purpose or merchantability. Nor shall the author or the publisher be liable for any special, consequential, or exemplary damages resulting, in whole or in part, directly or indirectly, from the reader's use of, or reliance upon, this material or subsequent revisions of this material.

---

Pearson Education Ltd.
Pearson Education Singapore Pte. Ltd.
Pearson Education Canada, Ltd.
Pearson Education—Japan

Pearson Education Australia Pty. Limited
Pearson Education North Asia Ltd.
Pearson Educación de Mexico, S.A. de C.V.
Pearson Education Malaysia Pte. Ltd.

PEARSON
Prentice
Hall

10 9 8 7 6 5 4 3 2 1
ISBN-13: 978-0-13-159227-8
ISBN-10:    0-13-159227-0

I dedicate this book to the women I love,
my mother Lillian,
my wife Judith Ellen,
and my daughter Allison Julia.

# WHAT USERS ARE SAYING....

"*Autodesk® Architectural Desktop 2006: A Comprehensive Tutorial* differs from most ADT publications because author Ed Goldberg—an architect—focuses on learning the basic tools necessary for productively using ADT, rather than trying to cover every tool and feature available. He offers a thorough explanation of each selected tool or feature and how you can use it in your ADT projects."

Patrick Davis, Contributing Editor, *Cadalyst* magazine

"Ed Goldberg writes a well-organized software guide in the same direct and lucid style he employs in his many magazine articles on this subject. As an architect trained in an era when pencils and pens were standard equipment in the design studio, he understands how to approach a design problem, proceeding from conception and modeling through technical drawing and specification to construction. His book is a valuable asset for those of us with similar backgrounds who wish to maintain a 'hands-on' relationship with the documents produced by our practice, but are often frustrated by the necessity of continually learning new software."

Michael J. Linehan, AIA, Architect. Director, Facilities Management, Johns Hopkins University School of Public Health

"As a practicing and teaching architect, I appreciate Ed Goldberg's practical approach to writing for the architectural CAD community. Architectural Desktop is a very deep program, yet this book is written in a way that makes it easy to teach. Because Ed is a practicing architect, he understands what is involved in the process of designing and documenting buildings. To him it's not just computer programming and architectural theory: his book 'makes it real.' His new book is a welcome addition to my classroom."

Dean R. Camlin, AIA
President
DEAN ROBERT CAMLIN & ASSOCIATES, INC.
CAD Instructor at Carroll Community College in Westminster, MD

"Mr. Goldberg handles a complex subject in an easy-to-understand style that will have you working more efficiently immediately. He covers virtually every aspect of creating a complete 3D building model using Architectural Desktop 2004. Thanks to a well-thought-out design, this book will be a handy reference long after you've completed the tutorials."

Art Liddle, Architect. Editor, *Inside AutoCAD Journal* (former editor of *Cadalyst* magazine)

"Ed Goldberg's easy-to-follow, tutorial approach to ADT applies the program tools from an architect's perspective. While Autodesk's program manual contains useful operational information, it doesn't provide the professional in the field with a workflow methodology. Ed's book fills this gap, beautifully. Thanks, Ed!"

Louis Chibbaro, CAD Manager; Perkins & Will Architects, NYC

# THE NEW AUTODESK DESIGN INSTITUTE PRESS SERIES

Pearson/Prentice Hall has formed an alliance with Autodesk® to develop textbooks and other course materials that address the skills, methodology, and learning pedagogy for the industries that are supported by the Autodesk® Design Institute (ADI) software products. The Autodesk Design Institute is a comprehensive software program that assists educators in teaching technological design.

## Features of the Autodesk Design Institute Press Series

**JOB SKILLS**—Coverage of computer-aided drafting job skills, compiled through research of industry associations, job websites, college course descriptions, and the Occupational Information Network database, has been integrated throughout the ADI Press books.

**PROFESSIONAL** and **INDUSTRY ASSOCIATIONS INVOLVEMENT**—These books are written in consultation with and reviewed by professional associations to ensure they meet the needs of industry employers.

**AUTODESK LEARNING LICENSES AVAILABLE**—Many students ask how they can get a copy of the AutoCAD® software for their home computer. Through a recent agreement with Autodesk®, Prentice Hall now offers the option of purchasing textbooks with either a 180-day or a 1-year student software license agreement for AutoCAD. This provides adequate time for a student to complete all the activities in the book. The software is functionally identical to the professional license, but is intended for student personal use only. It is not for professional use.

For more information about this book and the Autodesk Student Portfolio, contact your local Pearson Prentice Hall sales representative, or contact our National Marketing Manager, Jimmy Stephens, at 1-800-228-7854 x3725 or at Jimmy_Stephens@prenhall.com. For the name and number of your sales rep, please contact Prentice Hall Faculty Services at 1-800-526-0485.

# FEATURES OF AutoCAD® ARCHITECTURE 2008

This text presents a modern approach to using AutoCAD® Architecture. That is, it addresses advances in technology and software evolution and introduces commands and procedures that reflect a modern, efficient use of AutoCAD® Architecture 2008. Features include:

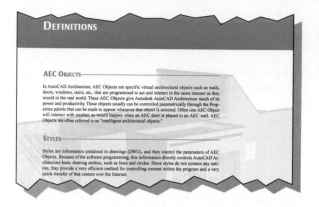

A "Getting Started" section at the beginning of the book provides essential information, preparing users for the guided tutorial on AutoCAD Architecture 2008, including Definitions, Concepts, Abbreviations, and more.

Section Objectives, a bulleted list of learning objectives for each chapter, provide users with a road map of important concepts and practices that will be introduced in the chapter.

Sections and Tutorials present Tool Palettes in the order in which they are commonly used.

A New to 2008 icon flags features that are new to the 2008 version of the AutoCAD Architecture software, creating a quick "study guide" for instructors who need to familiarize themselves with the newest features of the software to prepare for teaching the course. Additional details about these new features can be found in the Online Instructor's Manual.

---

**Converting the Mass Object into a Roof Slab**

16. Recreate the **Mass Object** you created in the previous exercise, but do not section it this time.
17. Change to the **Top View.**
18. Place a **Mass Object** cylinder 1'-6" radius by 4'-0" high in the center of the sloping **Mass Object** you created.
19. Change to the **SW Isometric View** (see Figure 1-32).
20. Select the sloping **Mass Object, RMB,** and select **Boolean > Subtract** from the contextual menu that appears.
21. When the **Command line** reads **Select objects to subtract,** select the cylinder, and press **Enter** on your keyboard.
22. Enter **Y** (Yes) in the **Command line** to the question **Erase layout geometry?** and press **Enter** on your keyboard to complete the command.

**Note:**
The Convert tools were greatly enhanced in Architectural Desktop 2007. One word of caution, though: the Convert from Mass Object to Wall, Slab, and Roof Slab is technically a "REPLACE." This means that the converted or "Replaced" object will be placed on the Wall, Slab, or Roof Slab layers, but these objects cannot be modified like real Walls, Slabs, or Roof Slabs. This exercise demonstrates the conversion from Mass Object to Roof Slab, and methods for making holes in the slab.

TIP, NOTE, and FOR MORE DETAILS boxes highlight additional helpful information for the student.

---

**Exercise 2-6:** Using the AEC MODIFY Tool to Modify Spaces

**Using the Trim Option**

1. Start a new drawing using the AEC Model (Imperial Stb) template.
2. Change to the **Model Layout.**
3. Change to the **Top View.**
4. Select the **Space** object icon from the **Design** tool palette, and place a 10' × 10' Standard-style space object in the Drawing Editor.
5. Select the space object you just placed to activate its grips.
6. Drag the space object to 30' × 30', and press the **Esc** key to deselect the grips.
7. **RMB** in the **Drawing Editor** and select **AEC Modify Tools > Trim** from the contextual menu that appears (see Figure 2-21).
8. Select the space object and press **Enter.**
9. Select a point to the left of the space object, drag your cursor as shown in Figure 2-22, and click your mouse button. This creates your **Trim** line.

Exercises throughout the chapters provide step-by-step walk-through activities for the student, allowing immediate practice and reinforcement of newly learned skills.

## INSTRUCTOR RESOURCES

An online Instructor's Manual and PowerPoints are available to qualified instructors for downloading. To access supplementary materials online, instructors need to request an instructor access code. Go to *www.prenhall.com,* click the **Instructor Resource Center** link, and then click **Register Today** for an instructor access code. Within 48 hours after registering, you will receive a confirming e-mail, including an instructor access code. Once you have received your code, go to the site and log on for full instructions on downloading the materials you wish to use.

# Preface

This book has been organized into an introductory part, "Getting Started," and two main parts: "Sections," typically made up of several tutorial exercises that illustrate commands, and "Putting It All Together," which uses the knowledge gleaned from the sections to create a building.

The exercises in this book have been designed as tutorials for most of the major commands and routines used in operating AutoCAD Architecture 2008. Rather than require the student to read a great deal of verbiage and theory, this book was designed to use the "hands-on" method of learning, with each exercise guiding the student through the typical use of the commands for a subject. It is suggested that the student perform the exercises first before attempting to use the program to design a building. It is also suggested that the student perform the sections in the order presented, as they often add information for later exercises. Even if a student understands a particular command, he or she should complete that exercise either to gain new insight or to compare operator strategy. This book assumes a general knowledge of standard AutoCAD or AutoCAD LT up to Release 2008. Students without knowledge of Paperspace and Modelspace will be at a very great disadvantage. It is also important that the student have a good understanding of the Windows operating system and be able to quickly navigate the various navigation trees in that system.

Because buildings are so complex, and the variations are so numerous, 3D Computer-Aided Architectural Design (CAAD) programs such as AutoCAD Architecture are not inherently easy to use. In my opinion, AutoCAD Architecture, previously Autodesk Architectural Desktop, has never been a program for the computer or CAD novice. Because of its complexity, one can become very frustrated when first approaching its multitude of commands, even though the programmers have gone to great effort to make this software user-friendly.

**This author believes that the sign of a good operator depends on several fundamental working values:**

- Use the least number of keystrokes for a particular operation. Do not use the full typed name of a command if the command can be performed with a letter alias.

- Use the space bar on the keyboard while operating the program instead of the **Enter** key, except when inserting text.

- Use a strategy of operating this program as one would play a game of chess, thinking several moves ahead, and never moving backwards unless absolutely necessary.

## Acknowledgments

I want to acknowledge all the wonderful and dedicated people at the Building Systems Division of Autodesk in Manchester, New Hampshire, for their professional assistance, their excellent and creative work, and for their friendship. Special thanks go to Julian Gonzalez, Bill Glennie, Dennis McNeal, and Anna Oscarson.

I again want to thank Art Liddle, past editor of *CADALYST,* who introduced me to this excellent program and gave me my first opportunity to write for *CADALYST* magazine. I would also like to thank the following reviewers: Rita A. Hawkins Ph.D., Missouri State University; Susan Sherod, Santa Ana College; Robert Ho, Mt. San Antonio College; Stephen Huff, High Point University; Garry Allen Perryman, Mercer County Community College.

| Text Element | Example |
|---|---|
| **Key terms**—Bold and italic on first mention (first letter lowercase) in the body of the text. Brief glossary definition in margin following first mention. | Views are created by placing *viewport* objects in the paper space layout. |
| **AutoCAD commands**—Bold and uppercase. | Start the **LINE** command. |
| **Toolbar names, menu items, and dialog box names**—Bold and follow capitalization convention in AutoCAD toolbar or pull-down menu (generally first letter capitalized). | The **Layer Manager** dialog box<br><br>The **File** pull-down menu |
| **Toolbar buttons and dialog box controls/ buttons/input items**—Bold and follow capitalization convention of the name of the item or the name shown in the AutoCAD tooltip. | Choose the **Line** tool from the **Draw** toolbar.<br><br>Choose the **Symbols and Arrows** tab in the **Modify Dimension Style** dialog box.<br><br>Choose the **New Layer** button in the **Layer Properties Manager** dialog box.<br><br>In the **Lines and Arrows** tab, set the **Arrow size:** to **.125.** |
| **AutoCAD prompts**—Dynamic input prompts are italic. Command window prompts use a different font (Courier New) and are boldface. This makes them look like the text in the command window. Prompts follow capitalization convention in AutoCAD prompt (generally first letter capitalized). | AutoCAD prompts you to *Specify first point:*<br><br>AutoCAD prompts you to *Specify next point or⤶*.<br><br>`Specify center point for circle or [3P/2P/Ttr (tan tan radius)]:` |
| **Keyboard input**—Bold with special keys in brackets. | Type **3.5 <Enter ⤶>**.<br><br>In the **Lines and Arrows** tab, set the **Arrow size:** to **.125.** |

# Contents

# Definitions

## AEC Objects

In AutoCAD Architecture, AEC Objects are specific virtual architectural objects such as walls, doors, windows, stairs, etc., that are programmed to act and interact in the same manner as they would in the real world. These AEC Objects give Autodesk AutoCAD Architecture much of its power and productivity. These objects usually can be controlled parametrically through the Properties palette that can be made to appear whenever that object is selected. Often one AEC Object will interact with another, as would happen when an AEC door is placed in an AEC wall. AEC Objects are often referred to as "intelligent architectural objects."

## Styles

Styles are information contained in drawings (DWG), and they control the parameters of AEC Objects. Because of the software programming, this information directly controls AutoCAD Architecture basic drawing entities, such as lines and circles. Since styles do not contain any entities, they provide a very efficient method for controlling content within the program and a very quick transfer of that content over the Internet.

## Multi-view Blocks

Although there is a plethora of AEC or programmed content, there is always need for specialized content. Here, AutoCAD Architecture provides a variation on its standard "Block" system known to users of AutoCAD and AutoCAD LT. Multi-view blocks allow the user to place content in one view and have the appropriate view of that content appear in other views at the same time. Although multi-view blocks don't have the intelligence, they can increase productivity greatly. AutoCAD Architecture 2008 includes many routines that depend on multi-view blocks. An exercise in the creation of multi-view blocks is given in this book.

## Tool Palettes

Common to Architectural Desktop 2004, 2005, 2006, 2007, and now AutoCAD Architecture 2008, these palettes can be sized, renamed, modified, and moved. Most of the major architectural routines are represented as icons or pictures, and they can be implemented by either dragging into or clicking in the Drawing Editor from these palettes. The developers of the program have replaced most of the standard toolbars and icons with this method in order to optimize the drawing environment for maximum productivity.

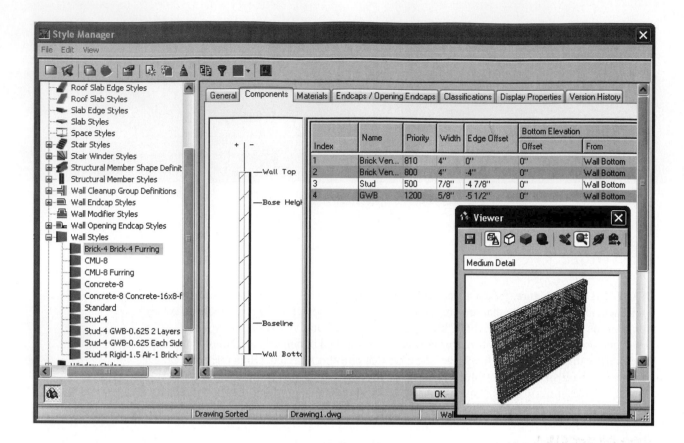

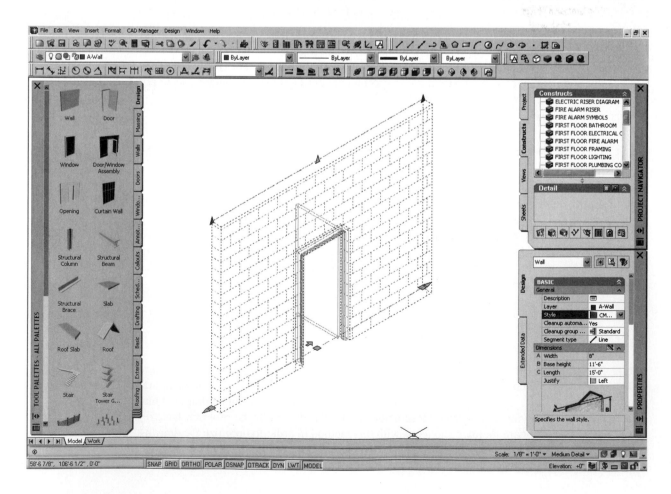

## CHECK BOXES

Check boxes indicate the on or off state of available options. If they are in a group, several check boxes can be selected at the same time.

## RADIO BUTTONS

Radio buttons (the name comes from the button selectors on car radios) indicate the on or off state of available options. Only one button in a group of buttons can be chosen.

## CONTEXTUAL MENUS

Contextual (context-sensitive) menus became popular when Microsoft introduced Windows 95. AutoCAD Architecture 2008 makes extensive use of these menus to control options and subcommands of various components. Contextual menus typically are summoned by clicking the right mouse button on a specific object, entity, or spot in the interface. Through programming, the appropriate menu or "context" will appear for that object at that point in its command structure. As an example, clicking the right mouse button on a door within a wall will provide all the commands available for the door and its relationship to the wall.

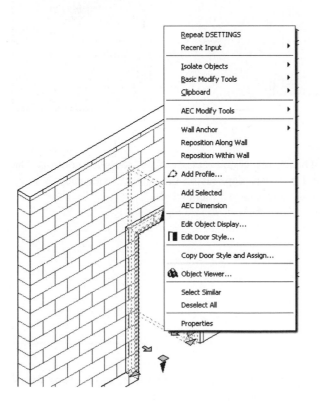

## Dynamic Input

Dynamic input offers a group of features that allow the user to view the **Command line** at the cursor.

    ***Pointer input.***    Allows you to key commands "into the pointer," which displays a small "pop-up" replacing the cursor until the command entry is finished. This allows keyboard commands previously entered on the command line to be entered "on the fly." If you type L for line entering, it will cause "L" to display in a pop-up, and as soon as you press **Enter,** the **Line** command will begin.

    ***Dimension input.***    Allows direct entry of dimensions at the cursor or on dynamic object dimensions during grip editing. The value entered is displayed and can be edited in a pop-up at the cursor location.

    ***Dynamic prompts.***    Messages that display at the cursor location to lead you through command sequences. One of the first things any AutoCAD Architecture user learns is *Read the command line prompts.* Along with prompts, the command line often presents a range of options for each stage in a given command. The default option is presented as a dynamic prompt, and pressing the keyboard "Down arrow" will present a pick list of all the other appropriate options.

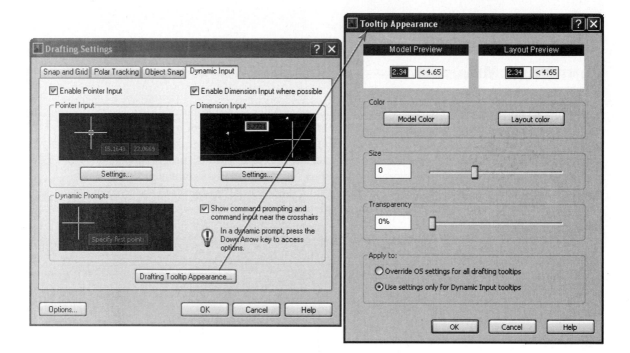

## The Dashboard

The Dashboard is organized into control panels that contain sets of related tools and controls. The number of tool panels displayed on the Dashboard depends on the current workspace, but can also be displayed or hidden using the Dashboard shortcut menus.

    The list of available control panels includes the following:

- 2D Draw
- 3D control panel
- 3D Navigation
- Lights control panel
- Visual styles control panel
- Materials control panel
- Render control panel

You can open the Dashboard by entering **dashboard** in the **Command line,** and pressing **Enter** on the keyboard, or by selecting **Window** > **Dashboard** from the **Main** menu.

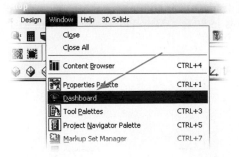

The Dashboard panels give you quick access to basic functionality. They normally appear in their collapsed state when you first open a drawing. If you move your cursor over the panel's icon, two vertical down arrows appear. Clicking on these arrows will expand the panels to reveal all their functions.

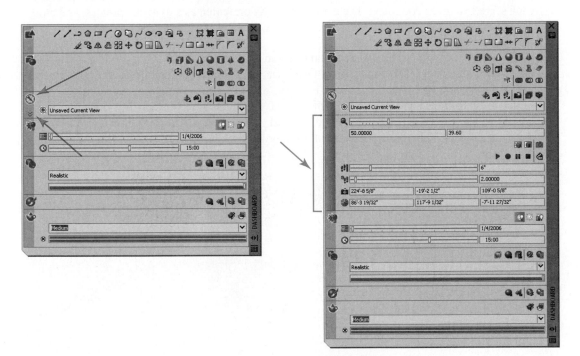

***2D Draw Panel.***    In this panel you can create a range of objects, from simple lines and circles to spline curves and ellipses.

***3D Control Panel.***    In this panel you can create 3D solids and surfaces from scratch or from existing objects. These solids and surfaces can then be combined to create solid models. 3D objects can also be represented by simulated surfaces (3D thickness), as a wireframe model, or as a mesh model.

*3D Navigation.*    In this panel you have the tools to display different views so that you can see and verify the 3D effects in your drawing. These tools include a 3D rotation tool, camera tool, walk-through tool, and animation tool.

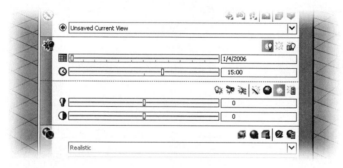

*Light Control Panel.*    This panel contains a Sun light and Sun locator as well as point lights, spotlights, and distant lights to achieve the effects you want. When you work in a viewport with a 3D shaded view, the default lighting is from two distant sources that follow the viewpoint as you move around the model. All faces in the model are illuminated so that they are visually discernible. You can control brightness and contrast, but you do not need to create or place lights yourself. Default lighting must be turned off in order to display lighting from user-created lights or the sun.

*Visual Style Control Panel.*    The Visual Styles Manager has controls for the visual styles available in the drawing, and the Face settings, Environment settings, and Edge settings. The Face settings control the appearance of faces in a viewport. These include the Highlight Intensity button, which controls the size of highlights on faces without materials, the Opacity Face button, which controls the opacity or transparency of faces, Lighting Quality, which sets the lighting to show faces on the model or not (Smooth is the default), and Materials, which controls whether materials and textures are displayed.

*Materials Control Panel and Materials Library.* Use this panel to attach a material to an object or a face. You drag the material from the tool palette onto the objects. At the same time, the material is added to the drawing, and it is displayed as a swatch in the **Materials** window.

When you create or modify a material in the **Materials** window, you can drag the swatch directly onto objects in the drawing or drag it onto the active tool palette to create a material tool.

Wood and marble are available as procedural maps in the **Materials** window. The grain is included and you can modify it and change the colors.

A library of more than 300 materials and textures is included with the product. The materials are on tool palettes and all are displayed with a checkered underlay.

*Render Control Panel.* From the **Render Preset** drop menu, you can also open the **Render Presets Manager** dialog box where you can create or alter custom render presets.

If you require more control, you can expand the **Render** dashboard by clicking the teapot icon in the gray board.

The controls on the expanded **Render** dashboard give you access to more advanced rendering features and settings including:

- Access to the **Environment** dialog box where you can set fog and depth-of-field effects.
- Open the **Render Settings** palette to make more advanced settings.
- Display the **Render** window to view images and render history entries that are saved with the current drawing.
- Adjust the image quality to render more or less detailed images.
- Specify a storage location, file name and file format to save your images when you're done rendering.
- Set the output resolution for your renderings.

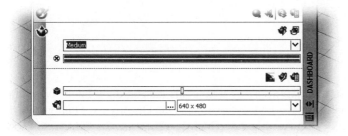

# Concepts

As with previous versions of AutoCAD Architecture, this new release uses three different concepts for eventually creating documentation. These concepts are the mass model concept, the space-planning concept, and the virtual building concept. Of course, you can always operate AutoCAD Architecture 2008 as a typical 2D electronic CAD drafting program, but that really negates the benefits of the virtual building features and eliminates much of the intrinsic volumetric information endemic to the virtual building.

## THE MASS MODEL

The mass model concept is based on a modeling tradition called "massing model" used by many architects. In that system, the architect or designer makes a cardboard, wood, or clay "study model" of the building. These small models often show the relationship between parts of the structure while also indicating scale and the effect of light and shadow on the facades. Typically the architect would create more sophisticated models later while creating the construction documents.

In AutoCAD Architecture 2008, you can make very sophisticated virtual massing models. These massing models can then be sliced into "floorplates" or horizontal sections from which walls can be generated. These walls are the connection point between the massing model and the construction documentation in AutoCAD Architecture 2008.

## SPACE PLANNING

The space-planning concept is one that has been used by architects and designers for years. In this concept, rectangles and circles represent building program areas. The designer then places these forms in relationship to each other to create "flow diagrams." After the relationships have been established, they are then used to help create the form of the structure. In AutoCAD Architecture 2008, the developers took this one step farther by combining a 3D component with the relationships. Every space planning object also contains information about floor-to-ceiling heights, and floor-to-floor heights. After the space planning has been completed, the space plan can be converted automatically into three-dimensional walls into which doors, windows, and so on can be added. These three-dimensional walls can then form the basis for construction documents. Besides being the basis for construction documents, the space plan can be culled for space information that can be transferred to data base programs.

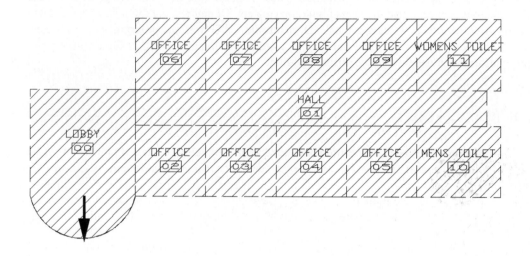

## THE VIRTUAL BUILDING MODEL

The virtual or 3D model differs from standard electronic drafting with the concept of placing components of a building much as one would place objects in the real world. Instead of drawing lines and circles, one places doors, windows, walls, roofs, and so on, which can be controlled or modified parametrically and relate to each other as they would in the real world. To this end AutoCAD Architecture 2008 has a myriad of parametric tools. The virtual building concept has been greatly discussed by architects and designers and is generally accepted as the direction in which CAAD is progressing. AutoCAD Architecture 2008 and its previous releases have always been considered leaders in this trend.

## AutoCAD Architecture 2008 Feature Summary———

This Feature Summary provides an overview of the new functionality in AutoCAD Architecture 2008.

This release of AutoCAD Architecture supports an easier transition for new users to AutoCAD Architecture (such as the operator moving from AutoCAD) as well as addressing the needs of the existing user. The objective of this release is to begin simplifying the core interactions and experiences of AutoCAD Architecture. This includes:

*Making graphical editing of object display as simple as changing AutoCAD linework*

*Making Project Navigator more intuitive by reducing interaction complexity and barriers to adoption*

*Creating tools and workflows that support and add value to AutoCAD functionality*

The high-level features of AutoCAD Architecture 2008 include the following:

**Documentation**

_Annotation scaling

_Spaces

   _Auto-Generate Space user interface

   _Automatic associative spaces

   _Surface opening improvements

   _Area calculation standards

_MasterFormat 2004 content

**Graphical Editing**

_Object Display user interface

_Global drawing cut plane discoverability

**Project Workflow**

_Drawing Compare

_View-to-sheet synchronization

**Visualization**

_Photometric lighting

_Sun/Sky systems

_Procedural materials

_Material editing interface

**Additional Improvements**

_Startup experience

_Performance enhancements

_Structural member trim plane

The following sections deal with each of these features in detail.

### Documentation

*Annotation Scaling.*    AutoCAD Architecture has long provided proper scaling of annotations during placement of annotations such as tags. In the 2008 release these annotation objects will scale appropriately when the scale changes per viewport. When you annotate drawings in model space, the process of scaling annotations is performed automatically in various layout viewports and in model space. Objects that can be designated as annotative include text, leaders, dimensions, field codes, hatches, blocks, Tags, Mview blocks, attribute definitions, and tables. You no longer need to use tedious and error-prone methods such as duplicating your annotations or blocks to display them at different scales in the same drawing.

*Spaces.*

**Auto-Generate Space User Interface.**   In AutoCAD Architecture 2008 the ability to generate spaces automatically from objects and linework has now been integrated into the Space tool. No longer is it necessary to utilize the previously separate dialog box. This also provides the advantage of prespecifying various options, such as style, to help streamline space creation.

**Automatic Associative Spaces.**   Architectural Desktop 2007 provided the ability for spaces to be associative to the objects (walls, slabs, curtain walls, etc.) that surround them. This eliminated tedious steps of updating space objects when boundaries change.

**Surface Openings.**   Openings on space surfaces can be important for calculations when the drawing is used in Autodesk Building Systems or other building applications. You can add openings to the surfaces of extruded 3D spaces and 3D freeform spaces. You can manually add openings to nonassociative spaces, while openings in an associative space are automatically determined by the openings in the bounding objects.

**Area Calculation Standards.**   Together with the additional capabilities of volumetric and associative spaces in Architectural Desktop 2007, AutoCAD Architecture 2008 adds support for area calculation standards, such as BOMA (US), SIS, and DIN 277 (German). Built-in rules automatically offset the gross, usable, and net boundaries during object creation and editing based on spatial adjacencies. The available rules are set for the drawing on the Options > AEC Object Settings tab.

*MasterFormat 2004.*   Many users are beginning to use the updated MasterFormat 2004 edition on their building design and construction projects. AutoCAD Architecture now provides content, detail components, and keynote databases that are configured for The Construction Specifications Institute's MasterFormat 2004.

## Object Enhancements

*Display Modification.*   The new Display tab in the Properties palette provides direct graphic feedback after modification of an object or its components. This reduces the steps needed to change graphic appearance, leverages a similar interaction with the basic AutoCAD objects, and reduces mystery and unexpected results of working with objects.

*Global Cut Plane Discoverability.*   Cut plane is a basic concept in architectural drafting; it determines what to display on the plan. In previous releases, changing the global cut plane entailed opening the Display Manager, picking the right display configuration, switching to the Cut Plane tab and then finally changing the setting. In AutoCAD Architecture 2008, the current cut plane setting is displayed on the drawing window status bar. By simply clicking on the value, you can quickly change the height without having to open the Display Manager.

# PROJECT WORKFLOW

## Drawing Compare for Subscription Customers

The Drawing Compare feature will allow you to:

- visually compare versions of drawings
- compare by object properties
- compare DWG-to-DWG or an entire Xref'd hierarchy
- compare structural members exported from Autodesk® Revit Structure against AutoCAD Architecture

**This new feature is a reviewing tool and will not merge or update the drawings being compared.**

## Project Navigator Enhancements

*Launch Project from APJ.*    You can now launch a Project Navigator project by double clicking on the .APJ file from within Windows Explorer or a shortcut created on your desktop.

*Views Control Sheets.*    By selecting an option in the Project Setup dialog, changes in a View drawing's layer display carry over to its corresponding Sheet View layer display. The Sheet View layer states will resolve to and display the same as the layer states in the View drawing.

*Layer States and Overrides.*    In AutoCAD Architecture 2008, Layer Snapshots, found only in AutoCAD Architecture, are now combined with Layer States from the AutoCAD platform, simplifying the overall toolset. Additionally, you can move and hide columns in the Layer Properties Manager to control the information displayed in it. Several new columns provide information and control over additional layer properties and overrides that can be assigned to layout viewports. The Layer States Manager, which you can now access outside the Layer Properties Manager, provides powerful features for managing and editing saved layer states. You can also display objects differently in selected layout viewports while retaining their original layer properties in model space and in other layout viewports. With layer property overrides, you no longer need to use tedious and error-prone methods such as duplicating geometry on separate layers or making copies of xrefs. Instead, you can use the Layer Properties Manager to set overrides for color, linetype, lineweight, and plot style for each layout viewport.

## Visualization

With AutoCAD Architecture 2008, the Mental Ray rendering engine has replaced the core rendering capabilities of AutoCAD, and therefore AutoCAD Architecture. AutoCAD Architecture 2008 has continued the work on this core rendering environment with the goal of building the most-needed capabilities used in VIZ Render into the main AutoCAD Architecture workspace. This now provides a single in-process rendering environment for creating highly photo-realistic renderings, based on real-world photometric indoor and outdoor lighting, procedural materials, more robust material editing, and inherent interoperability with AutoCAD and the AutoCAD family of products.

*Photometric Lights and Luminaries.*    You can use photometric light sources to illuminate scenes for more physically correct rendered images. With photometric light sources, you can specify real-world values. For example, if you need to use fixtures with 75-watt light bulbs, you set the light source to 75 watts.

*Procedural Maps and Advanced Lighting.*    With additional procedural maps and advanced lighting overrides for materials, you can achieve more realistic results than from texture maps alone. Advanced lighting overrides let you adjust lighting parameters such as light emission, reflectance, and color bleeding for greater realism.

## Additional Improvements

*Startup Experience.*    This feature helps new users to AutoCAD Architecture be productive within their first 3 hours using the product, by focusing on learnability and discoverability of critical concepts. There are eight training videos along with links to the Getting Started Guide, a User Interface Overview, the New Features Workshop, and an AutoCAD to AutoCAD Architecture comparison chart.

*Structural Member Trim Plane.*    This feature provides a member style setting to control the automatic updating of trim planes after grip editing members. This feature also provides an object level setting such that the individual members can override the member style automatically trim setting.

*Performance Improvements.*    Boosting performance has been a focus for AutoCAD Architecture 2008.

*Case Improvement.*    The File Open example test case has improved from 31 seconds to 24 seconds, except for when FIELDEVAL is used to avoid update on open or plot. File Open when using Project Standards in the example test case improved by 75%, from more than 10 minutes to 2 minutes 36 seconds.

Improvement in Plot Preview with Project-based Callouts is remarkable when there are many field codes/callouts in a sheet, and when files are located on a slow network. The example test case improved from 6 minutes to 75 seconds.

Zoom Performance has improved when zooming in and out in an isometric view.

Selecting objects in a drawing, especially when creating large selection sets of objects in a drawing at one time, now is performed more quickly.

Editing a tread/riser of a custom stair improved approximately 8 times (from ~500 ms to ~65 ms).

When changing the Display Configuration in a single viewport on a Layout tab with multiple viewports, only that viewport is regenerated. Previously, all viewports would be regenerated. With 10 viewports on a Layout, this represents a 90% reduction in time.

Section and Elevation Generation has improved approximately 30%.

# AutoCAD 2008 Changed Commands

The following commands have either changed in, or been removed from, AutoCAD 2008.

**3DCONFIG** Added plot emulation and texture compression options.

**–3DCONFIG** Added plot emulation and texture compression options (*Command prompt version*).

**ATTDEF** Added support for annotative scaling.

**–ATTDEF** Added support for annotative scaling (*Command prompt version*).

**ATTEDIT** Multiple-line attribute support.

**BATTMAN** Added support for annotative scaling.

**BLOCK** Added support for annotative scaling.

**–BLOCK** Added support for annotative scaling (*Command prompt version*).

**CHPROP** Added support for annotative scaling.

**CUI** Added dashboard panel customization and some enhancements for customizing toolbars.

**DASHBOARD** Added access to the Customize User Interface from the shortcut menu.

**DIMANGULAR** Added the Quadrant option.

**DIMDIAMETER** Added the Extension line option.

**DIMJOGGED** Added the Extension line option.

**DIMRADIUS** Added the Extension line option.

**DIMSTYLE** Added a new tolerance alignment option, a size option for linear jog, and break spacing.

**–DIMSTYLE** Command prompt version of DIMSTYLE (*Command prompt version*).

**DISTANTLIGHT** Modified to support entering photometric properties.

**EATTEXT** Now activates the DATAEXTRACTION command rather than the Attribute Extraction wizard.

**–EATTEXT** Command prompt version of the EATTEXT command (*Command prompt version*).

**ETRANSMIT** Added support for visual fidelity.

**HATCH** Added support for annotative scaling.

**–HATCH** Added support for annotative scaling (*Command prompt version*).

**HATCHEDIT** Added support for annotative scaling.

**–HATCHEDIT** Added support for annotative scaling (*Command prompt version*).

**INSERT** Added support for annotative scaling.

**–INSERT** Added support for annotative scaling (*Command prompt version*).

**–LAYER** Added an option to import layer states from drawings. The Edit option now includes Material and Description suboptions, the Import option now includes DWG/DWS/DWT formats, and the Export option includes the LAY file format (*Command prompt version*).

**MATCHCELL** Added support for double line borders, border linetypes, and new cell formats.

**MTEXT** Added support for annotative scaling.

**–MTEXT** Added support for annotative scaling (*Command prompt version*).

**MVIEW** When used on a layout, a new option, Layer, removes all layer property override values and resets them back to their corresponding global properties.

**OPTIONS** Added the Maintain Visual Fidelity check box to the Open and Save tab as well as the Display Drawing Status Bar check box to the Display tab.

**PASTESPEC** Enhanced for pasting Microsoft Excel data from the clipboard to create a data link to this information immediately.

*PLOT* Affected by the hardware configuration settings Plot Emulation and Texture Compression.

*POINTLIGHT* Start and end limits for attenuation are supported with the Direct 3D driver; also added prompting for area-sampled shadow options and photometric prompting.

*QSELECT* Added support for annotative scaling.

*SPELL* Now checks words in dimensions and zooms into words being corrected; added an option to ignore words that contain numbers or special characters.

*SPOTLIGHT* Start and end limits for attenuation are supported with the Direct 3D driver; also added prompting for area-sampled shadow options and photometric prompting.

*STYLE* Added support for annotative scaling.

*–STYLE* Added support for annotative scaling (*Command prompt version*).

*TABLE* Added From Style and Data Link branches.

*–TABLE* Added From Style and Data Link branches (*Command prompt version*).

*TABLESTYLE* Defines a new table style.

*TEXT* Added support for annotative scaling.

*VIEW* Modified to support the new sky background option, when applicable.

*–VPORTS* Added option, Layer, removes all layer property override values and resets them back to their corresponding global properties (*Command prompt version*).

*XCLIP* Added the Invert option.

## REMOVED OR OBSOLETE COMMANDS

*ASSIST* Opens Quick Help in the Info palette, which provides context-sensitive information.

*ASSISTCLOSE* Closes Quick Help and the Info palette.

# AutoCAD 2008 System Variable Changes

## NEW SYSTEM VARIABLES

***3DCONVERSIONMODE*** Converts material and light definitions.

***3DSELECTIONMODE*** Controls the selection precedence of visually overlapping objects when using 3D visual styles.

***ANNOALLVISIBLE*** Hides or displays annotative objects that do not support the current annotation scale.

***ANNOAUTOSCALE*** Updates annotative objects to support the annotation scale when the annotation scale is changed.

***ANNOTATIVEDWG*** Specifies whether or not the drawing will behave as an annotative block when inserted into another drawing.

***ATTIPE*** Controls the display of the in-place editor used to create multiline attributes.

***ATTMULTI*** Controls whether multiline attributes can be created.

***AUTODWFPUBLISH*** Controls whether the AutoPublish feature is on or off.

***CANNOSCALE*** Sets the name of the current annotation scale for the current space.

***CANNOSCALEVALUE*** Returns the value of the current annotation scale.

***CMLEADERSTYLE*** Determines the current multileader style.

***COPYMODE*** Controls whether the COPY command repeats automatically.

***DATALINKNOTIFY*** Controls the notification for updated or missing data links.

***DGNFRAME*** Determines whether DGN underlay frames are visible or plotted in the current drawing.

***DGNOSNAP*** Controls object snapping for geometry in DGN underlays.

***DIMANNO*** Indicates whether or not the current dimension style is annotative.

***DXEVAL*** Controls when data extraction tables are compared against the data source, and if the data is not current, displays an update notification.

***HPMAXLINES*** Controls the maximum number of hatch lines that will generate.

***LAYEREVAL*** Controls when the Unreconciled New Layer filter list in the Layer Properties Manager is evaluated for new layers.

***LAYERNOTIFY*** Specifies when an alert displays for new layers that have not yet been reconciled.

***LAYLOCKFADECTL*** Controls the dimming for objects on locked layers.

***LIGHTINGUNITS*** Controls whether generic or photometric lights are used, and indicates the current lighting units.

***LIGHTSINBLOCKS*** Controls whether lights contained in blocks are used when rendering.

***LINEARBRIGHTNESS*** Controls the global brightness level of the drawing when using default lighting or generic lights.

***LINEARCONTRAST*** Controls the global contrast level of the drawing when using default lighting or generic lights.

***LOGEXPBRIGHTNESS*** Controls the global brightness level of the drawing when using photometric lighting.

***LOGEXPCONTRAST*** Controls the global contrast level of the drawing when using photometric lighting.

***LOGEXPDAYLIGHT*** Controls whether exterior daylight is used for photometric lighting.

***LOGEXPMIDTONES*** Controls the global mid tones level of the drawing when using photometric lighting.

***MSLTSCALE*** Scales linetypes displayed on the model tab by the annotation scale.

***PERSPECTIVECLIP*** Determines the location of eyepoint clipping.

***PUBLISHCOLLATE*** Controls whether plotting a sheet set, multi-sheet plot file, or plot spool file can be interrupted by other plot jobs.

***RENDERUSERLIGHTS*** Controls whether user lights are translated during rendering.

***SAVEFIDELITY*** Controls whether the drawing is saved with visual fidelity.

***SELECTIONANNODISPLAY*** Controls whether alternate scale representations are temporarily displayed in a dimmed state when an annotative object is selected.

***SETBYLAYERMODE*** Controls which properties are selected for SETBYLAYER.

***TABLETOOLBAR*** Controls the display of the Table toolbar.

***TEXTOUTPUTFILEFORMAT*** Provides Unicode text file output options.

***VPLAYEROVERRIDES*** Indicates if there are any layers with viewport (VP) property overrides for the current layout viewport.

***VPLAYEROVERRIDESMODE*** Controls whether layer property overrides associated with layout viewports are displayed and plotted.

***VSFACEHIGHLIGHT*** Controls whether layer property overrides associated with layout viewports are displayed and plotted.

## CHANGED SYSTEM VARIABLES

***AFLAGS*** Added a value for the new Multiple Lines mode.

***DCTMAIN*** Displays the three-letter keyword of the current main spelling dictionary.

***DIMSCALE*** Automatically set to 0 when an annotative dimension style is made current.

## REMOVED OR OBSOLETE SYSTEM VARIABLES

***ASSISTSTATE*** Indicates whether the Info palette that displays Quick Help is active or not.

# Questions and Answers about AutoCAD Architecture 2008

The following information was gleaned from Autodesk Press releases. The author has selected this information to answer questions that might be in readers' minds.

*Has the User Interface Changed for AutoCAD Architecture?* Not really; the user interface for AutoCAD Architecture 2008 continues the improvements seen in Architectural Desktop 2004, 2005, 2006, and 2007, and it will be quite familiar to users of those products. The streamlined user interface first introduced with Autodesk Architectural Desktop 2004 improves on traditional CAD design software and earlier versions of Architectural Desktop in terms of look and feel and overall functionality. Highly visual, simpler, and more intuitive, the interface helps you increase productivity using process-focused tools that make the software easier to use. With less focus on dialog boxes and more emphasis on designing directly in the workspace, the design tools in the software are easily accessible. Furthermore, enhanced tool palettes, the Properties palette, and the new Content Browser complement this redesigned workspace to help you work more efficiently.

*Are AutoCAD Architecture and Autodesk® Revit® Files Interoperable?* **Yes.** You can exchange drawing information (2D DWG files) between AutoCAD Architecture and the Autodesk Revit software through their respective Export to AutoCAD features.

*Can I Export More than One Architectural Desktop File at a Time?* **Yes.** With AutoCAD Architecture 2008, you can export multiple Architectural Desktop files.

Enhanced e-transmit functionality allows users to transmit multiple entire projects, sheet sets, and specific DWGs.

*What Is the Autodesk AEC Object Enabler?* The Autodesk AEC Object Enabler is a free downloadable and distributable utility that gives AutoCAD users functionality and design flexibility through the power of Autodesk Architectural Desktop objects. With the proper version of the AEC Object Enabler, any AutoCAD 2000, AutoCAD 2000i, AutoCAD 2002, AutoCAD 2004, AutoCAD 2005, AutoCAD 2006, AutoCAD 2007, or AutoCAD 2008 user can have full compatibility with Autodesk Architectural Desktop objects. The AEC Object Enabler is included with AutoCAD 2005. For more information and to download the AEC Object Enabler, go to **www.autodesk.com/aecobjecten.**

*Will Autodesk Continue to Develop Autodesk Architectural Desktop?* **Yes.** With well over 550,000 Autodesk Architectural Desktop licenses worldwide, AutoCAD Architecture 2008 clearly continues to be a powerful AutoCAD-based solution for architectural customers.

*Is a Network Version of AutoCAD Architecture Available?* **Yes.** Autodesk Architectural Desktop software uses standard Autodesk network license management. For more information, see "Platforms, System Requirements, and Network" later in this section.

*What Is Building Information Modeling, and How Does It Apply to AutoCAD Architecture?* Building Information Modeling (BIM) is an innovative approach to building design, construction, and management introduced by Autodesk in 2002. BIM delivers high-quality information about project design scope, schedule, and cost when you need it and how you need it, dramatically helping reduce inefficiencies and risk throughout the building process. The ability to keep this information up to date and accessible in an integrated digital environment gives architects, engineers, builders, and owners a clear overall vision of their projects. It also contributes to the ability to make better decisions faster, helping raise the quality and increase the profitability of projects. Although building information modeling is not itself a technology, it does require suitable technology to be implemented effectively. Examples of some of these technologies, in increasing order of effectiveness, include

- CAD
- Object CAD
- Parametric Building Modeling

With a high level of effort, CAD-based software can be used to achieve some of the benefits of BIM. With some effort, so can object CAD–based software. Parametric Building Modeling (PBM) software offers the highest level of effectiveness with the least effort, but it also requires a full commitment to building information modeling (a new way of working). There is no other way to use PBM to support a traditional drafting workflow.

AutoCAD Architecture is built on object CAD technology, adding intelligent architectural and engineering objects to the familiar AutoCAD platform. It can be used to deliver BIM benefits with significantly less effort than CAD technology. Since it is built on AutoCAD, however, it can also be used very productively for design and documentation in a traditional drafting or CAD-based workflow unrelated to BIM. For more information about BIM and Autodesk's strategy for the application of information technology to the building industry, please see Autodesk's white paper on the subject at **www.autodesk.com/bim.**

*What Are Intelligent Architectural Objects?*     The ObjectARX® technology used in AutoCAD Architecture enables you to create intelligent architectural objects that know their form, fit, and function and behave according to their real-world properties. This technology improves software performance, ease of use, and flexibility in design. Intelligent architectural objects respond directly to standard AutoCAD editing commands in the same way that common AutoCAD drawing objects (such as lines, arcs, and circles) do. Yet they also have the ability to display according to context and to interact with other architectural objects. Object-based technology transforms ordinary geometry into intelligent architectural objects whose behavior models that of physical objects.

*What Is the Significance of Door, Wall, Window, and Other Architectural Objects?*     These intelligent objects improve design productivity and efficiency because they behave according to the specific properties or rules that pertain to them in the real world.

Architectural objects thus have a relationship to one another and interact with each other intelligently. For example, a window has a relationship to the wall that contains it. If you move or delete the wall, the window reacts appropriately. In addition, intelligent architectural objects maintain dynamic links with construction documents and specifications, resulting in more accurate and valuable project deliverables that can be used to manage a building throughout its lifecycle. When someone deletes or modifies a door, for example, the door schedule is updated automatically.

*Will AutoCAD Architecture and Autodesk Revit Be Combined into a Single Product in the Future?*     **No.** AutoCAD Architecture is based on the AutoCAD platform. Autodesk Revit is based on an entirely different technology and principle of operation. Thus, the products cannot be combined, and Autodesk has no plans to do so.

*What Is the Significance of 3D in AutoCAD Architecture?*     Because the objects in AutoCAD Architecture describe real-world building components, both 2D and 3D representations can be created automatically, and either one can be used to view or edit the model. This conveniently and smoothly integrates 2D and 3D functionality and allows exploration of design ideas within CAD in a fashion similar to the way architects and designers envision their designs. For example, you can quickly and easily create 3D massing studies in the initial phases of the design process to explore multiple design scenarios. Or you can develop a floor plan in 2D and then immediately see a perspective view of it in 3D. You can even use 3D to visually check for any type of interference in your design.

Additionally, AutoCAD Architecture has introduced many features that allow you to work in 3D easily. 3D also provides you with exportable geometric information that can be used for other applications to perform functions like energy analysis.

*Has 2D Functionality Been Enhanced in AutoCAD Architecture 2008?* **Yes.** The software's intelligent objects and architectural tools provide important benefits for 2D design development and construction documentation. You have all the functionality of AutoCAD plus powerful architectural design and drafting tools, including a detailing toolkit that vastly accelerates the production of construction details. Therefore, you can create key project deliverables more efficiently and accurately.

*Is AutoCAD Architecture 2008 Compatible with Earlier Releases of Autodesk Architectural Desktop?* Earlier versions of Architectural Desktop are forward compatible with the current release; i.e., designs created in earlier versions of Autodesk Architectural Desktop easily migrate to the current release of AutoCAD Architecture. AutoCAD Architecture 2008 is backward compatible with Architectural Desktop 2004, 2005, 2006, and 2007 at the object level (AEC Objects used in Architectural Desktop). Architectural Desktop 2007, 2006, 2005, and 2004 are *not* backward compatible at the object level with earlier releases of Architectural Desktop, but files created in these versions of the software can be saved as DWG files to be read by versions of Autodesk Architectural Desktop based on AutoCAD 2000, AutoCAD 2000i, and 2002 platforms.

*Will My Third-Party Applications Work with the Current Release of AutoCAD Architecture 2008?* Your existing third-party applications may or may not be compatible with the current release of AutoCAD Architecture. Contact your independent software supplier for details. For more information about the availability of third-party applications compatible with the current release of AutoCAD and AutoCAD Architecture, visit **www.autodesk.com/partnerproducts.**

*Is AutoCAD Architecture Compatible with Industry Foundation Classes (IFCs)?* **Yes.** IAI-certified support for IFCs is currently provided in AutoCAD Architecture.

*AutoCAD Architecture 2008 Has AutoCAD 2008 as its Foundation. Has the AutoCAD 2008 Drawing File Format (DWG) Changed from the AutoCAD 2007 Products, as It Did Between AutoCAD 2000 and AutoCAD 2005?* **No.** The AutoCAD 2008 DWG file format has not changed from the AutoCAD 2007, format. The AutoCAD 2007 file format was updated and is different from the AutoCAD 2006 DWG file format. This new format was necessary to provide performance enhancements, smaller file sizes, presentation graphics, and drawing security.

*Can I Run AutoCAD Architecture 2008 Side by Side with Other AutoCAD Platform-based Applications?* **Yes.** You can install the current release of AutoCAD Architecture 2008 side by side with any other AutoCAD 2000i–, AutoCAD 2002–, AutoCAD 2004 –, AutoCAD 2005–, AutoCAD 2006–, AutoCAD 2007, or AutoCAD 2008–based product. These products include Autodesk Building Systems, Autodesk Mechanical Desktop, AutoCAD Mechanical, Autodesk Land Desktop, Autodesk Map, and AutoCAD LT® software.

*How Can I Find Technical Support Information for AutoCAD Architecture 2008?* You can learn about all support options from your local Autodesk Authorized Reseller or Distributor. Visit **autodesk.com/support** and find a knowledge base of commonly asked support questions. Also, you can ask questions and read information about the use of Autodesk products in the peer-to-peer discussion groups on **discussion.autodesk.com.** Autodesk hosts topical discussion groups about specific products, and about general topics, such as drafting techniques and customization. Alternatively, Autodesk software manuals and documentation are a great source of answers to your support questions.

*How Do I Obtain Direct Technical Support?*    Autodesk® Subscription is the best way to keep your design tools and learning up to date. In the United States and Canada, for an annual fee you get the latest versions of your licensed Autodesk software, web support direct from Autodesk, self-paced training options, and a broad range of other technology and business benefits. You must purchase a subscription at the time you purchase or upgrade an Autodesk product. For more information, contact your Autodesk Authorized Reseller or visit **autodesk.com/subscription.**

Autodesk Systems Centers (ASCs) and Autodesk Authorized Resellers also provide support services for AutoCAD Architecture software and all other Autodesk products. In the United States and Canada, call 800-964-6432 to locate an ASC or reseller near you, or visit **autodesk.com/reseller.** You can find a complete list of support options from Autodesk at **autodesk.com/support.**

*Can I Rely on My AutoCAD Knowledge to Use AutoCAD Architecture? How Quickly Can I Learn the New Features in AutoCAD Architecture?*    AutoCAD Architecture builds on the speed, performance, and familiarity of AutoCAD, so AutoCAD users have a strong foundation from which to learn AutoCAD Architecture.

*Where Do I Find Training Courses for AutoCAD Architecture 2008?*    Training courses are available from Autodesk Professional Services as well as at Autodesk Authorized Training Center (ATC®) locations and Autodesk Authorized Resellers. Training courses are available through Autodesk Professional Services, and include Autodesk Virtual Classroom Training (online, instructor-led), custom training to match your organization's specific needs, as well as Autodesk Classroom Training. To obtain more information about Autodesk's training services, visit **www.youlearn.com.**

Other helpful training resources include the online discussion groups you can access through the AutoCAD Architecture Communication Center. The Communication Center also features industry-specific news, tips and tricks, product updates, and AutoCAD Architecture software manuals and online documentation.

*Should I Get Training with This Release?*    Although AutoCAD Architecture takes advantage of your existing knowledge of AutoCAD software, some training is recommended. Training improves productivity, increases return on investment, and enhances your AutoCAD Architecture knowledge.

*What Consulting Services Are Available for AutoCAD Architecture 2008?*    Autodesk Consulting provides customer consulting offerings for project assessments, process audits, implementation services, networking setup, application porting, and other custom services to help you get the best possible return on your investment in Autodesk technology. For more information on Autodesk Consulting, contact your Autodesk Account Executive or your local Autodesk Authorized Reseller; or visit **autodesk.com/consulting.**

## PLATFORMS, SYSTEM REQUIREMENTS, AND NETWORK

*Do I Need to Buy New Hardware to Run AutoCAD Architecture 2008?*    Following are the minimum hardware and operating system requirements for running AutoCAD Architecture.

### Description Minimum Requirement

*Operating System*

- Microsoft® Vista
- Microsoft® Windows 2000 Professional, SP3, or later
- Windows XP Professional, SP1, or later
- Windows XP Home Edition, SP1, or later
- Windows XP, Tablet PC Edition

Windows 95, 98, and NT are no longer supported.

*CPU.*   Intel® Pentium® 4 or AMD K7 with 1.4-GHz processor

*RAM.*   512 MB (1 GB recommended)

*Hard Disk Space.*   650 MB free and 75 MB swap space

*Display Resolution.*   1024 × 768 with True Color

***I'm Upgrading from Architectural Desktop 2004, but My Hardware Does Not Meet the Minimum Requirements for This Release; Can I Still Use the Current Release of AutoCAD Architecture Effectively?***   **Yes**—if you are using AutoCAD Architecture Desktop strictly for drafting and design. On hardware that does not meet the minimum system requirements, however, you should avoid using certain features that may cause below-optimal performance. These features include VIZ Render and Materials with surface hatching enabled.

***Are There Any Changes to the Licensing for Stand-Alone Seats?***   **Yes.** SafeCast is now the stand-alone licensing technology used in Autodesk products worldwide. For customers in the United States and Canada, this is a change in the stand-alone licensing.

Why change SafeCast? CD-Secure and SafeCast store licensing information on the user's hard drive, typically on the hard disk. Examining re-authorization statistics, it became clear that a number of technical issues with storing information on the hard drive could be resolved by implementing a new feature of SafeCast.

What will this feature do instead? This feature will store a duplicate set of licensing information in the computer's registry. For the types of errors that render the hard-drive storage ineffective, there will now be a fallback location in the registry, which will allow the licensing system to continue without error.

***Where Can I Purchase AutoCAD Architecture?***   AutoCAD Architecture is available worldwide. Contact your local Autodesk Authorized Reseller or Distributor for more information. To locate one near you, visit **http://usa.autodesk.com.**

AutoCAD Architecture is also available through the Autodesk online store at **http://usa. autodesk.com.**

***Is AutoCAD Architecture Being Released as an English-Only Product?***   **No.** This product will be released worldwide. Versions of this product will be available in a wide of range of languages and with localized content in many countries. For information on product availability contact your local Autodesk Authorized Reseller or Autodesk Systems Center (ASC).

***Is Subscription Available for AutoCAD Architecture?***   **Yes.** Subscription is available in most countries around the world for many of Autodesk's products including AutoCAD Architecture. Autodesk Subscription is the best way to keep your design tools and learning up to date. In the United States and Canada, for an annual fee you get the latest versions of your licensed Autodesk software, web support direct from Autodesk, self-paced training options, and a broad range of other technology and business benefits. You must purchase a subscription at the time you purchase or upgrade an Autodesk product. For more information, contact your Autodesk Authorized Reseller or visit **http://usa.autodesk.com.**

# Installing AutoCAD Architecture 2008

AutoCAD Architecture 2008 ships with three CDs labeled 1 of 3, 2 of 3, and 3 of 3. Installing AutoCAD Architecture 2008 is relatively easy. Just follow these directions.

1. Insert the disk labeled 1 of 3 in your CD drive and close the CD tray.
2. If your Windows Operating system is set for **Autorun,** the CD will begin to self-load.
3. If the CD does not self-load, go to the next step.
4. In the Windows Desktop, select the **Start** button, and pick the Run icon to bring up the Windows **Run** dialog box.
5. In the Windows **Run** dialog box, press the **Browse** button, and select the CD drive letter (labeled ACD-A 2008-1).
6. In the ACD-A 2008-1 directory on the CD drive, select **Setup,** and press the **OK** open button to return to the **Run** dialog box.
7. In the **Run** dialog box, press the **OK** button to start the installation process.

**Be prepared to wait for several seconds until the main AutoCAD Architecture 2008 screen appears (see the figure below).**

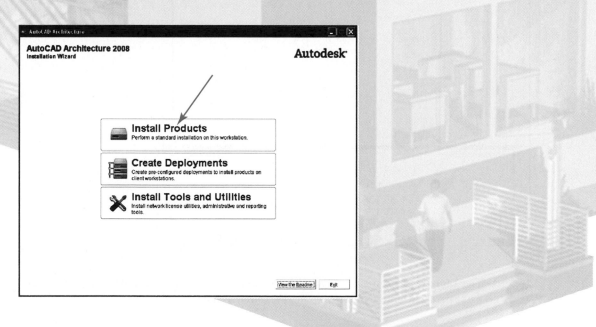

In the main AutoCAD Architecture 2008 installation screen, press **Install Products** to move to the next screen.

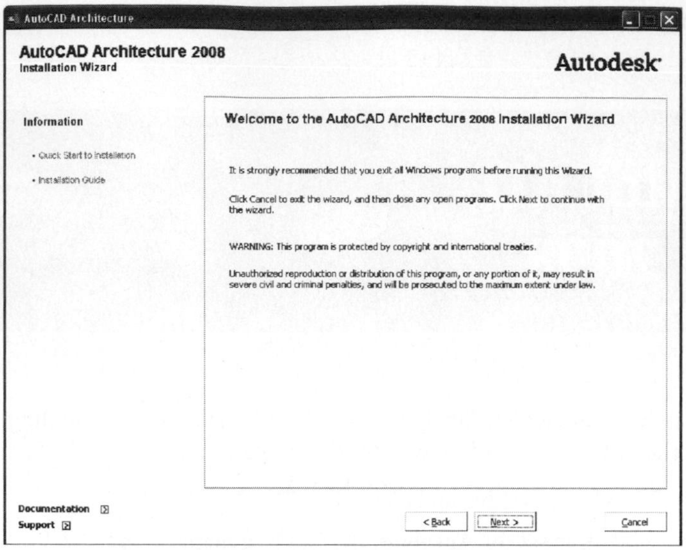

8. Close all Windows programs, and press the **Next** button to move to the next screen.

9. In the next screen, check the **AutoCAD Architecture** and **DWF Viewer** check boxes, and then press the **Next** button to move to the next screen.

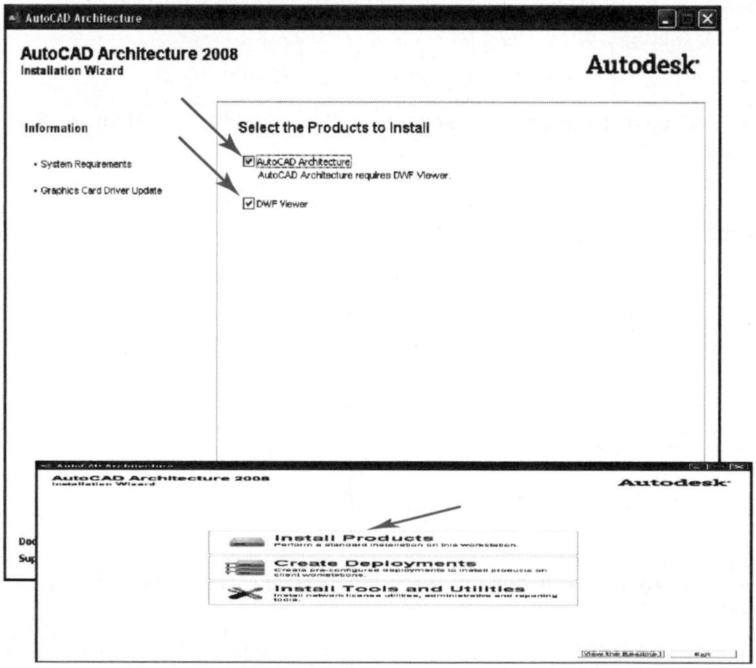

10. The **License Agreement** screen will now appear. Select the **I Accept** radio button, and press the **Next** button to bring up the **Personalize the Products screen.**

11. In the **Personalize the Products** screen, fill in your information, and press the **Next** button to bring up the **Review – Configure – Install** screen.

12. In the **Review – Configure – Install** screen, you will see the programs that will be installed, listed on the left.

13. In the **Review – Configure – Install** screen, press the **Configure** button to bring up the configuration tabs. In the **AutoCAD Architecture** tab, you can select the **Stand-alone license** or **Network license** radio buttons.

14. In the **DWF Viewer** tab, you can select a location other than the default location for installation of the DWF Viewer.

15. After completing the configuration options, press the **Configuration Complete** button to return to the **Review – Configure – Install** screen. In this screen press the **Install** button to start the installation process.

16. When installation is complete, the **Installation Complete** screen will appear. Press the **Finish** button to finalize the installation.

## HARDWARE/SOFTWARE REQUIREMENT NOTES

It is recommended that non–English language versions of AutoCAD Architecture be installed on an operating system with a user interface language that matches the Windows® XP Professional, Service Pack 2 (or later), Windows XP Home, Service Pack 2 (or later), Windows XP Tablet PC, Service Pack 2 (or later), or Windows 2000, Service Pack 4 (or later) operating system code page of the AutoCAD Architecture language. A code page provides support for character sets used in different languages. You must have administrative permissions to install AutoCAD Architecture. You cannot install AutoCAD Architecture if Microsoft Internet Explorer 6.0 with Service Pack 1 (or later) is not installed on the installation workstation. You can download Internet Explorer from the Microsoft website: Microsoft Internet Explorer 6.0, Service Pack 1 (or later) Web browser **http://www.microsoft.com/downloads/.**

Processor Pentium® 4—1.4 GHz (minimum). Pentium 4—3.4 GHz (recommended), RAM 1 GB (minimum), 2 GB (recommended). Requires a Windows-supported display adapter. 1024 × 768 with True Color (minimum) NVIDIA Quadro FX 1400 recommended by the author for shadows and quick 3D response.

# Abbreviations

In order to make this book easier to understand, shortcut abbreviations are often used. The following list codifies those abbreviations.

## PLEASE READ BEFORE PROCEEDING

**ACD-A**   Refers to AutoCAD Architecture 2008

**Activate a field** Refers to selecting a selection made up of a sentence.

**Activate a viewport**   Refers to clicking in a viewport to make it the active viewport.

**ADT**   Refers to Autodesk Architectural Desktop.

**AEC Objects**   Refers to any AutoCAD Architecture 2008 intelligent object such as walls, stairs, schedules, etc.

**Ancillary**   Refers to space between the ceiling and the floor above.

**Browse**   Refers to searching through the file folders and files.

**Contextual menu**   Refers to any menu that appears when an object or entity is selected with a **Right Mouse Button (RMB).**

**Dialog box**   Refers to any menu containing parameters or input fields.

**Display tree**   Refers to a Microsoft Windows folder listing consisting of + and − signs. If a + sign appears, then the listing is compressed with more folders available.

**Drawing editor**   Refers to the drawing area where drawings are created.

**Drop-down list**   Refers to the typical Windows operating system list with arrow. When selected, a series of options appear in a vertical list.

**DWG**   Refers to an Architectural Desktop Drawing.

**Elevation View**   Refers to **Front, Back, Right,** or **Left Views,** perpendicular to the ground plane.

**Layouts**   Refers to drawing areas. All layouts except the **Model Layout** can be broken down into **Paper Space** viewports. More layouts can be added.

**Plan View**   Refers to looking at a building from the **Top View.**

**Press the Enter button**   Refers to any **Enter** button in any dialog box on the screen.

**Press the Enter key**   Refers to the keyboard **Enter** key (the **space bar** will usually act as the **Enter** key, except when entering dimensions, text, or numerals).

**Press the OK button**   Refers to any **OK** button in any dialog box on the screen.

**RMB**   Refers to clicking using the **Right Mouse Button.** This is most often used to bring up contextual menus.

**Tooltips**   Refers to the information that appears when the cursor is held momentarily over an icon.

**Viewports**   Refers to **Paper Space** viewports.

Note:
Architectural Desktop has been renamed AutoCAD Architecture for 2008.

# Tool Palettes

AutoCAD Architecture 2008 ships with 18 default tool palettes and the **Properties** palette in place. These can be easily modified or deleted, or new palettes can be added.

## BRINGING UP THE TOOL PALETTES

The tool palettes can be brought up by three methods:

1. Typing **toolpalettes** in the **Command line.**
2. Pressing **Ctrl + 3** on the keyboard.
3. Selecting the **Tool Palettes** icon.

## RESIZING THE PALETTE

You can resize the tool palettes by moving your cursor to the cut corner at the bottom of the palettes. Your cursor will change to a "double arrow." Click, hold, and drag vertically and horizontally to resize, as shown in the figure below.

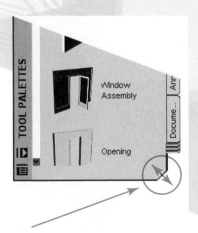

If you have more tool palettes than are showing, a "stair step" icon will appear at the bottom of the last tab name. (See the figure below.)

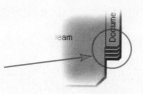

If you click on the "stair step" icon, a menu will appear that you can use to select all the tool palettes, as shown in the figure below.

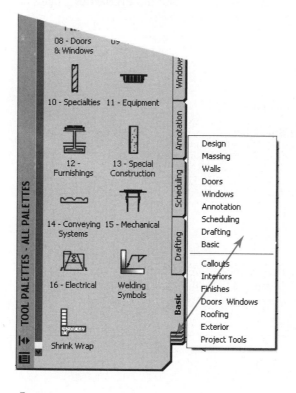

## AUTO-HIDE

Because the palettes cover some of the Drawing Editor, there is a control called **Auto-hide** that opens and closes the palette when the cursor is moved over its surface. The following figures show the icon used to turn **Auto-hide** on or off.

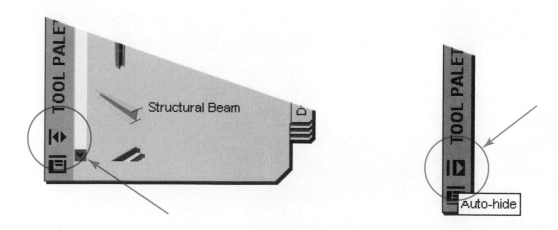

# TOOL PALETTES PROPERTIES

The **Tool Palettes Properties** give access to options necessary to control the size, location, and appearance of the palettes. **Tool Palettes Properties** also allow for creation and renaming of palettes. (See the figures below.)

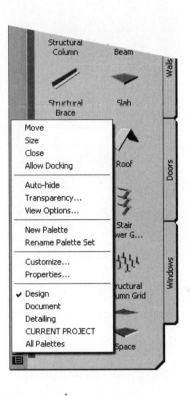

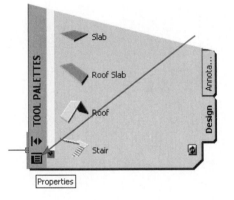

## Allow Docking

Allows the palette to attach to the sides of the Drawing Editor.

## Transparency

Makes the palette transparent, allowing entities on the Drawing Editor to be seen.

## View Options

Changes the sizes of the **Tool Palette** icons, as shown in the next figure.

**View Options**                    ?  ✕

Image size:

View style:

◯ Icon only

◯ Icon with text

⦿ List view

Apply to:

Current Palette

    OK              Cancel

## New Palette

Creates new palettes.

## Rename Palette Set

Renames the entire set of palettes.

## Customize

Groups, adds, deletes, and renames tool palettes.

1. Select the **Customize Palettes** option from the **Tool Palette** contextual menu to bring up the **Customize** dialog box.

2. In the **Customize** dialog box, select the **Tool Palettes** tab.

3. **RMB** in the **Tool Palettes** list to bring up the contextual menu for creating, renaming, and deleting tool palettes.

4. **RMB** in the **Palette Groups** list to bring up the contextual menu for creating or deleting tool palette groups.

5. Select a palette group, **RMB** to bring up the contextual menu for creating, renaming, deleting, and making a tool palette group current.

6. Drag and drop selections from **Tool Palettes** into **Palette Groups.**

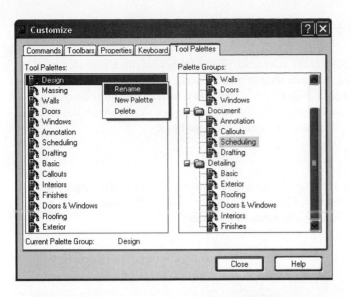

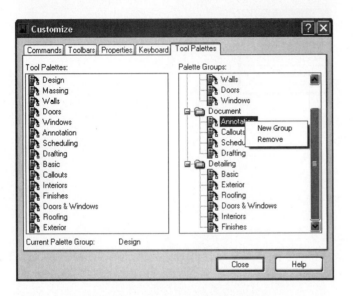

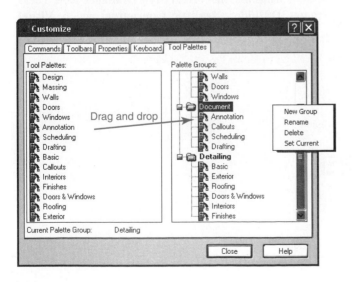

# VISUAL STYLES

Again in AutoCAD Architecture 2008 is the advanced **Visual Styles** palette with new rendering capability and real-time shadowing. A visual style is a collection of settings that control the display of edges and shading in a viewport. With this new capability, instead of using commands and setting system variables, you change the properties of the visual style. You can see the effect in the viewport as soon as you apply a visual style or change its settings.

## The Visual Styles Toolbar

The new **Visual Styles** toolbar replaced the old Architectural Desktop 2006 **Shading** toolbar. In order to activate the **Visual Styles** toolbar, **RMB** on an empty space in the toolbar area, and select **ACD** > **Visual Styles** from the contextual menu that appears.

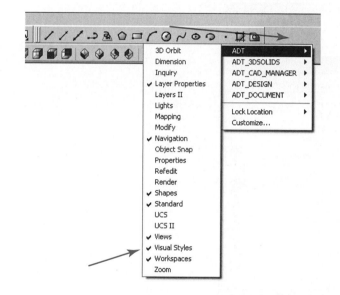

The **Visual Styles** toolbar includes five style icons and the **Visual Style Manager** icon. These icons are the **2D Wireframe, 3D Wireframe, 3D Hidden, Realistic, Conceptual,** and the **Visual Style Manager.**

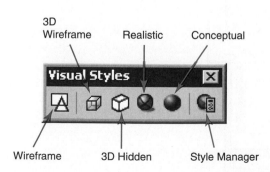

## The Five Visual Styles

The Wireframe, 3D Wireframe, and 3D Hidden styles produce the same result as those in Architectural Desktop 2007, and previous versions. The new rendering styles for AutoCAD Architecture 2008 are the **Realistic** and **Conceptual** styles. Wireframe is the standard 2D display that has been with AutoCAD and Architectural Desktop from the beginning. 3D Wireframe displays 3D objects with all lines displayed. Wireframe 3D Hidden displays objects with all visible lines displayed as continuous lines, and all hidden lines displayed as dashed or not displayed lines. The Conceptual style displays objects in a flat shaded manner with all lines displayed. Finally, Realistic displays objects realistically with all materials showing. Both the Realistic and Conceptual styles are capable of real-time shadowing if one of the Autodesk certified video cards is installed in your system.

**Exercise 1:** Creating a Sample Structure to Visualize the Styles

1. Select **File** > **New** in the **Main** menu to bring up the **Select Template** dialog box.
2. In the **Select Template** dialog box, pick the AEC Model (Imperial Stb) template, and press the **Open** button to create a new drawing.
3. From the **Walls** tool, select the **Brick-4 Brick-4 furring** wall tool, and place an enclosure 9'-0" high similar to that shown in the following drawing.
4. Select the **Roof** tool from the **Design** tool palette, and place a roof on the enclosure.
5. Select doors and windows from the **Door** and **Window** tool palettes, and insert them in the walls.

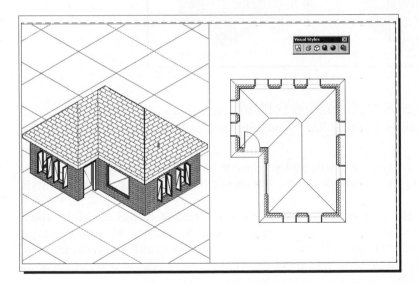

**Testing the Different Visual Styles**

6. Change to the **SW Isometric View.**
7. Select the **3D Wireframe** icon in the **Visual Styles** toolbar; this makes everything transparent and you can see inside the building.
8. Select the **3D Hidden** icon. In this style, nothing is transparent.
9. Select the **Conceptual** style. This style has a flat appearance, and the default setting shows the "triangulations" that create the faces.
10. Finally, select the **Realistic** style. This is the most realistic Visual Style, and will display your building with materials applied.
11. The styles you just selected are the default settings, but all these styles are configurable.

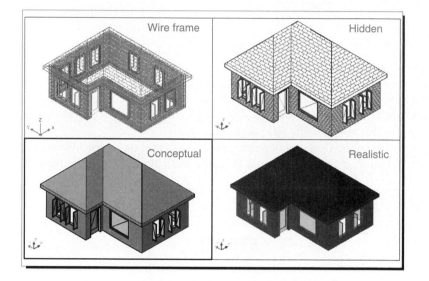

**Exercise 2:** Understanding and Modifying the Visual Styles

Now that you have seen the default Visual Styles, let's take a look at modifying the styles.

1. Select the last icon on the **Visual Styles** toolbar to bring up the **Visual Style Manager.** (You can also type **visualstyles** in the **Command line** to bring up the **Visual Style Manager.**)
2. At the top of this manager, you find five large icons; each represents one of the Visual Styles. When you select one of the icons, you will find the configurable settings for that style. Below and to the right of these icons are three smaller icons for creating, applying, and exporting a Visual Style. Except for the Wireframe style, the other styles are really selected variations and settings of a basic template.

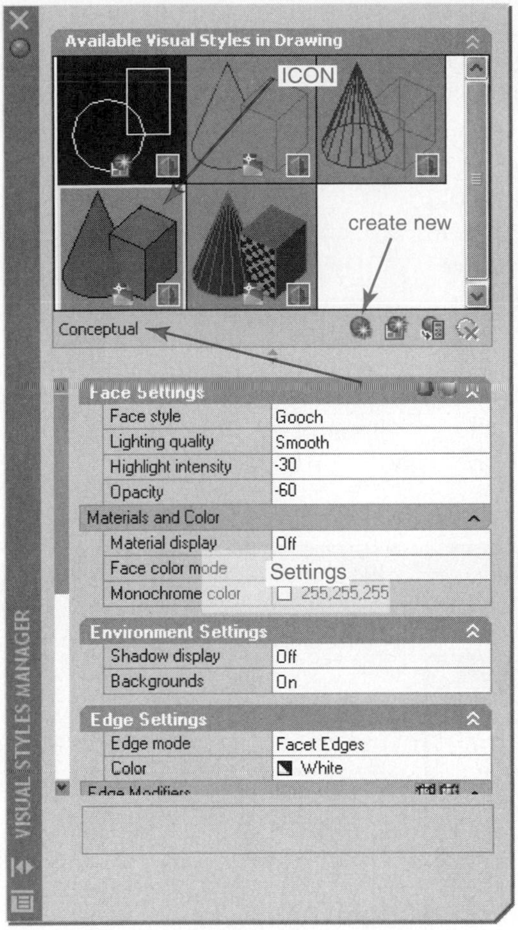

The Visual Styles Manager panel showing:

**Available Visual Styles in Drawing**

ICON, create new

Conceptual

| Face Settings | |
|---|---|
| Face style | Gooch |
| Lighting quality | Smooth |
| Highlight intensity | -30 |
| Opacity | -60 |

| Materials and Color | |
|---|---|
| Material display | Off |
| Face color mode | Settings |
| Monochrome color | 255,255,255 |

| Environment Settings | |
|---|---|
| Shadow display | Off |
| Backgrounds | On |

| Edge Settings | |
|---|---|
| Edge mode | Facet Edges |
| Color | White |
| Edge Modifiers | |

3. Set the view to **SW Isometric.**
4. **RMB** on any style icon and select **Create New Visual Style** from the contextual menu that appears to bring up the **Create New Visual Style** dialog box.
5. In the **Create New Visual Style** dialog box, enter **TEST VISUAL STYLE** in the name field, and press the **OK** button to create a new style.
6. Select and drag the **NEW TEST STYLE** icon from the **Visual Styles Manager** into the Drawing Editor.

The view will now be set to the **NEW TEST STYLE.**

7. In the settings area, select the **Material display** field, and select **Materials** from the drop-down list.
8. The walls of the structure turn Brick brown.
9. Select the same field in the **Visual Styles Manager** again, and this time, select **Materials and Textures.**

Now the walls show the brick texture.

## Exercise 3: Shadows

The third category in the **Visual Styles Manager** is **Environmental Settings.** This is where you select the **Shadow** display field.

1. Select **Full shadows** from the drop-down list.
2. If you want to check what existing video card you have and the features it supports, you can open the **Adaptive Degradation and Performance Tuning** dialog box by entering **3dconfig** in the **Command line,** and pressing the **Enter** key on your keyboard. In this dialog box, press the **View Tune Log** button to bring up the **Performance Tuner Log.** This log will tell you which features are supported.

**Note:**
If you don't see shadows, you may not have an Autodesk Certified Video card. There are only 11 video cards that are certified, and they are all made either by NVIDIA or ATI.

3. Type **dashboard** in the **Command line** to bring the **Dashboard** dialog box.
4. In the **Dashboard** dialog box, expand the **Light control panel.**
5. In the **Light control panel,** select the **Edit the Sun** icon to open the **Sun Properties** dialog box.
6. In the **Sun Properties** dialog box, select **On** from the **Status** drop-down list at the top of the dialog box.

**Note:**
You will get a warning asking if you want the default viewport lighting turned off; select **YES.**

## WORKSPACES

This feature allows you to create sets of menus, toolbars, and palettes that are grouped and organized so that you can work in a custom drawing environment. When you use a workspace, only the menus, toolbars, and palettes that are relevant to a task are displayed.

To create a new workspace, place all your toolbars, palettes, and so on in place and select the **Save Current As . . .** option to open the **Save Workspace** dialog box. In the dialog box, enter the name of the new workspace.

Select the **Workspace settings...** option to bring up the **Workspace Settings** dialog box.

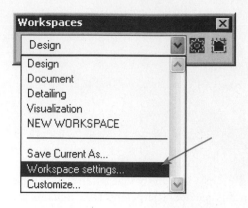

In the **Workspace Settings** dialog box, you can set the workspace to be your "Home Workspace," and check the check boxes to select the workspaces to be displayed in the **Workspaces** drop-down list.

This author suggests that you select the **Automatically save workspace changes** radio button to have the workspace automatically save any changes you make in the workspace in which you are working.

# The Properties Palette

The **Properties** palette changes depending on the AEC Object or entity that is selected. All the properties of the selected object can be changed in this palette. The palette also contains the **Quick Select** icon; this is very useful in selecting objects, especially when several objects are located together.

## BRINGING UP THE PROPERTIES PALETTES

The **Properties** palettes can be brought up by three methods:

1. Typing properties in the **Command line.**
2. Pressing **Ctrl + 1** on the keyboard.
3. Double-clicking any AEC Object or entity (see the figure below).

| No selection | | |
|---|---|---|
| **General** | | |
| Color | ByLayer | |
| Layer | 0 | |
| Linetype | ByLayer | |
| Linetype scale | 1.00000 | |
| Lineweight | ByLayer | |
| Thickness | 0" | |
| **3D Visualization** | | |
| Material | ByLayer | |
| Shadow display | Casts and Receives… | |
| **Plot style** | | |
| Plot style | ByLayer | |
| Plot style table | Aec Standard.stb | |
| Plot table attached to | Model | |
| Plot table type | Named without tran… | |
| **View** | | |
| Center X | 160'-5 23/32" | |
| Center Y | 97'-0 1/4" | |
| Center Z | 0" | |
| Height | 195'-3 3/32" | |
| Width | 358'-8 11/16" | |
| **Misc** | | |
| Annotation scale | 1/8" = 1'-0" | |
| UCS icon On | Yes | |
| UCS icon at origin | No | |
| UCS per viewport | Yes | |
| UCS Name | | |
| Visual Style | 2D Wireframe | |

Design    Display    Extended Data    PROPERTIES

## QUICK SELECT

The **Quick Select** toggle icon allows you to filter and select from any of the AEC objects or entities presently in the Drawing Editor. To use this filter, select the **Quick Select** icon at the top right of the **Properties** palette to bring up the **Quick Select** dialog box.

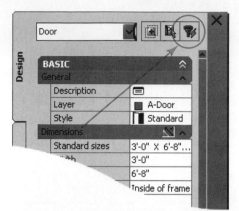

# PICKADD Toggle

The **PICKADD** toggle turns the PICKADD system variable on and off. When PICKADD is on, each object selected, either individually or by windowing, is added to the current selection set. When PICKADD is off, selected objects replace the current selection set.

# Select

Click to deselect a selection.

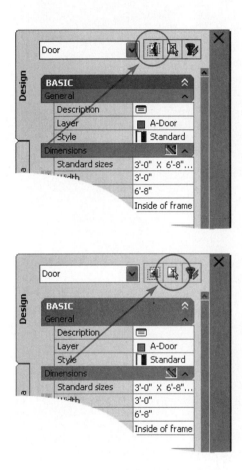

## OBJECT DISPLAY TAB

The **Display** tab gives you access to all the components of an object (see the figure below).

For example, a door object has five display components by default: Door Panel, Frame, Stop, Swing, and Glass. (Many display components correspond directly to the physical components of the object, but some, like Swing, do not.) For each of these display components, the drawing default settings specify the relevant display properties as appropriate for the drawing type. In the case of doors, the default settings specify that the Swing component is visible in plan and elevation views, but not in 3D views.

To change the display using this tab, you select an object display component (like a hatch or a boundary), and then select or enter a new value for the display property you want to change (such as color, visibility, or lineweight). The results are immediately visible in the drawing area for the current display representation and can be applied to other display representations that use the same component. You can also apply style or object overrides by changing the value of **Display controlled by.**

**Note:**
To hide the Display tab (or show it if it is currently hidden), enter the following command at the command line: AecChange Display tab Status.

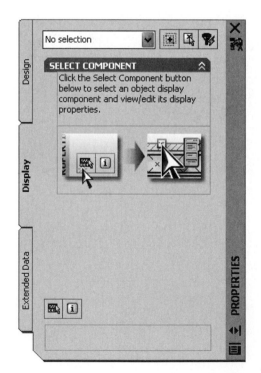

1. Place an AEC Object (the **CMU-8 Rigid – 1.5 Air-2 Brick-4 Furring-2** wall has been used for this example).
2. With the **Properties** palette open, change to the **Display** tab.

3. In the **Display** tab select the **Select Component** icon at the lower left of the tab, and select the CMU hatch. Notice that the Display tab becomes populated with component fields.)

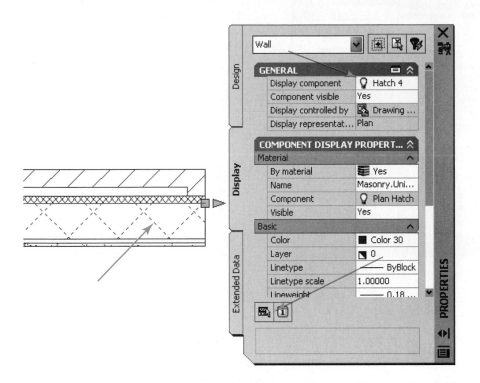

The **Display component** field in the **GENERAL** group will display the component selected, and the **Component visible** field will read **Yes** or **No** depending on whether it is visible or not.

4. Change the **Component visible** drop-down list to **No.** A warning dialog box will appear Press the **Yes** button, and the hatch disappears.

If you select the **Display component** field in the **GENERAL** group, you can select any of the other components of the wall.

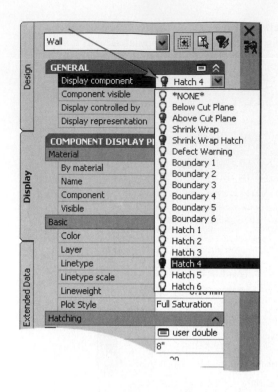

You can also control the component display by **Material.**

5. Return the **Hatch 4 Component Visible** to **Yes** to make it visible.

6. Select the **Name** drop-down list under the **COMPONENT DISPLAY PROPERTIES**> **Material** category.

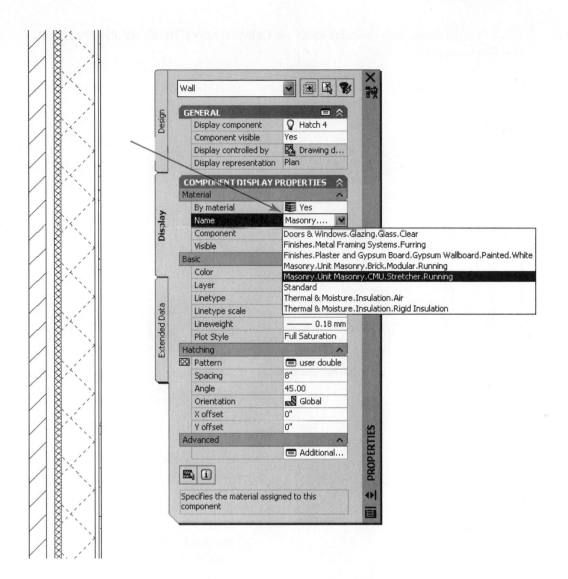

The drop-down list will show the **Material** assigned to that component.

**Note:**

If the value of **By material** is **Yes**, only that setting and the **Component visible** setting will be applied to the selected display representations. If the value of **By material** is **No**, all of the display property settings for the component will be applied to the selected display representations.

7. Select the **Color** drop-down list under the **COMPONENT DISPLAY PROPERTIES>
Basic** category.

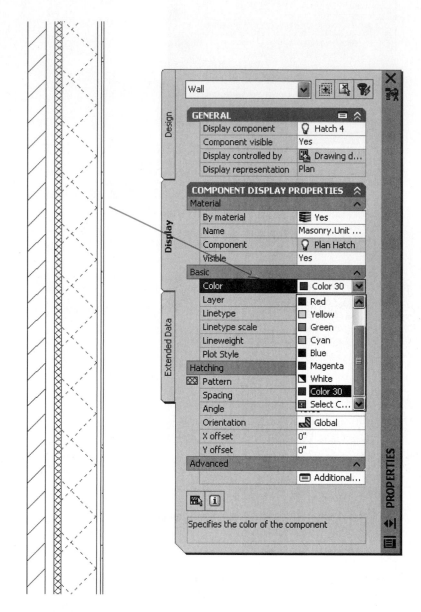

The drop-down list allows you to change the color, linetype, lineweight, and plot style of the component.

**Note:**
Change the color for screen clarity, or if you are using colors to control printer lines.

8. Change the color to **Blue.** Again you will get the warning dialog box telling you that modifying the **Material** definition will affect all objects to which this material is applied.

9. Press the **Yes** button, and return to the Drawing Editor.

10. Select the **Pattern** field under the **COMPONENT DISPLAY PROPERTIES** > **Hatching** category.

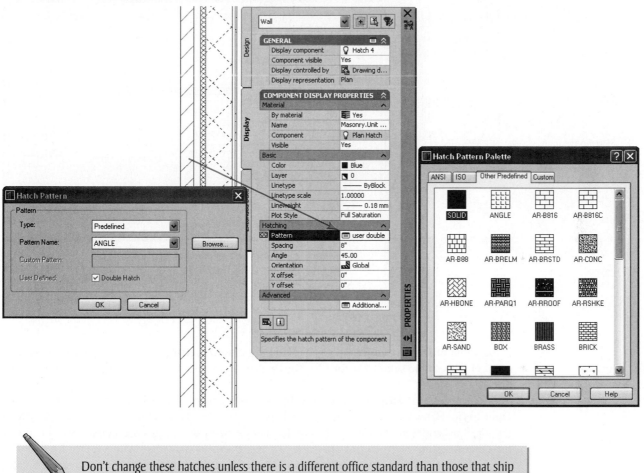

TIP  Don't change these hatches unless there is a different office standard than those that ship with AutoCAD Architecture.

Here you can change the hatch pattern, size, rotation, and so on for a component.

11. Select the **Additional properties** field under the **COMPONENT DISPLAY PROP-ERTIES**> **Advanced** category. This brings up the **Display Properties** dialog box (more information on using this dialog box in a later section).

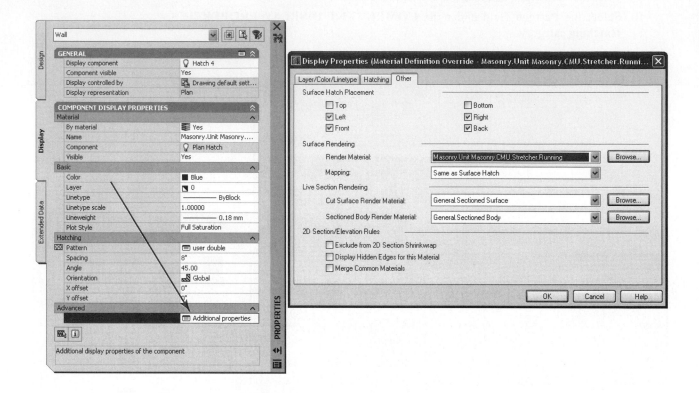

If the value of **Display controlled by** is **Drawing default setting,** then your changes will apply to all objects of the same type for which no overrides are in effect (for example, all doors in the drawing).

If the value of **Display controlled by** is <object type>Style:<style name> (for example: **Door Style: Hinged - Single)**, changes will apply to all objects with the specified style for which no object overrides are in effect. This is called a style override; it takes precedence over the drawing default setting.

If the value of **Display controlled by** is **This object,** this is called an object override; it takes precedence over either the drawing default setting or the style.

# The Content Browser

The Content Browser locates all your AEC tools such as walls, windows, and doors. You drag your tools into your tool palettes using Autodesk's idrop technology. You can also drag AEC content back into your tool palettes to create new tools. After creating a new tool palette, it is a good idea to drag a copy of the tool palette back into the **My Tool Catalog** folder in the Content Browser to save a copy of the palette.

## BRINGING UP THE CONTENT BROWSER

The Content Browser can be brought up by three methods:

1. Typing **aeccontentbrowser** in the **Command line.**
2. Pressing **Ctrl + 4** on the keyboard.
3. Selecting the **Content Browser** icon (see the figure below).

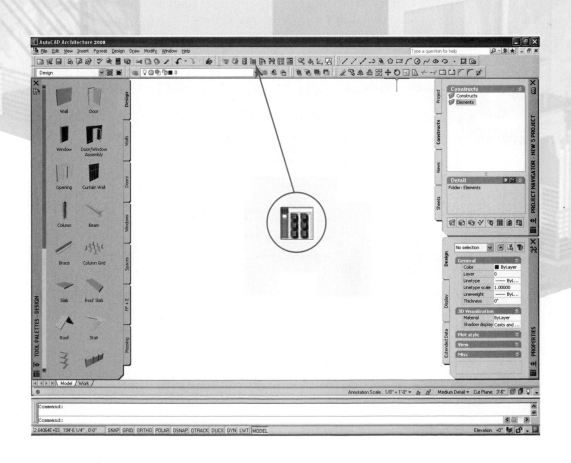

The Content Browser starts off with the Catalog Library, which contains several catalogs (see the following figure).

Click the Modify Library View Options icon to open the Content Browser Preferences dialog box. Here you can set the number of Catalog rows and new Catalog types.

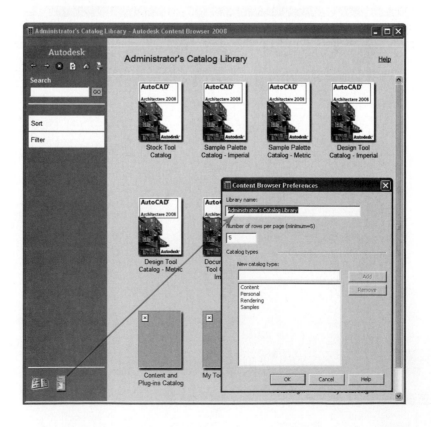

Click the **Add or Create a Catalog** icon to open the **Add Catalog** dialog box. Here you can create a new **Catalog** or add an existing **Catalog** from a location such as a **website.**

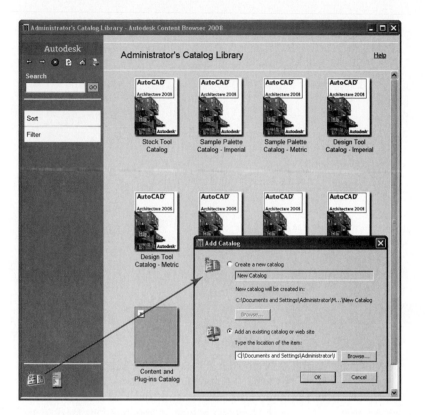

You drag content from the Catalog folders into your tool palettes, as shown in the figure below. (Make sure **Auto-hide** is turned off when you do this.)

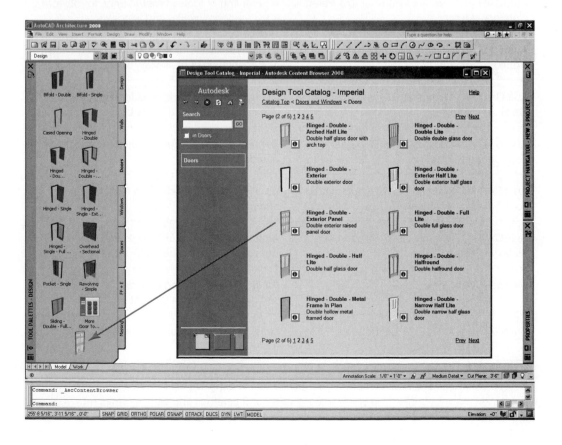

You can also create a tool by just dropping an ADT Object from the drawing to a tool palette, a style from **Style Manager** to a tool palette, or a piece of AEC Content from the **Custom** tab in the **DesignCenter.**

**Note:**
Some objects use fixed images like the Schedule Tool, AEC Dimension Tool, and the Layout Object Tools.

The following tool catalogs are supplied with the program:

| Catalog Name | Contents |
|---|---|
| Stock Tool Catalog | A catalog that contains the standard, stock tools in AutoCAD Architecture 2008 |
| AutoCAD Architecture 2008 Sample Palette Catalog—Imperial | A sampling of tools in imperial units for objects such as doors, walls, and windows. |
| AutoCAD Architecture 2008 Sample Palette Catalog—Metric | A sampling of tools in metric units for objects such as doors, walls, and windows |
| AutoCAD Architecture 2008 Tool Catalog—Imperial | Content tools in imperial units for design and documentation of multi-view blocks and symbols |
| AutoCAD Architecture 2008 Tool Catalog—Metric | Content tools in metric units for design and documentation of multi-view blocks and symbols |
| AutoCAD Architecture 2008 Documentation Tool Catalog—Imperial | Content tools in imperial units for annotation and documentation |
| AutoCAD Architecture 2008 Documentation Tool Catalog—Metric | Content tools in metric units for annotation and documentation |
| AutoCAD Architecture 2008 Render Material Catalog | Architectural render materials for use with AutoCAD Architecture 2008 |
| My Tool Catalog | An empty tool catalog provided so that you can create your own tool set |
| AutoCAD Architecture 2008 Plug-ins | Links to third-party plug-ins for AutoCAD Architecture 2008 |

You cannot add or remove items from the Autodesk-supplied tool catalogs, but you can create your own tool catalogs. You can also copy other tool catalogs and website links into your catalog library.

# The Open Drawing Menu

The **Open Drawing Menu** icon is located at the bottom left of the AutoCAD Architecture 2008 interface (see the figure below).

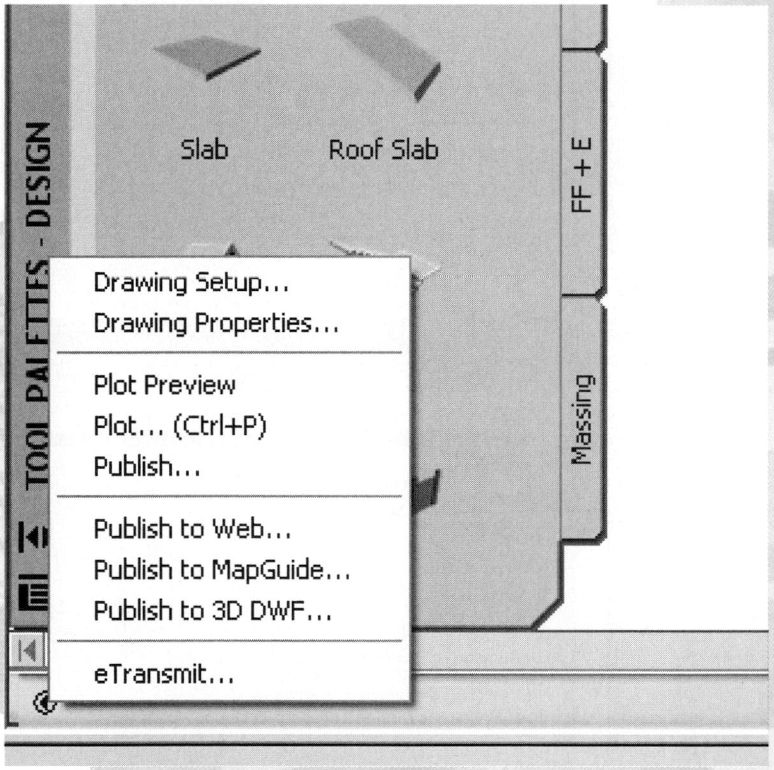

# DRAWING SETUP

Selecting **Drawing Setup** brings up the **Drawing Setup** dialog box with tabs to set drawing units, scale, layers, and display. The **Drawing Setup** dialog box can also be accessed from the **Format** menu in the **Main** toolbar (see the figures below).

# PUBLISH—DWF PUBLISHER

Selecting **Publish** brings up the **Publish** dialog box (see the figure below). In this dialog box, press the **Publish Options** button to select the publish options for the DWFs (see the figure below).

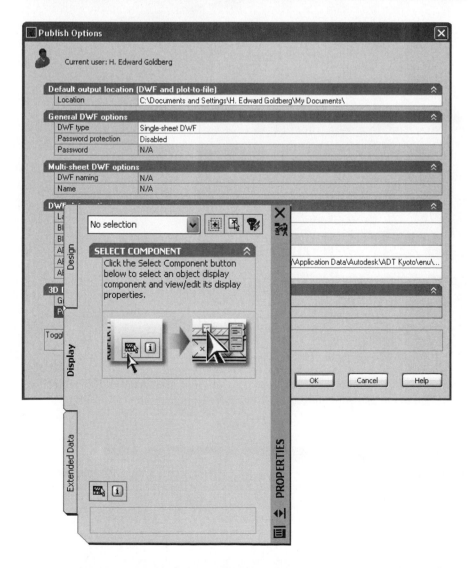

## PUBLISH TO WEB

Selecting **Publish to Web** from the **Open Drawing** menu opens the **Publish to Web** wizard to create a Web page with i-drop capability. For this tutorial, select the **Create New Web Page** radio button and press the **Next** button.

**Note:**
This feature creates a Web page containing examples of drawings that you wish to display on the Internet. Before using this feature, make sure that you display your building in the drawing as you wish to have it shown. If you have zoomed in and saved your drawing, it will display as zoomed in. Also, either create a new named layout, or rename the Model layout to the name that you wish to have displayed on the Web page (this will not be necessary if you want to publish sheets).

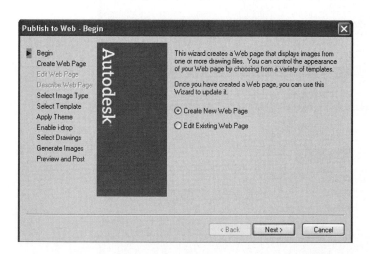

You will probably get the following message telling you that only a saved drawing can be published. If you want to publish your current drawing, save it and press the **OK** button.

The **Publish to Web** drawing selection dialog box will now appear. Browse to select a drawing that you wish to have on the Web page. After selecting a file from the **Publish to Web** dialog box, press the **Open** button to move to the next dialog box (**Create Web Page**).

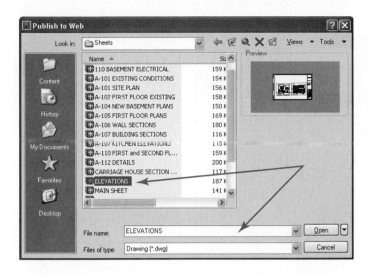

In the top field of the **Create Web Page** dialog box, enter a unique name for the web page. In the next field browse to a location on your computer and create a new file folder and location for the web page. Press the **Next** button to move to the **Select Image Type** dialog box.

In the **Select Image Type** dialog box, select **JPEG** (the most popular picture format). If you want people to be able to download DWFs, choose **DWF** from the drop-down list. Select a size for the images from the Image size drop-down list, and press the **Next** button to move to the **Select Template** dialog box.

In the **Select Template** dialog box, select one of the four templates listed (this author chose the **List plus Summary** template). Press the **Next** button to move to the **Apply Theme** dialog box.

In the **Apply Theme** dialog box, select a color theme from the drop-down list (this author chose **Autumn Fields**). Press the **Next** button to move to the **Enable i-drop** dialog box.

In the **Enable i-drop** dialog box, check the **Enable i-drop** check box if you wish to add DWF i-drop drag-and-drop capability to your Web page. This will allow users to drag DWFs directly into their copy of AutoCAD or AutoCAD Architecture. Press the **Next** button to move to the **Select Drawings** dialog box.

In the top drop-down list of the **Select Drawings** dialog box, browse to the location of your project on your computer, and choose another drawing to publish on your page from the **Publish to Web** dialog box that appears. After choosing a file, press the **Open** button to return to the **Select Drawings** dialog box. Select a layout from the **Layout** drop-down list, and press the **Add** button to add the drawing to the **Image list.** Repeat until you have several drawings listed, and then press the **Next** button to move to the **Generate Images** dialog box.

In the **Generate Images** dialog box, select the **Regenerate images for drawings that have changed** radio button, and then press the **Next** button to move to the **Preview and Post** dialog box. (This may take a few moments while the drawings are brought up and regenerated.)

In the **Preview and Post** dialog box, press the **Preview** button to see the Web page in your Web browser. After viewing, close the Web page, press the **Post Now** button, and find a location for the files. Upload the files to your own website.

## PUBLISH TO MAPGUIDE

If you have MapGuide installed, you can deploy MapGuide GIS and digital design data applications on the Internet, on your intranet, or in the field.

## PUBLISH TO 3D DWF

Selecting **Publish to 3D DWF** from the **Open Drawing** menu takes you to the **Export 3D DWF** dialog box where you select a location to place the DWF.

After saving the DWF, a message appears asking if you wish to view the DWF.

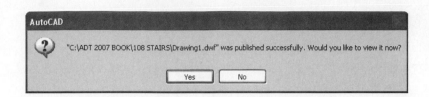

If you press the **Yes** button, the Autodesk DWF Viewer appears with your DWF.

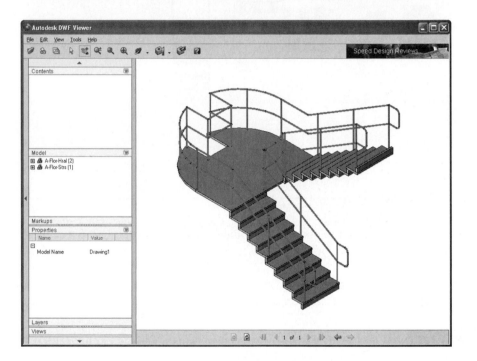

By opening the **Views** section, you can select a view.

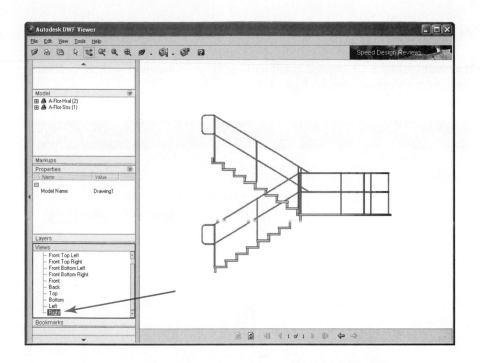

By selecting the **Cross Section** icon at the top of the **DWF Viewer,** you can section the object.

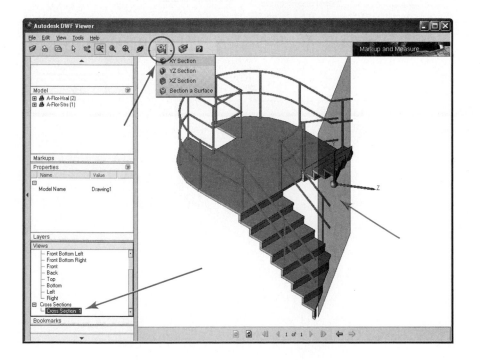

## eTRANSMIT

Selecting **eTransmit** creates a compressed email package of your drawings with all necessary files. It also includes a transmittal (see the figure below).

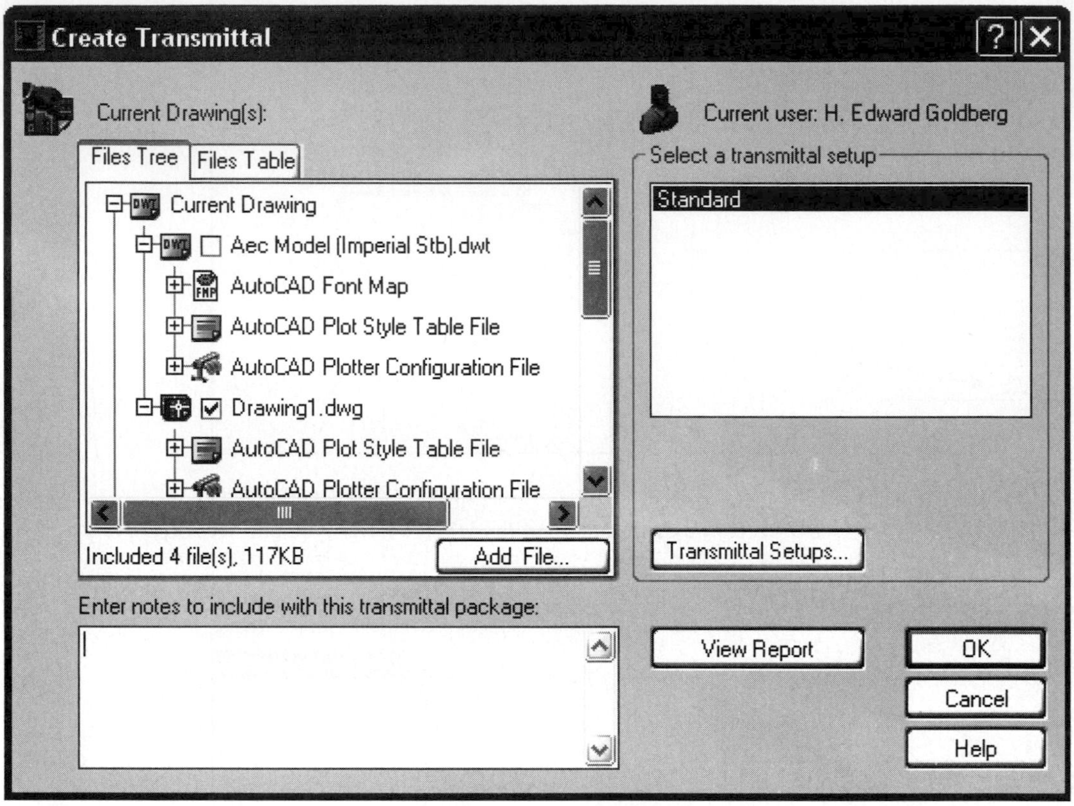

# Massing/Mass Elements and Groups

# 1

## *Section* Objectives

- Learn how to create a massing object.
- Learn how to modify a massing object.
- Create and attach slice plates (floor slices).
- Modify the massing object after applying the slice plates.
- Change the slice plates into space boundaries, and then into walls.
- Learn how to use the **Drape** tool to create contour massing models.

Massing objects can be dragged or inserted either from the **Design Tool** palette, or by typing **MassElementAdd** on the **Command line.**

## MASSING AND MASS MODELING

Computerized mass modeling replicates the design system frequently used by architects to design large buildings. The initial design studies for these buildings are often modeled in clay or wood first. These small models generally show the relationship between parts of the building while indicating scale as well as how light and shadow react with the facades. Mass modeling is meant to be a quick process, akin to the building blocks we all played with as children.

With AutoCAD Architecture 2008 the concept of mass modeling takes yet another step. With the new Convert tools, mass modeling takes on a new importance for creating unusually shaped Roof and Floor Slabs as well as articulated Space objects.

The **Massing** tool palette comes with 14 preconfigured primitives (3D shapes). The primitives can be dragged or inserted into your drawing from the tool palette. The size of the primitive can be preset or can be modified when inserting. This can be determined by selecting yes or no from the **Specify on Screen** drop-down list in the **Properties** tool palette when inserting the primitive. Selecting and pulling on grips or changing parameters in the **Properties** tool palette associated with massing can easily modify each primitive's size and shape.

Building models can be made from Mass primitives that can be grouped together in a **Mass Group.** These primitives can then be individually changed to quickly change the Building model. After the building model has been created, floor slices can be created from the model. These floor slices can be used as a basis for area and space studies, or for eventually generating walls. Using this method, one can model a building and reuse the model for the basis of construction documents.

The following exercises are designed to give you a hands-on feel for using the **Massing** feature of the program. After doing these exercises, you should explore all the primitives, and try making new ones using the **Extrusion and Revolution** feature as well as the **Convert to Mass Element** tool that converts solid models and AEC Objects into mass elements.

### Exercise 1-1: Creating a Massing Object

1. Start a new drawing using the AEC Model (Imperial Stb) template.
2. Change to the **Model Layout.**
3. Change to the **NE Isometric View.**

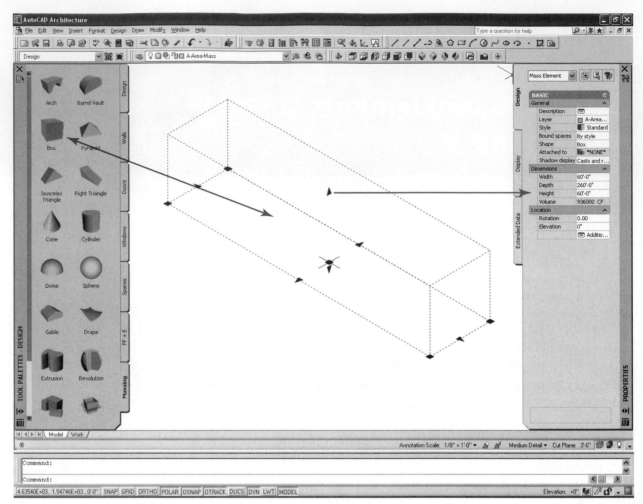

**Figure 1–1**

4. Select the **Massing** tool palette.
5. Drag the **Box Primitive** massing icon to the drawing area or click once on the **Box** icon and move your cursor to the drawing area. *Don't click in the drawing area yet!* Move your cursor to the closed **Properties** toolbar to open it (see Figure 1–1).
6. When the **Properties** toolbar opens, notice a blue asterisk icon (settable option upon insertion) next to the **Specify on screen** option. Select **No** from the drop-down list (this will allow you to preset the **Width, Depth,** and **Height** of the box). Set the Width to **60′**, Depth to **260′**, and Height to **60′** (see Figure 1–2).

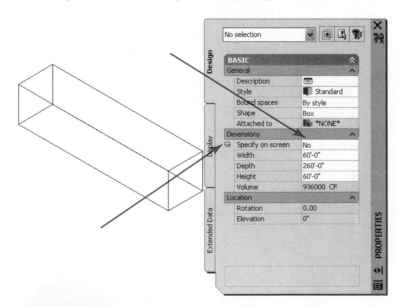

**Figure 1–2**

7. Once the size properties have been set, click to locate the **BOX** primitive, and then press **Enter** twice to accept the default rotation and close the command. Save this file.

## Exercise 1-2: Modifying a Massing Object

1. Select the primitive to activate its grips, and then select **Free Form** from the **Shape** drop-down list to make the massing box editable (see Figure 1–3).

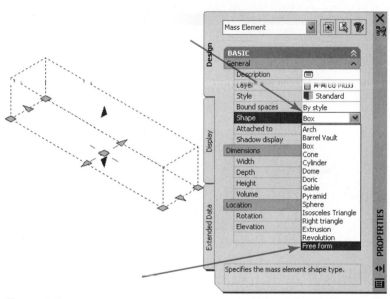

**Note:**
Before the massing primitive has been changed to a free form, it can be adjusted in the standard ACD-A 2009 manner by activating grips and entering dimensions, or pulling on the grips.

**Figure 1–3**

2. Select the free form, and move your cursor over the "dot," right-mouse-click, and select **Split Face** from the contextual menu (see Figure 1–4).

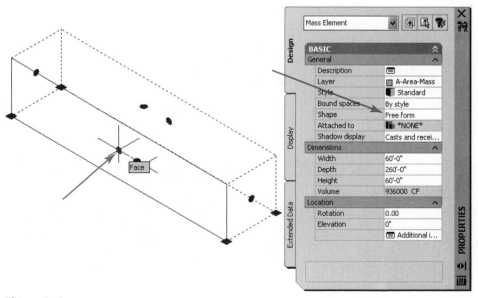

**Figure 1–4**

You can recognize an editable free form shape because its grips will be changed to dots. Selecting the dots will select the faces of the free form massing object (see Figure 1–5).

3. Set your **OSNAP** settings to **Endpoint** and **Perpendicular.**
4. Enter **fro** in the **Command line** and click on the upper right corner of the face.
5. Move the cursor to the left along the top of the face, and then enter **80′** in the **Command line** and press **Enter.**

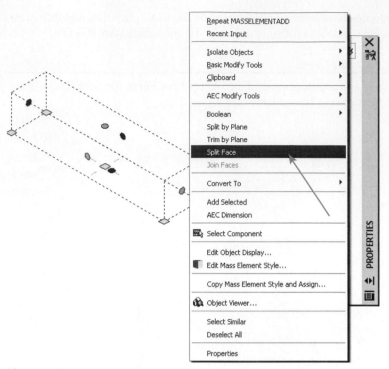

Repeat MASSELEMENTADD
Recent Input                           ▶

Isolate Objects                        ▶
Basic Modify Tools                     ▶
Clipboard                              ▶

AEC Modify Tools                       ▶

Boolean                                ▶
Split by Plane
Trim by Plane
Split Face
Join Faces

Convert To                             ▶

Add Selected
AEC Dimension

Select Component

Edit Object Display...
Edit Mass Element Style...

Copy Mass Element Style and Assign...

Object Viewer...

Select Similar
Deselect All

Properties

PROPERTIES

**Figure 1–5**

6. Finally, move your cursor down to the lower edge of the face until the **Perpendicular Osnap** icon appears, and then click to split the face. Press the **Esc** key to complete the command (see Figure 1–6).

Select the control dot on the new face to see your FACE options. Grab the control dot and drag the face. There are six adjustments that can be made to the faces. These are selected by pressing the **Ctrl** key on the keyboad as you drag (see Figure 1–7).

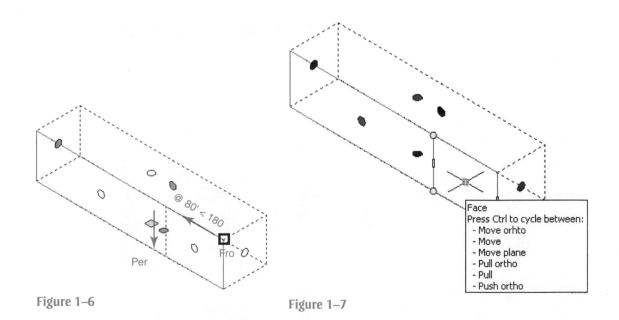

@ 80' < 180

Per

Fro

Face
Press Ctrl to cycle between:
 - Move orhto
 - Move
 - Move plane
 - Pull ortho
 - Pull
 - Push ortho

**Figure 1–6**

**Figure 1–7**

Figure 1–8 shows illustrations of different variations. It also illustrates moving edges. Pushing or pulling on the vertical tabs that appear at the edges can move these edges.

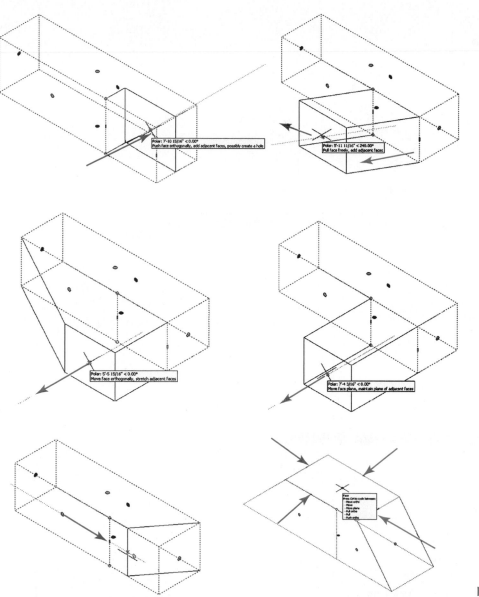

Figure 1–8

By using various primitives and adjusting them by splitting, pushing, pulling, and moving their faces, you can quickly create a mass model of your proposed building.

Now continue on to the next step in the hands-on tutorial.

7. Pull on the dot and press the **Ctrl** key on your keyboard until the face pulls forward.
8. Enter **60′** in the **Command line** and press **Enter** (see Figure 1–9).
9. Drag another box massing object into the drawing area.
10. This time, similar to Step 6, select **YES** from the drop-down list next to the **Specify on screen** option on the **Properties** tool palette. (This will now allow you to adjust your massing object while placing it.)
11. Make sure your **End Point Osnap** is active.
12. Place a box massing object on top of the massing object that has been modified previously.
13. With the new box massing object selected, **RMB** and select **Boolean > Union** from the contextual menu (see Figure 1–10).

You have now created a modified massing object made from two massing objects (see Figure 1–11).

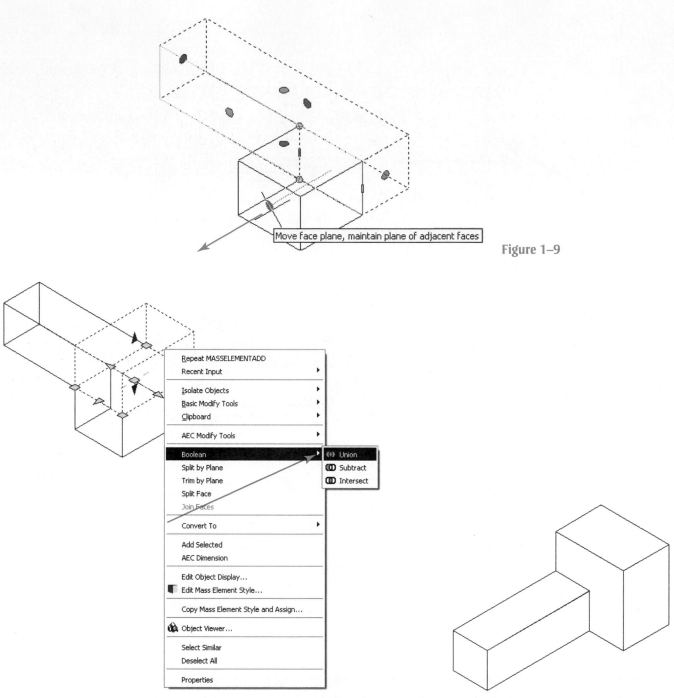

Figure 1–9

Figure 1–10

Figure 1–11

**Exercise 1-3:** Creating and Attaching Slice Plates (Floor Slices)

1. Select the **Massing** tool palette, and select the **Slice** icon (see Figure 1–12).
2. Click in the **Top** viewport.
3. Enter 11 in the **Command line** and press **Enter.**
4. Select a spot near the massing model, and then place a second to create a rectangle.
5. Accept the default **Rotation (0.00),** accept **Starting height (0″),** and set the distance between slices to 10′-0″. Then press the **Enter** key to complete the command.
6. Select all the markers with a window crossing, **RMB,** and select **Attach Objects** from the contextual menu that appears.
7. Select the massing object that you created in the previous section and press **Enter.**

You have now created 11 slice plates (floor slices) in your massing object (see Figure 1–13).

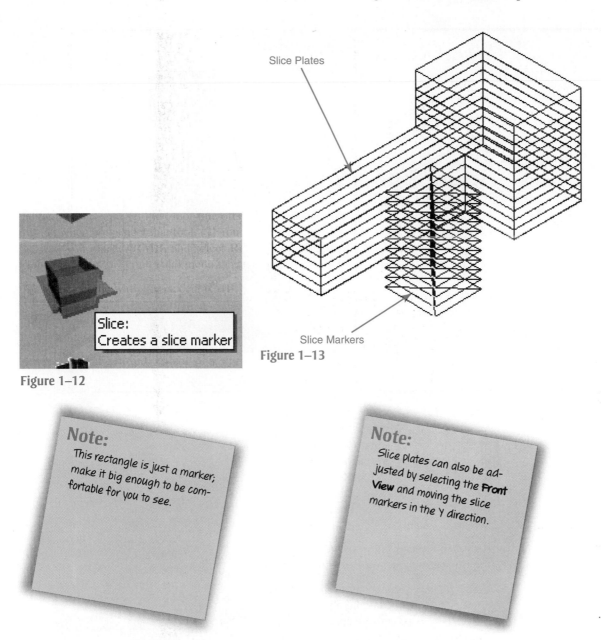

Figure 1–12

Figure 1–13

**Note:** This rectangle is just a marker; make it big enough to be comfortable for you to see.

**Note:** Slice plates can also be adjusted by selecting the **Front View** and moving the slice markers in the Y direction.

8. Change to the **NW Isometric View** and select the topmost slice marker.
9. **RMB** and select **Set Elevation** from the contextual menu.
10. Enter **115′** in the **Command line** and press **Enter** (note that the topmost slice plate moves downward). Save this file.

## HIDING THE SLICE MARKERS

1. Select one of the slice markers, **RMB,** and select **Edit Object Display** from the contextual menu that appears to bring up the **Object Display** dialog box.
2. Double-click on the word **General** to bring up the **Display Properties** dialog box.
3. Turn the **Cut Plane** and **Outline** visibility off, and then press the **OK** buttons on the dialog boxes to complete the command and return to the Drawing Editor.

**Exercise 1-4:** Modifying the Massing Object After Applying the Slice Plates

1. Select another box massing object from the **Massing** tool palette, and give it a 30′ width, 60′ depth, and 60′ height.
2. Place the new object as shown in Figure 1–14.

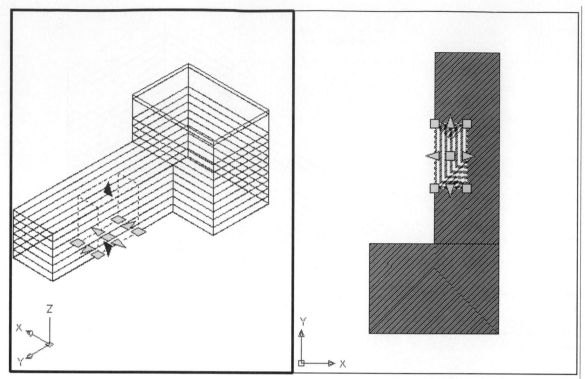

**Figure 1–14**

3. Select the original massing object, **RMB,** select **Boolean > Subtraction** from the contextual menu, and select the new massing object.
4. Enter **Y** (Yes) in the **Command line** to erase the layout geometry.

Notice that the slice plates follow the new outline created by the Boolean subtraction (see Figure 1–15).

5. Using the massing object modification techniques, modify the massing object.
6. Create new massing objects and Boolean them to the original object.

**Note:**
If you have trouble selecting the massing objects because you keep selecting the slice plates instead, you can temporarily turn off the visibility of their layer.

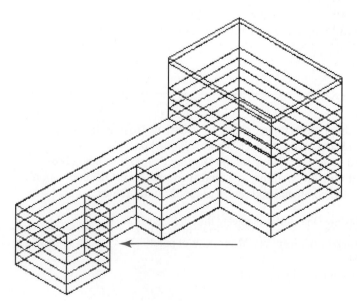

**Figure 1–15**

The slice plates will always follow the modified massing object (massing model) (see Figure 1–16).

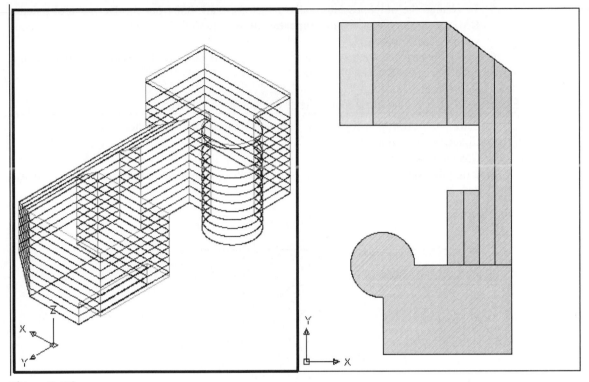

**Figure 1–16**

7. **RMB** in an empty space in the Drawing Editor, select **Object Viewer** from the contextual menu, and select the massing object.
8. Turn on **Perspective** and **Flat Shaded** to see the model (see Figures 1–17 and 1–18). Save the file.

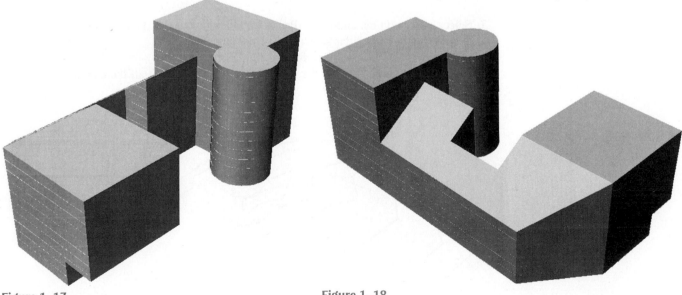

**Figure 1–17**                                      **Figure 1–18**

**Exercise 1-5:** Changing the Slice Plates into Walls

1. Use the previous exercise's file.
2. Change to the **Model Layout,** and then change to the **SW Isometric View.**

3. Make sure the slice markers are visible.
4. Select all the slice markers, **RMB,** and select **Convert to Polyline** from the contextual menu that appears. The slices will be converted to polylines.
5. To change the polylines into walls, select the wall tool from the **Design** tool palette, **RMB,** and select **Apply Tool Properties to** > **Linework.** The slices have now been converted to wall objects.
6. While the new walls are still selected, move your cursor over the **Properties** palette, and enter **10′** in the **Base** height field.

## Exercise 1-6: Using the Drape Tool to Create Contour Massing Models

1. Start a new drawing using the AEC Model (Imperial Stb) template.
2. Change to the **Model Layout.**
3. Change to the **Top View.**
4. Using the **Rectangle** and **Polyline** tools from the **Draw** menu, draw and modify until you get a drawing similar to that in Figure 1–19.

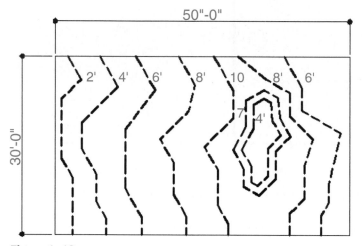

**Figure 1–19**

5. Select each polyline, and in the **Properties** palette, change the elevation of each of the polylines to the elevations shown in Figure 1–19.
6. Change to the **SW Isometric View** (see Figure 1–20).
7. Select the **Drape Tool** from the **Massing** tool palette, select all the contours, and press **Enter.**

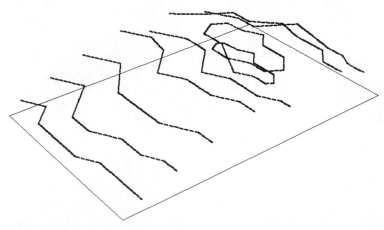

**Figure 1–20**

8. Enter **Y** (Yes) to erase the selected contours.
9. Select two opposite corners of the bottommost modified rectangle, and press **Enter.**
10. Accept the mesh size of 30, and press **Enter.**
11. Enter **12″** in the **Command line** for the base thickness and press **Enter** to complete the command.
12. Press the **Conceptual** icon in the **Visual Styles** toolbar to shade the contour model (see Figure 1–21). If the **Visual Styles** toolbar is not available, **RMB** an empty area of the toolbars to bring up the **ACD-A** contextual menu, and check the Visual Styles.

Figure 1–21

## Sectioning the Contour Mass Model by a Plane

13. Change to the **Front View.**
14. Press the **2D Wireframe** icon in the **Visual Styles** toolbar.
15. Place a rectangle as shown in Figure 1–22.
16. Change to the **Top View,** and move the rectangle so that it bisects the Contour model.
17. Change to the **SW Isometric View.**
18. Select the contour model, **RMB,** and select **Split by Plane** from the contextual menu that appears.
19. Enter **3** (three points) in the **Command line,** and press the **Enter** key on your keyboard.
20. Pick the three points numbered in Figure 1–23.
21. Move the sectioned Contour Mass as shown in Figure 1–24 and erase the rectangle.

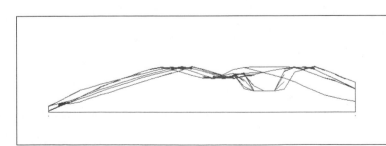

Figure 1–22

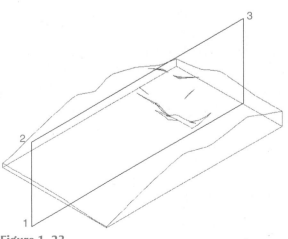

Figure 1–23

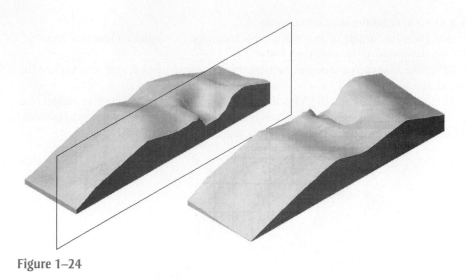

**Figure 1–24**

## Exercise 1-7: Using the Drape Tool to Create a Slope on a Flat Slab

Commercial buildings often have flat roofs and depend on sloped external rigid insulation to create the drainage slopes.

1. Start a new drawing using the AEC Model (Imperial Stb) template.
2. Change to the **Top View.**
3. Using the **Rectangle** tool from the **Draw** menu, draw a 40′ × 30′ rectangle.
4. Place a line from the midpoint of one 40′ side to the midpoint of the other 40′ side (see Figure 1–25).

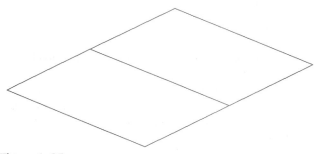

**Figure 1–25**

5. Copy the rectangle 24″ in the Z direction (see Figure 1–26).

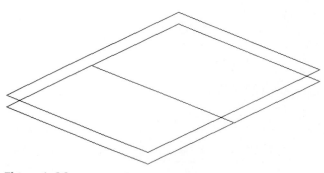

**Figure 1–26**

6. Change to the **SW Isometric View.**
7. With the **End Point** and **Mid Point** Osnaps set, draw a **3D polyline** as shown in Figure 1–27.

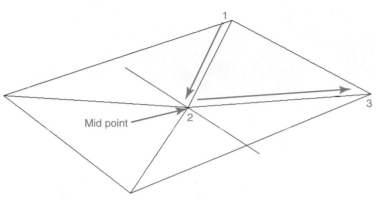

**Figure 1–27**

8. Repeat or **mirror** the 3D polyline; the result should appear in the **Front** view as shown in Figure 1–28.

**Figure 1–28**

9. In the **SW Isometric View,** select the **Drape Tool** from the **Massing** tool palette, select the two 3D polylines you created, and press **Enter** on your keyboard.
10. Enter **Y** (Yes) to erase the polylines, and press **Enter** on your keyboard.
11. Enter **N** (No) in the **Command line** when asked to **Generate regular mesh,** and press **Enter** on your keyboard.
12. Enter **N** (No) in the **Command line** when asked to **Generate rectangular mesh,** and press **Enter** on your keyboard.
13. Enter **12″** in the **Command line** when asked to **Enter base thickness,** and press **Enter** on your keyboard to create the sloping **Mass Element.**

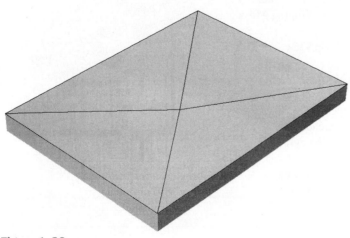

**Figure 1–29**

14. Using the **Split by Plane** method shown in the previous exercise, split the roof slab in half to see the slope (see Figure 1–30).

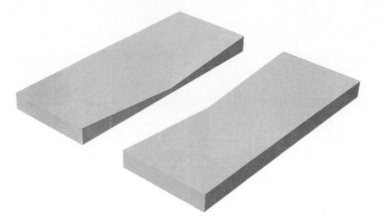

**Figure 1–30**

15. By selecting the faces of the Mass Element with the **Face UCS** icon, you can see that you truly have a sloped element (see Figure 1–31).

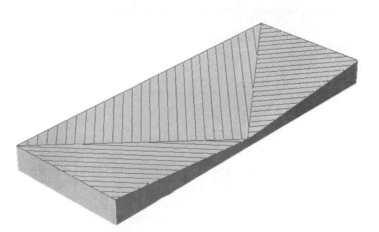

**Figure 1–31**

## Converting the Mass Object into a Roof Slab

16. Recreate the **Mass Object** you created in the previous exercise, but do not section it this time.
17. Change to the **Top View.**
18. Place a **Mass Object** cylinder 1'-6" radius by 4'-0" high in the center of the sloping **Mass Object** you created.
19. Change to the **SW Isometric View** (see Figure 1–32).
20. Select the sloping **Mass Object, RMB,** and select **Boolean > Subtract** from the contextual menu that appears.
21. When the **Command line** reads **Select objects to subtract,** select the cylinder, and press **Enter** on your keyboard.
22. Enter **Y** (Yes) in the **Command line** to the question **Erase layout geometry?** and press **Enter** on your keyboard to complete the command.

**Note:**

The Convert tools were greatly enhanced in Architectural Desktop 2007. One word of caution, though: the Convert from Mass Object to Wall, Slab, and Roof Slab is technically a "REPLACE." This means that the Converted or "Replaced" object will be placed on the Wall, Slab, or Roof Slab layers, but these objects cannot be modified like real Walls, Slabs, or Roof Slabs. This exercise demonstrates the conversion from Mass Object to Roof Slab, and methods for making holes in the slab.

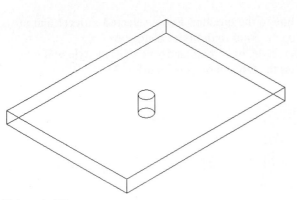

Figure 1–32

The sloping Mass Object now has a hole in it (see Figure 1–33).

23. Select the sloping **Mass Object, RMB,** and select **Convert To** > **Roof Slab** from the contextual menu that appears (see Figure 1–34).

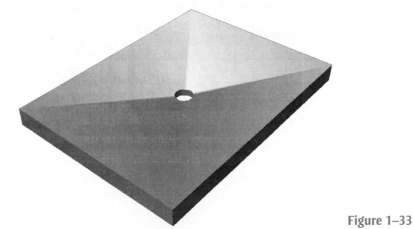

Figure 1–33

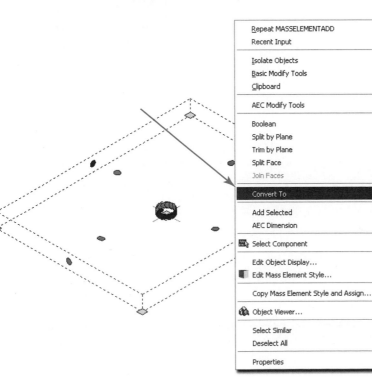

Figure 1–34

24. Enter **Y** (Yes) in the **Command line** to the question **Erase selected object?** and press **Enter** on your keyboard to bring up the **Roof Slab Styles** dialog box.

25. Unless you have created a roof slab style, only the Standard roof slab style will appear. Select the **Standard** style, and press the **OK** button (see Figure 1–35).

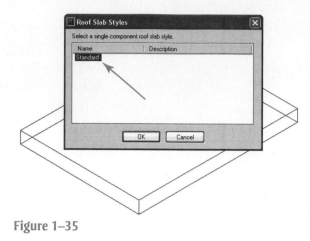

Figure 1–35

Your sloping **Mass Object** converts (replaces) into a **Roof Slab** object.

# Space Objects

## 2

## Section
## Objectives

- Learn how to create a **2D Space Object** and label it with a **Space Tag.**
- Know how to create a **Simple 3D Space Plan** with **Space Objects,** and create a **Space Evaluation** report.
- Learn how to create a **Freeform Space Object,** and use the **Space Zone Manager.**
- Learn how to convert **Mass Elements** to **Freeform Space Objects,** and use the **Space/Zone Manager.**
- Use the **Space Generate** tool.
- Use the **AEC Modify Trim** option.
- Use the **AEC Modify Divide** option.
- Use the **AEC Modify Merge** option.
- Use the **AEC Modify Crop** option.
- Know how to use the space object grip features.

Space objects create a sophisticated space-planning system and data extraction system.

Space objects can contain Property Set Data that can be retrieved automatically and read in AEC schedules. They can also be used to control and generate ceiling and floor slabs.

The space object represents either 2D or contained 3D space. If it is a 3D space, it includes floor and ceiling thickness, floor-to-ceiling heights, elevation, and ancillary space heights. All the aforementioned attributes can be modified easily. The space object contains wall area information.

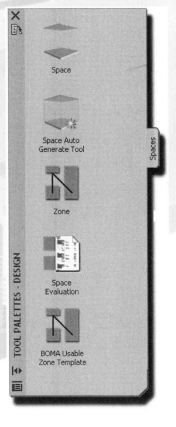

## SPACE OBJECTS PROPERTIES TOOL PALETTE

| Number | Name | Purpose |
|--------|------|---------|
| 1 | Style | Select from available space styles |
| 2 | Name | Name of the space |
| 3 | Tag | Drop-down list to select tags on insert |
| 4 | Associative | Yes or No if the space has been made associative to walls |
| 5 | Offset boundaries | Drop-down list specifies how the Net, Usable, and Gross boundaries are offset from the space object—Manually or by Style |

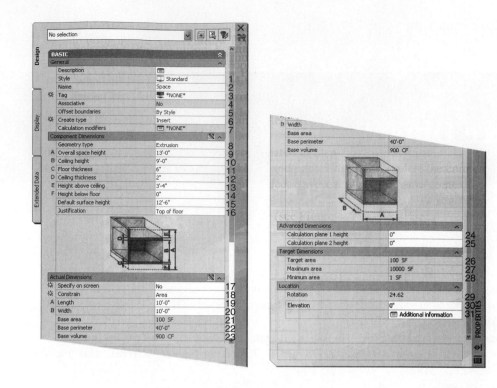

| 6 | Create type | Drop-down list specifies by Insert (by style), by rectangle, or by polygon |
|---|---|---|
| 7 | Calculation modifiers | Calculation styles that mathematically modify space areas |
| 8 | Geometry type | 2D or Extrusion—Extrusion is 3D Space object |
| 9 | Overall space height | If Geometry Type is Extrusion—Top of Space to Bottom of Space Object |
| 10 | Ceiling height | If Geometry Type is Extrusion—Floor to bottom of ceiling |
| 11 | Floor thickness | Floor thickness |
| 12 | Ceiling thickness | Ceiling thickness |
| 13 | Height above ceiling | Distance above top of ceiling to top of Space object |
| 14 | Height below floor | Distance from bottom of floor to bottom of Space object |
| 15 | Default surface height | Specifies the default surface height to be used by all surfaces whose height is not overridden. The default is the sum of the combined height of Floor thickness, Ceiling thickness, Height above ceiling, and Height below floor. Setting the Default Surface height will change the ceiling height to the entered value minus the remaining values, and keeping the remaining values constant. |

| 16 | Justification | Insertion option for Top of floor, Bottom of floor, or Bottom of Space below floor |
| 17 | Specify on screen | Change length, width, area by dragging on screen |
| 18 | Constrain | Constrain dragging of object to only **Area, Length, Width,** or **None** |
| 19 | Length | Preset length value of space object |
| 20 | Width | Preset width value of space object |
| 21 | Base area | Preset area value of space object |
| 22 | Base perimeter | Displays the base perimeter of the space |
| 23 | Base volume | Displays the base volume of the space |
| 24 | Calculation plane 1 height | Use this procedure to set calculation of either or both of the cut planes available for 3D freeform spaces. These can be useful for rooms under a roof where the space area can be calculated only for the parts of a space with a specific height. Calculation planes can be automatically scheduled. |
| 25 | Calculation plane 2 height | |
| 26 | Target area | Target area for space |
| 27 | Maximum area | Maximum area for space |
| 28 | Minimum area | Minimum area for space |
| 29 | Rotation | Rotation angle of space object |
| 30 | Elevation | Elevation of space object |
| 31 | Additional information | Launches the Additional Information Worksheet with more structural member information |

**Exercise 2-1:** Creating a 2D Space Object and Labeling It with a Space Tag

1. Start a new drawing using the AEC Model (Imperial Stb) template.
2. Change to the **Model Layout.**
3. Change to the **Top View.**

## Creating a NAMED SPACES Property Set Definition

4. Select **Format** > **Style Manager** from the **Main** menu to bring up the **Style Manager.**
5. In the **Style Manager,** expand the **Documentation Objects** folder, **RMB** on **Property Set Definitions,** and select **New** from the contextual menu that appears.
6. Name the new **Property Set Definition NAMED SPACES.**
7. In the **NAMED SPACES** Property Set Definition, change to the **Applies To** tab.
8. In the **Applies To** tab, select the **Clear All** button, and then place a check in the **Space** check box.
9. Change to the **Definition** tab, and select the **Add Automatic Property Definition** icon to bring up the **Automatic Property Source** dialog box.

10. In the **Automatic Property Source** dialog box, place checks in the **Name, Length,** and **Width** check boxes, and press the **OK** buttons to return to the Drawing Editor (see Figure 2–1).
11. Press **OK** to complete the command and return to the Drawing Editor.

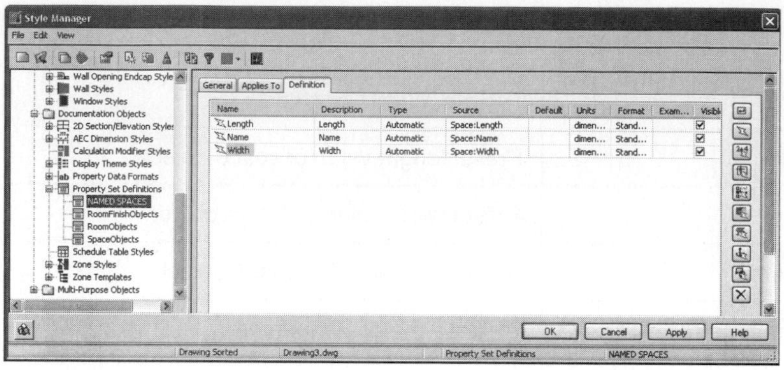

Figure 2–1

## Creating the Spaces

12. Select **Format** > **Style Manager** to bring up the **Style Manager** dialog box.
13. Expand the **Architectural Objects** folder, **RMB** on **Space Styles,** and select **New** from the contextual menu that appears.
14. Create several new **Space** styles and call them **LOBBY, HALL, OFFICE, MALE TOILET,** and **FEMALE TOILET.**
15. Select each style you created, **RMB,** and select the **Design Rules** tab.
16. In the **Design Rules** tab, set your **Target - Area**, **Length,** and **Width**.

This will be your target size of your space, and starting length and width.

17. Set the following:

   a. **LOBBY - 240 SF, Length = 15′-0″, Width = 16′-0″**
   b. **HALL - 250 SF, Length = 50′-0″, Width = 5′-0″**
   c. **OFFICE - 100 SF, Length = 10′-0″, Width = 10′-0″**
   d. **MALE TOILET - 120 SF, Length = 12′-0″, Width = 10′-0″**
   e. **FEMALE TOILET - 120 SF, Length = 12′-0″, Width = 10′-0″**

18. Click on the **Space** icon on the **Spaces** tool palette, and move your cursor over the **Properties** tool palette to open it.
19. Set the following:

   a. Style = **LOBBY**
   b. Name = **MAIN LOBBY**
   c. Tag = **Aec3_Room_Tag**
   d. Create Type = **Insert**
   e. Geometry type = **2D**
   f. Specify on screen = **Yes**
   g. Constrain = **Area**
   h. Length = **15′-0″**
   i. Width = **16′-0″**

> **Note:**
> When you are inserting the space, you can enter **D** (Drag point) in the **command line,** and press the **Enter** key on your computer to change the space insertion point.

20. Click in the **Drawing Editor** and press **Enter** twice to place the space.
21. Enter **C** (Centered) to place the tag in the center of the space, and press the **Enter** key on your keyboard twice to complete the command, and place the space with a tag.
22. Repeat steps 18–20 for the rest of the spaces, naming them as you add them.
23. Repeat the **OFFICE** eight times.

You now have tagged space objects (see Figure 2–2). Save this drawing.

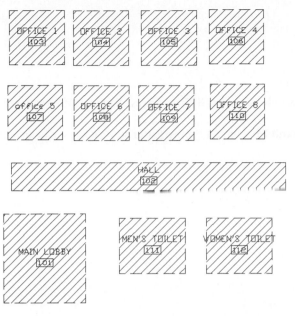

Figure 2–2

**Exercise 2-2:** Creating a Simple 3D Space Plan with Space Objects, and Creating a Space Evaluation Report

## Creating the 3D Space Plan

1. Use the previous exercise.
2. Change to the **Top View.**
3. Select the **Space** icon from the **Spaces** tool palette.
4. Move your cursor over the **Properties** palette to open it.
5. Set the following:

    a.   Style = **LOBBY**
    b.   Name = **LOBBY**
    c.   Tag = **Aec3_Room_Tag**
    d.   Create type = **Insert**
    e.   Geometry type = **Extrusion**
    f.   Ceiling height = **14′-0″**
    g.   Floor thickness = **4″**
    h.   Ceiling thickness = **2″**
    i.   Height above ceiling = **0″**
    j.   Justification = **Top of floor**
    k.   Specify on screen = **No**
    l.   Constrain = **\*NONE\***
    m.   Length = **15′-0″**
    n.   Width = **15′-0″**

6. Click in the **Drawing Editor** and press **Enter** twice.
7. Place the Room Tag.
8. Again select the **Space** icon from the **Spaces** tool palette.
9. In the **Properties** palette set the following:

    a.   Style = **HALL**
    b.   Name = **HALL**
    c.   Tag = **Aec3_Room_Tag**
    d.   Create type = **Insert**
    e.   Geometry type = **Extrusion**

    f.  Ceiling height = **8′-0″**
    g.  Floor thickness = **4″**
    h.  Ceiling thickness = **0″**
    i.  Height above ceiling = **0″**
    j.  Justification = **Top of floor**
    k.  Specify on screen = **No**
    l.  Constrain = **\*NONE\***

10. Click in the **Drawing Editor** to the right of the **LOBBY** and press **Enter** on the keyboard twice.
11. Enter **C** (Centered) in the **Command line,** and press the **Enter** key on the keyboard to place the Room Tag.
12. Again select the **Space** icon from the **Spaces** tool palette.
13. In the **Properties** palette set the following:

    a.  Style = **OFFICE**
    b.  Name = **OFFICE 1**
    c.  Tag = **Aec3_Room_Tag**
    d.  Create type = **Insert**
    e.  Geometry type = **Extrusion**
    f.  Ceiling height = **9′-0″**
    g.  Floor thickness = **4″**
    h.  Ceiling thickness = **0″**
    i.  Height above ceiling = **0″**
    j.  Justification = **Top of floor**
    k.  Specify on screen = **No**

14. Click in the **Drawing Editor** adjacent to the **HALL** and press **Enter** on the keyboard twice.
15. Place the Room Tag.
16. Repeat Steps 13–15 seven more times.
17. If the offices you placed have a subnumber after the name, select all the offices you placed and change the name in the **Properties** palette to **OFFICE.**
18. Again select the **Space** icon from the **Spaces** tool palette.
19. In the **Properties** palette set the following:

    a.  Style = **MALE TOILET**
    b.  Name = **MENS TOILET**
    c.  Tag = **Aec3_Room_Tag**
    d.  Create type = **Insert**
    e.  Geometry type = **Extrusion**
    f.  Ceiling height = **8′-0″**
    g.  Floor thickness = **4″**
    h.  Ceiling thickness = **0″**
    i.  Height above ceiling = **0″**
    j.  Justification = **Top of floor**
    k.  Specify on screen = **No**

20. Click in the **Drawing Editor** adjacent to the **HALL** and press **Enter** on the keyboard twice.
21. Place the Room Tag.
22. Again select the **Space** icon from the **Spaces** tool palette.
23. In the **Properties** palette set the following:

    a.  Style = **FEMALE TOILET**
    b.  Name = **WOMENS TOILET**
    c.  Tag = **Aec3_Room_Tag**
    d.  Create type = **Insert**
    e.  Geometry type = **Extrusion**
    f.  Ceiling height = **8′-0″**

g.  Floor thickness = **4″**
h.  Ceiling thickness = **0″**
i.  Height above ceiling = **0″**
j.  Justification = **Top of floor**
k.  Specify on screen = **No**

24.  Click in the **Drawing Editor** adjacent to the **HALL** and press **Enter** on the keyboard twice.
25.  Place the Room Tag.
26.  Select the **Lobby** grip shown in Figure 2–3, and drag it downwards.

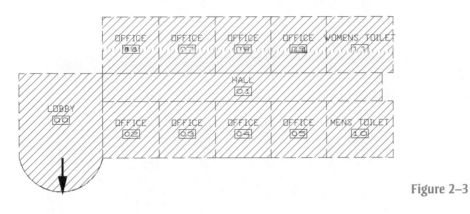

Figure 2–3

27.  Press the **Ctrl** key on the keyboard twice, enter **6′** in the **Command line,** and press the **Enter** key on your keyboard to curve the face of the **LOBBY** Space object. **Save the file** (see Figure 2–4).

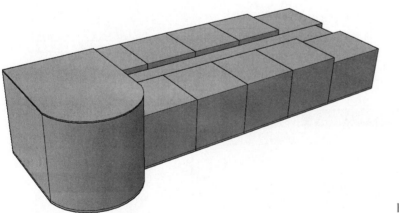

Figure 2–4

## Creating the 3D Space Evaluation Report

28.  Use the previous exercise.
29.  Select the **Space Evaluation** tool from the **Scheduling** tool palette to bring up the **Space Evaluation** dialog box.
30.  In the **Space Evaluation** dialog box, check all the check boxes for the spaces that you wish to report.
31.  Press the **Evaluation Options** button to bring up the **Evaluation Properties** dialog box.
32.  In the **Evaluation Properties** dialog box, check the check boxes shown in Figure 2–5, and press the **OK** button to return to the **Space Evaluation** dialog box.
33.  In the **Space Evaluation** dialog box, press the **Export Evaluation to Text Format** icon to bring up the **Open Template** dialog box (see Figure 2–6).
34.  In the **Open Template** dialog box, select the **Space Evaluation** template, and press the **Open** button.

Figure 2–5

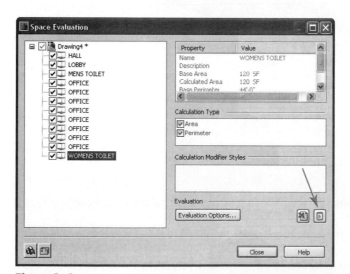

Figure 2–6

35. At the AutoCAD warning, press the **No** button to *not* set this template as the default.
36. Save the file as **TEST EVALUATION** in a convenient location on your computer.
37. Go to the location where you saved the evaluation, and double-click on the file to open it (see Figure 2–7).

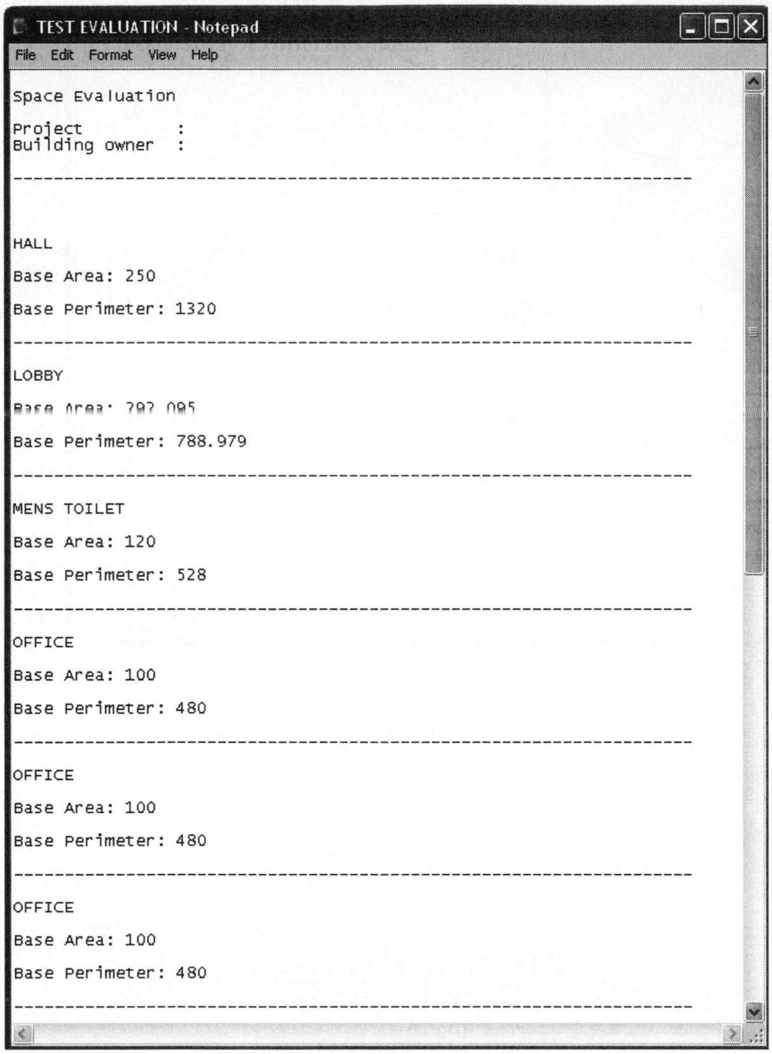

```
 TEST EVALUATION - Notepad                              [_][□][X]
File  Edit  Format  View  Help
Space Evaluation                                              ▲

Project      :
Building owner  :
--------------------------------------------------------------


HALL

Base Area: 250

Base Perimeter: 1320
--------------------------------------------------------------

LOBBY

Base Area: 787.095

Base Perimeter: 788.979
--------------------------------------------------------------

MENS TOILET

Base Area: 120

Base Perimeter: 528
--------------------------------------------------------------

OFFICE

Base Area: 100

Base Perimeter: 480
--------------------------------------------------------------

OFFICE

Base Area: 100

Base Perimeter: 480
--------------------------------------------------------------

OFFICE

Base Area: 100

Base Perimeter: 480
--------------------------------------------------------------     ▼
◄                                                            ►
```

**Figure 2–7**

---

**Exercise 2-3:** Creating a Freeform Space Object; Using the Space/Zone Manager

The Freeform space object differs from the Extrusion space object by the fact that it assumes unusual 3D shapes. These shapes can be created by converting Mass Elements to Spaces, or by creating a totally bounded area comprised of AEC Objects such as walls, slabs, and roofs. Once the Freeform object has been created, it can be evaluated using the Space/Zone Manager.

For this exercise, you will have to understand how to create Roofs and Slabs. You might wait until you have tried those exercises.

### Creating a Freeform Space from Bounding AEC Objects

1. Start a new drawing using the AEC Model (Imperial Stb) template.
2. Change to the **Top View.**
3. Select the **Brick-4 Brick-4** wall from the **Walls** tool palette, and create a **15′ × 15′** enclosure **8′-0″** high.
4. Select the **Slab** tool from the **Design** tool palette and place a **6″** slab as shown in Figure 2–8.
5. Change to the **Top View,** and select the **Roof** tool from the **Design** tool palette.
6. Move your cursor over the **Properties** palette to open it.
7. In the **Properties** palette, set the **Plate height** to **7′-11″**.
8. Return to the **Top** view.

> **Note:**
> The slab must be completely enclosed inside the walls, or extend to the exterior of the walls, for it to be a bounding object.

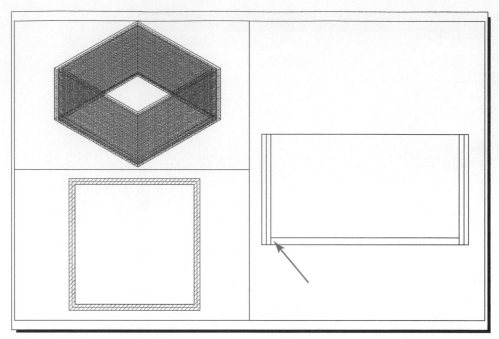

**Figure 2–8**

9. Select the **Space Auto Generate Tool** from the **Design** tool palette to bring up the **Generate Spaces** dialog box.
10. In the **Generate Spaces** dialog box, change the **Type** to **Freeform**.
11. Select the **Tag Settings** button to open the **Tag Settings** dialog box.
12. In the **Tag Settings** dialog box, uncheck all the check boxes, and press the **OK** button to return to the **Generate Spaces** dialog box.
13. Enter **A** (generate All) in the **Command line,** and press the **Enter** key on the keyboard to create the **Freeform Space object.**
14. Press the **Close** button on the **Generate Spaces** dialog box.
15. Select the **Freeform Space object** you just created, **RMB,** and select **Isolate Objects > Isolate Objects** from the contextual menu that appears to hide everything but the Space object.

> **Note:**
> Setting the **Plate height** to 7"-11" closes the bounding. Any dimension less than the plate height of the wall will work (see Figure 2–9).

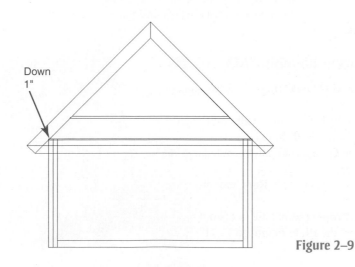

Down 1"

**Figure 2–9**

16. Change to the **SW Isometric** view.
17. Select the Space object, and change its color to **White** by selecting the color from the **Properties** tool bar (see Figure 2–10).
18. Select the Space object, **RMB**, and select **Space/Zone Manager** from the contextual menu that appears to bring up the **Space/Zone Manager.**
19. In the **Space/Zone Manager,** check only the **Show Space Surfaces** check box.

**Note:**
This author changes the Space object to White because the surface indicators in the Space/Zone Manager are a red color similar to that of the Space object. This author is red-green color blind, and cannot see the surface indicators unless the Space object is a different color.

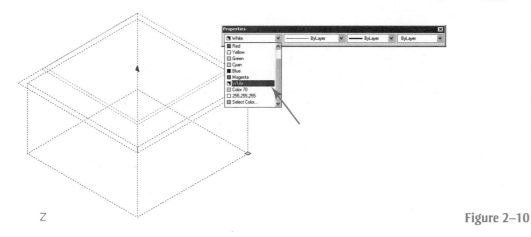

Figure 2–10

20. Notice as you select a **Surface** in the **Space/Zone Manager,** that surface will be indicated in red outline, and the area will be indicated in the **Space/Zone Manager** (see Figure 2–11).

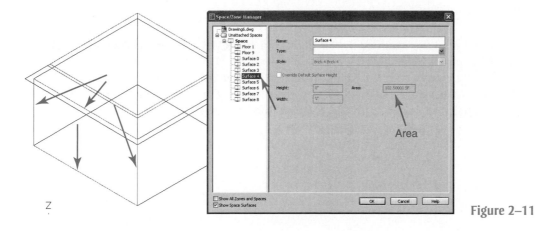

Figure 2–11

**Exercise 2-4:** Converting Mass Elements to Freeform Space Objects; Using the Space/Zone Manager

Converting is very powerful in AutoCAD Architecture 2008. You can convert from 3D Solid models to Mass objects, and then to Space objects. This then gives the designer the ability, through the Space/Zone Manager, to evaluate surface areas of unusual spaces.

1. Start a new drawing using the AEC Model (Imperial Stb) template.
2. Change to the **Top View.**
3. Select the **Box** tool from the **Massing** tool palette, and move your cursor over the **Properties** palette to open it.

4. In the **Properties** palette, set the **Shape** to **Free Form, Specify on screen** to **No,** and **Width**, **Depth**, and **Height** to **40′-0″.**

5. Click in the **Drawing Editor** to place the **Free Form**, and press the **Enter** key on your keyboard twice to finish the command.

6. Select the **Free Form,** and select the round grip on the top surface to activate the edge grips.

7. Grab the edge grip, and drag it and click as shown in Figure 2–12.

8. Select the **Free Form**, **RMB,** and select **Edit in Place** from the contextual menu that appears.

9. While in **Edit in Place** mode, you can convert it to a 3D Solid, and then press the **Save All Changes** icon (see Figure 2–13).

10. While you are in **3D Solid** mode, you can modify the space object.

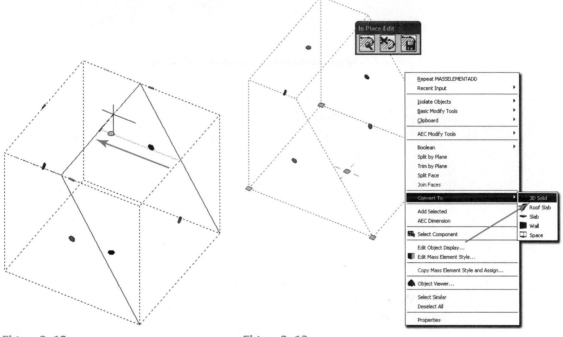

Figure 2–12                    Figure 2–13

11. Once you have modified the **3D Solid,** you can **RMB** and convert the object back to a Mass object (see Figure 2–14).

12. Finally, convert it from a **Mass Element** to a **Space** object.

13. Select the **Space** object, **RMB,** and select **Space/Zone Manager** from the conceptual menu that appears to bring up the **Space/Zone Manager** dialog box.

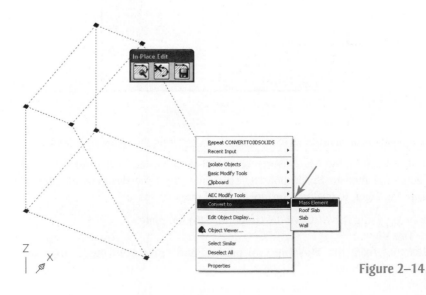

Figure 2–14

14. In the **Space/Zone Manager** dialog box, expand the **Space** tree.
15. As you select each surface in the **Space/Zone Manager** dialog box, its surface is high-lighted in the **Space** object, and its area appears in the dialog box (see Figure 2–15).

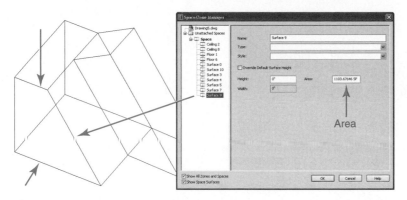

Area

Figure 2–15

**Exercise 2-5:** Using the Space Generate Tool

1. Start a new drawing using the Architectural Building Model and View (Imperial - ctb) template.
2. Change to the **Model Layout.**
3. Change to the **Top View.**
5. Using lines, polylines, and a circle, create the 2D drawing shown in Figure 2–16.
6. Select the **Space Generate** tool from the **Design** tool palette, and move your cursor over the **Properties** palette to open it.
7. In the **Properties** palette, select the **Aec7_Room_Tag** from the **Tag** drop-down list, and **Generate** from the **Create type** drop-down list (see Figure 2–17).

**Note:**
The **Space Generate** tool was called the **Space Auto Generate** tool in previous Architectural Desktop versions.

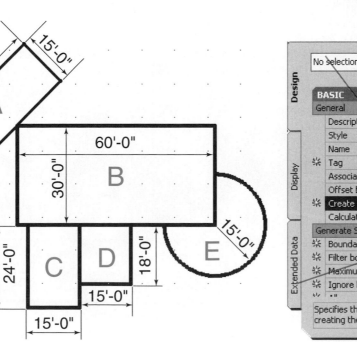

Figure 2–16

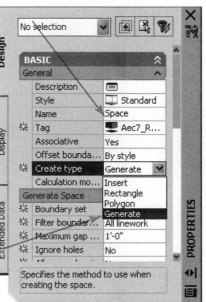

Figure 2–17

8. Click inside rectangle **A** that you have drawn to create a space object with tag.
9. Enter **G** (Generate All) in the **Command line,** and press the **Enter** key on your keyboard. The remaining rectangles will create tagged spaces (see Figure 2–18).

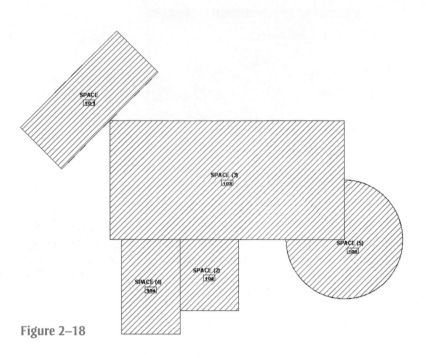

**Figure 2–18**

10. Select each space you have created (not the tag), and move your cursor over the **Properties** palette to open it.
11. In the **Properties** palette, change the name in the **Name** field to a unique name (the author used **ANNEX**).
12. In the **Properties** palette, change the height above the ceiling for each space (make it a different height) (see Figures 2–19 and 2–20).

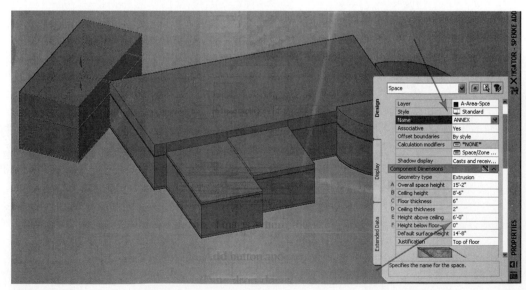

**Figure 2–19**

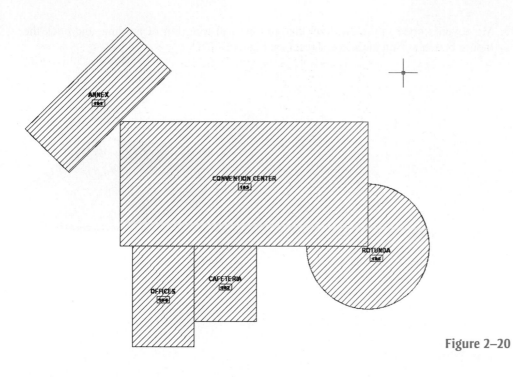

Figure 2–20

## Exercise 2-6: Using the AEC MODIFY Tool to Modify Spaces

### Using the Trim Option

1. Start a new drawing using the AEC Model (Imperial Stb) template.
2. Change to the **Model Layout.**
3. Change to the **Top View.**
4. Select the **Space** object icon from the **Design** tool palette, and place a 10′ × 10′ Standard-style space object in the Drawing Editor.
5. Select the space object you just placed to activate its grips.
6. Drag the space object to 30′ × 30′, and press the **Esc** key to deselect the grips.
7. **RMB** in the **Drawing Editor** and select **AEC Modify Tools** > **Trim** from the contextual menu that appears (see Figure 2–21).
8. Select the space object and press **Enter.**
9. Select a point to the left of the space object, drag your cursor as shown in Figure 2–22, and click your mouse button. This creates your **Trim** line.

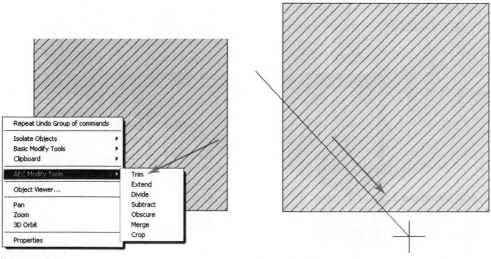

Figure 2–21                              Figure 2–22

10. Move your cursor in the direction that you wish to trim, left of the line, and click the mouse button to trim the space object (see Figure 2–23).

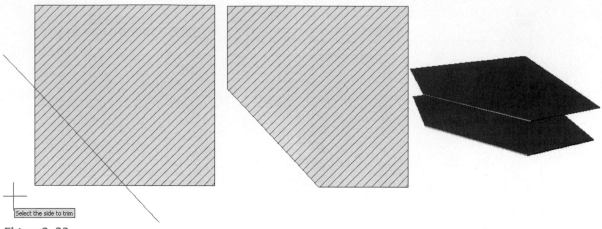

Select the side to trim

**Figure 2–23**

## Using the Divide Option

11. With the space object *not selected,* **RMB** in the **Drawing Editor** and select **AEC Modify Tools > Divide** from the contextual menu that appears.
12. Select the space object and then press **Enter.**
13. Select two points in a similar manner as in the **Trim** exercise.
14. Move one division to the right (see Figure 2–24).

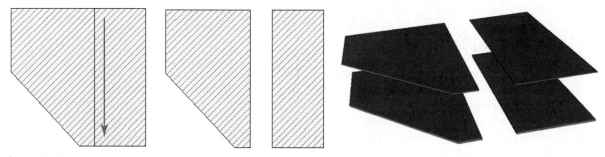

**Figure 2–24**

## Using the Subtract Option

15. From the **Draw** toolbar, place two rectangles and a circle as shown in Figure 2–25.

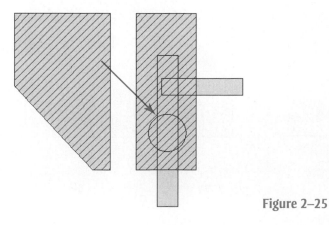

**Figure 2–25**

16. With the space object *not selected,* **RMB** in the **Drawing Editor** and select **AEC Modify Tools > Subtract** from the contextual menu that appears.
17. Select the right object division and press **Enter.**
18. Select the rectangles and the circle and then press **Enter.**
19. Enter **Y** (Yes) in the **Command line** and press **Enter** (see Figure 2–26).

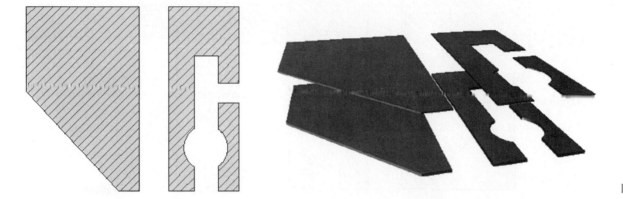

Figure 2–26

## Using the Merge Option

20. From the **Draw** toolbar, place two rectangles and a circle as shown in Figure 2–27.
21. With the space object *not selected,* **RMB** in the **Drawing Editor** and select **AEC Modify Tools > Merge** from the contextual menu that appears.
22. Select the right object division and press **Enter.**

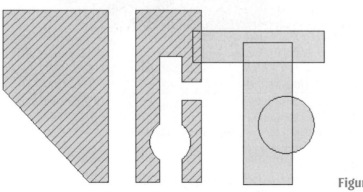

Figure 2–27

23. Select the rectangles and the circle and then press **Enter.**
24. Enter **Y** (Yes) in the **Command line** and press **Enter** (see Figure 2–28).

Figure 2–28

## Using the Crop Option

25. From the **Draw** toolbar, place a rectangle and circle as shown in Figure 2–29.
26. With the space object *not selected,* **RMB** in the **Drawing Editor** and select **AEC Modify Tools > Crop** from the contextual menu that appears.

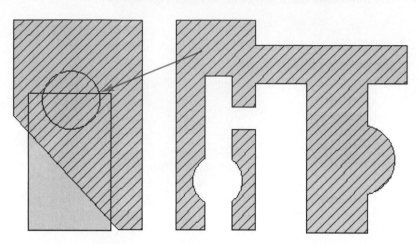

Figure 2–29

27. Select the space object division and press **Enter.**
28. Select the rectangle and the circle and then press **Enter.**
29. Enter **Y** (Yes) in the **Command line** and press **Enter** (see Figure 2–30).

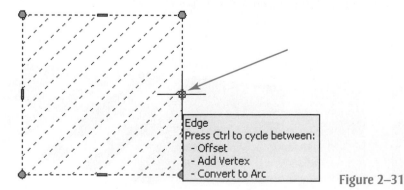

Figure 2–30

**Exercise 2-7:** Using the Space Object Grip Features

## Adding and Removing a Vertex

1. Start a new drawing using the AEC Model (Imperial Stb) template.
2. Change to the **Model Layout.**
3. Change to the **Top View.**
4. Select the **Space** object icon from the **Design** tool palette, and place a 10′ × 10′ Standard-style space object in the Drawing Editor.
5. Select the space object to activate its grips.
6. Move your cursor over the right **Edge** grip to show the grip's "tool tip" (see Figure 2–31).

Figure 2–31

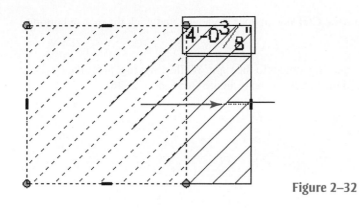

Figure 2–32

7. Select the right **Edge** grip, and drag to the right (see Figure 2–32).
8. While dragging, press the **Ctrl** key on your keyboard to place the grips in **Add vertex** mode (see Figures 2–33 and 2–34).
9. Move your cursor over the new vertex to show the vertex's tool tip (see Figure 2–35).

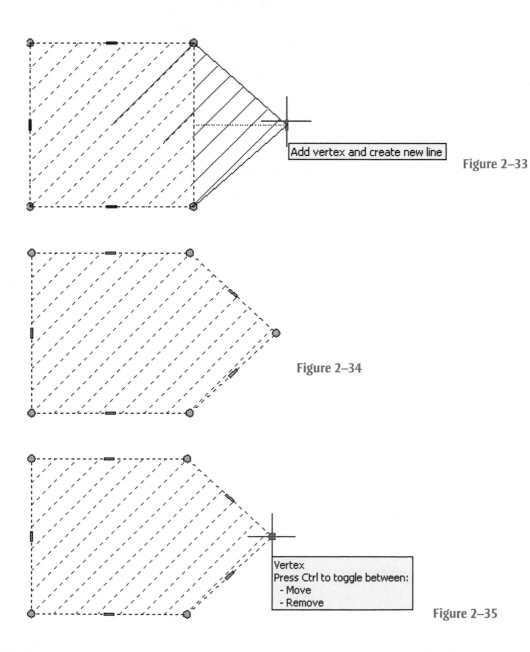

Add vertex and create new line

Figure 2–33

Figure 2–34

Vertex
Press Ctrl to toggle between:
- Move
- Remove

Figure 2–35

10. Select the new vertex, press the **Ctrl** key on your keyboard, and click the mouse button to remove or move the vertex.
11. Remove the vertex.
12. Click the right **Edge** grip again and drag it to the right. While dragging, press the **Ctrl** key on your keyboard twice and then click to create an arc (see Figure 2–36).

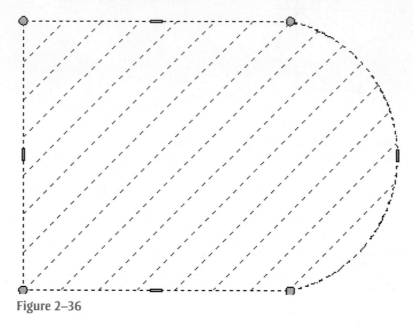

**Figure 2–36**

# Walls

# 3

## *Section* Objectives

- Learn how to place a wall object.
- Learn how to change walls by dynamically pulling on grips.
- Know how to create **wall sweeps.**
- Know how to create wall endcaps using **Calculate Automatically.**
- Use **plan modifiers.**
- Use **body modifiers.**
- Use the **Roof/Floor** line option.
- Use **interference conditions.**
- Know how to use **Cleanups—Applying 'T' Cleanup** and **Wall Merge.**
- Learn how to edit wall styles.

Wall objects can be dragged or inserted either from the **Design** tool palette, or by typing **walladd** in the **Command line.**

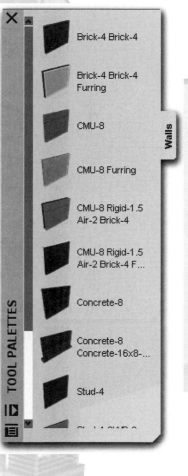

## WALLS

Wall objects are the basis of all buildings; they enclose space and give the building its character. Because buildings require a vast variety of wall types and configurations, these objects have become very sophisticated in AutoCAD Architecture 2008.

In order to understand how to use AutoCAD Architecture 2008's wall objects, we must first understand some basic AutoCAD Architecture 2008 wall object conventions. Among these conventions are **Base Height, Baseline, Roofline Offset from Base Height, Floor Line Offset from Baseline,** and **Justification** (see Figure 3–1).

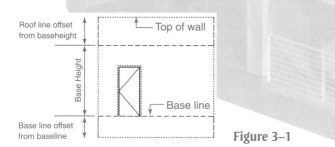

Figure 3–1

## Wall Objects Properties Tool Palette

AutoCAD Architecture 2008 contains controls and routines for modifying the shape of the wall itself. These include **Wall Sweeps, Wall Endcaps and Opening Endcaps, Plan Modifiers, Body Modifiers, Modifications to the Roof/Floor lines,** and **Interference Conditions.**

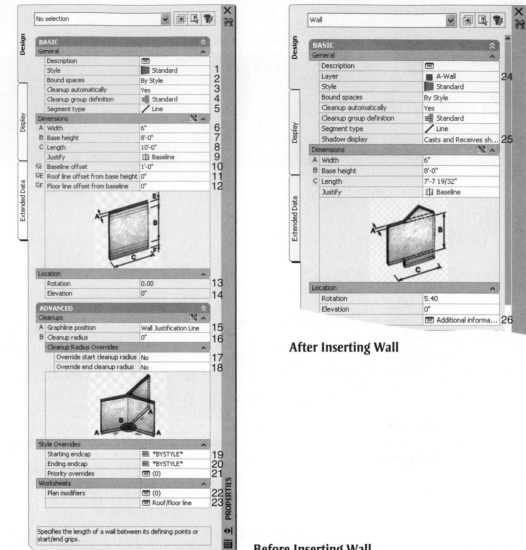

**After Inserting Wall**

**Before Inserting Wall**

| Number | Name | Purpose |
|--------|------|---------|
| 1 | Style | Change this to change to another style such as 12″ brick and block, etc. |
| 2 | Bound spaces | By Style, Yes, No for bounding Associative spaces |
| 3 | Cleanup automatically | Change to Yes or No if you want the wall to join with similar components of intersecting walls |
| 4 | Cleanup group definition | Change to Style allowing Wall Cleanup between host and xref drawings and/or allowing objects anchored to walls in other cleanup groups to be moved or copied to walls in this cleanup group |
| 5 | Segment type | Change to either Line or Arc to create linear or curved walls |
| 6 | Width | Set the width for nonpreset walls |
| 7 | Base Height | Set a new base height |

| Number | Name | Purpose |
|--------|------|---------|
| 8 | Length | Set a new wall length |
| 9 | Justify | Change whether the wall is placed and references from the left, center, right, or baseline of the wall |
| 10 | Baseline offset | Wall offset from baseline in plan |
| 11 | Roof line offset from | Offset down from base height |
| 12 | Floor line offset from baseline | Offset from floor—good for elevated walls |
| 13 | Rotation | Rotation angle for the wall |
| 14 | Elevation | Elevation of the baseline of the wall |
| 15 | Graphline position | Specifies the graphline position—either at Justification line or center line of wall |
| 16 | Cleanup radius | Specifies the radial distance from a wall endpoint within which other walls will be connected |
| 17 | Override start cleanup | Overrides the cleanup radius at a wall start point (No or Yes). Yes will bring up radius field. |
| 18 | Override end cleanup | Overrides the cleanup radius at a wall end point (No or Yes). Yes will bring up radius field. |
| 19 | Starting endcap | Drop-down list for wall start endcap profile |
| 20 | Ending endcap | Drop-down list for wall end endcap profile |
| 21 | Priority overrides | Displays the wall component priority override dialog box |
| 22 | Plan modifiers | Displays the wall Plan modifier dialog box, which controls the location of plan modifiers |
| 23 | Roof/floor line | Displays the Roof/Floor line dialog box, which allows for wall vertex editing |
| 24 | Layer | Change this to place the wall on another layer |
| 25 | Shadow display | Casts and Receives, Casts shadows, Receives shadows, Ignore shadows |
| 26 | Additional information | Launches the Additional Information Worksheet with more wall location information |

## Exercise 3-1: Placing a Wall Object

1. Start a new drawing using the AEC Model (Imperial Stb) template.
2. Change to the **Model Layout.**
3. Change to the **Top View.**
4. Select the **Wall** icon from the **Design** tool palette and drag your cursor over the **Properties** palette to open the palette.

Here you will find all the size parameters that you can change upon insertion of a wall.

**Note:**
The blue asterisks are called "Add" icons, and they represent properties that are available only when adding an object.

5. Set the following in the **Properties** palette:

   a. Style = **Standard**
   b. Width = **6″**
   c. Base Height = **8′-0″**
   d. Justify = **Left**
   e. Roof line offset from base height = **4′-0″**
   f. Floor line offset from base line = **-3′-0″**

6. Click in the drawing area and drag a 10′-0″-long wall, and click a second time to complete the command.
7. Change to the **SW Isometric View** (see Figure 3–2).

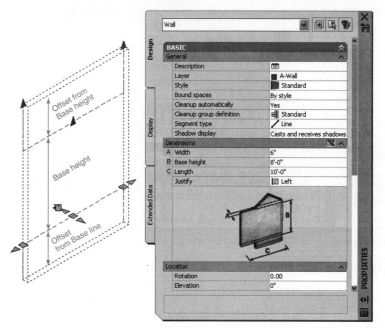

Figure 3–2

---

**Exercise 3-2:** Changing Walls by Dynamically Pulling on Grips

Example: Dynamically changing the roof offset

1. Select the wall to activate its grips.
2. Move your cursor over the leftmost top grip, and notice the tool tip.
3. Select the grip and move your cursor upward.
4. Tab to change the magenta-colored dimension selection.
5. Enter **8′-0″** for the overall dimension of the roof offset, and press the **Enter** key to complete the command (see Figure 3–3).

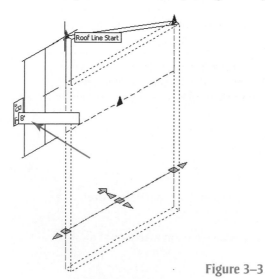

Figure 3–3

## Exercise 3-3: Creating Wall Sweeps

1. Create a new drawing, and change to the **Top View.**
2. Select the **CMU-8 Furring** icon from the **Walls** tool palette, and drag your cursor over the **Properties** palette to open the palette.
3. Place a new wall with the following properties:

    a. Style = **CMU-8 Furring**
    b. Width = **9-1/2"**
    c. Base Height = **10'-0"**
    d. Justify = **Left**
    e. Roof line offset from base height = **0**
    f. Floor line offset from base line = **0**

4. Change to the **NW Isometric View.**
5. Select the wall, **RMB,** and select **Sweeps > Add** from the contextual menu that appears to bring up the **Add Wall Sweep** dialog box.
6. In the **Add Wall Sweep** dialog box enter the following:

    a. Wall Component = **CMU**
    b. Profile Definition = **Start from scratch**
    c. New Profile Name = **TEST SWEEP PROFILE**

7. Press the **OK** button. Select a location on the wall for editing, and a blue field with grips will appear (see Figure 3–4).
8. Grab the lower grip of the blue field, drag it in the direction of 180 degrees, enter **2'-0"** in the **Command line,** and press **Enter** (see Figure 3–5).
9. Select the **Rectangle** icon from the **Draw** menu and place a rectangle as shown in Figure 3–6.

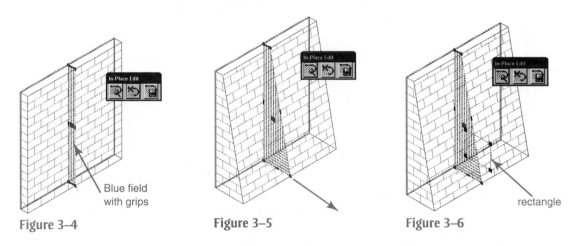

Figure 3–4                    Figure 3–5                    Figure 3–6

10. Select the blue field, **RMB,** and select **Add Ring** from the contextual menu that appears.
11. Select the rectangle, enter **Y** (Yes) in the **Command line,** and press **Enter.**
12. Accept **Join** in the **Command line** and press **Enter.**
13. Press the **Save All Changes** icon in the **In-Place Edit** dialog box to complete the command and create the new wall sweep (see Figure 3–7).
14. Select the wall again, **RMB,** and select **Sweeps > Edit Profile In Place** from the contextual menu that appears.
15. Select a place on the wall to bring up the blue **Edit Profile In Place** field.
16. Select the edge grip of the **Edit Profile In Place** field as shown in Figure 3–8.
17. Drag the grip to the right, and press the **Ctrl** key on your keyboard twice to convert the edge to an arc.
18. Click the mouse button to complete the command.
19. **RMB** on the blue **Edit Profile In Place** field, and select **Save As New Profile** from the contextual menu that appears to bring up the **New Profile** dialog box.
20. Enter a new name for the new wall sweep profile, and press the **OK** button.

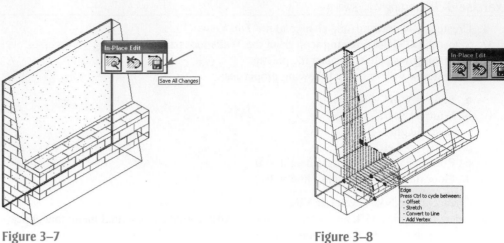

**Figure 3–7**                                                **Figure 3–8**

You have now created a new wall sweep (see Figure 3–9).

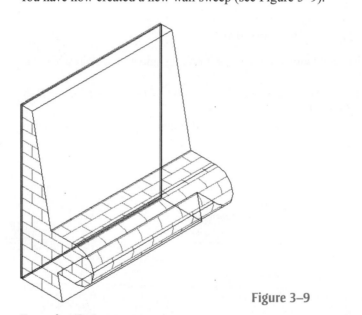

**Figure 3–9**

**Exercise 3-4:** Creating Wall Endcaps Using Calculate Automatically

1. Create a new drawing.
2. Change to the **Top View.**
3. Select the **CMU-8 Rigid-1.5 Air-2 brick 4 Furring 2** icon from the **Walls** tool palette and drag your cursor over the **Properties** palette to open the palette.
4. Place a new wall with the following properties:

    a. Style = **CMU-8 Rigid-1.5 Air-2 brick 4 Furring 2**
    b. Width = **1′-5″**
    c. Base Height = **10′-0″**
    d. Justify = **Left**
    e. Roof line offset from base height = **0**
    f. Floor line offset from base line = **0**

5. Zoom close to the left end of the wall (see Figure 3–10).

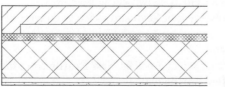

**Figure 3–10**

This will allow you to draw a new wall endcap on top of the existing wall.

6. Select **Format** > **Style Manager** from the **Main** menu to bring up the **Style Manager.**
7. In the **Style Manager,** left panel, expand the **Architectural Objects** folder.
8. In the **Architectural Objects** folder, expand the **Wall Endcap Styles.**
9. Click on the **CMU-8 Rigid-1.5 Air-2 brick 4 Furring 2** style to open it.

This endcap style will be in your **Style Manager** because you placed a CMU-8 Rigid-1.5 Air-2 brick 4 Furring 2 wall that uses this endcap style. For your own information, compare the endcap style in the **Style Manager** with the end of the wall you placed (see Figure 3–11); then close the **Style Manager** dialog box.

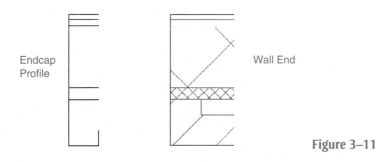

Endcap
Profile

Wall End

Figure 3–11

10. Select the **Polyline** icon from the **Draw** menu, and trace in a counterclockwise direction a new polyline for the end of each component in the wall.

This author has moved the wall away and moved each polyline to illustrate how they were created (see Figure 3–12).

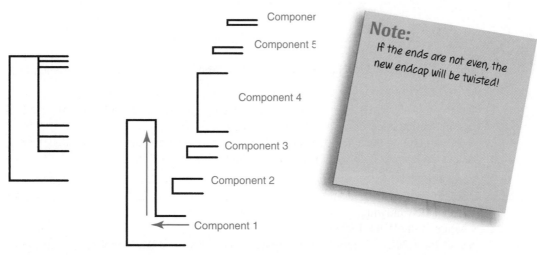

Componer

Component 5

Component 4

Component 3

Component 2

Component 1

**Note:**
If the ends are not even, the new endcap will be twisted!

Figure 3–12

11. Place a line that crosses all your new polylines as shown in Figure 3–13, and trim all ends of the polylines so that they are even.
12. Erase the trim line.
13. Move the original wall near the new polylines (see Figure 3–14).
14. Select the wall, **RMB,** and select **End Caps** > **Calculate Automatically** from the contextual menu that appears.
15. Select all your new polylines with a window crossing and press **Enter.**
16. Enter **Y** (Yes) in the **Command line** to erase the polylines and press **Enter.**
17. In response to **Modify Current Endcap Style,** enter **N** (No) in the **Command line** and press **Enter.**

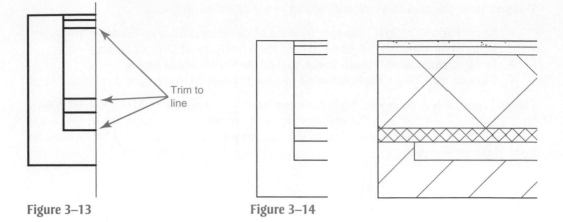

**Figure 3–13**                                    **Figure 3–14**

18. In response to **Apply the new wall endcap style to this end as,** enter **O** (Override) in the **Command line** and press **Enter** to bring up the **New Endcap Style** dialog box.
19. In the **New Endcap Style** dialog box, enter **ENDCAP TEST** and press the **OK** button.

Your wall will now have your new endcap, and the new endcap style will appear in the **Style Manager** (see Figure 3–15).

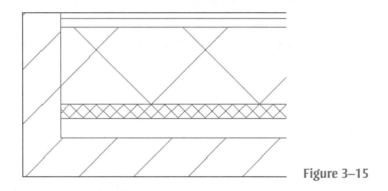

**Figure 3–15**

To change your endcap back to the original or to place your new endcap on the other end of the wall, do the following:

20. Select the wall, **RMB**, and select **Endcaps** > **Override Endcap Style** from the contextual menu that appears.
21. Select a point on the end of the wall to bring up the **Select an Endcap Style** dialog box.
22. Select the endcap style you wish to replace and press the **OK** button.

## Exercise 3-5: Using Plan Modifiers

1. Create a new drawing.
2. Change to the **Work Layout.**
3. Select the **CMU-8 Rigid-1.5 Air-2 brick 4** icon from the **Walls** tool palette, and drag your cursor over the **Properties** palette to open the palette.
4. Place a new 10′-long wall in the **Top View** with the following properties:

   a. Style = **CMU-8 Furring**
   b. Width = **1′-3-1/2″**
   c. Base Height = **10′-0″**
   d. Justify = **Left**
   e. Roof line offset from base height = **0**
   f. Floor line offset from base line = **0**

5. Place an open polyline as shown in Figure 3–16.
6. Select the wall, **RMB,** and select **Plan Modifiers** > **Convert Polyline to Wall Modifier** from the contextual menu that appears.

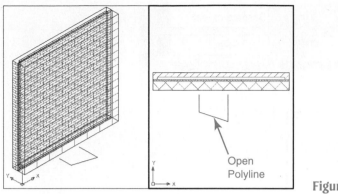

Figure 3–16

7. Select the polyline, enter **Y** (Yes) in the **Command line**, and enter **TEST WALL MODI-FIER** in the **New Wall Modifier Style Name** dialog box that appears.
8. The **Add Wall Modifier** dialog box now appears. Press the **OK** button to end the command and add the wall modifier (see Figure 3–17).

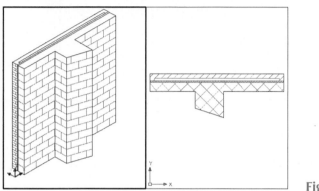

Figure 3–17

9. To modify the modifier, double-click the wall to bring up the **Properties** palette.
10. Scroll down to the bottom of the **Properties** palette, and click on **Plan Modifiers** to bring up the **Wall Modifiers** dialog box (see Figure 3–18).

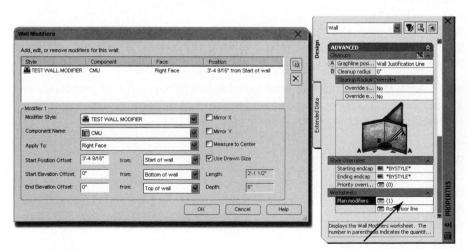

Figure 3–18

11. Place the dimensions shown in Figure 3–19.
12. Press **OK** and see the result (see Figure 3–20).

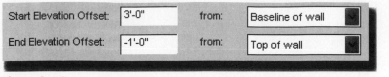

| | | | |
|---|---|---|---|
| Start Elevation Offset: | 3'-0" | from: | Baseline of wall |
| End Elevation Offset: | -1'-0" | from: | Top of wall |

**Figure 3–19**

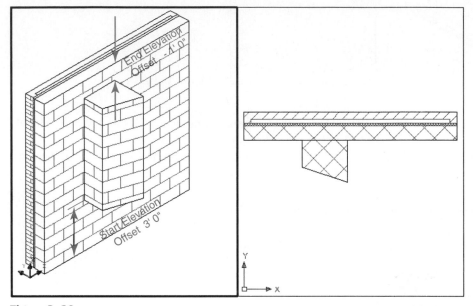

**Figure 3–20**

**Exercise 3-6:** Using Body Modifiers

1. Clear the previous exercise.
2. Change to the **Work Layout.**
3. Select the **Wall** icon from the **Design** tool palette, and drag your cursor over the **Properties** palette to open the palette.
4. Place a new 10′-long wall in the **Top View** with the following properties:

   a. Style = **Standard**
   b. Width = **12**
   c. Base Height = **10′-0″**
   d. Justify = **Left**
   e. Roof line offset from base height = **0**
   f. Floor line offset from base line = **0**

5. Select the **Arch Massing** object from the **Massing** tool palette, and drag your cursor over the **Properties** palette to open the palette.
6. Place the **Massing** object with the following properties:

   a. Style = **Standard**
   b. Width = **5′-6″**
   c. Depth = **3′-0″**
   d. Height = **3′-0″**
   e. Radius = **2′-0″**
   f. Elevation = **2′-0″**

7. Place it as shown in Figure 3–21.
8. Select the wall, **RMB,** and select **Body Modifiers > Add** from the contextual menu that appears.
9. Select the massing object and press **Enter** to bring up the **Add Body Modifier** dialog box.
10. Select **Subtractive** from the **Operation** drop-down list, and check the **Erase Selected Object(s)** check box (see Figure 3–22).

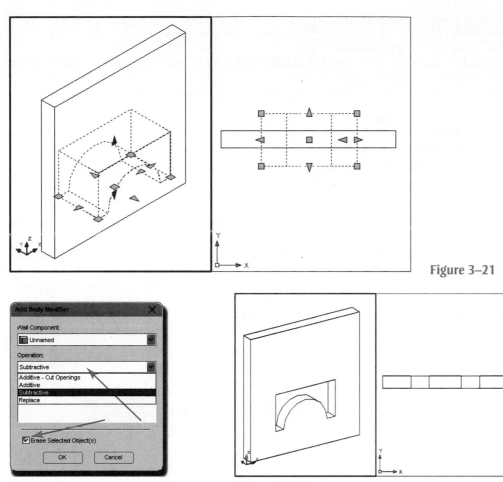

Figure 3–21

Figure 3–22

Figure 3–23

11. Finally, press the **OK** button to complete the command and add the body modifier (see Figure 3–23).

If you now wish to change the component you added or adjust the **Operation,** do the following:

12. Double-click the wall to activate the **Properties** palette.
13. Click on the **Body modifiers** field under **Worksheets** near the bottom of the palette to open the **Body Modifiers** worksheet.
14. In the **Body Modifiers** worksheet, select a new **Operation** or **Component** from the **Component** or **Operation** drop-down list (see Figure 3–24).

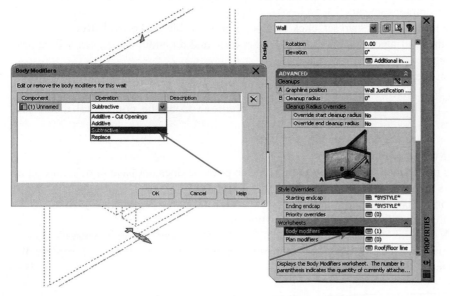

Figure 3–24

**Exercise 3-7:** Using Roof/Floor Line Option

1. Clear the previous exercise.
2. Select the **Wall** icon from the **Design** tool palette, and drag your cursor over the **Properties** palette to open the palette.
3. Place a new 10'-long wall in the **Top View** with the following properties:

   a. Style = **Standard**
   b. Width = **6**
   c. Base Height = **10'-0"**
   d. Justify = **Left**
   e. Roof line offset from base height = **0**
   f. Floor line offset from base line = **0**

4. Select the **NE Isometric** icon from the **Views** toolbar to change to the **NE Isometric** view.
5. Select the wall, **RMB**, and select **Roof/Floor Line > Edit in Place** from the contextual menu that appears to apply a blue editing field on the wall (see Figure 3–25).
6. Select the blue field, **RMB,** and select **Add Gable** from the contextual menu that appears.
7. Select the roof line—the wall adds a gable (see Figure 3–26).
8. Select the wall so the blue field reappears, **RMB,** and select **Add Step** from the contextual menu that appears. The wall adds a step (see Figure 3–27).

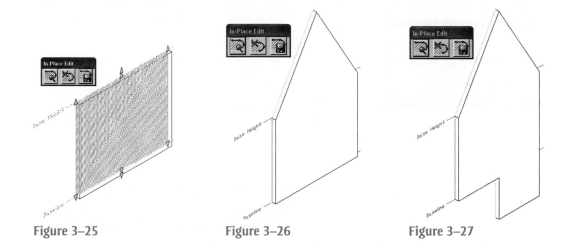

Figure 3–25                    Figure 3–26                    Figure 3–27

9. Select the wall so the blue field reappears, **RMB,** and select **Add Vertex** from the contextual menu that appears.
10. With the near Object Snap set, click on a point on the gable, and press **Enter.**
11. Select the wall again so the blue field reappears, and an additional vertex will appear where you clicked.
12. Drag on the vertex to change the wall and click to change the shape of the wall (see Figure 3–28).
13. Select the blue field, **RMB,** and select **Remove** from the contextual menu that appears.
14. Click on the gable to remove it.
15. Change to the **Front View.**
16. Place a polyline as shown in Figure 3–29. The polyline does not have to be on the same plane as the wall, only parallel to the plane of the wall.
17. **RMB** on the blue field and select **Project to Polyline** from the contextual menu.
18. Select the top of the wall, then select the polyline.
19. Enter **N** (No) in the **Command line,** and press the **Enter** key on your keyboard.
20. Press the **Save All Changes** icon in the **In-Place Edit** toolbar to complete the command.

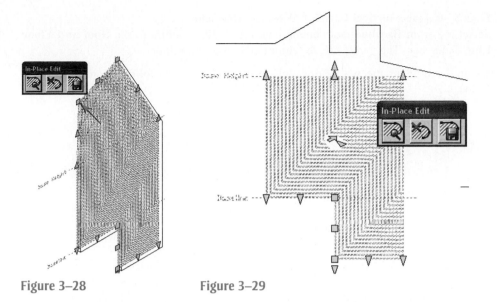

Figure 3–28                    Figure 3–29

21. Change to the **SW Isometric View,** and press the **Hidden** icon in the **Shading** toolbar (see Figure 3–30).
22. Double-click the wall you just edited to bring up its **Properties** palette.
23. Scroll down to the last field on the palette called **Roof/floor line.**
24. Click on the **Roof/floor line** field to bring up the **Roof and Floor Line** dialog box (see Figure 3–31).

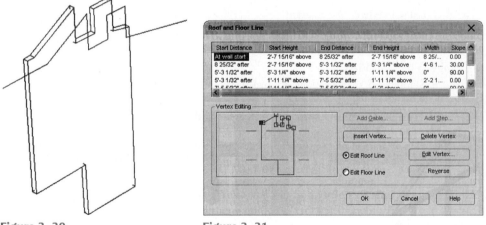

Figure 3–30                    Figure 3–31

25. Select the **Edit Floor Line** radio button, and select the vertex shown in Figure 3–32.
26. In the **Roof and Floor Line** dialog box, press the **Edit Vertex** button to bring up the **Wall Roof/Floor Line Vertex** dialog box (see Figure 3–33).

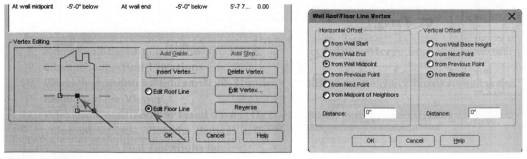

Figure 3–32                    Figure 3–33

27. Enter **3′-0″** in the **Vertical Offset > Distance** data field.
28. Select the **from Baseline** radio button, and press **OK** to return to the **Roof and Floor Line** dialog box. Then press **OK** to return to the Drawing Editor.

You have now modified the wall floor line through the Roof/Floor dialog boxes (see Figure 3–34).

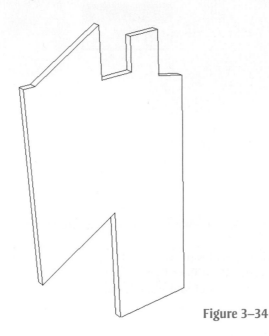

Figure 3–34

**Exercise 3-8:** Using Interference Condition

1. Start a new drawing using the AEC Model (Imperial Stb) template.
2. Change to the **Model Layout.**
3. Change to the **Top View.**
4. Place a Standard 6″-wide, 10′-0″-high, 10′-0″-long wall. Baseline = 0, roofline = 0, floorline = 0
5. From the **Design** tool palette, select the **Stair** icon and place a Standard, Straight 3′-0″-wide stair with a height of 10′-0″ (see Figure 3–35).

If you don't understand how to place stairs, see Section 8, Stairs, for exercises on placing and modifying stair objects.

6. Select the wall, **RMB,** and select **Interference Condition > Add** from the contextual menu that appears.

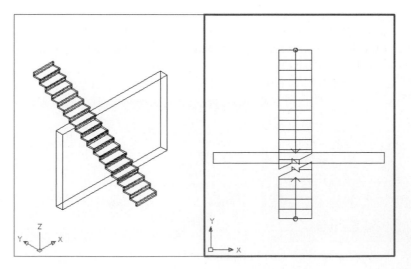

Figure 3–35

7. Select the stair you placed and press **Enter.**
8. Enter **S** (Subtractive) in the **Command line** and press **Enter.**

The interference area located above the stair and set in the stair **Properties** palette is removed from the wall (see Figure 3–36).

9. Double-click the stair to bring up its **Properties** palette.
10. Scroll down to **Interference > Headroom height.**
11. Change the headroom height to **4′**, and notice the change in the interference condition in the wall (see Figure 3–37).

Wall interference conditions will work in concert with any intelligent AutoCAD Architecture AEC Object.

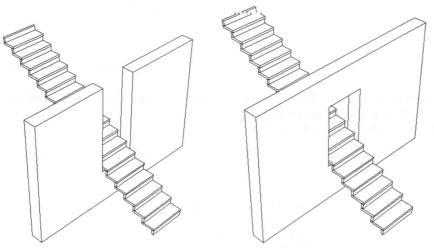

Figure 3–36                          Figure 3–37

---

**Exercise 3-9:** Cleanups—Apply 'T' Cleanup, and Wall Merge

1. Start a new drawing using the AEC Model (Imperial - Stb) template.
2. Change to the **Model Layout.**
3. Change to the **Top View.**
4. Place a Standard 6″-wide, 10′-0″-high, 10′-0″-long wall.
5. Select the walls, **RMB,** and select **Add Selected** from the contextual menu that appears.
6. Place another wall perpendicular to the first as shown in Figure 3–38.
7. Select the vertical wall segment, **RMB,** and select **Cleanups > Apply 'T' Cleanup** from the contextual menu that appears.
8. Select the horizontal wall to create the 'T' cleanup (see Figure 3–39).

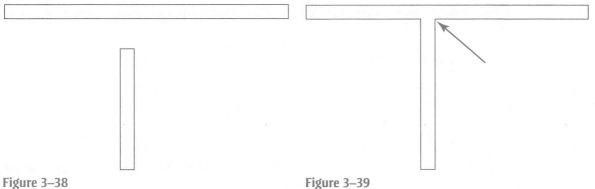

Figure 3–38                          Figure 3–39

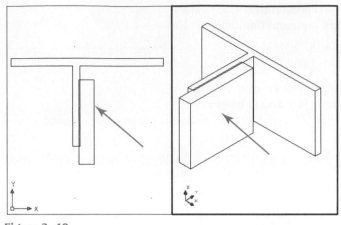

**Figure 3–40**

9. Add another vertical wall adjacent to the vertical wall; make the adjacent wall 24″ and overlapping it (see Figure 3–40).
10. Select the new wall segment, **RMB,** and select **Cleanups** > **Add Wall Merge Condition** from the contextual menu that appears.
11. Select the first walls and press **Enter.**

The wall is now merged into one wall, but the new segment can still be adjusted and moved separately (see Figure 3–41).

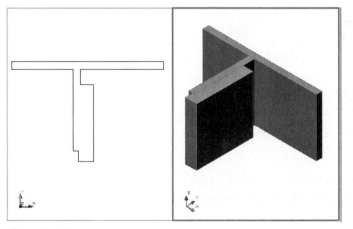

**Figure 3–41**

---

**Exercise 3-10:** Editing Wall Styles

---

## Base Height, Baseline, Edge, and Floor Line Concepts (see Figure 3–42)

In this exercise, you learn how to create a wall and foundation using the components shown in Figure 3–43.

### Creating the Wall Style

1. Start a new drawing using the AEC Model (Imperial Stb) template.
2. Change to the **Model Layout.**
3. Change to the **Top View.**
4. Select the **Wall** tool from the **Design** toolbar, and place a standard wall 8′ high and 10′ long.
5. Select the wall you just placed, **RMB,** and select **Copy Wall Style and Assign** from the contextual menu that appears.

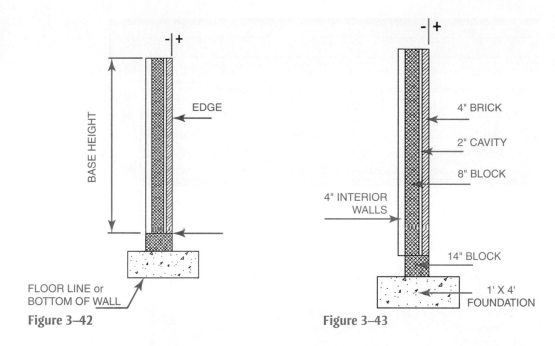

Figure 3–42                          Figure 3–43

This will create a copy of the wall style with the name Standard [2], and open its **Wall Style Properties** dialog box.

    6. In the **Wall Style Properties** dialog box, select the **General** tab.
    7. In the **General** tab, in the **Name** field, change the name to **TESTWALL.**
    8. Change to the **Components** tab, and open the floating **Viewer** (see Figure 3–44).

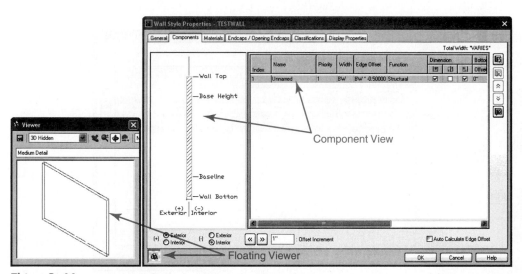

Figure 3–44

    9. In the **Components** tab, press the **Add Component** icon six times to create a total of seven components.
  10. Rename the components from top to bottom—BRICK, CAVITY, CMU, WOOD STUD, .5″ GYP BOARD, 14″ CMU, and FOOTING (see Figure 3–45).
  11. Select the **Width** drop-down list for the BRICK component, and set the **Width** to **4″**, and **Base Width** to **0″** (see Figure 3–46).
  12. Select the other components and set their fields to those shown in Figures 3–47 and 3–48.

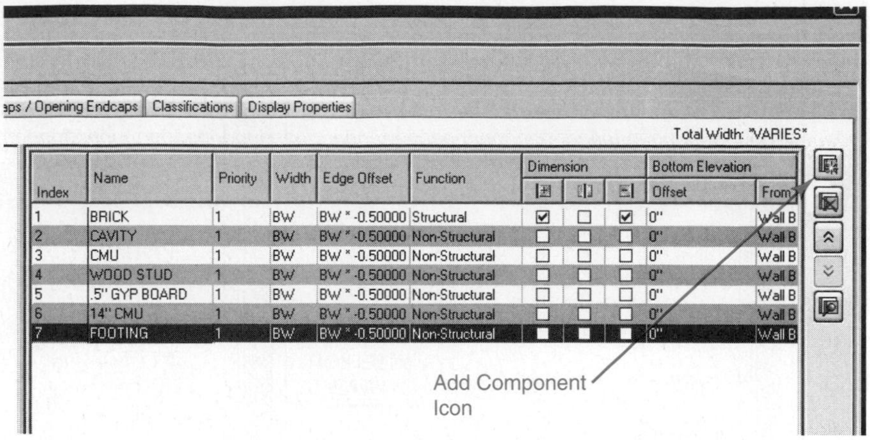

**Figure 3–45**

Add Component
Icon

**Figure 3–46**

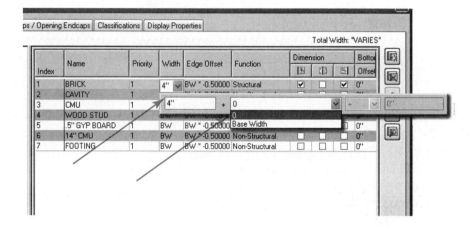

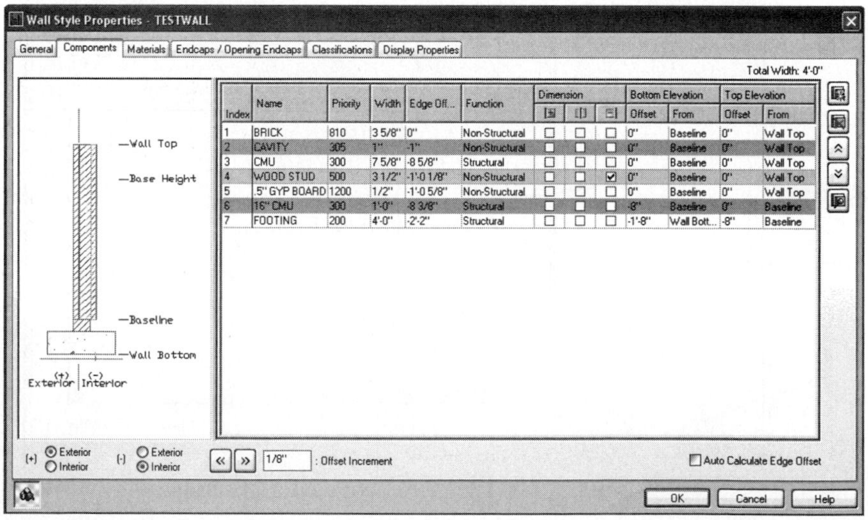

**Figure 3–47**

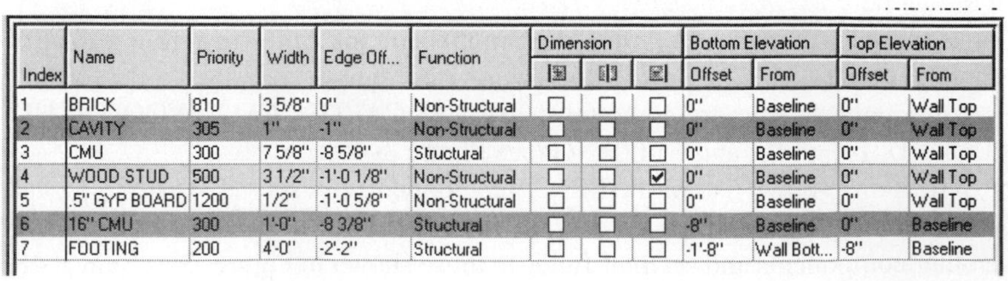

**Figure 3–48**

13. Press the **OK** button to close the **Wall Style Properties** dialog box. The wall you placed in step 4 now reflects the changes you created in the TESTWALL style.

14. Change to the **Right** view, and notice that the Footing is not showing. This is because you must set the Floor line offset (Figure 3–49).

There are three ways to set the Floor line offset. (1) You can set the Floor line offset in the **Properties** palette as you are placing the wall. (2) You can drag the wall style you created into a tool palette, select the tool, **RMB,** and set the Floor line offset so that it is set when you select that tool. (3) You can select the wall you placed, **RMB,** and select **Roof/Floor line** > **Modify Floor line** from the contextual menu that appears. We will do the third.

**Note:**
BW signifies Base Width, and it is the size that you set for the total width of a wall in the **Properties** palette. When using components, you usually turn the BW off by entering 0".

15. Select the wall you placed, **RMB,** and select **Roof/Floor line** > **Modify Floor line** from the contextual menu that appears.

16. Enter **O** (Offset) in the **Command line,** and press the **Enter** key on your keyboard.

17. Enter **-1'-8″** in the **Command line,** and press the **Enter** key on your keyboard. The footing appears (see Figure 3–49).

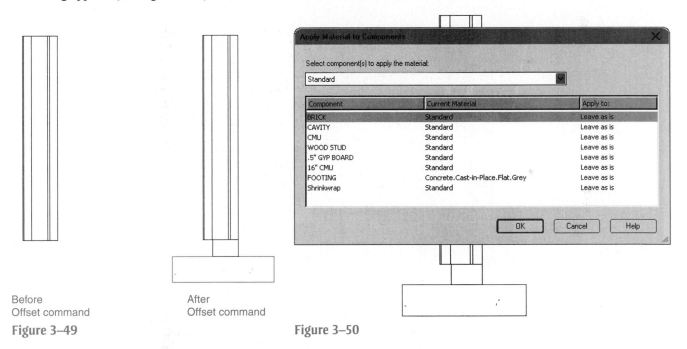

Before
Offset command

**Figure 3–49**

After
Offset command

**Figure 3–50**

## Applying the Component Materials and Associated Hatches

18. Select the **Material** tool from the **Design** menu, and select the **TESTWALL** you created in the previous exercise to bring up the **Apply Material to Components** dialog box (see Figure 3–50).

19. Select the **BRICK** component, select **Masonry.Unit Masonry.Brick.Modular. English** from the **Select components(s) to apply the material** drop-down list, and select **Object Override** from the **Apply to** drop-down list (see Figure 3–51).

20. Press the **OK** button to apply the material and its associated hatches (see Figure 3–52).

21. Finish applying the rest of the materials (see Figure 3–53).

When showing walls, the footings are usually shown with hidden lines. To do this, do the following:

22. Change to **Top View,** select the **TESTWALL. RMB,** and select **Edit Wall Style** from the contextual menu that appears to bring up the **Wall Style Properties** dialog box.

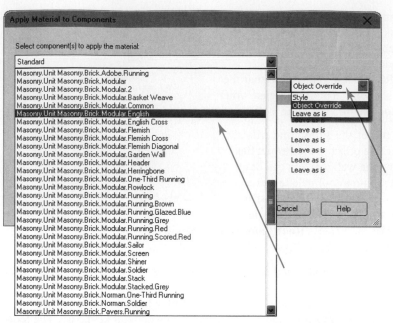

Figure 3–51

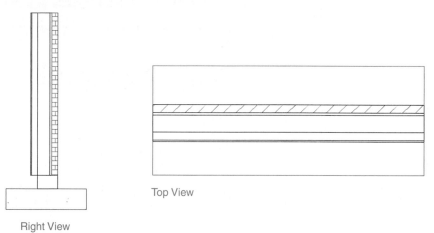

Top View

Right View

Figure 3–52

23. In the **Wall Style Properties** dialog box, change to the **Display Properties** tab.
24. In the **Display Properties** tab, select the **Plan Display Representation,** and check its **Style Override** check box to bring up the **Display Properties (Wall Style Override)** dialog box.
25. In the **Display Properties (Wall Style Override)** dialog box, select the **Below Cut Plane Display Component,** change its Linetype to **HIDDEN 2,** and press the **OK** buttons to return to the Drawing Editor.

The **Top View** of the wall now shows the footing with a hidden line (see Figure 3–54).

**FOR MORE INFORMATION**     Before we move on, please take a look at the explanations of the different columns in the Components tab.

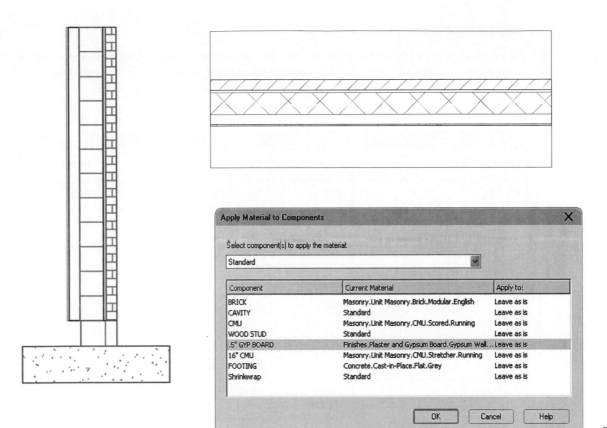

Figure 3–53

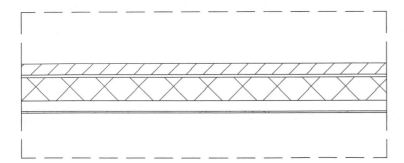

Figure 3–54

## Priorities—Cleanup Priorities

The component priority determines how each wall component cleans up with the components of an intersecting wall. The lower the component index number, the higher the priority of the component when it intersects other walls. Below is a list of recommended index numbers.

| Component | Index | Component | Index |
|---|---|---|---|
| Air Gap | 700 | Concrete | 200 |
| Air Gap (Brick/Brick) | 805 | Concrete (Footing) | 200 |
| Air Gap (CMU/CMU) | 305 | Glass | 1200 |
| Air Gap (Stud/Stud) | 505 | GWB | 1200 |
| Brick | 800 | GWB (X) | 1200, 1210, 1220, 1230 |
| Brick Veneer | 810 | Insulation (CMU/Brick, Stud/Brick) | 600 |
| Bulkhead | 1800 | Metal Panel | 1000 |
| Casework - Backsplash | 2030 | Precast Panel | 400 |
| Casework - Base | 2010 | Rigid Insulation (Brick) | 404 |
| Casework - Counter | 2020 | Siding | 900 |
| Casework - Upper | 2000 | Stucco | 1100 |
| CMU | 300 | Stud | 500 |
| CMU Veneer | 350 | Toilet Partition | 3000 |

**Edge Offset**—Offset of edge of component in relationship to the Baseline in Plan View.

**Function**—Either Structural or Non-Structural. This is useful when setting up dimension styles so that you can define that only Structural or all wall components should be dimensioned.

**Dimension**—Dictates the side on which you wish to dimension the component.

**Bottom and Top Elevation Offsets**—Dictates the offsets from Wall Top, Base Height, Baseline, and Wall Bottom.

The final TESTWALL is shown in Figure 3–55.

**Figure 3–55**

# Windows

**4**

## *Section* **Objectives**

- Know how to place a Window object using **Reference.**
- Know how to place a Window object using **Offset/Center.**
- Learn how to change window sizes with grips.
- Learn how to add a profile (change window shape).
- Learn how to move the window vertically, within the wall, and along the wall.
- Know how to edit window styles.

## WINDOWS

Windows are important objects in every building. In AutoCAD Architecture 2008, a window is an AEC object that interacts with walls or door and window assemblies just as it would in a real building. After a window is placed in a wall or door and window assembly, the window is constrained to the object and cannot move outside it. Windows can be anchored to specific locations in walls or door and window assemblies; when the wall or door and window assembly moves or changes size, the location of the window in that object stays constant. If you wish, a window can also be a freestanding object by pressing the **Enter** key on your keyboard while placing the window in space.

Window objects can be dragged or inserted either from the **Design** tool palette, by clicking **RMB** on a wall, or by typing **window add** on the **Command line.**

Windows can be placed directly into walls by right-clicking on the wall and selecting **Insert > Window** from the contextual menu, or by selecting from the **Windows** or **Design** tool palettes and pressing **Enter.**

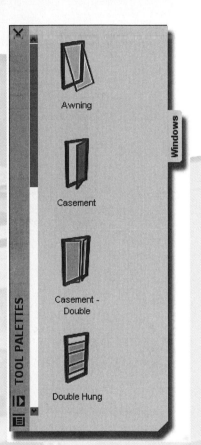

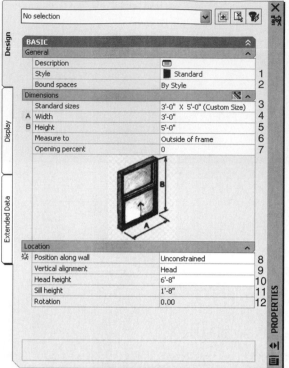

**Before Insertion of Window**          **After Insertion of Window**

| Number | Name | Purpose |
|--------|------|---------|
| 1 | Style | Change this to change to another style such as Casement, etc. |
| 2 | Bound spaces | By Style, Yes, No for bounding Associative spaces |
| 3 | Standard sizes | Select from a list of preset sizes |
| 4 | Width | Change width of window |
| 5 | Height | Change height of window |
| 6 | Measure to | Set width and height to inside or outside of window frame |
| 7 | Opening percent | Set amount that window is open in model and elevation view |
| 8 | Position along wall | Set to **Offset/Center** or **Unconstrained;** Offset/Center wall automatically offsets a set distance from the wall ends, or inserts at center of wall. |
| 9 | Vertical alignment | Set to **Head** or **Sill;** this will govern on insert |
| 10 | Head height | Set elevation for top of window if **Vertical alignment** is set to **Head** |
| 11 | Sill height | Set elevation for bottom of window if **Vertical alignment** is set to **Sill** |
| 12 | Rotation | Rotation angle for the window |

| Number | Name | Purpose |
|--------|------|---------|
| 13 | Layer | Change this to place the window on another layer |
| 14 | Shadow display | Casts and Receives, Casts Shadows, Receives shadows, Ignore shadows |
| 15 | Additional Information | Launches the Additional Information Worksheet with more window location information |

**Exercise 4-1:** Placing a Window Object Using Reference

1. Start a new drawing using the AEC Model (Imperial Stb) template.
2. Change to the **Model Layout.**
3. Set the **Object Snap** to **End Point.**
4. Change to the **Top View.**
5. Place a standard wall 10'-0" long, 10'-0" high, and 6" thick. (See Section 3, "Walls," for information on how to place walls.)
6. Select the **Double Hung** icon from the **Windows** tool palette and drag your cursor over the **Properties** palette to open it.
7. Enter the following data:

   a. Style = **Double Hung**
   b. Width = **3'-0"**
   c. Height = **5'-0"**
   d. Measure to = **Outside of Frame**
   e. Position along wall = **Unconstrained**
   f. Vertical alignment = **Head**
   g. Head height = **6'-8"**

8. Select the wall and enter **RE** (Reference point) in the **Command line.**
9. Select the left corner of the wall, move the cursor to the right (0°), and enter **3'** on the keyboard. Then press **Enter** to place the window 3'-0" from the left wall corner (Figure 4–1).

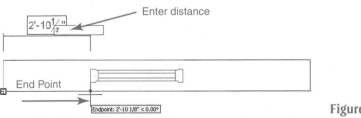

Figure 4–1

**Exercise 4-2:** Placing a Window Object Using Offset/Center

1. Erase the window in the previous exercise.
2. Turn off all Object Snaps.
3. Select the **Double Hung** icon from the **Windows** tool palette and drag your cursor over the **Properties** palette to open it.
4. Enter the following data:

   a. Style = **Double Hung**
   b. Width = **3'-0"**
   c. Height = **5'-0"**
   d. Measure to = **Outside of Frame**
   e. Position along wall = **Offset/Center**

    f. Automatic Offset = **6″**

    g. Vertical alignment = **Head**

    h. Head height = **6′-8″**

5. Select the wall near the left end of the wall, click the mouse, and press **Enter** to complete the command and place the window.

The window will be placed 6″ from the left end of the wall (see Figure 4–2).

> **Note:**
> By pressing the **Tab** key you can cycle the 6″ dimension and enter an overriding dimension.

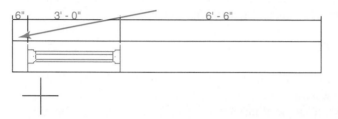

**Figure 4–2**

6. Again, select the **Double Hung** icon from the **Windows** tool palette and drag your cursor over the **Properties** palette to open it.

7. Select the wall near the center of the distance left between the previous window placement and the right-hand wall end. Click the mouse, and press **Enter** to complete the command and place the window.

The window will be placed at the center of the distance between the second window and the right end of the wall (see Figure 4–3).

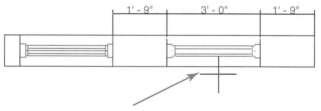

**Figure 4–3**

**Exercise 4-3:** Changing Window Size with Grips

1. Select a window to activate its grips, and drag to the right (0°). If the window has sizes listed in its **Window Styles Properties > Standard Sizes,** it will snap at gray lines in plan. These are sizes listed in the aforementioned **Properties** (see Figure 4–4).

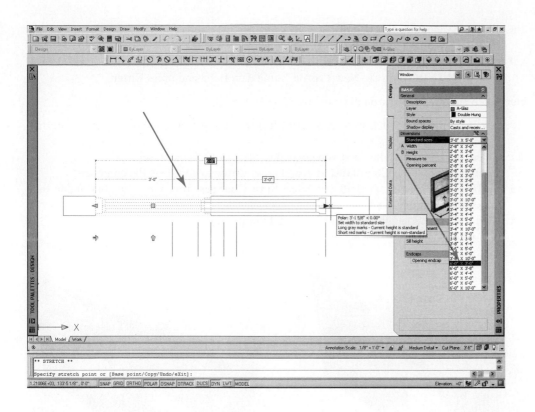

Figure 4–4

## Exercise 4-4: Adding a Profile

1. Erase the previous exercise.
2. Place a Standard wall 15'-0" long, 10'-0" high, and 6" thick.
3. Select the **Pivot Horizontal** icon from the **Windows** tool palette and drag your cursor over the **Properties** palette to open it.
4. Enter the following data:

   a. Style = **Pivot Horizontal**
   b. Width = **5'-0"**
   c. Height = **4'-0"**
   d. Measure to = **Outside of Frame**
   e. Position along wall = **Unconstrained**
   f. Vertical alignment = **Head**
   g. Head height = **6'-8"**

5. Place the window 2'-0" from the left edge of the wall.
6. Change to the **Front View.**
7. Place a closed polyline as shown in Figure 4–5.

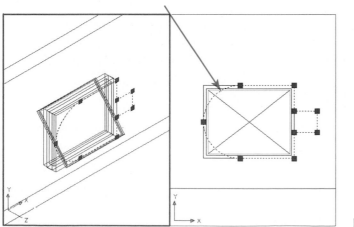

Figure 4–5

8. Select the window, **RMB,** and select **Add Profile** from the contextual menu that appears to bring up the **Add Window Profile** dialog box.
9. Select **Start from scratch** from the **Profile Definition** drop-down list, enter **TEST PIVOT WINDOW** in the **New Profile Name** data field, and press **Enter.**

A blue hatch field will appear on the window.

10. **RMB** on the blue hatch field and select **Replace Ring** from the conceptual menu that appears.
11. Select the closed polyline that you created in Step 7 of this exercise.
12. Enter **Y** (Yes) in the **Command line,** and press **Enter** to complete the command.
13. **RMB** on the blue hatch field and select **Save Changes** from the contextual menu that appears (see Figure 4–6).
14. Mirror the window in the **Front View** (see Figure 4–7).

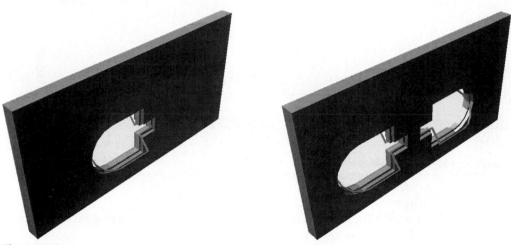

Figure 4–6                         Figure 4–7

15. Delete the windows you just created.
16. Select the **Double Hung** icon window from the **Windows** tool palette, and place a 5′-high by 3′-wide window constrained to the center of the wall (see Figure 4–8).

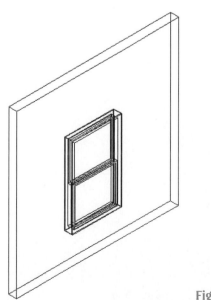

Figure 4–8

17. Select the window, **RMB,** and select **Add Profile** from the contextual menu that appears to bring up the **Add Window Profile** dialog box.
18. At the **Add Window** dialog box, select **Start from scratch** from the **Profile Definition** drop-down list, enter **Curved Top window** in the **New Profile Name** data field, and press the **Enter** key.

As with the editing of the previous window, a blue hatch field will appear on the window.

19. Click on the top **Edge** grip, and drag upwards (see Figure 4–9).
20. Press the **Ctrl** key on your keyboard twice, and click the mouse key.

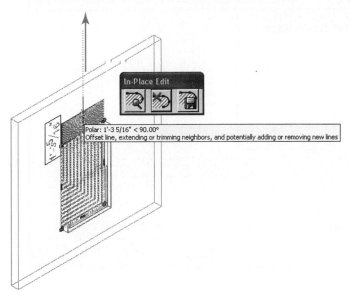

Figure 4–9

21. Press the **Save All Changes** icon in the on-screen **In-Place Edit** dialog box.

You have now created a double hung window with a curved top (see Figure 4–10).

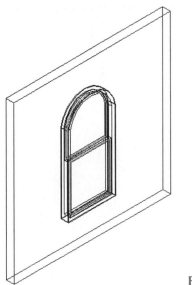

Figure 4–10

22. Select **Format > Style Manager** from the **Main** menu.
23. Expand the **Multi-Purpose Objects** folder.
24. Expand **Profiles**.

25. Double-click on **Curved Top Window** to bring up the **Profile Definitions Properties** dialog box (see Figure 4–11).

Notice that the window profile you created in place is now in your Style Manager.

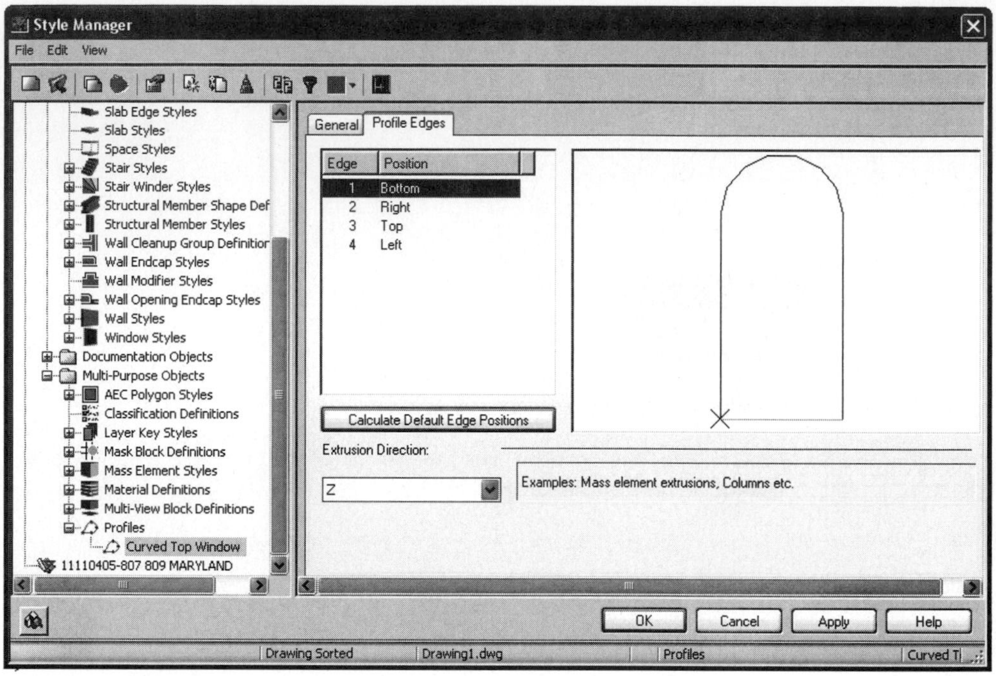

**Figure 4–11**

**Exercise 4-5:** Modifying Window Height

1. Use the previous exercise.
2. Change to the **Front View.**
3. Select the window to activate its grips.
4. Pick and move the square grip at the bottom of the window; a yellow dialog field appears (see Figure 4–12).

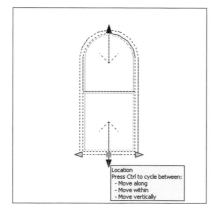

**Figure 4–12**

5. Press the **Ctrl** key until the dialog field reads **Move Vertically.**
6. Press the **Tab** key until the data field turns magenta in color.
7. Enter **3′-0″** in the **Command line** and press **Enter.**

The window will move vertically and be 3′-6″ above the wall baseline.

8. Activate the square grip at the bottom of the window again.
9. Press the **Ctrl** key until the dialog field reads **Move Along.**
10. Enter **3′-0″** in the **Command line** and press **Enter.**

The window will move horizontally 3′-0″ in the direction that the grip was moved.

11. Change to the **Top View.**
12. Activate the square grip at the center of the window.
13. Press the **Ctrl** key until the dialog field reads **Move Within.**
14. Move the grip vertically.
15. Enter **2″** in the **Command line** and press **Enter.**

The window will move vertically within the wall 2″ in the direction the grip was moved. Save this file.

## Exercise 4-6: Editing Window Styles

1. Use the previous exercise.
2. Change to the **Front View.**
3. Select the window, **RMB,** and select **Edit Window Style** from the contextual menu that appears to bring up the **Window Style Properties** dialog box.
4. Select the **Dimensions** tab.

This is where you set the **Frame Width** and **Depth.** Check the **Auto-Adjust** check box if you want the frame depth to match the wall in which it has been inserted.
The **Sash Width** and **Depth** plus the **Glass Thickness** are also located in the **Dimensions** tab.

5. Select the **Floating Viewer** icon at the lower left corner of the **Window Style Properties** dialog box to bring up the **Viewer.**
6. In the **Viewer,** select the **Gouraud Shaded** icon in the top **Viewer** toolbar (see Figure 4–13).
7. Enter the following data in the entry fields:

   a. Frame Width = **1″**
   b. Frame Depth = **12″**
   c. Sash Width = **4″**
   d. Sash Depth = **4″**

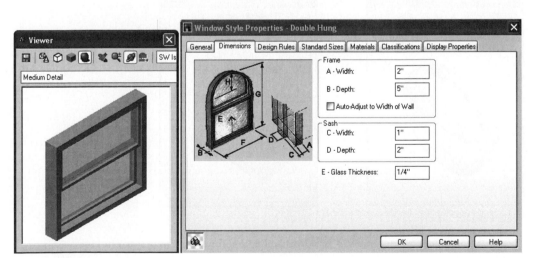

Figure 4–13

Press **Enter** after entering the last data field, and note the change in window in the **Viewer** (see Figure 4–14).

8. Reset the data fields to the following:

    a. Frame Width = **2″**
    b. Frame Depth = **5″**
    c. Sash Width = **1″**
    d. Sash Depth = **2″**

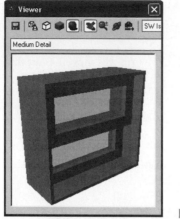

Figure 4–14

9. Select the **Design Rules** tab.
10. Select the **Predefined** radio button; select **Round** from the **Predefined** drop-down list, and **Awning-Transom** from the **Window Type** drop-down list.

Note the change in window in the **Viewer** (see Figure 4–15).

11. Select the **Use Profile** radio button, and select **TEST PIVOT WINDOW** from its drop-down list (**TEST PIVOT WINDOW** was the profile created in Step 9 of Exercise 4–4, "Adding a Profile").

Note the change in window in the **Viewer** (see Figure 4–16).

Figure 4–15

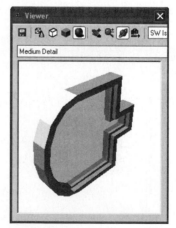

Figure 4–16

12. Change to the **Standard Sizes** tab.

The **Standard Sizes** tab is where standardized windows are entered. These sizes allow you to change windows interactively as shown in the following steps.

13. Press **OK** to close the **Window Style Properties** dialog box.
14. Change to the **Top View.**
15. Double-click on the window to bring up its **Properties** palette.

16. Set the style to **Double Hung,** and allow the palette to close.
17. Select the window's right arrow grip, and drag it to the right.

You will see a yellow dialog field explaining the gray and red marks that appear above the window. These marks are "snap" points corresponding to the preset width sizes set in the **Standard Sizes** tab of the **Window Style Properties** dialog box (see Figure 4–17).

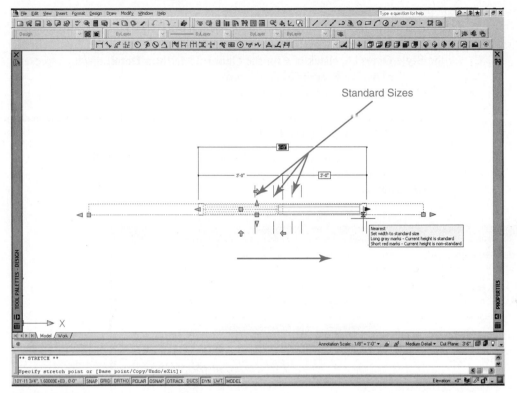

**Figure 4–17**

18. **RMB** on the window again and select **Edit Window Style** from the contextual menu that appears.
19. Change to the **Materials** tab.
20. Activate the **Frame** field, and click on the **Material Definition** drop-down list (see Figure 4–18).

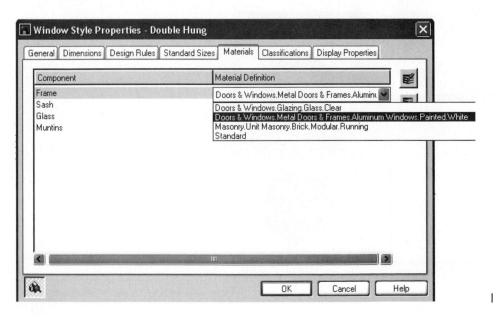

**Figure 4–18**

Four preset materials are shipped with the program. If you need more materials, you need to add and edit a new material.

21. To add and edit a new material, press the **Add New Material** icon at the right side of the **Materials** tab.
22. Enter a new name for the new material in the **New Material** data field that appears, and press **OK.**
23. Activate the **New Material** field in the **Material Definition** column, and select the **Edit Material** icon above the **Add Material** icon to bring up the **Material Definition Properties** dialog box.
24. Check the **Style Override** check box for the **General Medium Detail** display representation to open the **Display Properties** dialog box.
25. Select the **Other** tab (see Figure 4–19).

In the **Other** tab you can control the placement of hatches on surfaces, and **Browse** for materials made in the VIZ Render module (see Figure 4–20).

26. Press the **OK** buttons until you return to the **Window Style Properties** dialog box.
27. Change to the **Display Properties** tab.
28. Select the **Elevation** field.

**Figure 4–19**

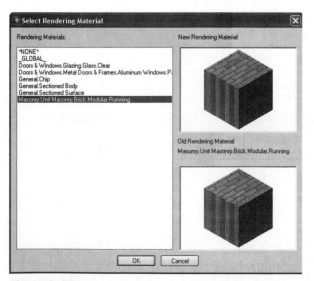

**Figure 4–20**

29. Press the **Edit Display** icon at the upper right side of the **Display Properties** tab to bring up the **Display Properties** dialog box.
30. Select the **Muntins** tab.
31. Press the **Add** button to bring up the **Muntins Block** dialog box.
32. Select the **Prairie - 12 Lights** from the **Pattern** drop-down list, check the **Clean Up Joints** and **Convert to Body** check boxes, and then press the **OK** buttons to close the command and view the window (see Figures 4–21 and 4–22).

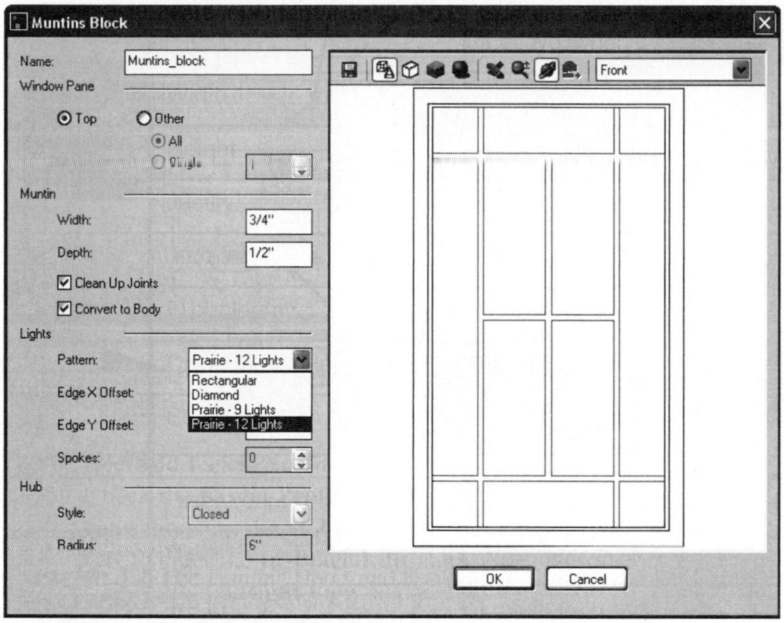

Figure 4–21

Figure 4–22

# Doors

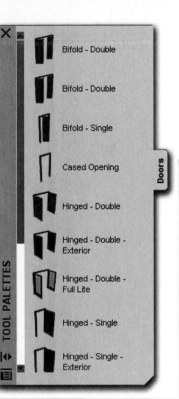

## Section Objectives

- Learn how to place a door object using **Reference.**
- Learn how to place a door object using **Offset/Center.**
- Learn how to change door size and swing location with grips.
- Know how to control the door swing angle.
- Learn how to add a profile (change door panel shape).
- Add a doorknob.
- Move the door within the wall and along the wall.
- Know how to edit door styles.
- Know how to use the **Materials** tab.

Wall objects can be dragged or inserted either from the **Design** tool palette, or by typing **dooradd** in the **Command line.**

## DOORS

In AutoCAD Architecture 2008, door objects are totally customizable. All is possible in this program—from customizing the size and shape of the door or the size and shape of the jamb to including side lights, mullions, and/or a sill. As with other features of this program, a premade library of door styles greatly enhances productivity.

It is hoped that manufacturers will jump on the AutoCAD Architecture bandwagon and place their door styles on the Web. If they do this, you will be able to quickly **idrop** or update your catalogs with premade doors and door accessories. If this happens and the manufacturer makes changes, you will be able to update your catalogs and drawings automatically directly from the Internet.

Doors can be placed directly into walls by right-clicking on the wall and selecting **Insert > Door** from the contextual menu or by selecting from the **Doors** or **Design** tool palettes and pressing **Enter.**

| Number | Name | Purpose |
|--------|------|---------|
| 1 | Style | Change this to change to another style, such as **Double Doors** |
| 2 | Standard sizes | Select from a list of preset sizes in the **Door Style** dialog box |
| 3 | Width | Set custom width |

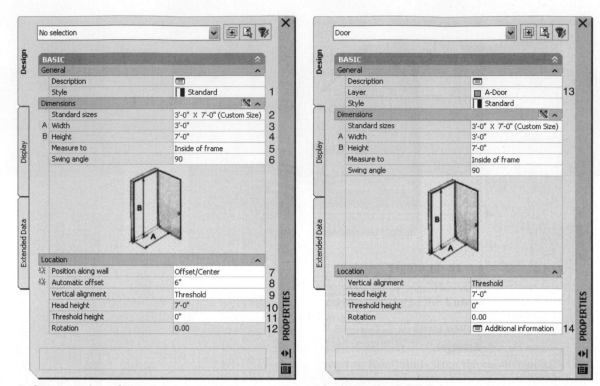

**Before Insertion of Door**                    **After Insertion of Door**

| 4 | Height | Set custom height |
|---|---|---|
| 5 | Measure to | Set width and height to measure inside of frame or outside of frame |
| 6 | Swing angle | Set door swing opening 0° to 90° |
| 7 | Position along wall | **Unconstrained** (any placement); **Offset/Center** (set offset from ends of wall or midpoint of wall) |
| 8 | Automatic offset | Set distance for offset from wall end if **Position along** is set to **Offset/Center** |
| 9 | Vertical alignment | Set to head height or threshold governs |
| 10 | Head height | Head height above wall baseline if **Vertical Alignment** is set to **Head** |
| 11 | Threshold height | Head height above wall baseline if **Vertical Alignment** is set to **Threshold** |
| 12 | Rotation | Rotation angle for the door |
| 13 | Layer | Change this to place the door on another layer |
| 14 | Additional information | Launches the Additional Information Worksheet with more door location information |

**Exercise 5-1:** Placing a Door Object Using Reference

1. Start a new drawing using the AEC Model (Imperial Stb) template.
2. Change to the **Model Layout.**

3. Change to the **Top View.**
4. Set the Object Snap to **End Point.**
5. Place a Standard 10′-long, 10′-high wall.
6. Select any door from the **Doors** tool palette and drag your cursor over the **Properties** palette to open the palette.
7. Enter the following data:

    a. Style = **Standard**
    b. Width = **3′-0″**
    c. Height = **6′-8″**
    d. Measure to = **Outside of Frame**
    e. Swing angle = **90**
    f. Position along wall = **Unconstrained**
    g. Vertical alignment = **Head**
    h. Head height = **6-8″**
    i. Threshold height = **0″**

8. Select the wall and enter **RE** (Reference point) in the **Command line.**
9. Select the left corner of the wall, move the cursor to the right (0°), and enter **5′** on the keyboard. Press **Enter** to place the door 5′-0″ from the left wall corner (see Figure 5–1).

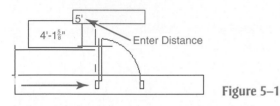

**Figure 5–1**

## Exercise 5-2: Placing a Door Object Using Offset/Center

1. Erase the door in the previous exercise.
2. Turn off all Object Snaps.
3. Select any door icon in the **Doors** tool palette and drag your cursor over the **Properties** palette to open it.
4. Enter the following data:

    a. Style = **Standard**
    b. Width = **3′-0″**
    c. Height = **6′-8″**
    d. Measure to = **Outside of Frame**
    e. Position along wall = **Offset/Center**
    f. Automatic Offset = **6″**
    g. Vertical alignment = **Head**
    h. Head height = **6′-8″**
    i. Threshold = **0**

5. Select the wall near the left end of the wall, click the mouse, and press **Enter** to complete the command and place the door.

> **Note:**
> By pressing the **Tab** key, you can cycle the **6″** dimension and enter an overriding dimension.

The door will be placed 6″ from the left end of the wall (see Figure 5–2).

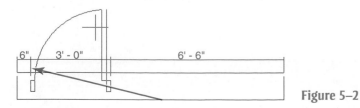

**Figure 5–2**

**Exercise 5-3:** Changing Door Size and Swing Location with Grips

1. Select the door to activate its grips and drag the green arrow on the right door edge to the right (0°). If the door has sizes listed in its **Door Styles Properties > Standard Sizes,** it will snap at gray lines in plan.
2. To add doors to the **Standard Sizes** menu, **RMB** on the door and select **Edit Door Style** from the contextual menu that appears to bring up the **Door Style Properties** dialog box.
3. Select the **Standard Sizes** tab.
4. Press the **Add** button to bring up the **Add Standard Size** dialog box (see Figure 5–3).
5. Add the four doors shown in Figure 5–4 to the **Standard Sizes** tab, and close the **Door Style Properties** dialog box by pressing the **OK** button.

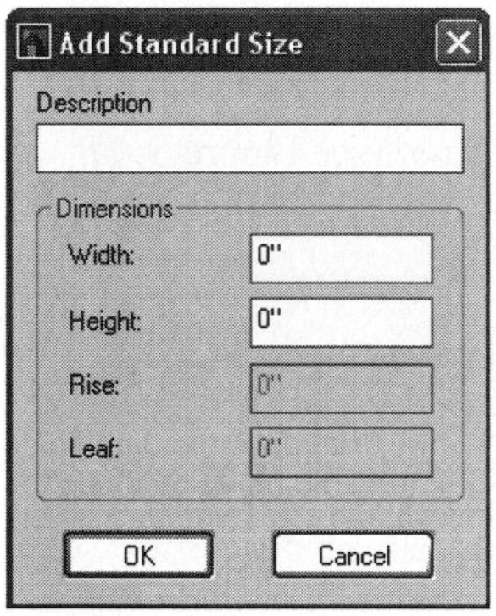

Figure 5–3

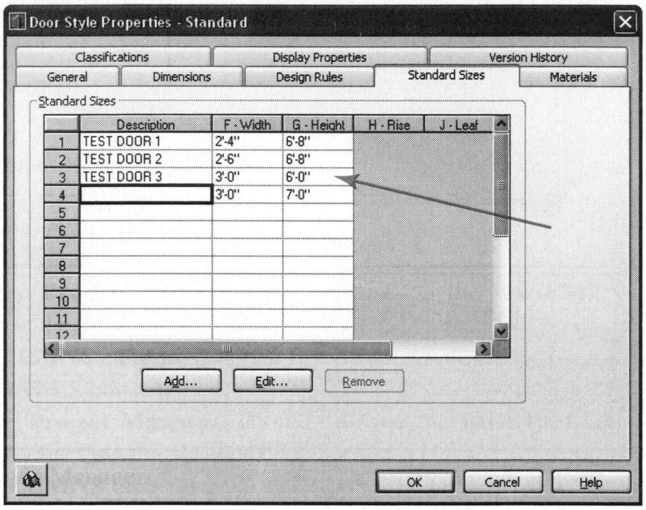

Figure 5–4

6. Again, select the door to activate its grips and drag to the right (0°). The door will now snap to the sizes you added in the **Standard Sizes** tab (see Figure 5–5).
7. Select the arrow grip shown in Figure 5–6 to flip the door swing in different directions. Save this file.

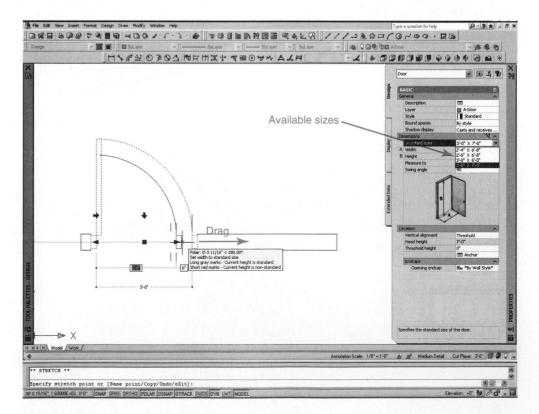

Figure 5–5

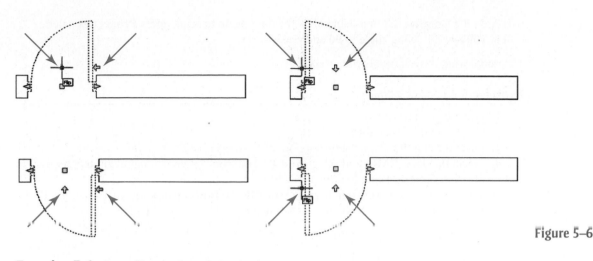

Figure 5–6

## Exercise 5-4: Controlling the Door Swing Angle

1. Using the previous exercise, change to the **SW Isometric view.**

Notice that although the swing shows open in **Top View** (Plan), the door swing is closed in the **SW Isometric (Model View).** AutoCAD Architecture ships from the developer with the doors closed in **Model View** (see Figure 5–7).

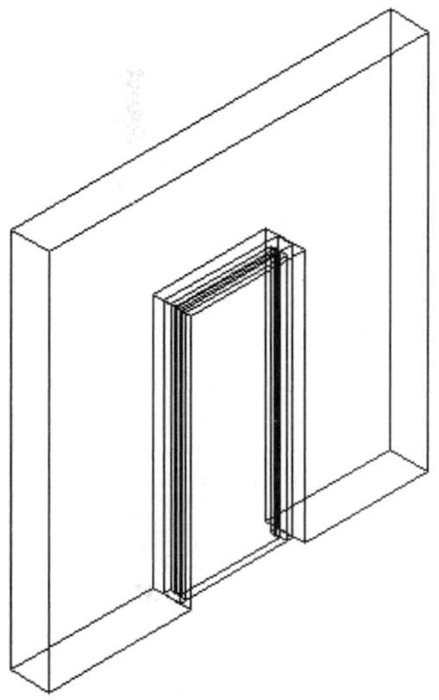

2. Double-click the door to bring up its **Properties** palette.
3. Notice that the swing angle is 90.
4. Change the swing angle to **45,** and press **Enter.** Note that nothing happens in the isometric or model view (the plan view will show a change).

Nothing happens because there is a model override set at **0,** which prevents the door's **Properties** palette from controlling the door swing angle. To allow control from the **Properties** palette do the following:

5. Select the door, **RMB,** and select **Edit Door Style** from the contextual menu that appears to bring up the **Door Style Properties** dialog box.
6. Select the **Display Properties** tab.
7. Double-click the **Model** field (don't check the style **Override** check box because that would only control the door selected, and not all the doors) to bring up the **Display Properties** dialog box.
8. Select the **Other** tab.
9. *Clear* the **Override Open Percent** check box, and press the **OK** buttons until you return to the Drawing Editor (see Figure 5–8).

Figure 5–7

The **Override Open Percent** check box overrides the **Properties** palette. You can also change the door swing to a straight swing in the **Other** tab.

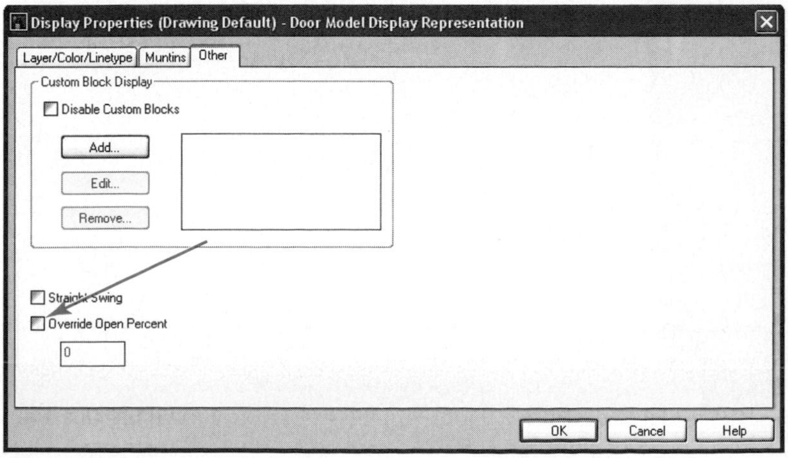

Figure 5–8

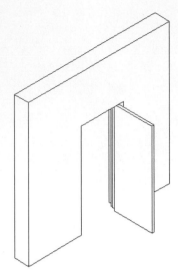

**Figure 5–9**

10. In the Drawing Editor, double-click the door again to bring up its **Properties** palette.
11. Change the swing angle to **90** and press **Enter.**

The door swing is open (see Figure 5–9).

**Exercise 5-5:** Adding a Profile

1. Use the previous exercise.
2. Change to the **Front View.**
3. Place the closed polyline shown in Figure 5–10 over the door.
4. Select the door, **RMB,** and select **Add Profile** from the contextual menu that appears to bring up the **Add Door Profile** dialog box.
5. Select **Start from scratch** from the **Profile Definition** drop-down list, enter **TEST PIVOT DOOR** in the **New Profile Name** data field, and press **Enter.**

A blue hatch field will appear on the door (see Figure 5–11).

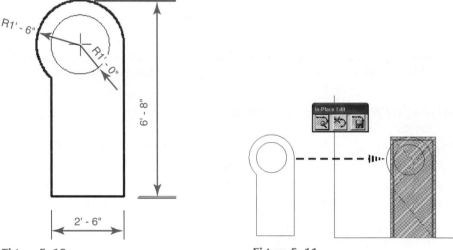

**Figure 5–10**                    **Figure 5–11**

6. **RMB** on the blue hatch field and select **Replace ring** from the conceptual menu that appears.
7. Select the closed polyline that you created in Step 3 of this exercise.
8. Enter **Y** (Yes) in the **Command line** and press **Enter.**
9. **RMB** again on the blue hatch field and select **Add ring** from the contextual menu that appears.
10. Select the 1′-0″ circle that you created with the polyline in Step 3 of this exercise.
11. Again enter **Y** (Yes) in the **Command line,** and press **Enter** to complete the command.
12. Change to the **NE Isometric View** and select the **Hidden** icon from the **Shading** toolbar.
13. **RMB** on the blue hatch field and select **Save Changes** from the contextual menu that appears (see Figure 5–12).

Save this exercise.

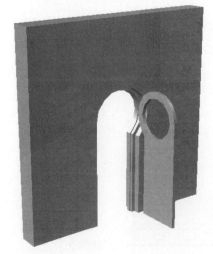

**Figure 5–12**

## Exercise 5-6: Adding a Doorknob

1. Use the previous exercise.
2. Draw the closed polyline shown in Figure 5–13.
3. Select **Door** > **Pulldowns** > **3D Solids Pulldown** from the **Main** toolbar to place the **3D Solids** menu group on the **Main** toolbar.
4. Now, select **3D Solids** > **Revolve** from the **Main** toolbar and revolve 360° (see Figure 5–14).
5. Select **Mirror** to mirror the knob (see Figure 5–15).

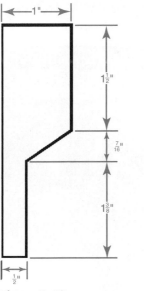

Figure 5–13

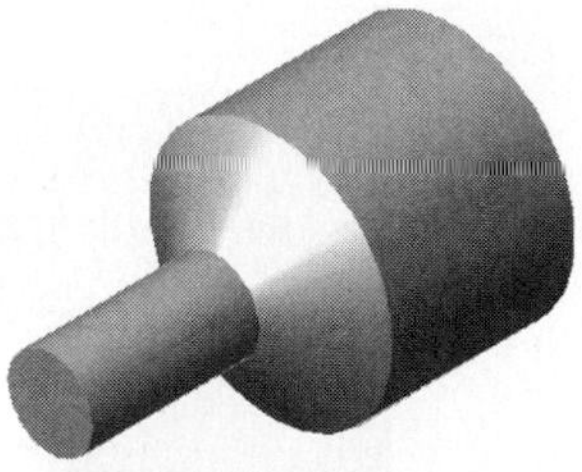

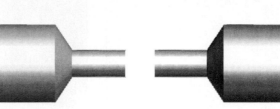

Figure 5–14

Figure 5–15

6. Select **Format** > **Blocks** > **Block Definition** from the **Main** toolbar to bring up the **Block Definition** dialog box.
7. Create two blocks named **KNOB1** and **KNOB2**.
8. Select the door you created in the previous exercise, **RMB,** and select **Edit Door Style** from the contextual menu that appears to bring up the **Door Style Properties** dialog box.
9. Select the **Display Properties** tab.
10. Double-click on the **Elevation** field to bring up the next **Display Properties** dialog box.
11. Select the **Other** tab.
12. Press the **Add** button to bring up the **Custom Block** dialog box (see Figure 5–16).

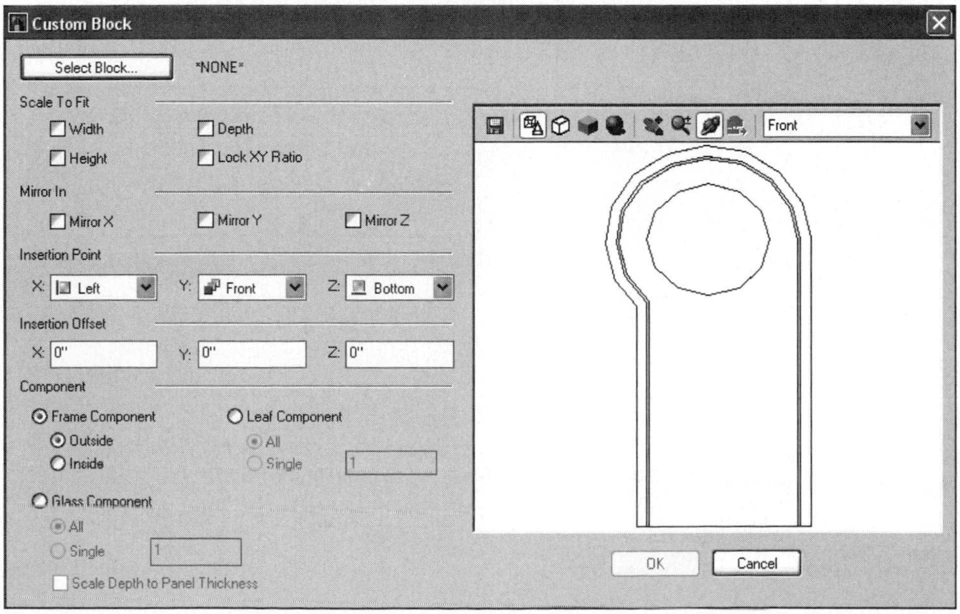

Figure 5–16

13. Select the **Select Block** button to bring up the **Select A Block** dialog box.
14. Select **KNOB1** and press the **OK** button.
15. Use the settings shown in Figure 5–17 to move KNOB1 into position in the **Front View,** and then press the **OK** button to return to the **Display Properties** dialog box > **Other** tab.
16. Select the **Add** button to again bring up the **Custom Block** dialog box.
17. Press the **Select Block** button, this time select **KNOB 2,** and press **OK** to return to the **Custom Block** dialog box.
18. Use the same settings for KNOB2 that you used for KNOB1, and press the **OK** buttons until you return to the Drawing Editor (see Figure 5–18).

Save this file.

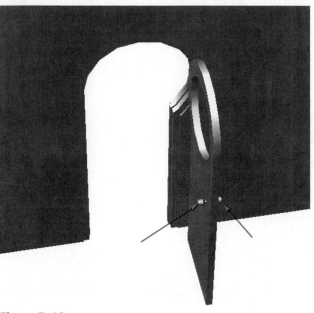

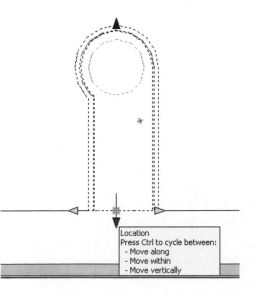

Figure 5–17                                    Figure 5–18

---

**Exercise 5-7:** Moving the Door Vertically, Within the Wall, and Along the Wall

1. Use the previous exercise.
2. Change to the **Front View.**
3. Select the door to activate its grips.
4. Activate the square grip at the bottom of the door—a yellow dialog field appears (see Figure 5–19).

Figure 5–19

8. Select the **Other** tab (see Figure 5–23).
9. In the **Display Properties** dialog box, press the **OK** buttons until you return to the **Door Style Properties** dialog box.
10. Change to the **Display Properties** tab.
11. Select the **Elevation** field.
12. Press the **Edit Display** icon at the upper right side of the **Display Properties** tab to bring up the **Display Properties** dialog box.
13. Select the **Muntins** tab.
14. Press the **Add** button to bring up the **Muntins Block** dialog box.

**Note:**
In the **Other** tab, you can control the placement of hatches on surfaces, and browse for materials made in the VIZ Render module (see Figure 5–24).

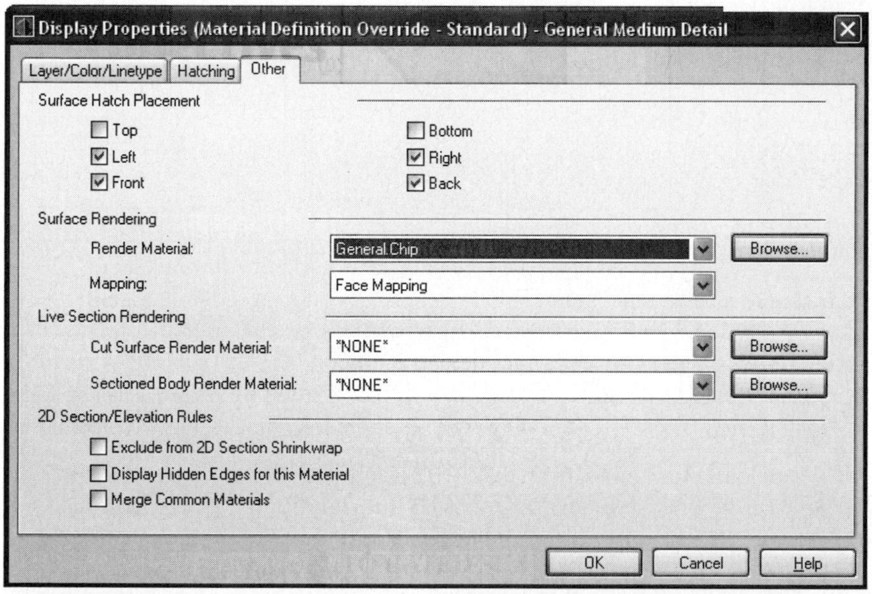

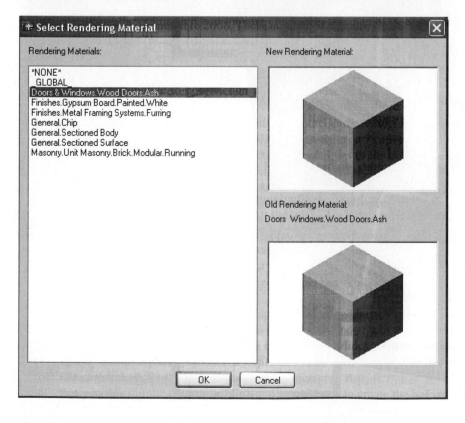

Figure 5–23

Figure 5–24

15. Select the **Prairie – 12 Lights** from the **Pattern** drop-down list, check the **Clean Up Joints** and **Convert to Body** check boxes, and then press the **OK** buttons to close the command and view the door (see Figures 5–25 and 5–26).

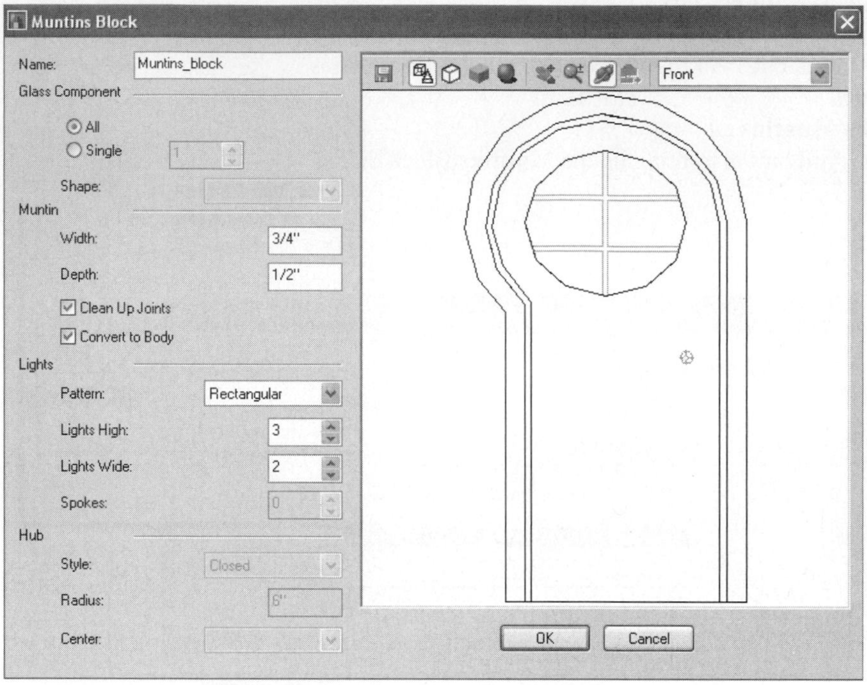

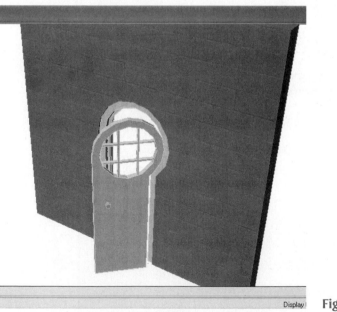

**Figure 5–25**

**Figure 5–26**

### Exercise 5-10: Using In-Place Edit

1. Start a new drawing using the AEC Model (Imperial Stb) template.
2. Change to the **Model Layout.**
3. Change to the **Top View.**
4. Place a Standard 10′-long, 10′-high wall.
5. Place a Standard 3′-wide × 7′-high door constrained to the center of the wall.
6. Change to the **NW Isometric View.**

7. Select the door, **RMB**, and select **Add Profile** from the contextual menu that appears to bring up the **Add Door Profile** dialog box.
8. Select **Start from scratch** from the **Profile Definition** drop-down list, enter **CURVED TOP door** in the **New Profile Name** data field, and press **Enter.**

As with the editing of the previous door, a blue hatch field will appear on the door.

9. Click on the top **Edge** grip and drag upward (see Figure 5–27).
10. Press the **Ctrl** key on your keyboard twice and click the mouse key.
11. Press the **Save All Changes** icon in the **In-Place Edit** dialog box.

You have now created a double-hung door with a curved top (see Figure 5–28).

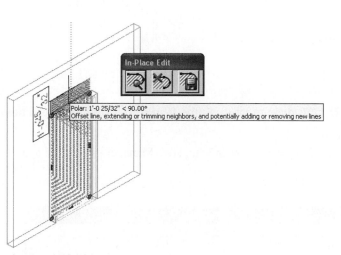

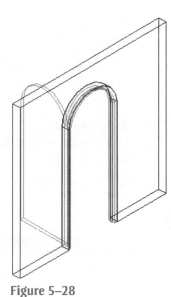

Figure 5–27                                          Figure 5–28

12. Change to the **Front View.**
13. Select the door, **RMB,** and again select **Edit Profile In Place** from the contextual menu that appears.

The blue hatch fields will appear on the door again.

14. Click on the left hand edge grip, and press the **Ctrl** key to change to **Add vertex** mode.
15. Move vertically downward and click the mouse button to add a new edge grip and vertex (see Figure 5–29).

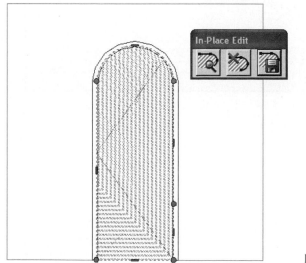

Figure 5–29

16. Select the new edge grip, drag to the right, and click the mouse button (see Figure 5–30).
17. Press the **Save All Changes** icon in the **In-Place Edit** dialog box.
18. Select **Format > Style Manager** from the **Main** menu.
19. Expand the **Multi-Purpose Objects** folder.

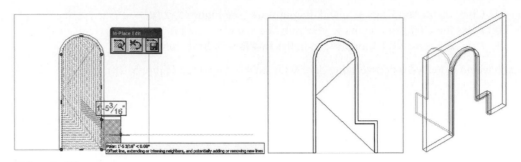

Figure 5–30

20. Expand **Profiles.**
21. Double-click on **CURVED TOP door** to bring up the **Profile Definitions Properties** dialog box.

Notice that the door profile you created in place is now in your Style Manager (see Figure 5–31).

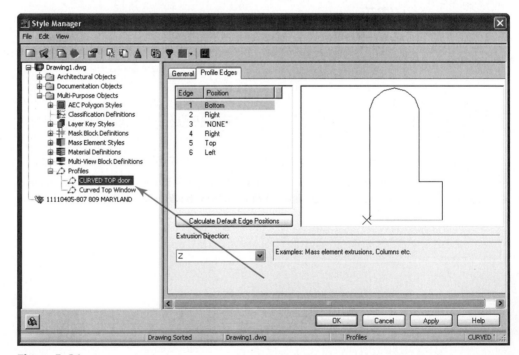

Figure 5–31

# Curtain Walls

# 6

## Section Objectives

- Know how to create a **Curtain Walls** tool palette.
- Learn how to place a curtain wall.
- Learn how to set miter angles.
- Learn how to use the **Roof Line/Floor Line** command.
- Learn how to apply tool properties to a layout grid.
- Learn how to apply tool properties to an elevation sketch.
- Know how to edit a grid in place.
- Know how to edit curtain wall styles.
- Apply curtain walls to faces.
- Add doors to curtain walls.

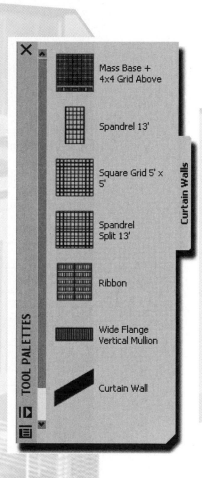

**Curtain Wall** objects can be dragged or inserted from the **Design** tool palette or by typing **curtainwall add** in the **Command line.**

Curtain Wall objects can serve many purposes in AutoCAD Architecture 2008. Originally created to represent storefront and nonbearing perimeter walls, Curtain Wall objects can be easily modified to represent many different kinds of walls. Their unique feature is their modifiable grid that can contain 3D solids, AEC polygons, and door and window assemblies. Curtain Wall objects can even be modified to represent roof and floor trusses, with the curtain wall's parametrically changeable frames representing the truss members.

Besides being created from direct numerical input, **Curtain Wall** objects can be generated from **layout grids** and elevation **sketches.**

Once created, the resultant curtain wall styles can be applied to existing walls (the Curtain Wall object will replace the wall) or applied to a **reference base curve** (the curtain wall will use a curve on the ground plane as a basis for its shape in **Plan View**).

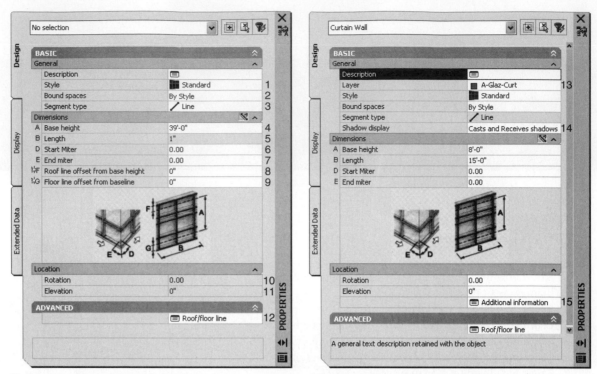

**Before Insertion of Curtain Wall**          **After Insertion of Curtain Wall**

| Number | Name | Purpose |
|--------|------|---------|
| 1 | Style | Select from available curtain wall styles |
| 2 | Bound spaces | By Style, Yes, No for bounding Associative spaces |
| 3 | Segment type | Choose Line or Arc for a linear or curved wall, respectively |
| 4 | Base height | Get height of curtain wall |
| 5 | Length | Present length value of curtain wall object |
| 6 | Start miter | Miter of curtain wall frame at corner, at start of wall (in degrees) |
| 7 | End miter | Miter of curtain wall frame at corner, at start of wall (in degrees) |
| 8 | Roof line offset from base height | Any part of the curtain wall above the Base height such as parapet, gable end, etc. |
| 9 | Floor line offset from baseline | Any part of the curtain wall below the floor line |
| 10 | Rotation | Rotation of curtain wall |
| 11 | Elevation | Height above level |
| 12 | Roof/floor line | Vertex modifications for roof or floor line |
| 13 | Layer | Change this to place the curtain wall on another layer |
| 14 | Shadow display | Casts and Receives, Casts shadows, Receives shadows, Ignore shadows |
| 15 | Additional information | Launches the Additional Information Worksheet with more wall location information |

## Exercise 6-1: Creating a Curtain Walls Tool Palette

1. Select the **Content Browser** icon from the **Navigation** toolbar to bring up the Catalog Library in the Content Browser (see Figure 6–1).
2. In the Catalog Library, double-click the **Design Tool Catalog - Imperial** catalog to open it (see Figure 6–2).
3. Double-click on the area shown in Figure 6–3 to open the pages with all the tool folders.
4. Change to **Page 2,** select the **Curtain wall** folder, open it, and drag all the curtain walls to a new tool palette labeled **Curtain Walls.**

Figure 6–1

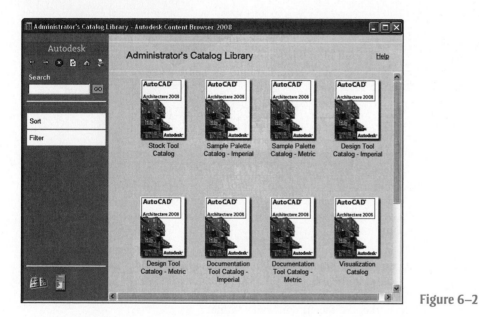

Figure 6–2

Figure 6–3

## Exercise 6-2: Placing a Curtain Wall

1. Start a new drawing using the AEC Model (Imperial Stb) template.
2. Change to the **Model Layout.**
3. Change to the **Top View.**
4. Turn the **ORTHO** button on.
5. Click on the **Curtain Wall** icon on the **Design** tool palette and move your cursor over the **Properties** tool palette to open it.
6. Set the following parameters:

   a.  Style = **Standard**
   b.  Segment type = **Line**
   c.  Base height = **10′-0″**

7. Click to set the curtain wall start point, drag your cursor to the right, enter **10′-0″** in the **Command line,** and press **Enter.**
8. Move your cursor vertically and again enter **10′-0″** in the **Command line.**
9. Press **Enter** twice to finish the command.

You have now created two joined sections of curtain wall.

**Exercise 6-3:** Setting Miter Angles in the Contextual Menu and the Start and End Miters in the Curtain Wall Properties Toolbar

1. Press the **SE Isometric View** icon on the **Views** toolbar.
2. Press the **Flat Shaded** icon on the **Shading** toolbar to shade the curtain walls.
3. Select one of the segments of curtain wall and **RMB** to bring up the **Curtain Wall** contextual menu.
4. Select **Edit Object Display** to bring up the **Object Display** dialog box.
5. Select the **Display Properties** tab, and then select the **Model** display representation, and click the **Edit Display Properties** icon to bring up the **Display Properties** dialog box (see Figure 6–4).
6. Open the **Layer/Color/Linetype** tab, and turn the **Default Infill** light off. Press all the **OK** buttons in the dialog boxes to return to the Drawing Editor.

Notice that your curtain walls now have no glass (infill) showing.

7. Zoom close to the top corner joint between the two sections of curtain wall (see Figure 6–5).

**Figure 6–4**

**Figure 6–5**

8. Select a section of curtain wall, **RMB,** select **Set Miter Angles** from the **Curtain Wall** contextual menu, and then select the other section of curtain wall (see Figure 6–6).

You have now mitered the corners of the curtain wall's frame.

If you select one of the curtain wall sections to bring up its **Properties** tool palette, you will see that its **Start Miter** or **End Miter** has been set. The vertical part of the frame can also be mitered, as we will see later.

**Figure 6–6**

9. Click each section of curtain wall separately to bring up its **Properties** tool palettes and check the **End Miter** for the left section, and the **Start Miter** for the right section.

The **End Miter** for the left section should now read **45,** and the right section of the curtain wall should read **315.**

10. Erase everything in the Drawing Editor.
11. Again, click on the **Curtain Wall** icon on the new **Curtain Walls** tool palette and move your cursor over the **Properties** tool palette to open it. This time, enter the **Start** and **End** miter values you got in the previous exercise.
12. Click to set the curtain wall start point, drag your cursor to the right, enter **10′-0″** in the **Command line,** and press **Enter.**
13. Move your cursor vertically, and again enter **10′-0″** in the **Command line.**
14. Enter **OR** (ORTHO) in the **Command line** and press **Enter.**
15. Drag your cursor to the left and click in response to the **Command line** "Point on wall in direction of close."

You have now created a four-wall enclosure with mitered corners (see Figure 6–7). Save this file.

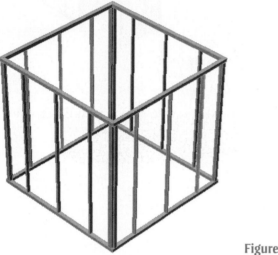

Figure 6–7

**Exercise 6-4:** Using the Roof Line/Floor Line Selections in the Contextual Menu

1. Using the walls from the previous exercise, select a wall, **RMB,** and select **Roof Line/Floor Line > Edit In Place** from the contextual menu that appears (see Figure 6–8).

When editing a curtain wall in place, an **In-Place Edit** toolbar will appear in the Drawing Editor, and blue shading will appear over the wall. This shading shape can be modified and saved back to the curtain wall (see Figure 6–9).

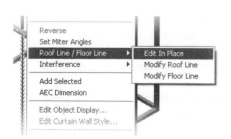

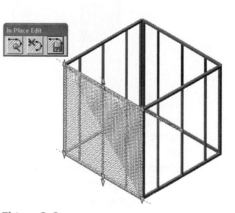

Figure 6–8                                    Figure 6–9

2. Select the blue shading, **RMB,** and select **Add Step** from the contextual menu that appears.
3. Select the floor line of the curtain wall. The curtain wall steps (see Figure 6–10). Repeat Step 2, this time picking **Add Gable** (see Figure 6–11).

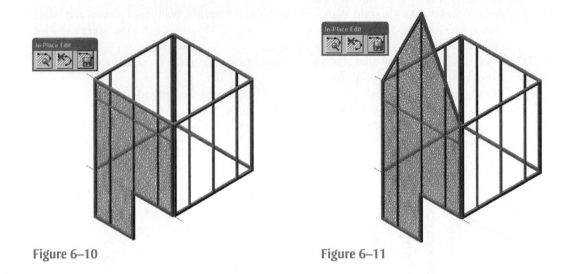

Figure 6–10                          Figure 6–11

4. Select the blue shading again, **RMB,** and select **Reverse** from the contextual menu that appears.
5. Select the floor line of the curtain wall.

The curtain wall step will reverse (see Figure 6–12).

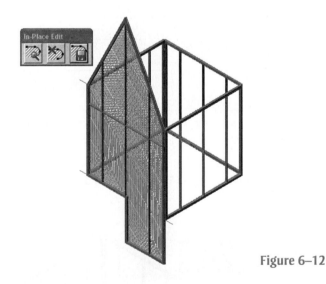

Figure 6–12

6. Select the **Left View** icon from the **Views** toolbar to change to the **Left View.**
7. Select the **Polyline** icon from the **Shapes** toolbar, and draw a polyline as shown in Figure 6–13. The polyline does not have to be in the same plane or touch the curtain wall.
8. Select the blue shading again, **RMB,** and select **Project to Polyline** from the contextual menu that appears.
9. Select the polyline that you just drew, enter **Y** for Yes in the **Command line,** and press **Enter.**

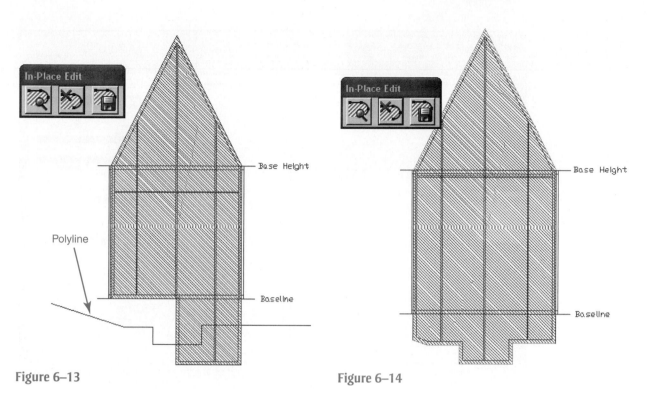

**Figure 6–13**                                    **Figure 6–14**

The curtain wall changes shape to match the polyline (see Figure 6–14).

   10.  Press the **Save All Changes** icon in the **In-Place Edit** toolbar to save the changes.

Save this file.

## Exercise 6-5: Applying Tool Properties to a Layout Grid

   1.  Start a new drawing using the AEC Model (Imperial Stb) template.
   2.  Change to the **Work Layout.**
   3.  Create two viewports, one showing the **Top** view and the other showing the **NW Isometric** view.
   4.  Press the **Content Browser** icon in the **Main** toolbar or enter **Ctrl + 4** on the keyboard to bring up the Content Browser.
   5.  In the Content Browser, select the **Stock Tool Catalog** to open it.
   6.  Open the **Parametric Layout & Anchoring** folder.
   7.  Drag the **Layout Grid 2D** icon into the **Curtain Walls** tool palette you created, and then close the **Stock Tool Catalog.**
   8.  Select the **Layout Grid 2D** icon, and move your cursor over the **Properties** palette to open the palette.
   9.  Enter the following:

   a.  Shape = **Rectangular**
   b.  Boundary = ***NONE***
   c.  Specify on screen = **No**
   d.  X-Width = **30′-0″**
   e.  Y-Depth = **15′-0″**
   f.  (For X axis) Layout type = **Space evenly**
   g.  Number of bays = **6**
   h.  (For Y axis) Layout type = **Space evenly**
   i.  Number of bays = **3**

   10.  Place the grid in the **Top View** viewport, and press the **Enter** key twice to complete the command (see Figure 6–15).
   11.  Select the layout grid, **RMB,** and select **X-Axis > Layout Mode** from the contextual menu that appears.

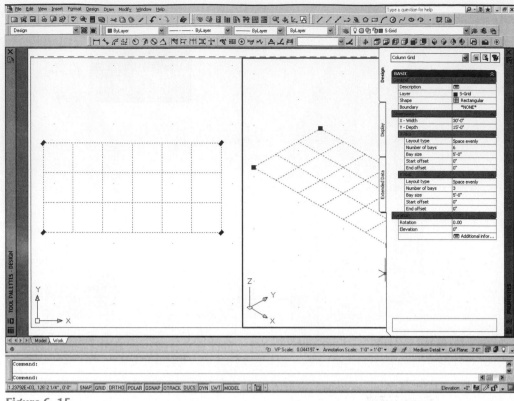

**Figure 6–15**

12. Enter **M** (Manual) in the **Command line,** and press **Enter.**
13. Select the layout grid again, and move some of the grips in the X direction to change the layout (see Figure 6–16).

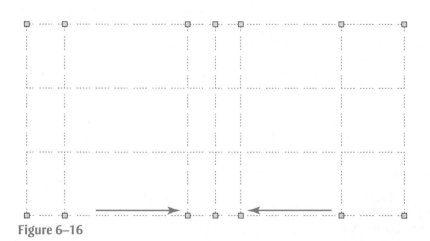

**Figure 6–16**

14. **RMB** on the **Layout Square Grid 5′ × 5′** icon and select **Apply Tool Properties to > Layout Grid** from the contextual menu that appears.
15. Select the layout grid, enter **Y** (Yes) in the **Command line,** and press **Enter.**
16. Enter **V** (Vertical) in the **Command line** (to make the verticals one piece and the horizontals segments) and press **Enter.**
17. Give the curtain wall a new name in the **Curtain Wall Style Name** dialog box that appears and press **Enter** to create the new curtain wall (see Figure 6–17).

Save this exercise.

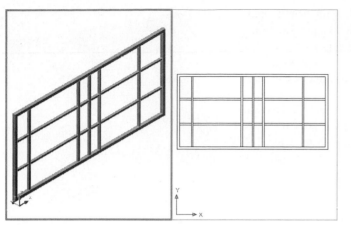

**Figure 6–17**

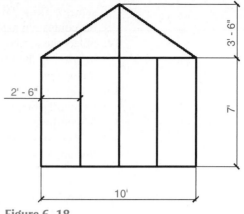

**Figure 6–18**

**Exercise 6-6:** Applying Tool Properties to an Elevation Sketch

1.  Start a new drawing using the AEC Model (Imperial Stb) template.
2.  Change to the **Work Layout.**
3.  Select the **Front View** and create the line drawing shown in Figure 6–18.
4.  **RMB** on the **Square Grid 5′ × 5′ Curtain Wall** icon from the **Curtain Walls** tool palette you created to bring up its contextual menu.
5.  Select **Apply Tool Properties to > Elevation Sketch** from the contextual menu.
6.  Select the line drawing you made in Step 3 of this exercise, and press **Enter** twice.
7.  Enter **Y** (Yes) in the **Command** line when asked to erase the geometry, and press **Enter** to create the curtain wall.

Your line work will now create a curtain (see Figure 6–19).

8.  Select the new curtain wall, **RMB,** and select **Infill > Show Markers** from the contextual menu that appears.

The cell markers will now become visible (see Figure 6–20).

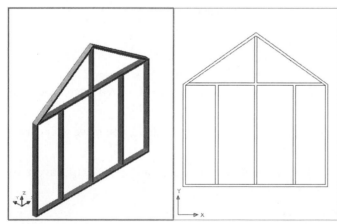

**Figure 6–19**

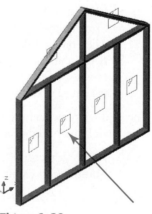

**Figure 6–20**

9.  Select the new curtain wall again, **RMB,** and select **Infill > Merge** from the contextual menu that appears.
10. When the **Command line** reads, "Select cell A," select the leftmost cell marker, and press **Enter.**
11. When the **Command line** reads, "Select cell B," select the next cell marker, and press **Enter.**

The two curtain wall divisions merge into one cell.

12. Repeat Steps 8, 9, and 10 to merge the upper cell (see Figure 6–21).

13. Select the curtain wall again, **RMB,** and select **Infill > Override Assignment** from the contextual menu that appears.
14. Select the leftmost marker and press **Enter** to bring up the **Infill Assignment Override** dialog box.
15. Check the **Bottom** check box and press **OK** to remove the bottom frame (see Figure 6–22).
16. Select the curtain wall again, and select **Infill > Hide Markers** from the contextual menu that appears.

**Note:**
For clarity, the author has removed the display of the window (infill) itself in these illustrations.

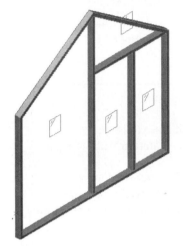

**Figure 6–21**

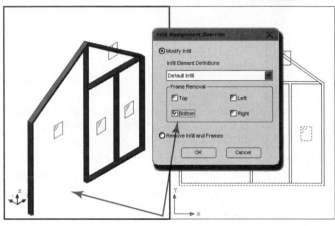

**Figure 6–22**

## Exercise 6-7: Editing a Grid in Place

1. Start a new drawing using the AEC Model (Imperial Stb) template.
2. Change to the **Model Layout.**
3. Change to the **Top View.**
4. Place a Square Grid 5′ × 5′ curtain wall 10′ high and 15′ long.
5. Change to the **Front View.**
6. Click on the curtain wall to activate its grips.
7. Click on the **Edit Grid** grip (see Figure 6–23).
8. **RMB** and select **Division in place** from the contextual menu that appears.
9. Move your cursor over to the left edge of the grid making sure that a red hatch appears in the entire grid, and click (see Figure 6–24).

The grid will now be in Auto Grid Bay Spacing mode (you can see this if you move your cursor over the left middle edge arrow.

10. **RMB** on the grid to bring up the contextual menu that appears, and select **Convert To Manual** (see Figure 6–25).

When you select **Convert To Manual,** + and − icons appear.

11. Select the + icon to add a horizontal mullion (see Figure 6–26).
12. Select the **Exit Editing Grid** icon to bring up the **Save Changes** dialog box, press the **New** button to bring up the **New Division Override** dialog box, enter **New Horizontal Mullion** in the **New Name** data field, and press **OK** to complete the command.
13. Repeat Steps 7–11, picking a vertical mullion and creating a **New Vertical Mullion** (see Figures 6–27 and 6–28).
14. Change the view to **SW Isometric View** and select the **Gouraud** icon in the **Shading** toolbar (see Figure 6–29).

Save this file.

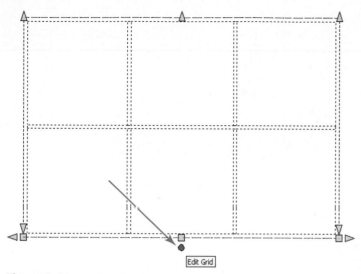

**Figure 6–23**

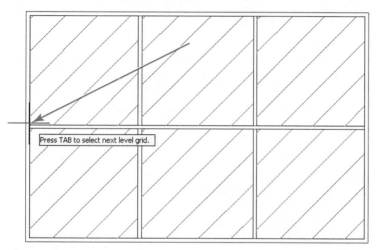

**Figure 6–24**

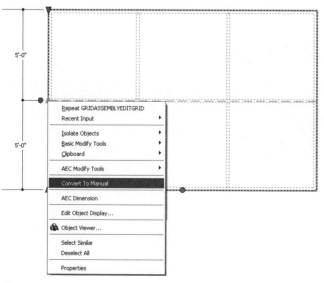

**Figure 6–25**

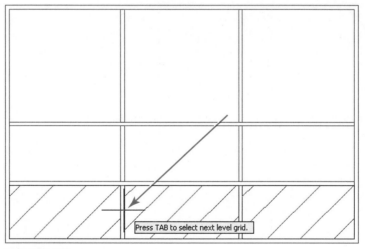

**Figure 6–26**

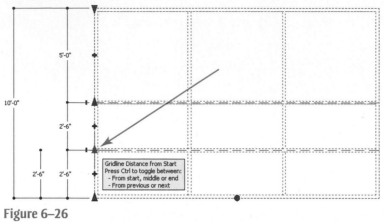

**Figure 6–27**

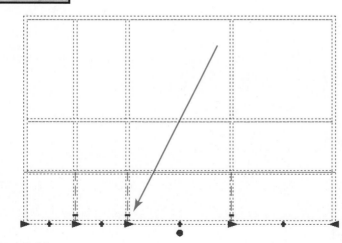

**Figure 6–28**

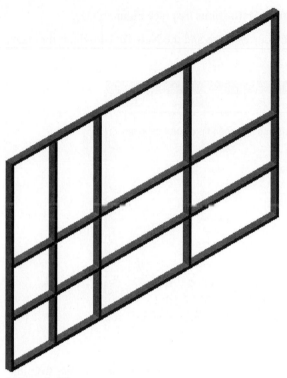

Figure 6–29

## Exercise 6-8: Editing Curtain Wall Styles

1. Use the previous exercise.
2. Select the curtain wall, **RMB,** and select **Edit Curtain Wall Style** from the contextual menu that appears to bring up the **Curtain Wall Style Properties** dialog box.
3. Select the **Design Rules** tab.
4. Select the **Floating Viewer** icon at the bottom left of the **Curtain Wall Style Properties** dialog box, and size it so that both the **Viewer** and the dialog box are open at the same time. Be sure to set the viewer in **SW Isometric** (see Figure 6–30).

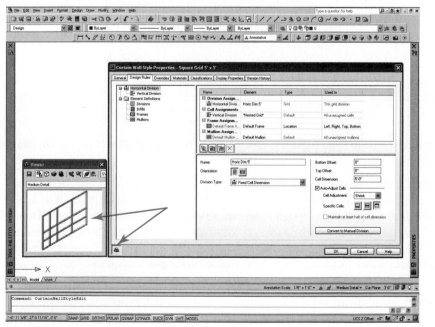

Figure 6–30

5. Select the **Divisions** icon in the **Element Definitions** tree (see Figure 6–31).

Note the divisions made and saved in the previous exercise and the **New Division** icon for creating divisions in this dialog box.

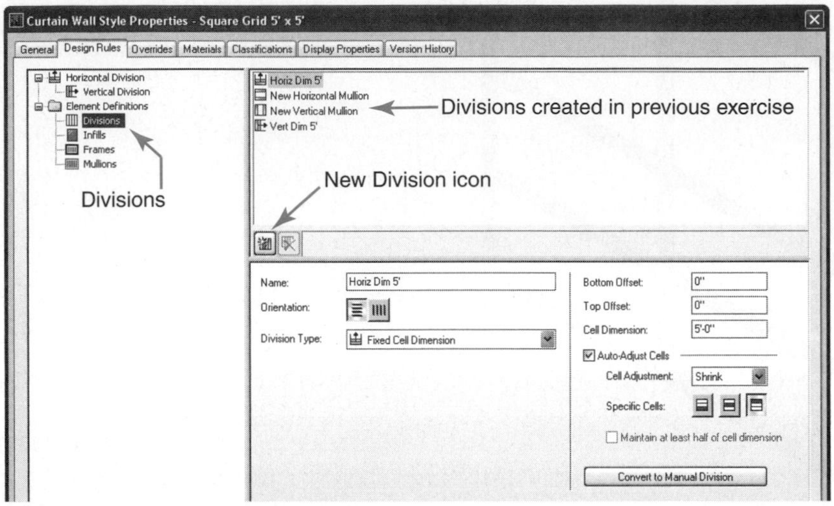

**Figure 6–31**

6. Select the **Horizontal Division** in the tree and select **New Horizontal Mullion** from the **Division Assignment** drop-down list shown in Figure 6–32.

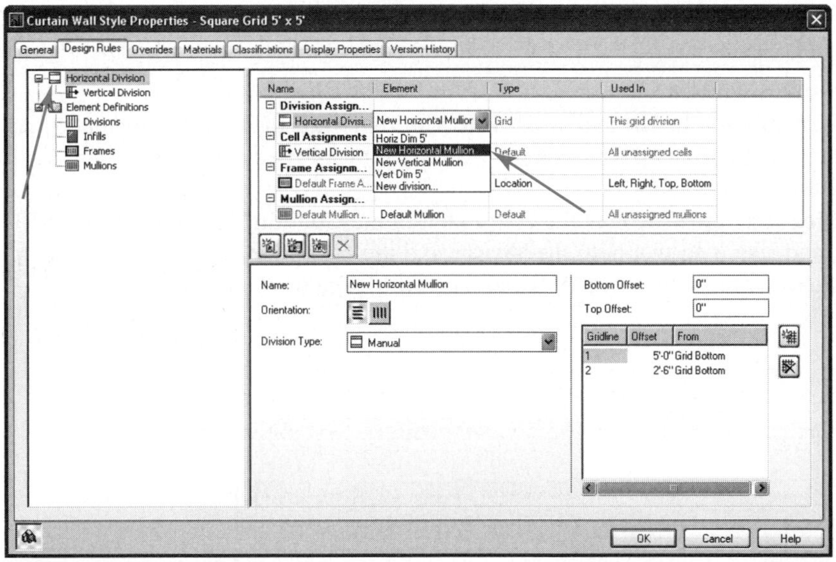

**Figure 6–32**

7. Select **Vertical Division** from the tree and select **New Vertical Mullion** from its **Division Assignment** drop-down list.

We will need a **Pivot - Horizontal** window for this next part of the exercise so use the **Content Browser** to drag a pivot window style into your drawing. To do this: Exit the **Style** dialog box, select the **Content Browser,** and then select the **Design Tool Catalog - Imperial.** In this catalog select **Doors and Windows** and then the **Windows** folder. From the Windows folder, drag the **Pivot - Horizontal** window onto your **Windows** tool palette. Place a **Pivot - Horizontal** window in the Drawing Editor or a spare wall so that the style and properties will be available in the **Properties** palette.

8. Select **Infills** from the tree, select the **New Infill** icon, name the new infill **Pivot Window,** select **Style** from the **Infill Type** drop-down list, and pick the **Pivot - Horizontal** style from the **Style** list (see Figure 6–33).

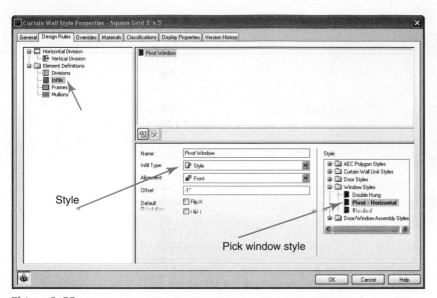

**Figure 6–33**

9. Select the boxed + symbol next to the **Horizontal Division** in the tree menu. This will drop the Vertical Division tree. Select **Vertical Division** from the tree, select the **New Cell Assignment** icon to create a new cell assignment, select **Pivot Window** from the **New Cell Assignment Element** drop-down list, and select **End** from the **Used In** drop-down list (see Figure 6–34).

**Figure 6–34**

10. Press the **OK** buttons to complete the command and return to the Drawing Editor.
11. Select a pivot window that you just installed in the curtain wall, **RMB,** and select **Edit Object Display** from the contextual menu that appears to bring up the **Object Display** dialog box.
12. Make sure the **Model** field is selected, select the **Display Properties** tab, and press the **Edit Display Properties** icon at the upper right to bring up the **Display Properties** dialog box.
13. Select the **Other** tab.
14. Set the **Override Open Percent** to **30,** and press the **OK** buttons in all the dialog boxes to return to the Drawing Editor (see Figure 6–35).

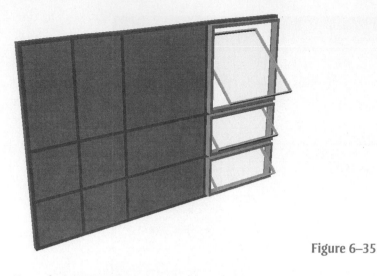

**Figure 6–35**

## Exercise 6-9: Applying Curtain Walls to Faces

1. Start a new drawing using the AEC Model (Imperial Stb) template.
2. Select the **Box** tool from the **Massing** tool palette, and place a **6′-0″**-wide, **4′-0″**-deep, and **7′-0″**-high mass element in the Drawing Editor.
3. Change to the **SW Isometric** view.
4. Double-click the mass element to open the **Properties** palette, and select **Free Form** from the **Shape** drop-down list.
5. With the mass element in **Free Form** mode, select the element, **RMB,** and select **Split by Plane** from the contextual menu that appears.
6. Enter **3** (three points) in the **Command line,** and press the **Enter** key on your keyboard.
7. With the endpoint and nearest Osnaps set, select the points shown in Figure 6–36 in the order shown to create a split plane.
8. Select the top mass form and delete it. You have now created the mass element for placing faces in this exercise (see Figure 6–37).

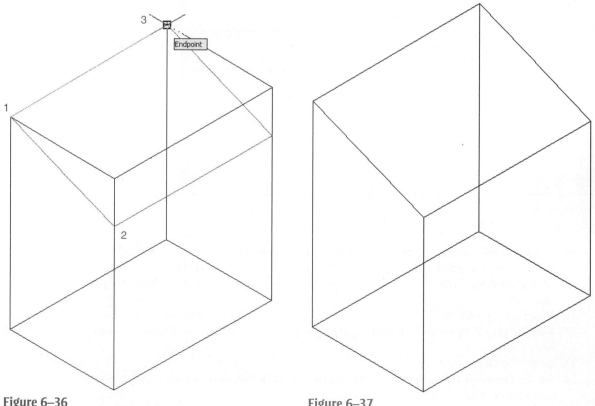

**Figure 6–36**                      **Figure 6–37**

9. Select the **Curtain Wall** tool in the **Design** tool palette, **RMB,** and select **Apply Tool Properties to > Faces** from the contextual menu that appears.
10. Move your cursor over the front face of the mass element until a red hatch appears on that face; then click the cursor to bring up the **Convert to Curtain Walls** dialog box.
11. In the **Convert to Curtain Walls** dialog box, select **Standard,** and press the **OK** button to place the curtain wall on the front face (see Figures 6–38 and 6–39).

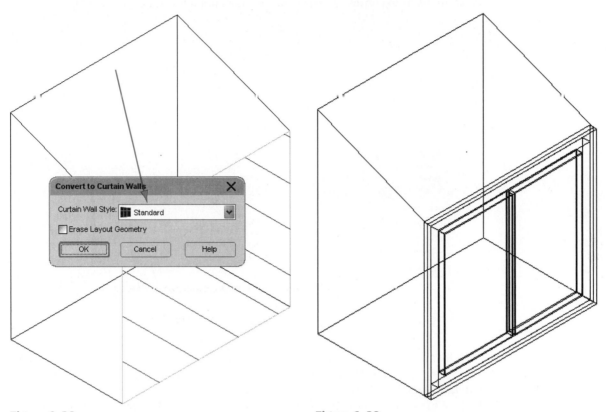

Figure 6–38                              Figure 6–39

12. Zoom in and observe that the midpoint of the curtain wall frame extrusion has been placed on the face of the mass element, and that there is an extra inner frame (see Figure 6–40).

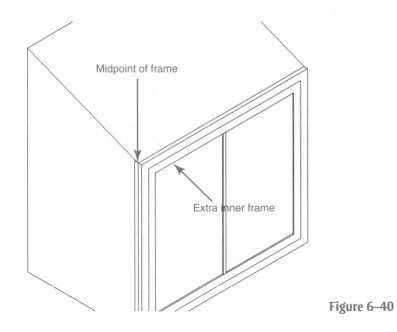

Figure 6–40

To correct this, do the following:

13. Select the curtain wall you just placed, **RMB,** and select **Design Rules > Save to Style** from the contextual menu that appears to bring up the **Save Changes** dialog box.
14. In the **Save Changes** dialog box, press the **New** button to bring up the **New Curtain Wall Style** dialog box.
15. In the **New Curtain Wall Style** dialog box, enter **FRONT,** and press the **OK** buttons to close all the dialog boxes and return to the Drawing Editor (see Figure 6–41).

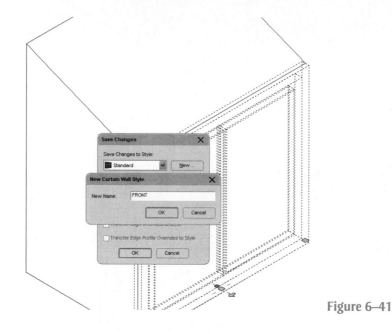

**Figure 6–41**

16. Now that you have changed the curtain wall you placed to **FRONT,** select it, **RMB,** and select **Edit Curtain Wall Style** from the contextual menu that appears to open the **Curtain Wall Style Properties** dialog box for this style.
17. In the **Curtain Wall Style Properties** dialog box, select the **Design Rules** tab.
18. In the **Design Rules** tab, in the left pane, click **Unnamed** at the top of the tree, and expand the **Frame Assignments** in the right pane.
19. Under **Frame Assignments** select the **Default Frame Assignment** field, click to the right of (**Left, Right, Top, Bottom**) in the **Used In** column and select the button that appears to bring up the **Frame Location Assignment** dialog box.
20. In the **Frame Location Assignment** dialog box, *uncheck* all the check boxes, and press the **OK** button to return to the **Curtain Wall Style Properties** dialog box (see Figure 6–42). This will remove the extra inner frame.
21. In the **Curtain Wall Style Properties** dialog box, in the right pane, set the Default Frame **Width** to **2″** and depth to **5″.** Finally, set the **"Y" Offset** to **2-1/2″.** This will move the 5″-deep frame forward from the point. Press the **OK** button to close the dialog box and return to the Drawing Editor (see Figure 6–43).
22. Repeat Steps 9–21 for the left, right, and top faces using **Design Rules > Save to Style** to save them as **LEFT, RIGHT,** and **TOP.** (For the LEFT style you will have to set the **"Y" Offset** to − **2-1/2″.**) See Figure 6–44.

**Exercise 6-10:** Adding Doors to Curtain Walls

1. Start a new drawing using the AEC Model (Imperial Stb) template.
2. Change to the **Top** view.
3. Select the **Curtain Wall** tool from the **Design** tool palette, and move your cursor over the **Properties** palette to open it.
4. In the **Properties** palette set the **Style** to **Standard,** and **Base height** to **10′** and place a curtain wall 8′ long in the Drawing Editor.
5. Change to the **Front** view.

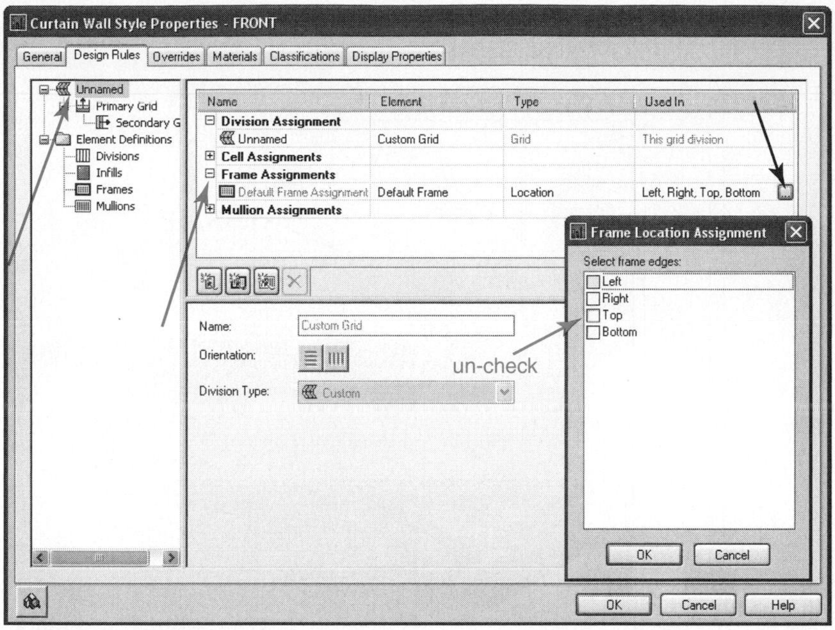

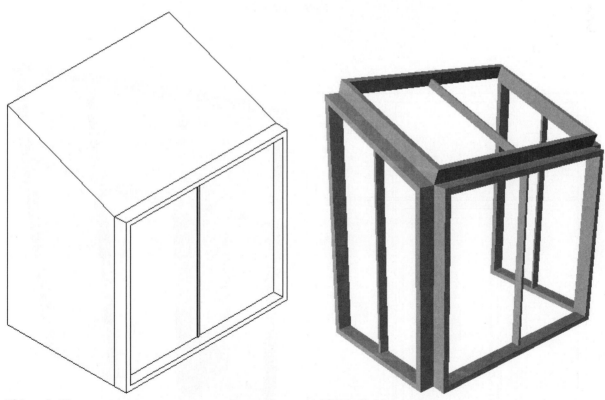

Figure 6–42

Figure 6–43                                    Figure 6–44

6. Using the techniques shown in Exercise 6-7, "Editing a Grid in place," edit the curtain wall to resemble that shown in Figure 6–45.

7. Select the **Hinged–Single–Full Lite** door from the **Doors** tool palette, and select the curtain wall—the cell markers will appear.

8. Move your cursor over the center cell until a red hatch appears, and click to bring up the **Add Infill** dialog box.

9. In the **Add Infill** dialog box, select the **Add as Cell Override** radio button, select the **New Infill** radio button, enter **TEST DOOR** in the **New Infill** field, and check the

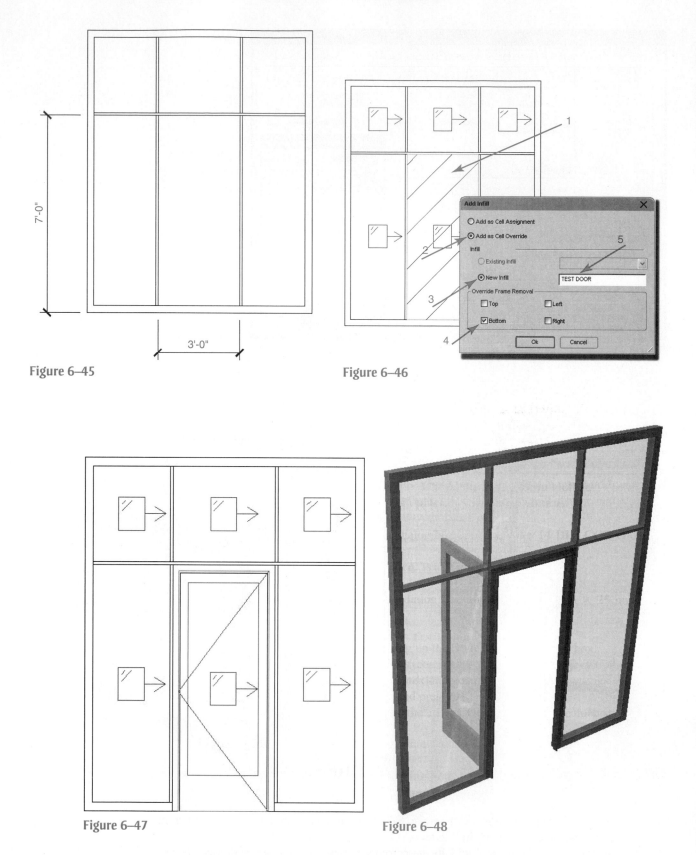

**Figure 6–45**

**Figure 6–46**

**Figure 6–47**

**Figure 6–48**

**Bottom** check box in the **Override Frame Removal** (to remove the frame below the door). Press the **OK** button to complete the command and place the door (see Figures 6–46, 6–47, and 6–48).

This same process can be done for doors, windows, and door and window assemblies.

# Door and Window Assemblies

# 7

## Chapter Objectives

- Create a **Primary Grid** for a **Door/Window Assembly.**
- Learn how to create a door style for double doors.
- Know how to assign doors to a **Door/Window Assembly** infill.
- Test the partially complete **Door/Window Assembly.**
- Know how to add sidelites.
- Know how to size the frame of a **Door/Window Assembly.**
- Remove the sill of a **Door/Window Assembly.**
- Learn how to use a **Door/Window Assembly.**

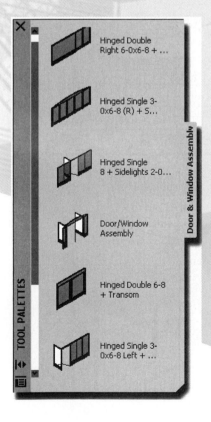

Door/window assemblies provide a grid or framework for the insertion of windows or doors that are commonly used in the design of storefront windows. With this framework, you can create complex window or door assemblies for insertion in a wall or as repetitive elements of the curtain wall.

Window assemblies insert like doors and windows, and they are customized by using the same methods used to create curtain walls.

## Exercise 7-1: Creating a Primary Grid

1. Start a new drawing using the AEC Model (Imperial Stb) template.
2. Change to the **Model Layout.**
3. Select **Format** > **Style Manager** from the **Main** menu to bring up the **Style Manager.**
4. Select **Architectural Objects** > **Door/Window Assembly Styles.**
5. Select the **Door/Window Assembly Styles** icon, **RMB,** and select **New** from the contextual menu that appears.
6. Name the new style **TEST DRWIN ASSEM STYLE.**
7. Double-click on the **TEST DRWIN ASSEM STYLE** icon to bring up the **Door/Window Assembly Style Properties** dialog box.
8. Select the **Floating Viewer** icon and place the **Viewer** adjacent to the **Door/Window Assembly Style Properties** dialog box on the screen (see Figure 7–1).

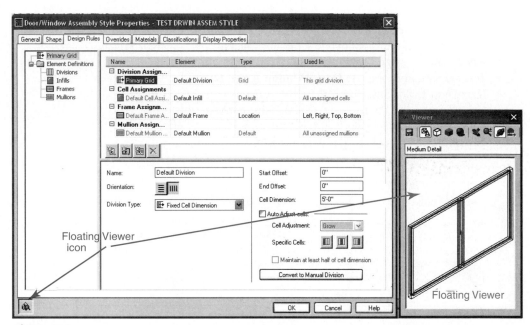

**Figure 7–1**

9. Change to the **Design Rules** tab.
10. Select the **Divisions** icon and follow the directions in Figure 7–2.
11. Select the **Primary Grid** icon, and change its **Element** to the **DOUBLE DOORS DIVISION** that you just created (see Figure 7–3).

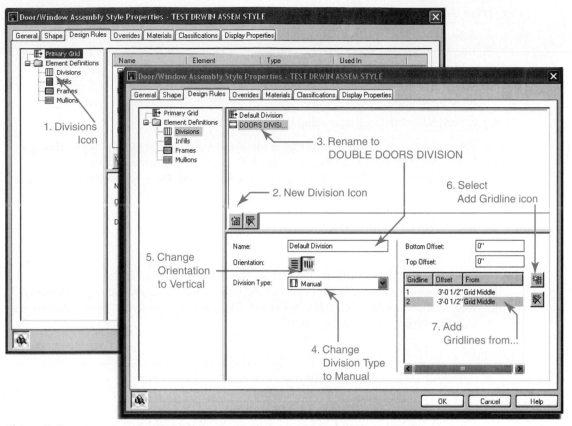

Figure 7–2

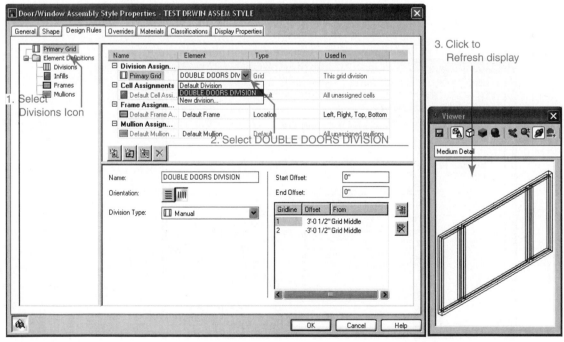

Figure 7–3

**Exercise 7-2:** Creating a Door Style for Double Doors

1. Select the **Content Browser** icon to bring up the **Content Browser.**
2. Locate the **Design Tool Catalog – Imperial** > **Doors and Windows** > **Doors** > **Page 3** folder.
3. In the **Page 3** folder, locate the **Hinged-Single** door.
4. Drag the **Hinged-Single** door onto your **Design** toolbar.

Now you need a Double Door style using this door.

5. Select **Format** > **Style Manager** from the **Main** menu to bring up the **Style Manager.**
6. Locate the **Architectural Objects** > **Door Styles** > **Hinged-Single** icon.
7. Double-click on the **Hinged-Single** icon to bring up the **Door Styles Properties** dialog box.
8. Change to the **Dimensions** tab.
9. Set the **Frame A- Width** to 0″.

This makes the door frameless.

10. In the **Door Styles Properties** dialog box, change to the **Design Rules** tab.
11. Select **Double** from the **Door Type** list, and press **OK** to return to the **Style Manager.**
12. Rename the door **DOUBLE HINGED SINGLE,** and then press the **Apply** and **OK** buttons to return to the Drawing Editor.

**Exercise 7-3:** Assigning Doors to a Door/Window Assembly Infill

1. Select the **Infills** icon and follow the directions in Figure 7–4.
2. After creating the **DOUBLE DOORS** infill, press the **Primary Grid** icon again, and follow the directions in Figure 7–5.
3. Click on the **New Nested Grid** icon below the **Primary Grid** icon and follow the directions in Figure 7–6.
4. Press **OK** to return to the Drawing Editor.

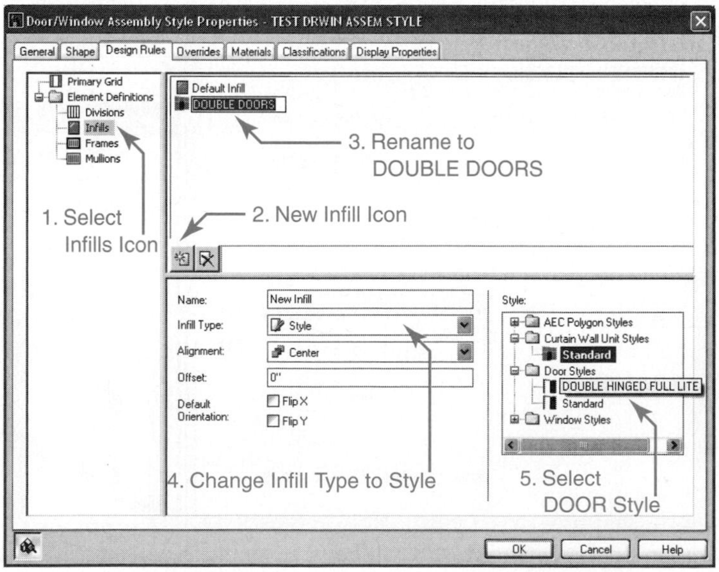

Figure 7–4

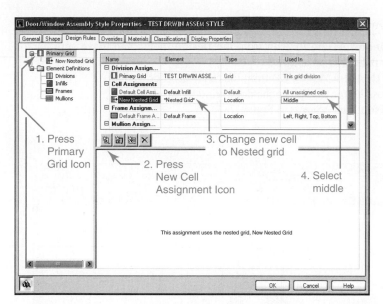

**Figure 7–5**

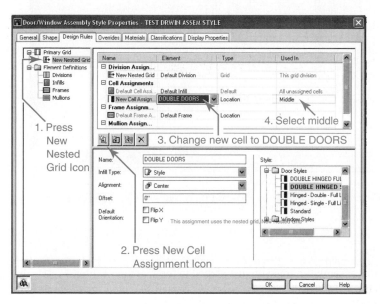

**Figure 7–6**

**Exercise 7-4:** Testing the Partially Complete Door/Window Assembly

1. Select the **Door/Window Assembly** icon from the **Design** menu, and move your cursor over the **Properties** palette to open it.
2. Select **TEST DRWIN ASSEM STYLE** from the **Style** drop-down list.
3. In the **Top View,** press **Enter,** and place the door/window assembly.
4. Change to the **SW Isometric View** (see Figure 7–7).

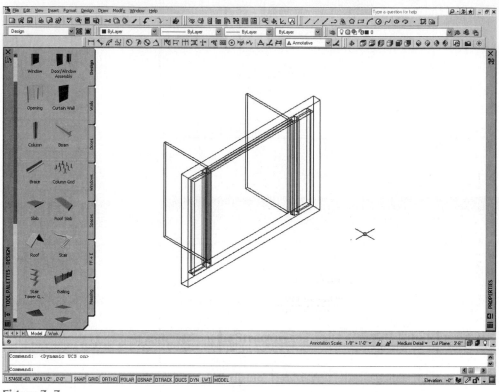

**Figure 7–7**

**Exercise 7-5:** Adding Sidelites

1. Select the door/window assembly frame you just placed in the Drawing Editor, **RMB,** and select **Edit Door/Window Assembly Style** from the contextual menu that appears to bring up the **Door/Window Assembly Style Properties** dialog box.
2. Select the **Design Rules** tab again.
3. Select the **Primary Grid** icon and follow the directions in Figure 7–8.
4. Select the **SIDELITE GRID** icon below the **Primary Grid** icon and follow the directions in Figure 7–9.
5. Select the **Infill** icon and create another infill called **BASE** with a panel thickness of 1′-0″ (see Figure 7–10).

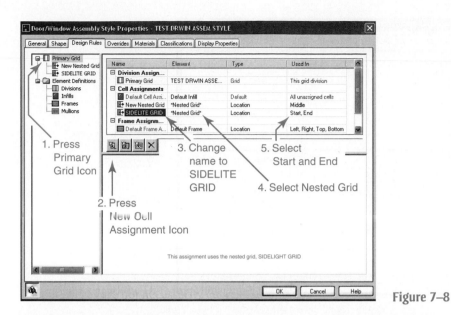

1. Press Primary Grid Icon

2. Press New Cell Assignment Icon

3. Change name to SIDELITE GRID

4. Select Nested Grid

5. Select Start and End

This assignment uses the nested grid, SIDELIGHT GRID

**Figure 7–8**

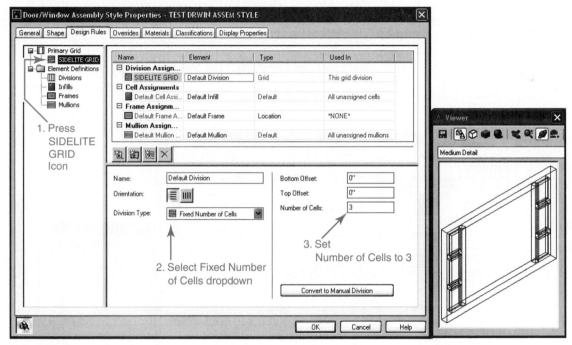

1. Press SIDELITE GRID Icon

2. Select Fixed Number of Cells dropdown

3. Set Number of Cells to 3

**Figure 7–9**

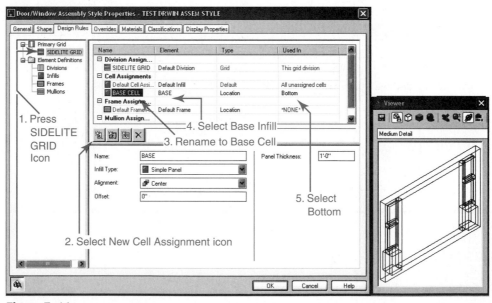

Figure 7–10

6. Select the **SIDELITE GRID** icon below the **Primary Grid** and follow the directions in Figure 7–11.

Figure 7–11

## Exercise 7-6: Sizing the Frame of a Door/Window Assembly

1. Click on the **Frames** icon, change the **Width** to 2″ and the **Depth** to 6″, and press **OK** to return to the Drawing Editor (see Figure 7–12).

**Figure 7–12**

**Exercise 7-7:** Removing the Sill of a Door/Window Assembly and Changing the Sidelite

1.  Select the door/window assembly frame, **RMB,** and select **Infill > Show Markers** from the contextual menu that appears (see Figure 7–13).
2.  Select the frame again, **RMB,** and select **Infill > Override Assignment** from the contextual menu that appears.

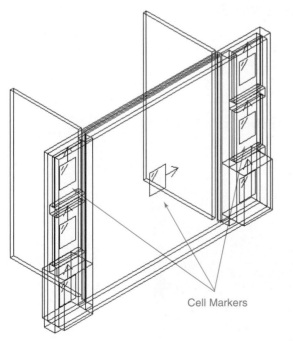

Cell Markers

**Figure 7–13**

3.  Select the cell marker in the center of the door opening, and press **Enter** to bring up the **Infill Assignment Override** dialog box.
4.  Check the **Frame Removal - Bottom** check box (see Figure 7–14).

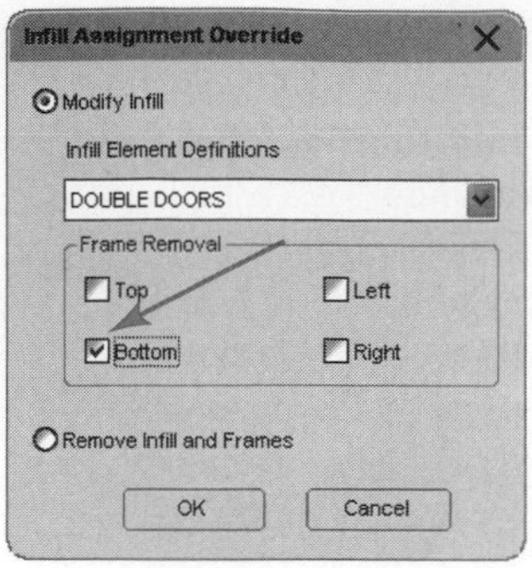

**Infill Assignment Override** ✕

◉ Modify Infill

Infill Element Definitions

DOUBLE DOORS ▾

Frame Removal

☐ Top          ☐ Left

☑ Bottom       ☐ Right

○ Remove Infill and Frames

[ OK ]    [ Cancel ]

**Figure 7–14**

5. Press **OK** to remove the sill and return to the Drawing Editor.
6. Select the frame again, **RMB,** and select **Infill > Merge** from the contextual menu that appears.
7. Select the top two cells in each sidelite to merge the top cells.
8. Select the frame again, **RMB,** and select **Infill > Hide Markers** from the contextual menu that appears.

You now have created a new custom door/window assembly. Save this file.

**Exercise 7-8:** Using the New Custom Door/Window Assembly

1. Use the previous file.
2. Change to the **Top View.**
3. Select the **Wall** icon from the **Design** tool palette, and place a 20'-0"-long Standard wall 8" thick and 10'-0" high.
4. Select the **Door/Window Assembly icon** from the **Design** tool palette.
5. Move your cursor over the **Properties** palette to open it.
6. Select the following:

   a. Style = TEST DRWIN ASSEM STYLE
   b. Position along the wall = **Offset/Center**
   c. Vertical alignment = **Sill**
   d. Sill Height = **0"**

7. Click on the wall to place the assembly (see Figure 7–15).

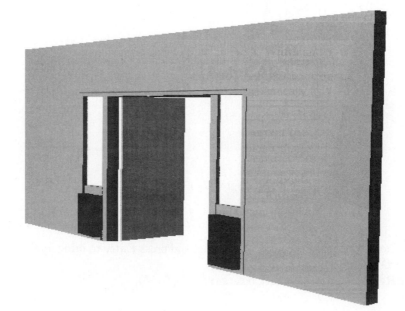

**Figure 7–15**

# Stairs

# 8

## *Chapter* Objectives

- Learn how to set **AEC Object Settings.**
- Know how to make a **Stairs** tool palette.
- Learn how to place a stair object.
- Modify a stair with stair grips.
- Learn how to change an AEC Stair object style.
- Know how add a stair rail object.
- Know how to edit a stair style.
- Know how to place a multilanding stair.
- Understand interference conditions for stairs.
- Learn how to anchor a second stair to an existing landing.
- Learn how to project a stair edge to a polyline.
- Learn how to project a stair edge to a wall or AEC Object.
- Generate a polyline from a stair object.
- Know how to create a stair tower.
- Create and modify a **Custom Stair** from linework.

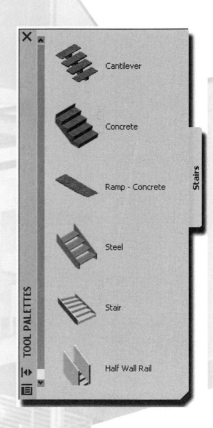

Stair objects can be dragged or inserted either from the **Design** tool palette or by typing **stair add** in the **Command line.**

Stairs are an important part of almost every project, and it is here that designers often make mistakes. AutoCAD Architecture 2008 stair and railing systems aid in the productivity and accuracy of these objects. Because of the complexity and variance of stairs, there is a multitude of settings. Once understood and preset, placing and modifying stairs is quite easy.

Stairs styles are controlled by three factors: style, shape, and turn type. The Content Browser contains eight different preset styles. They are Standard, Cantilever, Concrete, Steel, Half Wall Rail, Ramp Concrete, Ramp Concrete-Curb, and Ramp-Steel. As with the other styles in this program, there are many controls available for the styles in the **Stair Styles** dialog box. By creating your own styles, stairs can be placed into a project quickly and efficiently.

## PROPERTIES PALETTE

**Before Insertion of Stair**

| No selection | | |
|---|---|---|
| **BASIC** | | |
| General | | |
| Description | ▤ | |
| Style | Standard | 1 |
| Shape | Multi-landing | 2 |
| Turn type | 1/2 landing | 3 |
| Vertical Orientation | Up | 4 |
| Dimensions | | |
| A Width | 3'-8" | 5 |
| B Height | 10'-0" | 6 |
| Justify | Center | 7 |
| Terminate with | Riser | 8 |
| Flight length | Distance | 9 |
| Calculation rules | ▤ Tread | 10 |
| C Straight length | 15'-7" | 11 |
| D Riser count | 18 | 12 |
| E Riser | 6 21/32" | 13 |
| F Tread | 11" | 14 |
| Rise/tread calculation | 2'-0 11/32" | 15 |
| Location | | |
| Rotation | 0.00 | 16 |
| Elevation | 0" | 17 |
| **ADVANCED** | | |
| Floor Settings | | |
| A Top offset | 0" | 18 |
| C Bottom offset | 0" | 19 |
| Flight Height | | |
| Minimum Limit type | *NONE* | 20 |
| Maximum Limit type | *NONE* | 21 |
| Interference | | |
| Headroom height | 7'-0" | 22 |
| Left Clearance | 0" | 23 |
| Right Clearance | 0" | 24 |
| Worksheets | | |
| | ▤ Components | 25 |
| | ▤ Landing extensions | 26 |

**After Insertion of Stair**

| Stair | | |
|---|---|---|
| **BASIC** | | |
| General | | |
| Description | ▤ | |
| Layer | A-Flor-Strs | 27 |
| Style | Standard | |
| Shape | Straight | |
| Vertical Orientation | Up | |
| Shadow display | Casts and Receives sh... | 28 |
| Dimensions | | |
| A Width | 3'-8" | |
| B Height | 10'-0" | |
| Justify | Center | |
| Terminate with | Riser | |
| Calculation rules | ▤ Tread | |
| C Straight length | 15'-7" | |
| D Riser count | 18 | |
| E Riser | 6 21/32" | |
| F Tread | 11" | |
| Rise/tread calculation | 2'-0 11/32" | |
| Location | | |
| Rotation | 0.00 | |
| Elevation | 0" | |
| | ▤ Additional informat... | |
| **ADVANCED** | | |
| Floor Settings | | |
| A Top offset | 0" | |
| C Bottom offset | 0" | |
| Flight Height | | |
| Minimum Limit type | *NONE* | |
| Maximum Limit type | *NONE* | |
| Interference | | |
| Headroom height | 7'-0" | |
| Left Clearance | 0" | |
| Right Clearance | 0" | |
| Worksheets | | |
| | ▤ Components | |
| | ▤ Landing extensions | |

| Number | Name | Purpose |
|---|---|---|
| 1 | Style | Select from available stair styles |
| 2 | Shape | U-shaped, Multi-landing, Spiral, Straight |
| 3 | Turn type | ½ landing, ½ turn, ¼ landing, ¼ turn |
| 4 | Vertical Orientation | Specifies whether the stair goes up or down from the level when it is inserted |
| 5 | Width | Width of stair |
| 6 | Height | Height of stair vertically |
| 7 | Justify | Right, Center, or Left insertion points |
| 8 | Terminate with | Terminate with Riser, Tread, or Landing |
| 9 | Flight length | Length of stair horizontally—by tread or distance |
| 10 | Calculation rules | Brings up **Calculation Rules** dialog box |
| 11 | Straight length | Length of stair set by **Calculation Rules** dialog box |
| 12 | Riser count | Amount of risers calculated by stair-calculation rules |
| 13 | Riser | Riser height calculated by stair-calculation rules |
| 14 | Tread | Length of tread set by **Calculation Rules** dialog box |
| 15 | Rise/tread calculation | Calculation formula used by stair-calculation rules |
| 16 | Rotation | Rotation of stair |
| 17 | Elevation | Starting elevation of stair |
| 18 | Top offset | Floor-surface depth at the top of the stairs |
| 19 | Bottom offset | Floor-surface depth below first riser |
| 20 | Minimum Limit type | Riser or flight height minimums |
| 21 | Maximum Limit type | Riser or flight height maximums |
| 22 | Headroom height | Used to control interference with slab above the stair |
| 23 | Left Clearance | Used to control clearance at the left side of the stair |
| 24 | Right Clearance | Used to control clearance at the right side of the stair |
| 25 | Components | Information on tread and riser thickness, nosing length, etc. |
| 26 | Landing extensions | Information on landings |
| 27 | Layer | Change this to place the stair on another layer |
| 28 | Shadow display | Casts and Receives, Casts shadows, Receives shadows, Ignore shadows |

Before beginning to use the stair object, **AEC Object Settings** must be set for the stairs.

### Exercise 8-1: Setting the AEC Object Settings for Stairs

1. Select **Format > Options** from the **Main** toolbar to bring up the **Options** dialog box.
2. Select the **AEC Object Settings** tab (see Figure 8–1).
3. In the **Stair Settings** area select **Flight & Landing Corners** from the **Node Osnap** drop-down list and **Finished Floor to Floor** from the **Measure Stair Height** drop-down list (see Figure 8–2).

**Figure 8–1**

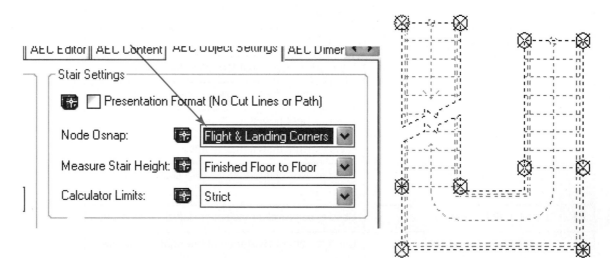

**Figure 8–2**

### Exercise 8-2: Making a New Stairs Tool Palette

1. Create a new tool palette, and name it **Stairs.**
2. Select the **Content Browser** icon from the **Main** toolbar to launch the Content Browser.
3. In the **Design Tool Catalog - Imperial,** locate the **Stairs** folder in the **Stairs and Railings** folder.
4. Drag all the stairs into the new tool palette you created.

## Exercise 8-3: Placing a Stair

1. Start a new drawing using the AEC Model (Imperial Stb) template.
2. Change to the **Model Layout.**
3. Change to the **Top View.**
4. Select the **Stair** icon in the **Stairs** tool palette you created and drag your cursor over the **Properties** palette to open it.
5. Set the following:

    a. Shape = **U-shaped**
    b. Turn type = **1/2 landing**
    c. Horizontal Orientation = **Clockwise**
    d. Vertical Orientation = **Up**
    e. Width = **3'-0"**
    f. Height = **10"**
    g. Top offset = **0"**
    h. Top depth = **10"**
    i. Bottom offset = **0"**
    j. Bottom depth = **10"**
    k. Headroom height = **7'-0"**
    l. Side clearance = **0**

6. Click in the viewport and drag the stair to the right, enter **10'** in the **Command line** and press **Enter** twice to complete the command and create the stair (see Figure 8–3).

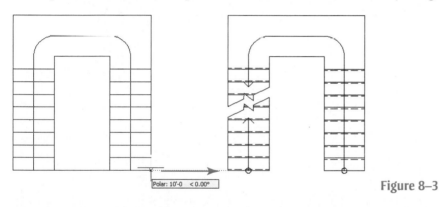

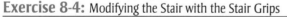

Figure 8–3

## Exercise 8-4: Modifying the Stair with the Stair Grips

1. Select the stair object to activate the stair. Select the **Edit Edges** button to activate the stair grips. Place and modify six stairs using Figures 8–4 through 8–9 as examples. After placing

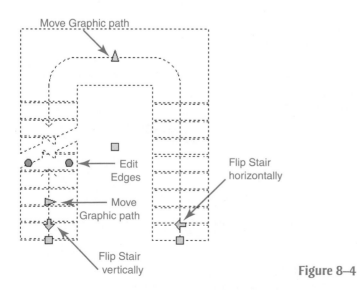

Figure 8–4

each stair, change to the **SW Isometric View** to examine your stair. Save this DWG as STAIR.

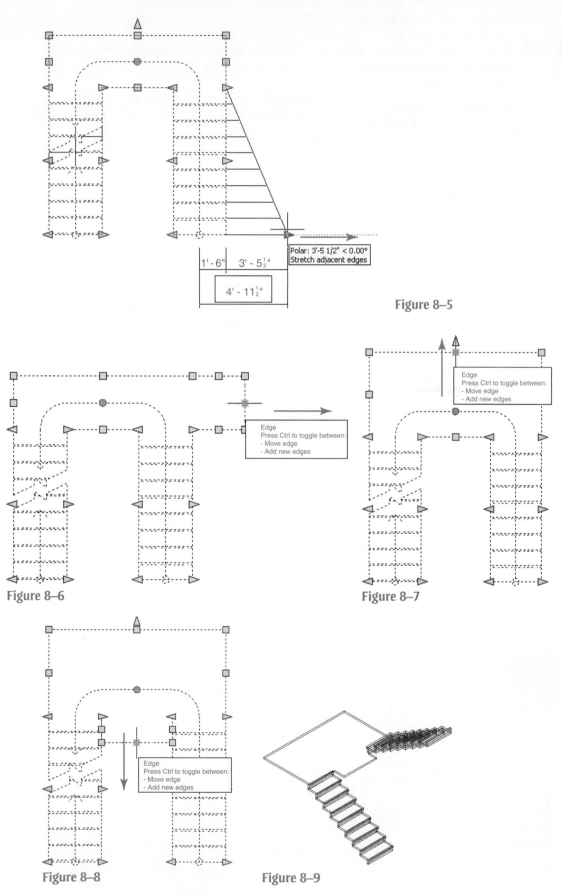

Polar: 3'-5 1/2" < 0.00°
Stretch adjacent edges

1' - 6"     3' - 5$\frac{1}{2}$"

4' - 11$\frac{1}{2}$"

**Figure 8–5**

Edge
Press Ctrl to toggle between:
- Move edge
- Add new edges

**Figure 8–6**

Edge
Press Ctrl to toggle between:
- Move edge
- Add new edges

**Figure 8–7**

Edge
Press Ctrl to toggle between:
- Move edge
- Add new edges

**Figure 8–8**

**Figure 8–9**

## Exercise 8-5: Changing Stair Styles

1. Change to the **SW Isometric View.**
2. In your new **Stairs** tool palette, **RMB** on the **Half Wall Rail** icon and select **Apply Tool Properties to Stair** from the contextual menu that appears.
3. Select your stair, and press **Enter** to complete the command.
4. **RMB** in an empty space in the Drawing Editor, and select **Object Viewer** from the contextual menu that appears.
5. Select the stair, and press **Enter** to open the **Object Viewer** with the stair.
6. Expand the **Object Viewer,** and select the **Perspective** and **Flat Shaded** icons to display the stair in perspective and color (see Figure 8–10).
7. Close the **Object Viewer** to return to the Drawing Editor.
8. Repeat this process with all the other stair styles in your **Stairs** tool palette. Save the file.

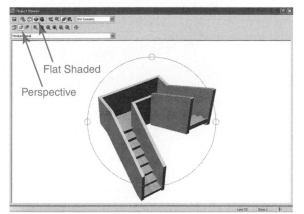

**Figure 8–10**

## Exercise 8-6: Adding a Stair Rail

Modifying railings is explained in Section 9, "Railings."

1. Change your stair back to the Stair style by **RMB** and applying that style to your stair.
2. Select the stair, **RMB,** and select **Add Railing** from the contextual menu that appears.
3. Move your cursor over the closed **Properties** palette to open it.
4. Click on the **\* Attached to** drop-down list, and select **Stair flight** (see Figure 8–11).

**Note:**
If you have difficulty placing the rails in 3D or if the rails don't appear, change to **Top View**, and place the rails in that view.

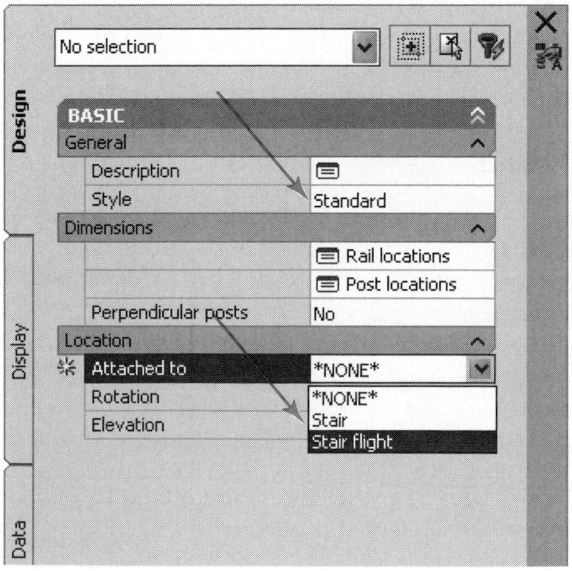

**Figure 8–11**

5. Select the lower corners of the lower stair flight to place a rail (see Figure 8–12).
6. Remove the stair rails and repeat this using the **Stair** and **NONE** options in the **Properties** palette.

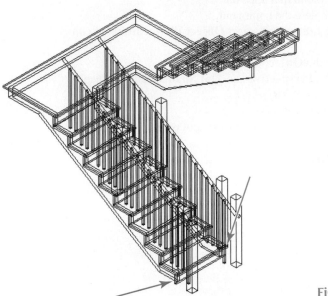

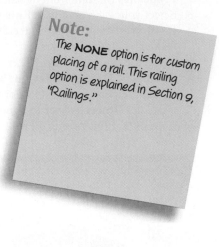

Note:
The **NONE** option is for custom placing of a rail. This railing option is explained in Section 9, "Railings."

Figure 8–12

## Exercise 8-7: Editing a Stair Style

This can also be done through the Style Manager.
1. Select your stair, **RMB,** and select **Edit Stair Style** from the contextual menu that appears to bring up the **Stair Styles** dialog box.
2. Select the **Design Rules** tab. This is where the **Riser Height, Tread Depth,** and the stair calculator are located (see Figure 8–13).

Figure 8–13

3. Change to the **Stringers** tab. This is where the stair stringers are added, removed, and modified.
4. In the **Stringers** tab, press the **Add** button and create a left stringer with the following settings:

   a. **Housed** option from the **Type** drop-down list
   b. D - Total = **12″**
   c. F - Total = **12″**

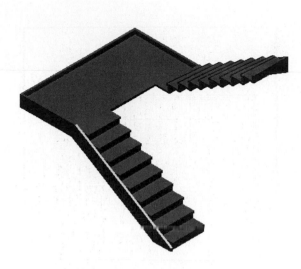

Figure 8–14

d.  E - Waist = **6″**
e.  F - Total = **12″**

5.  Press **OK** to return to the Drawing Editor and see the stair changes (see Figure 8–14).
6.  Select the stair, **RMB,** and open the **Stair Styles** dialog box again.
7.  Select the **Components** tab. This is where modifications to the tread, riser, and land-ing thicknesses are controlled. This is also where tread nosing length and straight or sloping risers are controlled. (Sloping risers are typically used on steel and concrete stairs.)
8.  Select the **Landing Extensions** tab. This is where modifications are made relating to the landings.
9.  Select the **Materials** tab. This is where the materials for the stair are set.
10. Select the **Display Properties** tab. This is where modifications are made relating to the display of stair components in different views.

## Exercise 8-8: Placing a Multilanding Stair

1.  Erase the stair in the previous exercise.
2.  Change to the **Top View.**
3.  Select the **Stair** icon from your **Stairs** tool palette.
4.  Drag your cursor over the **Properties** palette to open it.
5.  Set the following:

a.  Shape = **Multi-landing**
b.  Turn type = **1/2 landing**
c.  Vertical Orientation = **Up**
d.  Width = **3′-0″**
e.  Height = **10″**
f.  Top offset = **0″**
g.  Top depth = **10″**
h.  Bottom offset = **0″**
i.  Bottom depth = **10″**
j.  Headroom height = **7′-0″**
k.  Side clearance = **0**

6.  Click in the viewport and drag the stair vertically (90°) until 7/18 appears to the left of the stair, and click again; this starts the landing.
7.  Continue to move the cursor in the direction of 90°, enter **5′** in the **Command line,** and press **Enter;** this establishes the end of the landing.
8.  Drag the cursor to the right (0°) until 18/18 appears above the stair, and click the mouse to complete the stair.
9.  Change to the **SW Isometric View** and press the **Flat Shaded** icon in the **Shading** toolbar (see Figure 8–15). Save this file.

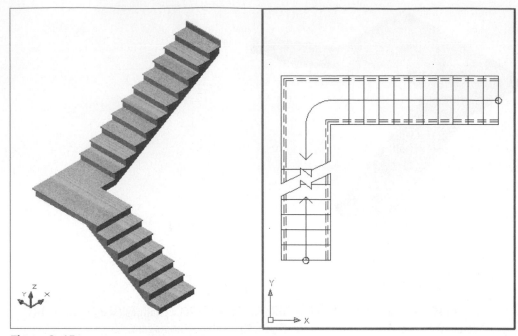

**Figure 8–15**

### Exercise 8-9: Interference Conditions

1. Using the stair from the previous exercise, change to the **Top View.**
2. Place a 20′-high wall as shown in Figure 8–16.
3. Select the wall, **RMB,** and select **Interference Condition > Add** from the contextual menu that appears.
4. Select the lower stair flight, and press **Enter.**
5. Enter **S** (Subtractive) in the **Command line** and press **Enter** to complete the command.

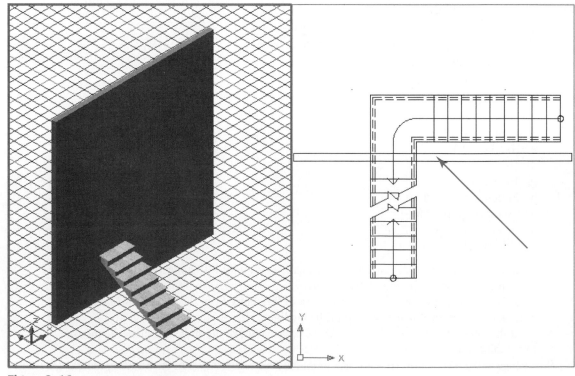

**Figure 8–16**

The wall is cut by the stair (see Figure 8–17), and the interference distance above the stair is set in the stair properties under **Interference Headroom height** (see Figure 8–18).

**Note:**
Stair interference conditions are also available for slabs.

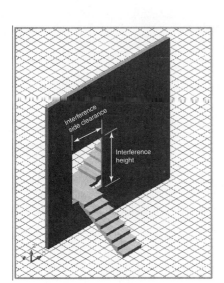

Figure 8–17

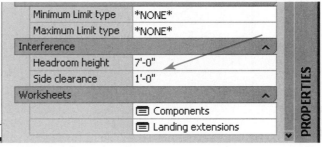

Figure 8–18

**Exercise 8-10:** Anchoring a Second Stair to an Existing Landing

1. Use the stair created in Exercise 8-8, "Placing a Multi-landing Stair."
2. Change to the **Work Layout.**
3. Change to the **Top View.**
4. Create a new straight Standard stair with **Vertical Orientation** set to **Up** (see Figure 8–19).
5. Select the original stair, **RMB,** and select **Stair landing Anchor > Anchor to Landing** from the contextual menu that appears.
6. Select the second stair.

**Note:**
Once anchored, the new stair might not be in the right location. If you drag the new stair around the landing, it will stop at different locations, similar to a door or window that is anchored to a wall.

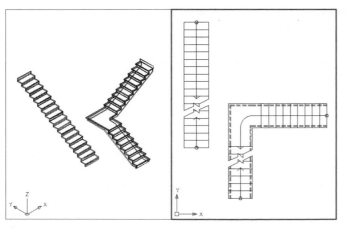

Figure 8–19

7. Select the first stair's landing to attach the second stair to the landing.
8. Once it is attached, you can change to the **Top View** and move the second stair into a desired location (see Figure 8–20).

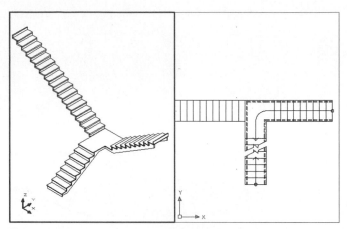

**Figure 8–20**

**Exercise 8-11:** Projecting a Stair Edge to a Polyline

1. Start a new drawing using the AEC Model (Imperial Stb) template.
2. Change to the **Model Layout.**
3. Change to the **Top View.**
4. Select the **Polyline** icon from the **Draw** toolbar and draw the shape shown in Figure 8–21.

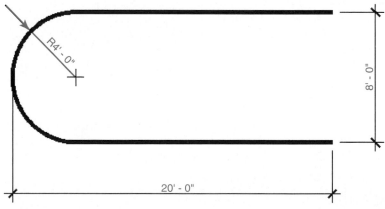

**Figure 8–21**

5. Select the **Stair** icon from the **Stairs** tool palette and add a U-shaped stair 8′ high inside the polyline as shown in Figure 8–22.
6. Select the stair, **RMB,** and select **Customize Edge > Project** from the contextual menu that appears.
7. In the **Top View** select the front of the stair landing, select the curved part of the polyline, and then press **Enter** to project the landing (see Figure 8–23).

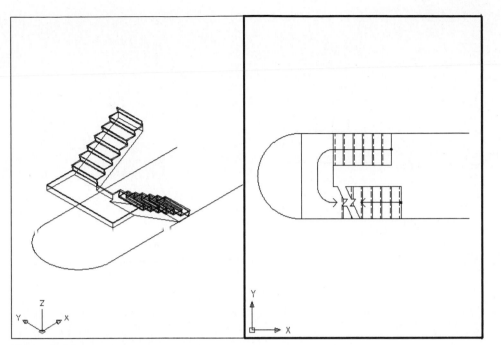

**Figure 8–22**

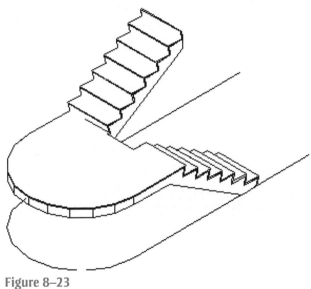

**Figure 8–23**

## Exercise 8-12: Projecting a Stair Edge to a Wall or AEC Object

1. Using the previous exercise, select the polyline to activate its grips.
2. Select an end grip, and modify the polyline as shown in Figure 8–24.
3. Select the **Wall** icon from the **Design** tool palette, **RMB,** and select **Apply Tool Properties to > Linework.**
4. Select the polyline and press **Enter.**
5. Enter **Y** (Yes) in the **Command line,** and press **Enter** to create the wall.
6. While the wall is still selected, move your cursor over the **Properties** palette to open it.
7. Set the following:

   a. Style = **CMU-8 Rigid-1.5 Air-2 Brick-4**
   b. Base height = **8″-0′**
   c. Justify = **Left**

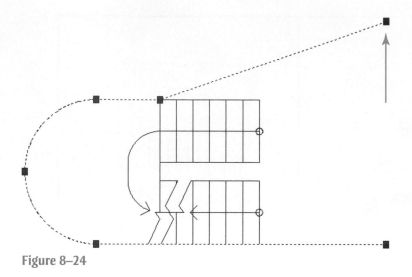

Figure 8–24

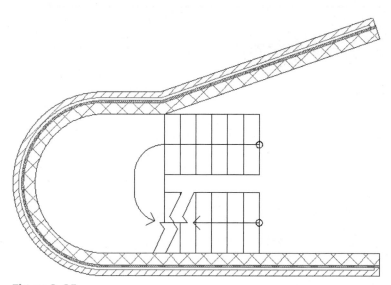

Figure 8–25

You now have a stair within a masonry enclosure (see Figure 8–25).

8. Select the stair, **RMB,** and select **Customize Edge > Project** from the contextual menu.
9. Select the right-hand edge of the stair run, select the wall opposite it, and then press **Enter** to complete the command.

The stair run projects itself to the wall (see Figure 8–26).

**Note:**

If you don't have the CMU-8 Rigid-1.5 Air-2 Brick-4 style in your **Walls** tool palette, you can find it in the AutoCAD Architecture Design Tool Catalog- Imperial > Walls > CMU > Page 4.

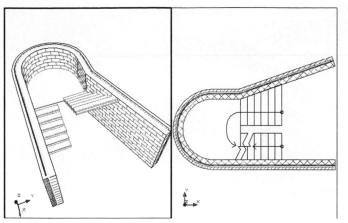

Figure 8–26

## Exercise 8-13: Generating a Polyline from a Stair Object

The **Generate Polyline** command is very useful when you have created a stair, and need a polyline to create walls, or to create an opening in a slab.

1. Use the previous exercise.
2. Erase the walls leaving just the stair.
3. Select the **Slab** icon from the **Design tool** palette, and place a Standard 6″, Direct-mode,
   top-justified slab underneath the stair as shown in Figure 8–27.

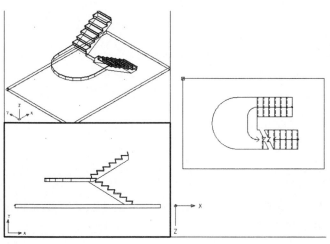

Figure 8–27

4. Select the stair, **RMB,** and select **Customize Edge > Generate Polyline** from the contextual menu that appears.
5. Select the outer edge of the stair, repeat Step 4, and touch the inside of the lower stair run.
   Press **Enter** to complete the command, and then place a line at the inner edge of the stair
   run (see Figure 8–28).
6. Select the **Layers** icon from the **Object Properties** toolbar and **Freeze** the **Stair** layer
   (A-Flor-Strs) to hide the stair.
7. Using **Extend** and **Trim,** clean up the polylines created by the **Generate Polyline** option
   of **Customize Edges** in Steps 4 and 5.
8. Type **Pedit** in the **Command line** and create two polylines as shown in Figure 8–29.
9. Select the slab object, **RMB,** and select **Hole > Add** from the contextual menu that appears.
10. Select the closed polyline, and press **Enter.**
11. Enter **Y** (Yes) in the **Command line** and press **Enter** to create the hole in the slab.

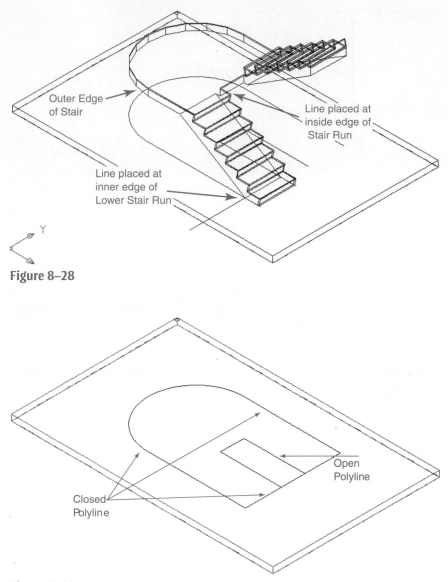

Outer Edge of Stair

Line placed at inside edge of Stair Run

Line placed at inner edge of Lower Stair Run

**Figure 8–28**

Open Polyline

Closed
Polyline

**Figure 8–29**

You have now made a hole in the slab exactly matching the stair through the use of the **Generate poly** option of the **Customizing Edge** command.

## Finishing the Stairway

12. Unfreeze the stair layer to unhide the stair.
13. Select the **Wall** icon from the **Design** tool palette, **RMB,** and select **Apply Tool Properties to > Linework** from the contextual menu that appears.
14. Select the open polyline, enter **Y** (Yes) in the **Command line,** and press **Enter** to create a wall.
15. While the wall is still selected, move your cursor over the **Properties** palette to open it.
16. Set the following:

    a. Style = **Standard**
    b. Width = **6″**
    c. Base height = **8′-0″**
    d. Justify = **Left**

You have now created a stair, a slab, and walls (see Figure 8–30).

17. Select the **Railing** icon from the **Design** tool palette, and move your cursor over the **Properties** palette to open it.

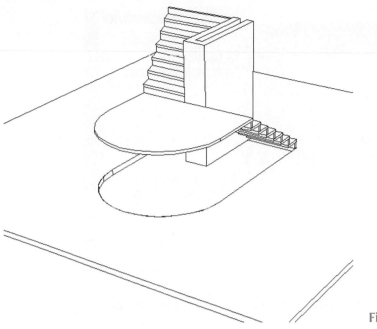

Figure 8–30

18. Select the following:

    a. Style = **Standard**
    b. Attached to = **Stair**
    c. Side offset = **2″**
    d. Automatic placement = **Yes**

19. Select the stair to create the railing; then press **Enter** to complete the command.

## Exercise 8-14: Creating a Stair Tower

You create a stair tower from one stair, which is replicated on selected levels in the building. You can create a stair tower with all stair shapes except spiral. The floor-to-floor height and starting elevation of each stair are adjusted to match those for each selected level. The X, Y coordinates for each stair start point are fixed.

> **Note:**
> To create a stair tower, the stair must be in a construct with multiple levels.

1. Select **File > Project Browser** from the **Main** menu to bring up the **Project Browser** dialog box.
2. Select the **New Project** icon at the bottom left of the dialog box, and create a new project. Name the new project **STAIR TOWER TEST,** and press the **OK** button.
3. Press the **Close** button in the **Project Browser** dialog box to bring up the **Project Navigator** dialog box.
4. Select the **Edit Levels** icon in the **Levels** icon to bring up the **Levels** dialog box.
5. Press the **Add Level** icon five times to create five levels. Set the **Floor Elevations** and **Floor to Floor Heights** as shown in Figure 8–31, and press the **OK** button to return to the Drawing Editor.
6. In the **Project Navigator,** select the **Constructs** tab, **RMB** on the **Constructs** icon, and select **New > Construct** from the contextual menu that appears to bring up the **Add Construct** dialog box.
7. Enter **STAIR TOWER** in the **Name** field.
8. Check all check boxes in the **Division** column and press the **OK** button (see Figure 8–32).
9. In the **Project Navigator,** select the **Constructs** tab and double-click on the **STAIR TOWER** construct you just created to open it in the Drawing Editor.

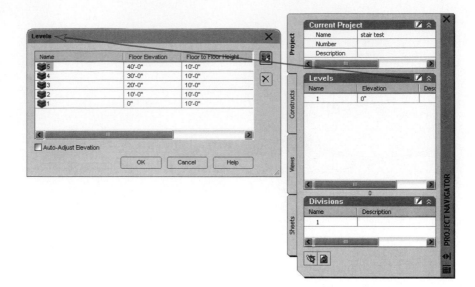

Figure 8–31

10.  Place a Standard U-shaped stair with the following property settings:

    a.  Shape = **U-shaped**
    b.  Turn type = **1/2 landing**
    c.  Horizontal Orientation = **Clockwise**
    d.  Vertical Orientation = **Up**
    e.  Width = **3′-0″**

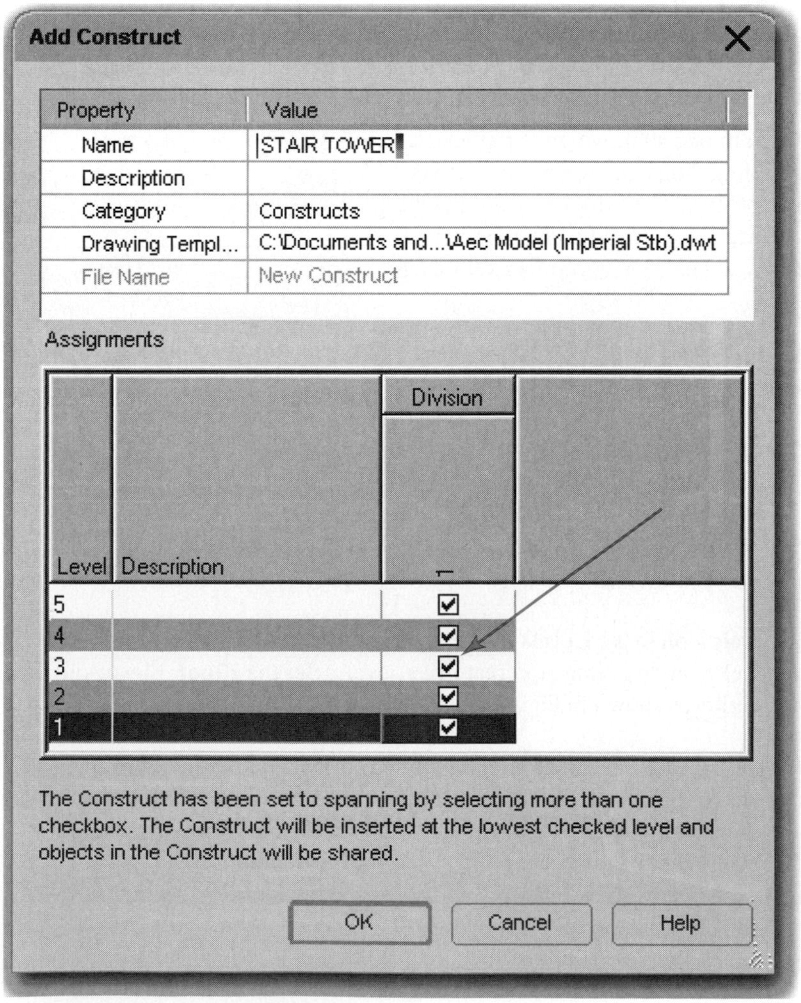

Figure 8–32

f.  Height = **10″**

g.  Justify = **Outside**

h.  Top offset = **0″**

i.  Top depth = **10″**

j.  Bottom offset = **0″**

k.  Bottom depth =**10″**

l.  Headroom height = **7′-0″**

m.  Side clearance = **0″**

11.  Make the overall width of the stair **7′-0″.**

12.  Place an 8′ × 12″ rectangle as shown in Figure 8–33.

13.  In the **Design** tool palette, **RMB** on the **Slab** tool, and select **Apply Tool Properties to > Linework and Walls.**

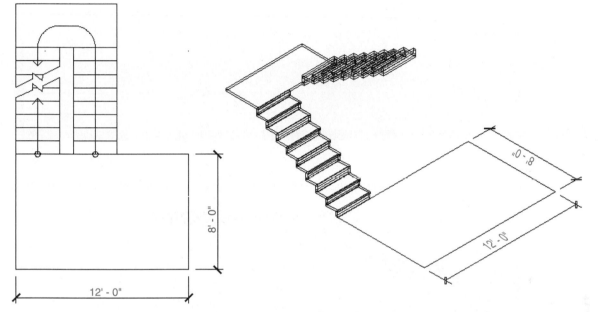

Figure 8–33

14.  Select the rectangle you just created and press **Enter.**

15.  Enter **Y** (Yes) in the **Command line** and press **Enter.**

16.  Enter **P** (Protected) in the **Command line** and press **Enter.**

17.  Enter **10′** in the **Command line** and press **Enter.**

18.  Enter **T** (Top) in the **Command line** and press **Enter.**

You have now placed a slab at the top of the stair (see Figure 8–34).

19.  Change to the **SW Isometric View.**

20.  In the **Design** tool palette, select the **Stair Tower Generate** tool, select the stair and then the slab you just created, and press **Enter** to bring up the **Select Levels** dialog box (see Figure 8–35).

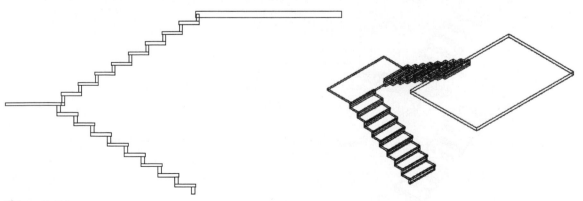

Figure 8–34

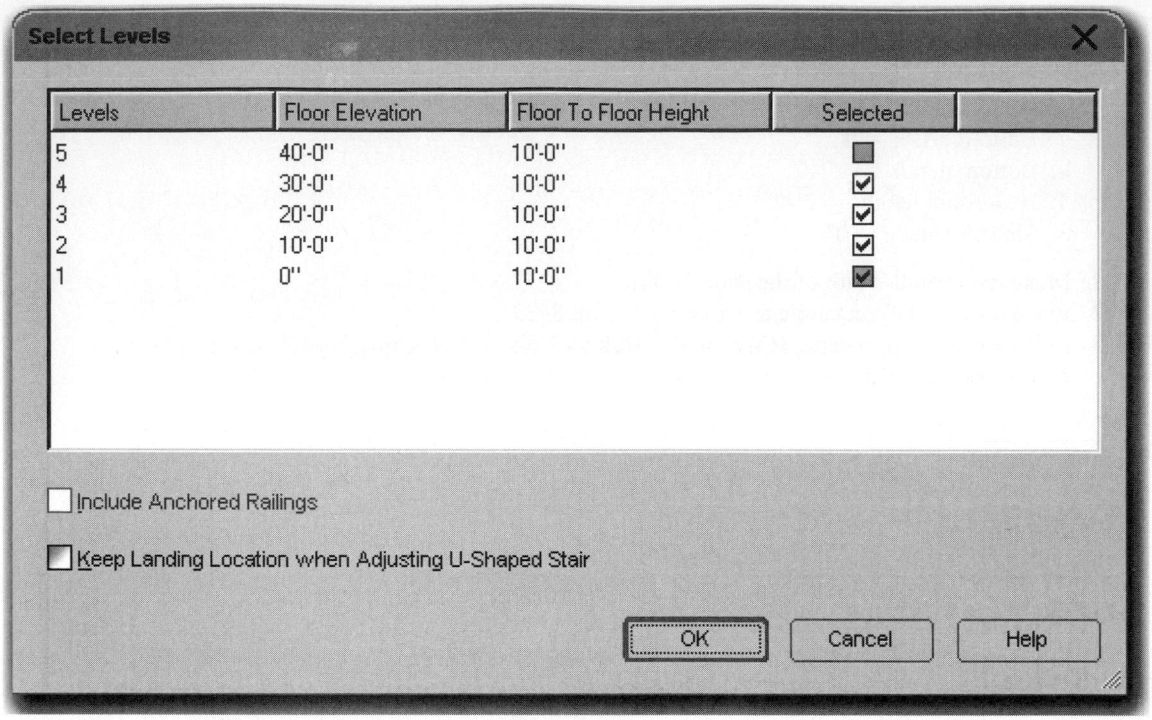

**Select Levels**

| Levels | Floor Elevation | Floor To Floor Height | Selected | |
|--------|-----------------|-----------------------|----------|---|
| 5 | 40'-0'' | 10'-0'' | ☐ | |
| 4 | 30'-0'' | 10'-0'' | ☑ | |
| 3 | 20'-0'' | 10'-0'' | ☑ | |
| 2 | 10'-0'' | 10'-0'' | ☑ | |
| 1 | 0'' | 10'-0'' | ☑ | |

☐ Include Anchored Railings

☐ Keep Landing Location when Adjusting U-Shaped Stair

[ OK ]    [ Cancel ]    [ Help ]

**Figure 8–35**

21. Press the **OK** button in the **Select Levels** dialog box to generate the stair tower (see Figure 8–36).

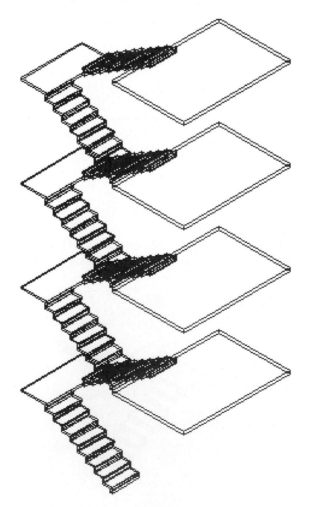

**Figure 8–36**

## Exercise 8-15: Creating and Modifying a Custom Stair from Linework

This is the option to create custom stairs by creating some of the parameters with linework.

The stair outline component of a custom stair is delineated by the left and right stair sides, the nosing of the first tread, and the front of the last tread or landing.

Stair stringers can be selected as linework, or they can be automatically generated by AutoCAD Architecture. After you create a custom stair, you can replace stringer paths. You can add or modify stringers by editing the stair style. The current stair properties govern the appearance of stair components in various representations.

You can create the linework for your custom stair using lines, polylines, or arc segments. All tread lines must intersect with the sides of the stair.

Linework for custom stairs can represent the following components:

- Left and right stair sides (required)
- Stair path (optional)
- Left, right, and center stair stringers (optional)
- First tread at current level (required)
- Remaining treads (required)

1. Start a new drawing using the AEC Model (Imperial Stb) template.
2. Change to the **Top View.**
3. Select the **Line** tool from the **Draw** toolbar.
4. Create the outline shown in Figure 8–37.
5. Using the **Offset** command, offset the left and right lines 6″—these will become the **Left** and **Right Stringer paths** (see Figure 8–38).
6. Again using the **Offset** command, offset the left lines 2′-6″—this will become the **Stair Path** (see Figure 8–39).

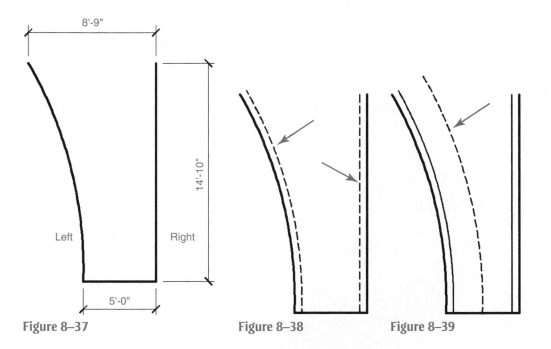

Figure 8–37                    Figure 8–38            Figure 8–39

7. Again using the **AEC Modify Tools > Array** command, offset the left lines' bottom line 11″—these will become the **Stair treads.**
8. Extend the treads to the left outline (see Figure 8–40).
9. Select the **Stair** tool from the **Design** tool palette, **RMB,** and select **Apply Tool Properties to > Linework** from the contextual menu that appears.
10. Select the **Left** and then the **Right** outline, respectively, and then press **Enter** on your keyboard.
11. Select the **Stair Path** you created.
12. Select the **Left Stringer Path,** and then the **Right Stringer Path,** and then press **Enter** on your keyboard.

13. Select the bottom tread, and then select the remaining treads (you can use a "crossing window" to select them all at the same time).
14. Press the **Enter** key on your keyboard to bring up the **Convert to Stair** dialog box.
15. In the **Convert to Stair** dialog box, set the **Stair Style** (accept **Standard** for this exercise).
16. Set the **Height** to **9′-0″, Terminate with > Landing,** check the **Erase Layout Geometry** check box, and then press the **OK** button to return to the Drawing Editor and create the custom stair (see Figure 8–41).

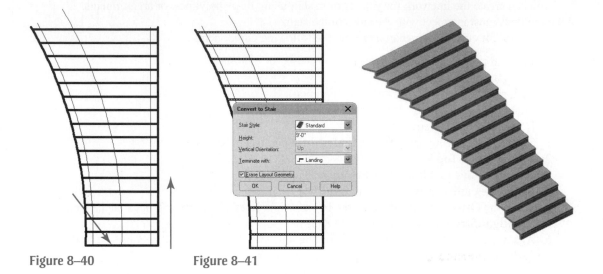

Figure 8–40                    Figure 8–41

17. Change to the **SW Isometric** view.
18. Select the stair you created, **RMB,** and select **Copy Stair Style and Assign** from the contextual menu that appears to bring up the **Stair Styles** dialog box.
19. In the **Stair Styles** dialog box, change to the **General** tab, and rename this new Stair Style **CUSTOM TEST STAIR.**
20. Change to the **Stringers** tab, and add two **2″**-wide **Saddled** stringers, aligned **Left** and **Right.**
21. Press **OK** to return to the Drawing Editor (see Figure 8–42).

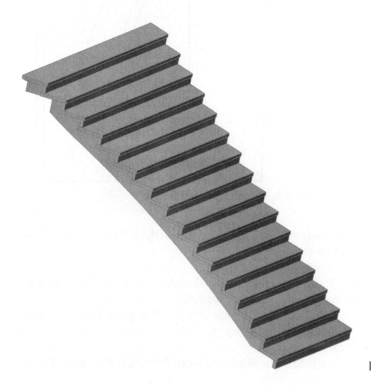

Figure 8–42

22. Select the stair, **RMB,** and select **Modify Custom Stair > Edit Tread/Riser** from the contextual menu that appears.
23. Press the round grip on the bottom tread to expose the tread edge grips.
24. Grab the edge grip, drag it to the right, press the **Ctrl** key on your keyboard, enter **9″** in the **Command line,** and then press the **Enter** key on your keyboard. Repeat on the other side of the bottom tread (see Figure 8–43).

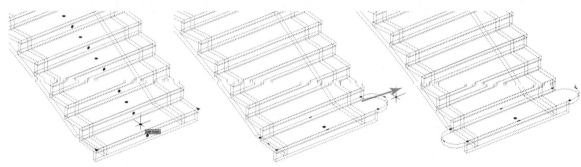

**Figure 8–43**

25. Select the round grip on top of the tread to exit the **tread edit** mode, and enter the adjacent lower riser mode.
26. Grab the arrows that appear above the tread, and move them in the direction shown in Figure 8–44.

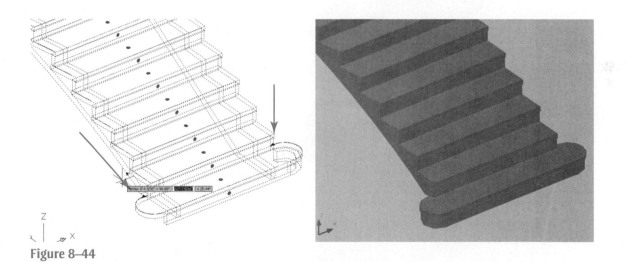

**Figure 8–44**

27. Change to the **Top** view.
28. Place a **Polyline** set for **Arc** as shown in Figure 8–45.

This will be the shape and placement for the stringer.

29. Again select the stair, **RMB,** and select **Modify Custom Stair > Replace Stringer Path** from the contextual menu that appears.
30. Enter **L** (Left Stringer) in the **Command line,** and press **Enter** on your keyboard.
31. Select the polyline you just placed, and press **Enter** on your keyboard.
32. Enter **X** (Exit) in the **Command line,** and press **Enter** on your keyboard.

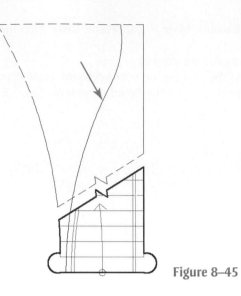

**Figure 8–45**

33. Change to a 3D view, and take a look at the left stringer.

The stair is shown in transparency so that the modified stringer can be viewed  (Figure 8–46).

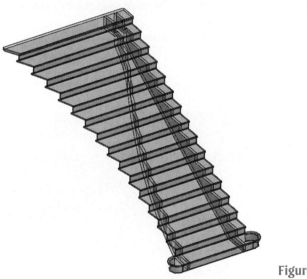

**Figure 8–46**

# Railings

# 9

## Chapter *Objectives*

- Make a **Railing** tool palette.
- Learn how to place a **Railing.**
- Learn how to edit a **Railing Style.**
- Know how to modify balusters.
- Add a railing to a stair and stair flight.
- Add a railing to a landing.
- Add a railing and landing support—**Anchor to Object.**
- Learn how to create a railing using a polyline.
- Know how to edit a **Railing Profile** in place.

## RAILINGS

Stairs and porches must have rails. AutoCAD Architecture 2008 has an excellent parametric railing feature. Railings are AEC Objects that interact with stairs and other objects such as slabs. You can add railings to existing stairs, or you can create freestanding railings. Railings can have guardrails, handrails, posts, balusters, and one or more bottom rails. Additionally, you can add custom blocks to railings in order to create a railing with a nontypical detail. This feature has not changed significantly from prior release of this program, which attests to its completeness.

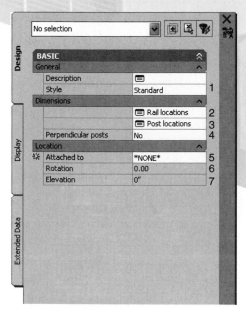

**Before Insertion of Railing**

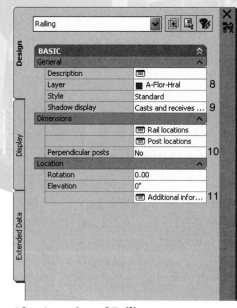

**After Insertion of Railing**

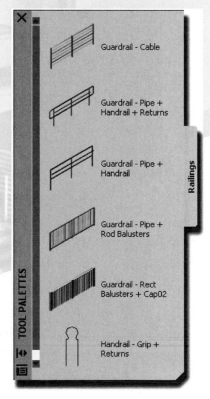

| Number | Name | Purpose |
|--------|------|---------|
| 1 | Style | Select from available railing styles |
| 2 | Rail locations | Set locations of rails fixed by Style |
| 3 | Post locations | Set locations of posts fixed by Style |
| 4 | Perpendicular Posts | Yes or No—perpendicular to carriage |
| 5 | Attached to | Set None, Stair, or Stair Flight |
| 6 | Rotation | Set rotation of railing |
| 7 | Elevation | Set elevation of railing from level |
| 8 | Layer | Change this to place the railing on another layer |
| 9 | Shadow display | Casts and Receives, Casts shadows, Receives shadows, Ignore shadows |
| 10 | Perpendicular Posts | Yes or No |
| 11 | Additional information | Launches the Additional Information Worksheet with more railing locations information |

## Exercise 9-1: Making a New Railing Tool Palette

1. Create a new tool palette, and name it **Railings.**
2. Select the **Content Browser** icon from the **Main** toolbar to launch the Content Browser.
3. In the **Architectural Desktop Design Tool Catalog - Imperial,** locate the **Railings** folder in the **Stairs and Railings** folder.
4. From the **Railings** folder, drag all the railings into the new tool palette you created.
5. Click and hold on the tab of your new tool palette and drag a copy to **My Tool Catalog** into the Content Browser.

## Exercise 9-2: Placing a Railing

1. Start a new drawing using the AEC Model (Imperial Stb) template.
2. Change to the **Model Layout.**
3. Change to the **Top View.**
4. Select any **Railing** icon in the **Railings** tool palette you created and drag your cursor over the **Properties** palette to open it.
5. In the **Properties** palette, select **Standard** from the **Style** drop-down list and **\*NONE\*** from the **Attached to** drop-down list.
6. Click in the Drawing Editor, drag your cursor to the right (0°), enter **10′** in the **Command line,** and press **Enter** three times to complete the command.

**Note:**
When you select **\*NONE\***, you can use your railing as a fence, porch rail, and so on.

You have now placed a 10′-0″ -long Standard railing.

## Exercise 9-3: Editing a Railing Style

1. Select the railing you placed in the previous exercise, **RMB,** and select **Edit Railing Style** from the contextual menu that appears to bring up the **Railing Styles** dialog box.
2. Press the **Floating Viewer** icon to bring up the **Viewer.**

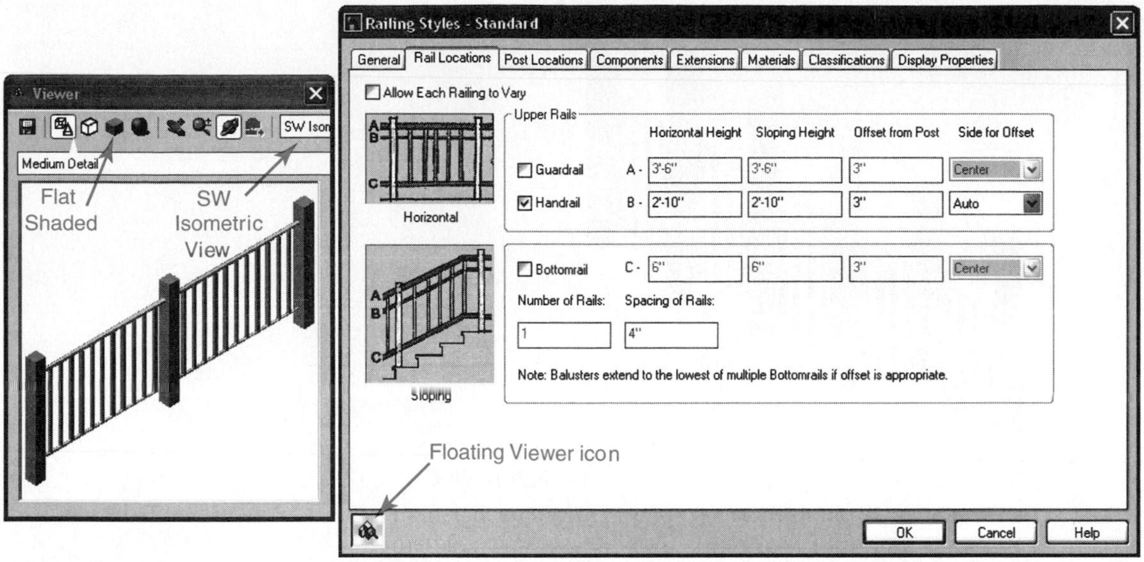

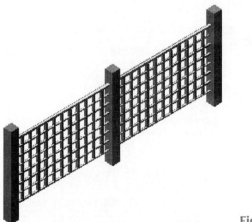

Figure 9–1

3. Resize the **Viewer** so that both the **Viewer** and the **Railing Styles** dialog boxes are side by side and open at the same time. In the **Viewer,** set the drop-down list to the **SW Isometric View,** and press the **Flat Shaded** icon (see Figure 9–1).

4. In the **Railing Styles** dialog box, select the **Rail Locations** tab.

5. Check and uncheck **Guardrail, Handrail,** and **Bottomrail** check boxes and view the changes in the **Viewer.**

6. Change the **Side for Offset** by clicking on the **Side for Offset** drop-down lists and view the changes in the **Viewer.**

7. Enter **8** in the **Number of Rails** value entry field, and **4″** in the **Spacing of Rails** value entry field. Press **Enter,** and view the changes in the **Viewer** (see Figure 9–2).

Figure 9–2

8. Reset to all the original settings.

9. Change to the **Post Locations** tab.

10. Check and uncheck the **Guardrail, Handrail,** and **Bottomrail** check boxes and view the changes in the **Viewer.**

11. Check and uncheck the **Fixed Posts, Dynamic Posts,** and **Balusters** check boxes and value entry fields. View the changes in the **Viewer.**

12. Change to the **Post Locations** tab.

13. Check the **Fixed Posts** check box, and change the value in the **Extension of ALL Posts from Top Railing** value entry field to **18″.**

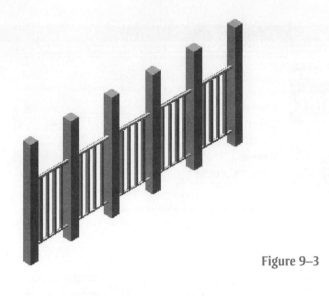

Figure 9–3

14. Check the **Dynamic Posts** check box, and change the value in the **Maximum Center to Center Spacing** value entry field to **2'-0".** View the changes in the **Viewer** (see Figure 9–3).
15. Reset to all the original settings.
16. Change to the **Components** tab.
17. Select the **D - Fixed Post** field.
18. Select **\*circular\*** from the drop-down list under **Profile Name,** and press **Enter.** Set its width to **1'-0",** and again press **Enter.**
19. View the changes in the **Viewer** (see Figure 9–4).

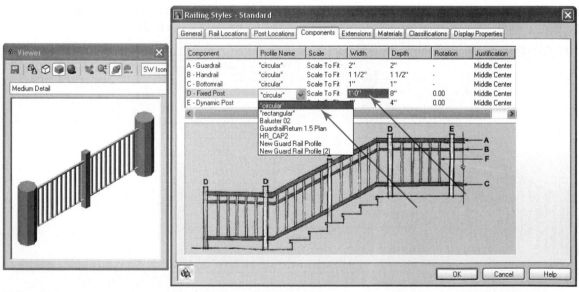

Figure 9–4

20. Reset to all the original settings.
21. Change to the **Extensions** tab.

The settings in this tab are used to set the extensions to the railings when the rails are connected to stairs. These extension dimensions are usually governed by the building codes (see Figure 9–5).

22. Change to the **Materials** tab.

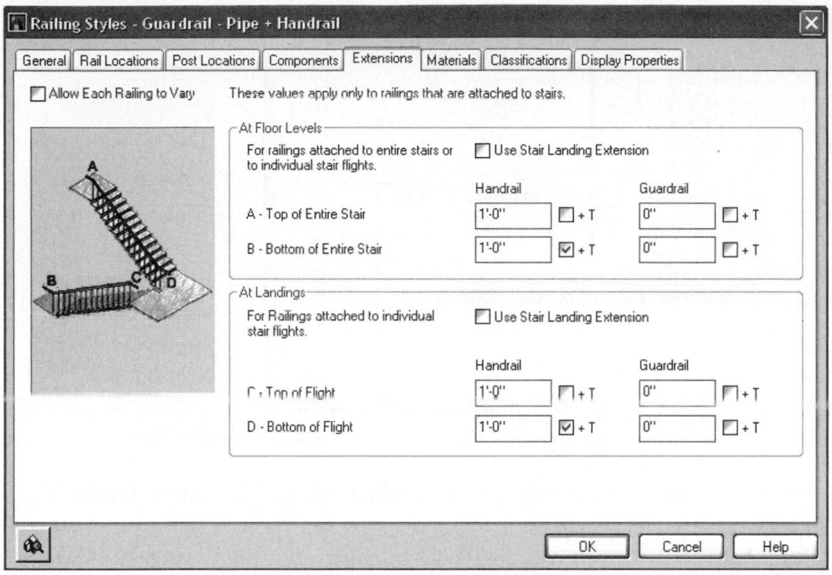

Figure 9–5

23. Select the **Fixed Post** field and press the **Edit Material** icon to bring up the **Material Definition Properties** dialog box. Press the **Edit Display Properties** icon to bring up the **Display Properties** dialog box (see Figure 9–6).

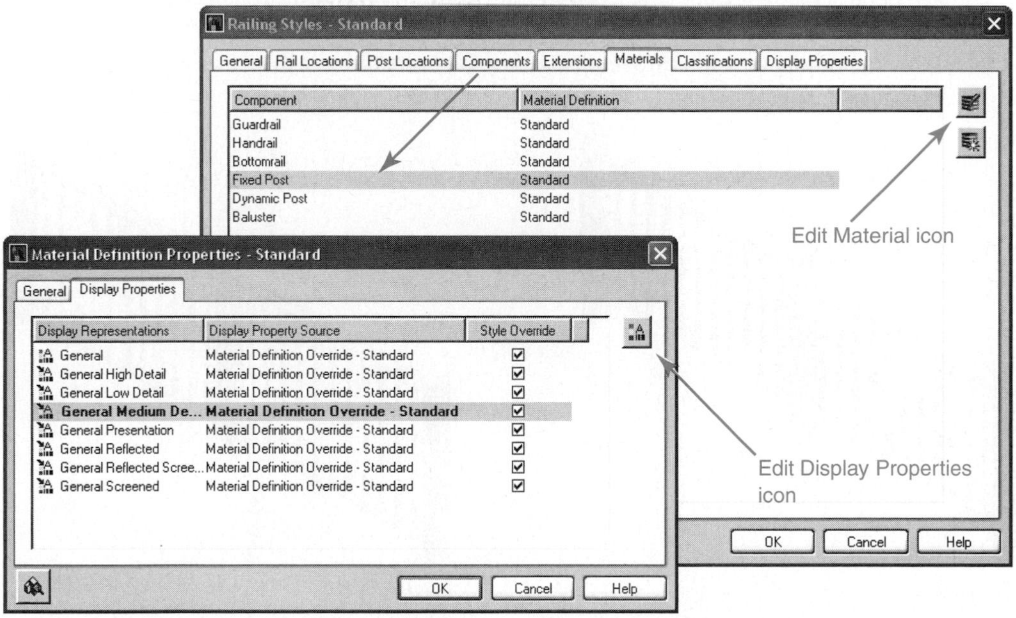

Figure 9–6

24. Select the **Other** tab. Select **Woods & Plastics** > **Architectural Woodwork** > **Wood Stairs and Railings** > **Ash** from the **Surface Rendering - Rendering Material** drop-down list (see Figure 9–7).

25. Press the **OK** buttons in the **Display Properties** and **Material Definition Properties** dialog boxes to return to the **Railing Styles** dialog box. View the material changes in the **Viewer** (see Figure 9–8).

**Exercise 9-4:** Modifying Balusters

1. Return to the Drawing Editor.
2. **RMB** on the **Guardrail - Wood Balusters 02** icon in the **Railings** tool palette you created, and select **Apply Tool Properties to** > **Railing** from the contextual menu that

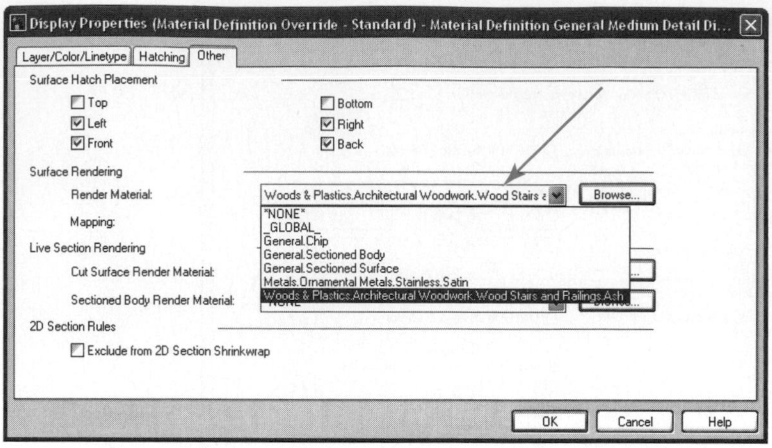

Figure 9–7

appears. (If this railing style is not available in the tool palette, get it from the **Design Tool Catalog - Imperial.**)

3. Select the railing that you placed in Exercise 9-2, "Placing a Railing," and press **Enter.**

The railing changes to the new railing style.

4. Select the railing again, **RMB,** and select **Edit Railing Style** from the contextual menu that appears to bring up the **Railing Styles** dialog box.
5. Press the **Floating Viewer** icon to bring up the **Viewer.**
6. Again resize the **Viewer** so that the **Viewer** and **Railing Styles** dialog box are side by side, and open at the same time. In the **Viewer,** set the drop-down list to the **SW Isometric View,** and press the **Flat Shaded** icon.
7. View the railing (see Figure 9–9).

Figure 9–8

Figure 9–9

8. In the **Railing Styles** dialog box, select the **Display Properties** tab and press the **Edit Display Properties** icon to bring up the **Display Properties** dialog box. Select the **Other** tab (see Figure 9–10).
9. Press the **Remove** button to remove the Baluster 02 block.
10. Press **OK** and view the railing in the **Viewer** again. This time the balusters are the default balusters (see Figure 9–11).

If you press the **Edit** button in the **Display Properties** dialog box, you can add your own balusters made from 3D solid model or surface model blocks.

**Exercise 9-5:** Adding a Railing to a Stair and Stair Flight

1. Start a new drawing using the Model (Imperial Stb) template.
2. Change to the **Work Layout.**
3. Change to the **Top View.**

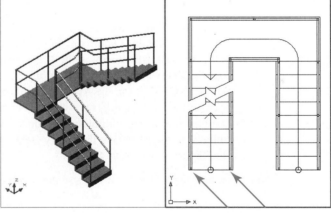

Figure 9–10

4.  Place a Standard-style U-shaped stair with 3'-0"-wide stair flights, a total of 9'-0" overall in width, and 10' height.
5.  Select the **Guardrail** icon in the **Railings** tool palette you created and move your cursor over the **Properties** palette to open it.
6.  Select **Stair** from the **Attached to** drop-down list.
7.  Select the outside side and inside side of the stair to place the rail (see Figure 9–12).

Figure 9–11

Figure 9–12

8.  Erase the railing, and repeat this process using the **Stair flight** option from the **Attached to** drop-down area of the **Properties** palette (see Figure 9–13).

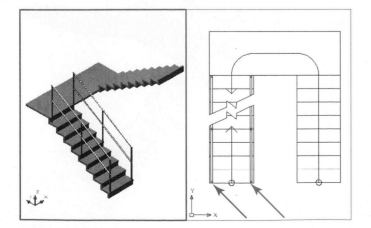

Note:
You can add a railing to a stair in the **3D View**, but it is easier in the **Top View**.

Figure 9–13

**Exercise 9-6:** Adding a Railing to a Landing

1. Erase the previous railing.
2. Activate the **SW Isometric View.**
3. Type **UCS** in the command line and press **Enter** twice to make sure the **SW Isometric View** is in the World UCS.
4. Measure the railing landing. Type **ID** in the command line, press **Enter,** and snap to any top corner of the landing. Read the Z dimension (5′-0″ for my landing). See Figure 9–14.

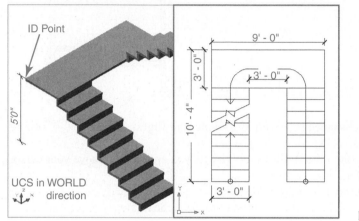

Figure 9–14

5. Activate the **Top View.**
6. Turn the **End Point Osnap** on.
7. Select the **Guardrail** icon in the **Railings** tool palette you created and move your cursor over the **Properties** palette to open it.
8. Select ***NONE*** from the **Attached to** drop-down list.
9. Start at the corner, and place a rail as shown in Figure 9–15.
10. Double-click on the railing to bring up the **Properties** palette for the railing.
11. Enter **5′** in the **Elevation** data entry field—the railing will move to the top of the landing (see Figure 9–16). Save the file.

You can return to the **Top View** and use the **Stretch** command to adjust the railing lengths.

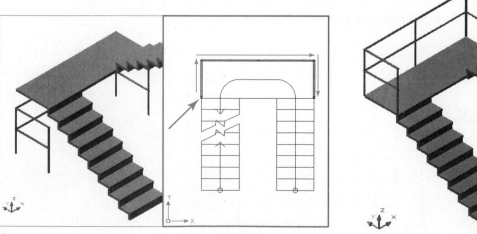

Figure 9–15

Figure 9–16

**Exercise 9-7:** Adding a Railing and Landing Support—Anchor to Object

1. Undo the previous exercise to Step 9.
2. Select the railing, **RMB,** and select **Railing Anchor > Anchor to Object** from the contextual menu that appears.
3. Select the landing and press **Enter.**
4. Enter **Y** (Yes) in the command line and press **Enter.**
5. Enter **F** (Follow surface) in the command line and press **Enter.** Save the file.

The railing moves to the top of the landing, but the posts extend to the ground (see Figure 9–17).

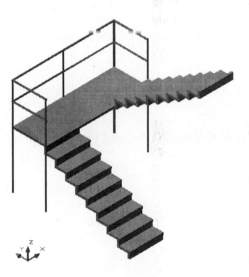

Figure 9–17

**Exercise 9-8:** Creating a Railing Using a Polyline

1. Clear the Drawing Editor.
2. Using the **Polyline** tool, create the shape shown in Figure 9–18.

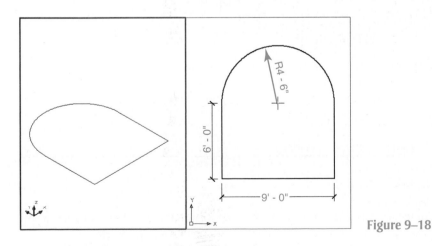

Figure 9–18

3. **RMB** on the **Guardrail - Cable** icon in your **Railings** palette and select **Apply Tool Properties to > Polyline** from the contextual menu that appears.
4. Select the polyline and press **Enter.**
5. Enter **Y** (Yes) in the **Command line** to erase the layout geometry and press **Enter** to create the railing (see Figure 9–19).

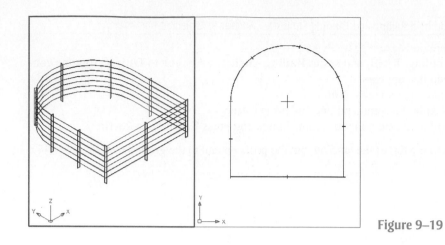

Figure 9–19

6. Select the railing, **RMB,** and select **Edit Railing Style** from the contextual menu that appears to bring up the **Railing Styles** dialog box.
7. Select the **Post Locations** tab.
8. Check the **Dynamic Posts** check box and enter **1′-0″** in the **Maximum Center to Center Spacing** data entry field.

Your railing changes to include more posts (see Figure 9–20).

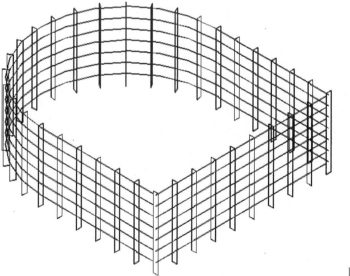

**Figure 9–20**

### Exercise 9-9: Editing a Railing Profile in Place

1. Clear the Drawing Editor.
2. Change to the **Model Layout.**
3. Change to the **Top View.**
4. Select the **Guardrail - Wood balusters 01 Railing** icon in the **Railings** tool palette you created and drag your cursor over the **Properties** palette to open the palette.
5. Select **Standard** from the **Style** drop-down list and **\*NONE\*** from the **Attached to** drop-down list.
6. Click in the Drawing Editor, drag your cursor to the right (0?), enter **12′** in the **Command line,** and press **Enter** three times to complete the command.
7. Change to the **Right View.**
8. In the **Right View,** select the railing, **RMB,** and select **Edit Profile In-Place** from the contextual menu that appears.

9. Select the top rail of the railing. You will get an AutoCAD message that the profile shape must be converted. Press the **Yes** button.
10. The top rail end will turn light blue with magenta grips (see Figure 9–21).

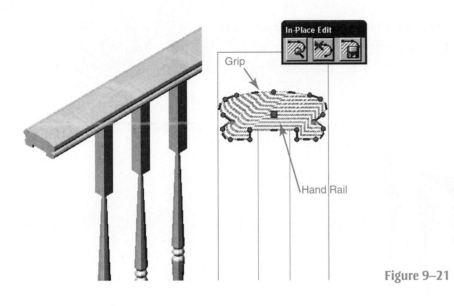

Figure 9–21

You can drag on the grips to edit the profile, or do the following:

11. Draw a circle and a rectangle similar to those shown in Figure 9–22.
12. Select the blue-shaded top rail, **RMB,** and select **Add Ring** from the contextual menu that appears.
13. Select the circle you drew in Step 11, enter **Y** (Yes) in the **Command line,** and press **Enter.**

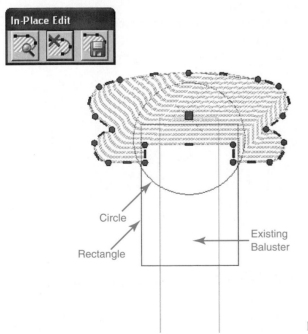

Figure 9–22

14. Enter **J** (Join) in the **Command line** and press **Enter.**
15. Repeat Steps 12–14 of this exercise for the rectangle.
16. Select the blue-shaded top rail again, **RMB,** and select **Save As New Profile** from the contextual menu that appears to bring up the **New Profile** dialog box.
17. In the **New Profile** dialog box, type the name **TEST RAIL PROFILE,** and press the **OK** button.

You have now edited the top rail in place (see Figure 9–23).

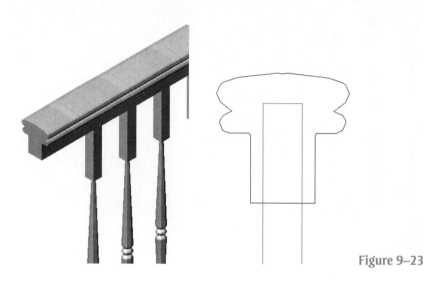

Figure 9–23

18. Select the top rail you just created, **RMB,** and again select **Edit Profile In-Place** from the contextual menu that appears.
19. Select the top rail, and again the top rail end will turn light blue with magenta grips.
20. Grab the lower right **Edge** grip, drag to the right, and press the **Ctrl** button on your keyboard until the tool tip message reads **Convert line to arc,** and click the mouse button (see Figure 9–24).
21. Repeat the process for the lower left **Edge** grip.
22. **RMB** in the blue field and select **Save As New Profile** from the contextual menu that appears to bring up the **New Profile** dialog box.

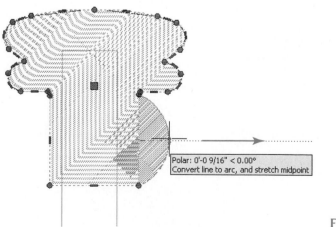

Figure 9–24

23. In the **New Profile** dialog box, type the name **TEST RAIL PROFILE 2**, and press the **OK** button to create the new profile (see Figure 9–25).

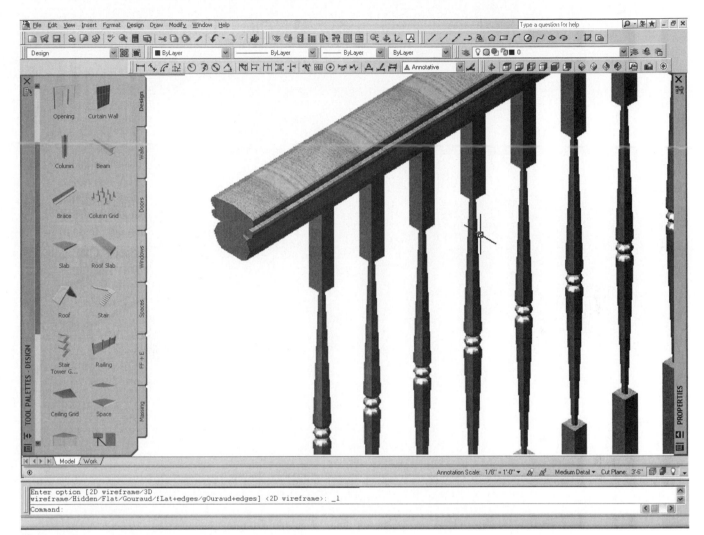

**Figure 9–25**

## 10

# Roofs and Roof Slab Objects

## *Section* Objectives

- Make a **Roof** and **Roof Slabs** tool palette.
- Learn how to place a **Roof** object.
- Know how to modify a **Roof** object.
- Learn how to edit a roof edge.
- Learn how to **Convert to Roof** and changing Segments (smoothing round roofs).
- Use the **Convert to Roof Slabs** command.
- Use the **roofslabmodifyedges** command.
- Know how to use **Apply Tool Properties.**
- Know how to cut a hole in a roof slab.
- Learn how to add edge profiles in place.
- Know how to create a **Roof Dormer.**

## ROOFS

Every building has a roof, and AutoCAD Architecture 2008 has an excellent roof tool. Roofs are AEC Objects that you can use to model an entire multiple-face roof surface. You can create roofs independently of other objects, or you can place a roof on a shape defined by a polyline or by a closed set of walls. After creating the roof, you can change its overall dimensions and slope, or edit its edges and faces individually. For more flexibility in customizing a roof, you can also convert the roof object into a collection of individual roof slabs.

## ROOF PROPERTIES PALETTE

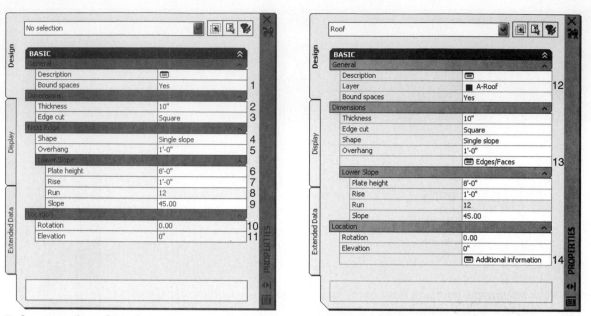

**Before Insertion of Roof**          **After Attachment of Roof**

| Number | Name | Purpose |
|--------|------|---------|
| 1 | Bound spaces | By Style, Yes, No for bounding Associative spaces |
| 2 | Thickness | Thickness of the roof structure |
| 3 | Edge cut | Square (perpendicular to the roof) or Plumb (parallel to the walls) |
| 4 | Shape | Single slope, Double slope, or Gable |
| 5 | Overhang | Distance beyond roof edge |
| 6 | Lower Slope—Plate height | Height at roof plate |
| 7 | Lower Slope—Rise | Vertical rise per foot dimension |
| 8 | Lower Slope—Run | Horizontal dimension |
| 9 | Lower slope—Slope | Angle in degrees of slope |
| 10 | Rotation | Rotation of roof on insertion |
| 11 | Elevation | Height above level |
| 12 | Layer | Change this to place the roof on another layer |
| 13 | Edges/Faces | Displays the Roof Edges worksheet for changing edges and faces |
| 14 | Additional information | Launches the Additional Information Worksheet with more Roof location information |

# ROOF SLAB PROPERTIES PALETTE

**Before Inserting of Roof Slab**

**After Insertion of Roof Slab**

| Number | Name | Purpose |
|--------|------|---------|
| 1 | Style | Style created in the Style Manager |
| 2 | Bound spaces | By Style, Yes, No for bounding Associative spaces |
| 3 | Mode | Projected (elevated) or Direct (at 0 elevation) |
| 4 | Thickness | Thickness of the roof structure |
| 5 | Vertical offset | Offset from wall top |
| 6 | Horizontal offset | Offset from wall edge |
| 7 | Justify | Top, Center, Bottom, Slopeline |
| 8 | Base height | Height above 0 elevation |
| 9 | Direction | Direction of slope |
| 10 | Overhang | Distance beyond roof edge |
| 11 | Baseline edge | Edge type at baseline |

*(Continued)*

| Number | Name | Purpose |
|---|---|---|
| 12 | Perimeter edge | Edge type at perimeter |
| 13 | Slope—Rise | Vertical height per foot dimension |
| 14 | Slope—Run | Horizontal run per foot dimension |
| 15 | Slope | Slope angle in degrees |
| 16 | Rotation | Rotation of roof slab |
| 17 | Elevation | Elevation of roof slab from level |
| 18 | Layer | Change this to place the roof slab on another layer |
| 19 | Shadow display | Casts and Receives, Casts shadows, Receives shadows, Ignore shadows |
| 20 | Edges | Displays the Slab Edges worksheet for changing edges |
| 21 | Hold fascia elevation | Adjust edges when rotating roof slab by adjusting overhang or by adjusting baseline height |
| 22 | Additional information | Launches the Additional Information Worksheet with more Roof slab location information |

## Exercise 10-1: Making a New Roof and Roof Slabs Tool Palette

1. Create a new tool palette, and name it **Roof & Roof Slabs.**
2. Select the **Content Browser** icon from the **Main** toolbar to launch the Content Browser.
3. In the **Desktop Stock Tool Catalog** locate the **Roof in Architectural Object Tools.**
4. Drag all the roof objects into the new tool palette you created.
5. In the **Design Tool Catalog - Imperial,** locate the **Roof Slabs** folder in the **Roof and Roof Slabs** folder.
6. Drag all the roof slabs into the new tool palette you created.
7. Click and hold on the tab of your new tool palette and drag a copy to **My Tool Catalog** into the Content Browser.

Roofs are intelligent AEC Objects. There are several ways to place them and many controls to modify them. It is probably easiest to place a roof and then modify it rather than set the roof controls before placement.

Do the following exercise to experience how to add, convert, and modify roof objects.

## Exercise 10-2: Placing a Roof Object

1. Start a new drawing using the AEC Model (Imperial Stb) template.
2. Change to the **Model Layout.**
3. Change to the **Top View.**
4. Using the wall object, place the floor plan shown in Figure 10–1. Make the walls **Standard** style **6″** wide and **9′-0″** high.
5. Set **Object Snap** to **End Point.**
6. Select the **Roof** icon in the **Roof and Roof Slabs** tool palette you created and drag your cursor over the **Properties** palette to open it.

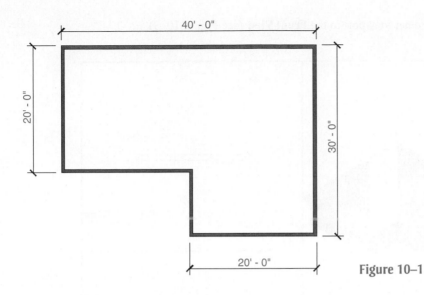

Figure 10–1

7. Set the following:

   a. Thickness = **10″**

   b. Edge cut = **Square**

   c. Shape = **Single slope**

   d. Overhang = **1′**

   e. Plate height = **9′-0″**

   f. Rise = **1′-0″**

   g. Run = **12**

   h. Slope = **45.00**

8. Starting at the top left outside corner shown in Figure 10–2, move clockwise until you get back to the last point shown in the figure. Then press **Enter** or the space bar on your keyboard. You have now placed a roof object.

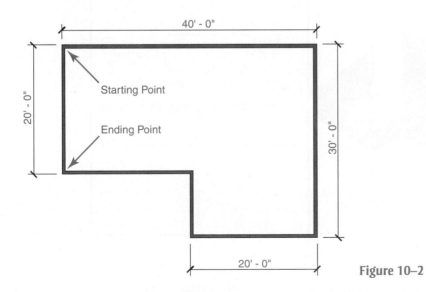

Figure 10–2

## Exercise 10-3: Modifying a Roof Object

1. Change to the **Work Layout,** and zoom extents in both viewports. Change the left viewport to the **SW Isometric View.**

2. In the **SW Isometric View,** select the **Flat Shaded, Edges On** icon from the **Shade** menu to shade the **SW Isometric View.**

3. Change the other viewport to the **Front View** (see Figure 10–3).

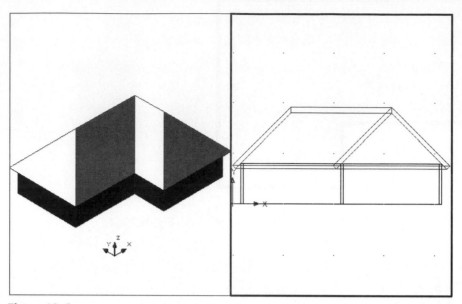

Figure 10–3

4. Double-click on the roof to bring up its **Properties** palette.
5. In the **Properties** palette, change the **Shape** to **Double,** and the **Upper slope's Upper height** to **12′,** and **Slope** to **55.00.** Notice the change to the roof (see Figure 10–4).
6. In the **Front View** viewport, zoom close to the edge of the roof.

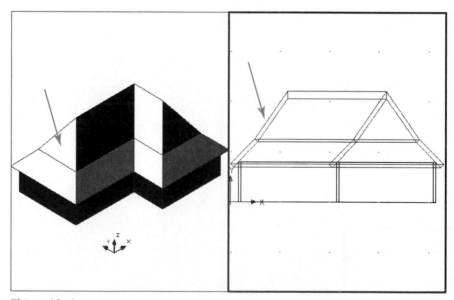

Figure 10–4

7. Again, double-click on the roof to bring up its **Properties** palette.
8. Change the **Edge cut** to **Plumb,** and notice the change (see Figure 10–5).

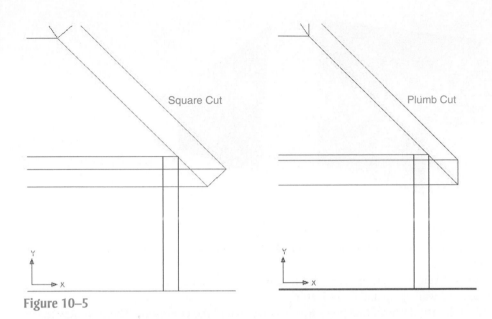

**Figure 10–5**

<u>**Exercise 10-4:** Editing a Roof Edge</u>

1. Double-click and reset the roof object to single slope in the **Properties** palette.
2. Select the roof, **RMB,** and select **Edit Edges/Faces** from the menu that appears.
3. Select a roof edge and press **Enter** to bring up the **Roof Edges and Faces** dialog box (see Figure 10–6).

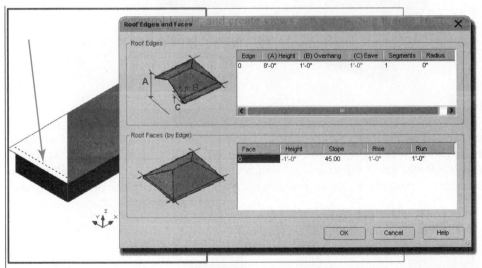

**Figure 10–6**

4. Set **Slope** to **90,** and press **OK** to return to the Drawing Editor.

The roof now has a gable end, but there is no infill between the top of the lower end wall and the underside of the roof (see Figure 10–7).

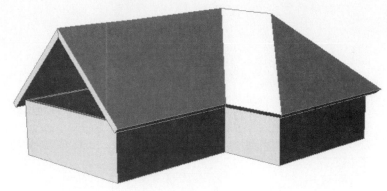

Figure 10–7

5. Select the end wall, **RMB,** and select **Modify Roof line** from the contextual menu that appears.
6. Enter **A** (Auto project) in the **Command line** and press **Enter.**
7. Select the wall again and press **Enter.**
8. Select the **Roof** object and press **Enter** twice to end the command. The wall now meets and closes the gable end (see Figure 10–8).

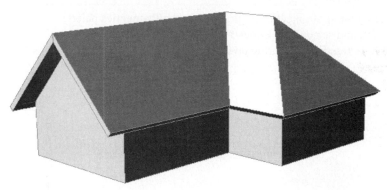

Figure 10–8

This same process can be done with a curtain wall (see Figure 10–9). To get this image you must select the **Design** tool palette, and select the **Curtain Wall** icon. **RMB** the icon, and select **Apply tool property to > Walls.** Select the appropriate wall, accept **Baseline** for the **Curtain wall baseline alignment,** enter **Y** (Yes) to erase layout geometry, and press the **Enter** key to complete the command.

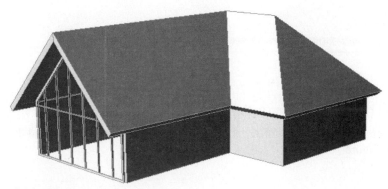

Figure 10–9

9. Change to the **Work Layout.**
10. In the **Top View** viewport, select the roof and pull on the vertex shown in Figure 10–10. You have now created a simple roof and roof overhang. Save this file.

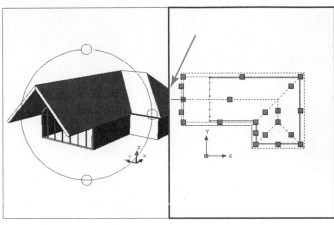

Figure 10–10

## Exercise 10-5: Changing Facets

Another way to create a roof is to use **Apply Tool Properties to.** In the following exercise **Apply Tool Properties to** was used because of the curved walls.

1. Create a new drawing.
2. Activate the **Top View** viewport.
3. Create the floor plan with 6″-wide walls 9′ high as shown in Figure 10–11.
4. Select the **Roof** icon from the **Roof and Roof Slabs** tool palette you created previously, **RMB,** and select **Apply Tool Properties to** from the contextual menu that appears.

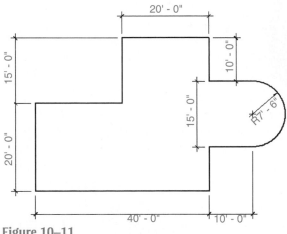

Figure 10–11

5. Select all the walls.
6. At the **Command line** question "Erase layout geometry?" type **N** (No) and press **Enter** to create a roof.
7. While the new roof is still lit (grips showing), move your cursor over the **Properties** palette to open it.
8. Change the **Edge Cut** to **Plumb,** and **Elevation** to **9′-0″** (see Figure 10–12).
9. Select the roof again, and move your cursor over the **Properties** palette to open it.

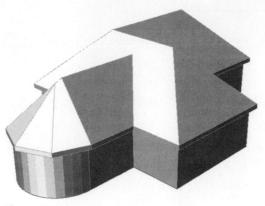

**Figure 10–12**

10. In the Properties palette, press the **Edges/Faces** button to open the **Roof Edges and Faces** dialog box.
11. In the **Roof Edges and Faces** dialog box, you will see **6** in the **Segments** column. Change this to **24,** and the curved section of the roof will become smoother.

Figure 10–13 shows the effects of increasing the **Segments** to **24.**

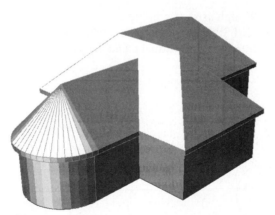

**Figure 10–13**

### Exercise 10-6: Converting to Roof Slabs

Converting roofs to slabs allows you the flexibility to adjust one slab or cut holes inherent in slabs. For pitched roofs it is often best to start with a standard roof object, and then convert it to roof slabs.

1. Use the previous exercise.
2. Select the roof, **RMB,** and select **Convert to Roof Slabs** from the contextual menu that appears.
3. Type **Y** (Yes) at the **Command line** question "Erase layout geometry" and press **Enter.** Accept the **Standard** roof, and again press **Enter** to complete the command.

> **Note:**
> Roofs can also be created by adding roof slab objects. This system is identical to that for creating slabs (see the exercises on creating, modifying, and editing slabs).

The roof color should now change, because the roof will now be made of roof slab objects and is now on the A-Roof-Slab layer.

## Exercise 10-7:  Roofslabmodifyedges

Although not documented in the manual, **roofslabmodifyedges** allows you to adjust all the roof slab edges at one time.

1. Use the previous exercise.
2. Type **Slabmodifyedges** in the **Command line** and press **Enter.**
3. Type **All** at the **Command line** request to select slabs to modify, and press **Enter.**
4. Select the **Baseline** option in the **Command line** and press **Enter.**
5. Enter **OV** (Overhang) in the **Command line** and press **Enter.**
6. Enter **3′-0″** in the **Command line,** and press **Enter.**

You have now adjusted the overhang for all the roof slab objects (see Figure 10–14).

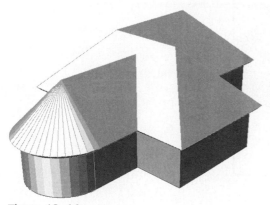

**Figure 10–14**

## Exercise 10-8: Applying Tool Properties to a Roof Slab

1. Select the roof slabs (this can be done by selecting the **Quick Select** icon at the top of the **Properties** palette to bring up the **Quick Select** dialog box and selecting **Roof Slab** from the **Object type** drop-down list).
2. **RMB** on any **Roof Slab** icon in the **Roof and Roof Slabs** toolbar that you created.
3. Select **Apply Tool Properties to > Roof Slab** from the contextual menu that appears and press **Enter.** Press the **Gouraud** icon in the **Shading** toolbar. Save this file.

The roof slabs change to the new applied roof slabs style, and the roof slab material is displayed (see Figure 10–15).

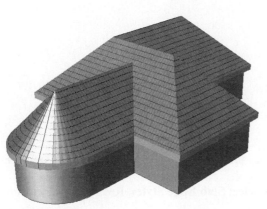

**Figure 10–15**

**Exercise 10-9:** Cutting a Hole in a Roof Slab

1. Zoom close to a roof slab in which you wish to place a hole.
2. Select the **Object UCS** icon from the **UCS** toolbar.
3. Select the roof slab in which you wish to place a hole.

The UCS now matches the surface of the roof slab.

4. Select the **Rectangle** icon in the **Draw** toolbar and place a rectangle on, over, or under the roof slab (see Figure 10–16).

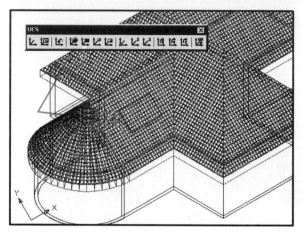

Figure 10–16

5. Select the roof slab in which you wish to place a hole, **RMB,** and select **Hole > Add** from the contextual menu that appears.
6. Select the rectangle created in Step 4, and press **Enter.**
7. Enter **Y** (Yes) in the **Command line** and press **Enter** to complete the command.

You have now created a hole in the roof slab (see Figure 10–17).

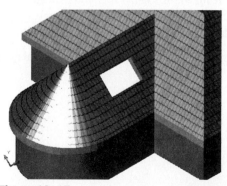

Figure 10–17

**Exercise 10-10:** Adding Edge Profiles in Place

1. Select **Format > Style Manager** from the **Main** toolbar to bring up the **Style Manager** dialog box.
2. Expand the **Architectural Objects** tree, select **Slab Edge Styles, RMB,** and select **New** from the contextual menu that appears.
3. Rename the new style to **SLAB EDGE TEST,** and press **OK** to return to the Drawing Editor.
4. Select a roof slab, **RMB,** and select **Add Edge Profiles** from the contextual menu that appears.
5. Select an edge of the roof slab, and a dialog box will appear (see Figure 10–18).

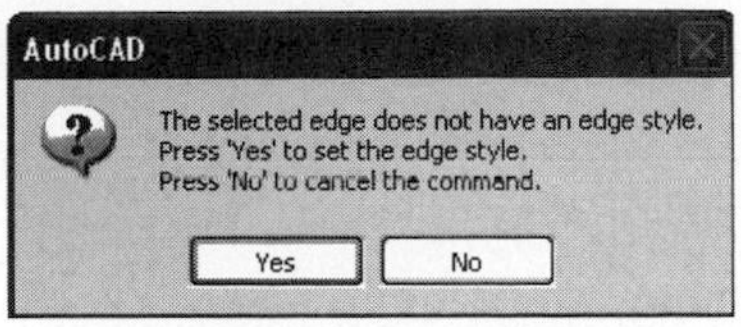

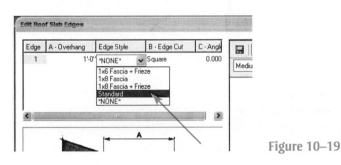

Figure 10–18

**Note:**

This dialog box may not appear, and you will immediately go to the **Edit Roof Slab Edges** dialog box shown in Figure 10–18.

6. Press the **Yes** button to bring up the **Edit Roof Slab Edges** dialog box.
7. Select **Standard** for the **Edge Style** and press **OK** (see Figure 10–19).

Figure 10–19

8. The **Add Fascia/Soffit Profiles** dialog appears.
9. Check the **Fascia Profile** check box, select **Start from scratch** from the drop-down list, enter the name **FASCIA PROFILE TEST** as the **New Fascia Profile Name,** and press **OK** to enter the **In-Place Edit** mode (see Figure 10–20).
10. Change to the **Right View,** and zoom close to the blue shading that signifies the **In-Place Edit** area.

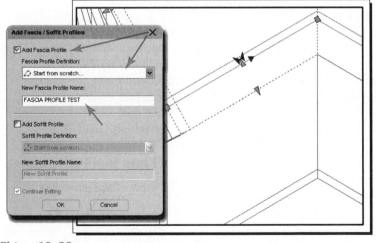

Figure 10–20

11. Create a gutter from a closed polyline as shown in Figure 10–21.

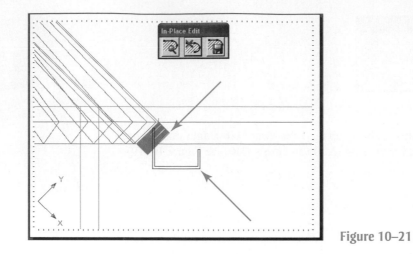

**Figure 10–21**

12. Select the blue area and grips will appear.
13. **RMB** on the blue area and select **Replace ring** from the contextual menu that appears.
14. Select the gutter drawn in Step 11, enter **Y** (Yes) in the command line, and press **Enter.**

The blue hatch will be replaced by the gutter in blue hatch.

15. Select the blue gutter, **RMB,** and select **Save Profile** from the contextual menu that appears.

The **FASCIA PROFILE TEST** is now the gutter.

## Exercise 10-11: Creating a Roof Dormer

Dormers are in vogue today, and AutoCAD Architecture 2008 has a command that aids in the creation of these objects.

1. Start a new drawing using the AEC Model (Imperial Stb) template.
2. Change to the **Model Layout.**
3. Change to the **Top View.**
4. Select the **Wall** icon from the **Design** tool palette, and create a 43′-0″ × 31′-wide structure 8′-0″ high with 6′-wide Standard walls.
5. Add a 15′ × 8′ enclosure 14′-0″ high with 6″-wide Standard walls.
6. Add a **Gable** roof to the 43′ × 31′ enclosure with a 30° slope (see Figure 10–22).

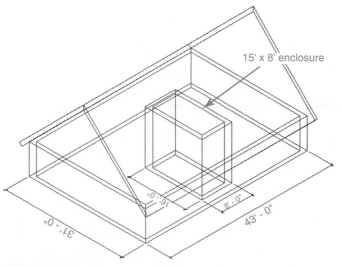

15' x 8' enclosure

**Figure 10–22**

7. Select the **Roof Slab** icon from the **Design** menu, **RMB,** and select **Apply Tool Properties to > Linework, Walls, and Roof** from the contextual menu.

8. Select the left wall of the 15′ × 8′ enclosure and press **Enter.**

9. Enter **N** (No) in the **Command line** and press **Enter.**

10. Enter **B** (Bottom) in the **Command line** and press **Enter.**

11. Enter **R** (Right) in the **Command line** and press **Enter.**

12. Enter **L** (Left) in the **Command line** and press **Enter** to create the first roof slab of the dormer (see Figure 10–23).

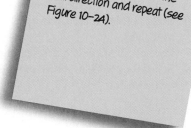

**Note:** Steps 11 and 12 may be reversed depending on which direction the walls were drawn.

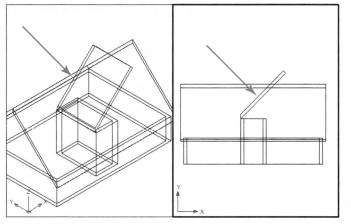

Figure 10–23

13. Again, select the **Roof Slab** icon from the **Design** menu, **RMB,** and select **Apply Tool Properties to > Linework, Walls, and Roof** from the contextual menu.

14. Select the right wall of the 15′ × 8′ enclosure and press **Enter.**

15. Enter **N** (No) in the **Command line** and press **Enter.**

16. Enter **B** (Bottom) in the **Command line** and press **Enter.**

17. Enter **L** (Left) in the **Command line** and press **Enter.**

18. Enter **R** (Right) in the **Command line** and press **Enter** to create the first roof slab of the dormer.

**Note:** If your roof slab doesn't follow the above rules, reverse the wall direction and repeat (see Figure 10–24).

19. Select both new roof slabs, and move your cursor over the **Properties** palette to open it.

20. Change the **Slope** to **25** (25°).

21. Select one of the roof slabs, **RMB,** and select **Miter** from the contextual menu.

22. Accept the default **<Intersection>** in the **Command line** and press **Enter.**

23. Select the lower part of the slab at the intersection of the two slabs, and then select the lower part of the other slab.

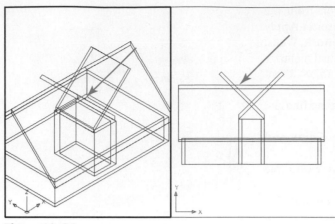

**Figure 10–24**

The two roof slabs will now miter, forming the roof of the dormer. This could also have been done with the roof object, making it a gable roof.

24. Change to the **Top View** and drag each roof slab 2'-0" (see Figure 10–25).

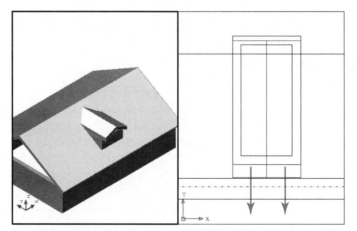

**Figure 10–25**

25. Select the main gable roof over the 43' × 31' enclosure, **RMB,** and select **Convert to Roof Slabs** from the contextual menu.
26. Enter **N** (No) in the **Command line,** and press **Enter** twice to change the roof object into roof slabs.
27. Press the **ESC** key to deselect the slabs.
28. Select the roof slab shown in Figure 10–26, **RMB,** and select **Roof Dormer** from the contextual menu.

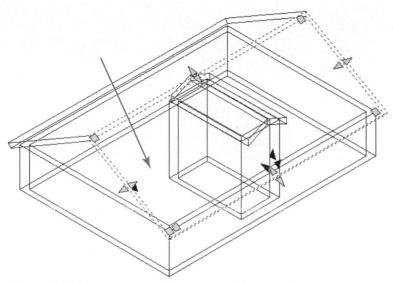

**Figure 10–26**

29. Select the 15′ × 8′ enclosure and its roof slabs and then press **Enter.**
30. Enter **Y** (Yes) in the **Command line,** and press **Enter** to form the dormer.
31. Erase any unneeded walls (see Figure 10–27).

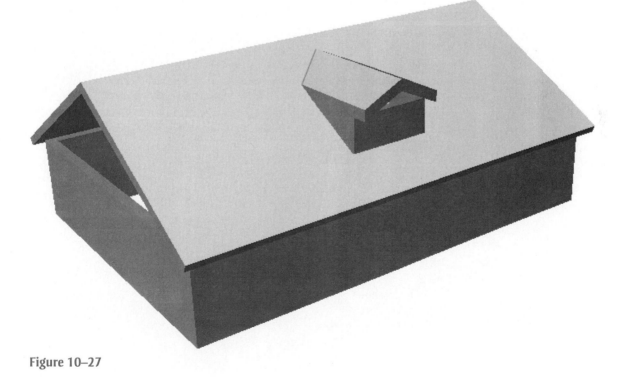

**Figure 10–27**

# Slabs and Slab Objects

# 11

## *Section* Objectives

- Use the **Convert Space Object to slab** option.
- Learn how to make a **Slabs** tool palette.
- Learn how to use **Direct Mode** and **Direction.**
- Know how to use **Projected** mode.
- Know how to apply tool properties to slabs.
- Learn how to cut slabs.
- Learn how to modify a slab object.
- Make a new edge from a profile.
- Know how to change a slab edge profile.

## SLABS

Slabs and roof slabs are AutoCAD Architecture objects that you use to model floors, roof faces, and other flat surfaces where edge conditions need to be specified. The slab or roof slab object is a three-dimensional (3D) body bounded by a planar polygon (perimeter) of any shape and has multiple edges. The object is defined by its perimeter, edge conditions, and style. Though they share many of the same properties, slabs and roof slabs represent separate style categories and tool types. For instance, you cannot apply the properties of a slab tool to an existing roof slab object. Slabs can be created in many ways. They can be extruded from polylines, lines, wall enclosures, or spaces. Slabs have many uses from floors and ceilings to counter tops. Because slabs are partially parametric, their thickness and rotation in many directions can be controlled from their **Properties** palette.

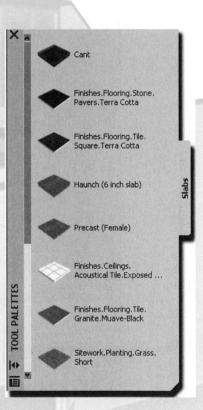

## SLAB PROPERTIES PALETTE

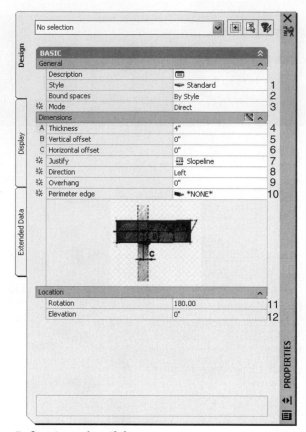

**Before Inserting Slab**          **After Inserting Slab**

| Number | Name | Purpose |
|--------|------|---------|
| 1 | Style | Select from available slab styles |
| 2 | Bound spaces | By Style, Yes, No for bounding Associative spaces |
| 3 | Mode | Specifies whether the slab is created in **Direct** or **Projected** modes |
| 4 | Thickness | Specifies the thickness of the slab |
| 5 | Vertical offset | Specifies the vertical offset of the slab |
| 6 | Horizontal offset | Specifies the horizontal offset of the slab while picking points |
| 7 | Justify | Specifies the slab justification—**Top, Bottom, Center,** or **Slopeline** |
| 8 | Direction | Specifies the **Left** or **Right** direction for the slab |
| 9 | Overhang | Distance of overhang; specifies the overhang depth for the slab |
| 10 | Perimeter edge | Specifies the edge style along the perimeter of the slab |

| Number | Name | Purpose |
|--------|------|---------|
| 11 | Rotation | Rotation reference angle for the slab |
| 12 | Elevation | Elevation of the slab |
| 13 | Layer | Change this to place the slab on another layer |
| 14 | Shadow Display | Casts and Receives, Casts shadows, Receives shadows, Ignore shadows |
| 15 | Edges | Displays the Slab Edges worksheet for changing edges |
| 16 | Additional information | Launches the Additional Information Worksheet with more slab location information |

## Exercise 11-1: Creating a New Slab Tool Palette

1. Create a new tool palette, and name it **Slab.**
2. Select the **Content Browser** icon from the **Main** toolbar to launch the Content Browser.
3. In the **Design Tool Catalog - Imperial,** locate the **Slabs** folder in the **Roof Slabs and Slabs** folder.
4. From the **Slabs** folder, drag all the slabs into the new tool palette you created.
5. Click and hold on the tab of your new tool palette and drag a copy to **My Tool Catalog** in the Content Browser.

## Exercise 11-2: Using the AutoCAD Architecture 2008 Convert Space Object to Slab Option to Create a Slab

1. Select **File > New,** and start a new drawing using the AEC Model (Imperial Stb) template.
2. Change to the **Top** or **Plan** view.
3. Select the **Wall** tool from the **Design** toolbar, and using a Standard 10′-high, 6″-wide wall, create the enclosure shown in Figure 11–1.

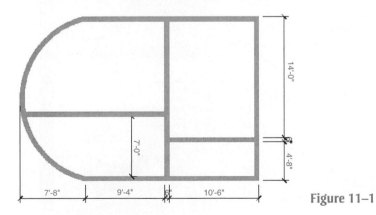

Figure 11–1

4. Select the **Space Auto Generate** tool from the **Design** tool palette, and move over one of the subenclosures of the enclosures you just created. The **Generate Spaces** dialog box will appear (Figure 11–2).
5. Click in each of the subenclosures of the enclosure, and then press the **Close** button in the **Generate Spaces** dialog box to return to the Drawing Editor. You have now created space objects in all the enclosures.
6. Change to the **SW Isometric View.**
7. Select one of the walls, **RMB,** and choose **Select Similar** from the contextual menu that appears to select all the walls.

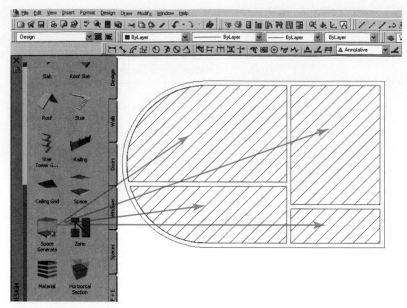

Figure 11–2

8. With all the walls selected, click on the **Isolate Objects** icon (lightbulb) at the lower right of the Drawing Editor, and select **Hide Objects** from the contextual menu that appears. The walls will now be hidden, showing only the space objects.

9. Select each space object individually, and move your cursor over the **Properties** palette to open the palette.

10. In the **Properties** palette, change the **Space height, Floor boundary thickness,** and **Ceiling boundary thickness** for every space (see Figure 11–3).

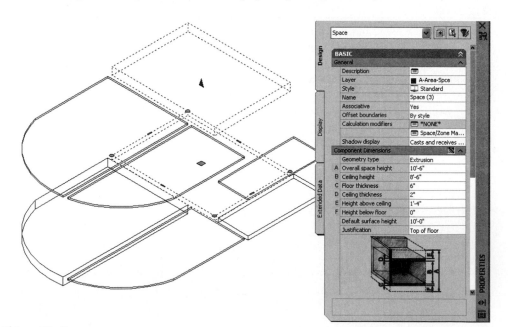

Figure 11–3

11. Select the **Slab** tool from the **Design** menu, **RMB,** and select **Apply Tool Properties to > Space** from the contextual menu that appears.

12. Select all the spaces, and press the **Enter** key on the keyboard to bring up the **Convert Space to Slab** dialog box.

13. In the **Convert Space to Slab** dialog, check the **Convert Ceiling to Slab, Convert Floor to Slab,** and **Erase Layout Geometry** check boxes, and then press the **OK** button to return to the Drawing Editor (see Figure 11–4).

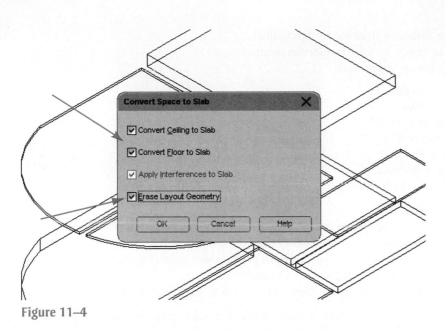

**Figure 11–4**

14. These slabs can now be treated as standard slab objects. They can be cut, have their elevations changed, have holes created in them, and be stretched and edited with vertices (see Figure 11–5).

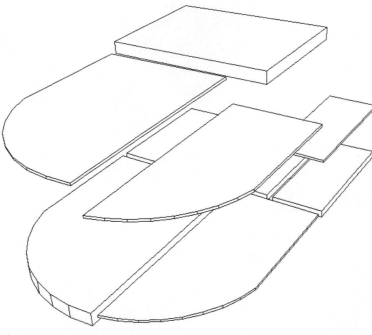

**Figure 11–5**

## Exercise 11-3: Using Direct Mode and Direction

Slabs can be either **Direct** or **Projected** modes. **Direct** mode allows you to place a flat slab, and **Projected** mode allows you to place a slab at a location in space with a given slope. **Direction** is used when using **Ortho Close.**

The first point establishes slab origin and pivot point. The first line establishes the base line.

1. Start a new drawing using the AEC Model (Imperial Stb) template.
2. Change to the **Model Layout.**
3. Change to the **Top View.**

4. Select the **Slab** icon from the **Design** toolbar.
5. Move your cursor over the **Properties** palette to open it.
6. Set the following parameters:

   a. Style = **Standard**
   b. Mode = **Direct**
   c. Thickness = **to 12″**
   d. Overhang = **0″**
   e. Mode = **Direct**
   f. Justify = **Bottom**
   g. Direction = **Left**

7. Set the first point of your slab.
8. Moving clockwise, set the second point at **10″** to the right.
9. Enter **O** (Ortho close) in the **Command line,** and press **Enter.**
10. Repeat Steps 5, 6, 7, 8, and 9 slightly below the first slab in the **Top** viewport, but change the direction arrow to the **Right** direction arrow.
11. Select each slab, and change the slope of each slab to **45** (45 degrees)

**Ortho Close** works differently for slabs than for walls. For slabs, only one line is drawn, so the direction arrow dictates in which direction the slab is cast (see Figures 11–6 and 11–7).

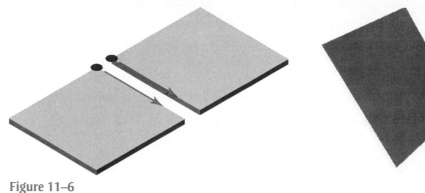

Figure 11–6

Figure 11–7

---

### Exercise 11-4: Projected Mode

1. Create a new drawing.
2. Again select the **Slab** icon from the **Design** tool palette.
3. Move your cursor over the **Properties** palette to open it.
4. Set the following parameters:

   a. Style = **Standard**
   b. Mode = **Projected**
   c. Thickness = **to 12″**
   d. Justify = **Bottom**
   e. Base height = **0**
   f. Direction = **Right**
   g. Overhang = **0″**

Notice that selecting the **Projected** mode causes the **Slope** option to now be available in the **Properties** palette.

5. In the **Properties** palette under **Slope,** set **Rise** to **6** and **Run** to **12.**
6. Set a point, and moving clockwise, set the second point at **10′** to the right.

Notice that the **Pivot** symbol is at your starting point. Also notice that selecting the **Projected** mode causes the **Slope** option to be available.

7. Enter **O** (Ortho close) in the **Command line,** and press the **Enter** key.
8. Repeat Steps 5, 6, and 7, but change the **Direction** to **Left** (see Figure 11–8).

You only change the **Rise** numbers. Leave **Run** at **12.000,** and the **Angle** will automatically calculate.

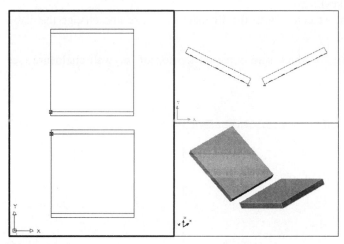

Figure 11–8

## Exercise 11-5: Applying Tool Properties to Slabs

**Convert to Slab** uses closed polylines or walls as a basis for creating slabs. You don't need closed walls to use **Convert to Slab;** one wall will work just fine. The default location for slabs created by **Convert to Slab** using walls is at the top of the wall.

1. Start a new drawing using the AEC Model (Imperial Stb) template.
2. Change to the **Model Layout.**
3. Make the left viewport **Top View,** and the right viewport **SW Isometric View.**
4. Change to the **Top View.**
5. Select the **Wall** icon from the **Design** tool palette.
6. Starting at the bottom left and moving clockwise, place an 8′ × 8′ enclosure 8′-0″ high (see Figure 11–9).

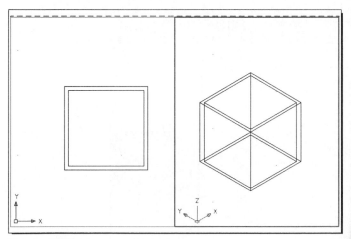

Figure 11–9

Note:
The first wall you pick becomes the pivot wall.

7. Select the **Slab** icon from the **Design** tool palette, **RMB,** and select **Apply Tool Properties to > Linework and Walls** from the contextual menu that appears.

8. In the **Top View,** select all the walls of the 8′ × 8′ enclosure starting at the bottom wall and moving counterclockwise.
9. In the **Command line,** accept **N** to leave the **Walls** in place.
10. For **Slab Justification,** select **Bottom;** for **Wall Justification,** select **Left;** for **Slope Direction,** select **Right** or **Left** (either is OK); and accept the **Standard** slab style by pressing the **Enter** key on the keyboard.
11. While the new slab is still selected, open the **Properties** palette and change the slab's thickness to 24″.

You have now placed a Standard 24″-thick slab object at the top of the wall enclosure (see Figure 11–10).

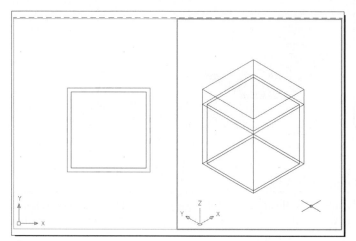

**Figure 11–10**

12. Repeat the above steps, changing the **Wall Justification, Slab Justification,** and **Slope Direction** until you feel comfortable with the controls.
13. Double-click the slab to open the **Properties** palette.
14. Set the **Slope Rise** to **12** (12″) (see Figure 11–11).

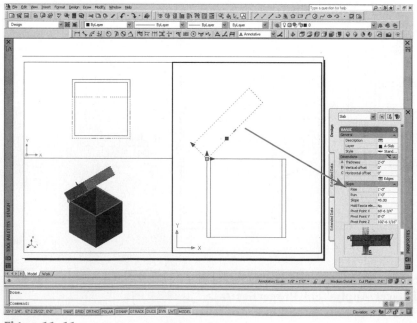

**Figure 11–11**

15. Select the slab, **RMB,** and select **Edit Slab Edges** from the contextual menu that appears to bring up the **Slab Edges** dialog box.
16. In the **Slab Edges** dialog box, change the **Edge Cut** to **Plumb** (see Figures 11–12 and 11–13).

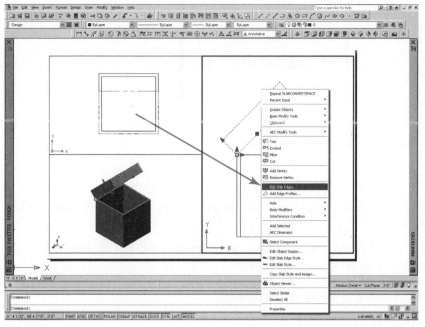

**Figure 11–12**

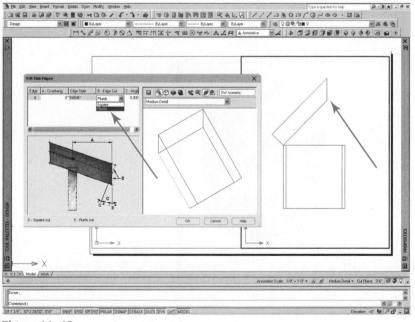

**Figure 11–13**

## Exercise 11-6: Cutting Slabs

1. Use the previous exercise.
2. Double-click the slab to open the **Properties** palette.
3. Set the **Slope Rise** to **0** (0″) to return the slab to a flat position (the changed edge is still plumb).
4. In the **Top View,** place and **Offset** several polylines as shown in Figure 11–14.

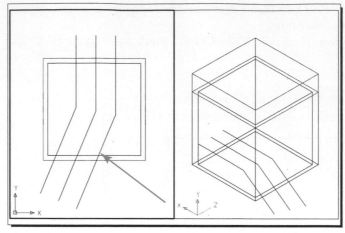

Figure 11–14

We are going to cut the slab with the polylines, even though the polylines are at 0″ elevation, and the slab is at 8′-0″ elevation.

5. Select the slab, **RMB,** and select **Cut** from the contextual menu that appears.
6. Select one of the polylines, and press **Enter.**
7. Enter **Y** (Yes) in the **Command line,** and press **Enter.**
8. Repeat Steps 5 through 7 for the other polylines.

You should now have three slab sections.

9. Select each slab section, and move your cursor over the **Properties** palette to open it.
10. Set the thickness for each section 8″ higher than the previous one (see Figure 11–15). Save this file.

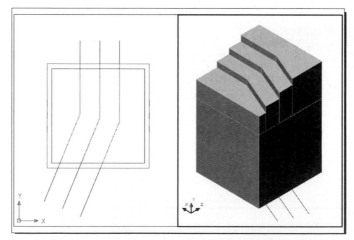

Figure 11–15

### Exercise 11-7: Making a New Edge from a Profile

1. Erase the slabs created in the previous exercise, and place a new 12″ slab starting at the upper left corner and moving clockwise.
2. Create a profile polyline shape by drawing the polyline shown in Figure 11–16.
3. Select the polyline, **RMB,** and select **Convert to > Profile Definition** from the contextual menu that appears.
4. Select the upper left corner of the polyline you just created.
5. Press **Enter** to bring up the **Profile Definition** dialog box.

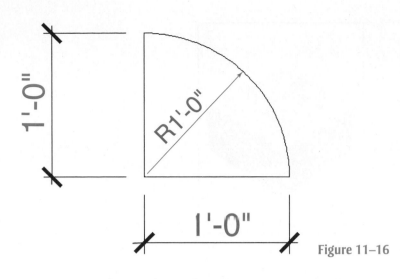

Figure 11–16

6. Enter **CURVED EDGE PROFILE,** and press the **OK** button.
7. Select **Format > Style Manager** to bring up the **Style Manager.**
8. Select **Architectural > Slab Edge Styles, RMB,** and select **New** from the contextual menu that appears.
9. Rename the new style **CURVED EDGE STYLE.**
10. Double-click on the **CURVED EDGE STYLE** icon you just created to bring up the **Slab Edge Styles** dialog box.
11. In the **Slab Edge Styles** dialog box select the **Design Rules** tab.
12. Check the **Fascia** check box, select **CURVED EDGE PROFILE** from the **Fascia Profile** drop-down list, and press the **OK** and **Apply** buttons to return to the Drawing Editor (see Figure 11–17).

Figure 11–17

13. Double-click the slab to bring up the **Properties** palette.
14. Select **Edges** to bring up the **Slab Edges** dialog box.
15. Select all the edges, select **CURVED EDGE STYLE** from the **Edge Style** drop-down list, and then press the **OK** button.

You have now placed a new curved edge on all the slab edges (see Figure 11–18).

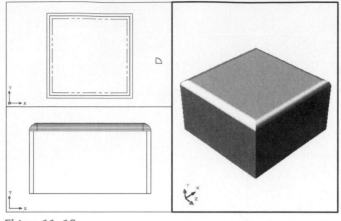

**Figure 11–18**

## Exercise 11-8: Changing the Slab Edge Profile

1. Return to the profile you created in the last exercise.
2. Add a rectangle as shown (see Figure 11–19).

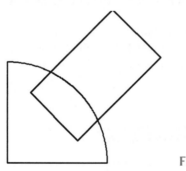

**Figure 11–19**

3. **RMB** on an empty place in the Drawing Editor, and select **AEC Modify Tools > Merge** from the contextual menu that appears.
4. Select the rectangle and press **Enter.**
5. Select the original profile and press **Enter.**
6. Enter **Y** (Yes) in the **Command line** and press **Enter** (see Figure 11–20).

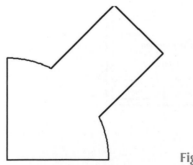

**Figure 11–20**

7. Select the changed profile, **RMB,** and select **Convert To > Profile Definition** from the contextual menu that appears.
8. Select the lower left corner of the profile and press **Enter.**

9. Enter **E** (Existing) in the **Command line,** and press **Enter** to bring up the **Profile Definitions** dialog box.
10. Select **CURVED EDGE PROFILE** (the one you created in the last exercise), and press **OK.**

The slab edge now reflects the changed profile (see Figure 11–21).

**Figure 11–21**

## Exercise 11-9: Multi-Component Slab Objects

Multi-component slab objects are created similarly to those multi-components in walls.

1. Start a new drawing using the AEC Model (Imperial Stb) template.
2. Change to the **Top View.**
3. Select the **Slab** tool from the **Design** toolbar, and place a **10′-0″ × 10′-0″** slab in the Drawing Editor.
4. Select the slab object you just created, **RMB,** and select **Copy Slab Style and Assign** from the contextual menu that appears to open the **Slab Styles** dialog box.
5. In the **Slab Styles** dialog box, change to the **General** tab.
6. In the **General** tab, change the name to **TEST MULTI_COMPONENT SLAB.**
7. Change to the **Components** tab, press the **Add Component** icon at the top left of the dialog box, and add two more components.
8. Name the **Components** starting at **Index 3 – SAND, WOOD,** and **CONCRETE** (see Figure 11–22).
9. Set the **Thickness** and **Thickness Offset** to those shown in Figure 11–23.
10. Change to the **Materials** tab.
11. In the **Materials** tab click on the **Add New Material** icon to bring up the **New Material** dialog box.
12. In the **New Material** dialog type **WOOD MATERIAL,** and press the **OK** button to return to the **Materials** tab.
13. In the **Materials** tab, now select **WOOD MATERIAL** from the **Material Definition** drop-down list opposite the **WOOD Component.**
14. Press the **Edit Material** icon to bring up the **Material Definition Properties** dialog box.

**Note:**
Positive Thickness offset is above the base. If you have difficulty figuring out the Thickness Offset, set the **Offset Increment** to a small size, and use the **Increment Slab Component** buttons. When setting the thicknesses, always set the **BT** (Base Thickness) to **0.**

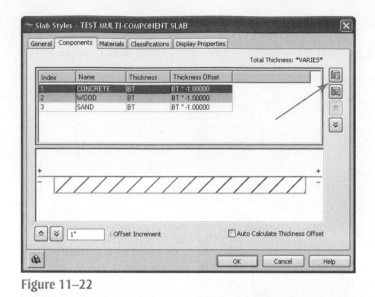

Figure 11–22

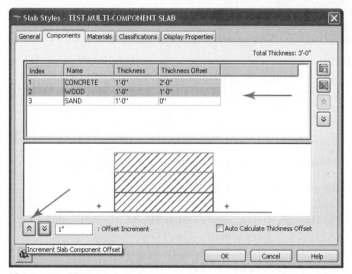

Figure 11–23

15. In the **Material Definition Properties** dialog box, double-click the **General Medium Detail Display Representation** to bring up the **Display Properties** dialog box.
16. In the **Display Properties** dialog box, change to the **Hatching** tab (see Figure 11–24).
17. In the **Hatching** tab, select the **Pattern** icon adjacent to **Section Hatch** to open the **Hatch Pattern** dialog box.
18. In the **Hatch Pattern** dialog box, select **Predefined** from the **Type** drop-down list to bring up the **Hatch Pattern Palette.**
19. In the **Hatch Pattern Palette,** change to the **Custom** tab.
20. In the **Custom** tab select the **Wood_3.pat,** and close the dialog boxes.
21. Repeat this process for **CONCRETE** and **SAND** materials.

## Testing the Slab

22. Change the Scale of the drawing to **1/4″ = 1′-0″.**
23. Select the **Section Mark A2T** from the **Callouts** tool palette, and click, drag, and click the section mark across the slab to bring up the **Place Callout** dialog box.
24. In the **Place Callout** dialog box, change the **Scale** to **1/4″ = 1′-0″,** press the **Current Drawing** icon, and place the section (see Figures 11–25 and 11–26). (Check Section 15, "Sections" if you are not sure how to do this.)

Figure 11–24

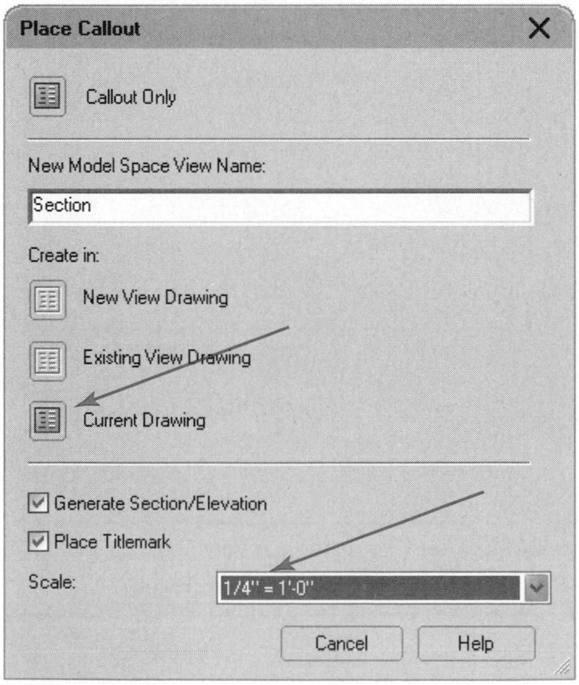

Place Callout

Callout Only

New Model Space View Name:

Section

Create in:

New View Drawing

Existing View Drawing

Current Drawing

☑ Generate Section/Elevation

☑ Place Titlemark

Scale:    1/4" = 1'-0"

Cancel    Help

Figure 11–25

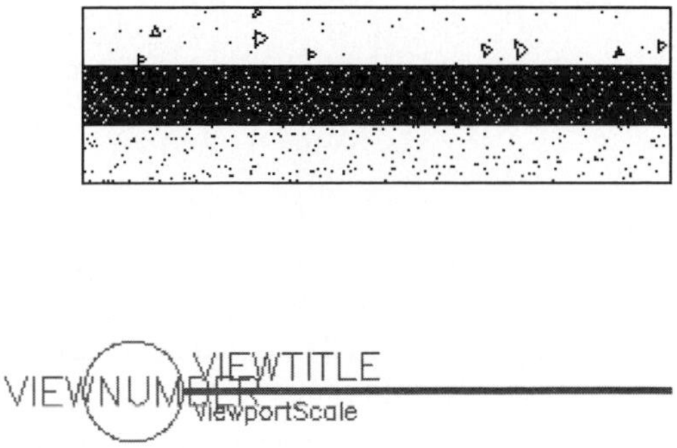

VIEWNUMBER    VIEWTITLE
ViewportScale

Figure 11–26

# Structural Members, Column Grids, Grids, and Anchors

# 12

- Learn how to make a **Structure** palette.
- Place a column and **Structural Column Grid.**
- Learn how to modify a **Structural Column Grid.**
- Create a **Structural Column Grid** from linework.
- Know how to place **Structural Beams** on **Structural Column Grids.**
- Know how to use the **Structural Beam "fill and array" options.**
- Learn how to modify structural members.
- Create a round composite concrete and steel column.
- Learn how to add bar joists.
- Learn how to label a grid.
- Know how to add and label a layout grid (2D).
- Create and use a **Layout Curve.**
- Know how to use a wall as a **Layout Curve.**
- Know how to use the **trim planes.**
- **Frame** floors and roofs using slabs and structural members.
- Create a custom structural member from linework, and apply a **Miter.**

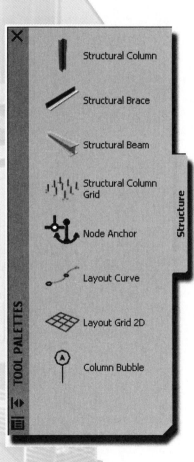

All buildings have a structural system. In the design of commercial buildings, the understanding and documentation of the structural system is of utmost importance. In AutoCAD Architecture, structural members give control over this phase of construction.

Structural members can be used as columns, beams, and braces, and can be configured in many ways not originally intended by the developers of the program. In reality, columns, beams, and braces are the same AEC Object used in different work planes. When understood, structural members can be some of the most important AEC Objects in your portfolio of tools.

Column grids are a variant on grids; they can be planar (flat) or volumetric (three-dimensional). Columns can be attached to any grid, but column grids can have columns attached upon input of the grid.

## BEAM PROPERTIES PALETTE

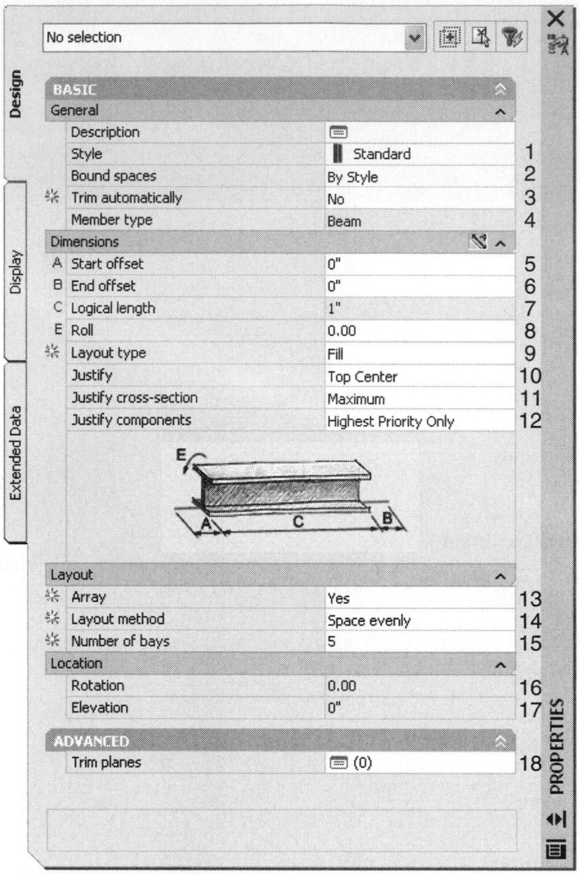

**After Inserting Beam**

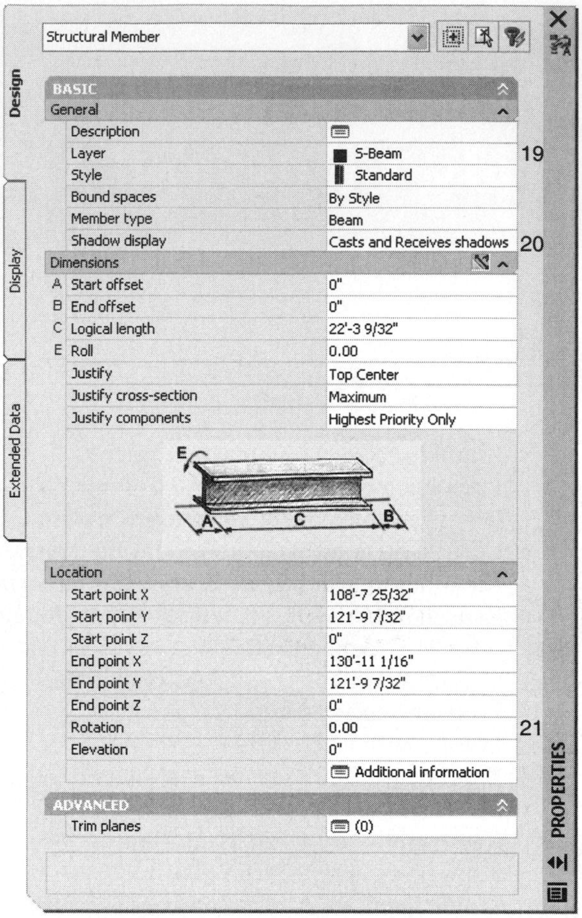

**Before Inserting Beam**

| Number | Name | Purpose |
|---|---|---|
| 1 | Style | Select from available structural member styles |
| 2 | Bound spaces | By Style, Yes, No for bounding Associative spaces |
| 3 | Trim automatically | Specifies whether to trim member ends against existing members |
| 4 | Member type | Beam (type chosen from tool palette) |
| 5 | Start offset | Distance offset from the start end of member |
| 6 | End offset | Distance offset from the end of member |
| 7 | Logical length | Actual length of structural member |
| 8 | Roll | Roll angle around the main axis through member |
| 9 | Layout type—Fill or Edge | Specifies whether to create new members along the hovered object's edges or within the area of the hovered object. |
| 10 | Justify | Insertion node location—Top Center, Bottom Center, etc. |

| 11 | Justify cross-section | Justify cross-section by Maximum or At Each Node |
|----|----------------------|--------------------------------------------------|
| 12 | Justify components | Justify components by Highest Priority Only or All |
| 13 | Array—Yes or No | Specifies whether to add multiple members as you drag. If Yes, Layout method and Number of bays appear. |
| 14 | Layout method | Space evenly or Repeat rule for member spacing |
| 15 | Number of bays | Number of bays |
| 16 | Rotation | Rotation of the structural member |
| 17 | Elevation | Elevation of the structural member |
| 18 | Trim planes | Planes used to modify end conditions of the structural member |
| 19 | Layer | Change this to place the slab on another layer |
| 20 | Shadow display | Casts and Receives, Casts shadows, Receives shadows, Ignore shadows |
| 21 | Additional information | Launches the Additional Information Worksheet with more structural member information |

## COLUMN PROPERTIES PALETTE

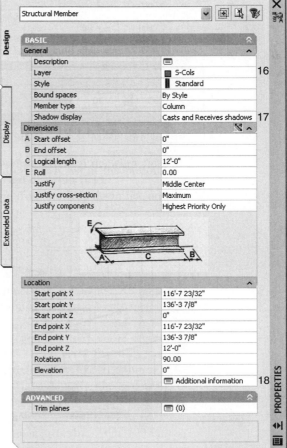

**Before Inserting Column**                    **After Inserting Column**

| Number | Name | Purpose |
|---|---|---|
| 1 | Style | Select from available structural member styles |
| 2 | Bound spaces | By Style, Yes, No for bounding Associative spaces |
| 3 | Trim automatically | Specifies whether to trim member ends against existing members |
| 4 | Member type | Column (type chosen from tool palette) |
| 5 | Start offset | Distance offset from the start end of member |
| 6 | End offset | Distance offset from the end of member |
| 7 | Logical length | Actual length of structural member |
| 8 | Roll | Roll angle around the main axis through member |
| 9 | Layout type—Fill or Edge | Specifies whether to create new members along the hovered object's edges or within the area of the hovered object. |
| 10 | Justify | Insertion node location—Top Center, Bottom Center, etc. |
| 11 | Justify cross-section | Justify cross-section by Maximum or At Each Node |
| 12 | Justify components | Justify components by Highest Priority Only or All |
| 13 | Rotation | Rotation of the structural member |
| 14 | Elevation | Elevation of the structural member |
| 15 | Trim planes | Planes used to modify end conditions of the structural member |
| 16 | Layer | Change this to place the slab on another layer |
| 17 | Shadow display | Casts and Receives, Casts shadows, Receives shadows, Ignore shadows |
| 18 | Additional | Launches the Additional Information Worksheet information with more structural member information |

## Exercise 12-1: Making a New Structure Tool Palette

1. Create a new tool palette named **Structure.**
2. Select the **Content Browser** icon from the **Main** toolbar to launch the **Content Browser.**
3. In the **Stock Tool Catalog** locate the **Structural Beam, Structural Brace, Structural Column,** and **Structural Grid Object** in the **Architectural Object Tools** folder.
4. From the **Architectural Object Tools** folder, drag the objects into the new tool palette you created.
5. In the **Stock Tool Catalog** locate the **Cell Anchor, Node Anchor, Layout Curve** and **Layout Grid (2D)** tools in the **Parametric Layout & Anchoring** folder, and drag these tools to the **Structure** palette you created.

6. Click and hold on the tab of your new tool palette and drag a copy to **My Tool Catalog** in the Content Browser.
7. In the **Sample Palette Catalog - Imperial,** locate the **Column Bubble** tool in the **Annotation** folder, and drag these tools to the **Structure** palette you created.

## Exercise 12-2: Placing a Column and Grid

1. Start a new drawing using the AEC Model (Imperial Stb) template.
2. Change to the **Work Layout.**
3. Erase the existing viewports.
4. Select **View > Viewports > 3 Viewports** from the **Main** menu.
5. Set the left viewport to **Top View,** the upper right to **Front View,** and the lower right to **SW Isometric.**
6. Activate the **Top View.**
7. Select **Structural Column Grid** from the **Structure** tool palette you created and drag your cursor over the **Properties** palette to open it.
8. Enter the following data:

    a.  Shape = **Rectangular**
    b.  Boundary = ***NONE***
    c.  Specify on screen = **No**
    d.  X - Width = **60′**
    e.  Y - Depth = **40′**
    f.  XAXIS Layout type = **Repeat**
    g.  Bay size = **20′-0″**
    h.  YAXIS Layout Type = **Repeat**
    i.  Bay size = **20′-0″**
    j.  Column Style = **Standard**
    k.  Column Logical Length = **10′-0″**
    l.  Justify = **Middle Center**

9. Click in the Drawing Editor in the **Top View** to place the grid and columns, and press **Enter** twice to complete the command (see Figure 12–1).

Save this file.

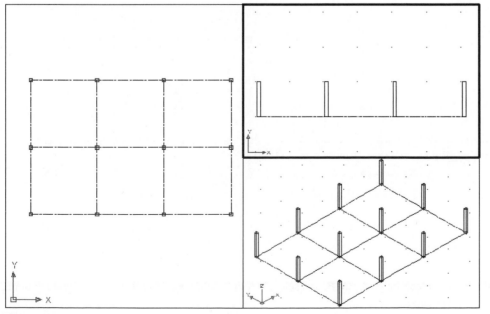

**Figure 12–1**

## Exercise 12-3: Modifying a Column Grid

1. Using the previous exercise, select the column grid and move your cursor over the **Properties** palette to open it.
2. In the **Properties** palette change the **X Axis** and **Y Axis Layout type** to **Manual.** This will allow you to drag the grid lines with your cursor and will also enable you to manually add guide lines (see Figure 12–2).

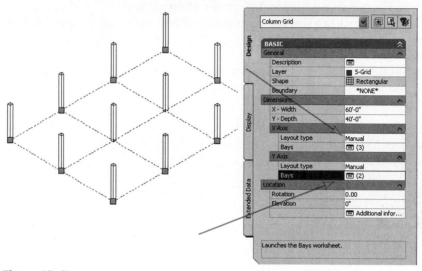

**Figure 12–2**

3. In the **Top View,** select the grid, and drag the middle left node **10′** in the **270** degree direction (see Figure 12–3).

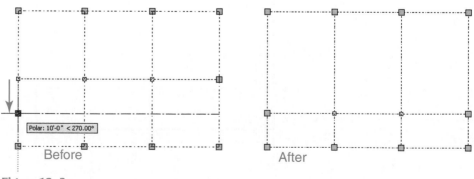

**Figure 12–3**

4. Again, select the grid, **RMB,** and select **Y Axis > Add Grid line** from the contextual menu that appears.
5. Enter **30′** in the **Command** line, and press the **Enter** key. This will add a new grid line **30′** from the lowest grid line (see Figure 12–4).

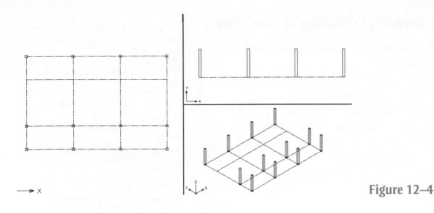

Figure 12–4

6. Select **Structural Column** from the **Design** tool palette, and place columns at the new grid nodes created by the new grid line. Save this file.

**Exercise 12-4:** Creating a Column Grid from Linework and Placement of Structural Columns

1. Start a new drawing using the AEC Model (Imperial Stb) template.
2. Using **Line** and **Arc,** create the line drawing shown in Figure 12–5.

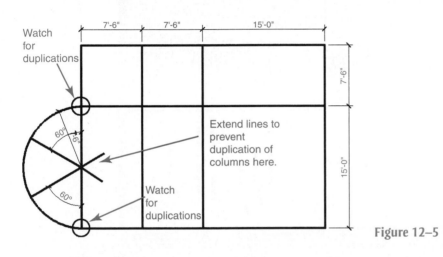

Figure 12–5

3. Select the **Structural Column Grid** tool from the **Design** tool palette, **RMB,** and select **Apply Tool Properties to > Linework.**
4. Select all the linework you created in Step 2, and press the **Enter** key on your keyboard.
5. Enter **Y** (Yes) in the **Command line** to erase the selected linework, and press the **Enter** key on your keyboard.

The linework changes into a Structural Column Grid with nodes (see Figure 12–6).

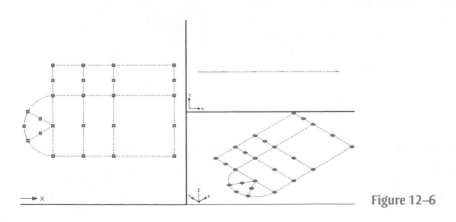

Figure 12–6

## Placing All the Structural Columns at One Time

6. Select the **Structural Column** tool from the **Design** tool palette.
7. Click on the column grid, and release the mouse button until you see the tool tip.
8. Press the **Ctrl** key on the keyboard until you see small red circles at the node points. When they appear, click the left mouse button again to place columns at all the grid nodes.
9. Press the **Esc** key on the keyboard to end the command (see Figure 12–7).

**Note:**
The placing of all the Structural Columns at one time can be used with all the creation methods for Structural Column Grids. **Be sure to turn OSNAP off to see the Ctrl tool tips for structural member placement.** Save this file.

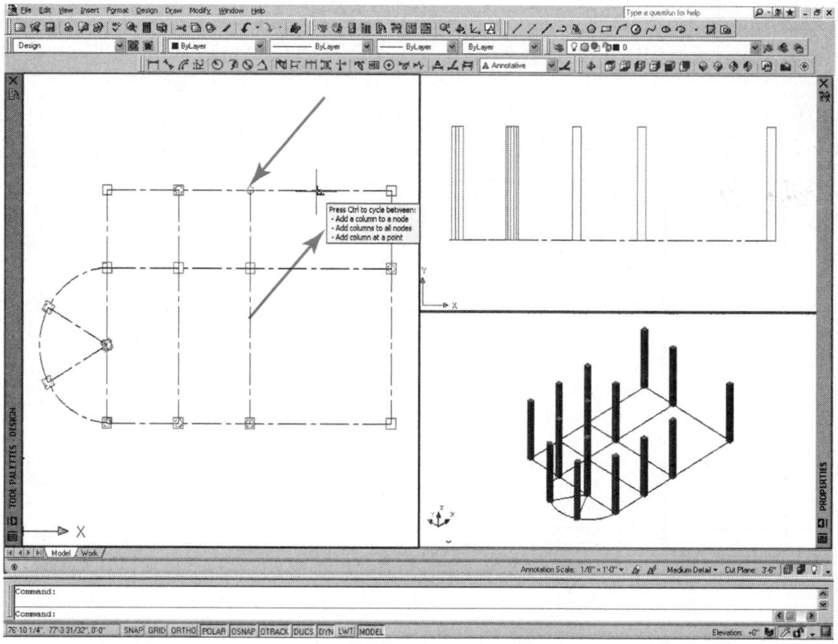

Figure 12–7

---

**Exercise 12-5:** Placing Beams on Structural Column Grids

1. Open the drawing for the first exercise in this chapter.
2. Activate the **Top View.**
3. Select the **Structural Beam** tool from the **De**    tool palette.
4. Move your cursor over the **Properties** palette open it.
5. In the **Properties** palette, select **Yes** from t **Trim Automatically** drop-down list and **Edg** from the **Layout Type** drop-down list.
6. Move your cursor over the Structural Column Grid (not at a column or node), and press the **Ctrl** key twice.

**Note:**
This feature will work only with Structural Column Grids and not with any other type of grid.

You will see that the beam expands to fill the entire grid line (see Figure 12–8).

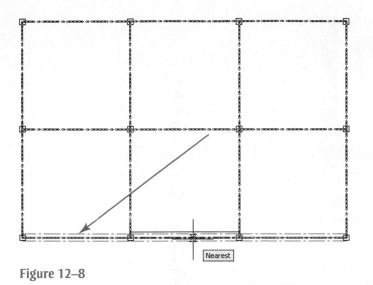

**Figure 12–8**

7.  Move your cursor over the Structural Column Grid (not at a column or node), and press the **Ctrl** key twice more.

You will see that the beam expands to fill all the grid lines.

8.  Click the left mouse button to place the beams (see Figure 12–9).

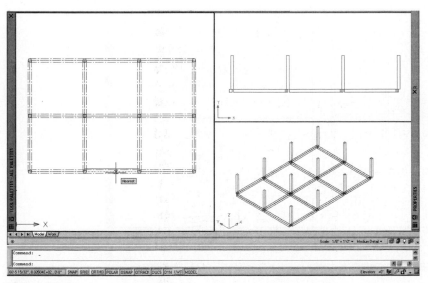

**Figure 12–9**

The default Structural Column that you placed on the Structural Column Grid is 12′-0″.

9.  Erase all the beams you placed.
10. Select the **Replace Z value with current elevation** icon at the bottom right of the Drawing Editor. This must be set before starting a placement command (see Figure 12–10).

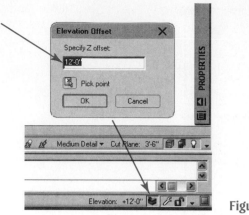

**Figure 12–10**

11. Select the **+0** to the left of the **Replace Z value with current elevation** icon you selected in Step 10 to bring up the **Elevation Offset** dialog box.
12. In the **Elevation Offset** dialog box, enter **12′-0″,** and press the **OK** button to return to the Drawing Editor.
13. Select the **Structural Beam** tool from the **Design** tool palette.
14. Move your cursor over the **Properties** palette to open it.
15. In the **Properties** palette, select **Yes** from the **Trim Automatically** drop-down list and **Edge** from the **Layout Type** drop-down list.
16. Repeat Steps 6–8 of this exercise to place beams at the top of the columns (see Figure 12–11).

Save this file.

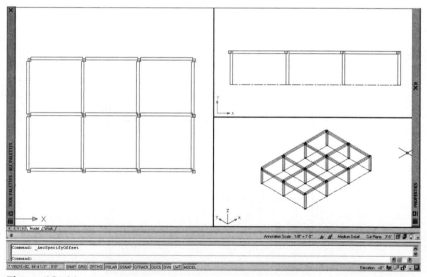

**Figure 12–11**

### Exercise 12-6: Using the Structural Beam "Fill and Array" Options

1. Use the drawing file from the previous exercise.
2. Select **Format > Structural members > Catalog** from the **Main** menu to bring up the **Structural Member Catalog** dialog box.
3. In the **Structural Member Catalog** dialog box, in the left pane, expand **Imperial,** then expand **Timber,** and finally expand **Nominal Cut Lumber.**
4. In the **Structural Member Catalog** dialog box, in the right pane, double-click on **2 × 4** to bring up the **Structural Member Style** dialog box.

5. In the **Structural Member Style** dialog box, press the **OK** button, and then close the **Structural Member Style** dialog box to return to the Drawing Editor (see Figure 12–12).

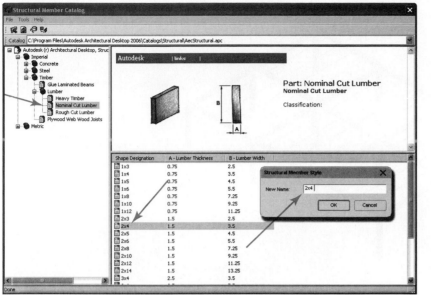

Figure 12–12

6. Select the **Structural Beam** tool from thc **Design** tool palette.
7. Move your cursor over the **Properties** palette to open it.
8. In the **Properties** palette, select **Yes** from the **Trim Automatically** drop-down list, **Fill** from the **Layout Type, Yes** from the **Array** drop-down list, **Space evenly** from the **Layout method** drop-down list, and insert **5** in the **Number of bays** field (see Figure 12–13).

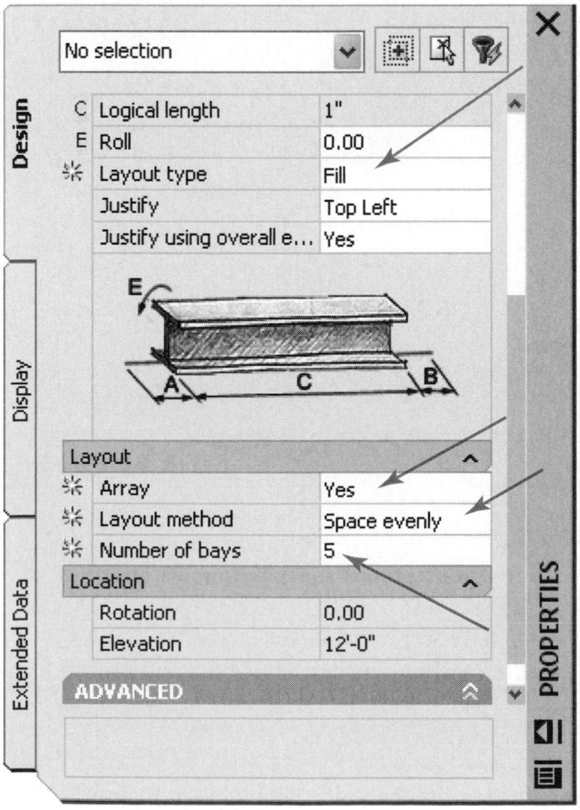

Figure 12–13

9. Move your cursor over the Structural Column Grid (not at a node or column), click the **Ctrl** key on your keyboard twice, and then click the left mouse button to place the beams as shown in Figure 12–14.

**Figure 12–14**

## Exercise 12-7: Modifying Structural Members

1. Use a window selection to select only the middle row of columns, and move your cursor over **Properties** palette to open it.
2. Set the **Logical length** to 14′-0″, and press **En**[
3. Select the **Structural Beam** icon from t **Structure** toolbar, set the **Style** to **Standar** and **Justify** to **Bottom Center.**
4. Click at the top of the first center column, the at the top of the second center column.
5. Repeat the above process with the top center nodes of the columns (see Figure 12–15).

**Note:**
Bottom center is the location of the grips now set for the beam.

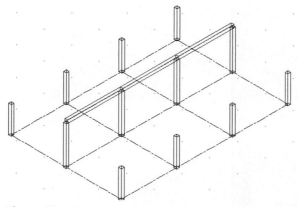

**Figure 12–15**

6. Repeat the process for the other columns to create the frame illustrated in Figure 12–16.

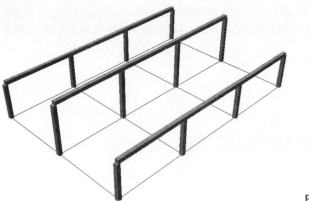

Figure 12–16

7. Select the end beams on the left and right sides, and move your cursor over the **Properties** palette to open it.
8. Set the **Start offset** to 2'-0" (see Figure 12–17).

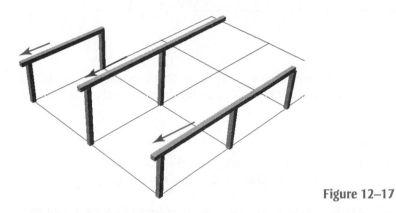

Figure 12–17

9. Repeat this process on the beams at the opposite end. Use +2'-0" for **End offset.**
10. Select **Format > Structural Member Catalog** from the **Main** toolbar.
11. Select **Imperial | Steel | AISC | Channels | MC, Miscellaneous Channels.**
12. Double-click the **MC12 × 10.6** channel.
13. When the **Structural Member Style** dialog box appears, accept the default **MC12 × 10.6** name (see Figure 12–18).

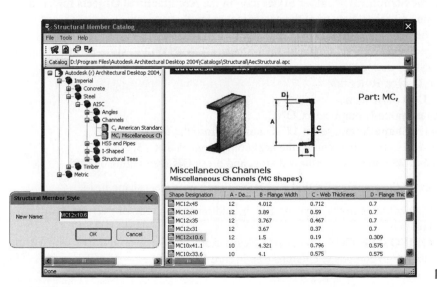

Figure 12–18

14. Select all the outer beams, **RMB,** and select **Properties** from the contextual menu. In the structural **Properties** dialog box, select the **Style** tab and change the style to **MC12 × 10.6** (see Figure 12–19).

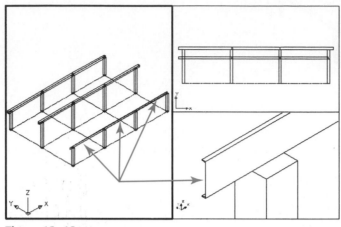

Figure 12–19

15. Repeat the above process for the beams on the other side. This time also change **Roll** to **180** and **Justification** to **Top Center.** This will cause the other channels to rotate 180° with the grip on the bottom.

**Exercise 12-8:** Creating a Round Composite Concrete and Steel Column

1. Select **Format > Structural Members > Catalog** from the **Main** toolbar.
2. Select **Imperial > Concrete > Cast - in place > Circular Columns.**
3. Double-click the 14″ diameter.
4. When the **Structural Member Style** dialog box appears, enter **14 DIA COL** and then press **OK.**
5. Select **Imperial | Steel | AISC | I Shaped, Wn Wide-Flange Shapes.**
6. Double-click **W6 × 25.**
7. When the **Structural Member Style** dialog box appears, accept **W6 × 25** and then press **OK.**
8. Close the **Structural Member Catalog.**
9. Select **Format > Style Manager** to bring up the **Style Manager** dialog box.
10. **RMB** on the **Structural Member Styles** icon in the **Architectural Objects** folder in the display tree and select **New** from the contextual menu that appears.
11. Rename the new style **COMPOSITE** and press **OK.**
12. Double-click on the icon adjacent to the new **COMPOSITE** style to bring up the **COMPOSITE** dialog box.
13. Select the **Design Rules** tab.
14. Press the **Edit Style** icon.
15. Name the **unnamed** component **CONC.**
16. Under **Start Shape Name,** select **14″-Diameter** from the drop-down list.
17. Press the **Add** button, and rename the next component **W6 × 25.**
18. Select **W6 × 25** under **Start Shape Name,** and press **OK** (see Figure 12–20).

You have now created the composite round concrete column with steel shape inside.

19. Select all the columns in the Drawing Editor, and move your cursor over the **Properties** palette to open it.
20. Select **COMPOSITE COL Structural Beam** from the **Style** drop-down list. All the columns change to composite columns (see Figure 12–21).

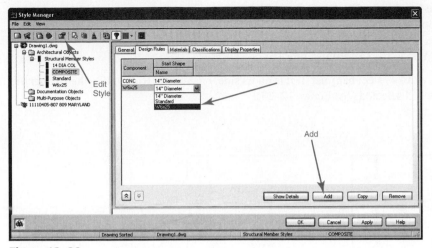

**Figure 12–20**

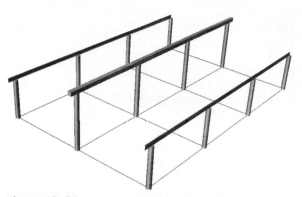

**Figure 12–21**

## Exercise 12-9: Adding Bar Joists

1. Select the **Content Browser** icon from the **Main** toolbar to launch the **Content Browser.**
2. In the **Design Tool Catalog - Imperial** locate the **Bar Joists** in the **Structural** folder.
3. From the **Bar Joists** folder, drag the **Steel Joist 24** into the **Structure** tool palette you created, and close the Content Browser.
4. Select **Line** from the **Draw** toolbar, and place a line from the middle beam to the top outside edge of the channel (see Figure 12–22).

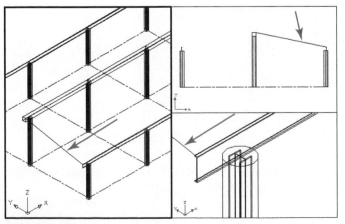

**Figure 12–22**

5. Select the **Steel Joist 24** icon from the **Structure** palette you created, **RMB,** and select **Apply Tool Properties to > Linework** from the contextual menu that appears.
6. Select the line you placed in Step 4 and press **Enter.**
7. Enter **Y** (Yes) in the **Command line** and press **Enter.**

The line changes to a 24″ steel bar joist. If it is on its side, change the **Roll** to **0** in the **Properties** palette while it is still selected (see Figure 12–23).

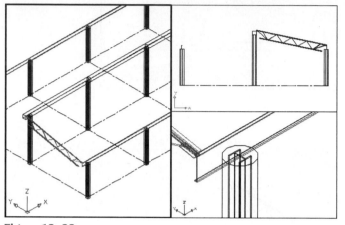

**Figure 12–23**

8. Change to the **Model Layout.**
9. Change to the **Left View,** and zoom window around the location of the joist seat and the channel (see Figure 12–24).

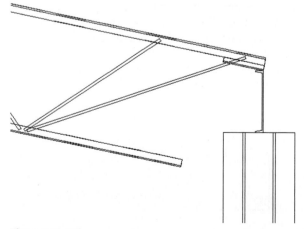

**Figure 12–24**

10. Select the bar joist, **RMB,** and select **Edit Member Style** from the contextual menu that appears to bring up the **Structural Member Style** dialog box.
11. Select the **Design Rules** tab. This is where you control the components of the bar joist.
12. Press the **Show Details** button at the bottom of the dialog box to expand the truss details.

13. Set the settings shown for the **TopChord** and **JoistSeat-End** and press **OK** (see Figure 12–25).

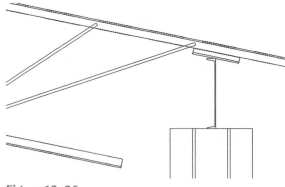

**Figure 12–25**

The bar joist top chord and joist seat change (see Fi 12–26).

14. Change to the **Top View.**
15. Select the bar joist, **RMB,** and select **AEC Mo ify Tools > Array** from the contextual menu th appears.
16. Select the front edge of the bar joist as an edge drag to the right, and enter **2′-0″** in the dynamic input field.

**Note:**
The author adjusted the titles in the details columns to the left, so some columns such as Mirror, Rotate, and Y and Z Offsets are not illustrated.

**Figure 12–26**

17. When you reach the last set of columns, click the left mouse again to complete the command (see Figure 12–27).

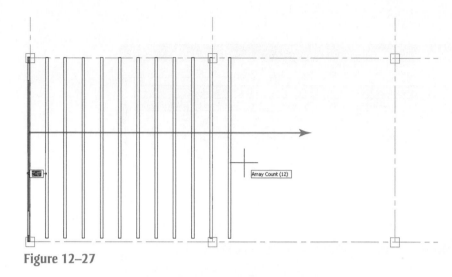

**Figure 12–27**

18. Mirror the bar joists to the other side of the structure, and you are finished (see Figure 12–28). Save this exercise.

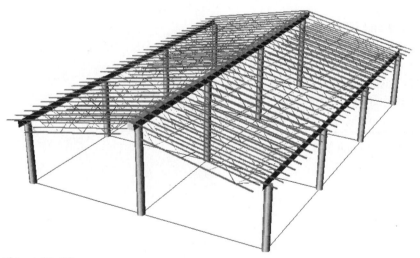

**Figure 12–28**

## Exercise 12-10: Labeling a Column Grid

1. Use the previous exercise.
2. Change to the **Top View.**
3. Select the **Layer Manager** icon from the **Layer Properties** toolbar to bring up the **Layer Manager.**
4. Turn the **S-Beam** and the **S-Cols** layers off, and press **OK** to return to the Drawing Editor.

The column grid will now be exposed.

5. Select the column grid, **RMB,** and select **Label** from the contextual menu that appears to bring up the **Column Grid Labeling** dialog box.
6. Select the **X-Labeling** tab.
7. In the **Number** list enter the letter **A** and press **Enter** to fill the other letters automatically.

8. Also do the following on the same tab:

   a. Check the **Automatically Calculate Values for Labels** check box.
   b. Select the **Ascending** radio button.
   c. Check the **Bottom** check box for **Bubble Parameters.**
   d. Enter **4′-0″** for **Extension** under **Bubble Parameters.**
   e. Check the **Generate New Bubbles On Exit** check box.

9. Change to the **Y - Labeling** tab.
10. In the **Number** list, enter the number **1** and press **Enter** to fill the other numbers automatically.
11. Also do the following in the same tab:

    a. Check the **Automatically Calculate Values for Labels** check box.
    b. Select the **Ascending** radio button.
    c. Check the **Right** check box for **Bubble Parameters.**
    d. Enter **4′-0″** for **Extension** under the **Bubble Parameters.**
    e. Check the **Generate New Bubbles On Exit** check box.

12. Press **OK** to return to the Drawing Editor (see Figure 12–29).

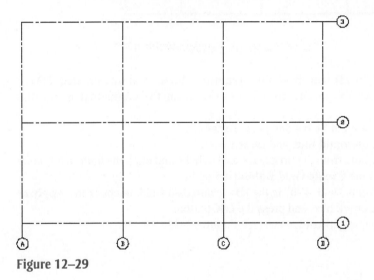

**Figure 12–29**

13. Select the bubble containing the letter **A** to activate its grips.
14. Drag the grip above the bubble to the right; the leader will follow (see Figure 12–30).

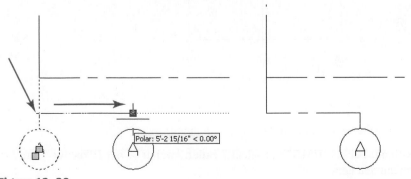

**Figure 12–30**

**Exercise 12-11:** Adding and Labeling a Layout Grid (2D)

1. Start a new drawing using the AEC Model (Imperial Stb) template.
2. Activate the **Top View.**
3. With various tools from the **Draw** menu, create the plan shown in Figure 12–31.

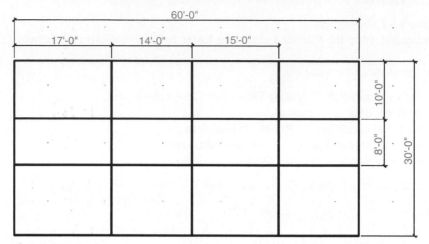

**Figure 12–31**

4. Select the **Layout Grid 2D** icon from the **Structure** palette that you created, **RMB,** and select **Apply Tool Properties to > Linework** from the contextual menu that appears.
5. Select the plan you created in Step 4 and press **Enter.**
6. Enter **Y** (Yes) in the **Command line,** and press **Enter.**
7. Select the **Column Bubble** from the **Structure** tool palette, and click the bottom left node of the plan to bring up the **Create Grid Bubble** dialog box.
8. Enter **A1** in the **Label** data field, **4'-0"** in the **Extension** data field, uncheck the **Apply at both ends of gridline** check box, and press the **OK** button.
9. Repeat for the following right-hand nodes (see Figure 12–32).

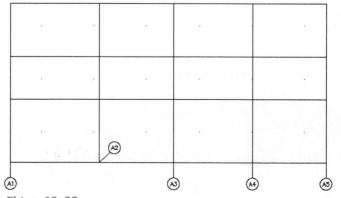

**Figure 12–32**

If a column bubble is misplaced or at an angle, do the following:

10. Select the column bubble, **RMB,** and select **Leader Anchor > Set Direction** from the contextual menu that appears.
11. For this example, enter **270°** and press **Enter** (see Figure 12–33).

Before

After

**Figure 12–33**

# LAYOUT CURVES

Layout curves are not necessarily curves. Straight lines and many AEC Objects such as walls, stairs, and doors can also be used as layout curves. If a line were placed on a wall, changed to a layout curve, and then moved vertically 24″ up the wall, attached content would move with the layout curve. If the wall had been used as a layout curve, the nodes would be at its base.

Use a layout curve to anchor objects along a path. You can define the following objects as layout curves:

- Walls
- Curtain walls
- Window assemblies
- Spaces
- Mass elements
- Roofs
- Lines
- Arcs
- Circles
- Ellipses
- Polygons
- Polylines
- Splines

**Exercise 12-12:** Creating and Using a Layout Curve

1. Start a new drawing using the AEC Model (Imperial Stb) template.
2. Select **Spline** from the **Draw** menu, and place a spline.
3. Select the **Layout Curve** icon from the **Structure** palette.
4. Select the spline, enter **S** (Space evenly) in the **Command line,** and press **Enter.**
5. Enter **5** in the **Command line** for the **Number** of nodes and press **Enter.**
6. Enter **0″** for **Start** and **End** offsets.
7. Change to the **SW Isometric View.**
8. Turn on the **Node** Object Snap.
9. Select **Structural Column** from the **Structure** tool palette, select one of the nodes on the spline, and click the mouse to place it.
10. Select **Node Anchor** from the **Structure** tool palette.
11. Enter **C** (Copy to each node) in the **Command line,** and press **Enter** as the object to be copied.
12. Select the column you placed and press **Enter.**

13. Select any other node on the spline and press **Enter.**
14. Enter **Y** (Yes) in the **Command line** and press **Enter.**

All the nodes on the spline now have columns (see Figure 12–34).

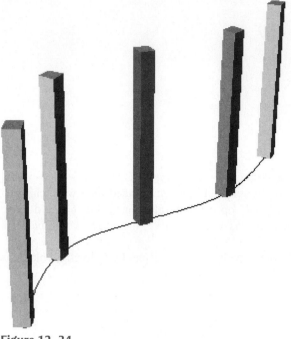

**Figure 12–34**

**Exercise 12-13:** Using a Wall as a Layout Curve

1. Use the previous drawing.
2. Select the **Wall** icon from the **Design** menu and place a **Standard** 15′-0″-long, 10′-high, 6″-wide wall.
3. Select the **Layout Curve** icon from the **Structure** palette, and select the wall you just created.
4. Enter **S** (Space evenly) in the **Command line,** and press **Enter.**
5. Enter **24″** for the **Start offset** and press **Enter.**
6. Enter **24″** for the **End offset** and press **Enter.**
7. Accept **3** as the **Number of nodes,** and press **Enter** to place the nodes.
8. Select the **Content Browser** icon from the **Main** toolbar and select and drag into the drawing the **Regular** drinking fountain from the **Design Tool Catalog - Imperial > Mechanical > Plumbing Fixtures >  Fountain** folder (see Figure 12–35).
9. Select the **Node Anchor** icon from the **Structure** palette.
10. Enter **C** (Copy to each node) in the **Command line** and press **Enter.**
11. Select the drinking fountain, and then select one of the nodes anchored to the wall.

The fountains are now anchored to the wall as the layout tools.

12. Select all the fountains and move your cursor over the **Properties** palette to open it.
13. Select the **Anchor** field to bring up the **Anchor** dialog box.
14. Change the **Insertion Offset Z** to **3′-0″,** the **Rotation Z** to **270,** and press **OK** to return to the Drawing Editor.

All the fountains move vertically up the wall 3′-0″ (see Figure 12–36).

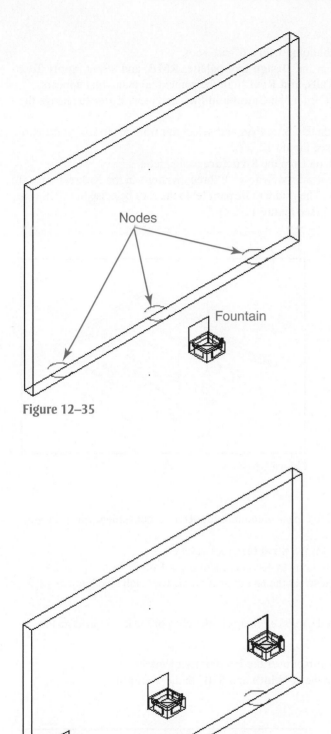

**Figure 12–35**

**Figure 12–36**

## Exercise 12-14: Layout Grid (2D)

1. Start a new drawing using the AEC Model (Imperial Stb) template.
2. Change to the **Model Layout.**

3. Change to the **Top View.**
4. Create a 40′-long × 30′-wide building with a 6″-rise roof.
5. Select the **Roof Slab** icon from the **Design** tool palette, **RMB,** and select **Apply Tool Properties to > Linework, Walls, and Roof** from the contextual menu that appears.
6. Select the roof object, enter **N** (No) in the **Command line,** and press **Enter** to change the roof object to roof slabs.
7. Select the **Object UCS** from the **UCS** toolbar, and select the front roof slab. Make sure the **ucsicon** OR **option** is on (see Figure 12–37).
8. Select the **Layout Grid (2D)** icon from the **Structure** tool palette.
9. Center a 15′ × 10′ grid on the front roof slab with three divisions in the X direction and two divisions in the Y direction. The grid will lie parallel to the roof because the UCS was set parallel to the roof in Step 7 (see Figure 12–38).

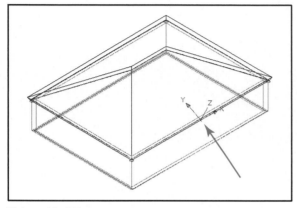

**Figure 12–37**

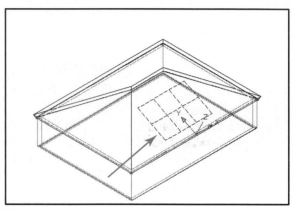

**Figure 12–38**

10. Place a 5′-0″-high × 1′-0″-radius mass element cylinder in a convenient place in your drawing.
11. Select the **Cell Anchor** icon from the **Structure** tool palette.
12. Type **C** at the **Command line** to copy to each cell, and press **Enter.**
13. Select the mass object, and then select the layout grid on the roof slab (see Figures 12–39 and 12–40).

Note in Figures 12–25 and 12–26 that the mass elements in the cells of the layout grid match the size of the grid.

14. Select the grid, and move your cursor over the **Properties** palette to open it.
15. Change the grid size to **5′-0″** in the **X-Width** and **5′-0″** in the **Y-Depth.**

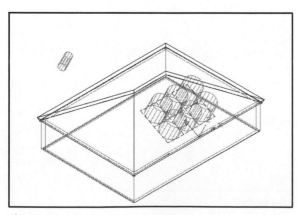

**Figure 12–39**

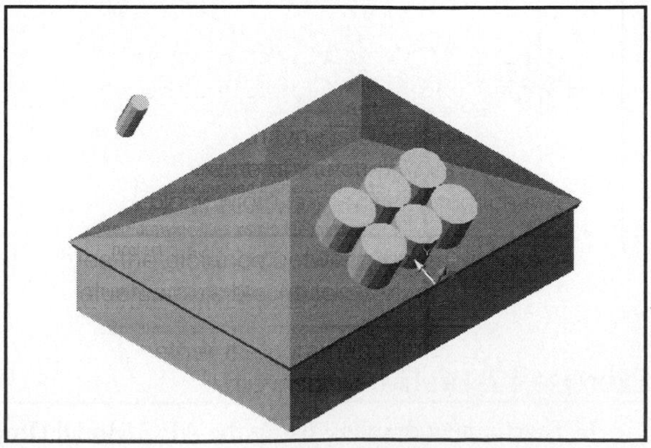

**Figure 12–40**

Note that the mass elements in the cells automatically change size (see Figures 12–41 and 12–42).

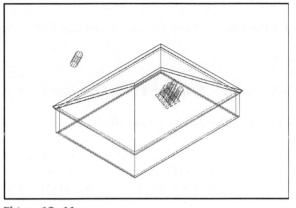

**Figure 12–41**

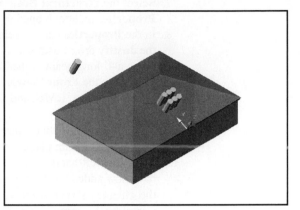

**Figure 12–42**

16. Place another grid on the roof; 9′ × 6′ will fit.
17. Select the **Node Anchor** icon from the **Structure** tool palette.
18. Enter **C** (Copy to each node) in the **Command line** and press **Enter.**
19. Select the mass element, and then select the layout grid (see Figure 12–43).

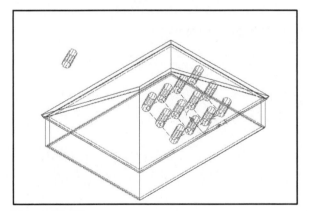

**Figure 12–43**

Note that the mass elements attached to the nodes of the layout grid. Moving or modifying the grid will then move the anchored objects.

The layout volume grid (3D) works and is modified in a similar manner to the 2D layout grid.

Experiment with all the different settings, and try anchoring and rotating different kinds of content to AEC Objects and AutoCAD entities. Don't forget that you can use the layout grid to put a series of skylights or windows on a roof or wall. **Save this file.**

### Exercise 12-15: Using the Trim Planes

1. Start a new drawing using the AEC Model (Imperial Stb) template.
2. Select **Format > Structural members > Catalog** from the **Main** menu to bring up the **Structural Member Catalog** dialog box.
3. In the **Structural Member Catalog** dialog box, expand **Timber** and then expand **Nominal Cut Lumber.**
4. In the right pane of the **Structural Member Catalog** dialog box, double-click on **2 × 6** to bring up the **Structural Member Style** dialog box.

5. Press the **OK** button to return to the right pane of the **Structural Member Catalog** dialog box. Close the **Structural Member Catalog.**
6. Change to the **Top View.**
7. Select the **Structural Beam** tool from the **Design** menu, and move your cursor over the **Properties** palette to open it.
8. In the **Properties** palette, select **2 × 6** from the **Style** drop-down list, and **Top Left** from the **Justify** drop-down list.
9. Place a 4′-long beam in the **Top** viewport.
10. Change to the **Front View.**
11. Select the beam, **RMB,** and select **Trim Planes > Edit Trim Planes** from the contextual menu that appears.
12. Notice the + signs that appear at the top ends of the beam; this signifies that you are ready to add an **Edit** trim plane.
13. Select the left-hand **+ sign** to add the plane, and the + changes to − meaning that you have now added the **Edit** trim plane, and are ready to make the edit. Grip the node, make the changes shown (Figure 12–44), and then press the **Esc** key on your keyboard to complete the command.

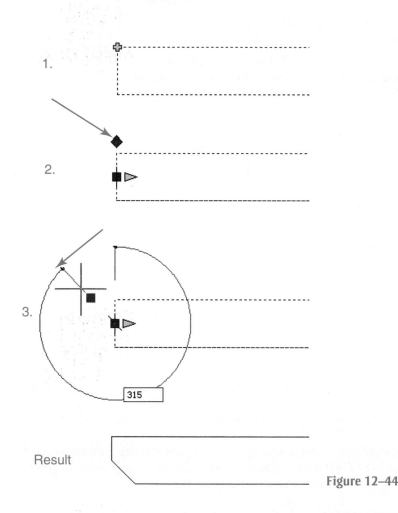

Figure 12–44

14. Select the beam again, **RMB,** and move your cursor over the **Properties** palette to open it.
15. At the very bottom of the **Properties** palette, under **ADVANCED,** click on **(1)** in the trim planes field to open the **Beam Trim Planes** dialog box.
16. In the **Beam Trim Planes** dialog box, enter **6″** in the **X** column, and press the **OK** button.

The trim plane can be controlled directly from the beam or through the **Beam Trim Planes** dialog box (see Figure 12–45).

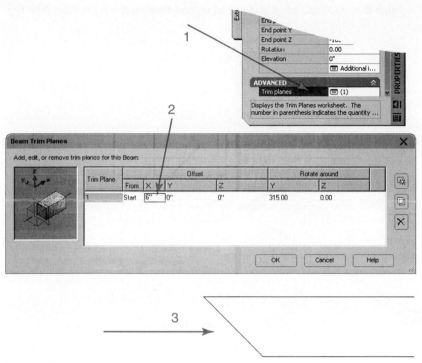

**Figure 12–45**

## Exercise 12-16: Framing Floors and Roofs Using Slabs and Structural Members

1. Start a new drawing using the AEC Model (Imperial Stb) template.
2. Select **Format > Structural members > Catalog** from the **Main** menu to bring up the **Structural Member Catalog** dialog box.
3. In the **Structural Member Catalog** dialog box, expand **Timber** and then expand **Plywood Web Wood Joists.**
4. In the right pane of the **Structural Member Catalog** dialog box, double-click on **10in Plywood Web Wood Joist** to bring up the **Structural Member Style** dialog box.
5. Press the **OK** button to return to the right pane of the **Structural Member Catalog** dialog box. Close the **Structural Member Catalog.**
6. Change to the **Top View,** select the **Wall** tool from the **Design** tool palette, and using a **9′-0″** high **Standard** wall place a **10′ × 20′** enclosure.

### Creating the Floor and Floor Framing

7. Select the **Space Auto Tool** from the **Design** tool palette, and place a **Standard** space in the enclosure.
8. Double-click the space you just created to open the **Properties** palette.
9. In the **Properties** palette, set the **Space height** to **10′-1/4″, Floor boundary thickness** to **1/2″, Ceiling boundary thickness** to **3/4″,** and **Elevation** to **1/2″.**
10. Select the **Slab** tool from the **Design** tool palette, **RMB,** and select **Apply Tool Properties to Space** from the contextual menu that appears.
11. Click on the space object you just created and adjusted, and press the **Enter** key on your keyboard to bring up the **Convert Space to Slab** dialog box.
12. In the **Convert Space to Slab** dialog box, check all the check boxes, and press the **OK** button to return to the Drawing Editor. The space object has been changed to slabs.
13. Change to the **SW Isometric View** to see the slabs you created.
14. Select the **Structural Beam** tool from the **Design** tool palette, and move your cursor over the **Properties** palette to open it.
15. In the **Properties** palette, set **Style** to **10in Plywood Web Wood Joist, Layout Type** to **Edge,** and **Justify** to **Top Left.**

16. Select the top slab that you created on the left edge, and then on the right edge (see Figure 12–46).

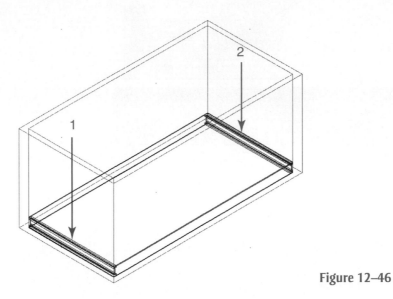

**Figure 12–46**

17. After placing the two end joists, again move your cursor over the **Properties** palette to open it.
18. In the **Properties** palette, set **Layout type** to **Fill, Array** to **Yes, Layout method** to **Repeat,** and **Bay side** to **2′-0″.**
19. Click on the side edge of the top floor slab you created to place the remaining joists (see Figure 12–47).

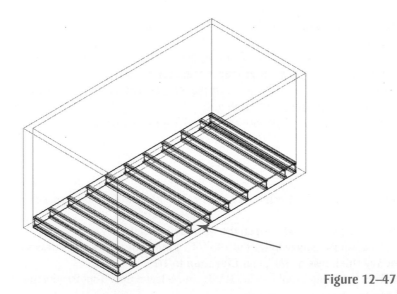

**Figure 12–47**

## Creating the Roof and Roof Framing

20. Select the **Roof** tool from the **Design** tool palette, **RMB,** and select **Apply Tool Properties to > Linework and Walls** from the contextual menu that appears.
21. Select all the walls; press the **Enter** key on your keyboard.
22. Press the **Enter** key on your keyboard again to not erase layout geometry.

A room appears on the enclosure. Press the **Esc** key to complete the command, and deselect the new roof (see Figure 12–48).

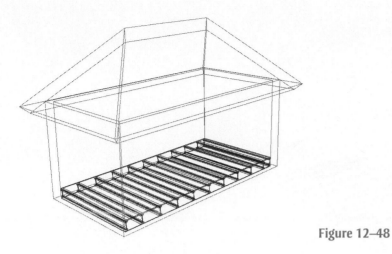

Figure 12–48

23. Change to the **Top View.**
24. Move the vertices as shown (see Figure 12–49) to create the roof shown (see Figure 12–50).

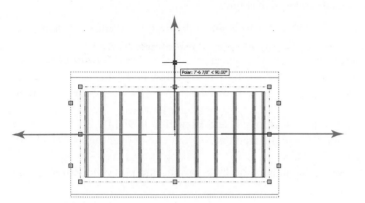

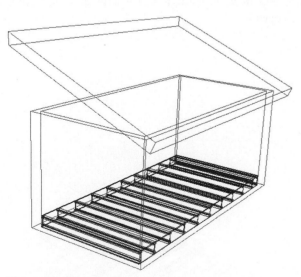

25. Select the three walls shown in Figure 12–51, **RMB,** and select **Roof/Floor Line > Modify Roof Line** from the contextual menus that appear.

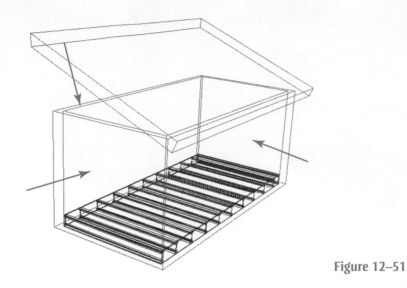

Figure 12–51

26. Enter **A** (Auto project) in the **Command line,** and press the **Enter** key twice.
27. Select the roof slab, and press the **Enter** key.

The walls now project to the underside of the slab (Figure 12–52).

28. Select the roof, **RMB,** and select **Convert to Roof Slabs** from the contextual menu that appears.
29. The **Convert to Roof Slabs** dialog box will appear, check the **Erase Layout Geometry** check box, and then press the **OK** button to return to the Drawing Editor.
30. With the new roof slab still selected, move your cursor over the **Properties** palette to open it.
31. In the **Properties** palette, set **Thickness** to **3/4″** and **Elevation** to **9′-11″.**
32. Select the **Face UCS** from the **UCS** toolbar, and move your cursor over the roof slab until a red hatch appears (Figure 12–53).
33. Click the lower right corner of the slab as the UCS origin, and press the **Enter** key to complete the command.

You have now set the UCS so that the roof trusses will be perpendicular to the roof slab you created.

34. Again, select the **Structural Beam** tool from the **Design** tool palette, and move your cursor over the **Properties** palette to open it.

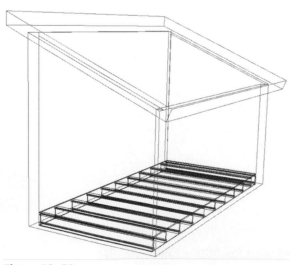

Figure 12–52

Figure 12–53

35. In the **Properties** palette, set **Layout type** to **Fill, Array** to **Yes, Layout method** to **Repeat,** and **Bay side** to **2′-0″.**
36. Click on the left edge of the roof slab to place the joists, and then press the **Esc** key to complete the command (Figure 12–54).

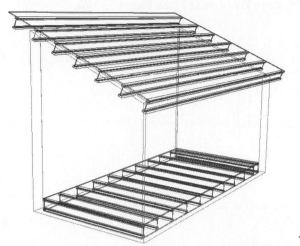

**Figure 12–54**

## Exercise 12-17: Creating a Custom Structural Member from Linework, and Applying a Miter

1. Start a new drawing using the AEC Model (Imperial Stb) template.
2. Select **Format > Structural members > Catalog** from the **Main** menu to bring up the **Structural Member Catalog** dialog box.
3. In the **Structural Member Catalog** dialog box, expand **Steel,** expand **AISC,** expand **I Shaped** and, then, **HP Bearing Piles.**
4. In the right pane of the **Structural Member Catalog** dialog box, double-click on **HP14 × 117** to bring up the **Structural Member Style** dialog box.
5. Press the **OK** button to return to the right pane of the **Structural Member Catalog** dialog box.
6. Select the line command from the **Draw** menu and create the drawing shown (see Figure 12–55).

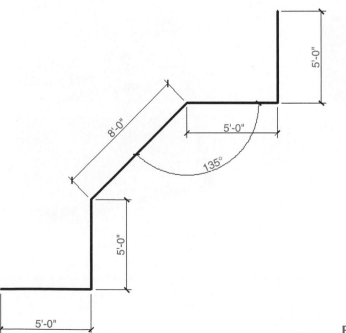

**Figure 12–55**

7. Select the **Structural Column** tool from the **Design** tool palette, **RMB,** and select **Apply Tool Properties to** from the contextual menu that appears.
8. The **Convert to Column** dialog box appears; check the **Erase Layout Geometry** check box, and press the **OK** button. The line drawing turns into structural members.
9. Select all the structural members, and move your cursor over the **Properties** palette to open it.
10. In the **Properties** palette, set the **Style** to **HP14 × 117** (see Figure 12–56).

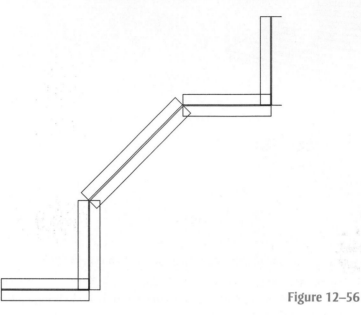

Figure 12–56

11. Select the top member, **RMB,** and select **Miter** from the contextual menu that appears.
12. Select the next member to miter the first to the second.
13. Press the **Enter** key on your keyboard to repeat the **Miter** operation, and select the next member.
14. Continue pressing the **Enter** key and selecting members until you have converted all the linework.
15. Change to the **SW Isometric View,** and press the **Flat Shaded, Edges On** icon in the **Shading** menu (see Figure 12–57).

Note:
Miter will not work with arc lines that have been converted to structural members.

Figure 12–57

## 13

# AEC Dimensions

## *Section* Objectives

- Learn how to set the text style.
- Know how to create a dimension style.
- Learn how to create an AEC dimension style.
- Use and modify an AEC dimension style.
- Dimension doors and windows with AEC dimension styles.
- Learn how to add a manual AEC dimension.
- Know how to detach objects from AEC dimensions.
- Understand AEC dimension chains.
- Understand the Dimension Wizard.

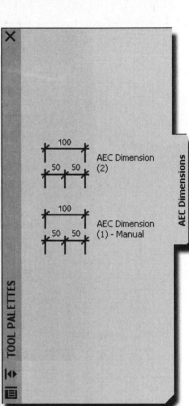

## AEC DIMENSIONS

AEC dimensions are automatic dimensions based on styles. Because there are so many variables in the dimension system, there are many dialog boxes. To make it easier, the developers have also added a Wizard to aid in variable setup.

Standard AutoCAD dimensions can be converted into AEC dimensions, and AEC dimensions can be mixed with the manual AEC and standard AutoCAD dimensioning systems.

AEC dimensions can dimension only AEC Objects such as walls, windows, stairs, structural members, and so on. If you add non-AEC objects to AEC Objects, you have to add manual dimension points to the automatic AEC dimension, or create manual AEC or standard AutoCAD dimensions.

The following table describes the differences in the three available dimensioning systems.

| AutoCAD Dimensions | Manual AEC Dimensions | AutoCAD Dimension Style |
|---|---|---|
| Logical dimension points taken from object | Manual dimension points taken from drawing | Manual dimension points taken from drawing |
| Dimension AEC objects | Dimension picked points in drawing | Dimension picked points in drawing |
| Associative toward building elements | Associative or nonassociative toward points, depending on user settings | Associative toward points |
| Dimension groups | Dimension groups | Single dimensions |
| Support superscripting, variable extension line length | Support superscripting, variable extension line length | Supports no superscripting, variable extension line length |
| Dimension texts cannot be edited | Dimension texts cannot be edited | Dimension texts can be edited |
| Defined by AEC dimension style and AutoCAD dimension style | Defined by AEC dimension style and AutoCAD dimension style | Defined by AutoCAD dimension style |

**TIP** Since the AEC dimensions are based on AutoCAD's standard dimensioning variables, it is imperative that you have a good understanding of that system and its operation. This includes an understanding of the relationship between dimensioning and Model - Paper space. This book assumes that understanding.

**Exercise 13-1:** Setting the Text Style

Before setting the dimension styles, change the **Standard** text style.

1. Start a new drawing using the AEC Model (Imperial Stb) template.
2. Select **Format > Text Style** from the **Main** toolbar to bring up the **Text Style** dialog box.
3. Select the **New** button and create a new style name called **NEW Text.**
4. Set the **NEW Text** font to **Arial** in the **Font Name** drop-down list, select **Bold** in the **Font Style** drop-down list, apply, and close (see Figure 13–1).

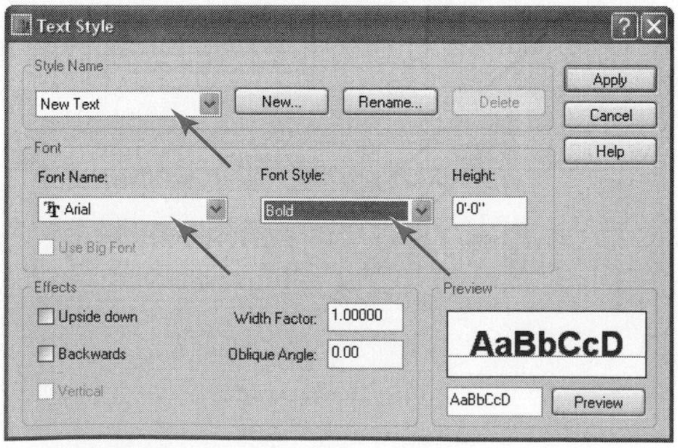

**Figure 13–1**

You have now created a Text style that you can use with AutoCAD Dimensions and AutoCAD Architecture AEC dimensions. Save this file.

## Exercise 13-2: Creating a Dimension Style

1. Select **Format  Dimension Style** from the **Main** toolbar to bring up the **Dimension Style Manager** dialog box.
2. Press the **New** button to bring up the **Create New Dimension Style** dialog box.
3. Set the following:

   a. New Style Name = **(Put your name here)**
   b. Start With = **Standard**
   c. Use for = **All dimensions**

4. Press the **Continue** button to bring up the **New Dimension Style** dialog box.
5. Select the **Text** tab.
6. Set the following:

   a. Text style = **NEW Text**
   b. Text height = **1/8"**
   c. Text Placement Vertical = **Above**
   d. Text Placement Horizontal = **Centered**
   e. Text Alignment = **Aligned with dimension line**

7. Change to the **Lines** tab.
8. Set the following:

   a. Extend beyond dim lines = **1/16"**
   b. Offset from origin = **1/16"**

9. Change to the **Symbols and Arrows** tab, and set the following:

   a. Arrowheads 1st = **Architectural tick**
   b. Arrowheads 2nd = **Architectural tick**
   c. Leader = **Closed filled**
   d. Arrow size = **1/16"**

10. Change to the **Fit** tab, and set **Use overall scale of:** to **48.0.**
11. Change to the **Primary Units** tab, and set the **Unit** format to **Architectural,** and press the **OK** button.
12. Press **Set Current,** and then press **OK** to close the dialog boxes and return to the Drawing Editor.

You have now set the AutoCAD dimension style for **NEW DIMENSION STYLE** dimensions.

## Exercise 13-3: Creating an AEC Dimension Style

1. Select **Format > AEC Dimension Styles** from the **Main** toolbar.
2. At the **Style Manager** dialog box, select the **New Style** icon in the top toolbar, and rename the new style **STUDENT's Name** (see Figure 13–2).

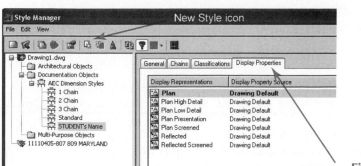

**Figure 13–2**

3. Select **STUDENT's Name,** and select the **Display Properties** tab.
4. Double-click on **Plan** in the **Display Representations** column to bring up the **Display Properties** dialog box.
5. Select the **Contents** tab.
6. Select **Wall** from **Apply to,** check the **Length of Wall** check box, check the **Chain 1** check box, and select **Wall Length** from the **Length of Wall** drop-down list (see Figure 13–3).
7. Select the **Other** tab, and select **STUDENT's Name,** at the **Dimension Style** drop-down list. Make sure the check boxes are unchecked, and then press the **OK** buttons to return to the Drawing Editor.

You have now created an AEC dimension style called **STUDENT's Name.** Save this file.

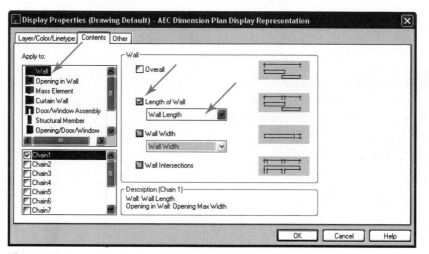

**Figure 13–3**

---

**Exercise 13-4:** Using and Modifying an AEC Dimension Style

1. Use the previous exercise.
2. Change to the **Work Layout.**
3. Clear the viewports and create one viewport.
4. Change to the **Top View.**
5. Change to **Paper space,** select the viewport frame, and move your cursor over the **Properties** palette to open it.
6. Set the following:

   a. Standard scale = **1/4″ = 1′-0″**

7. Change to **Model** space.
8. Select the **Wall** icon from the **Design** tool palette, and move your cursor over the **Properties** palette to open it.
9. Set the following settings:

   a. Style = **Standard**
   b. Width = **6″**
   c. Justify = **Left**

10. Create the walls shown in Figure 13–4. Don't include the dimensions shown.
11. Select all wall segments, **RMB,** and select **AEC Dimension** from the contextual menu that appears.
12. Move your cursor over the **Properties** palette to open it.
13. Set the **Style** to **STUDENT's Name** from the **Style** drop-down list.
14. Drag your cursor above the walls, and click to place dimensions for the walls.

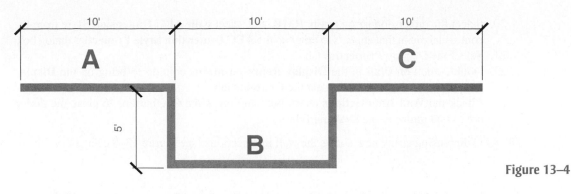

**Figure 13–4**

15. Select the dimension string you just placed, and a series of grips will appear (see Figure 13–5).

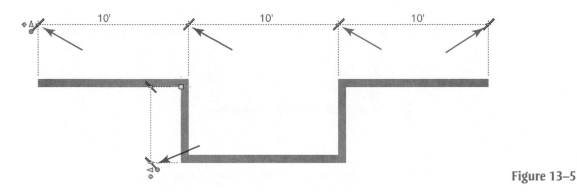

**Figure 13–5**

16. To remove a dimension extension line, press the adjacent negative (−) sign (see Figure 13–6).

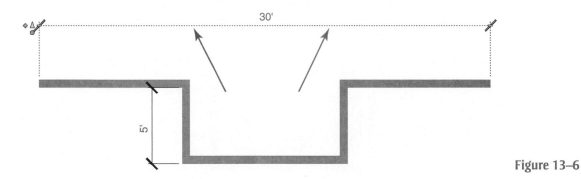

**Figure 13–6**

17. To add a dimension, press the plus (+) sign, enter **O** (Objects) or **P** (Pick points) in the **Command line,** and press the **Enter** key on your keyboard.
18. Pick the point on the object to which you wish to dimension, and press the **Enter** key on your keyboard.
19. Finally, pick the dimension line to add the dimension (see Figure 13–7).

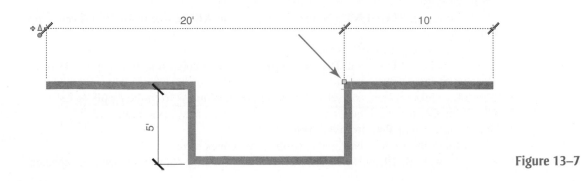

**Figure 13–7**

20. Select the dimension string again, **RMB,** and select **Edit AEC Dimension Style** from the contextual menu that appears to bring up the **AEC Dimension Style Properties** dialog box.
21. Select the **Display Properties** tab.
22. Double-click on **Plan** in the **Display Representations** column to bring up the **Display Properties** dialog box, and select the **Contents** tab.
23. Check the **Wall Intersections** check box, and press the **OK** buttons to close the dialog boxes and return to the Drawing Editor.

The AEC dimension string now shows the wall intersections (see Figure 13–8). Save this file.

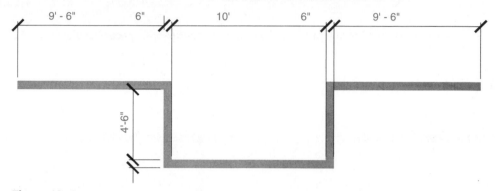

**Figure 13–8**

24. To move the extension line, select the dimension line, and press the round grip that appears. This will make arrow grips appear.
25. Move the arrows. You can also move the dimensions at the same time (see Figure 13–9).

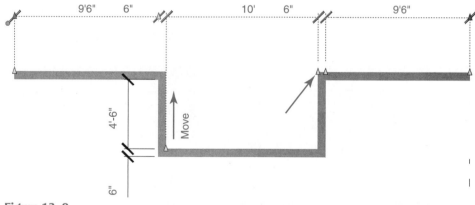

**Figure 13–9**

**Exercise 13-5:** Dimensioning Doors and Windows with AEC Dimension Styles

1. Start a new drawing using the AEC Model (Imperial Stb) template.
2. Select **Format > AEC Dimension Styles** from the **Main** toolbar again to bring up the **Style Manager.**
3. Double-click on **STUDENT's Name** to bring up the **AEC Dimension Style Properties** dialog box.
4. Select the **Display Properties** tab.
5. Double-click on **Plan** in the **Display Representations** column to bring up the **Display Properties** dialog box.
6. Select the **Contents** tab, and select **Opening/Door/Window** from the **Apply to** list.
7. Check the **Center** check box, and clear the other check boxes (see Figure 13–10).
8. Select **Opening in Wall** from the **Apply to** list.
9. Check the **Center** check box, and clear the other check boxes.
10. Select the wall, **RMB,** and select **Insert > Window** from the contextual menu that appears.

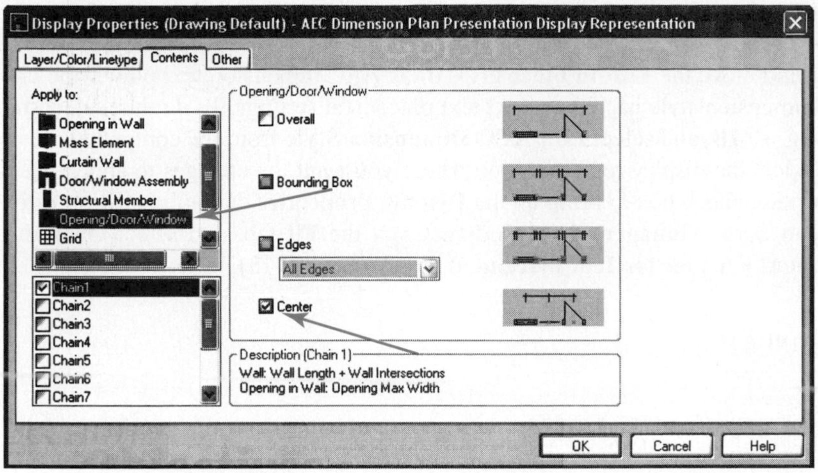

Display Properties (Drawing Default) - AEC Dimension Plan Presentation Display Representation

Layer/Color/Linetype | Contents | Other

Apply to:

Opening in Wall
Mass Element
Curtain Wall
Door/Window Assembly
Structural Member
Opening/Door/Window
Grid

☑ Chain1
☐ Chain2
☐ Chain3
☐ Chain4
☐ Chain5
☐ Chain6
☐ Chain7

Opening/Door/Window

☐ Overall

☑ Bounding Box

☑ Edges
All Edges

☑ Center

Description (Chain 1)
Wall: Wall Length + Wall Intersections
Opening in Wall: Opening Max Width

OK    Cancel    Help

Figure 13–10

11. In the **Properties** tool palette, make sure to check the **Automatic Offset/Center** check box, and insert a Standard 3′-wide, 5′-high window in the center of the wall.
12. Select all the walls, **RMB,** and select **AEC Dimension** from the contextual menu that appears.
13. Drag your cursor vertically above the horizontal walls, and click the mouse to place the dimension string.

The window will now be dimensioned by its center (see Figure 13–11).

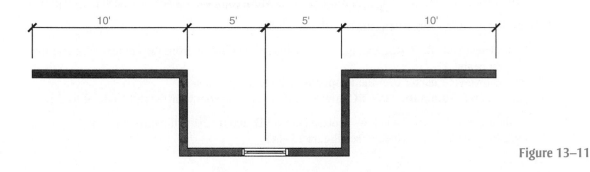

Figure 13–11

14. Select the dimension string again, **RMB,** and select **Edit AEC Dimension Style** from the contextual menu that appears to bring up the **AEC Dimensional Style Properties** dialog box.
15. Select the **Display Properties** tab.
16. Double-click on **Plan** in the **Display Representations** column to bring up the **Display Properties** dialog box.
17. Select the **Contents** tab, and select **Opening/Door/Window** from the **Apply to** list.
18. Check the **Center** check box, and clear the other check boxes (see Figure 13–12).

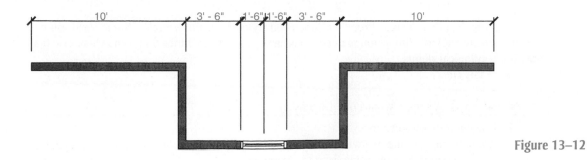

Figure 13–12

If there is some problem where dimension text overlaps, or if you want to modify the location of the text, you must do the following:

You can display and move the **Edit in Place** grips of an AEC dimension text only if the underlying AutoCAD dimension style has the correct text placement settings. To do this, select the AEC dimension string, **RMB,** and select **Edit AEC Dimension Style** from the contextual menu that appears. Then, select the display representation where you want the changes to appear, and check the **Style Override** check box to bring up the **Display Properties** dialog box. Click **Edit,** and in the **Dimension Style Manager,** click **Modify.** Click the **Fit** tab, and select **Over the dimension line, without a leader** for **Text Placement** (see Figure 13–13).

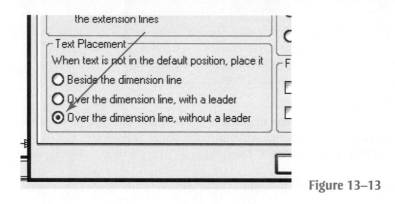

**Figure 13–13**

Now when you select the **Edit in Place** button for the AEC dimensions, a grip will appear on the dimension itself. You can grab that grip and move the dimension text anywhere you wish.

    19.  Move the window **24′-0″** to the left. (Use the **Move** command, or activate the window's grips.)

Note that the AEC dimensions move with the window.

    20.  Select wall **B, RMB,** and again select **Insert > Window** from the contextual menu that appears.
    21.  Move your cursor over the **Properties** palette to open it.
    22.  Set the **Automatic Offset/Center** to **18″,** and pick a spot near the right side of wall B.

You should now have two windows centered in wall B, and the AEC dimensions should show the dimensions for the new window (see Figure 13–14).

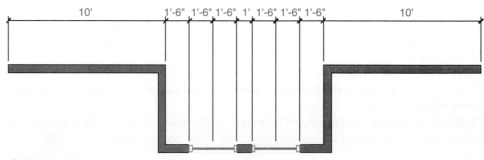

**Figure 13–14**

Explore the other Display Props for dimension styles. Save this exercise. Sometimes you will want to create an AEC dimension manually. Perhaps you want to dimension somewhere else than the built-in logical points.

Save this file.

## Exercise 13-6: Adding a Manual AEC Dimension

    1.  Use the previous exercise.
    2.  Zoom in close to the two windows inserted in the B wall.
    3.  Select **Format > Point Style** from the **Main** menu.

4. In the **Point Style** dialog box, select the **X** (see Figure 13–15).
5. Type **dimpointmode** in the **Command line,** and press the space bar or **Enter.**
6. Type **T** in the **Command line,** and press the space bar or **Enter.**

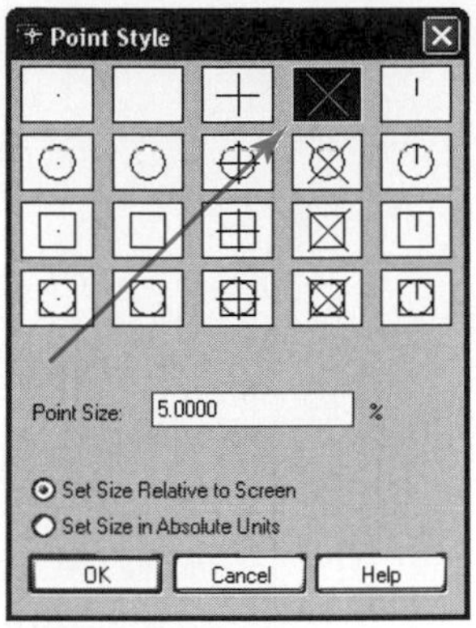

This sets the dimension points to transformable. Transformable dimension points move and are updated with the object; static points stay in place.

7. Set the **Intersection** Object Snap.
8. Select the **AEC Dimension (1) - Manual** icon from the **Annotation** tool palette.
9. Pick the two corners of the two window jambs, and press the space bar or **Enter.**
10. Pick a point to place the dimension string, and then pick a second point to complete the command (see Figure 13–15).
11. Select the **Move** icon from the **Modify** toolbar, and select the left window with a window marquee (see Figure 13–16), and move it to the left 1'-0". Repeat with the right window (see Figure 13–17).

**Figure 13–15**

You must move the points with the window to maintain the associative dimensions. Repeat Steps 7 through 11, but enter **S** (Static) when prompted for dimpointmode points. Note that the dimensions don't move.

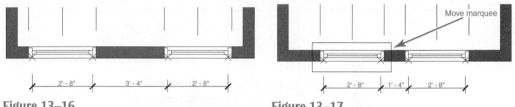

**Figure 13–16**          **Figure 13–17**

12. The point style you set in Step 6 will cause the points to show as X when you plot. To stop this, bring up the **Point Style** dialog box again, and change the point style to **NONE** (see Figure 13–18). Save this file.

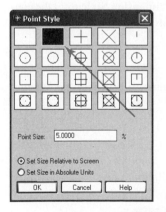

**Figure 13–18**

**Exercise 13-7:** Detaching Objects from AEC Dimensions

1. Use the previous exercise.
2. Zoom Extents (because the viewport is locked, the **Paperspace View** will zoom extents).
3. Select the AEC dimension string, **RMB,** and select the **Detach Objects** icon from the contextual menu that appears.
4. Select the top AEC dimension group (dimension string), and press the space bar or **Enter.**
5. Select the left window object, and press the space bar or **Enter** (see Figure 13–19).

You have now detached the left window from the top AEC Dimension Group. Save this file.

**Exercise 13-8:** AEC Dimension Chains

In order to clarify dimension strings, architects and architectural draftspeople often add additional dimension strings. AutoCAD Architecture 2008 calls these *chains.* The chain nearest the AEC Object is called "Chain1," the next is "Chain2," and so forth up to 10 chains.

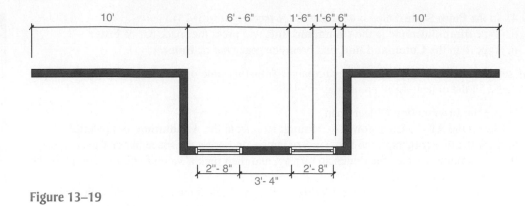

**Figure 13–19**

1. Use the previous exercise, and adjust the windows and AEC dimension settings to match Figure 13–20.

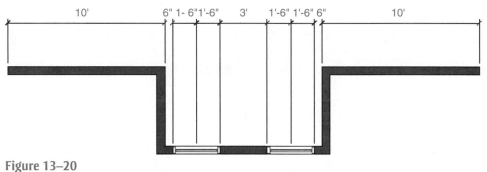

**Figure 13–20**

2. Select the AEC dimension string, **RMB,** and select **Edit AEC Dimension Style** from the contextual menu that appears to bring up the **AEC Dimensional Style Properties** dialog box.
3. Select the **Chains** tab.
4. Change the **Number of Chains** to **2.**
5. Change to the **Display Properties** tab.
6. Double-click on **Plan** in the **Display Representations** column to bring up the **Display Properties** dialog box.
7. Select the **Contents** tab.

Notice that two **Chain** check boxes now appear at the lower left of the **Contents** tab (see Figure 13–21).

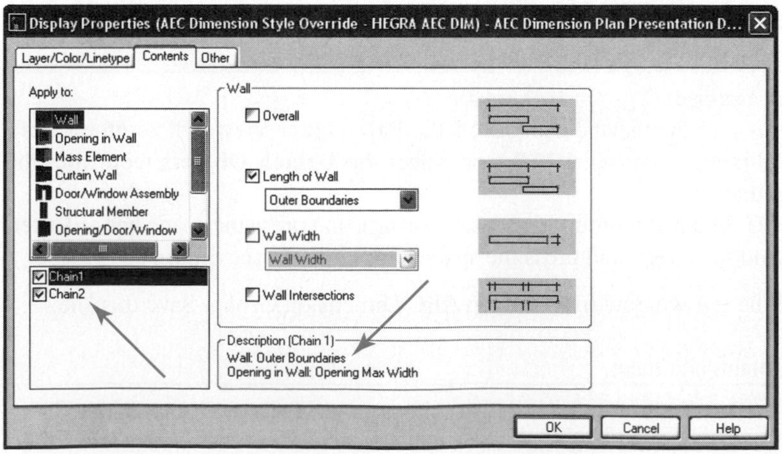

**Figure 13–21**

8. Activate the **Chain1** field, select the **Wall** icon in the **Apply to** field, and clear all the **Wall** check boxes.
9. Select the **Opening/Door/Window** icon in the **Apply to** field, and check the **Opening/Door/Window Center** check box.
10. Activate the **Chain2** field, select the **Wall** icon in the **Apply to** field, and check the **Length of Wall** check box.
11. Press the **OK** buttons to return to the Drawing Editor (see Figure 13–22).

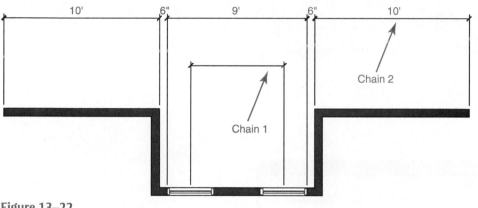

**Figure 13–22**

12. Select the AEC dimension string, **RMB,** and select **Add Dimension Points** and add a point to locate the windows.
13. Repeat Step 12, selecting **Remove Dimension Points,** and remove the two **Chain2** dimension extension lines to create the image shown in Figure 13–23.

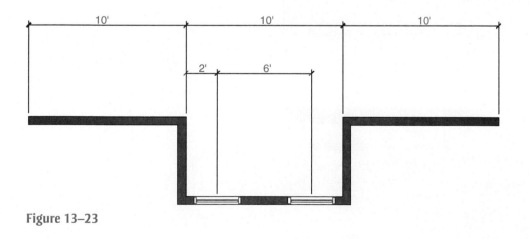

**Figure 13–23**

**Exercise 13-9:** The AEC Dimension Wizard

Although you can set the AEC Dimension display manually as shown at the beginning of this section, AutoCAD Architecture 2008 has provided a Wizard to aid you in setting the display.

Selecting the **Format > AEC Dimension Style Wizard** from the **Main** toolbar activates the dialog boxes shown in Figures 13–24 through 13–26.

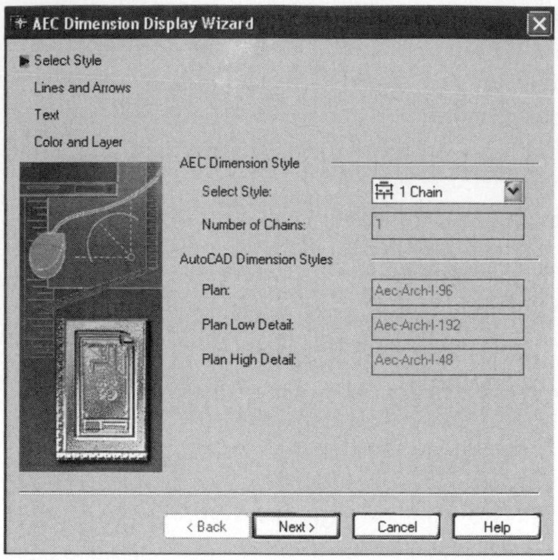

**Figure 13–24**

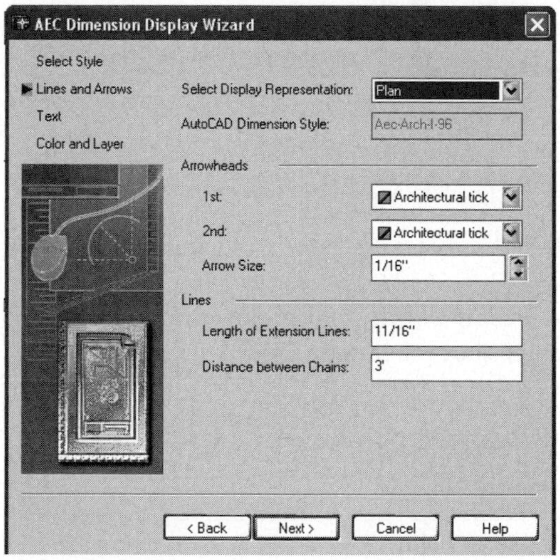

**Figure 13–25**

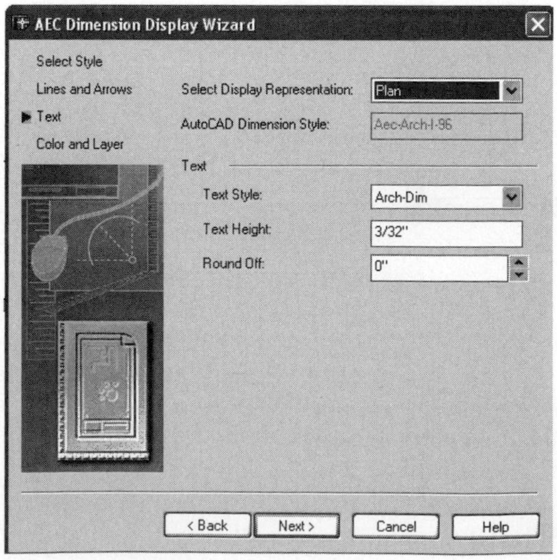

**Figure 13–26**

## *Section* Objectives

- Make a new **Elevations** tool palette.
- Learn how to create a simple building.
- Know how to make an **Elevation.**
- Know how to modify and update a **2D Elevation.**
- Understand how elevation subdivisions work.
- Know how to work with **Material Boundaries.**

## ELEVATIONS

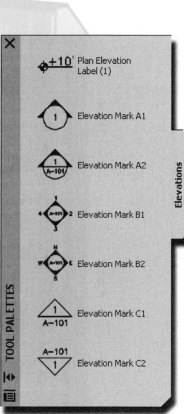

Architects and designers use elevations as a 2D representation of the front, side, and rear views of a building. Prior to AutoCAD Architecture and its use of the 3D model, these elevations were drawn using 2D tools. This was very error prone, and if a change were made to the plan, these changes would have to be manually changed in each elevation. In AutoCAD Architecture 2008, elevations are "extracted" from the 3D model. You create elevations of the building models in your drawings by first drawing an elevation line and mark, and then creating a 2D or 3D elevation based on that line. You can control the size and shape of any elevation that you create, and you can update an existing elevation when the objects included in the elevation are modified. 2D elevations are created with hidden and overlapping lines removed. You can control the appearance of 2D elevations by applying rules that are controlled by the style and display properties of the 2D elevation.

### Exercise 14-1: Making a New Elevation Tool Palette

1. Create a new tool palette and name it **Elevations.**
2. Select the **Content Browser** icon from the **Main** toolbar to launch the Content Browser.
3. Locate the **Documentation Tool Catalog - Imperial.**
4. Locate the **Callouts > Elevation Marks** folder.
5. Drag all the elevation marks into the new tool palette you created.
6. Click and hold on the tab of your new tool palette and drag a copy to **My Tool Catalog** in the Content Browser.

For the following exploration of elevations, first create a simple three-story building.

### Exercise 14-2: Creating a Sample Building for the Elevation Exercises

1. Start a new drawing using the AEC Model (Imperial Stb) template.
2. Change to **Top View,** and create the outline shown in Figure 14–1.
3. Select the **Wall** icon from the **Design** tool palette, **RMB,** and select **Apply Tool Properties to > Linework** from the contextual menu that appears.

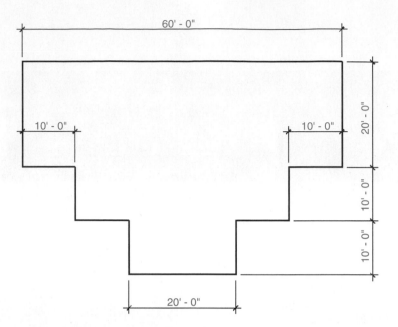

**Figure 14–1**

4. Select the outline you created.
5. Enter **Y** (Yes) in the **Command line** to erase the geometry, and press **Enter** to create walls from the outline.
6. While the walls are still selected, move your cursor over the **Properties** palette to open it.
7. Set the following:

    a. Style = **Standard**
    b. Wall Width = **8″**
    c. Base Height = **10′-0″**
    d. Justify = **Baseline**

8. Save the drawing as **Floor 1.**
9. Save the drawing two more times as **Floor 2** and **Floor 3.**
10. Open **Floor 3,** select the **Roof** icon from the **Design** tool palette, **RMB,** and select **Apply Tool Properties to > Linework and Walls** from the contextual menu that appears.
11. Select all the walls in the **Floor 3** drawing.
12. Enter **N** (No) in the **Command line,** and press **Enter** to create the roof.
13. While the roof is still selected, move your cursor over the **Properties** palette to open it.
14. Set the roof to the following:

    a. Thickness = **10″**
    b. Edge cut = **Square**
    c. Shape = **SingleSlope**
    d. Plate height = **10′-0″**
    e. Rise = **6″**

15. Save **Floor 3.**
16. Start a new drawing and save it as **Composite.**
17. Using **Insert > Xref Manager** from the **Main** toolbar, **Attach** the three floors at Z elevation of 0′ for Floor 1, 10′ for Floor 2, and 20′ for Floor 3 in the Composite drawing.

You have now created the building in Figure 14–2.

18. Select **Floor 1** in the **Composite** drawing, **RMB,** and select **Edit Xref in place** from the contextual menu that appears to bring up the **Reference Edit** dialog box.
19. Press **OK** to return to the Drawing Editor.
20. Select different walls in the floor, **RMB,** and insert windows and a door.
21. Press the **Save back changes to reference** icon in the **Refedit** dialog box, and press the **OK** button that appears.
22. Repeat for each floor until you have a building similar to that shown in Figure 14–3. Save this exercise.

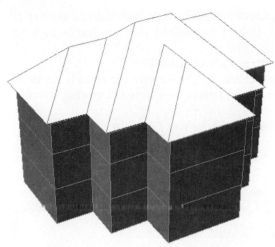

**Figure 14–2**

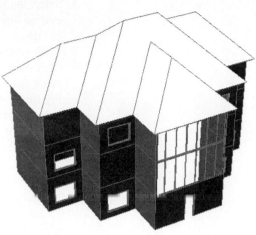

**Figure 14–3**

## Exercise 14-3: Making an Elevation

Using the previous exercise, select the **Composite** drawing.

1. Select the **Model Layout**, activate the **Top View,** and then pan the building to the left until it takes up a little less than half the page. Change the scale to **1/8″ = 1′-0″** in the **Scale** pop-up list (see Figure 14–4).

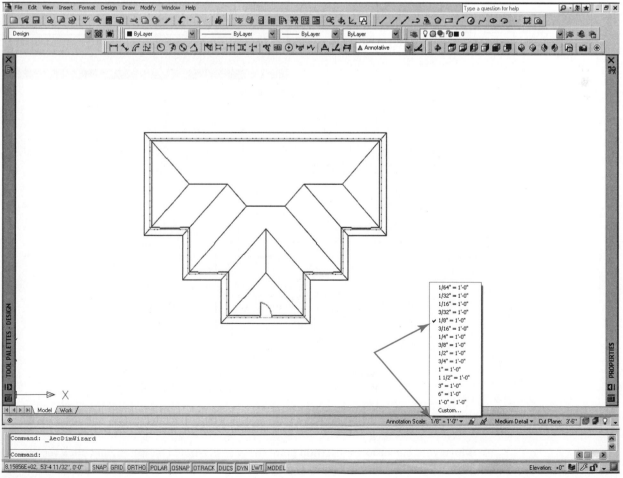

**Figure 14–4**

2. Select the **Elevation Mark A1** from the **Elevations** tool palette, and click and place an elevation line starting at the lower center in front of the building. Drag your cursor as shown in Figure 14–5.
3. Click your mouse again to bring up the **Place Callout** dialog box.
4. Check the **Generate Section/Elevation** check box. Make sure the scale is set to the same scale you set in the **Scale** pop-up list, and press the **Current Drawing** icon (see Figure 14–6).
5. Select the region of the elevation you wish to generate (see Figure 14–7).

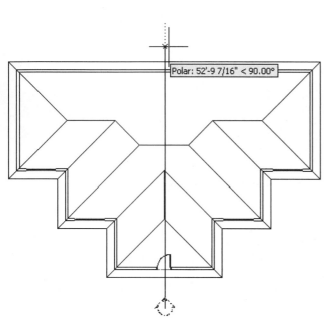

**Figure 14–5**

**Figure 14–6**

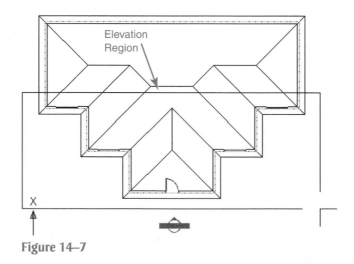

**Figure 14–7**

6. Move your cursor to an insertion point for your generated elevation, and click the mouse button. Your elevation will now appear (see Figure 14–8). Save this exercise.

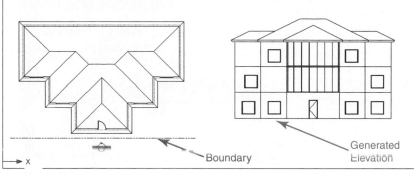

**Figure 14–8**

**Exercise 14-4:** Modifying and Updating the 2D Elevation

1. Open the **Composite** drawing from the previous exercise.
2. Change to the **SW Isometric View.**
3. Select the first floor in the Composite drawing, **RMB,** and select **Edit Xref in place** from the contextual menu that appears to bring up the **Reference Edit** dialog box.
4. Press **OK** to return to the Drawing Editor.
5. Select the front wall of the first floor, **RMB,** and insert windows on either side of the front door.
6. In the **Refedit** dialog box, press the **Save back changes to reference** icon button, and press **OK** at the AutoCAD message.
7. Change back to the **Top View,** and select the 2D elevation that you created.
8. **RMB** the 2D elevation, and select **Refresh** from the contextual menu that appears.

The 2D elevation now reflects the changes made in the 3D model (see Figure 14–9). Save this exercise.

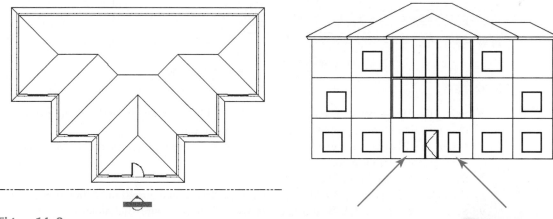

**Figure 14–9**

**Exercise 14-5:** Understanding Subdivisions

1. Using the previous exercise, select the elevation line object to open the **Properties** palette.
2. Click in the **Subdivisions** field to open the **Subdivisions** dialog box.
3. Press the **Add** button, add a 10′-0″ subdivision, and press **OK** to return to the Drawing Editor.

You have now created Subdivision 1 (see Figure 14–10).

4. Move the Subdivision 1 line so that the front extension of the building is within the first subdivision (see Figure 14–11).

**Note:**
Once you have a subdivision, you can select the elevation and move the subdivision with grips.

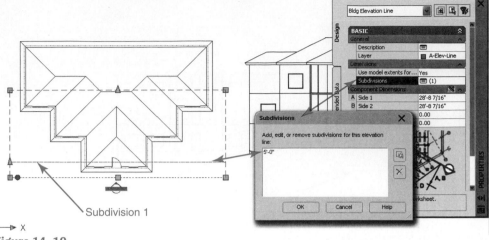

Subdivision 1

X

**Figure 14–10**

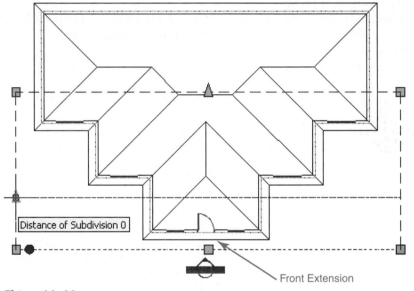

Distance of Subdivision 0

Front Extension

**Figure 14–11**

5. Select the 2D elevation, **RMB,** and select **Edit Object Display** from the contextual menu that appears to bring up the **Object Display** dialog box.
6. Select the **Display Properties** tab, and check the **Override** check box to bring up the **Display Properties** dialog box.
7. Select the **Layer/Color/Linetype** tab.
8. Change the Subdivision 1 **Color** to **blue,** select **OK,** and close all the dialog boxes.
9. Select the elevation, **RMB,** and select **Refresh** from the contextual menu.

You have now changed Subdivision 1 to a blue color. Anything between the defining line and Subdivision 1 will be blue in the elevation. You can also set the line width to be different in a subdivision (see Figure 14–12).

10. Select the elevation line object, **RMB,** and add two more subdivisions.
11. In the **Top View,** move the topmost boundary to the back of the building.
12. Select the elevation, **RMB,** and again select **Edit 2D Section/Elevation Style** from the contextual menu that appears.
13. Change the Subdivision 2 **Color** to **green,** and the Subdivision 3 **Color** to **black** (black will say "white" in the dialog box). Change the **Lineweight** of Subdivision 3 to **.30 mm,** select **OK,** close all the dialog boxes, and return to the Drawing Editor (see Figure 14–13).
14. Select the elevation line to activate it, and using the grips (be sure your Object Snap is turned off) move the subdivisions to look like Figure 14–14.

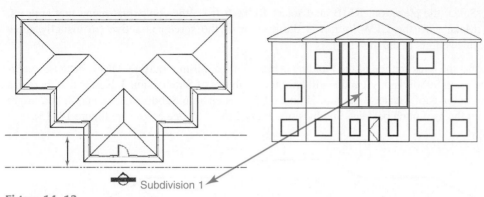

**Figure 14–12**

**Figure 14–13**

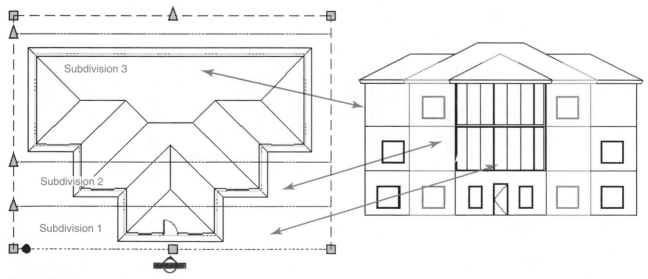

**Figure 14–14**

15. Select the elevation, **RMB,** and select **Refresh** from the contextual menu that appears. Make sure the **LTW** button at the bottom of the screen is active (to visually show lineweights in the drawing).

Notice that the back outline of the building is black with a .30-mm outline. This is because everything between Subdivisions 2 and 3 will have the attributes of Subdivision 3. Notice that there is a problem at the roof. Because the roof is pitched, it crosses both Subdivisions 2 and 3. You might also want the roof pitch between Subdivisions 1 and 2 to be all one color (see Figure 14–15).

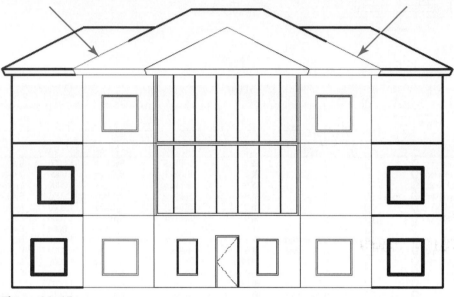

**Figure 14–15**

To fix these problems, you will use the **Linework > Edit** command.

16. Select the 2D elevation, **RMB,** and select **Linework > Edit** from the contextual menu that appears (see Figure 14–16).
17. Select the segment of lines that you wish to edit, and erase them.

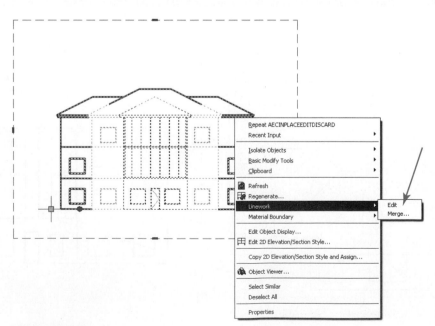

**Figure 14–16**

18. Using the **Line** command, replace the line with new lines (see Figure 14–17).
19. After placing the new lines, press the **Save All Changes** icon in the **In-Place Edit** dialog box shown in Figure 14–17.

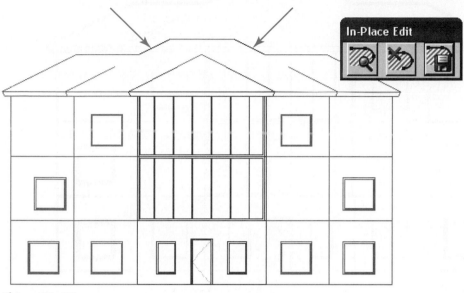

**Figure 14–17**

20. Select the elevation again, **RMB,** and select **Linework > Merge** from the contextual menu that appears.
21. Select the two lines you just placed and press **Enter.**
22. The **Select Linework Component** dialog box will now appear.
23. Select **Subdivision 3** from the **Linework Component** drop-down list, and press the **OK** button (Figure 14–18).

The lines will merge with the subdivision lines and have the same lineweight (see Figure 14–19).

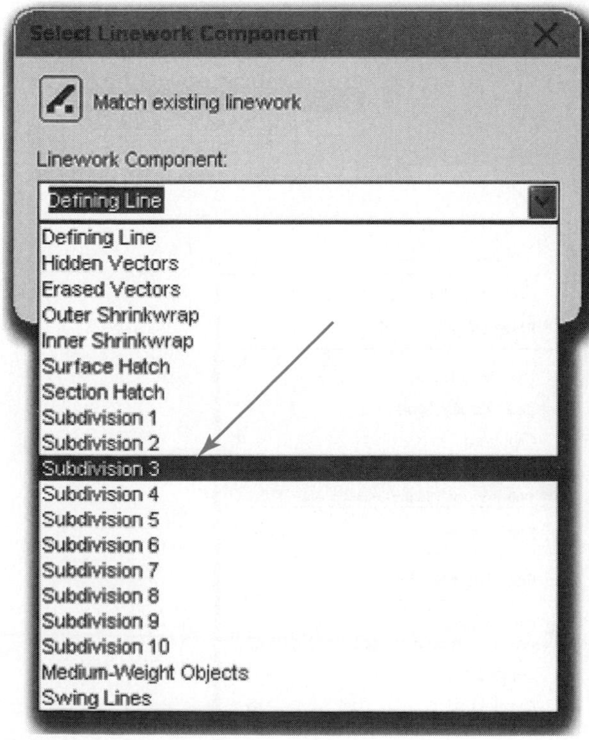

**Figure 14–18**

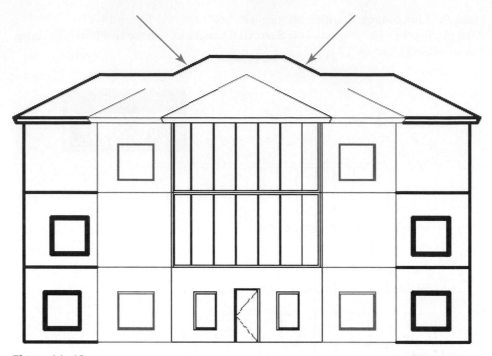

**Figure 14–19**

To fix the roof pitch between Subdivisions 1 and 2, do the following:

24. Select the elevation again, **RMB,** and select **Linework > Edit** from the contextual menu that appears.
25. Select the two lines at the top of the front roof pitch, **RMB,** and select **Modify Component** from the contextual menu that appears (see Figure 14–20).
26. The **Select Linework Component** dialog box will appear again.
27. Select **Subdivision 1** from the **Linework Component** drop-down list, and press the **OK** button. The lines will now turn blue to match Subdivision 1.

Add the remaining lines, select **Linework > Edit,** and complete the elevation. Save this file.

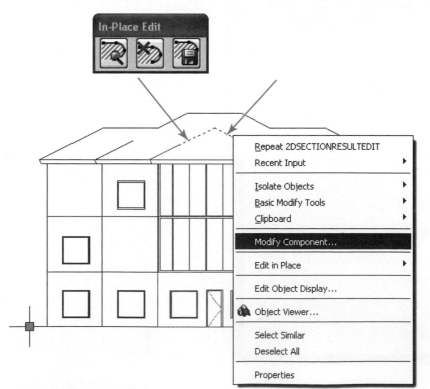

**Figure 14–20**

**Exercise 14-6:** Working with Material Boundaries

1. Close the Composite drawing.
2. Reopen the drawings for Floors 1, 2, and 3.
3. In each drawing, select all the walls, **RMB** on the **Brick4 Brick 4** icon in the **Walls** tool palette and select **Wall** from the option that appears. The walls will turn into brick walls.
4. Save all the drawings you just changed, and reopen the Composite drawing. All the walls in the building model are now brick.
5. Select the generated elevation, **RMB,** and select **Refresh** from the contextual menu that appears. The elevation now contains brick walls (see Figure 14–21).
6. Zoom in close to the generated elevation, and using the polyline command, create the closed polyline shown in Figure 14–22.

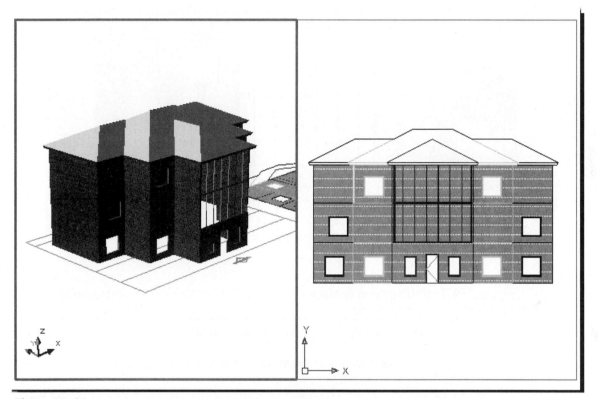

**Figure 14–21**

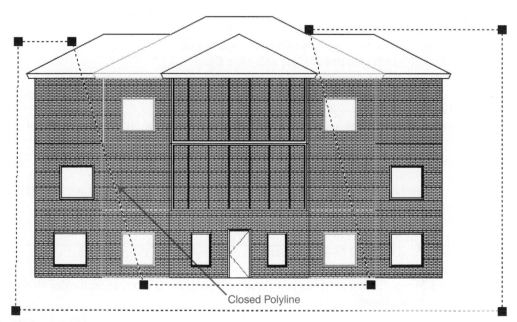

Closed Polyline

**Figure 14–22**

7. Select the generated elevation, **RMB,** and select **Material Boundary > Add** from the contextual menu that appears.
8. Select the closed polyline, enter **Y** (Yes) in the **Command line,** and press **Enter** to bring up the **2D Section/Elevation Material Boundary** dialog box.
9. Select **Limit** from the **Purpose** drop-down list, and **Surface Hatching Only** from the **Apply to:** drop-down list.
10. Press the **OK** button to create the material boundary (see Figure 14–23).

**Figure 14–23**

**Exercise 14-7:** Showing Common Materials as One Surface and Showing Objects Hidden Behind Other Objects in Generated Elevations

1. Start a new drawing using the AEC Model (Imperial Stb) template.
2. Change to the **Top View.**
3. Select the **Concrete-8** icon from the **Walls** tool palette and create a 10′ × 10′ enclosure 8′ high.
4. Select the **Slab** icon from the **Design** tool palette, **RMB,** and select **Linework and Walls** from the contextual menu that appears.
5. Select all the walls of the enclosure you just created and press **Enter.**
6. Enter **N** (No) in the **Command line** and press **Enter.**
7. Enter **B** (Bottom) in the **Command line** and press **Enter.**
8. Enter **R** (Right) in the **Command line** and press **Enter.**
9. Enter **L** (Left) in the **Command line** and press **Enter.**
10. Select the slab you have just created, move your cursor over the **Properties** palette to open it, and set the **Thickness** to **8″,** and **Elevation** to **0.**
11. Change to the **Front View** and using the **Array** command, array your enclosure and slab three rows high (see Figure 14–24).
12. Change to the **Top View** and, using the **Elevation Mark A1,** generate an elevation in the current drawing. Notice the floor division lines (see Figure 14–25).
13. Select **Format > Material Definitions** from the **Main** menu to bring up the **Style Manager.**
14. Double-click on **Concrete.Cast-in-place.Flat** to bring up the **Material Definition Properties** dialog box.
15. Double-click on **General Medium Detail** to open the **Display Properties** dialog box.
16. Change to the **Other** tab.
17. Check the **Merge Common Materials** check box, press the **OK** button, and close all the dialog boxes (see Figure 14–26).

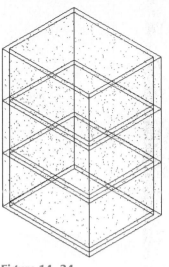

**Figure 14–24**

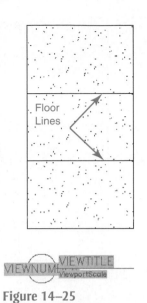

**Figure 14–25**

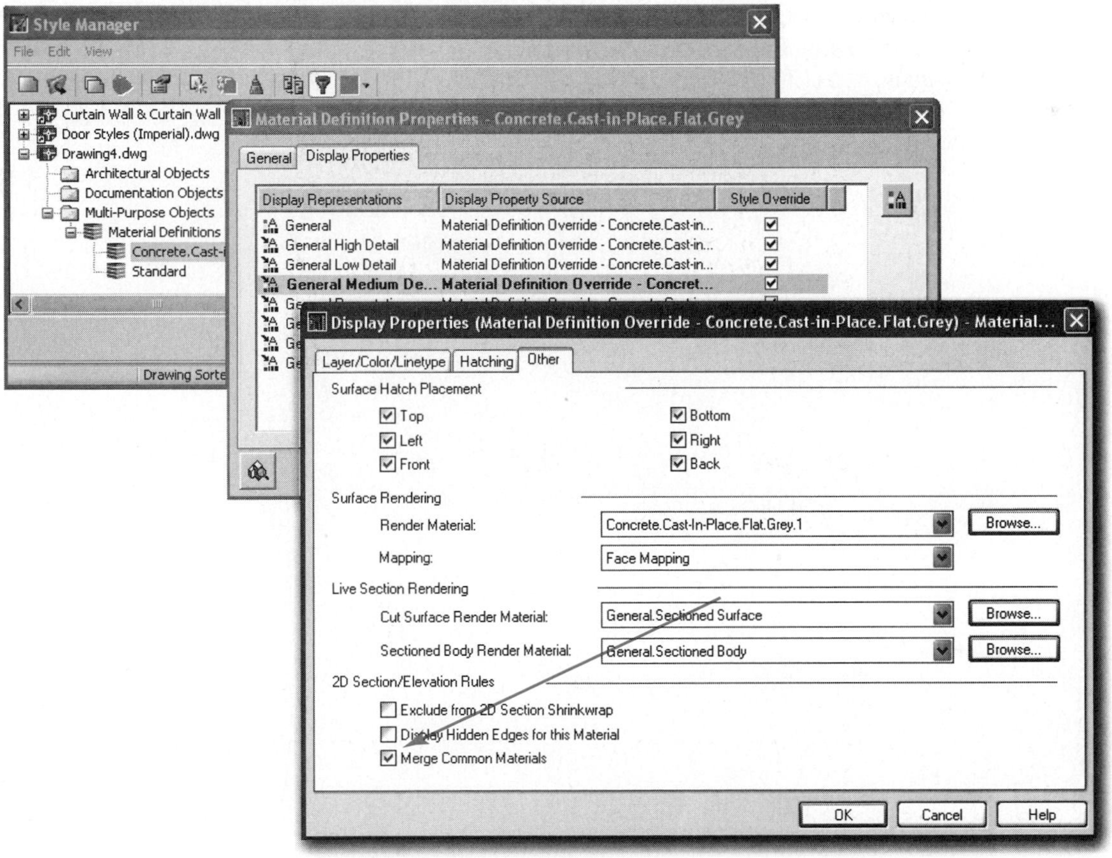

**Figure 14–26**

18. Select the generated elevation, **RMB,** and select **Refresh** from the contextual menu that appears. The floor lines disappear (see Figure 14–27).

19. Repeat Steps 13–17, this time checking the **Display Hidden Edges for this Material** check box in the **Display Properties** dialog box.

20. Again, select the generated elevation, **RMB,** and select **Refresh** from the contextual menu that appears. The hidden wall lines appear (see Figure 14–28).

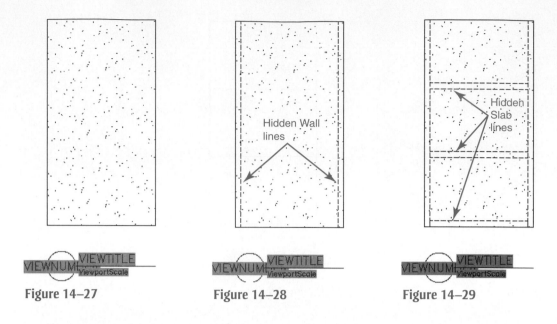

**Figure 14–27**          **Figure 14–28**          **Figure 14–29**

21. Because the slabs are using standard material, repeat Steps 13 through 17, selecting the standard material and checking the **Display Hidden Edges for this Material** check box in the **Display Properties** dialog box.

22. Again, select the generated elevation, **RMB,** and select **Refresh** from the contextual menu that appears. The hidden slab lines appear (see Figure 14–29).

# Sections

# 15

## Objectives

- Make a new **Section** tool palette.
- Learn how to create a simple building.
- Know how to place a **Section Object.**
- Know how to **Generate a Section.**
- Know how to change the section arrow appearance.
- Understand **Live Section definitions.**
- Create a sample building for a **Live Section.**
- Learn how to create a **Live Section.**
- Learn how to modify a **Live Section.**

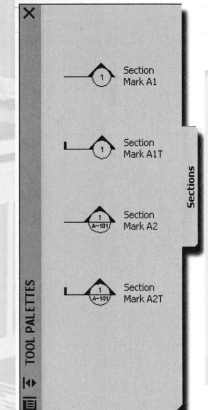

## SECTIONS

There are two different types of sections you can create in AutoCAD Architecture: Standard sections and Live sections.

Live sections cut only in Model Views and are limited to the following AEC Objects only:

- Walls
- Doors, windows, and door and window assemblies
- Mass elements and mass groups
- Stairs and railings
- Roofs and roof slabs
- Spaces and space boundaries
- Curtain wall layouts and units
- Structural members

**Exercise 15-1:** Making a New Section Tool Palette

1. Create a new tool palette, and name it **Section.**
2. Select the **Content Browser** icon from the **Main** tool bar to launch the Content Browser.
3. Locate **Documentation Tool Catalog - Imperial.**
4. Locate the **Callouts > Section Marks** folder.
5. Drag all the section marks into the new tool palette you created.
6. Click and hold on the tab of your new tool palette and drag a copy to **My Tool Catalog** in the Content Browser.

For the following exercise create a sample residence.

## Exercise 15-2: Creating a Sample Building

1. Start a new drawing using the AEC Model (Imperial Stb) template.
2. Change to the **Model Layout.**
3. Change to the **Top View,** select the **Wall** icon from the **Design** tool palette, and move your cursor over the **Properties** palette to open it.
4. Set the following:

   a. Style = **Standard**
   b. Wall Width = **8″**
   c. Base Height = **8′-0″**
   d. Justify = **Baseline**

5. Place the walls as shown in Figure 15–1.
6. Select the **Roof** icon from the **Design** tool palette, **RMB,** and select **Apply Tool Properties to > Linework and Walls** from the contextual menu that appears.
7. Select all the walls in your drawing.
8. Enter **N** (No) in the **Command line,** and press **Enter** to create the roof.
9. While the roof is still selected, move your cursor over the **Properties** palette to open it.
10. Set the roof to the following:

    a. Thickness = **10″**
    b. Edge cut = **Square**
    c. Shape = **SingleSlope**
    d. Plate height = **8′-0″**
    e. Rise = **12″**

11. Select the **Slab** icon from the **Design** tool palette, **RMB,** and select **Apply Tool Properties to > Linework and Walls** from the contextual menu that appears.
12. Again, select all the walls in your drawing, and press **Enter.**
13. Enter **N** (No) in the **Command line** and press **Enter.**
14. Enter **T** (Top) in the **Command line** and press **Enter.**
15. Enter **R** (Right) in the **Command line** and press **Enter** twice to place the slab.
16. While the slab is still selected, move your cursor over the **Properties** palette to open it.
17. Set the following:

    a. Style = **Standard**
    b. Thickness = **4″**
    c. Elevation = **0′**

18. Select the **Quick Select** icon in the **Properties** palette, select all the walls, and press **OK.**
19. With the walls selected, **RMB** anywhere in the Drawing Editor, and select **Insert > Window** from the contextual menu that appears.
20. Place 2′ × 4″-high Standard windows on each wall as shown in Figure 15–2.

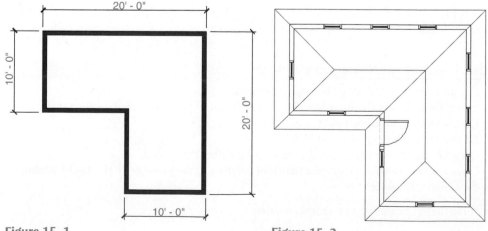

**Figure 15–1**     **Figure 15–2**

21. With the walls still selected, **RMB** anywhere in the Drawing Editor, and select **Insert > Door** from the contextual menu that appears.
22. Place a 3'-0" × 6'-8"-high Standard door as shown in Figure 15–2.

## Exercise 15-3: Placing the Standard Section Object

1. Select the **Section Mark A1** from the **Section** tool palette, click and drag through a window, and then click again through another window.
2. Press **Enter,** move your cursor in the view direction you wish to cut the section, and click the mouse button to bring up the **Place Callout** dialog box.
3. Name the view, check the **Generate Section/ Elevation** check box, set the **Scale** to **1/8' = 1'-0",** and press the **Current Drawing** icon.
4. Move your cursor to an insertion point for the generated section, and click the mouse button to create the generated section.

> **Note:**
> If you want to show the section object constantly in the Drawing Editor, do the following:

   a. Select the section line, **RMB,** and select **Edit Object Display** from the contextual menu that appears to bring up the **Object Display** dialog box.
   b. Check the **Object Override** check box for the **Plan** display representation to bring up the **Display Properties** dialog box.
   c. Turn on the visibility of the boundary, press **OK,** and close all the dialog boxes to return to the Drawing Editor (see Figure 15–3).

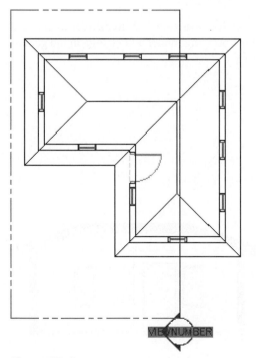

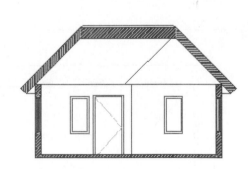

**Figure 15–3**

## Exercise 15-4: Reversing the Section Direction

1. Select the section line, **RMB,** and select **Reverse** from the contextual menu that appears.
2. Using the **Mirror** command, select the direction arrow and view number and reverse them.
3. Select the generated section, **RMB,** and select **Refresh** from the contextual menu that appears (see Figure 15–4).

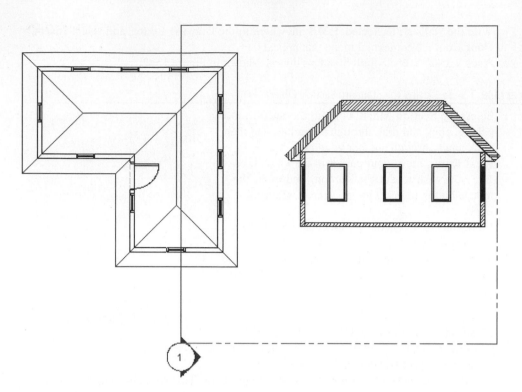

**Figure 15–4**

## Exercise 15-5: Modifying the Section

1. Reverse the section again.
2. Double-click the roof to open the **Properties** palette.
3. Change the **Rise** to **4″.**
4. Select the generated section, **RMB,** and select **Refresh** from the contextual menu that appears. Notice that anything you change in the building model will change in the generated section when you refresh it (see Figure 15–5).

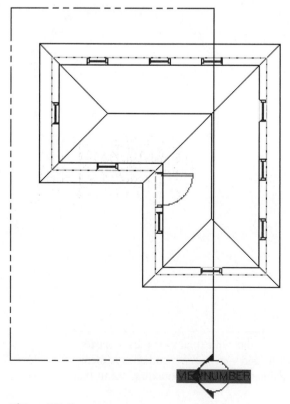

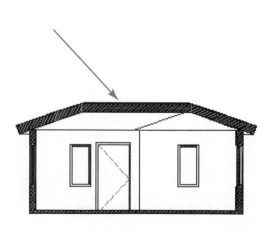

**Figure 15–5**

**Exercise 15-6:** Customizing the Section Arrow Appearance

1. Select the **VIEWNUMBER** text, **RMB,** and select **Edit Block in-place** from the contextual menu that appears to bring up the **Reference Edit** dialog box.
2. Press **OK** to return to the Drawing Editor.
3. Erase the circle and add a rectangle (see Figure 15–6).
4. Press the **Save back changes to reference** icon in the **Refedit** dialog box that appeared near the arrow.
5. Select the direction arrow, **RMB,** and select **Edit Block in-place** from the contextual menu that appears to bring up the **Reference Edit** dialog box.
6. Press **OK** to return to the Drawing Editor.
7. Erase the existing arrow and add a new arrow. You could even add your company logo. You now have a custom section line object arrow (see Figure 15–7).

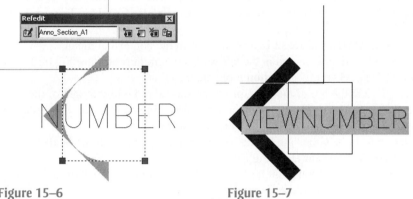

Figure 15–6                 Figure 15–7

## LIVE SECTIONS

Unlike generated sections, Live sections retain the original objects after sectioning, can set display properties for all objects in a section, and can set hatching for section boundaries.

Live section AEC Objects consist of six components (see Figure 15–8).

- **Cutting boundary:** Outside limit of the section (section line)
- **Hatch:** Graphic indication of area inside the cutting boundary

**Note:**
Each new Live section is displayed in a separate display configuration created specifically for that section. See the explanation of display configurations in this book.

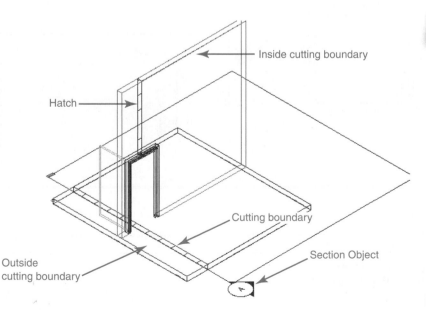

Figure 15–8

- **Inside cutting boundary:** Remaining object cut by cutting boundary *inside* cutting boundary
- **Outside cutting boundary:** Remaining object cut by cutting boundary *outside* cutting boundary
- **Inside full body:** Object completely *inside* section
- **Outside full body:** Object completely *outside* section

Before a Live section or any section can be created, a section mark or section line must be placed in your drawing to identify where the section is to take place.

### Exercise 15-7: Creating a Sample Building for a Live Section

1. Start a new drawing using the AEC Model (Imperial Stb) template.
2. Change to the **Top View.**
3. Select the **CMU-8 Rigid-1.5 Air-2 Brick-4 Furring Wall** icon from the **Walls** tool palette in the **Autodesk Architectural Desktop Sample Palette Catalog - Imperial,** and create a 10'-0" × 10'-0" enclosure.
4. Select the left wall, **RMB,** and select **Insert Door** from the contextual menu.
5. Place a 3'-0" Standard door centered in the left wall, swinging inward (see Figure 15–9).
6. Select **Section Mark A1** from the **Section** tool palette.
7. Place the start point at the left of the door, place the second point to the right of the right wall, and press **Enter.** Move your cursor in the view direction you wish to cut the section, and click the mouse button to bring up the **Place Callout** dialog box.
8. Name the view, check the **Generate Section/Elevation** check box, set the **Scale** to **1'/8" = 1'-0",** and press the **Current Drawing** icon.
9. Move your cursor to an insertion point for the generated section, and click the mouse button to create a generated section (see Figure 15–10).

It is a good idea to show the section object constantly in the Drawing Editor (follow the directions mentioned in Exercise 15-3, "Placing the Standard Section Object").

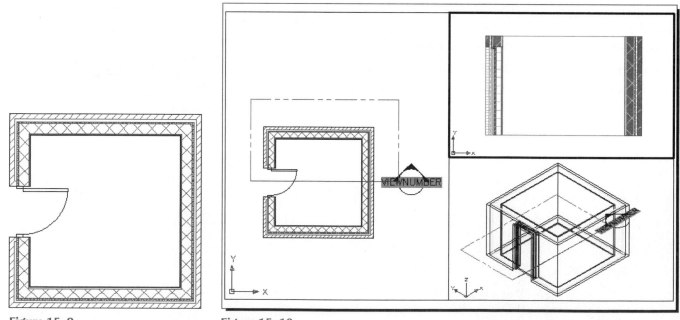

Figure 15–9                    Figure 15–10

### Exercise 15-8: Creating a Live Section

1. Use the previous exercise.
2. Change to the **Work Layout.**

3.  Select the section object (the cutting plane), **RMB,** and select **Enable Live Section** from the contextual menu that appears.

A 3D sectioned model of the enclosure appears in the Isometric view (see Figure 15–11).

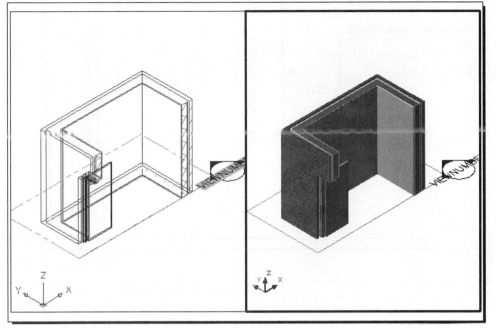

Figure 15–11

4.  Place one viewport of the enclosure in **Top View** and the other in **Front View.**
5.  Change to the **Front View.**
6.  Select the **Hidden** icon in the **Shading** toolbar to display the Live section in hidden display.
7.  Notice that the sectioned view displays symbols of all the materials set for the wall components (see Figure 15–12).

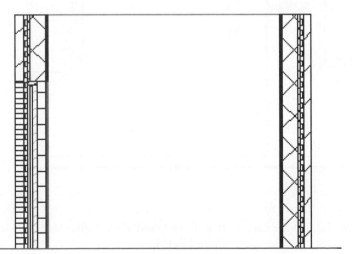

Figure 15–12

8.  Double-click on the front wall to open its **Properties** palette.
9.  Change the **Style** to **Standard.**
10. Return to the Drawing Editor, and notice that the front wall in the **Top View (Plan View)** has changed (see Figure 15–13).
11. Open the Content Browser (by pressing **Ctrl + 4**).
12. Add the **Bow Window Set** from the **Design Tool Catalog** to your tool palette.
13. Click the **Bow Window Set** icon in your tool palette, and select the wall illustrated in Figure 15–14.

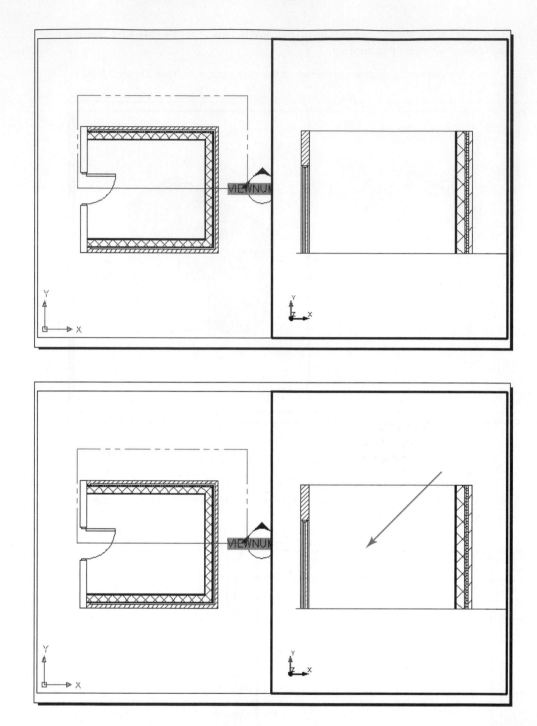

Figure 15–13

Figure 15–14

14. Insert the **Bow Window Set** into the Live section in the **Front View.** Notice that the window now also appears in the **Top View** (see Figure 15–15).

All the AEC components in a Live section such as door size, hatching, and so on, can be changed in the section and will reflect in the 2D plan drawing.

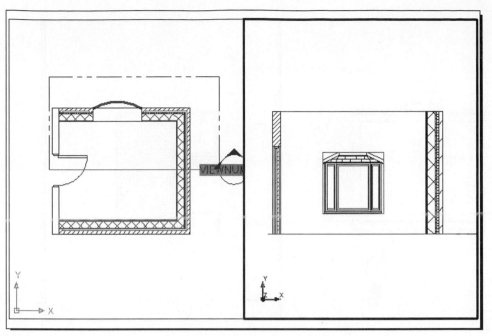

**Figure 15–15**

## Exercise 15-9: Modifying a Live Section

1. Select the section line object and move it so that it does not pass through the door. See that the Live section changes (see Figure 15–16).
2. Select the section line object and rotate it. See that the Live section changes (see Figure 15–17).

Using the Live section concept, you can adjust your sections automatically, even in another drawing, by changing the plan or changing the Live section.

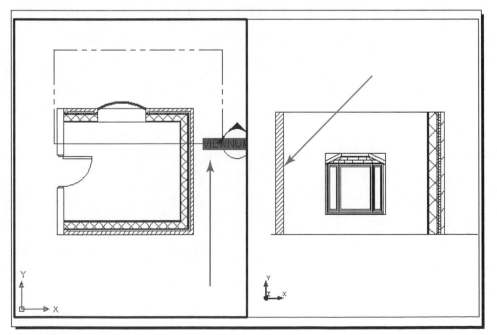

**Figure 15–16**

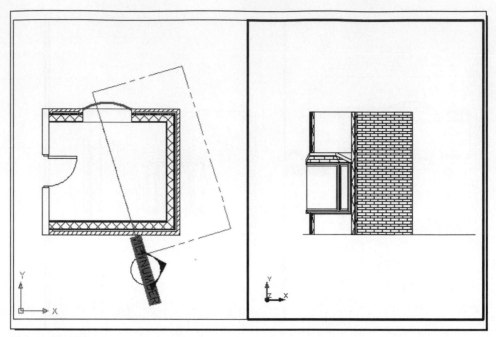

**Figure 15–17**

# Drawing Management

# 16

## Section Objectives

- Understand the Drawing Management concept.
- Know how to use the **Project Browser.**
- Learn how to create constructs and elements in the **Project Navigator.**
- Learn how to work with constructs and elements in the **Project Navigator.**
- Learn how to assign constructs and elements in the **Project Navigator.**
- Create views in the **Project Navigator.**
- Create plotting sheets in the **Project Navigator.**

AutoCAD Architecture 2008's Drawing Management feature automates the building design and document process. With this feature, all your project document files are codified in a central location from which you can call up and modify any drawing. This feature allows you to manage projects, automatically control levels, and create views and sheets. See Figure 16–1.

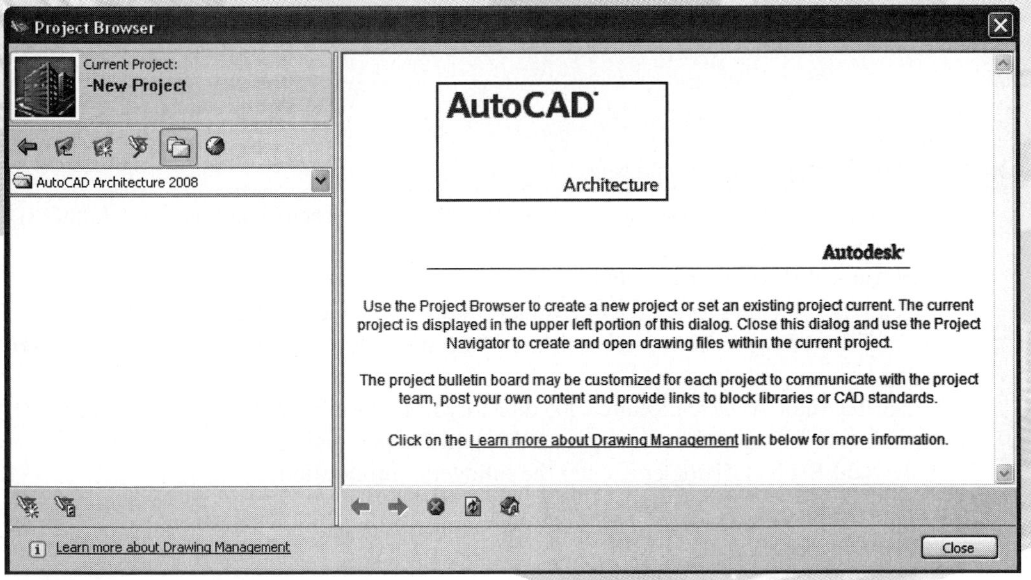

Figure 16–1

In reality, the Drawing Management feature is an advanced form of external referencing (XREF), which has been a feature of AutoCAD and Architectural Desktop for many releases. Using XML programming in conjunction with XREF, the programmers have created a very comprehensive system for automating this process.

Because the Drawing Management system is so closely related to the XREF system, those who understand how to use the conventional XREF will find this advanced feature easily comprehensible. For those who are totally new to AutoCAD or AutoCAD Architecture, this author suggests that you first read the online help on XREF before going on to the Drawing Management system.

## THE DRAWING MANAGEMENT CONCEPT

The Drawing Management system is based on a hierarchy starting with the project, which is made of constructs, elements, views, and plot sheets. Through sophisticated automated XREF commands, elements are XREFed into constructs, which are XREFed into views and then XREFed into plot sheets. See Figure 16–2.

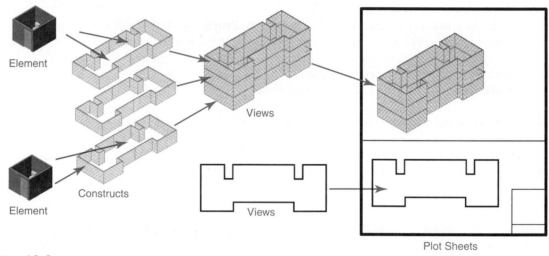

**Figure 16–2**

### Exercise 16-1: Using the Project Browser

1. In Windows Explorer, create a Microsoft Windows file directory and name it AutoCAD Architecture 2008.
2. Start AutoCAD Architecture 2008.
3. Start a new drawing using the AEC Model (Imperial Stb) template.
4. Select **File > Project Browser** from the **Main** menu to bring up the **Project Browser** dialog box.
5. Locate the AutoCAD Architecture 2008 directory from the drop-down list (see Figure 16–3).
6. Press the **Add Project** icon to bring up the **Add Project** dialog box.
7. In the **Add Project** dialog box, enter the following information:

    a. Number = **100**
    b. Name = **TEST PROJECT**
    c. Description: **3 Story Building**
    d. Check the **Create from template project** check box, and get the AutoCAD Architecture Template Project (Imperial) file from Documents\All Users\Application Data\-Autodesk\AutoCAD Architecture 2007\enu\Template.

8. After entering the information, press the **OK** button to return to the **Project Browser** dialog box.
9. In the **Project Browser** dialog box, **RMB** on **TEST PROJECT** you just created, and select **Project Properties** from the contextual menu to bring up the **Modify Project** dialog box.

Figure 16–3

10. In the **Modify Project** dialog box, enter the following additional information as shown (see Figure 16–4).

   a. Bulletin Board = (Any Intranet or leave Default directory)
   b. Project Image = (Any small GIF image or leave Default directory)
   c. Prefix Filenames with Project Number = **Yes** (from drop-down list)
   d. Use Relative Xref Paths = **Yes**
   e. Tool Palette File Location = Accept the default
   f. Tool Palette Storage Type = Accept the default
   g. Tool Content Root Path = Accept the default

| | |
|---|---|
| Number | 100 |
| Name | TEST PROJECT |
| Description | 3 STORY BUILDING |
| Project Path | C:\AutoCAD Architecture 2008\TEST PROJECT |
| Constructs Path | C:\AutoCAD Architecture 2008\TEST PROJECT\Constructs |
| Elements Path | C:\AutoCAD Architecture 2008\TEST PROJECT\Elements |
| Views Path | C:\AutoCAD Architecture 2008\TEST PROJECT\Views |
| Sheets Path | C:\AutoCAD Architecture 2008\TEST PROJECT\Sheets |
| Bulletin Board | C:\Program Files\AutoCAD Archit...\Sample Project Bulletin Board.htm |
| Project Image | C:\Program Files\AutoCAD Architecture ...\Default_Project_Image.bmp |
| Prefix Filenames with Project ... | Yes |
| Use Relative Xref Paths | Yes |
| Match Sheet View Layers to ... | No |
| Tool Palette File Location | C:\AutoCAD Architecture 2008\TEST PROJECT\ |
| Tool Palette Storage Type | Per user workspace catalog |
| Tool Content Root Path | C:\AutoCAD Architecture 2008\TEST PROJECT |
| Tool Catalog Library | |
| Default Construct Template | C:\Documents and Settings\All Users\...\Aec Model (Imperial Stb).dwt |
| Default Element Template | C:\Documents and Settings\All Users\...\Aec Model (Imperial Stb).dwt |

Project Details:                    Edit

Project Details Component Databases:     Add/Remove

Project Keynote Databases:          Add/Remove

Project Standards:                  Configure

OK    Cancel    Help

Figure 16–4

    h. Tool Catalog Library = Accept the default

    i. Default Construction Template = (accept default—AEC Model (Imperial Stb))

    j. Default Element Template = (accept default—AEC Model (Imperial Stb))

    k. Default Model View Template = (accept default—AEC Model (Imperial Stb))

    l. Default Section/Elevation View Template = (accept default—AEC Model (Imperial Stb))

    m. Default View Template = (accept default—AEC Model (Imperial Stb))

    n. Display Only Project Detail Component Databases = **No**

    o. Display Only Project Keynote Databases = **No**

11. Press **Edit** to bring up the **Project Details** dialog box. Here you can add information such as telephone numbers, billing addresses, and owner's representative (see Figure 16–5)

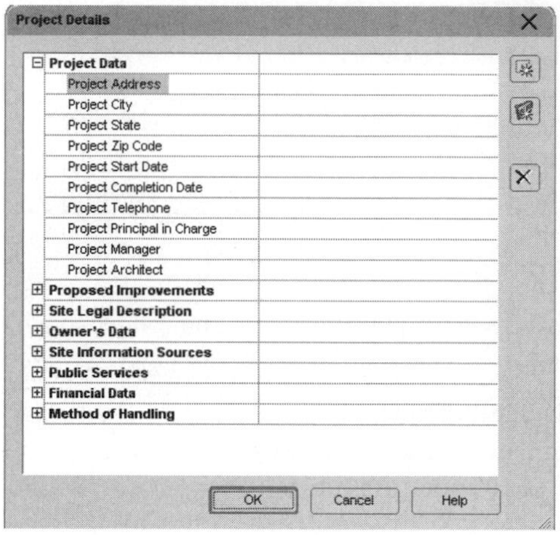

**Note:**
If **Set Project Current** is grayed out, then you have already set this project as current. After you create more projects, you will be able to change from project to project by setting different projects current.

**Figure 16–5**

12. Press the **OK** buttons to return to the **Project Browser.**
13. **RMB** on **TEST PROJECT** in the list and select **Set Project Current** from the contextual menu that appears.

The project will now appear in the Project Browser's header (see Figure 16–6).

14. Press the **Close** button in the **Project Browser** to return to the Drawing Editor, and automatically bring the **Project Navigator** palette into the Drawing Editor if it is not already there. The **Project Navigator** palette will now contain the TEST PROJECT (see Figure 16–7).

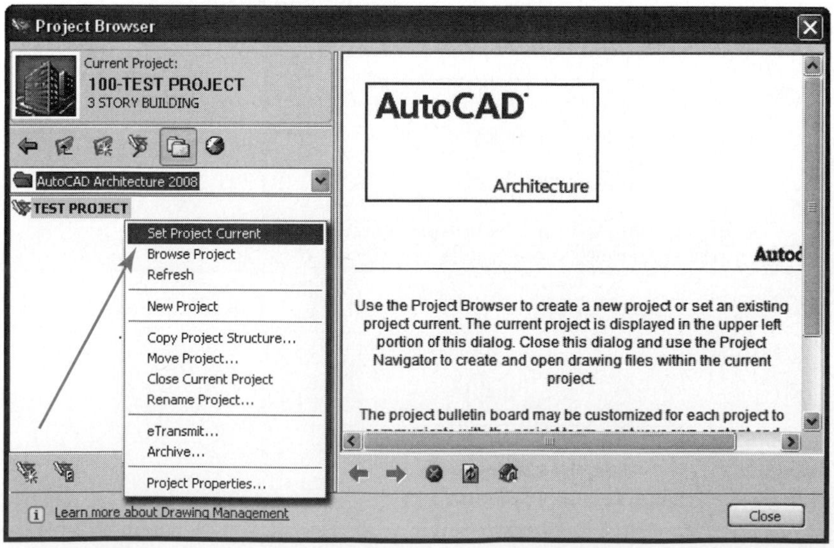

**Figure 16–6**

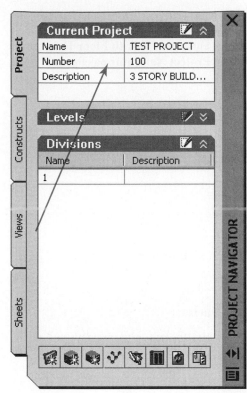

**Figure 16–7**

> **Note:**
> When you create a new project, using the Template Project (Imperial).apj file, a new empty tool palette will also be automatically created with the name of that project. You can drag all the tools you need from the Content Browser, and whenever you set that project current, the tool palette associated with that particular project will appear. Regardless, you will still have access to all the standard palettes, which can be accessed by pressing the **Tool Palette Properties** icon at the lower left of the tool palette.

**Exercise 16-2:** Creating Constructs and Elements in the Project Navigator

This project will have three floors with a basement. The second and third floors will each have two apartments, and the apartments will have bathrooms.

1. In the **Project** tab, select the **Edit Levels** icon in the top right corner of the levels information to bring up the **Levels** dialog box (see Figure 16–8).

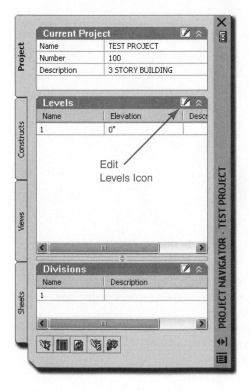

**Figure 16–8**

2. In the **Levels** dialog box, press the **Add Levels** icon, create four levels, and enter the information as shown in Figure 16–9. Be sure to check the **Auto-Adjust Elevation** check box so that the **Floor Elevation** adjusts when you enter the **Floor to Floor Height.**
3. In the **Levels** dialog box, press **OK** to return to the **Project Navigator** palette.

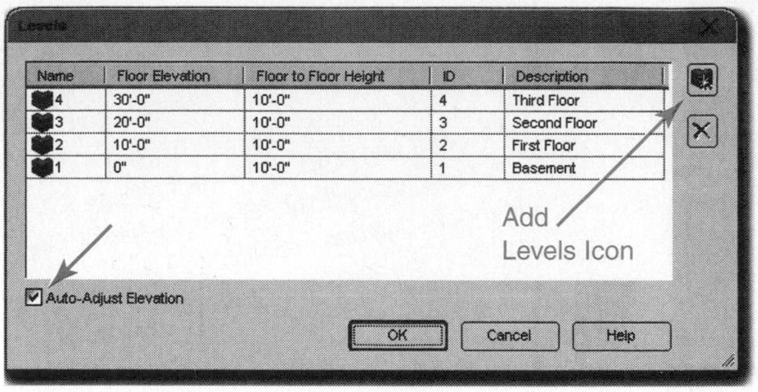

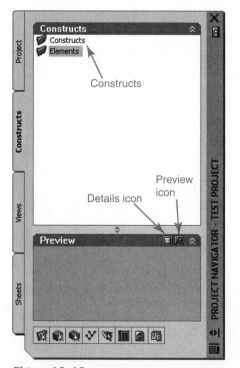

**Figure 16–9**

4. In the **Project Navigator** palette, select the **Constructs** tab.

The **Constructs** tab contains the **Constructs** and **Elements** folders, plus preview and detail screens to view their contents (see Figure 16–10).

**Figure 16–10**

5. In the **Constructs** tab, select the **Constructs** folder, **RMB,** and select **New > Construct** from the contextual menu that appears to bring up the **Add Construct** dialog box.
6. Enter **BASEMENT WALLS** in the **Name** field.
7. Check the **Basement** check box and press **OK** (see Figure 16–11).
8. In the **Constructs** tab, select the **Elements** folder, **RMB,** and select **New > Element** from the contextual menu that appears to bring up the **Add Element** dialog box.
9. Enter **COLUMN GRID** in the **Name** field and press **OK.**

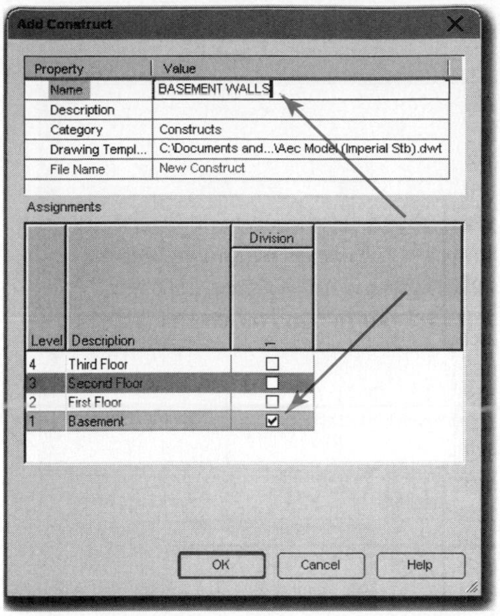

Figure 16–11

10. Create new elements, and name them **APARTMENT WALLS** and **BATH ROOM** (see Figure 16–12).

Save this file.

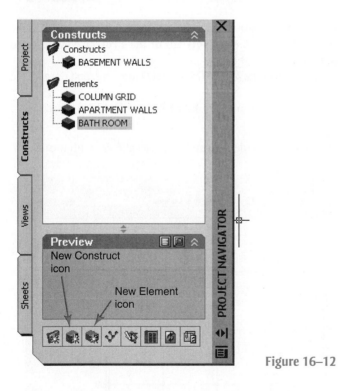

Figure 16–12

## Exercise 16-3: Working with Constructs and Elements in the Project Navigator

1. After the constructs and elements have been labeled, double-click on the **Column Grid** icon to bring up the **COLUMN GRID** drawing.
2. In the **COLUMN GRID** drawing, change to the **Top View**, and place a structural column grid 120′ wide by 60′ deep with 20′-0″ bays in both directions, and 10′ columns.
3. Select the column grid, **RMB,** and select **Label** from the contextual menu that appears.
4. Label the bottom and right of the grid with letters and numbers, respectively (see Figure 16–13).
5. Press **Ctrl + S** (**File > Save**) to save the drawing.

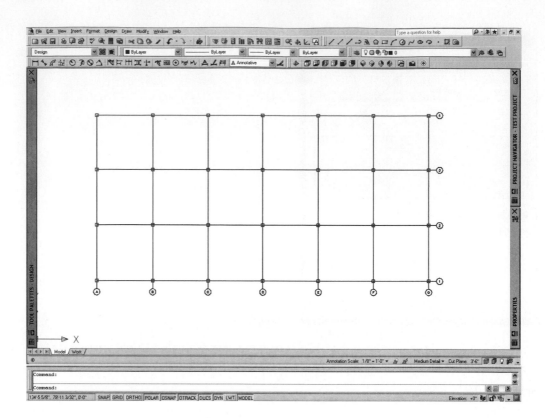

**Figure 16–13**

6. Move your cursor over the **Project Navigator** palette (to open it) and double-click on the icon next to **BASEMENT WALLS** in the **Constructs** tab of the **Project Navigator** to open the **BASEMENT WALLS** drawing.
7. Open the **Project Navigator** again, select the **COLUMN GRID** drawing, and drag it into the **BASEMENT WALLS** drawing.

The grid you made previously will now be XREFed into the **BASEMENT WALLS** drawing.

8. Turn the **Node** Object Snap on.
9. Using the **Node** snap, place Standard 12″-wide, 10′-high walls as shown in Figure 16–14.

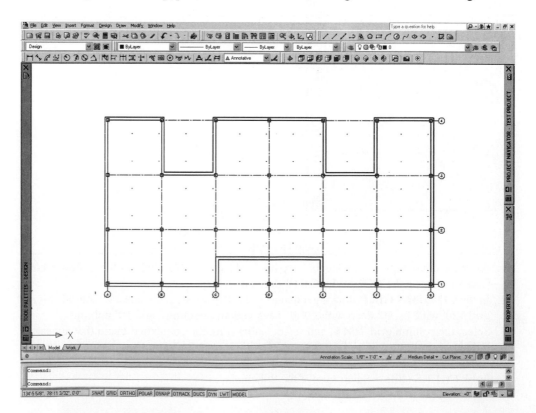

**Figure 16–14**

10. Delete the **COLUMN GRID** XREF and save the **BASEMENT WALLS** drawing.
11. Move your cursor over the **Project Navigator** palette to open it, select the **BASEMENT WALLS** construct, **RMB,** and select **Copy Construct to Levels** from the contextual menu that appears to bring up the **Copy Construct to Levels** dialog box.
12. Check the **First Floor, Second Floor,** and **Third Floor** check boxes, and then press **OK.**

The **Project Navigator Constructs** tab now contains three copies of the basement walls labeled **BASEMENT WALLS (2), (3), and (4)** (see Figure 16–15).

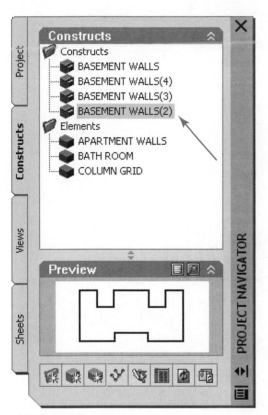

Figure 16–15

13. Select the **BASEMENT WALLS (2), (3), and (4),** and rename them **FIRST FLOOR WALLS, SECOND FLOOR WALLS,** and **THIRD FLOOR WALLS,** respectively.
14. Change to the **Views** tab in the **Project Navigator.**
15. Press the **Add View** icon to bring up the **Add View** dialog box.
16. Select the **General View** radio button (see Figure 16–16).
17. Press **OK** to bring up the **Add General View** dialog box.
18. Enter **TOTAL PERSPECTIVE** in the **Name** field and press **Next.**
19. In the next dialog box, check all **Level** check boxes and press **Next** again.
20. In the next dialog box, make sure that all the check boxes are checked, and press **Finish** to return to the Drawing Editor.

A new view called **TOTAL PERSPECTIVE** will now appear in the **Views** tab of the **Project Navigator.**

21. Double-click on **TOTAL PERSPECTIVE** in the **Views** tab to open it in the Drawing Editor.
22. Select the **Hidden** icon on the **Shading** toolbar, change to the **SW Isometric View,** and save the drawing (see Figure 16–17).

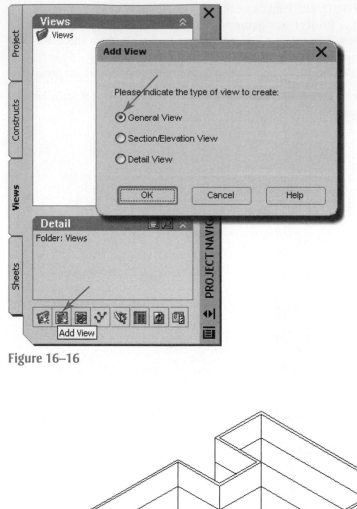

Figure 16–16

Figure 16–17

23. Change back to the **Constructs** tab in the **Project Navigator.**
24. Double-click on **APARTMENT WALLS** under **Elements** to bring up the **APARTMENT WALLS** drawing in the Drawing Editor.
25. Drag the **SECOND FLOOR WALLS** construct into the **APARTMENT WALLS** drawing.
26. Select the **Standard** wall from the **Design** tool palette, and place 4″-wide × 8′-high walls and 3′-0″ doors as shown in Figure 16–18.

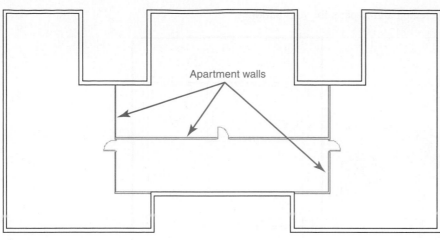

Apartment walls

**Figure 16–18**

27. In the **APARTMENT WALLS** drawing, delete the **SECOND FLOOR WALLS** XREF and save the **APARTMENT WALLS** drawing.
28. In the **Constructs** tab of the **Project Navigator,** create two new elements called **COLUMNS** and **FLOORS.**
29. In the **Constructs** tab, double-click **COLUMN GRID** to bring up the **COLUMN GRID** drawing in the Drawing Editor.
30. In the **COLUMN GRID** drawing, select all the columns, **RMB,** and select **Node Anchor > Release** from the contextual menu that appears.
31. Again, select all the columns, and select **Edit > Cut** from the **Main** menu, and then close and save the **COLUMN GRID** drawing.
32. In the **Constructs** tab of the **Project Navigator,** double-click on **COLUMNS** to open the **COLUMNS** drawing in the Drawing Editor.
33. Select **Edit > Paste to Original Coordinates** from the **Main** menu, and save the **COLUMNS** drawing.
34. Double-click on the **FLOORS** element to bring it up in the Drawing Editor.
35. Drag the **BASEMENT** construct into the **FLOORS** element drawing in the Drawing Editor.
36. Enter **BPOLY** in the **Command line** and press **Enter.**
37. Click in the middle of the **BASEMENT WALLS** that have been XREFed into the **FLOORS** construct to create a polyline.
38. Delete the **BASEMENT WALLS** XREF from the **FLOORS** element drawing leaving only the polyline.
39. RMB the **Slab** tool in the **Design** tool palette, and select **Apply Tool Properties to > Linework and Walls** from the contextual menu that appears.
40. Select the polyline you just created and press **Enter.**
41. Enter **Y** (Yes) in the **Command line** and press **Enter.**
42. Enter **D** (Direct) in the **Command line** and press **Enter.**
43. Enter **B** (Bottom) in the **Command line** and press **Enter.**

You have now created the floor slab.

44. While the slab is still selected, change its Thickness to **4″** in the **Properties** palette.
45. Save the **FLOORS** element drawing.
46. Open the **Project Navigator** again, and double-click on the **BATH ROOM** icon under the **Elements** folder to bring up the **BATHROOM** drawing in the Drawing Editor.
47. In the **BATHROOM** drawing, create a 10′-0″ square enclosure using Standard 4″-wide × 8′-0″-high walls.
48. Select one wall, **RMB,** and insert a Standard door 2′-6″ wide by 6′-8″ high.
49. Place a vanity, toilet, and spa tub from the **Design Tool Catalog – Imperial > Mechanical > Plumbing Fixtures** catalog.
50. Select the **Ceiling Grid** icon from the **Design** tool palette, center a 2′-0″ × 2′-0″ ceiling grid at 7′-6″ elevation, and save the file (see Figure 16–19).

You have now created all the parts for your building.

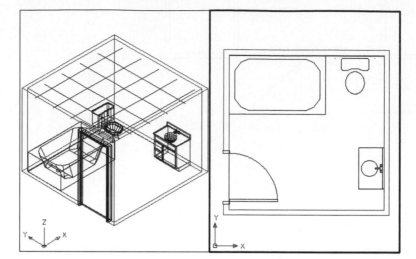

Figure 16–19

## Exercise 16-4: Putting the Elements and Constructs Together

1. In the **Constructs** tab of the **Project Manager,** double-click on the **BASEMENT WALLS** construct to open it in the Drawing Editor.
2. Drag the **FLOORS** and **COLUMNS** elements into the **BASEMENT WALLS** construct, and save the **BASEMENT WALLS** construct file.
3. In the **Constructs** tab of the **Project Manager,** double-click on the **FIRST FLOOR WALLS** construct to open it in the Drawing Editor.
4. Drag the **FLOORS** and **COLUMNS** elements into the **FIRST FLOOR WALLS** construct, and save the **FIRST FLOOR WALLS** construct file.
5. In the **Constructs** tab of the **Project Manager,** double-click on the **SECOND FLOOR WALLS** construct to open it in the Drawing Editor.
6. Drag the **FLOORS, COLUMNS, APARTMENT WALLS,** and **BATH ROOM** elements into the **SECOND FLOOR WALLS** construct.
7. In the **SECOND FLOOR WALLS** construct, copy the **BATH ROOM** element twice, arrange as shown in Figure 16–20, and save the file.

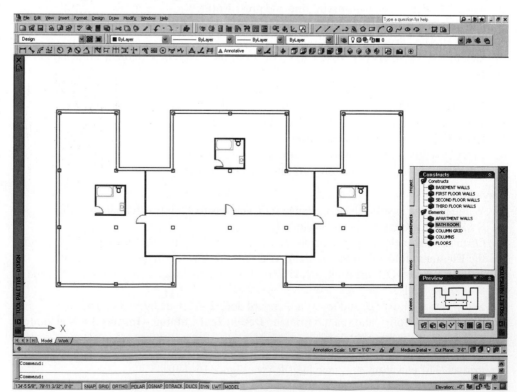

Figure 16–20

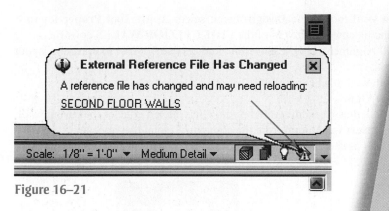

Figure 16–21

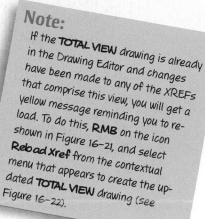

**Note:**
If the **TOTAL VIEW** drawing is already in the Drawing Editor and changes have been made to any of the XREFs that comprise this view, you will get a yellow message reminding you to re-load. To do this, **RMB** on the icon shown in Figure 16–21, and select **Reload Xref** from the contextual menu that appears to create the up-dated **TOTAL VIEW** drawing (see Figure 16–22).

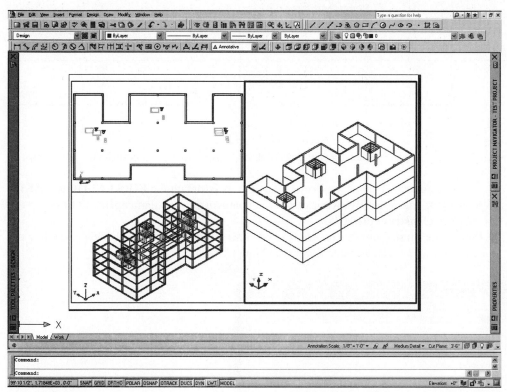

Figure 16–22

8. Select the apartment walls and bathrooms you just dragged into the **SECOND FLOOR WALLS** drawing.

9. While selected, open the **Properties** palette and set the Insertion point Z to **4″** (this places these elements on top of the 4″-thick FLOORS).

10. Repeat Steps 5 to 9 of this for the third floor walls, and save that file.

11. In the **Views** tab of the **Project Navigator,** double-click on **TOTAL VIEW** to open it in the Drawing Editor.

**Exercise 16-5:** Modifying the Constructs and Their Effects on the Views

1. In the **Constructs** tab of the **Project Navigator,** double-click on the **FIRST FLOOR WALLS** construct to open it in the Drawing Editor.

2. **RMB** the **Curtain Wall** tool in the **Design** menu, select **Apply Tool Properties to > Walls,** and select the indented front wall of the **FIRST FLOOR WALLS** construct.
3. For the curtain wall alignment, choose **Baseline**, and choose **Y** (Yes) to erase the layout geometry.
4. Drag the new curtain wall to a height of 35′.
5. Change to the **Front View.**
6. Select the curtain wall, press the **Edit Grid** button, click the left edge of the curtain wall, **RMB,** and select **Convert to Manual** from the contextual menu that appears.
7. Adjust the curtain wall as shown in Figure 16–23 and save its in-place edit changes.

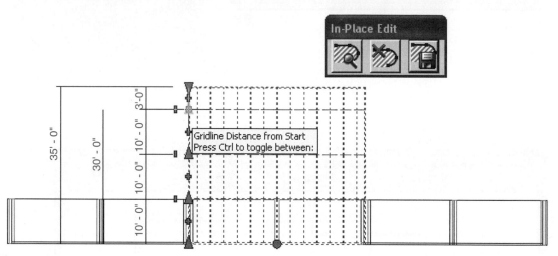

**Figure 16–23**

The curtain wall needs to span the first, second, and third floors. To coordinate these, do the following:

8. In the **Constructs** tab of the **Project Navigator, RMB** on the **FIRST FLOOR WALLS** construct, and select **Properties** from the contextual menu that appears to bring up the **Modify Construct** dialog box.
9. Select the **First Floor, Second Floor,** and **Third Floor** check boxes. This will allow the curtain wall to span all three floors (see Figure 16–24).

**Figure 16–24**

10. Save the **FIRST FLOOR WALLS** construct.
11. Open the **SECOND FLOOR WALLS** and **THIRD FLOOR WALLS** constructs, delete their front indented walls, and save those files.
12. In the **Views** tab of the **Project Navigator,** double-click on the **Total View** to bring it up in the Drawing Editor (see Figure 16–25, shown in three views for clarity).

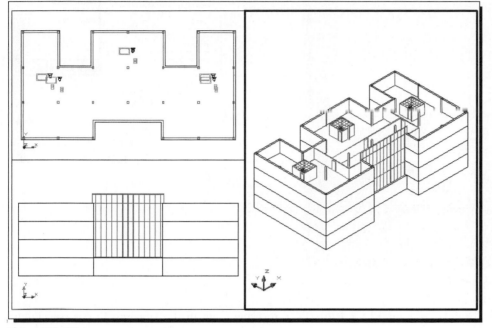

**Figure 16–25**

## Exercise 16-6: Creating Named Views and Plotting Sheets

1. In the **Views** tab of the **Project Navigator,** double-click on the **TOTAL VIEW** to open it in the Drawing Editor.
2. Change to the **SW Isometric View,** and set the scale to $1/8'' = 1'-0''$ from the **Scale** drop-down list at the bottom right of the Drawing Editor.
3. Select **View > Named Views** from the **Main** menu to bring up the **View** dialog box.
4. Select the **New** button to bring up the **New View** dialog box.
5. Enter **SW PERSPECTIVE** in the **View Name** field, select the **Define Window** radio button, select the building with a window selection, and click the mouse to return to the **New View** dialog box, and press **OK** and close the dialog boxes to return to the Drawing Editor.
6. Change to the **Front View,** and repeat the previous process naming the view **FRONT VIEW.**
7. Change to the **Top View,** and again repeat the process naming the view **TOP VIEW.**
8. Save the **Total View.**

> **Note:**
> If the **Total View** is already in the Drawing Editor and changes have been made to any of the XREFs that comprise this view, you will get a yellow message reminding you to reload.

Notice that in the **Views** tab of the **Project Navigator,** the **TOTAL VIEW** drawing contains your new named views (see Figure 16–26).

9. In the **Sheets** tab of the **Project Navigator**, RMB on **Plans,** and select **New > Sheet** from the contextual menu that appears (see Figure 16–27).
10. Enter **A-001** in the **Number** field, enter **TEST PROJECT** in the **Sheet title** field, and press **OK** to add the sheet to the **Plans** folder in the **Sheet** tab.

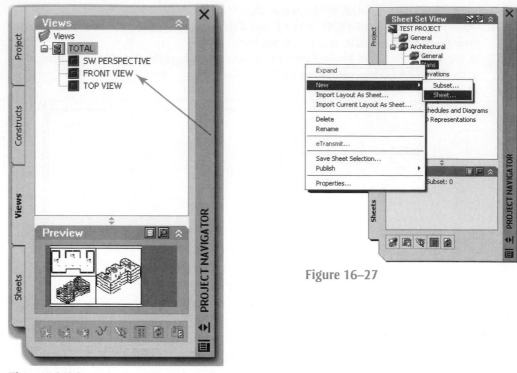

Figure 16–26

Figure 16–27

11. Double-click on **TEST PROJECT** to bring it up in the Drawing Editor (see Figure 16–28).

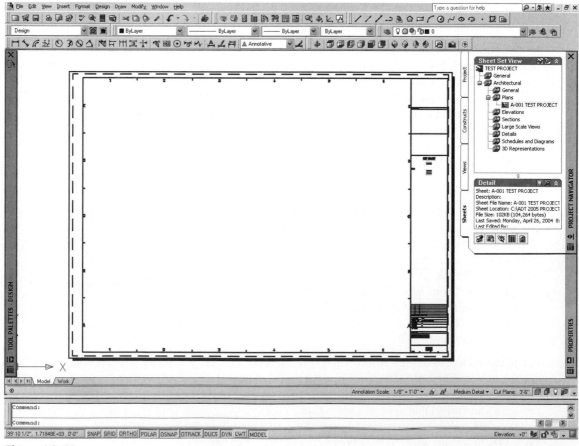

Figure 16–28

12. While the **TEST PROJECT** drawing is showing in the Drawing Editor, change to the **Views** tab in the **Project Navigator** and drag the **SW ISOMETRIC, FRONT,** and **TOP Views** into the **TEST PROJECT** drawing.

While dragging, you can **RMB** and select a scale for the view from a drop-down list (see Figure 16–29).

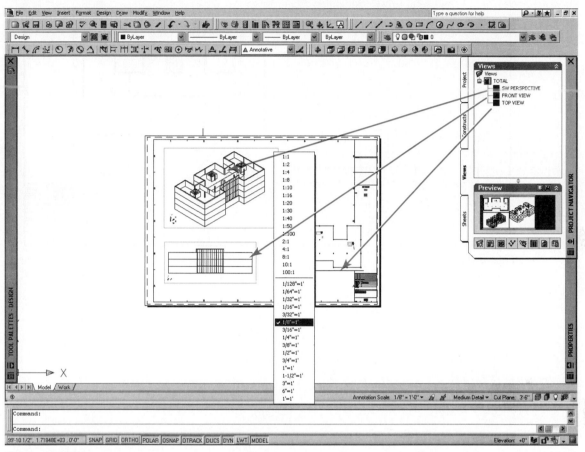

**Figure 16–29**

You have now completed your plot sheet (see Figure 16–30). You will learn more ways to insert views into sheets in Section 17, "Callouts and Annotation Scaling".

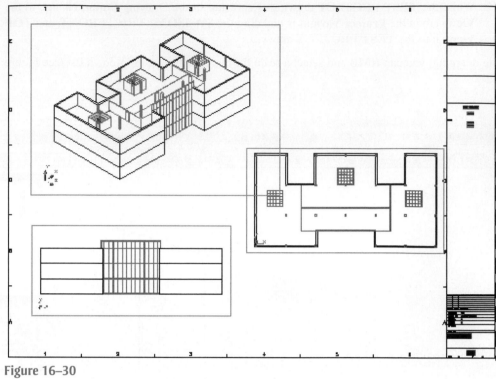

**Figure 16–30**

# Callouts and Annotation Scaling  17

## Section Objectives

- Create plotting sheets in the **Project Navigator.**
- Create a new project with the **Project Browser.**
- Learn how to create a new construct in the **Project Navigator.**
- Learn how to create elevations with the **MARK A3 Elevation** callout.
- Learn how to create details with the **Detail Boundary** callout.
- Learn how to place elevations in an **ELEVATION SHEET.**
- Learn how to place details into a **DETAIL SHEET.**
- Learn how to place floor plans in a **PLAN SHEET.**
- Understand the automated **ANNOTATION SCALING CONCEPT.**
- Know how to use the **AUTOMATED SCALING** feature.

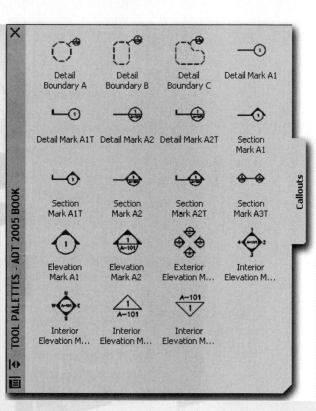

Callouts and Annotation Scaling are very important productivity features in AutoCAD Architecture 2008. These automated annotation tools allow you to coordinate sections and elevations througout a drawing set, as well as maintin the size of annotations regardless of changes in drawing scale. Because callouts and Annotation Scaling operate in conjunction with project management and the sheet sets, it is a good idea to review those sections before doing these exercises.

In the last two sections you learned about elevations and sections as well as elevation and section objects. In those exercises, you placed the elevation or section with a callout. In this section, you will learn the new advanced coordination capabilities of the callouts.

With AutoCAD Architecture 2008, details, elevations, and sections are views of the building model and part of the construction documentation. They can be created with callouts. Callout tools create a callout that is referenced to a model space view containing a user-defined part of the building model, such as a section, an elevation, or a detail. They are coordinated across the complete construction document set with the help of projects and sheet sets.

The following callout tools are provided with AutoCAD Architecture 2008.

A detail callout tool with a circular boundary that optionally can insert a title mark. The callout symbol has field placeholders for the sheet number and a detail number, which are resolved when the detail is placed on the sheet.

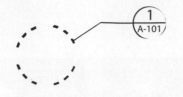

A detail callout tool with a rectangular boundary that optionally can insert a title mark. The callout symbol has field placeholders for the sheet number and a detail number, which are resolved when the detail is placed on the sheet.

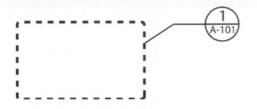

A detail callout tool with a free-form boundary that optionally can insert a title mark. The callout symbol has field placeholders for the sheet number and a detail number, which are resolved when the detail is placed on the sheet.

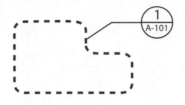

A detail tool with a leader line. The callout symbol has a field placeholder for the detail number that gets resolved when the detail is placed on the sheet.

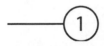

A detail tool with a leader line and tail. The callout symbol has a field placeholder for the detail number that gets resolved when the detail is placed on the sheet.

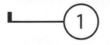

A detail tool with a leader line. The callout symbol has field placeholders for the detail number and the sheet number, which are resolved when the detail is placed on the sheet.

A detail tool with a leader line and tail. The callout symbol has field placeholders for the detail number and the sheet number, which are resolved when the detail is placed on a sheet.

A single elevation mark tool. The elevation mark has a field placeholder for the elevation number that gets resolved when the elevation is placed on the sheet.

A single elevation mark tool. The elevation mark has field placeholders for the elevation number and the sheet number, which are resolved when the elevation is placed on the sheet.

A four-way interior elevation mark tool in the format 1/2/3/4. The elevation mark's callout symbol has a field placeholder for the sheet number that gets resolved when the elevations are placed on the sheet.

A four-way interior elevation mark tool in the format N/E/S/W. The elevation mark's callout symbol has a field placeholder for the sheet number that gets resolved when the elevations are placed on the sheet.

A four-way exterior elevation mark tool in the format 1/2/3/4. The elevation mark's callout symbol has field placeholders for the detail number and the sheet number, which get resolved when the elevations are placed on the sheet.

A single interior elevation mark tool. The elevation mark contains field placeholders for the sheet number and the elevation number, which are resolved when the elevation is placed on the sheet.

A single interior elevation mark tool with inverted text. The elevation mark contains field placeholders for the sheet number and the elevation number, which are resolved when the elevation is placed on the sheet.

A single section mark tool with a leader line. The section mark contains a field placeholder for the section number that gets resolved when the section is placed on the sheet.

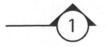

A single section mark tool with a leader line and a tail. The section mark contains a field placeholder for the section number that gets resolved when the section is placed on the sheet.

A single section mark tool with a leader line. The section mark contains field placeholders for the section number and the sheet number, which are resolved when the section is placed on the sheet.

A section mark tool with a leader line in a tail. The section mark contains field placeholders for the section number and the sheet number, which are resolved when the section is placed on the sheet.

A double section mark tool with a section line. The section marks contain field placeholders for the section number and the sheet number, which are resolved when the section is placed on the sheet.

## THE CALLOUT METHODOLOGY

Callouts are meant to work within the AutoCAD Architecture Drawing Management system. They automatically will reference the drawings in which they are placed. This automatic referencing system is said to be "resolved" when a view is placed on a plotting sheet. *Callouts are meant to work only with 2D details and 2D elevations.*

### Exercise 17-1: Creating a New Project with the Project Browser

1. Using the **Windows Explorer** or **My Computer,** create a new folder called **CALLOUTS.**
2. Select **File > Project Browser** from the **Main** menu to bring up the **Project Browser.**
3. Locate the **CALLOUTS** folder from the drop-down list and select the **New Project** icon to bring up the **Add Project** dialog box.
4. Enter the number **001** in the **Number** field, **CALLOUTTEST** in the **Name** field, and press **OK** to return to the **Project Browser** (see Figure 17–1).

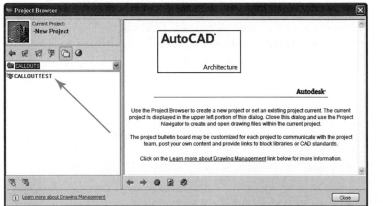

Figure 17–1

5. In the **Project Browser, RMB** on **CALLOUTTEST,** select **Set Project Current** from the contextual menu that appears, and press the **Close** button to close the **Project Manager** and bring in the **Project Navigator.**

In order for the Drawing Management system to work, you must have a drawing file in the Drawing Editor. This file is a dummy file and will not be used. The term *dummy file* refers to the fact that a file must be in the Drawing Editor for the menu bars to appear.

### Exercise 17-2: Creating Plotting Sheets in the Project Navigator

1. In the **Project Navigator,** change to the **Sheets** tab.
2. In the **Sheets** tab of the **Project Navigator,** select the **Plans** icon, and then press the **Add Sheet** icon to bring up the **New Sheet** dialog box.

3. Enter **A-101** in the **Number** field, **PLAN SHEET** in the **Sheet title** field, and press **OK.**

4. In the **Sheets** tab of the **Project Navigator,** select the **Elevations** icon, and then press the **Add Sheet** icon to bring up the **New Sheet** dialog box.

5. Enter **A-201** in the **Number** field, **ELEVATION SHEET** in the **Sheet title** field, and press **OK.**

6. In the **Sheets** tab of the **Project Navigator,** select the **Details** icon, and then press the **Add Sheet** icon to bring up the **New Sheet** dialog box.

7. Enter **A-401** in the **Number** field, **DETAILS SHEET** in the **Sheet title** field, and press **OK** (see Figure 17–2).

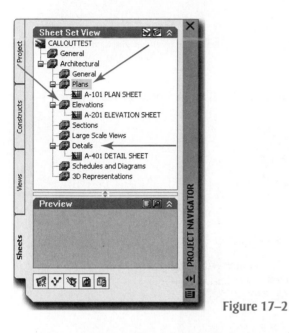

**Figure 17–2**

**Exercise 17-3:** Creating a New Construct in the Project Navigator

1. In the **Project Navigator**, change to the **Constructs** tab.

2. Select the **Add Construct** icon to bring up the **Add Construct** dialog box.

3. Enter **STAIR** in the **Name** field, and press **OK** to return to the Drawing Editor.

4. In the **Constructs** tab of the **Project Navigator,** double-click on the STAIR drawing you created in the previous step to bring that drawing into the Drawing Editor.

5. In the Drawing Editor place a wall with windows, a door, and a stair similar to that shown in Figure 17–3.

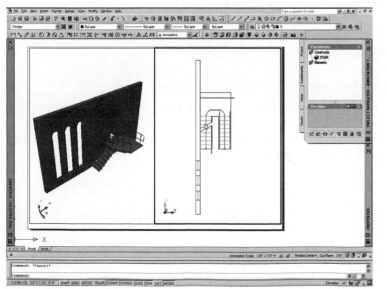

**Figure 17–3**

**Exercise 17-4:** Creating a New Plan View Drawing in the Project Navigator

1. In the **Project Navigator,** change to the **Views** tab.
2. Select the **Add View** icon to bring up the **Add View** dialog box.
3. Select the **General View** radio button, and press **OK** to open the **Add View** dialog box.
4. Enter **STAIR PLAN,** and press the **Next** button to bring up the **Context** screen.
5. Check the **Level** check box, and press the **Next** button to bring up the **Content** screen.
6. Make sure the **STAIR CONSTRUCT** check box is checked—this will add the stair construct to your STAIR PLAN drawing. Finally, press the **Finish** button in the **Content** screen

to return to the Drawing Editor, and create the STAIR PLAN drawing (see Figure 17–4).

**Note:** The STAIR PLAN drawing will contain the stair created in **STAIR** in the **Constructs** tab (it has been XREFed into the STAIR PLAN drawing automatically).

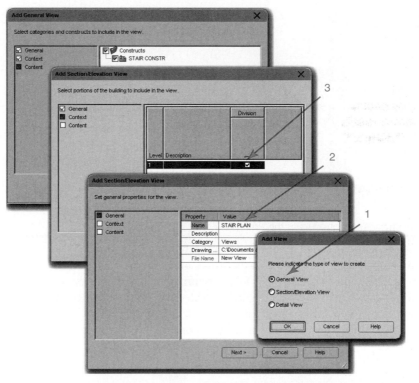

Figure 17–4

7. In the **Views** tab of the **Project Navigator,** double-click on the **STAIR Plan** icon to bring the **STAIR PLAN view** drawing into the Drawing Editor.

**Exercise 17-5:** Creating Elevations with the MARK A3 Elevation Callout

1. Select **Elevation Mark Elevation Mark A3** from the **Callouts** tool palette (see Figure 17–5).
2. In the STAIR PLAN drawing in the **Top View,** place a window selection around the stair construct and click to bring up the **Place Callout** dialog box.

Figure 17–5

3. Check the **Generate Section/Elevation** check box, select ½″ from the **Scale** drop-down list, and press the **New View** drawing icon to bring up the **Add Section/Elevation View** dialog box (see Figure 17–6).

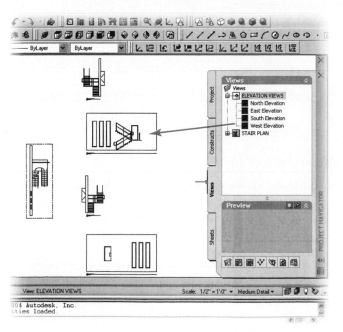

**Figure 17–6**

4. Enter **ELEVATION VIEWS** in the **Name** field (this will appear as the drawing file name in the **Project Navigator**), and press the **Next** button to bring up the **Context** screen.
5. Check the **Level** check box, and press the **Next** button to bring up the **Content** screen.
6. Make sure the **STAIR CONSTRUCT** check box is checked, and press the **Finish** button to return to the Drawing Editor.
7. In the Drawing Editor, click to the right of stair (where you click doesn't matter because you are creating the elevations in the new drawing file).
8. Move your cursor down 10″ vertically again (this will dictate the distance between the four elevations) and click your mouse button. The **Generate Elevation Progress** dialog screen will appear telling you when the elevations have been created in a new file.

Notice that the **ELEVATION VIEWS** file appears in the **Views** tab of the **Project Navigator.**

9. In the **Views** tab of the **Project Navigator,** double-click on the **ELEVATION VIEWS** file to bring that file up in the Drawing Editor (see Figure 17–7).

**Figure 17–7**

**Exercise 17-6:** Placing Elevation Views in the A-201 ELEVATION SHEET

1. In the **Sheets** tab of the **Project Navigator,** double-click the **A-201 ELEVATION SHEET** icon bring it up in the Drawing Editor.

2. In the **Project Navigator,** change to the **View** tab.

3. Drag the **ELEVATION VIEWS** icon into the **A-201 ELEVATION SHEET** that is open in the Drawing Editor.

4. Click a spot in the A-201 ELEVATION SHEET to place the first elevation. The other three elevations will appear in sequence automatically—place them also (see Fig-ure 17–8).

5. Press **Ctrl + S** on your keyboard or select **File > Save** from the **Main** menu to save the A-201 ELEVATION SHEET.

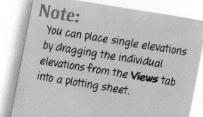

**Note:**
You can place single elevations by dragging the individual elevations from the **Views** tab into a plotting sheet.

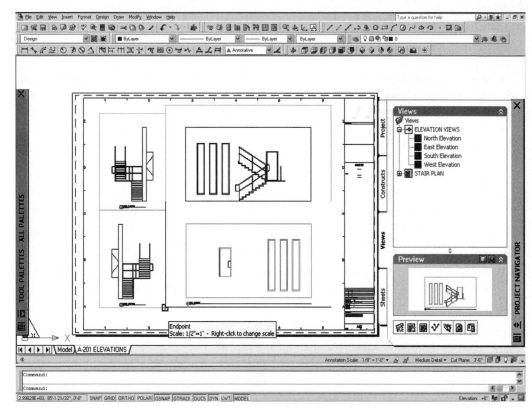

**Figure 17–8**

**Exercise 17-7:** Creating Details with the Detail Boundary Callout

1. In the **Project Navigator**, change to the **Views** tab and double-click the **East Elevation** to bring it up in the Drawing Editor.

2. Select the **Detail Boundary B** tool from the **Callouts** tool palette (see Figure 17–9).

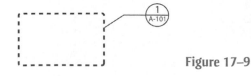

**Figure 17–9**

3. Click in the EAST ELEVATION drawing, and select with a window selection the area for your detail (see Figure 17–10).

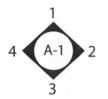

**Figure 17–10**

4. Move the leader line location and click to bring up the **Place Callout** dialog box.
5. Enter **DETAIL 1** in the **New Model Space View Name** field, uncheck the **Generate Section/Elevation** check box, select **1″ = 1′-0″** from the **Scale** drop-down list, and press the **New View** drawing icon to bring up the **Add Detail View** dialog box.
6. Enter **DETAILS** in the **Name** field (this will appear as the drawing file name in the **Project Navigator**) and press the **Next** button to bring up the **Context** screen.
7. Check the **Level** check box, and press the **Next** button to bring up the **Content** screen.
8. Make sure the **STAIR CONSTRUCT** check box is checked, and press the **Finish** button to return to the Drawing Editor.
9. In the Drawing Editor, click in the drawing to create the new detail view drawing.
10. In the **Views** tab, expand the DETAILS drawing that you just created to see the **DETAIL 1 View** (see Figure 17–11).

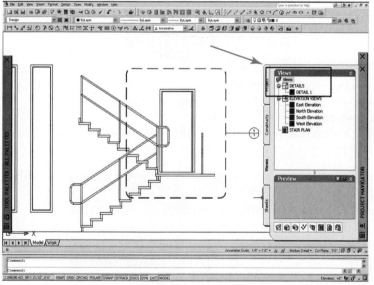

**Figure 17–11**

11. Repeat the previous process to create a new d... called **DETAIL 2.**
12. Press **Ctrl + S** on your keyboard or select **Fil** **Save** from the **Main** menu to save t **ELEVATION VIEWS** drawing.

**Note:**
You can place single details by dragging the individual details from the **Views** tab into a plotting sheet.

**Exercise 17-8:** Placing Details into the A-401 DETAIL SHEET

1. In the **Project Navigator,** change to the **Sheets** tab and double-click **A-401 DETAIL SHEET** to bring the A-401 DETAIL SHEET drawing into the Drawing Editor.
2. In the **Project Navigator,** change to the **Views** tab.

3. Drag the **DETAILS** icon into the A-401 ELEVATION SHEET that is open in the Drawing Editor.
4. Click a spot in the A-401 DETAIL SHEET to place the first detail. The other details will appear in sequence automatically—place them as well (see Figure 17–12).

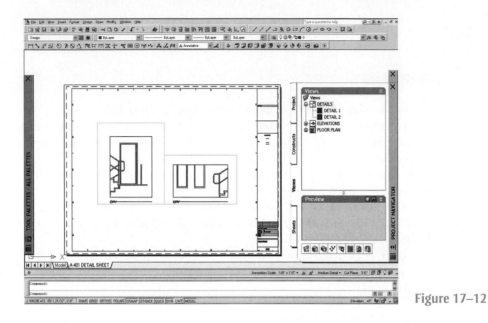

**Figure 17–12**

5. Press **Ctrl + S** on your keyboard or select **File > Save** from the **Main** menu to save the A-401 DETAIL SHEET.

**Exercise 17-9:** Placing the Floor Plan into the A-101 PLAN SHEET

1. In the **Project Navigator,** change to the **Sheets** tab and double-click **A-101 PLAN SHEET** to bring the A-101 PLAN SHEET drawing into the Drawing Editor.
2. In the **Project Navigator,** change to the **Views** tab.
3. Drag the **FLOOR PLAN** into the A-101 PLAN SHEET that is open in the Drawing Editor (see Figure 17–13).

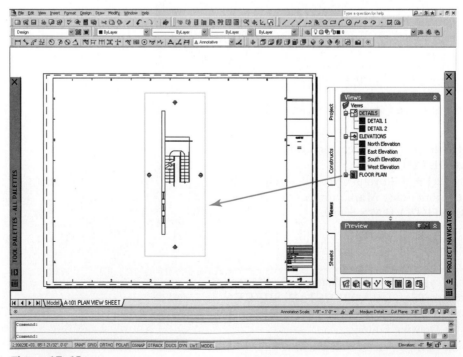

**Figure 17–13**

4. Press **Ctrl + S** on your keyboard or select **File > Save** from the **Main** menu to save the A-101 PLAN SHEET.

Close all the drawings.

In the **Sheets** tab, double-click on **A-101, A-201,** and **A-401,** and look at the callouts. The callout numbers have been coordinated automatically to the sheet, plan, elevation, and detail numbers (see Figures 17–14 through 17–17).

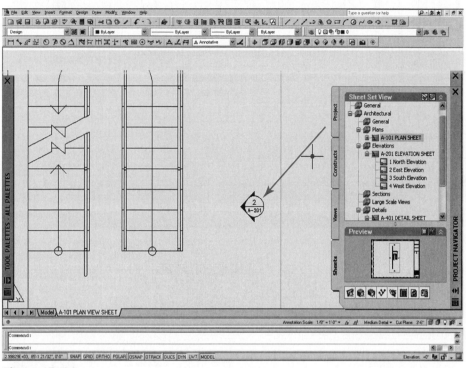

**Figure 17–14**

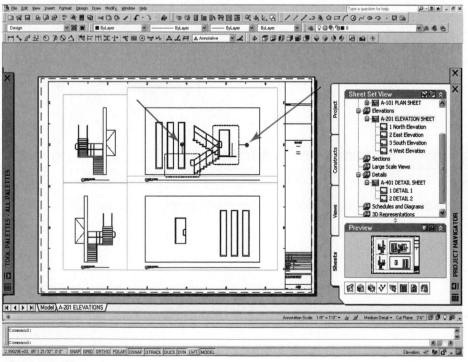

**Figure 17–15**

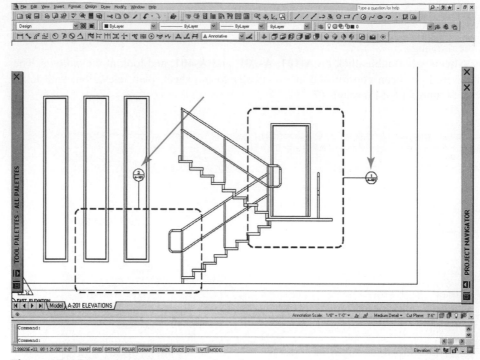

**Figure 17–16**

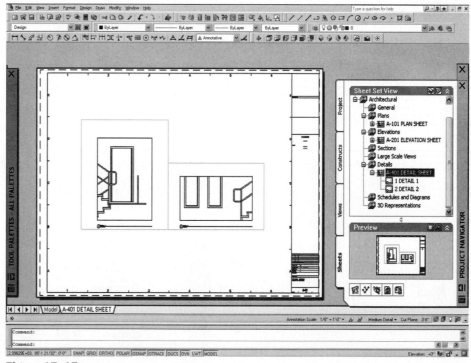

**Figure 17–17**

## ANNOTATION SCALING

Before AutoCAD Architecture 2008, changing scales was a chore. The new automated **annotation scaling** feature allows you to plot annotation at the same height or size regardless of the viewport zoom scale. Annotation scales can be associated with annotative objects such as Callouts so that these objects will be sized properly for the scale you set in paper space or on your plot sheet. You can also toggle on or off the display of annotation objects that do not participate in the current annotation scale.

An annotation tool is a customizable AutoCAD architecture tool for adding the following types of annotations to drawings:

- Multi-line text notes
- Symbol-based notes with attributes
- Reference keynotes
- Sheet notes
- Callouts

The following are annotation objects created by AutoCAD:

- Text
- MText
- Dimensions
- Leaders
- Block References
- Hatches

The following AutoCAD styles are also annotative:

- Text
- Dimensions
- Block Definitions
- MLeaders

### Exercise 17-10: Understanding the Automated Annotation Scaling Concept

1. Start a new drawing using the AEC Model (Imperial Stb) template. Make sure you are in model space.
2. Select **1/4″ =1′-0″** from the **Annotation Scale** drop-down list at the bottom of the **Drawing Editor** (see Figure 17–18).

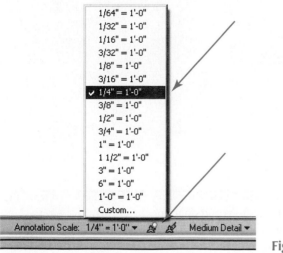

Figure 17–18

3. Select the **Brick-4 Brick-4** wall from the **Design** palette, and place a 10'-0" long wall in the **Drawing Editor**.
4. **RMB** on the wall you just created, and select **Insert > Door** from the contextual menu that appears (see Figure 17–19).

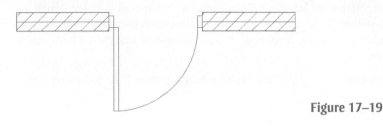

**Figure 17–19**

5. Select the wall, **RMB,** and select **AEC Dimension** from the contextual menu that appears.
6. Place an **AEC Dimension** string as shown in Figure 17–20.

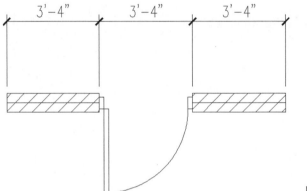

**Figure 17–20**

7. Change to the Document tool palette.
8. In the **Document** tool palette, change to the **Tags** tab.
9. In the **Tags** tab, select the **Door Tag**, select the door in the wall you created, and then press the **Enter** key on your keyboard three times to place the tag.

You have now placed annotation and dimensions at the 1/4" = 1'-0" scale (see Figure 17–21).

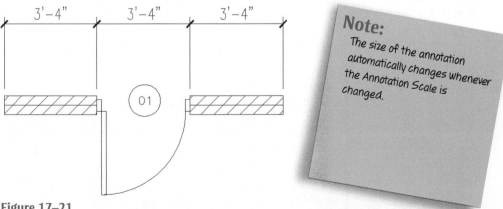

**Note:**
The size of the annotation automatically changes whenever the Annotation Scale is changed.

**Figure 17–21**

10. Select **1/8" = 1'-0"** from the **Annotation Scale** drop-down list at the bottom of the Drawing Editor, and notice that the dimensions and door tag change size.
11. Select **1/2" = 1'-0"** from the **Annotation Scale** drop-down list at the bottom of the Drawing Editor, and again notice that the dimensions and door tag change size (see Figure 17–22).

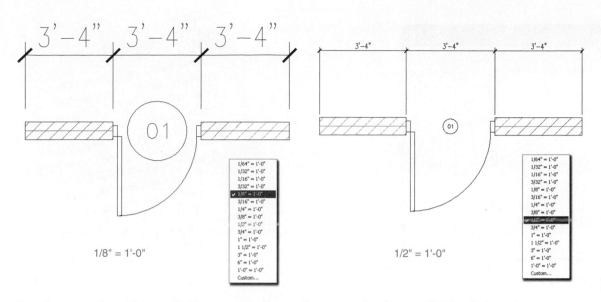

Figure 17–22

In order to see the various scaled annotations that you just created and are available, click on the annotations (see Figure 17–23).

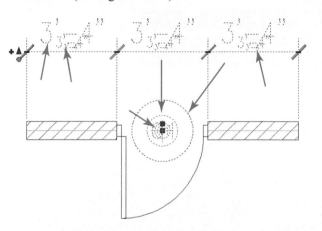

Figure 17–23

12. **RMB** on the Door tag you inserted previously, and select **Annotative Object Scale > Add/Delete Scales** from the contextual menu that appears to bring up the **Annotation Object Scale** dialog box (see Figures 17–24 and 17–25).

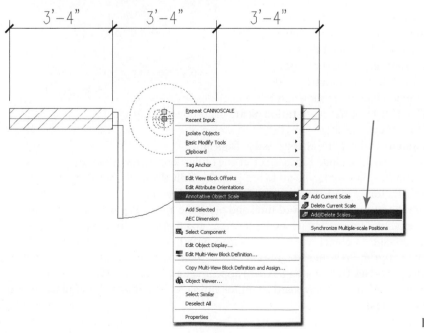

Figure 17–24

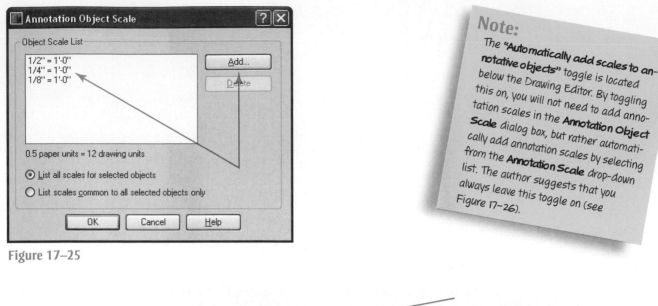

Figure 17–25

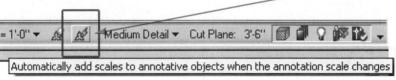

Figure 17–26

## Exercise 17-11: Utilizing the Automated Annotation Scaling Feature

1. Using the **Project Manager,** create a project called **ANNOTATION SCAL TEST.** For this exercise it is not necessa add levels.
2. In the **Project Navigator,** select **Constructs** tab, and create a new constr called **ANNOTATION CONSTRUCT**
3. Double click **ANNOTATION COI STRUCT** to bring it into the Drawin Editor.
4. Select the **Wall** tool from the **Design** too palette, and place a **15′ × 30′** rectangular enclosure in the Drawing Editor.
5. Select the **Door** and **Window** tools from the **Design** tool palette, and place doors and windows as shown in F

6. Select **1/4″ = 1′-0** from the **Annotation Scale** drop-down list at the bottom of the Drawing Editor.
7. In the **Document** tool palette, change to the **Tags** tab.
8. In the **Tags** tab, select the **Door Tag,** and select one of the doors in the enclosure you created.
9. Press the **Enter** key on your keyboard to bring up the **Edit Property Set Data** dialog box.
10. Press the **OK** button in the **Edit Property Set Data** dialog box.
11. Enter **M** (Multiple) in the **Command line,** and press the **Enter** key on your keyboard.
12. Select all the other doors with a window selection, and press the **Enter** key on your keyboard. The message "1 object was already tagged with the same tag. Do you want to tag it again?" will appear. Press the **No** button.
13. The **Edit Property Set Data** dialog box will appear again. Press the **OK** button, and then press the **Enter** key on your keyboard again to complete the command and place all the remaining door tags.

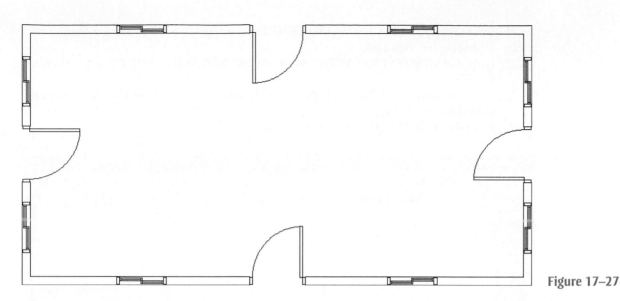

Figure 17–27

14. Repeat steps 7–13 for the window tags (see Figure 17–28).

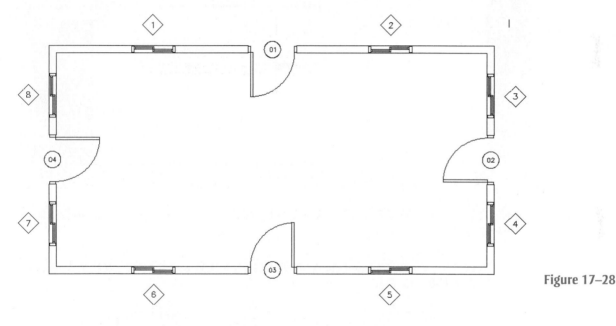

Figure 17–28

15. Turn on the **"Automatically add scales to annotative objects"** toggle.
16. Select **1/8″ = 1′-0, 1/2″ = 1′- 0,** and then **3/4″ = 1′-0″** from the **Annotation Scale** drop-down list at the bottom of the Drawing Editor.
17. Save the **ANNOTATION CONSTRUCT** file.
18. Change to the **Views** tab in the **Project Navigator.**
19. Create a new **View** drawing and name it **ANNOTATION VIEW.**
20. Make the **ANNOTATION CONSTRUCT** the contents of the **ANNOTATION VIEW.**
21. Double click **ANNOTATION VIEW** to bring it into the Drawing Editor.
22. Save the **ANNOTATION VIEW** file.
23. Change to the **Sheets** tab in the **Project Navigator.**
24. Create a new sheet named **001ANNOTATION SHEET.**

**Note:**
If you wish, you can turn off the **Edit Property Set Data** dialog box in the **AEC Contents** tab of the **Options** by unchecking the **Display Edit Property Data Dialog During Tag Insertion** check box. Leave this option checked if you want to add information while placing tags.

25. Double click on **001ANNOTATION SHEET** to bring it into the Drawing Editor.
26. Change to the **Views** tab.
27. Drag the **ANNOTATION VIEW** into the **001ANNOTATION SHEET** in the Drawing Editor.
28. Before placing the **ANNOTATION VIEW, RMB** and select **1/2″ = 1′-0″** from the scale drop-down list that appears.
29. Place the **ANNOTATION VIEW** (see Figure 17–29).

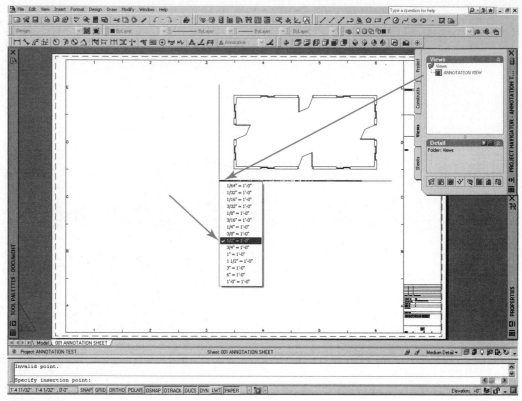

**Figure 17–29**

30. Repeat this process placing the **ANNOTATION VIEW** at **3/4″=1′0″, 1/4″ = 1′-0″,** and **1/8″ = 1′-0″** (see Figure 17–30).

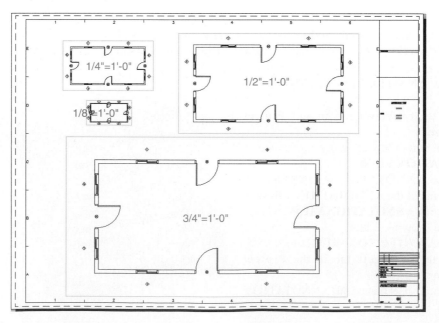

**Figure 17–30**

31. Zoom in on the views in the Sheet drawing, and notice that the annotation is always the same plot size although the drawing scales are different (see Figure 17–31).

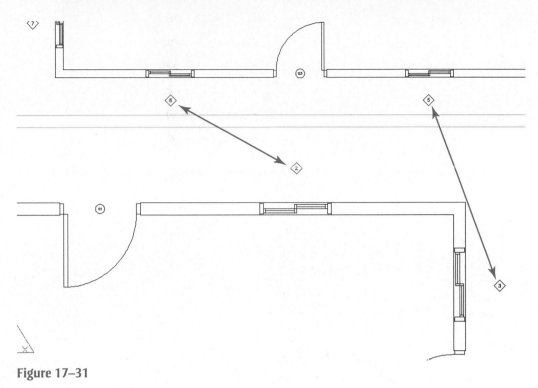

**Figure 17–31**

Save this file.

# Detail Components and the Detail Component Manager

# 18

## Section Objectives

- Understand the **Detail Component** concept.
- Create a wall detail using **Detail Components.**
- Learn how to place **Detail Components.**
- Learn how to place **Keynotes.**
- Learn how to use the **Detail Component Manager.**
- Know how to create new custom **Detail Components.**
- Know how to use the **Keynote Editor.**

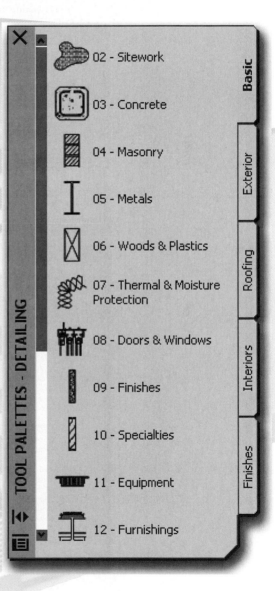

The Detailer has been around since the beginnings of Autodesk Architectural Desktop.

Detail components represent specific building materials and products and are made up of simple two-dimensional line work entities such as lines, polylines, arcs, circles, and hatches. In most cases, the detail component is a collection of such entities grouped as a block, which can be easily copied or moved as a single entity. The following are examples of detail components that are inserted as blocks:

- Bolt heads
- Fixed-length nails
- Section reviews of beams and columns
- Most selection views of framing members
- Units such as CMUs, bricks, and pavers
- Connectors
- Materials with reviews generated from interrelating parameters, for example, trusses, precast concrete, and hollow metal frames.

## Exercise 18-1: Inserting Detail Components

All detail components are inserted into drawings using the same basic tool, which performs the insertion routine associated with a selected component. Each detail component tool provided on the sample tool palettes represents a different configuration of the basic tool. You can activate the tool insertion tool in five different ways:

1. Click a detail component tool icon on a tool palette.
2. Click on the **Detail Component Manager** icon on the **Navigation** tool bar (see Figure 18–1), and select a component from the **Detail Component Manager** (see Figure 18–2).
3. Drag and drop a detail component that has been placed in a drawing from that drawing into a tool palette (see Figure 18–3).
4. Select a component in a drawing, **RMB,** and click **Add selected.** This reruns the tool with the same property settings used to insert the existing component, so that one can quickly insert additional copies of the same component.
5. Select a component in a drawing, **RMB,** and click **Replace selected.** This erases the selected component and reruns the tool with the same property settings used to insert the erased component. However, you can modify the tool to insert a different component by changing the component properties (**Category, Type, Description,** or **View**) on the **Properties** palette.

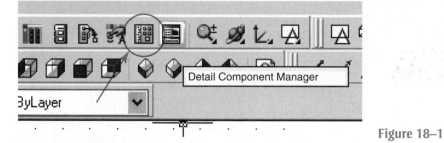

Figure 18–1

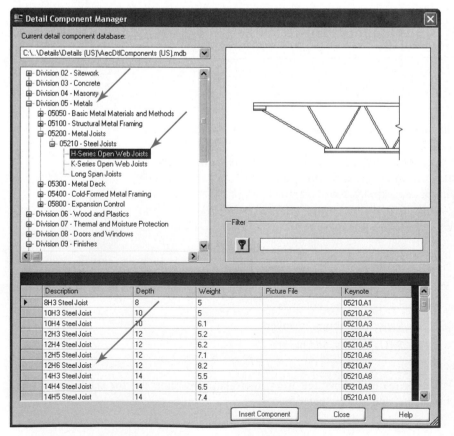

Figure 18–2

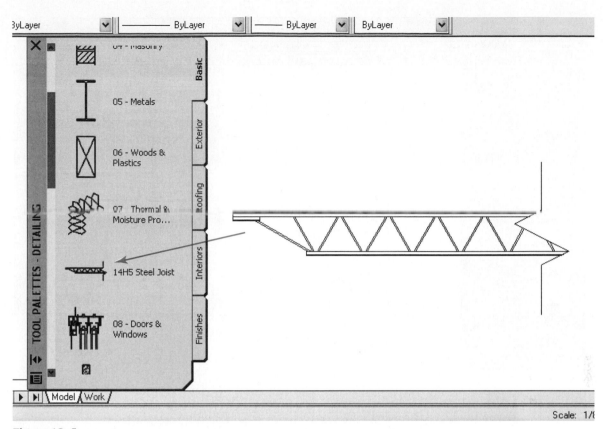

**Figure 18–3**

6. **RMB** on any **Detail Component** tool, and select **Detail Component Manager** from the contextual menu that appears to bring up the **Detail Component Manager.**

**Exercise 18-2:** Creating a Wall Detail Using Detail Components

1. Start a new drawing using the AEC Model (Imperial Stb) template.
2. Change to the **Top View.**
3. Click on the **03-Concrete** tool in the **Basic** tool palette of the **DETAILING** tool palettes.
4. Move your cursor over the **Properties** palette to open it, and set the settings shown in Figure 18–4.
5. In the **Description** field of the **Properties** palette, select the **6″ Slab With Haunch** option, and return to the Drawing Editor.
6. In the Drawing Editor, click and drag to the right, and then click again to establish the end of the slab.
7. Press **Enter** to complete the command (see Figure 18–5).

**TIP**

**Alternative Selection Method**
a. Select the **Detail Component Manager** icon from the **Navigation** toolbar to bring up the Detail Component Manager.
b. In the Detail Component Manager, select **Division 03-Concrete > 03310-Structural Concrete > Slabs with Optional Haunch.**
c. Press the **Insert Component** button to return to the Drawing Editor and begin to place the component.
d. Before placing the component, move your cursor over the **Properties** palette to open it, allowing you to modify all the options of your component (see Figure 18–6).

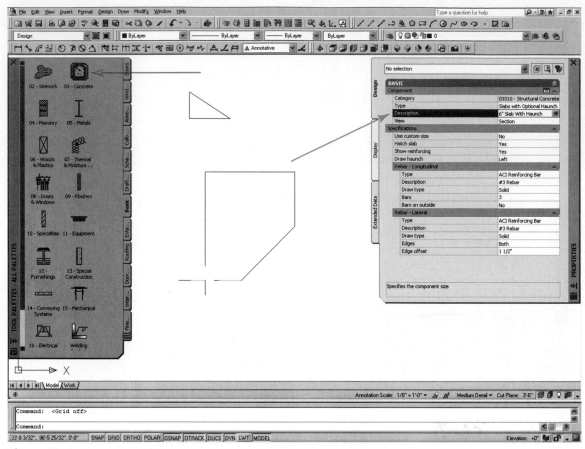

Figure 18–4

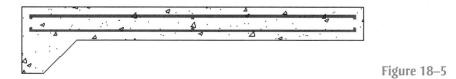

Figure 18–5

8. Click on the **04-Masonry** tool in the **Basic** tool palette of the **DETAILING** tool palettes.
9. Move your cursor over the **Properties** palette to open it, and set the settings shown in Figure 18–7.
10. Click at the left edge of the slab you just placed, drag vertically, enter **2′** in the **Command line** and press **Enter.** This will make a 2′-high masonry wall.
11. Select the **Detail Component Manager** icon from the **Navigation** toolbar to bring up the **Detail Component Manager.**
12. Select **Division 09110 - Non-Load Bearing Wall framing > Interior Metal Studs.**
13. Select **3-5/8″ Metal Stud,** and press the **Insert Component** button to return to the Drawing Editor.
14. In the **Properties** palette, set the **View** to **Elevation.**
15. Enter **L** (Left) in the **Command line** and press **Enter.**
16. With **Osnap** set to **Endpoint,** enter **fro** in the **Command line** and press **Enter.**
17. Enter **1″** in the **Command line** for the airspace, drag to the right, click again, drag vertically, enter **22-1/2″,** and press **Enter** to complete the command (see Figure 18–8).
18. In the **Detail Component Manager,** again select **Division 09110 - Non-Load Bearing Wall framing > Interior Metal Runner Channels,** and rotate and place runners at the top and base of the steel stud.

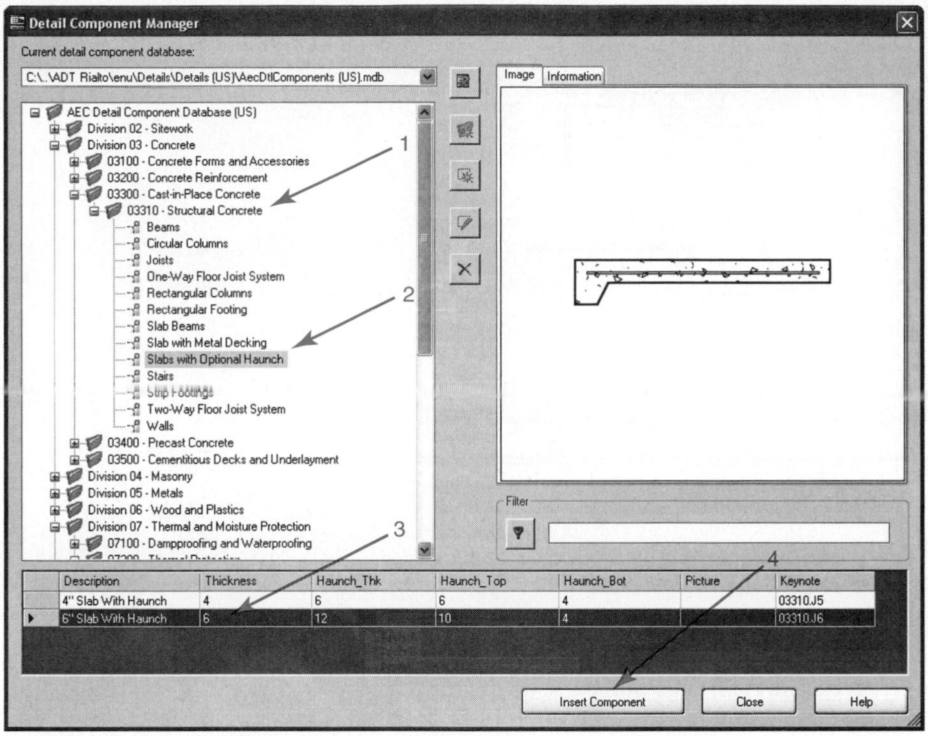

**Figure 18–6**

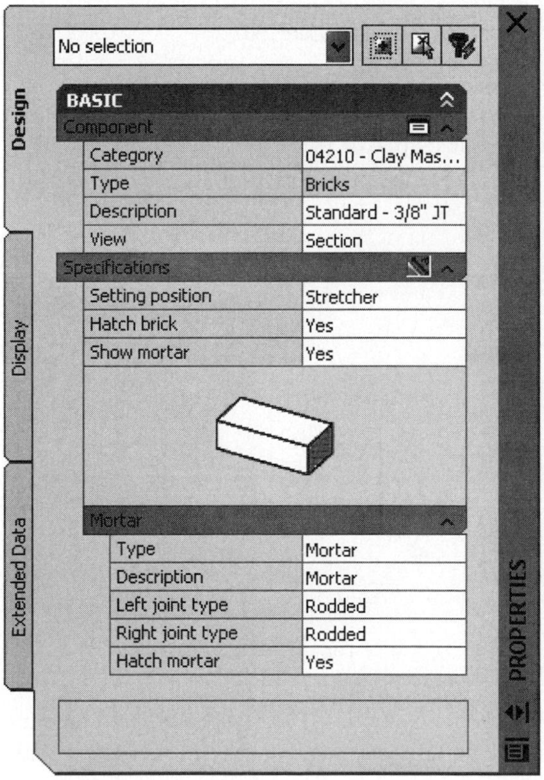

**Figure 18–7**

19. Click on the **06-Woods & Plastics** tool in the **Basic** tool palette of the **DETAILING** tool palettes.
20. Move your cursor over the **Properties** palette to open it, set the **Description** drop-down list to **2 × 4,** and **View** to **Section.**
21. Enter **R** (Rotate) in the **Command line** and press **Enter.**

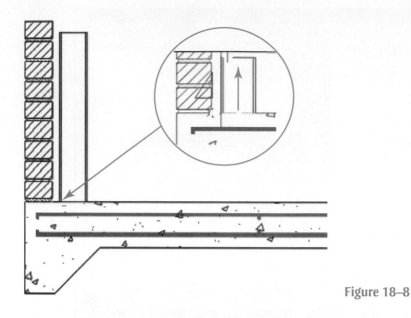

Figure 18–8

22. Enter **90** in the **Command line** and press **Enter.**
23. Place the bottom right edge of the 2 × 4 with the top right edge of metal stud and runner you placed previously.
24. Select the **Detail Component Manager** icon from the **Navigation** toolbar to bring up the **Detail Component Manager.**
25. Select **Division 08410 - Metal-Framed Storefronts** > **Front Double Glazed.**
26. Select **Storefront Sill at Finish,** and press the **Insert Component** button to return to the Drawing Editor.
27. Enter **B** (Base point) in the **Command line** and press **Enter.**
28. With **Osnap** set to **Endpoint,** click on the lower right corner of the storefront component.
29. Click on the top right of the 2 × 4 you previously placed (see Figure 18–9).

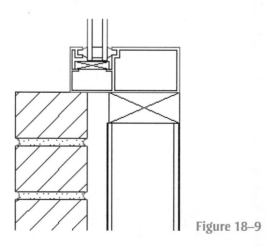

Figure 18–9

30. Click on the **09-Finishes** tool in the **Basic** tool palette of the **DETAILING** tool palettes.
31. Move your cursor over the **Properties** palette to open it, and select **1/2″ Gypsum Wall-board** from the **Description** field.
32. Enter **L** (Left) in the **Command line** and press **Enter.**
33. Click at the bottom right of the metal stud, and drag upwards to the midpoint of the right side of the storefront sill component.
34. Select the gypsum board you already placed, **RMB,** and select **Add Selected** from the contextual menu that appears.
35. Place a copy of 1/2″ gypsum wallboard on the left side of the metal stud.

You now need to cap the gypsum wallboard at the storefront component.

36. Select the **Detail Component Manager** icon from the **Navigation** toolbar to bring up the **Detail Component Manager.**
37. Select **Division 09270 - Gypsum Wall Board Accessories.**
38. Select **1/2″ J Casing Bead,** and press the **Insert Component** button to return to the Drawing Editor.
39. Enter **B** (Base point) in the **Command line** and press **Enter.**
40. With the **Endpoint Osnap** on, relocate the base point.
41. Enter **R** (Rotate) in the **Command line** and press **Enter.**
42. Enter **270** in the **Command line** and press **Enter.**
43. Place the casing bead as shown in Figure 18–10.
44. Click on the **07-Thermal & Moisture Protection** tool in the **Basic** tool palette of the **DETAILING** tool palettes.

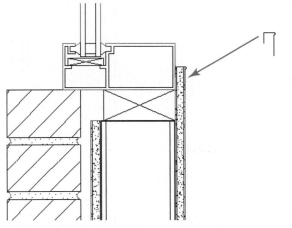

Figure 18–10

45. Move your cursor over the **Properties** palette to open it. Select **Batt Insulation** from the **Type** field, **3-1/2″ R-11 Fiberglass Batt Insulation** from the **Description** field, **Section** from the **View** field, and **Normal** from the **Density** field.
46. Click at the bottom center of the metal stud, drag upwards, and click again to place the insulation (see Figure 18–11).

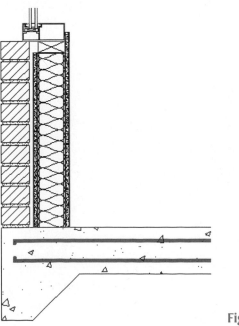

Figure 18–11

## Chamfer the Brick Sill

47. Select the brick directly below the storefront, **RMB,** and select **AEC Modify Tools >  Trim** from the contextual menu that appears.
48. Select two points for a trim plane and then select the side to trim (see Figure 18–12).

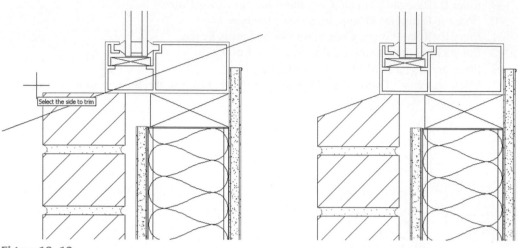

**Figure 18–12**

## Create Sill Flashing

49. Select the **Polyline** icon from the **Draw** toolbar, and create the flashing shown in Figure 18–13.
50. Select the **Detail Component Manager** icon from the **Navigation** toolbar to bring up the **Detail Component Manager.**
51. Select **Division 07620 - Sheet Metal Flashing.**
52. Select **Aluminum Flashing** from the list, and press the **Insert Component** button.
53. Select the polyline you just created and press **Enter** twice to complete the command. You have now applied aluminum flashing component information to the polyline that will control the keynote.

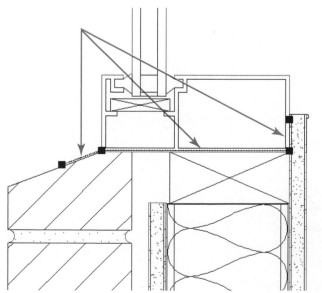

**Figure 18–13**

## Exercise 18-3: Keynoting

Keynoting is AutoCAD Architecture 2008's automated system for labeling detail components.

First you need to set your text style. This author prefers the Stylus BT text style because it looks like hand printing.

1. Select **Format > Text Style** from the **Main** menu to bring up the **Text Style** dialog box.
2. Select **Arch-Dim** from the **Style Name** drop-down list.
3. Select **Stylus BT** from the **Font Name** drop-down list, and close the **Text Style** dialog box.
4. Set the **Scale** drop-down list below the Drawing Editor to **1″= 1′-0″.**
5. Change to the **Document** tool palettes.
6. Select the **Reference Keynote** tool from the **Annotation** palette, **RMB,** and select **Properties** from the contextual menu that appears to bring up the **Tool Properties** dialog box.
7. Set the settings shown in Figure 18–14 and press the **OK** button.
8. Click on the storefront, select a point to start the keynote arrow, and then click a second point to place the keynote. The correct keynote for that particular detail component will appear on the drawing.
9. After placing the first keynote, press the space bar on your computer to repeat the keynote command for the next component.
10. Place all the keynotes (see Figure 18–15).

**Note:** By changing **Default text** to **?REFNOTE,** only the name of the material will be placed and not its CSI number.

**Note:** By setting **Mask background** to **No,** you will not see a gray background behind the keynote text.

**Tool Properties**

Refresh from:

Image:          Name:
09250.A1       Reference Keynote (Straight Leader)
               Description:
               Reference Keynote (Ke...        More Info

| BASIC | |
|---|---|
| **General** | |
| Layer key | ANNOBJ |
| Layer overrides | |
| Content type | MText |
| **Leader** | |
| Leader type | Straight |
| Leader dimen... | -- |
| Leader dimen... | -- |
| Limit points | -- |
| Maximum points | -- |
| **Text** | |
| Default text | ?REFNOTE |
| Angle | Force horizontal |
| Prompt for wi... | No |
| Always left ju... | -- |
| Left side atta... | -- |
| Right side att... | -- |
| Underline bot... | -- |
| Frame | -- |
| Mask backgro... | No |

Specifies an alternative layer key for the object

OK          Cancel          Help

**Figure 18–14**

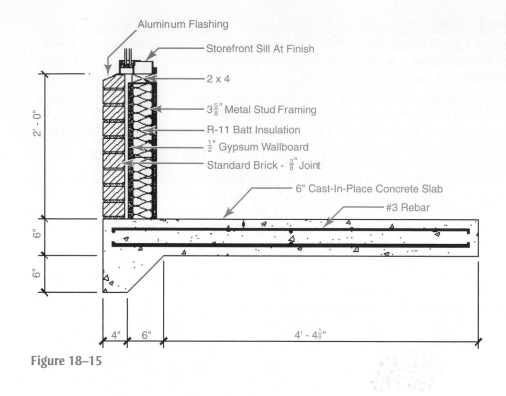

**Figure 18–15**

## THE COMPONENT EDITOR

A Component Editor has been added to enable you to create your own automated detail components. In order to automate these detail components you create a "recipe" of instructions using a worksheet called a *jig*. There are six jigs available. They are Stamp, Bookends, Linear Array, Surface, Surface Linetype, and Surface Top.

**Stamp Components jig** creates components that may need to be depicted multiple times at a particular orientation, such as nails or screws.

**Bookends Components jig** creates components, such as louvers and vents, that consist of a pattern repeated as a linear array but bounded by unique items at each end.

**Linear Array Components jig** creates components that consist of a pattern repeated as a linear array, such as shingles or corrugated sheet metal.

**Surface Components jig** creates components of a specific depth that have a hatch, such as base courses.

**Surface Linetype Components jig** creates components similar to surface components in that they have a specified depth and a rectangular boundary with user-specified start points and endpoints. Instead of a hatch-filled boundary, however, the surface linetype jig fills the boundary with a wide polyline of a specified linetype.

**Surface Top Components jig** creates components similar to surface components; however, they are components such as concrete topping, which is poured onto or bounded by another entity, which provides the bottom edge of the rectangle. Thus, the surface top jig draws only the top and side edges of the rectangle. Refer to the following table if you are adding a new detail component (or editing one that was created using the New Component option) and you want to define a recipe that uses a surface top jig to insert the component in the specified view.

Figure 18–16 shows a typical Detail Component jig, located in the **Parameters** tab of the component's properties.

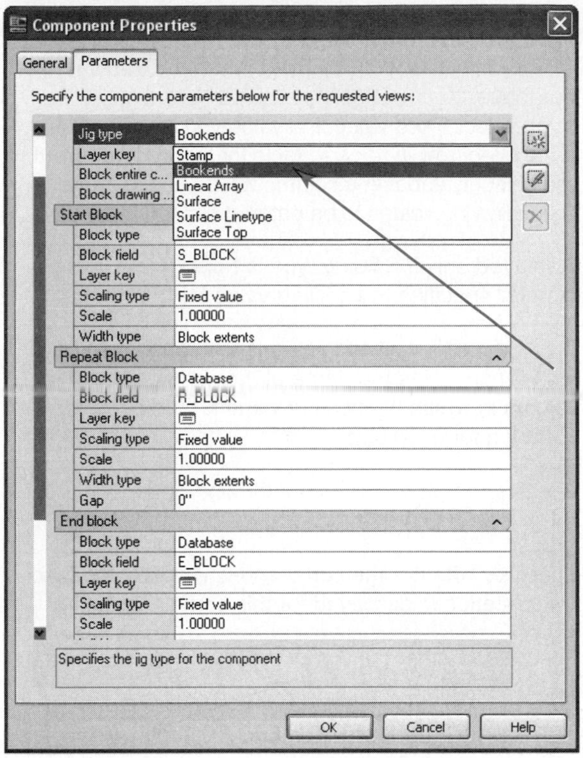

Figure 18–16

Listed below are the parameter names and descriptions for the six available Detail Component jigs.

## Parameters for Recipes Using Stamp Jigs

Stamp jigs are used to insert components that consist of a single block.

| Parameter Name | Description/Instructions |
|---|---|
| Layer key | Specifies the layer key for the layer to which the component will be assigned in the specified view. |
| Block drawing location | The name of the drawing file (a DWG, DWT, or DWS file) containing the blocks for the component table. |
| Block type | A drop-down list lets you specify either Fixed value or Database.<br>If you select Fixed value, the value you enter will apply to every row in the size table for this component. If you select Database, a column will be added to the table allowing values to be entered for individual sizes. |
| Block | Displayed only if Block type is Fixed value, this parameter specifies the block definition to be inserted for this component. |
| Block field | Displayed only if Block type is Database, this parameter specifies the name of the component table column in which the block to be inserted is specified for each size. |

| Scaling type | A drop-down list lets you specify either Fixed value or Database.<br>If you select Fixed value, the value you supply will apply to every row in the size table for this component. If you select Database, a column will be added to the table allowing values to be entered for individual sizes. |
|---|---|
| Scale | Displayed only if Scaling type is Fixed value, this parameter specifies the scaling value for the block. |
| Scale field | Displayed only if Scaling type is Database, this parameter specifies the name of the component table column in which the scaling value for the block is specified for each size. |
| Allow scaling | Specifies whether the command-line option for specifying scaling is displayed for this component. |
| Allow Rotation | Specifies whether the command-line option for specifying rotation is displayed for this component. |
| Allow X flip | Specifies whether the command-line option for flipping the block on its X axis is displayed for this component. |
| Allow Y flip | Specifies whether the command-line option for flipping the block on its Y axis is displayed for this component. |
| Allow Base point | Specifies whether the command-line option for specifying an alternate base point is displayed for this component. |

## Parameters for Recipes Using Bookends Jigs

Bookends jigs are used to insert components that consist of a pattern repeated as a linear array but bounded by unique items at each end. Thus, the recipe must define a start block, a repeat block, and an end block.

| Parameter Name | Description/Instructions |
|---|---|
| Layer key | Specifies the layer key for the layer to which the component will be assigned in the specified view. |
| Block entire component | Specifies whether the blocks comprising the component are inserted as a single block. |
| Block drawing location | Specifies the drawing file (a DWG, DWT, or DWS file) containing the blocks for the component table. |
| *Block type | Displayed only if Block type is Fixed value, this parameter specifies the block definition to be used for all sizes. |
| *Block field | Displayed only if Block type is Database, this parameter specifies the name of the component table column in which the block definition is specified for each size. |
| *Layer key | A drop-down list lets you specify either Fixed value or Database.<br>If you select Fixed value, the value you enter for the corresponding Scale parameter will apply to every row in this component's size table. If you select Database, a column (with the name specified for the corresponding |

| | |
|---|---|
| | Scale field parameter) will be added to the component table, allowing values to be entered for individual sizes. |
| *Scaling type | Specifies whether the command-line option for specifying scaling is displayed for this component. |
| *Scale | Displayed only if Scaling type is Fixed value, this parameter specifies the scaling value for the block. |
| *Scale field | Displayed only if Scaling type is Database, this parameter specifies the name of the component table column in which the scaling value for the block is specified for each size. |
| *Width type | A drop-down list lets you specify Fixed value, Database, or Block extents. If you select Fixed value, the value you enter for the corresponding Width parameter will apply to every row in the size table for this component. If you select Database, a column (with the name specified for the corresponding Width field parameter) will be added to the component table, allowing values to be entered for individual sizes. If you select Block extents, then block width is calculated dynamically as the block is inserted. |
| *Width | Displayed only if Width type is Fixed value, this parameter specifies the width for the block. |
| *Width field | Displayed only if Width type is Database, this parameter specifies the name of the component table column in which the block width is specified for each size. |
| Gap | Specifies the distance between repeat blocks. A negative value causes blocks to overlap. |
| Start prompt | Specifies the string to display for the start point prompt. |
| End prompt | Specifies the string to display for the endpoint prompt. |
| Block orientation | Specifies whether the block is oriented along the X axis or the Y axis. |
| Jig orientation | Specifies whether the jig is oriented along the X axis or the Y axis. |
| Allow X flip | Specifies whether the command-line option for flipping the block on its X axis is displayed for this component. |
| Allow Y flip | Specifies whether the command-line option for flipping the block on its Y axis is displayed for this component. |

## Parameters for Recipes Using Linear Array Jigs

Linear Array jigs are used to insert multiple copies of a block in a line along the X or Y axis.

| Parameter Name | Description/Instructions |
|---|---|
| Layer key | Specifies the layer key for the layer to which the component will be assigned in the specified view. |
| Block entire component | Specifies whether the blocks comprising the component are inserted as a single block. |

| | |
|---|---|
| Block drawing location | Specifies the drawing file (a DWG, DWT, or DWS file) containing the blocks for the component table. |
| Block type | A drop-down list lets you specify either Fixed value or Database. If you select Fixed value, the value you enter for the corresponding Block parameter will apply to every row in this component's size table. If you select Database, a column (with the name specified for the corresponding Block field parameter) will be added to the component table, allowing different block definitions to be specified for individual sizes. |
| Block | Displayed only if Block type is Fixed value, this parameter specifies the block definition to be used for all sizes. |
| Block field | Displayed only if Block type is Database, this parameter specifies the name of the component table column in which the block definition is specified for each size. |
| Scaling type | A drop-down list lets you specify either Fixed value or Database. If you select Fixed value, the value you enter for the corresponding Scale parameter will apply to every row in this component's size table. If you select Database, a column (with the name specified for the corresponding Scale field parameter) will be added to the component table, allowing values to be entered for individual sizes. |
| Scale | Displayed only if Scaling type is Fixed value, this parameter specifies the scaling value for the block for all sizes. |
| Scale field | Displayed only if Scaling type is Database, this parameter specifies the name of the component table column in which the scaling value for the block is specified for each size. |
| Width type | A drop-down list lets you specify Fixed value, Database, or Block extents. If you select Fixed value, the value you enter for the corresponding Width parameter will apply to every row in the size table for this component. If you select Database, a column (with the name specified for the corresponding Width field parameter) will be added to the component table, allowing values to be entered for individual sizes. If you select Block extents, then block width is calculated dynamically as the block is inserted. |
| Width | Displayed only if Width type is Fixed value, this parameter specifies the width for the block for all sizes. |
| Width field | Displayed only if Width type is Database, this parameter specifies the name of the component table column in which the block width is specified for each size. |
| Gap | Specifies the distance between repeat blocks. A negative value causes blocks to overlap. |
| Display count option | Specifies whether the command-line options for specifying a count are displayed. |
| Start prompt | Specifies the string to display for the start point prompt. |
| End prompt | Specifies the string to display for the endpoint prompt. |

| Count prompt | Displayed only if the Display count option parameter is Yes, this parameter specifies the command-line prompt to be displayed. |
| --- | --- |
| Block orientation | Specifies whether the block is oriented along the X axis or the Y axis. |
| Jig orientation | Specifies whether the jig is oriented along the X axis or the Y axis. |
| Allow X flip | Specifies whether the command-line option for flipping the block on its X axis is displayed for this component. |
| Allow Y flip | Specifies whether the command-line option for flipping the block on its Y axis is displayed for this component. |

## Parameters for Recipes Using Surface Jigs

Surface jigs are used to insert components that have a specified depth and a hatch-filled rectangular boundary with user-specified start points and endpoints.

| Parameter Name | Description/Instructions |
| --- | --- |
| Layer key | Specifies the layer key for the layer to which the component boundary will be assigned in the specified view. |
| Layer key (for hatching) | Specifies the layer key for the layer to which the component hatch infill will be assigned in the specified view. |
| Hatching type | A drop-down list lets you specify either Fixed value or Database.<br>If you select Fixed value, the value you enter for the corresponding Hatch alias parameter will apply to every row in this component's size table. If you select Database, a column (with the name specified for the corresponding Hatching parameter) will be added to the component table, allowing values to be entered for individual sizes. |
| Hatch alias | Displayed only if Hatching type is Fixed value, this parameter specifies the hatch alias (from the Hatches table for this database) for all sizes of the component. |
| Hatching | Displayed only if Hatching type is Database, this parameter specifies the name of the component table column in which the hatch is specified for each size. |
| Start prompt | Specifies the string to display for the start point prompt. |
| End prompt | Specifies the string to display for the endpoint prompt. |
| Allow X flip | Specifies whether the command-line option for flipping the block on its X axis is displayed for this component. |
| Allow Y flip | Specifies whether the command-line option for flipping the block on its Y axis is displayed for this component. |

## Parameters for Recipes Using Surface Linetype Jigs

Surface Linetype jigs are similar to Surface jigs in that they are used to insert components that have a specified depth and a rectangular boundary with user-specified start points and endpoints. Instead of a hatch-filled boundary, however, the Surface Linetype jig fills the boundary with a wide polyline of a specified linetype.

| Parameter Name | Description/Instructions |
| --- | --- |
| Layer key | Specifies the layer key for the layer to which the component boundary will be assigned in the specified view. |
| Linetype/Layer key | Specifies the layer key for the layer to which the component infill will be assigned in the specified view. |
| Linetype type | A drop-down list lets you specify either Fixed value or Database. If you select Fixed value, the value you enter for the corresponding Linetype parameter will apply to every row in this component's size table. If you select Database, a column (with the name specified for the corresponding Linetype field parameter) will be added to the component table, allowing values to be entered for individual sizes. |
| Linetype | Displayed only if Linetype type is Fixed value, this parameter specifies the linetype alias for all sizes of the component. |
| Linetype field | Displayed only if Linetype type is Database, this parameter specifies the name of the component table column in which the linetype is specified for each size. |
| Start prompt | Specifies the string to display for the start point prompt. |
| End prompt | Specifies the string to display for the endpoint prompt. |
| Allow X flip | Specifies whether the command-line option for flipping the block on its X axis is displayed for this component. |
| Allow Y flip | Specifies whether the command-line option for flipping the block on its Y axis is displayed for this component. |

## Parameters for Recipes Using Surface Top Jigs

Surface Top jigs are similar to Surface jigs in that they are used to insert components with a specified depth and a hatch-filled rectangular boundary. However, the Surface Top jig is designed for components such as concrete topping that is poured onto or bounded by another entity, which provides the bottom edge of the rectangle. Thus, the Surface Top jig draws only the top and side edges of the rectangle. Refer to the following table if you are adding a new detail component (or editing one that was created using the New Component option) and you want to define a recipe that uses a Surface Top jig to insert the component in the specified view.

| Parameter Name | Description/Instructions |
| --- | --- |
| Layer key | Specifies the layer key for the layer to which the component boundary will be assigned in the specified view. |
| Layer key (for hatching) | Specifies the layer key for the layer to which the component hatch infill will be assigned in the specified view. |

| Hatching type | A drop-down list lets you specify either Fixed value or Database. If you select Fixed value, the value you enter for the corresponding Hatch alias parameter will apply to every row in this component's size table. If you select Database, a column (with the name specified for the corresponding Hatching parameter) will be added to the component table, allowing values to be entered for individual sizes. |
|---|---|
| Hatch alias | Displayed only if Hatching type is Fixed value, this parameter specifies the hatch alias (from the Hatches table for this database) for all sizes of the component |
| Hatching | Displayed only if Hatching type is Database, this parameter specifies the name of the component table column in which the hatch is specified for each size. |
| Start prompt | Specifies the string to display for the start point prompt. |
| End prompt | Specifies the string to display for the endpoint prompt. |
| Allow X flip | Specifies whether the command-line option for flipping the block on its X axis is displayed for this component. |
| Allow Y flip | Specifies whether the command-line option for flipping the block on its Y axis is displayed for this component. |

## Exercise 18-4: Creating a New Custom Detail Component Block

1. Start a new drawing using the AEC Model (Imperial Stb) template.
2. Change to the **Top View.**
3. Select the line icon from the **Draw** menu, and create the detail of the siding shown (Figure 18–17) (do not include dimensions).
4. Select **Format > Blocks > Block Definition** from the **Main** menu to bring up the **Block Definition** dialog box.

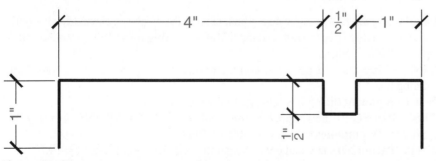

**Figure 18–17**

5. In the **Block Definition** dialog box, enter **TEST** in the **Name** field, and press the **Select objects** icon to return to the Drawing Editor.
6. In the Drawing Editor, select the detail you just drew, and press the **Enter** key on the keyboard to return to the **Block Definition** dialog box.
7. In the **Block Definition** dialog box, select the **Convert to block** radio button, and press the **Pick point** icon to return to the Drawing Editor.
8. In the Drawing Editor, select the lower left corner of the detail you drew to return to the **Block Definition** dialog box.
9. In the **Block Definition** dialog box, press the **OK** button to complete the command.
10. Save the drawing as **SIDING,** and close the drawing.

**Exercise 18-5:** Editing the Detail Component Database and Creating a Recipe Using the Linear Array Jig

1. Start a new drawing using the AEC Model (Imperial Stb) template.
2. Change to the **Top View.**
3. Select the **Detail Component Manager** icon from the **Main** menu to bring up the **Detail Component Manager** dialog box.
4. In the **Detail Component Manager** dialog box, select the **Edit Database** icon (see Figure 18–18).

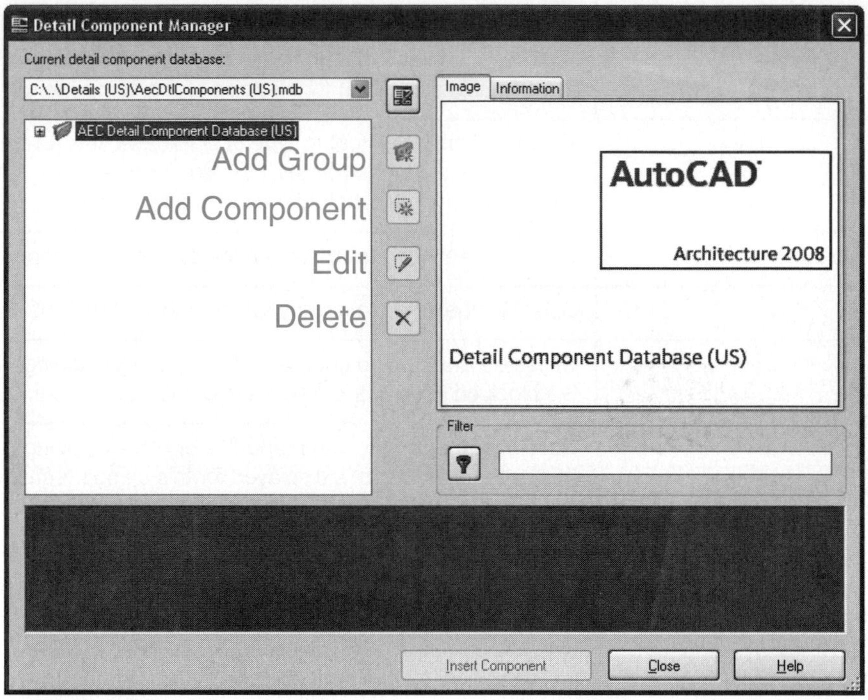

Figure 18–18

This will now light up the four lower icons.

5. In the **Detail Component Manager** dialog box, expand the database, expand **Division 07 - Thermal and Moisture protection,** expand **07400 - Roofing and Siding Panels,** and finally expand **07460 - Siding.**
6. With **07460 - Siding** selected, press the **Add Component** icon to bring up the **New Component** dialog box.
7. In the **New Component** dialog box, change to the **General** tab.
8. Enter **TEST SIDING** in the **Display Name** field; enter **TEST SIDING** in the **Table Name,** and **TESTComponent.xml** in the **Recipe** field.
9. Change to the **Parameters** tab, and enter the parameters shown in Figure 18–19.

Refer to the description of the **Parameters for Recipes Using Linear Array Jigs** described at the beginning of this section. Notice that the Jig type was set to **Linear Array,** the **Block drawing** is the drawing you created, and **TEST** is the name of the block you created in that drawing.

10. After you have entered the instructions to create the "recipe" in the Jig, press the **OK** button to close the **New Component** dialog box, and return to the **Detail Component Manager.**
11. At the bottom of the **Detail Component Manager,** enter **SIDING** in the **Description** column.
12. Press the **Close** button to close the **Detail Component Manager,** and return to the Drawing Editor.

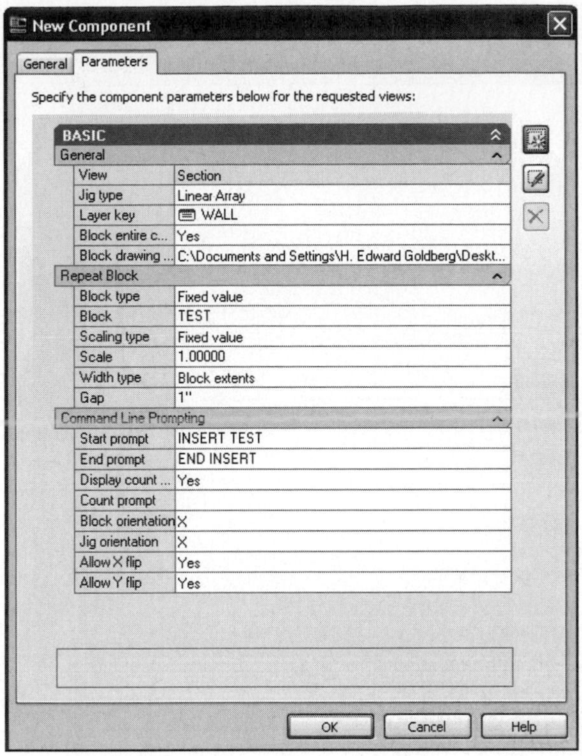

Figure 18–19

## Exercise 18-6: Testing the New Detail Component

1. Start a new drawing using the AEC Model (Imperial Stb) template.
2. Change to the **Top View.**
3. Select the **Detail Component Manager** icon from the **Main** menu to bring up the **Detail Component Manager** dialog box.
4. In the **Detail Component Manager,** expand the database, and select the **TEST SIDING** component you just created.
5. At the bottom of the **Detail Component Manager,** select the field to the left of **SIDING** in the **Description** column.
6. Select the **Insert Component** button at the bottom of the **Detail Component Manager** to return to the Drawing Editor.
7. With **Ortho** (on), click to start to place the **SIDING** component.
8. Enter **C** (Count) in the **Command line,** and press **Enter** on your keyboard.
9. Enter **6** in the **Command line,** and press **Enter** on your keyboard.
10. Click the mouse again to place the siding, and then press the **Esc** key to end the command.

You will have now placed six arrayed copies of your new SIDING detail component (see Figure 18–20).

Creating Detail Components is not difficult, but it does take some practice and patience. Remember to create the blocks first, and be sure to read the descriptions for all the different instructions in the Jigs.

Save this drawing.

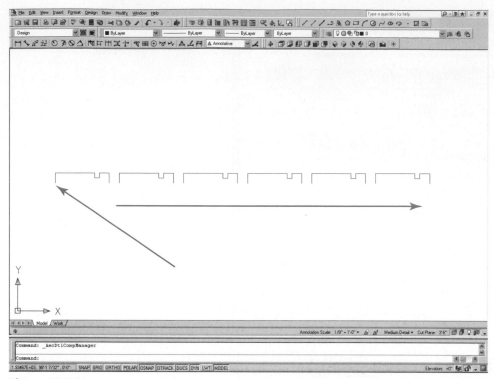

**Figure 18–20**

## THE KEYNOTE EDITOR

**Exercise 18-7:** Creating a New Keynote and Linking It to a Detail Component

1. Use the drawing from the previous exercise that contains the siding.
2. Change to the **Top View.**
3. Select **CAD Manager > Keynote Editor** from the **Main** menu to bring up the **Keynote Editor** dialog box.
4. In the **Keynote Editor,** browse for **C:\Documents and Settings\All Users\Application Data\Autodesk\ACD-A 2008\enu\Details\Details (US) \AecKeynotes (US).mdb** in the **Keynote Database** drop-down list at the top of the dialog box.
5. In the **Keynote Editor** dialog box, expand **Division 07 - Thermal and Moisture protection,** expand **07400 - Roofing and Siding Panels,** and finally expand **07460 - Siding.**
6. **RMB** on **07460 - Siding,** and select **New Keynote** from the contextual menu that appears to bring up the **Add Keynote** dialog box.
7. In the **Add Keynote** dialog box, enter **07460.A10** (for the Key) and **1″ Corrugated Steel 24 Ga** (for the Note), and press the **OK** button to return to the **Keynote Editor.**
8. In the **Keynote Editor,** press the **Save** button, and then press the **Close** button to return to the Drawing Editor.
9. Select the **Detail Component Manager** icon from the **Main** menu to bring up the **Detail Component Manager** dialog box.
10. In the **Detail Component Manager** dialog box, select the **Edit Database** icon.
11. Expand the database until you get to the **TEST SIDING** detail component that you created.
12. Double-click on **TEST SIDING** to bring up the **Component Properties** dialog box.

> **Note:**
> The Keynote Editor is located under the **CAD Manager** drop-down list. If it is not loaded, please refer to **Loading the CAD Manager** in the second exercise of Section 25.

13. In the **Component Properties** dialog box, press the **Select Keynote** button to bring up the **Select Keynote** dialog box.
14. In the **Select Keynote** dialog box, expand the keynotes until you get to the new keynote you just created.
15. Select the **07460.A10 - 1″ Corrugated Steel 24 Ga** keynote, and press the **OK** button to return to the **Component Properties** dialog box.
16. In the **Component Properties** dialog box, press the **OK** button to return to the **Detail Component Manager** dialog box.
17. In the **Detail Component Manager** dialog box, press the **Close** button to return to the Drawing Editor.

## Testing the New Keynote

18. Click the scale at the bottom right of the Drawing Editor, and select **11/2″ = 1′-0″** (see Figure 18–21).

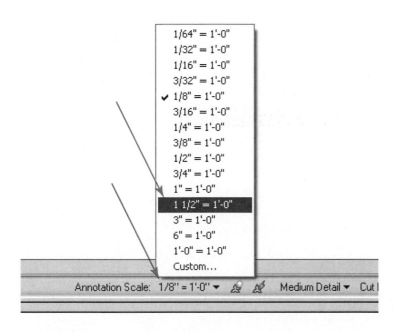

**Figure 18–21**

19. Select the **Reference Keynote (Straight leader)** tool from the **Annotation** tool palette.
20. Select one of the Siding components that you previously placed, click again on that component, move your cursor up in the direction of 90 degrees, and click again; then move your cursor in the 0 degree direction and click.
21. Press the **Enter** key to complete the tool and place the keynote (see Figure 18–22).

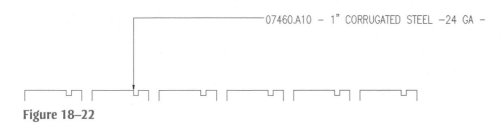

**Figure 18–22**

# Property Set Definitions and Property Sets

# 19

## Section Objectives

- Learn how to create a property set definition.
- Learn how to create and use an automatic property.
- Learn how to create and use a manual property.
- Learn how to create and use a formula property definition.
- Learn how to create and use the property data format.
- Add an **Anchor** property set definition.

AutoCAD Architecture 2008 uses property set definitions and property sets as means of codifying information concerning objects in the virtual building model.

# PROPERTY SET DEFINITION

A property set definition specifies the characteristics of a group of properties that can be tracked with an object. Each property has a name, description, data type, data format, and default value.

## Property Sets and Property Data

A property set is an object created from a property set definition. It contains a user-definable group of related object properties. When you attach a property set to an object or style, the property set becomes the container for the property data associated with the object. Property Data is similar to Block Attributes in AutoCAD.

## Automatic Properties

Automatic properties are built into objects and styles when they are created. Examples are width, length, height, and so on. They consist primarily of the physical properties of an object.

## Manual Properties

Manual properties are properties that are entered manually, such as manufacturer, price, and so on.

### Exercise 19-1: Adding the Automatic Properties

1. Start a new drawing using the AEC Model (Imperial Stb) template.
2. Select **Format > Style Manager** from the **Main** menu to bring up the **Style Manager.**
3. Expand the **Documentation Objects** folder.
4. **RMB** on **Property Set Definition,** to create a **New Style Property Set Definition.**
5. Name the new style **WALLPROPERTYSETDEFINITION** (see Figure 19–1).

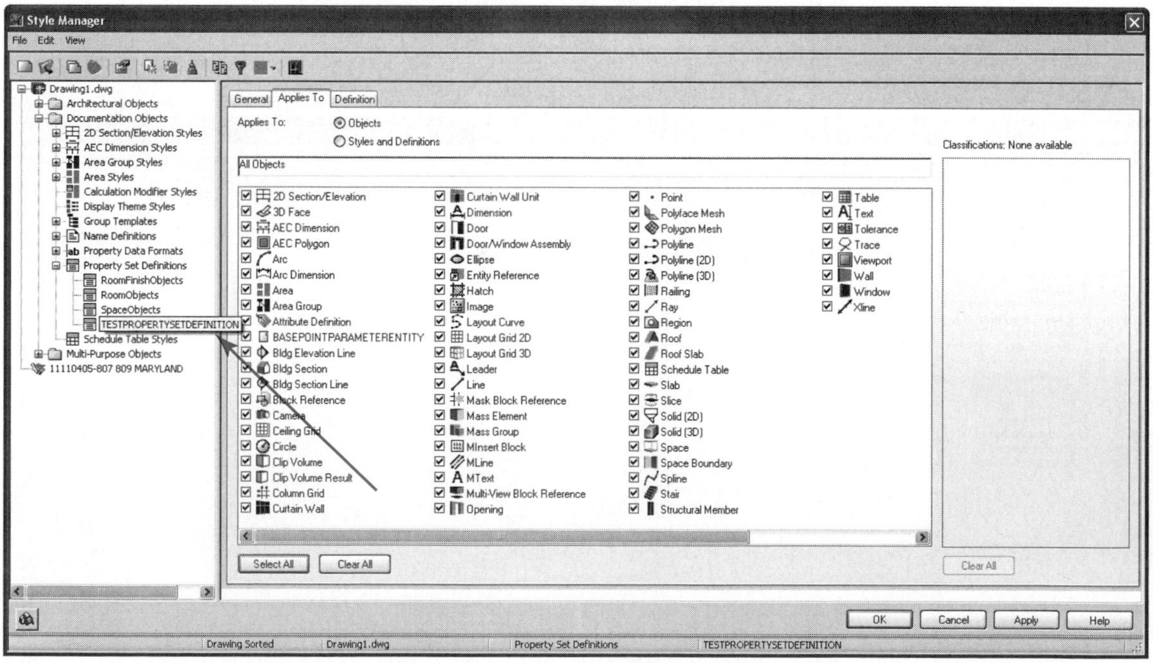

Figure 19–1

6. Select the **Applies To** tab.
7. Select the **Objects** radio button and press the **Select All** button. (Use this procedure to list the default auto properties only.)
8. Change to the **Definition** tab.
9. Select the **Add Automatic Property Definition** icon (see Figure 19–2).

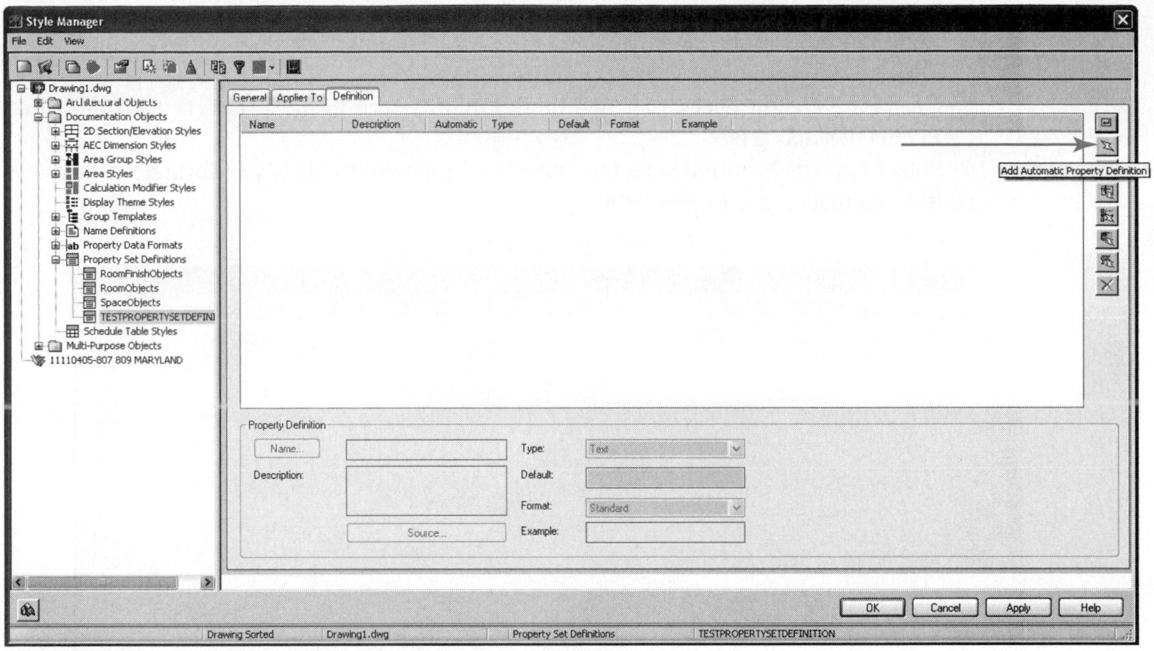

Figure 19–2

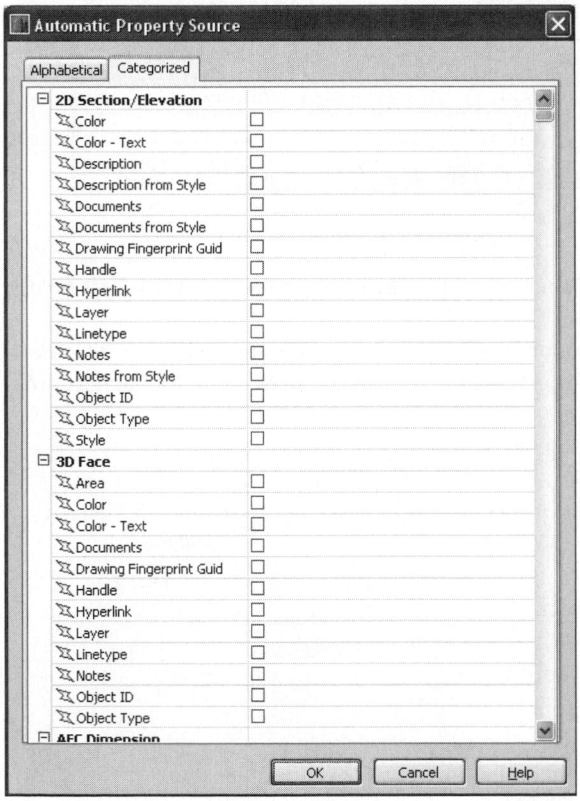

Figure 19–3

Because you have selected all the objects in the **Applies To** tab, you will get a warning message telling you that it will take some time to compile the list of data sources. Press the **Yes** button to proceed.

10. When the **Automatic Property Source** dialog appears, scroll through it to see all the properties available for all the objects (see Figure 19–3).
11. Press **Cancel** to return to the **Property Set Definition Properties** dialog box.
12. Change back to the **Applies To** tab.

13. Press the **Clear All** button, and then check the **Wall** check box.
14. Return to the **Definition** tab and press the **Add Automatic Property Definition** icon to bring up the **Automatic Property Source** dialog box.
15. Check the **Height** check box, and press **OK** to return to the **Property Set Definition Properties** dialog box.
16. Select **Length-Nominal** from the **Format** drop-down list. This will format the height in feet and inches (see Figure 19–4).

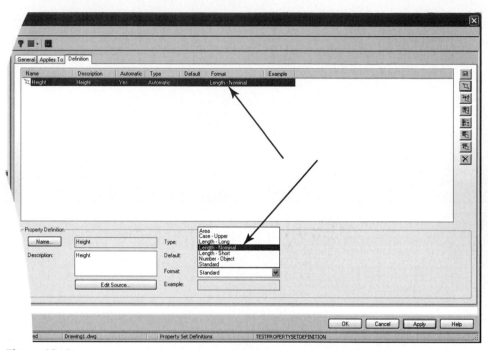

**Figure 19–4**

17. Repeat Steps 15–16, but this time hold down the **Shift** key and select **Area-Left Gross, Area-Left Net, Length,** and **Object Type.**
18. In the **Property Set Definition Properties** dialog box, set **Area-Left Gross** to **Standard** from the **Format** drop-down list. For **Area-Left Net,** select **Area** from the **Format** drop-down list.
19. In the **Property Set Definition Properties,** for **Length,** select **Length-Nominal** from the **Format** drop-down list. This will format the length in feet and inches. Press the **OK** button to return to the Drawing Editor.
20. In the Drawing Editor place a 15′-long wall (the style doesn't matter).
21. Double-click the wall you placed to open the **Properties** palette.
22. Change to the **Extended Data** tab.
23. Select the **Add Property Sets** icon to bring up the **Add Property Sets** dialog box (see Figure 19–5).
24. Press the **Select All** button.
25. Double-click the wall again to open the **Properties** palette again.
26. Again change to the **Extended Data** tab and notice that the height, length, and gross and net areas as well as object type are shown.

**Note:**
We are going to use the **Area-Left Gross** for a formula. If you use any property in a formula you must set its **Format** to **Standard.**

You will now be able to read any changes in the length, height, and gross and net areas of that wall in the **Extended Data** tab of the **Properties** palette (see Figure 19–6).

You can add as many automatic properties as you wish, and they will all appear in the **Properties** palette. Later you will be able to pull this data into a schedule object.

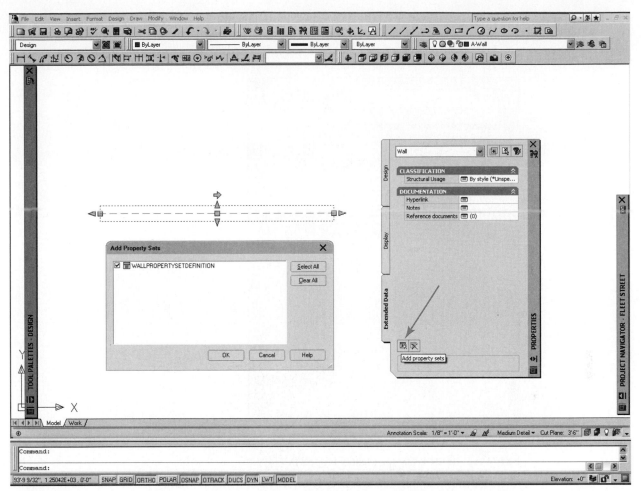

**Figure 19–5**

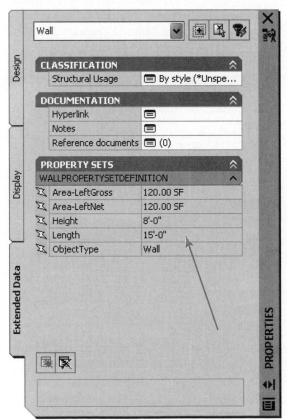

**Figure 19–6**

27. Select the wall, **RMB,** and insert a door in the wall.
28. Double-click on the wall to open the **Properties** palette. Notice that the **Area-LeftNet** field shows how much area has been subtracted by the door (see Figure 19–7).

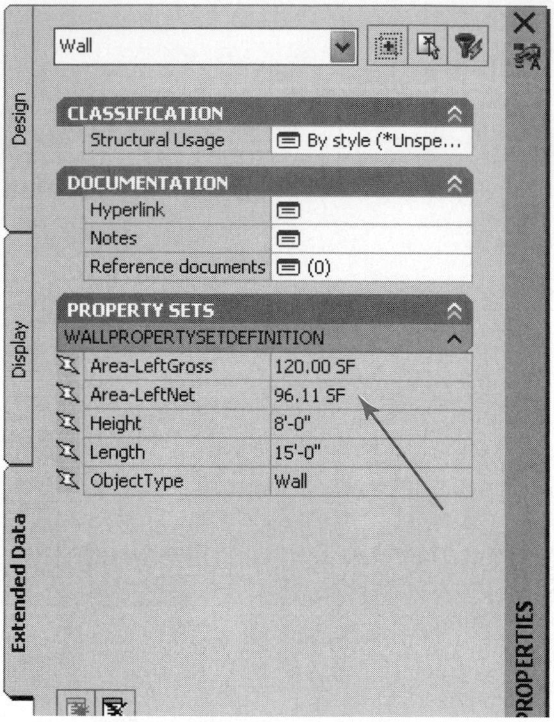

Figure 19–7

## Exercise 19-2: Using the Manual Properties

1. Using the previous exercise, select **Format > Style Manager** from the **Main** menu to bring up the **Style Manager.**
2. Expand the **Documentation Objects** folder, and click on **WALLPROPERTYSETDEF-INITION.**
3. Select the **Add Manual Property Definition** icon to bring up the **New Property** dialog box (see Figure 19–8).

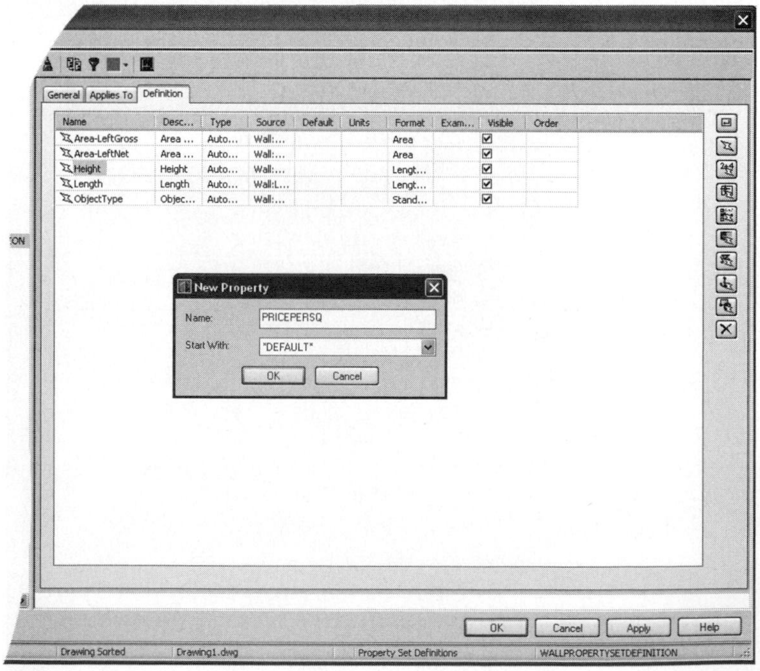

Figure 19–8

4. Enter **PRICEPERSQ** in the **Name** field, and press **OK** to return to the **Property Set Definition Properties** dialog box.
5. Set PRICEPERSQ's **Type** to **Real.**
6. Double-click the wall you placed in the previous exercise to open the **Properties** palette.
7. Change to the **Extended Data** tab.
8. You will now see a field called **PRICEPERSQ;** enter **2.5** in the field (see Figure 19–9).

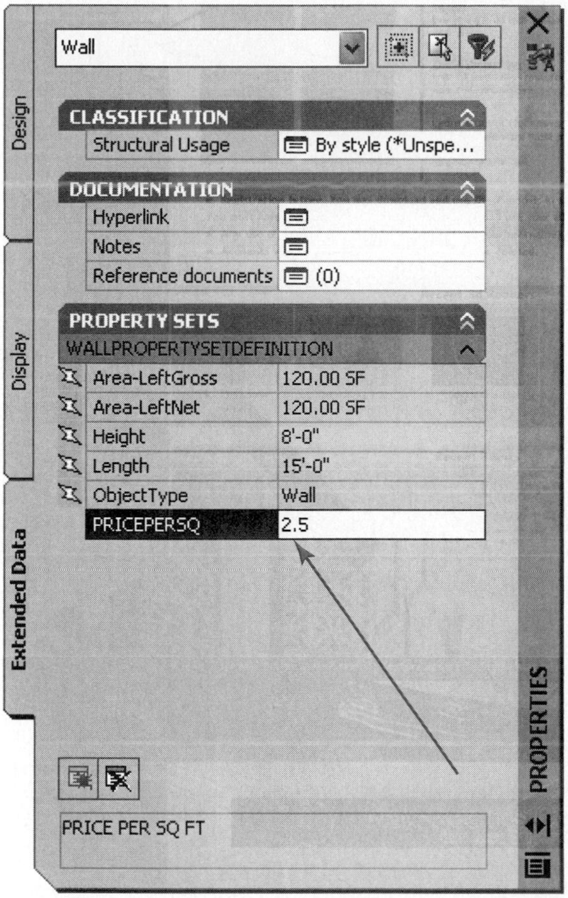

Figure 19–9

## Exercise 19-3: Using the Formula Property Definitions

1. Using the previous exercise, select **Format > Style Manager** from the **Main** menu to bring up the **Style Manager.**
2. Expand the **Documentation Objects** folder, and click on **WALLPROPERTYSETDEFINITION** to again bring up the **Property Set Definition Properties** dialog box.
3. Select the **Add Formula Property Definition** icon to bring up the **Formula Property Definition** dialog box (see Figure 19–10).
4. Enter **WALLCOST** in the **Name** field.
5. Double-click **Area-LeftGross** under **Insert Property Definitions;** then open **Operators > Arithmetic >** under **Insert VBScript** code and double-click the **x** (times) above. Finally, double-click **PRICEPERSQ** under **Insert Property Definitions.**

You have now created a formula that multiplies the area of the wall by the entered price per square foot (see Figure 19–11).

6. Press the **OK** buttons to close the dialog boxes.
7. Double-click on the wall in the Drawing Editor to open the **Properties** palette; notice that **WALLCOST** has been calculated, but it is not in dollars (see Figure 19–12).

To format **WALLCOST** in dollars, you will need a new property data format.

8. In the **Style Manager,** expand the **Documentation Objects** folder, **RMB** on **Property Data Formats,** and select **New** from the contextual menu that appears.

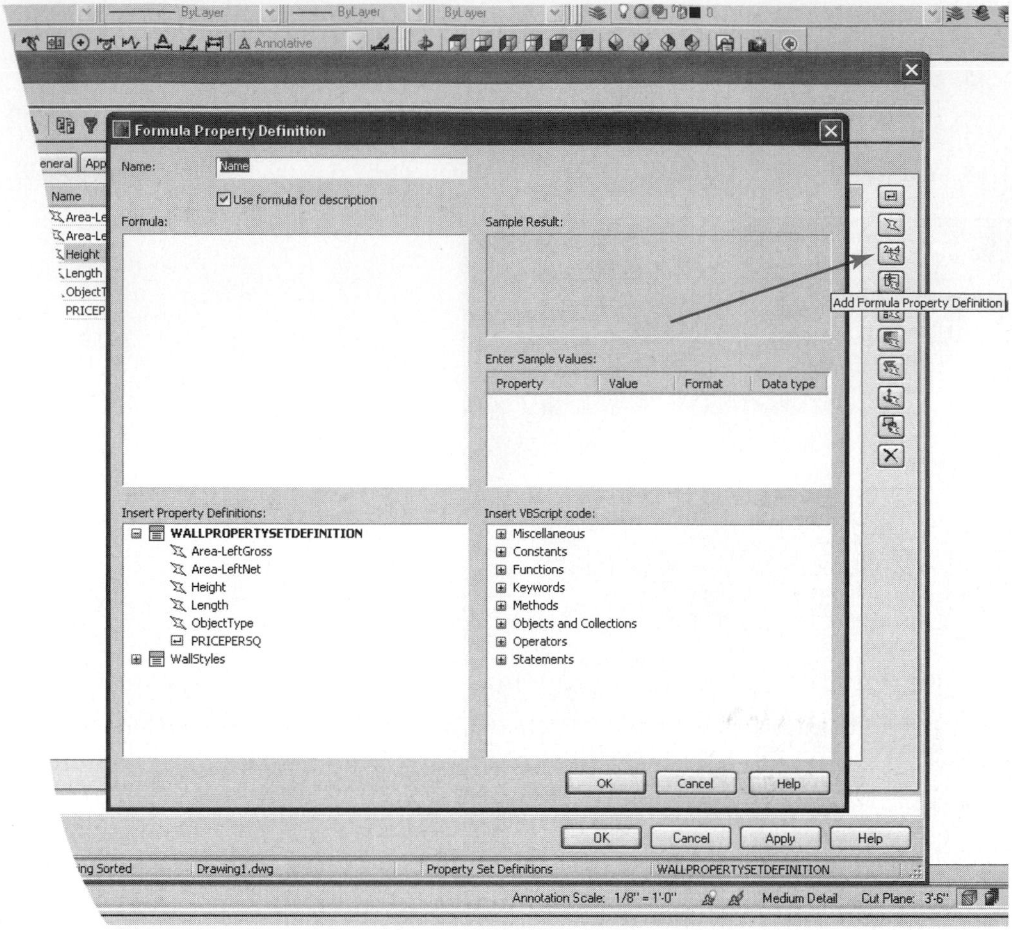


Figure 19–10

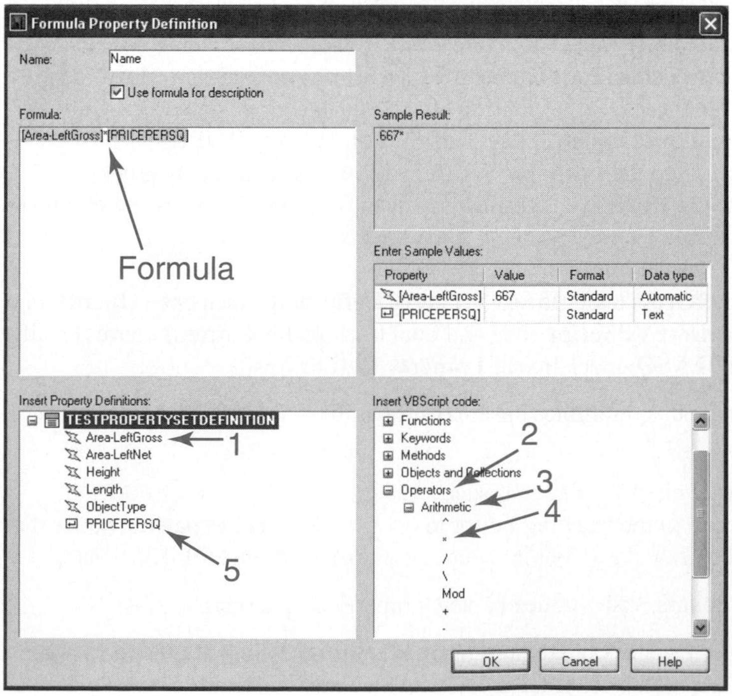


Figure 19–11

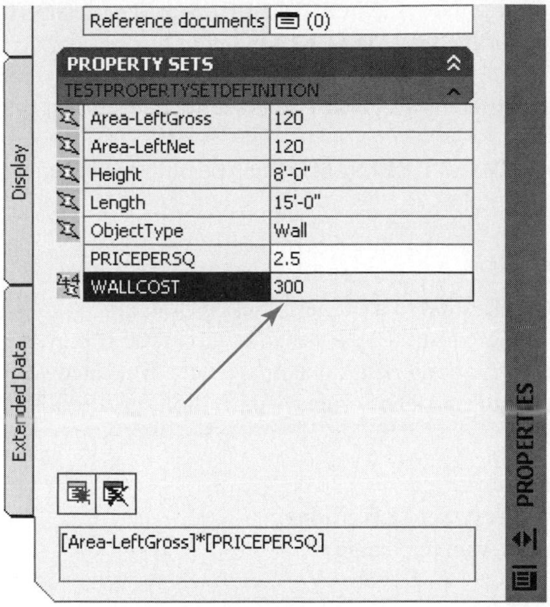

Figure 19–12

9. Name the new Property Data Format style **DOLLARS.**
10. Double-click on **DOLLARS** to bring up the **Property Data Format Properties** dialog box.
11. Change to the **Formatting** tab.
12. Enter **$** in the **Prefix** field, **Decimal** in **Unit Format,** and **0.00** in **Precision** (see Figure 19–13).
13. Press **OK** to return to the **Style Manager.**
14. Open up **WALLPROPERTYSETDEFINITION** again, and select **DOLLARS** (that will now be available) from the **Format** drop-down list for **WALLCOST.**
15. Now press the **OK** buttons to close all the dialog boxes and return to the Drawing Editor.
16. Again double-click on the wall to open the **Properties** palette.
17. Again change to the **Extended Data** tab.

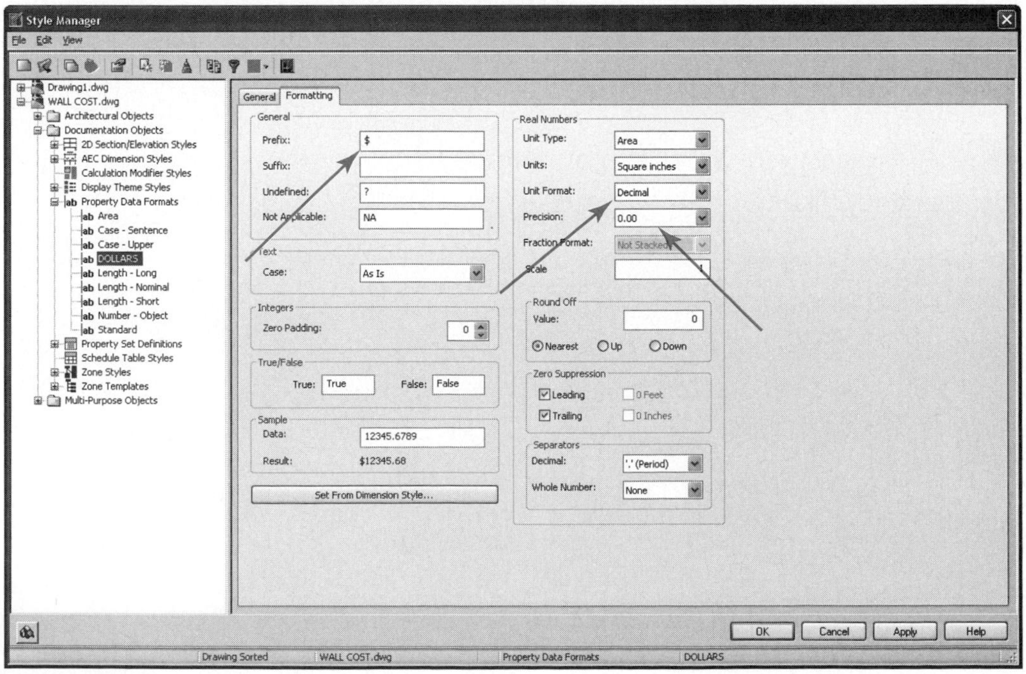

Figure 19–13

**WALLCOST** will now read **$300.00.** If you change the value in **PRICEPERSQ, WALLCOST** will change. If you change the length or height of the wall, **WALLCOST** will also reflect that change.

The best way to learn is to practice. Add different properties, and see their results in the **Properties** palette.

Save this drawing file as **WALLPROPERTYSETDEFINITION** to use with the schedule and schedule tags exercises in the following section.

### Exercise 19-4: Adding an Anchor Property Definition

Use this procedure to add an **Anchor** property definition to a Property Set Definition.

Anchor property definitions allow data that are shared by objects to be viewed if they are anchored to each other. For example, an anchor property of a door in a 2-hour fire-rated wall could display the 2-hour fire-rating of the wall with an anchor property definition specified. The information displayed cannot be edited directly.

1. On the **Format** menu, click **Style Manager.**
2. Expand **Documentation Objects > Property Set Definitions.**
3. Select the Property set definition that you want to change.
4. Click the **Definition** tab.
5. Click **OK.**
6. Enter a name for the **Anchor** property.
7. If you do not want to use the property name for the description, clear **Use property name for description.**
8. Select the property definitions to be associated with this property set.
9. Click **OK.**

# Schedules and Schedule Tags

# 20

## Section Objectives

- Create schedule tags and a **Schedules** tool palette.
- Learn how to create a schedule.
- Learn how to test a schedule.
- Learn how to modify a schedule.
- Learn how to schedule across drawings.
- Know how to place door and window tags.
- Learn how to place schedules.
- Use schedules to locate objects.
- Create and use custom schedules.
- Learn how to use the **Define Schedule Tag routine.**
- Know how to use the **Tool Catalog Generator.**

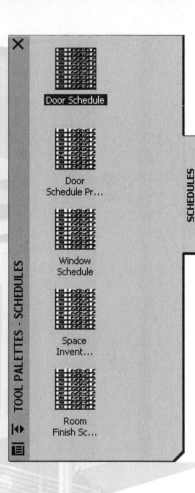

Drawing created in this section: **TESTWALLSCHEDULE.dwg**

Reference drawing: **WALLPROPERTYSETDEFINITION.dwg**

---

**Exercise 20-1:** Creating a Schedules Tool Palette and Copying Tools from the Content Browser

1. Create a new tool palette and name it **Schedules.**
2. Select the **Content Browser** icon from the **Main** toolbar to launch the **Content Browser.**
3. In the **Documentation Tool Catalog - Imperial,** locate the **Schedule Tables** folder.
4. Drag the **Door** and **Window** schedules and tags into the new tool palette you created.
5. In the **Autodesk Architectural Desktop Documentation Tool Catalog - Imperial,** locate the **Schedule Tags** folders.
6. Drag the **Door Tag** and **Window Tag** tags into the new tool palette you created.
7. Click and hold on the tab of your new tool palette and drag a copy to **My Tool Catalog** in the Content Browser.

This procedure backs up your custom tool palette.

Schedules work in concert with property set definitions, property data formats, and schedule tags.

**Exercise 20-2:** Creating a Wall Schedule

In order to create a new schedule, you will first have to create a Property Set Definition that can be tracked by a schedule. In Section 19, you created a property set definition called **WALL-PROPERTYSETDEFINITION.** For these exercises you will use that property set definition as a basis for your new schedule.

1. Start a new file based on the AEC Model (Imperial Stb) template.
2. Save the file as **TESTWALLSCHEDULE.**dwg (the finished schedule should be stored in a template or a **Standards** drawing file).
3. Select **Format > Style Manager** from the **Main** menu to bring up the **Style Manager.**
4. In the **Style Manager,** select the **Open Drawing** icon, and browse and open the **WALLPROPERTYSETDEFINITION** drawing you created in Section 19.

This will not open the drawing in the Drawing Editor, but rather it brings it into the Style Manager. To close this drawing, **RMB** on the drawing name in the left window, and select **Close** from the contextual menu that appears.

5. Expand the **Documentation Objects** folder of the **WALLPROPERTYSETDEFINI-TION.**dwg.
6. Expand the **Property Set Definitions** folder.
7. Drag **WALLPROPERTYSET** into the **Documentation Objects** folder of the **TEST-WALLSCHEDULE.**dwg.
8. Expand the **Property Data Formats** folder.
9. Drag **DOLLARS** into the **Property Data Formats** folder of the **TESTWALL-SCHEDULE.**dwg
10. Expand the **Documentation Objects** folder of the **TESTWALLSCHEDULE.**dwg.
11. **RMB** on **Schedule Table Styles,** and select **New** from the contextual menu that appears.
12. Name the new style **TESTWALLSCHEDULE.**
13. In the right screen of **TESTWALLSCHEDULE,** change to the **Applies To** tab.
14. Press the **Clear All** button, and then check the **Wall** check box (see Figure 20–1).

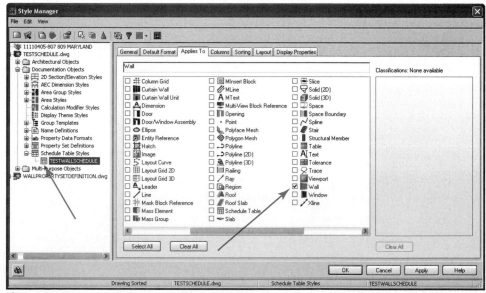

**Figure 20–1**

15. Change to the **Columns** tab.
16. Press the **Add Column** button to bring up the **Add Column** dialog box.
17. Change to the **Categorized** tab, and notice that it contains the properties that you set in the exercise on property set definitions in the previous section.
18. Select **WALLCOST,** enter **Cost of Walls** in the **Heading** field, select **DOLLARS** from the **Data Format** drop-down list, check the **Total** check box, and press **OK** (see Figure 20–2).

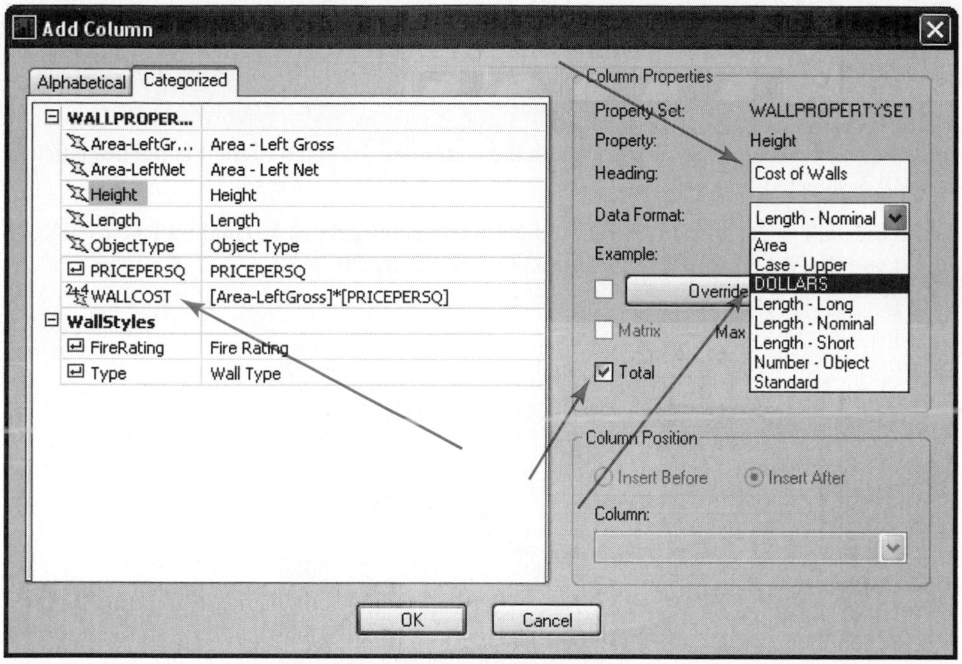

**Figure 20–2**

19. You will now return to the **Columns** tab of **TESTWALLSCHEDULE.**
20. In the **Columns** tab, check the **Include Quantity Column** check box to add a **Quantity** column (see Figure 20–3).

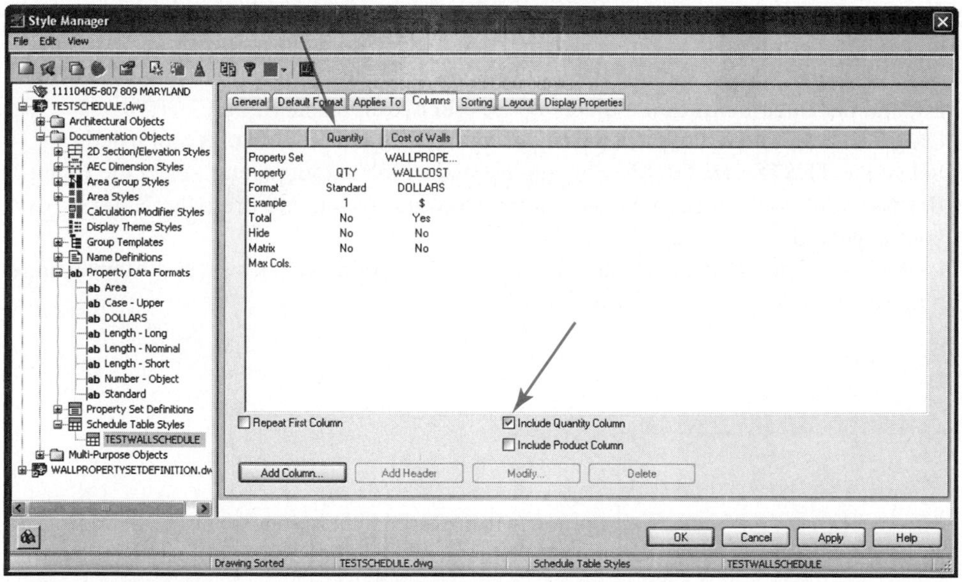

**Figure 20–3**

21. Press **OK,** and close all the dialog boxes to return to the Drawing Editor. Save this file as **TESTWALLSCHEDULE.**dwg.

## Exercise 20-3: Testing the New Schedule

1. Open the **TESTWALLSCHEDULE.**dwg from the previous exercise, select the **Brick-4 Brick-4 wall** from the **Walls** tool palette, and place a 15'-long wall 10' high in the Drawing Editor.
2. Double-click on the wall to open the **Properties** palette.
3. Change to the **Extended Data** tab.

4. Press the **Add Property Sets** icon at the lower left of the **Extended Data** tab, make sure the **WALLPROPERTYSETDEFINITION** check box is checked (see Section 19 for directions on doing this operation), and press the **OK** button to return to the Drawing Editor.

The property set information will now appear in the **Extended Data** tab of the **Properties** palette when the wall is selected.

5. With the wall selected, in the **Extended Data** tab, enter **2.5** ($2.50) in the **PRICEPERSQ** field and the **WALLCOST** will read **$375** (see Figure 20–4).

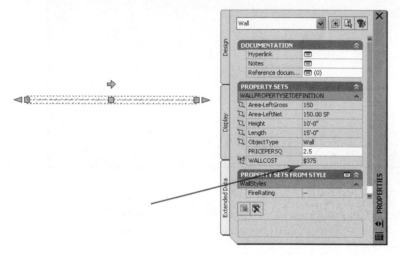

**Figure 20–4**

6. Open the **Schedules** tool palette you created in Exercise 20-1, and set **Auto-hide** to keep the palette open.
7. Select **Format > Style Manager** from the **Main** menu to bring up the **Style Manager.**
8. Expand the **Documentation Objects** folder > **Schedule Table Styles.**
9. Drag **TESTSCHEDULE** from the **Style Manager** into the **Schedules** tool palette.
10. Select the **TESTSCHEDULE** tool you just placed in the tool palette, select the **Brick-4 Brick-4 wall** you placed previously in the Drawing Editor, and press the **Enter** key on your keyboard.
11. In the **Top View,** click a placement point below the wall, and then press **Enter** again to place the schedule (see Figure 20–5).

15'–0"

| Schedule Table | |
|---|---|
| Quantity | Cost of Walls |
| 1 | $375 |
| | $375 |

**Figure 20–5**

Notice the size of the type in the schedule in relation to the size of the wall. This is because the default **Scale** button of the model layout is 1/8" = 1'-0", and **Plot Size** is 1/8". Refer to **Format > Drawing Setup > Scale** tab.

12. Delete the schedule you just placed, change the **Scale** at the bottom of the Drawing Editor to **1/4" = 1'-0",** and insert **TESTSCHEDULE** again.

Notice the size of the type in the schedule in relation to the size of the wall. This is because the scale of the model layout is now 1/4" = 1'-0" (see Figure 20–6).

**Figure 20–6**

13. Erase the first schedule you placed, leaving only the 1/4"-scale schedule.
14. Double-click the schedule to open the **Properties** palette.
15. In the **Design** tab, under **Update automatically,** select **Yes.** Under **Add new objects automatically,** also select **Yes.** Press the **Enter** key on your keyboard to ensure that the settings are set (see Figure 20–7).

**Note:**
Although Auto Updating is functional, projects with a large quantity of objects may experience a reduction in performance.

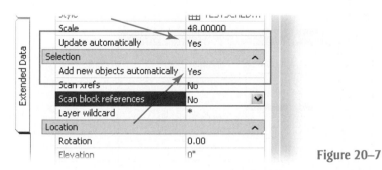

**Figure 20–7**

The schedule will now reflect automatically any additional walls having the same property set definition.

16. Press the **Esc** key to clear any selections in the Drawing Editor.
17. Select the wall, **RMB,** and select **Add Selected** from the contextual menu that appears.

Add more walls; the schedule automatically updates (see Figure 20–8). Save this file.

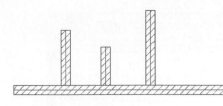

| Schedule Table | |
|---|---|
| Quantity | Cost of Walls |
| 1 | $375 |
| 1 | $99.36 |
| 1 | $69.29 |
| 1 | $134.19 |
| 4 | $677.84 |

Figure 20–8

**Exercise 20-4:** Modifying the Schedule—Text Appearance

1. Using the previous file **(TESTWALLSCHEDULE.dwg),** select **Format > Text Style** from the **Main** menu to bring up the **Text Style** dialog box.
2. Press the **New** button, and name the style **TESTTEXT.**
3. Select **Arial** from the **Font Name** drop-down list and **Bold** from the **Font Style** drop-down list.
4. Select **Standard** from the **Style Name** drop-down list, select **Arial** from the **Font Name** drop-down list, select **Regular** from the **Font Style** drop-down list, press the **Apply** button, and then press the **Close** button.
5. Select the schedule you placed in the Drawing Editor, **RMB,** and select **Edit Schedule Table Style** from the contextual menu that appears to bring up the **Schedule Table Style Properties** dialog box.
6. Select the **Layout** tab.
7. Enter **WALL Schedule** in the **Table Title** field, and press the **Title Override Cell Format** button to bring up the **Cell Format Override** dialog box.
8. Select **TESTTEXT** from the **Style** drop-down list (see Figure 20–9).

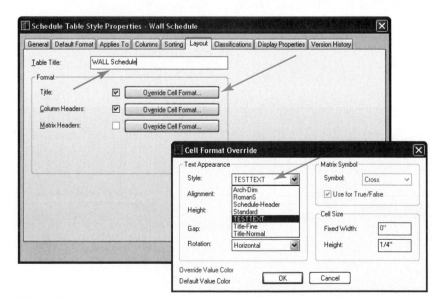

Figure 20–9

9. Press the **Column Headers Override Cell Format** button, select **TESTTEXT** from the **Style** drop-down list, and press the **OK** buttons to close all the dialog boxes and return to the Drawing Editor (see Figure 20–10).

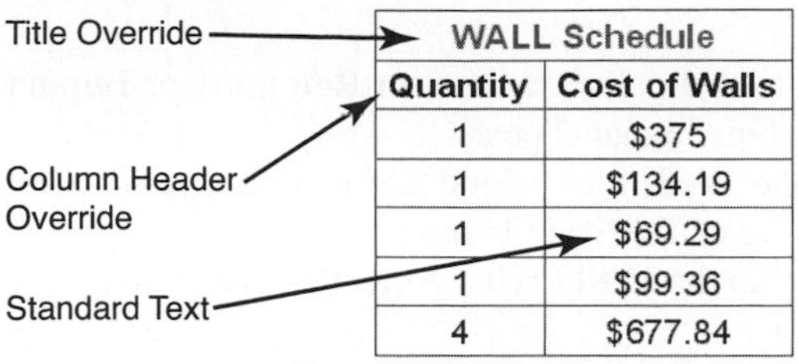

| WALL Schedule | |
|---|---|
| Quantity | Cost of Walls |
| 1 | $375 |
| 1 | $134.19 |
| 1 | $69.29 |
| 1 | $99.36 |
| 4 | $677.84 |

Title Override → (points to WALL Schedule)
Column Header Override → (points to Quantity / Cost of Walls)
Standard Text → (points to $69.29)

Figure 20–10

10. **RMB** on the **TESTSCHEDULE** in the Drawing Editor and select **Edit Schedule Table Style** from the contextual menu that appears to bring up the **Schedule Table Style Properties** dialog box.

## Adding a Column to the Schedule

11. Change to the **Columns** tab.
12. Press the **Add Column** button to bring up the **Add Column** dialog box.
13. Select **Wall Type** for **Type,** enter **WALL CODE** in the **Heading** field, press the **Insert Before** radio button, select **QTY** from the **Column** drop-down list, and press the **OK** buttons to return to the Drawing Editor (see Figure 20–11).

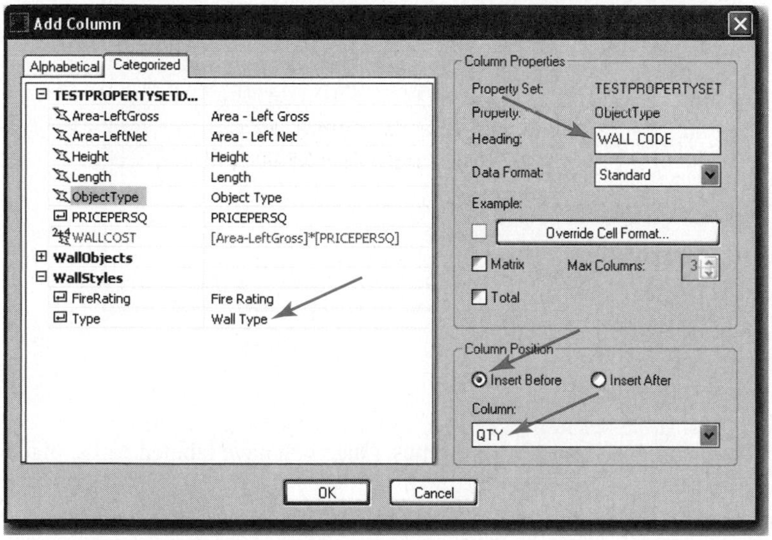

Figure 20–11

14. The **WALL Schedule** will now include a **WALL CODE** column, but it will not have codes. Because the types are a **Style**-based property, they are usually not predefined in the **Wall** styles out of the box (see Figure 20–12).

To label a wall, do the following (using CMU-8 as an example):

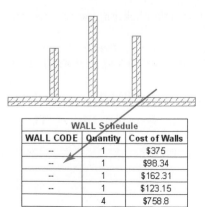

| WALL Schedule | | |
|---|---|---|
| WALL CODE | Quantity | Cost of Walls |
| -- | 1 | $375 |
| -- | 1 | $98.34 |
| -- | 1 | $162.31 |
| -- | 1 | $123.15 |
| | 4 | $758.8 |

Figure 20–12

## Method 1

    a. **RMB** on the **CMU-8** wall in the **Walls** tool palette and select **Reimport** or **Import CMU-8 Wall Style** from the contextual menu that appears.

    b. Again **RMB** on the **CMU-8** wall in the **Walls** tool palette and this time select **Wall Styles** from the contextual menu to bring up the **Style Manager.**

    c. Double-click the **CMU-8** wall to bring up the **Wall Style Properties** dialog box.

    d. Change to the **General** tab.

    e. Select the **Property Sets** button to bring up the **Edit Property Set Data** dialog box.

    f. Enter **A** in the **Type** field, and press the **OK** buttons to return to the Drawing Editor (see Figure 20–13).

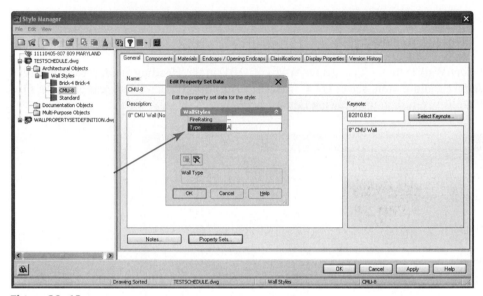

**Figure 20–13**

    g. Repeat Steps a–f for some of the other wall types. Once you have labeled walls, place the walls.

## Method 2

This method allows data to be pushed from the schedule to intelligent AEC Objects.

    a. Select schedule table in the drawing, **RMB,** and select **Edit Table Cell.**

    b. Click on the cell to be edited, input a value, and click the **OK** button.

    c. Press the **Enter** key to exit the **Edit Table Cell** command.

15. After placing some walls, select all the walls and double-click on one to open the **Properties** palette.

16. With all the walls still selected, select the **Extended Data** tab in the **Properties** palette.

17. Press the **Add property sets** icon and attach the **WALLPROPERTYSETDEFINITION** property set.

18. Enter **2.5** in the **PRICEPERSQ** field. Press the **Esc** key to clear the grips.

Your wall schedule is now complete (see Figure 20–14). Save this file as **TEST-WALLSCHEDULE.**

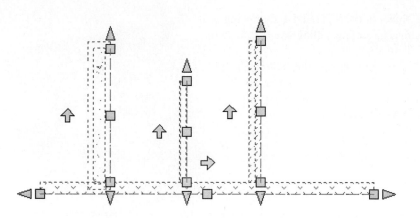

| WALL Schedule | | |
|---|---|---|
| **WALL CODE** | **Quantity** | **Cost of Walls** |
| A | 1 | $486.29 |
| D | 1 | $215.7 |
| C | 1 | $147.83 |
| B | 1 | $206.58 |
| | 4 | $1056.4 |

Figure 20–14

## Exercise 20-5: Scheduling across Drawings—Scheduling XREFs

Because schedules are not necessarily placed on the same page as the objects they are scheduling, AutoCAD Architecture's scheduling object has an option to schedule "across" drawings.

1. Using the previous file **(TESTWALLSCHEDULE)**, select **Edit > Cut** from the **Main** menu. Select all the walls and press **OK.** Your walls should disappear, and the schedule should clear.

2. Start a drawing using the AEC Model (Imperial Stb) template, and save it as **WALLS.** dwg.

3. In the WALLS drawing, select **Edit > Paste to Original Coordinates** from the **Main** menu to paste the walls that you previously cut from the **TESTWALLSCHEDULE** drawing into the WALLS drawing.

4. Press **Ctrl + S** to save the WALLS drawing. *This is essential.*

5. Double-click the schedule object in the **TESTWALLSCHEDULE** drawing to open its **Properties** palette.

6. In the **Properties** palette, select **Yes** from the **Schedule external drawing** field in the **ADVANCED** section. This will then show an **External drawing** field.

7. In the Select **External drawing** field, select **Browse** from the drop-down list, and locate the WALLS drawing (see Figure 20–15).

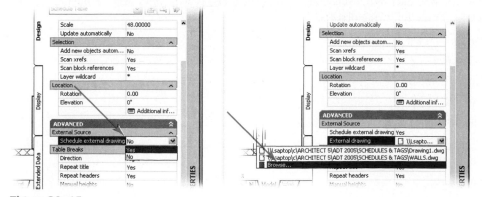

**Figure 20–15**

8. The schedule object in the **SCHEDULE** drawing will show a line across its surface telling you to update the schedule.

9. **RMB** on the schedule object and select **Update Schedule Table** from the contextual menu that appears. The schedule will now reflect the information from the **WALLS** drawing.

**Note:**
If you change any wall in the **WALLS** drawing and save that drawing, the **SCHEDULE** drawing will be able to show those changes upon updating. In AutoCAD Architecture 2008, updating can be done automatically through the sheet set (see Figure 20–16).

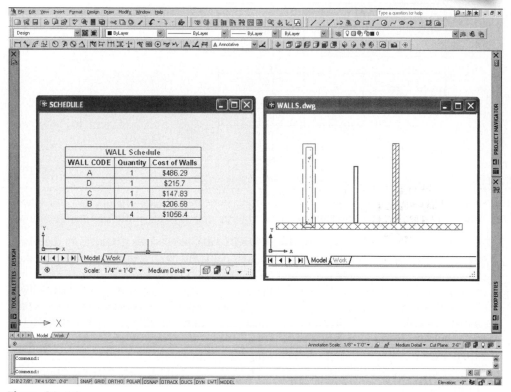

**Figure 20–16**

## Schedule Tags

In order to compile data into a schedule, objects must be tagged. AutoCAD Architecture 2008 contains tags for the following objects:

- Doors
- Windows
- Room numbers
- Room finishes
- Spaces
- Beams, braces, and columns
- Equipment
- Furniture
- Walls

## Exercise 20-6: Placing Door and Window Tags

1. Using the previous **TESTWALLSCHEDULE** drawing, erase everything, select the **Wall** icon in the **Design** tool palette, and create a 30' -0" × 20' -0"-wide enclosure. Make the walls Standard 6" wide, 8' high.
2. Select a wall, **RMB,** and select **Insert > Door** from the contextual menu.
3. Place a 3' -0"-wide Standard door in each wall.
4. Repeat Steps 2 and 3, placing 3' × 5' windows alongside the doors (see Figure 20–17).

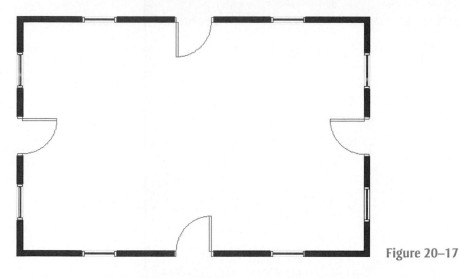

**Figure 20–17**

5. Set the **Scale** button for the correct scale that you want the drawing to be in the plot sheets. This will control the tag and annotation size.
6. Select the **Door Tag** icon from the **Schedules** tool palette you created, select the bottom-most door, and place the tag in the middle of the door opening.

The **Edit Property Set Data** dialog box will now appear. You can now change data such as **FireRating** (see Figure 20–18).

**Edit Property Set Data**

Edit the property set data for the object:

| DoorObjects | |
|---|---|
| Data source | Drawing1.dwg |
| DoorSize | 3'-0" x 6'-8" |
| FireRating | -- |
| FrameDepth | 5" |
| FrameMaterial | -- |
| FrameWidth | 2" |
| Glazing | -- |
| HeadDetail | -- |
| HeadHeight | 6'-8" |
| Height | 80 |
| HeightUniform... | 80 |

OK    Cancel    Help

**Figure 20–18**

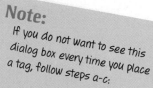

**Note:** If you do not want to see this dialog box every time you place a tag, follow steps a-c:

7. When you are finished, press **OK** in the dialog box to place the schedule tag.

   a. Select **Format > Options** to bring up the **Options** dialog box.
   b. Select the **AEC Content** tab.

c. Uncheck the **Display Edit Property Data Dialog During Tag Insertion** check box (see Figure 20–19).

8. Place door tags for the other doors.

9. Zoom close to the doors.

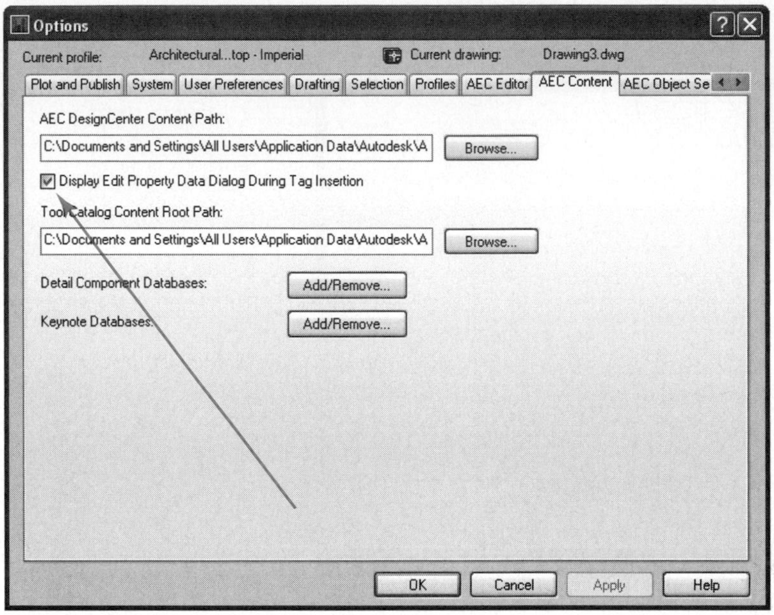

**Figure 20–19**

Notice that they are numbered incrementally automatically. To change the settings of the tag, do the following:

10. Select **Format > Style Manager** from the **Main** toolbar to bring up the **Style Manager** dialog box.

11. Select **Documentation Objects > Property Set Definitions > Door Objects.**

Property set definitions are groups of properties for particular objects that you want to manage in schedules. They can be automatic, deriving their values from the properties of objects, or user-defined.

12. In the Style Manager, select the **Definition** tab.

If you want to increment the objects' number system automatically, select **Number,** change its **Type** to **Auto Increment - Integer,** and set the start number as **Default.** The tags can also be created or modified to display the information defined in the property definition (see Figure 20–20).

13. Place window tags for the windows. If the tags don't increment automatically, change their setting in the property definition set for window objects. Save this file.

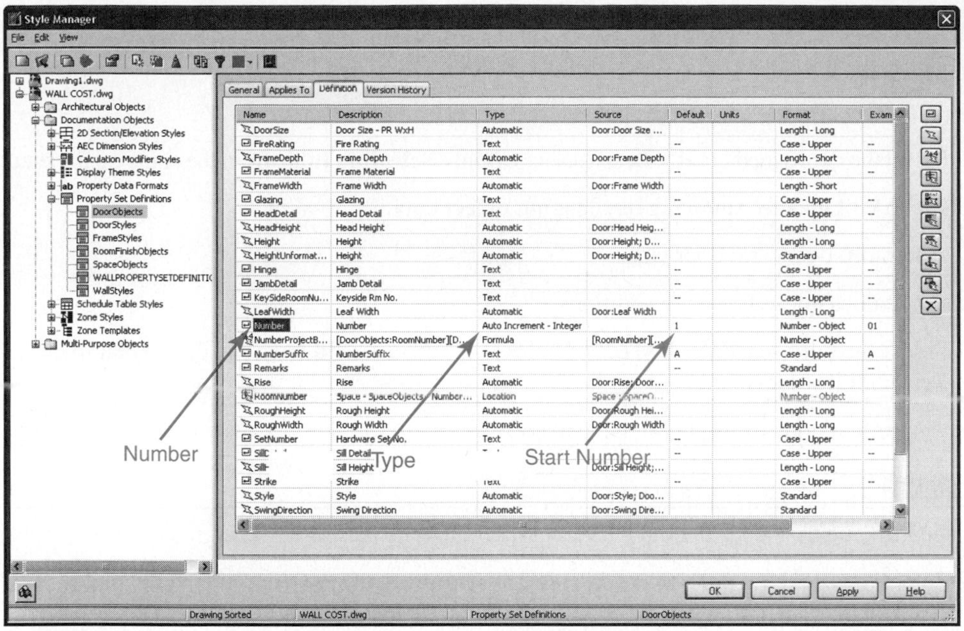


Figure 20–20

## Exercise 20-7: Placing Schedules

1. Using the previous **TESTWALLSCHEDULE** drawing, select the **Door Schedule** icon from the **Schedules** tool palette you created.
2. Move your cursor over the **Properties** palette to open it.
3. Set the following:
   a. Update automatically = **No** (for next exercise)
   b. Add new objects = **No** (for next exercise)
   c. Scan xrefs = **Yes**
   d. Scan block references = **Yes**
4. Select all the doors (this can be done with a selection window).
5. Click in a spot in the drawing to start the upper left corner of the schedule.
6. Press the space bar or **Enter** key when requested for the lower right corner.

Pressing **Enter** (AutoCAD Architecture calls it **Return** in the command line) causes the schedule to be scaled automatically at the size set by the drawing scale you set earlier.

7. Select all the doors and their tags, and press **Enter.**
8. Repeat Steps 1–5 for the **window schedule** (see Figure 20–21). Save this file.

**DOOR AND FRAME SCHEDULE**

| MARK | DOOR SIZE WD | DOOR SIZE HGT | DOOR SIZE THK | DOOR MATL | DOOR GLAZING | DOOR LOUVER WD | DOOR LOUVER HGT | FRAME MATL | FRAME EL | FRAME DETAIL HEAD | FRAME DETAIL JAMB | FRAME DETAIL SILL | FIRE RATING LABEL | HARDWARE SET NO | HARDWARE KEYSIDE RM NO | NOTES |
|---|---|---|---|---|---|---|---|---|---|---|---|---|---|---|---|---|
| 1 | 3'-0" | 6'-8" | 2" | -- | -- | 0" | 0" | -- | -- | -- | -- | -- | -- | -- | -- | -- |
| 2 | 3'-0" | 6'-8" | 2" | -- | -- | 0" | 0" | -- | -- | -- | -- | -- | -- | -- | -- | -- |
| 3 | 3'-0" | 6'-8" | 2" | -- | -- | 0" | 0" | -- | -- | -- | -- | -- | -- | -- | -- | -- |
| 4 | 3'-0" | 6'-8" | 2" | -- | -- | 0" | 0" | -- | -- | -- | -- | -- | -- | -- | -- | -- |

**WINDOW SCHEDULE**

| MARK | SIZE WIDTH | SIZE HEIGHT | TYPE | MATERIAL | NOTES |
|---|---|---|---|---|---|
| 1 | 3'-0" | 5'-0" | -- | -- | -- |
| 2 | 3'-0" | 5'-0" | -- | -- | -- |
| 3 | 3'-0" | 5'-0" | -- | -- | -- |
| 4 | 3'-0" | 5'-0" | -- | -- | -- |
| 5 | 3'-0" | 5'-0" | -- | -- | -- |
| 6 | 3'-0" | 5'-0" | -- | -- | -- |
| 7 | 3'-0" | 5'-0" | -- | -- | -- |
| 8 | 3'-0" | 5'-0" | -- | -- | -- |

Figure 20–21

## Exercise 20-8: Updating Schedules

1. Using the previous file, remove two of the doors.

Notice that a line appears across the schedule.

2. Select the door schedule, **RMB,** and select **Update Schedule Table** from the contextual menu.

The schedule will update, removing or changing object data.

3. Add more doors and door tags.

The schedule does not indicate the additions.

4. Select the door schedule, **RMB,** and select **Selection > Add** from the contextual menu.
5. Select all the doors and tags.

The door schedule updates, showing the new doors.

## Exercise 20-9: Using Schedules to Locate Objects

If you need to quickly locate an object listed in the schedule, do the following:

1. Select the door schedule, **RMB,** and select **Selection > Show** from the contextual menu.
2. Hold down the **Ctrl** key on the keyboard, and pick any number in a field.

The screen will zoom to the object in that field.

This feature will work across XREFs. This feature does *not* work with **Schedule external drawing.**

## Exercise 20-10: Exporting Schedules to Databases

If you have Microsoft Excel or a text editor such as Microsoft Word or even Windows Notepad software, you can export your schedules to these formats.

1. Select the door schedule, **RMB,** and select **Export** from the contextual menu to bring up the **Export Schedule Table** dialog box.
2. Select **Microsoft [Tab delimited] [*.xls]** from the **Output - Save As Type** drop-down list.
3. Browse to a convenient folder, and press **OK.**

You will be able to open the file in Microsoft Excel 95 and later.

4. If you set the **Output - Save As Type to Text [Tab delimited] [*.txt],** you will be able to open the file in any text editor (see Figures 20–22 and 20–23).

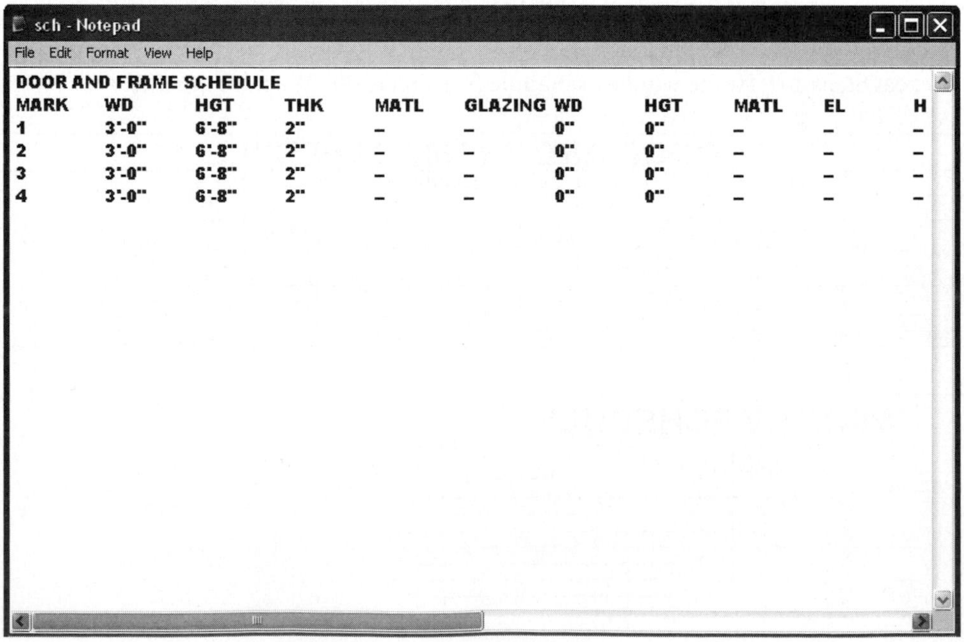

**Figure 20–22**

**Figure 20–23**

## Exercise 20-11: Creating and Using Custom Schedules

Schedules in AutoCAD Architecture are robust enough to permit scheduling normal AutoCAD entities such as circles in this exercise. This ability can often help keep track of objects while creating drawings.

### The Drawing

1. Start a new drawing using the AEC Model (Imperial Stb) template.
2. Place three circles in the drawing with radii of 2', 4', and 6'.

You are going to create a schedule that records information about the circles in your drawing. In order to make a schedule you will need to create a property set definition.

### The Property Set Definition

3. Select **Format > Style Manager** from the **Main** toolbar to bring up the **Style Manager** dialog box from the **Main** toolbar.
4. Expand the **Documentation Objects > Property Set Definitions.**
5. **RMB** on **Property Set Definitions,** and select **New** from the contextual menu to create a new property set definition.
6. Rename the new property set definition **CIRCLEPROPERTYSET.**
7. In the right pane of the **Style Manager,** select the **Applies To** tab.
8. Select the **Objects** radio button, and then select the **Clear All** button at the lower left of the dialog box. Check the **Circle** check box (see Figure 20–24).
9. In the right pane of the **Style Manager,** change to the **Definition** tab.
10. Press the **Add Manual Property Definition** icon button at the top right side of the dialog box to bring up the **New Property** dialog box.
11. Enter the word **NUMBER** in the **Name** section, and press **OK** (see Figure 20–25).
12. In the **Definition** tab, also set the **Type** to **Auto Increment - Integer** and **Default** to **1,** and **Format** to **Number - Object.**
13. Next, press the **Add Automatic Property Definition** icon button at the top right side of the **Style Manager** dialog box to bring up the **Automatic Property Source** dialog box.

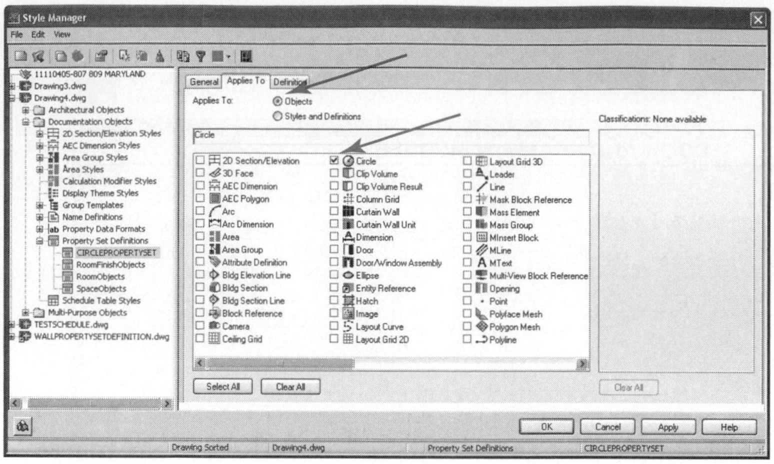

**Figure 20–24**

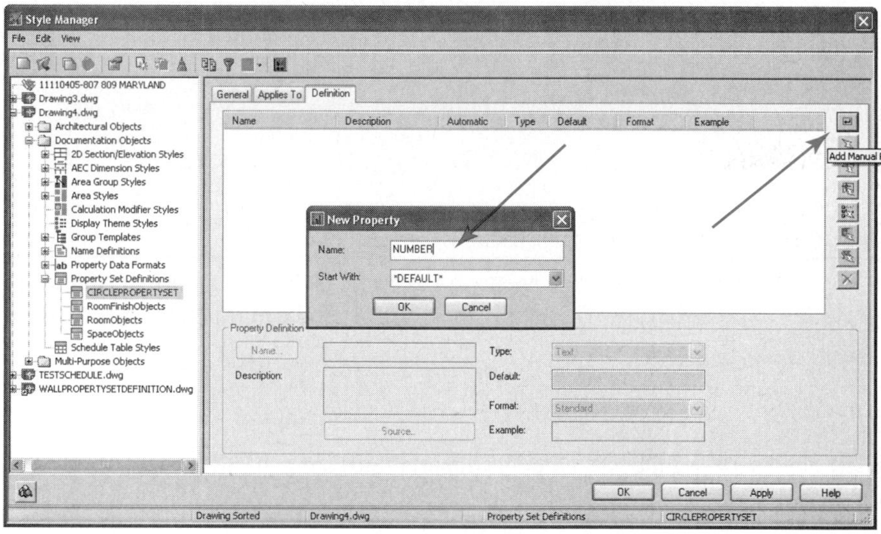

**Figure 20–25**

The **Automatic Property Source** dialog box shows all the properties of a circle.

14. Check the **Area** check box, and press **OK** to return to the **Property Set Definition Properties** dialog box (see Figure 20–26).

15. Add two more automatic property definitions called **Radius** and **Circumference,** and check their **Automatic Property Source** check boxes for **Radius** and **Circumference,** respectively.

16. Press the **Apply** button to apply all this to the **CIRCLEPROPERTYSET** property set definition.

You have now defined all the properties of circles that you wish to be recorded in a schedule.

## Creating the Table Style

17. Select **Format > Style Manager** from the **Main** menu to bring up the **Style Manager** dialog box.

18. Select **Document Objects > Schedule Table Styles.**

19. **RMB** on **Schedule Table Styles,** and select **New** from the contextual menu.

20. Name the new style **CIRCLESCHEDULE,** and press the **Apply** and **OK** buttons.

21. Change to the **Applies To** tab.

22. Press the **Clear All** button to clear the list, and then check the **Circle** check box.

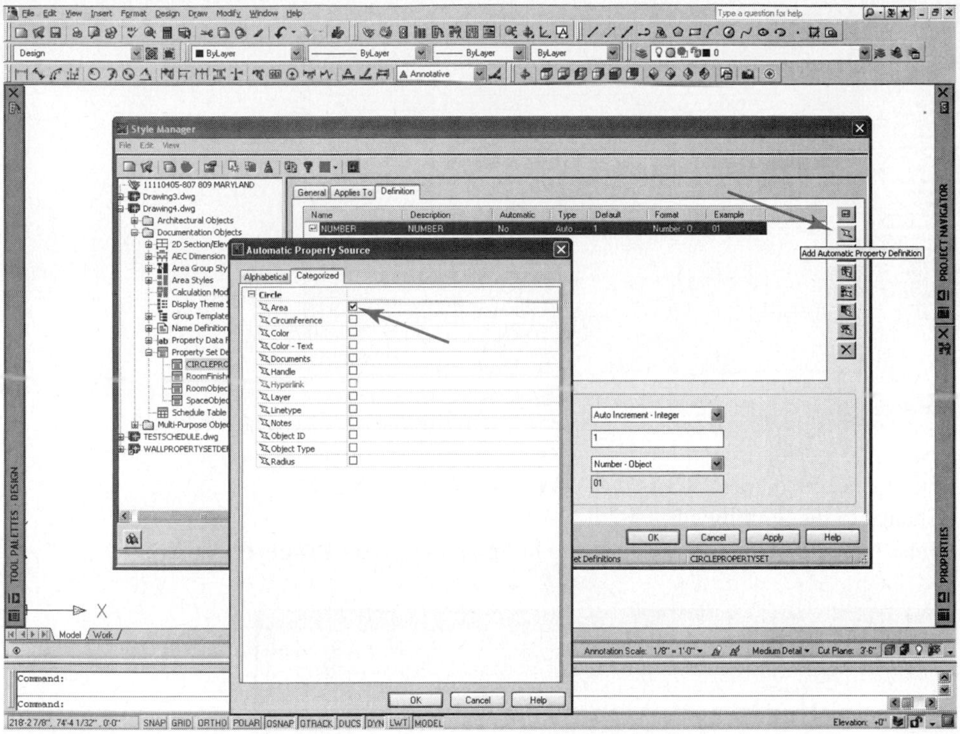

**Figure 20–26**

This tells the program that the schedule applies to circles and their properties.

23. Change to the **Columns** tab and press the **Add Column** button at the lower left to bring up the **Add Column** dialog box.

You should now see the property definition set you created in Steps 3–23.

24. Select the **NUMBER** property and press **OK** to return to the **Style Manager** dialog box (see Figure 20–27).

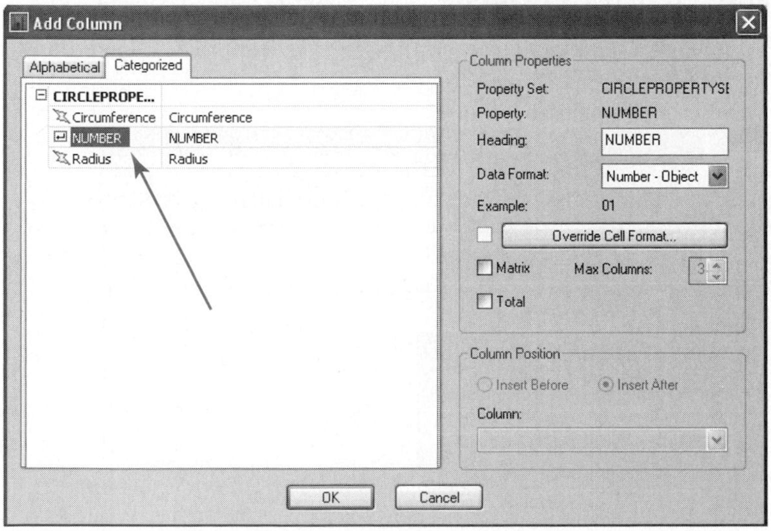

**Figure 20–27**

25. Returning to the **Style Manager** dialog box, again press the **Add Column** button.
26. Repeat the steps, adding columns named **Radius** and **Circumference** (see Figure 20–28).
27. Hold down the **Ctrl** key and select the **Radius** and **Circumference** headers.
28. Press the **Add Header** button.

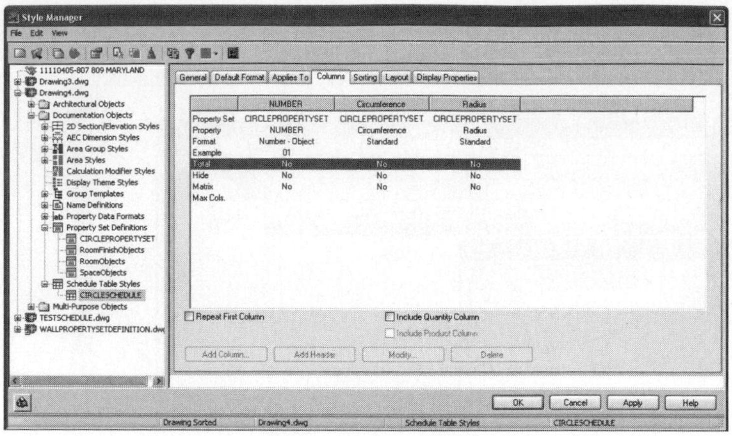

**Figure 20–28**

29. Enter a header name of **CIRCLE DATA** (see Figure 20–29).
30. Change to the **Sorting** tab.
31. Press the **Add** button at the top left to bring up the **Select Property** dialog box.

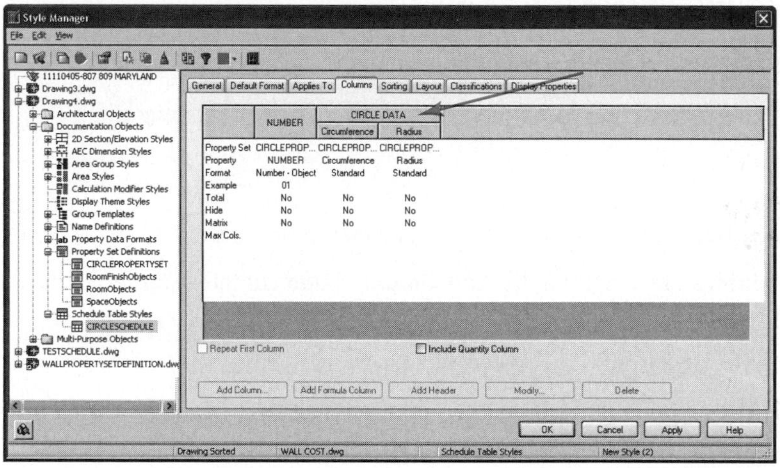

**Figure 20–29**

32. Select **CIRCLEPROPERTYSET:NUMBER,** and press **OK** (see Figure 20–30).
33. Repeat for all the other properties.
34. Change to the **Layout** tab.

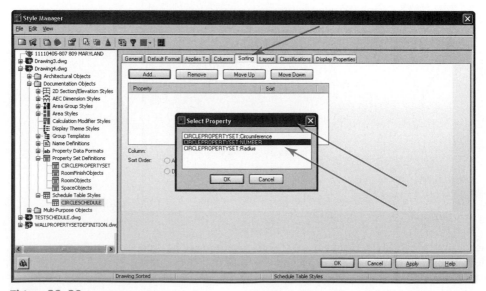

**Figure 20–30**

35. Enter a **Table Title** of **CIRCLE SCHEDULE,** and press **OK** to return to the Drawing Editor (see Figure 20–31). IMPORTANT: save this drawing now.

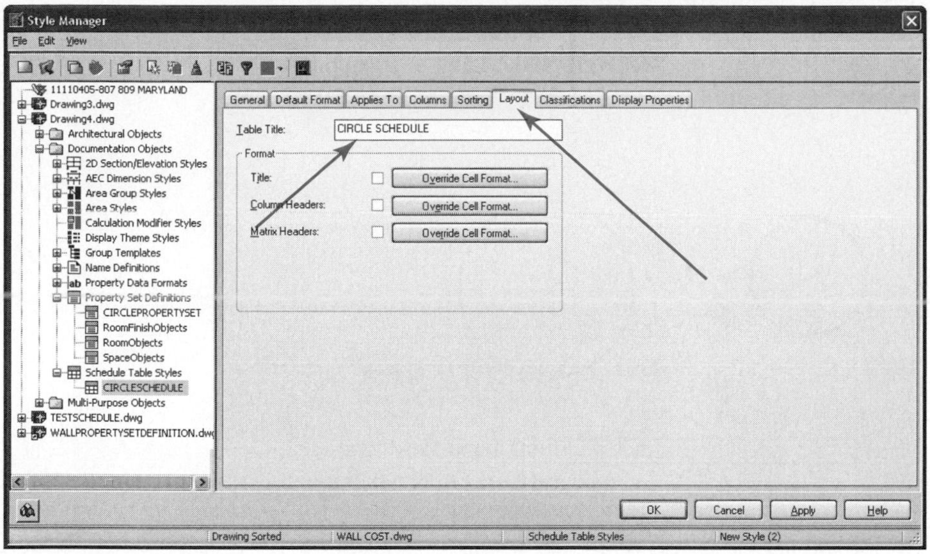

**Figure 20–31**

## Using the Custom Schedule

36. Open the **Schedules** tool palette you created in Exercise 20-1, and lock it open.
37. Select **Format > Style Manager** from the **Main** menu.
38. Expand the **Documentation Objects** folder.
39. Expand the **Schedule Table Styles.**
40. From the **Schedule Table Styles,** drag the **CIRCLESCHEDULE** table style you created into your **Schedules** tool palette.
41. In the **Style Manager,** press the **OK** button to return to the Drawing Editor.
42. Select the **CIRCLESCHEDULE** from the **Schedules** tool palette.
43. Move your cursor over the **Properties** palette to open it.
44. Select the following:

    a.  Style = **CIRCLESCHEDULE**
    b.  Add new objects automatically = **Yes**

45. Select all the circles in your drawing, and press **Enter.**
46. Place the upper left corner of the table, and press **Enter.**

> **Note:**
> Remember, pressing **Enter** after placing the upper left corner of a schedule table automatically places the table according to your annotation scale settings.

47. Select the schedule table you placed, **RMB,** and select **Add All Property Sets** from the contextual menu that appears.
48. The schedule table now reads the circumference and radius of each of the circles (see Figure 20–32).
49. Select one of the circles, and use grips to change its size.

Note that a line now appears across the schedule telling you that something has changed.

50. Select the schedule table, **RMB,** and select **Update Schedule Table** from the contextual menu that appears (see Figure 20–33).
51. In the Drawing Editor, add another circle.

Again a line appears across the schedule table. Update the schedule table, and note that the new circle shows up in the table, but its size is represented by question marks.

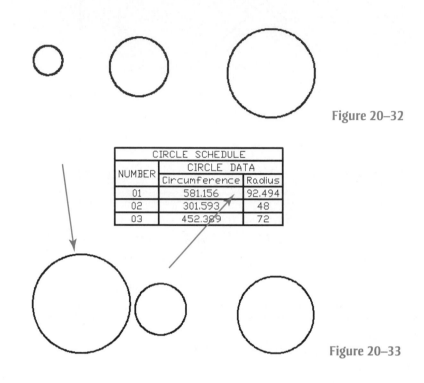

| CIRCLE SCHEDULE | | |
|---|---|---|
| NUMBER | CIRCLE DATA | |
| | Circumference | Radius |
| 01 | 150.796 | 24 |
| 02 | 301.593 | 48 |
| 03 | 452.389 | 72 |

Figure 20–32

| CIRCLE SCHEDULE | | |
|---|---|---|
| NUMBER | CIRCLE DATA | |
| | Circumference | Radius |
| 01 | 581.156 | 92.494 |
| 02 | 301.593 | 48 |
| 03 | 452.389 | 72 |

Figure 20–33

52. Select the schedule, **RMB,** and select **Add All Property Sets** from the contextual menu.
53. The new circle is now listed in the schedule.

## Exercise 20-12: Using the Define Schedule Tag Routine to Create Custom Schedule Tags

The **Define Schedule Tag** routine was developed to aid in the creation of automated custom schedule tags. Since **Tags** are **Multi-View Blocks,** the **Define Schedule Tag** routine is really an automated **Multi-View Block and Property Set Definition** integrator.

For this exercise, we are going to use the **Project Browser** and project management. If you have problems following the material, please review Section 16.

### Setting Up in Preparation for Creating a New Tag

1. Select **File > New** from the **Main** menu and create a new drawing using the AEC Model (Imperial Stb) template, and save it as **CUSTOMTAG.dwg.**
2. Use the **NEW AutoCAD Architecture 2008 PROJECTS** folder you created in Section 16.
3. Select **File > Project Browser** from the **Main** menu, browse and locate the **NEW AutoCAD Architecture 2008 PROJECTS** folder and then create a new project named **CUSTOM SCHEDULE TAGS.**
4. While still in the **Project Browser,** set the **CUSTOM SCHEDULE TAGS** project you just created,

**Note:**
In AutoCAD Architecture 2008, whenever you create a new project using the Template Project (Imperial) apj, you automatically create a new, empty tool palette specifically tied to that new project. Make sure that the tool palette is locked open. If you open the **Content Browser** icon at the bottom of the **Project Navigator,** you will find a Project Catalog also tied to the new project you just created (see Figure 20–35).

**current,** and close the **Project Browser** to bring up the **Project Navigator** and create the **SCHEDULE TAGS** tool palette (see Figure 20–34).

We are going to make a custom Door tag, so we will need to have a Door Object property set definition.

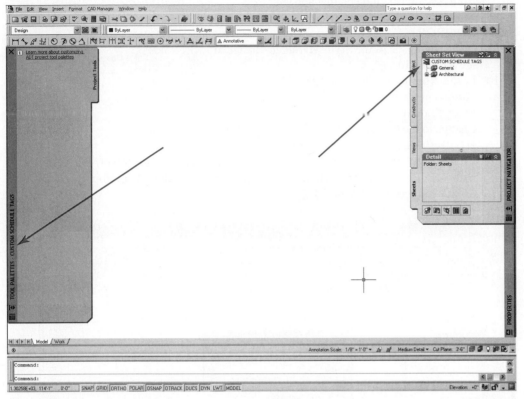

**Figure 20–34**

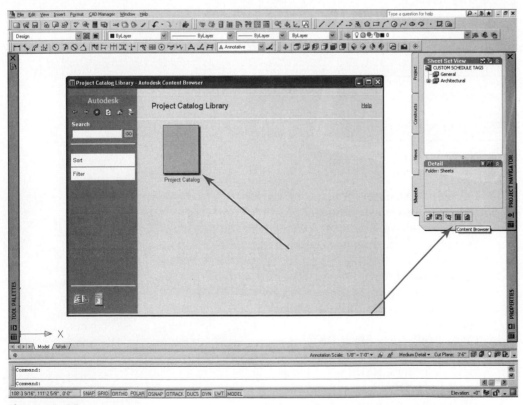

**Figure 20–35**

5. Select **Format > Style Manager** to bring up the **Style Manager** dialog box.
6. Expand the **Documentation Objects** folder, and then locate the **Property Set Definitions.**
7. **RMB** the **Property Set Definitions,** and select **New** from the contextual menu that appears.
8. Name the new **Property Set Definition - DOOROBJECT** (no spaces).
9. In the right pane of the **Style Manager,** change to the **Applies To** tag.
10. In the **Applies To** tab, select the **Objects** radio button, press the **Clear All** button, and then check the **Door** check box.
11. Change to the **Definition** tab, and select the **Add Manual Property Definition** icon to bring up the **New Property** dialog box.
12. In the **New Property** dialog box, enter **NUMBER,** and select **RoomObjects: Number** from the **Start With** drop-down list, and press the **OK** button to return to the **Style Manager** (see Figure 20–36).

**Note:**

This new **Content Browser** icon located in the **Project Navigator** is in addition to the standard **Content Browser** icon located in the **Main** menu or activated by **Ctrl + 4.** The standard **Content Browser** will bring down all the catalogs.

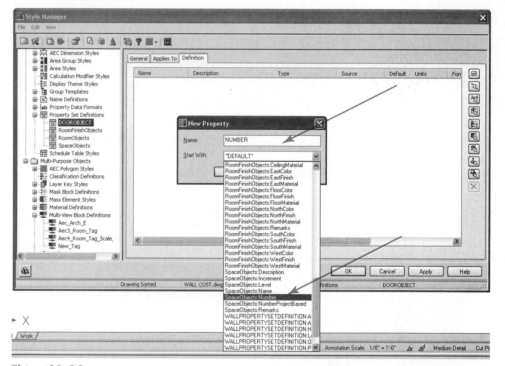

**Figure 20–36**

13. In the **Style Manager,** in the right pane, select **Auto Increment - Integer** from the **Type** drop-down list, enter **100** in the **Default** field, and **Number-Object** in the **Format** field.
14. In the **Style Manager,** in the left pane, expand the **Multi-Purpose Objects** folder, and select the **Multi-View Block Definitions.**
15. Under **Multi-View Block Definitions,** select each of the existing multi-view block definitions, **RMB,** select **Purge** to delete the definitions, and press the **OK** button to return to the Drawing Editor.

**Note:**

We are removing the existing multi-view block definitions because the AutoCAD Architecture 2008 Tool Catalog Generator that we will use in the next exercise will generate all the multi-view block definitions that will exist in this drawing as tags. For clarity in that exercise, we are removing those multi-view block definitions so that only the new tag that we will create in this exercise will show up in the catalog generated by the next exercise (see Figure 20–37).

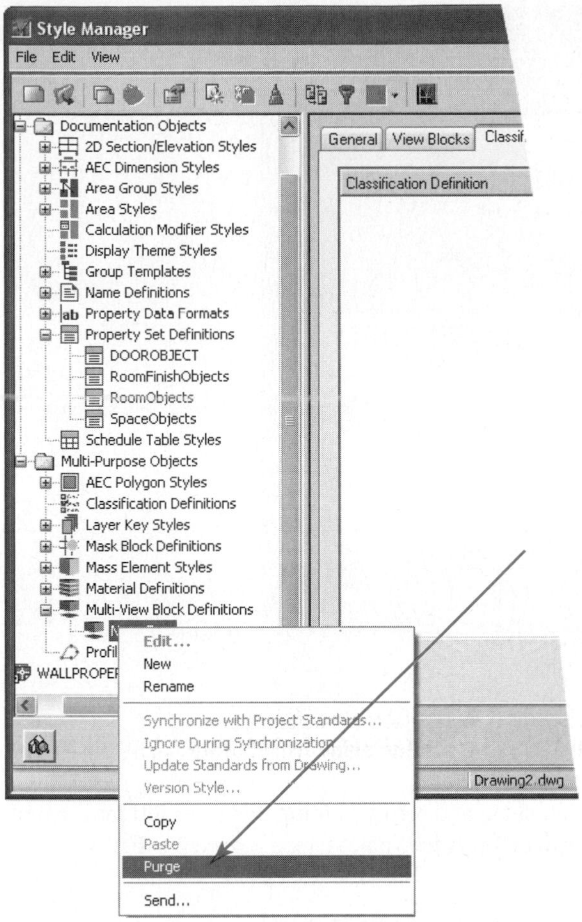

Figure 20–37

## Creating the New Tag Design

16. Refer to the previous drawing file.
17. Select the **Rectangle** icon from the **Draw** menu, and place a **2-1/2" × 2-1/2"** rectangle in the Drawing Editor.
18. Using the **Line** command from the **Draw** menu and the **Mtext** command, create the tag shown (Figure 20–38). **Save this file**—this is important!

This design is arbitrary; you can make any design you wish. The "A" is just a locator for the door number.

Figure 20–38

## Defining (Creating) the Tag Using the New Define Schedule Tag Routine

19. Select **Format > Define Schedule Tag** from the **Main** menu, and with a window marquee, select the tag design you just created.
20. With the tag design selected, press the **Enter** key on your keyboard to bring up the **Define Schedule Tag** dialog box.
21. In the **Define Schedule Tag** dialog box, name the tag **TEST_DOOR_TAG.**
22. In the "A" field select **Property** from the **Type** drop-down list.
23. In the "A" field select **DOOROBJECT** from the **Property Set** drop-down list.
24. In the "A" field select **NUMBER** from the **Property Definition** drop-down list.

Notice that **DOOROBJECT** is the Property Set Definition we created at the start of this exercise, and **NUMBER** is its Property (see Figure 20–39).

25. In the **Define Schedule Tag** dialog box, leave the **DOOR TAG** label as **Text** in the **Type** column. This is because the text **DOOR TAG** is just part of the design and will not pick up information from the door as will happen with the "A" when we use the tag.
26. In the **Define Schedule Tag** dialog box, press the **OK** button, select a point at the center of the tag design to define an insertion point, and return to the Drawing Editor.

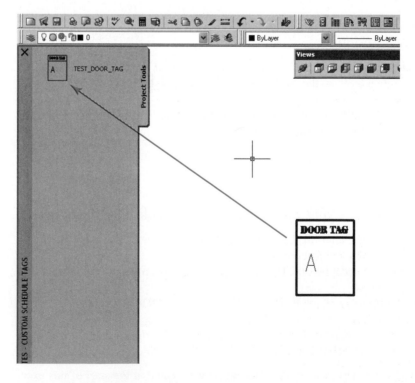

**Define Schedule Tag**

DOOR TAG

A

Name:
TEST_DOOR_TAG

Select Objects
6 items selected

| Label | Type | Property Set | Property Definition |
|-------|------|--------------|---------------------|
| DOOROBJE... | Property | DOOROBJECT | NUMBER |
| DOOR TAG | Text | -- | -- |

OK     Cancel     Help

**Figure 20–39**

27. Save the drawing—location doesn't matter.
28. Select the tag design, and notice that it is no longer made of separate parts, but is one object and has become a tag.
29. Move your cursor to the top of the tag, click, and, while holding down the left mouse button, drag the tag into your empty **Project Tools** tool palette (see Figure 20–40).

**Figure 20–40**

## Testing the New Tag

30. Select **Format > Style Manager** from the **Main** menu to bring up the **Style Manager.**
31. In the **Style Manager,** expand the **Multi-Purpose Objects** folder, and then locate the **Multi-View Block Definitions** folder. Notice that it now contains the **TEST_DOOR_TAG.**

32. Select the **Door** tool from the **Design** tool palette, and place a Standard door in your Drawing Editor.
33. With the door selected, move your cursor over the **Properties** palette to open it.
34. In the **Properties** palette, change to the **Extended Data** tab.
35. At the bottom left of the **Extended Data** tab, select the **Add Property Sets** icon to bring up the **Add Property Sets** dialog box.
36. In the **Add Property Sets** dialog box, make sure the **DOOROBJECT** check box is checked, and then press the **OK** button to return to the Drawing Editor (see Figure 20–41).

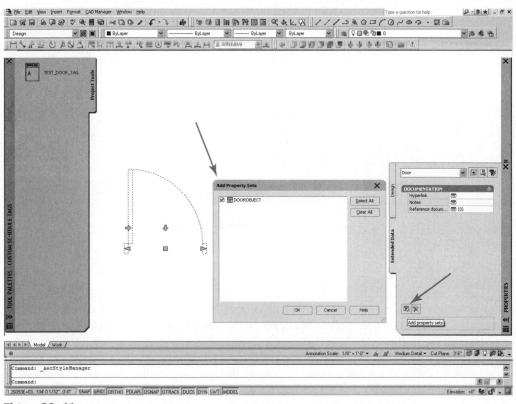

**Figure 20–41**

37. Copy the door four times.
38. Select the **Scale** drop-down list at the lower right of the Drawing Editor, and set the scale to drawing scale to **1/4" = 1' -0"**.
39. Select the **TEST_DOOR_TAG** tool that you placed in the **Project Tools** tool palette, and select the first door. Locate the tag at the middle of the door opening, and click the left mouse button to open the **Edit Property Set Data** dialog box. (Remember that this will appear each time because it has been set to do this in **Options > AEC Content.** See the note near Step 7 of Exercise 20-6, "Placing Door and Window Tags.")
40. In the **Edit Property Set Data** dialog box, press **OK** to return to the Drawing Editor, and place the first tag.
41. Enter **M** (Multiple) in the **Command line,** and press the **Enter** key on the keyboard.
42. Select the remaining doors, and again press the **Enter** key on the keyboard to bring up the **Edit Property Set Data** dialog box.
43. In the **Edit Property Set Data** dialog box, press the **OK** button to return to the Drawing Editor, and automatically label all the doors.

Notice that all the doors are incrementally numbered with your custom tag (see Figure 20–42).

Save this drawing file.

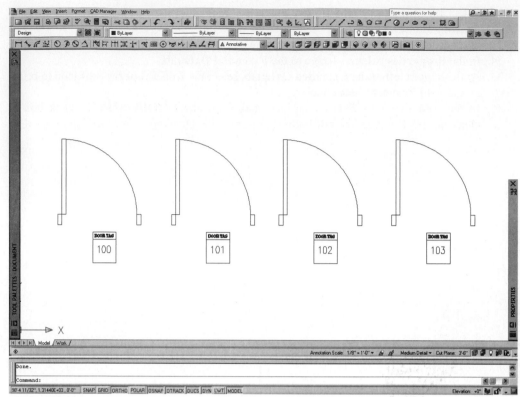

**Figure 20–42**

## Exercise 20-13: The Tool Catalog Generator

Catalogs are where we keep our AutoCAD Architecture 2008. The developers have created a tool that creates tool catalogs from **Styles, Mask Block Definitions, Multi-View Block Definitions,** and **Material Definitions.** The Tool Catalog Generator gets these Styles and Definitions from the Style Manager of selected drawings. If you are using a **Standards** drawing, you might want to generate your catalog from that drawing. Changing that drawing would allow you to change the tools in the existing catalogs.

The AutoCAD Architecture 2008 Tool Catalog Generator is located in the **CAD Manager Pulldown** on the **Main** menu. If it is not there, you will need to load it.

1. To load the **CAD Manager** select **Window > Pulldowns > CAD Manager,** and click **CAD Manager Pulldown** to load it. If it is already loaded, and you select **Window > Pulldowns > CAD Manager Pulldown,** you will see a check next to it. If you now click on **CAD Manager Pulldown,** you will remove the pulldown from the **Main** menu.
2. Select **File > Open,** and open the drawing you saved from the previous exercise.

Remember that we created this drawing on purpose, having only one **Multi-View Block Definition.**

3. Select **CAD Manager > Tool Catalog Generator** from the **Main** menu to bring up the **Populate Tool Catalog from Content Drawings** dialog box.
4. In the **Populate Tool Catalog from Content Drawings** dialog box, under **Catalog,** select the **Create a new catalog** radio button, and name the catalog **CUSTOM SCHEDULE TAGS.** Directly below this, press the **Browse** button to bring up the **Browse For Folder** dialog box and locate the **NEW AutoCAD Architecture 2008 PROJECTS > CUSTOM SCHEDULE TAGS** folder that you created at the start of the **Define Schedule Tag** routine exercise.
5. After you have located the folder, press the **OK** button in the **Browse For Folder** dialog box to return to the **Populate Tool Catalog from Content Drawings** dialog box.
6. In the **Populate Tool Catalog from Content Drawings** dialog box, press the **Clear All** button, and then check the **Multi-View Block Definitions** check box.

7. In the **Populate Tool Catalog from Content Drawings** dialog box, under **Content Source,** select the **Create from drawing** radio button. This tells the generator to generate the catalog from a drawing file.

8. Directly below the **Create from drawing** radio button, press the **Browse** button, and locate the drawing that you have been saving in the exercise on the **Define Schedule Tag** routine.

Finally, under **Tool Organization,** check the **Group tools by object type** check box, select the **Create tools in Categories** radio button, and then press the **OK** button at the bottom of the dialog box (see Figure 20–43).

The Tool Catalog Generator will now create the catalog file and return you to the Drawing Editor.

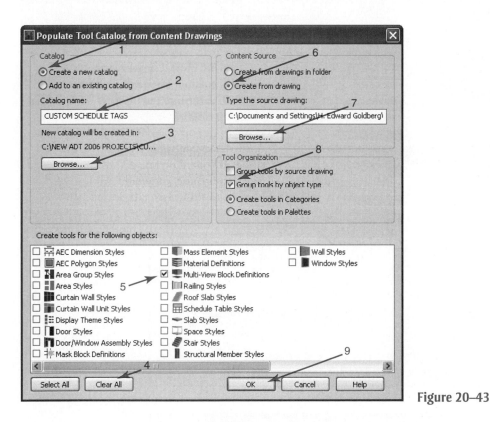

**Figure 20–43**

## Loading the Catalog in the Project Content Browser

9. Open the **Project Navigator,** and press the **Content Browser** at the bottom of the **Project Navigator** to bring up the **Content Browser** for the **CUSTOM SCHEDULE TAGS** project.

10. **RMB** in this **Content Browser,** and select **Add Catalog** from the contextual menu that appears to bring up the **Add Catalog** dialog box (see Figure 20–44).

11. In the **Add Catalog** dialog box, select the **Add an existing catalog or web site** radio button, and press the **Browse** button to open the **Browse for Catalog Files** dialog box.

12. In the **Browse for Catalog Files** dialog box, select the **CUSTOM SCHEDULE TAGS** catalog file **in the NEW AutoCAD Architecture 2008 PROJECTS > CUSTOM SCHEDULE TAGS** folder, and press the **Open** button (see Figure 20–45).

13. Again, open the **Project Navigator,** and press the **Content Browser** button at the bottom of the **Project Navigator** to bring up the **Content Browser** for the **CUSTOM SCHEDULE TAGS** project. The **CUSTOM SCHEDULE TAGS** catalog now appears in the **Content Browser** (see Figure 20–46).

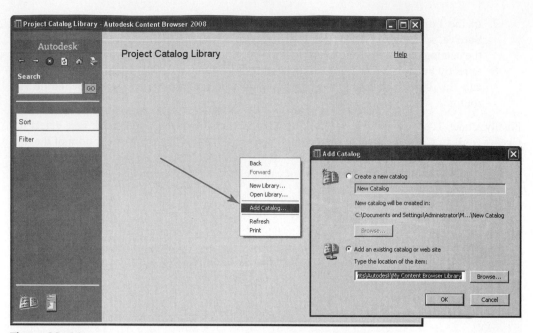

Figure 20–44

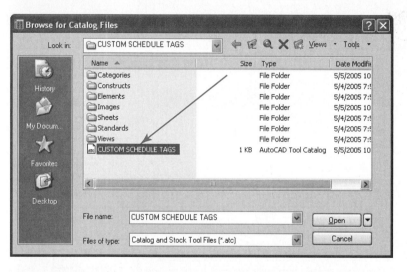

Figure 20–45

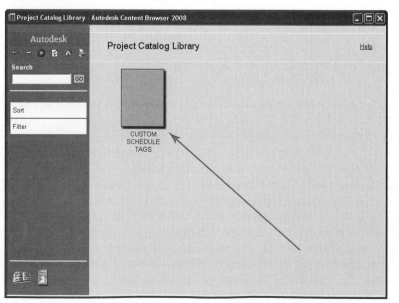

Figure 20–46

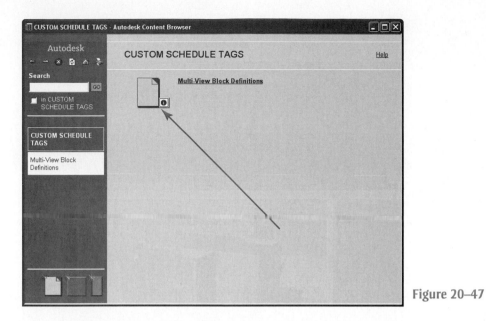

Figure 20–47

14. Click on the **CUSTOM SCHEDULE TAGS** catalog in the **Content Browser** to see the **Multi-View Block Definitions** folder (see Figure 20–47).
15. Finally, double-click on the **Multi-View Block Definitions** folder to see the **TEST_DOOR_ TAG** (see Figure 20–48).

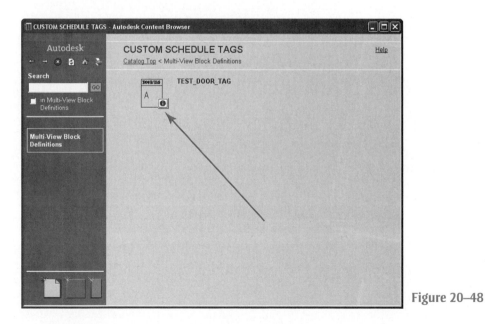

Figure 20–48

The **Content Browser** that is activated from the **Project Navigator** is always related to the project made current in the **Project Browser.** If you create catalogs with tools and connect them to the **Project Navigator Content Browser,** every time you change a project, the correct catalogs and tools for that project will be in the **Project Navigator Content Browser.** Besides this, the **Tool Palettes** are also automatically connected to the current project.

## 21

# Sheet Sets

## *Section* Objectives

- Learn how to create a **Sheet Set.**
- Learn how to modify a **Sheet Set.**
- Know how to test a new **Sheet Set.**

A sheet set is an ordered collection of sheets derived from several drawing files. You can manage, transmit, publish, and archive sheet sets as a unit.

## Exercise 21-1: Creating a New Sheet Set

1. Start a new drawing using the **AEC Model (Imperial Stb)** template.
2. Type **sheetset** in the **Command line** to bring up the **Sheet Set Manager.**
3. Select the drop-down list shown in Figure 21–1, and select **New Sheet Set** to bring up the **Begin** dialog box.

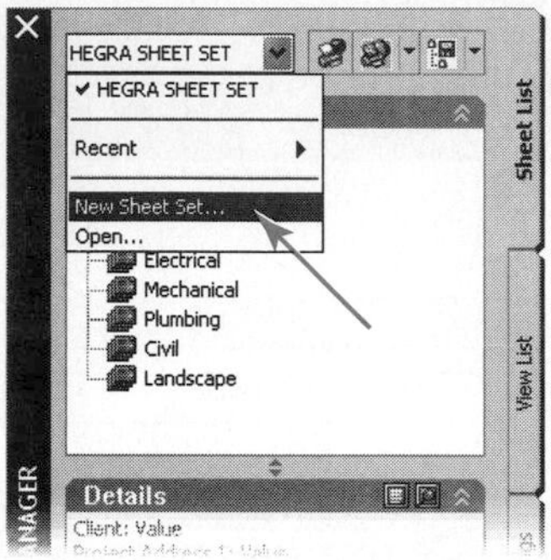

**Figure 21–1**

4. Select the **An example sheet set** radio button, and then press the **Next** button to bring up the **Sheet Set Example** dialog box.
5. Select the **Select a sheet set to use as an example** radio button, select **Architectural Imperial Sheet Set,** and then press the **Next** button to go to the **Sheet Set Details** dialog box (see Figure 21–2).

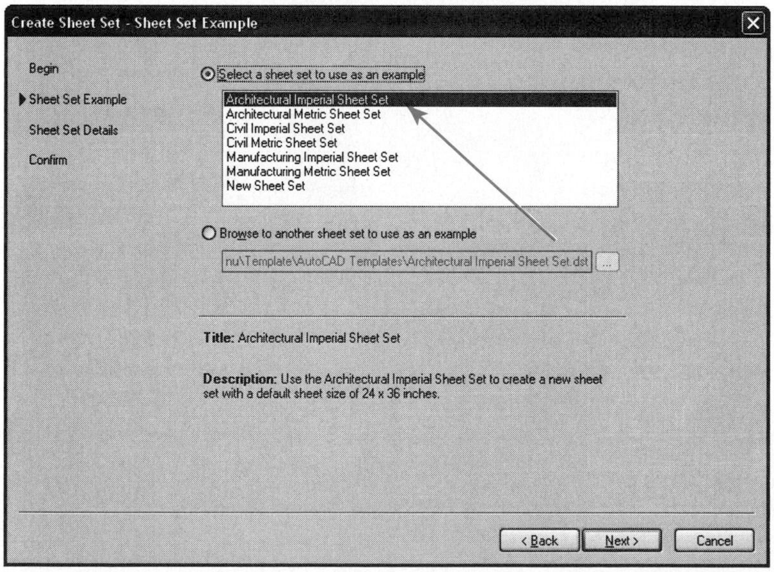

**Figure 21–2**

6. Name the sheet set **TEST SHEET SET.**
7. Press the **Sheet Set Properties** button at the bottom of the dialog box to bring up the **Sheet Set Properties** dialog box. In this dialog box, you can control the location of a custom drawing template, sheet storage, client and project, and so on (see Figure 21–3).
8. Press the **Edit Custom Properties** button to open the **Custom Properties** dialog box. Here you can also edit information on the client, address, and so on.
9. Press the **Add** button to bring up the **Add Custom Property** dialog box. Here you can add new places or make changes for information to be added automatically to the drawings.

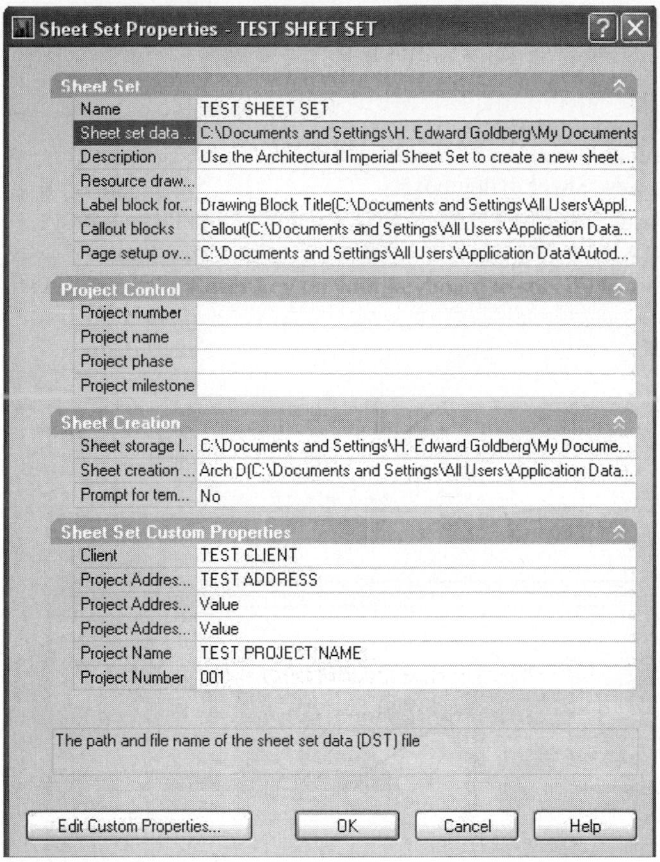

**Figure 21–3**

10. In the **Custom Properties** dialog box change the **Project Address 1** and **Project Address 2** to **TEST STREET** and **TEST CITY,** respectively (see Figure 21–4).
11. When you are finished, press the **OK** buttons to return to the **Sheet Set Details** dialog box. Press the **Next** button to go to the **Confirm** dialog box.
12. In the **Confirm** dialog box, if everything is OK, press the **Finish** button to create the sheet set. Save this file.

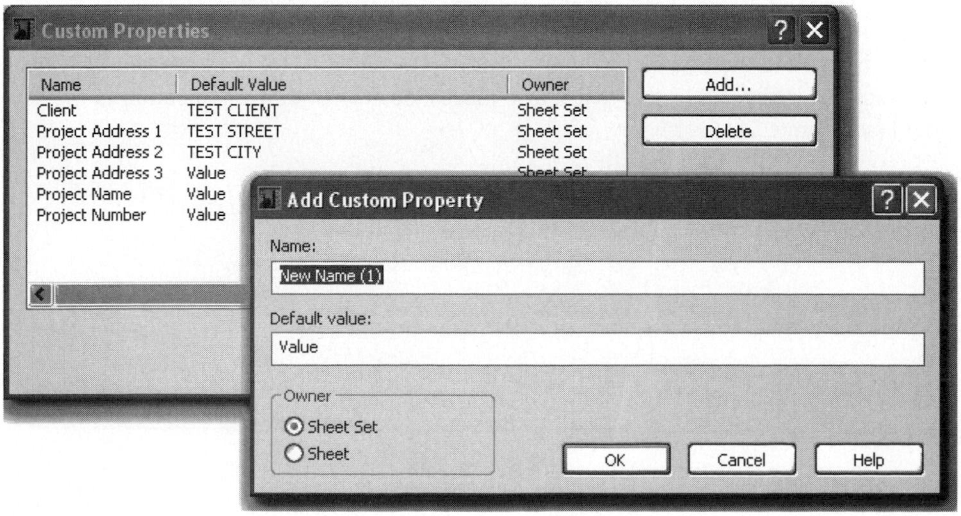

**Figure 21–4**

**Exercise 21-2:** Testing the New Sheet Set

1. Type **sheetset** in the **Command line** to bring up the **Sheet Set Manager.**
2. Select **Open** from the drop-down list.
3. Locate **TEST SHEET SET.**
4. Under **Sheets**, **RMB** on **Architectural,** and select **New Sheet** from the contextual menu that appears to bring up the **New Sheet** dialog box.
5. Enter **A-1** in the **Number** field, and **TEST ARCH SHEET** in the **Sheet title** field.
6. Press the **OK** button to return to the **Sheet Set Manager.**
7. Double-click on **A-1 - TEST ARCH SHEET** to bring up the new drawing (see Figure 21–5).

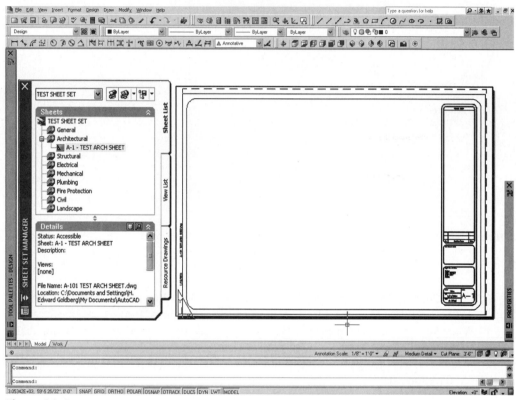

**Figure 21–5**

8. Zoom in close to the title block. Notice that it automatically contains the various values you dictated in the set. Notice that it also places the date of drawing creation in the date field (see Figure 21–6).

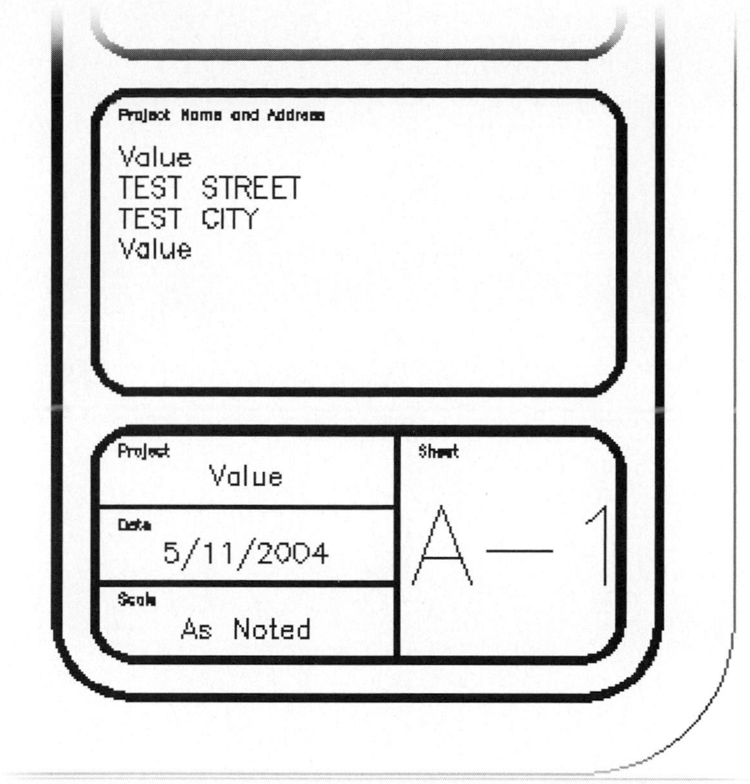

**Figure 21–6**

Although the sheet set command is included in AutoCAD 2008, it has been seamlessly integrated in AutoCAD Architecture 2008 in the **Project Navigator.** Adding a sheet and double-clicking on it to bring it up in the Drawing Editor is performed in the identical manner in the **Project Navigator** as was demonstrated in Section 16, "Drawing Management."

# Mask Blocks

## Section Objectives

- Understand the purpose of **Mask Blocks.**
- Know how to create, modify, and use **Mask Blocks.**

Mask blocks are two-dimensional blocks that mask the graphic display of AEC Objects in Plan View.

Mask blocks are often combined with AutoCAD objects such as lay-in fluorescent fixtures to mask the AEC ceiling grid. With a thorough understanding of mask blocks, you will probably find a myriad of uses for these objects.

**Exercise 22-1:** Creating a Custom Fluorescent Fixture Called New Fixture

1. Start a new drawing using the AEC Model (Imperial Stb) template.
2. Change to the **Model Layout.**
3. Change to the **Top View.**
4. Using the standard AutoCAD drawing commands, draw the ceiling fixture shown in Figure 22–1.
5. Enter **Pedit** in the **Command line,** select the outline, and join the outline into a closed polyline.
6. **RMB** anywhere in the Drawing Editor and select **Basic Modify Tools > Offset** from the contextual menu that appears.

**Note:**
If you don't know how to convert and join a line into a polyline, consult the AutoCAD 2008 help for **Polyline Edit (Pedit).**

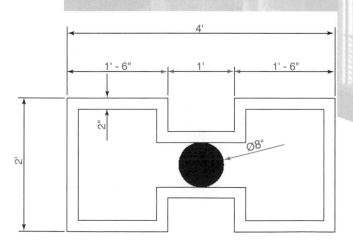

Figure 22–1

7. Enter **2″** in the **Command line,** and press **Enter** to create the 2″ outline shown in Figure 22–1.
8. Select **Format > Style Manager** from the **Main** toolbar to bring up the **Style Manager** dialog box.
9. Open the **Multi-Purpose** folder and double-click on the **Mask Block Definitions** icon.
10. Select the **New Style** icon from the **Main Style Manager** toolbar.
11. Rename the new style to **NEW LIGHT FIXTURE.**
12. Select the **NEW LIGHT FIXTURE** icon, and select the **Set From** icon from the **Main Style Manager** toolbar.
13. Select the outline when asked to **"Select a close polyline"** at the **Command line.**
14. Accept **N** when asked to "**Add another ring?"** at the **Command line.**
15. Make the insertion point for the mask the center point of the outline.
16. Select everything except the outline when asked to **"Select additional graphics"** at the **Command line.**
17. In the **Style Manager** dialog box, press the **Apply** button, and then press **OK.**

The outline will become the mask block, and the interior objects of the drawing will become the fixture graphics.

## Exercise 22-2: Testing the New Light Fixture Mask Block

1. Erase everything.
2. Create a 30′ × 30′ standard wall enclosure 10′ high.

For this exercise you will need to add the **Mask Block** tool to your **Design** tool palette, so do the following:

    a. Select the **Content Browser** icon from the **Main** toolbar to launch the Content Browser.
    b. Locate the **Stock Tool Catalog.**
    c. Locate the **Drafting Tools** folder.
    d. From the **Drafting Tools** folder, drag the **Mask Block** tool into your **Design** tool palette.

3. Select the **Rectangle** icon from the **Draw** toolbar, and place a rectangle inside the 30′ × 30′ enclosure you created (see Figure 22–2).

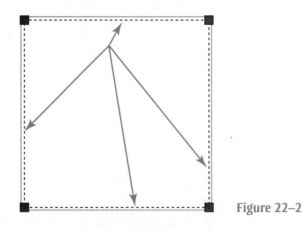

Figure 22–2

4. Change the **Display Configuration** to **Reflected.**
5. Select the **Ceiling Grid** icon from the **Design** tool palette, enter **S** (Set boundary) in the **Command line,** and press **Enter.**
6. Select the rectangle you placed in Step 3 of this exercise.
7. Move your cursor over the **Properties** palette to open it.
8. Set the following:
    a. Specify on screen = **No**
    b. X-Width = **40′**
    c. Y-Depth = **40′**
    d. XAxis Layout type = **Repeat**

e.  XAxis Bay size = **2'-0"**

f.  YAxis Layout type = **Repeat**

g.  YAxis Bay size = **4'-0"**

9.  Enter **SN** (Snap to center) in the **Command line,** press **Enter** twice, and then press the **Esc** key to complete the command.

You have now placed a centered ceiling grid, but it is located at elevation 0".

10.  Select the ceiling grid again, and move your cursor over the **Properties** palette to open it.

11.  Set the **Elevation** to **8'-0"** (see Figure 22–3).

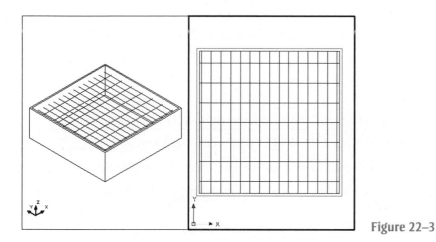

Figure 22–3

12.  Select the **Mask Block** tool icon that you placed in the **Design** palette.

13.  Move your cursor over the **Properties** palette to open it.

14.  Enter **R** (Rotation) in the **Command line,** enter **90,** and press **Enter.**

15.  Insert 12 copies of the mask block vertically.

16.  Insert two more copies horizontally (see Figure 22–4).

Notice that the horizontal mask blocks cross over a grid (see Figure 22–5).

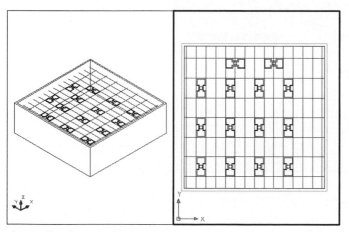

Figure 22–4

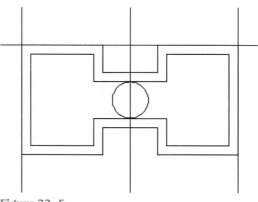

Figure 22–5

To correct this, do the following:

17.  Select the horizontal mass blocks you placed, **RMB,** and select **Attach Object** from the contextual menu that appears.

18.  Select the ceiling grid to bring up the **Select Display Representation** dialog box.

19.  Press **OK** to return to the Drawing Editor.

The grid is now masked by the NEW LIGHT FIXTURE mask block (see Figure 22–6). Save this file.

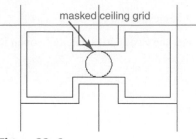

masked ceiling grid

**Figure 22–6**

**Exercise 22-3:** Using Create AEC Content to Place the New Light Fixture in the DesignCenter

1. Erase everything but one NEW LIGHT FIXTURE in the **Top View.**

The icon that will be used in the **DesignCenter** will be taken from the current view.

2. Select the **Format > AEC Content Wizard** from the **Main** toolbar to bring up the **Create AEC Content Wizard** dialog box.
3. Select the **Masking Block** radio button, press the **Add** button to add the **NEW LIGHT FIXTURE** mask block to the **Content File,** and press the **Next** button (see Figure 22–7).

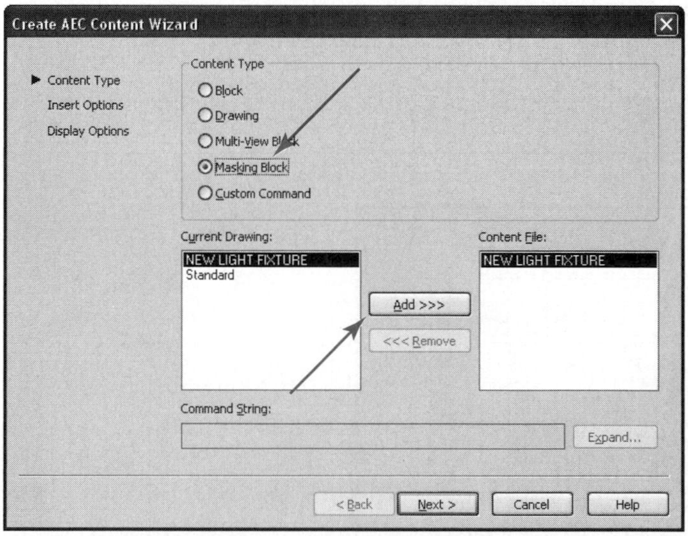

**Create AEC Content Wizard**

► Content Type
  Insert Options
  Display Options

Content Type
  ○ Block
  ○ Drawing
  ○ Multi-View Block
  ⊙ Masking Block
  ○ Custom Command

Current Drawing:
  NEW LIGHT FIXTURE
  Standard

Content File:
  NEW LIGHT FIXTURE

[Add >>>]
[<<< Remove]

Command String:

[Expand...]

[< Back] [Next >] [Cancel] [Help]

**Figure 22–7**

4. In **Insert Options,** press the **Select Layer Key** button to bring up the **Select Layer Key** dialog box.
5. Select **LIGHTCLG** under **Layer Key,** and press **OK** (see Figure 22–8).

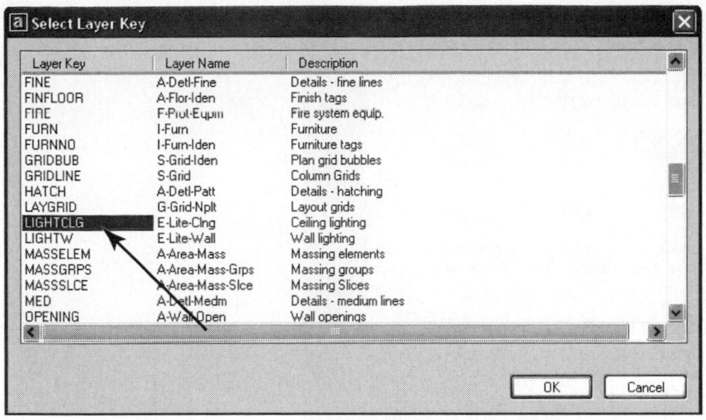

Figure 22–8

Selecting the **LIGHTCLG** layer key assures you that when you insert the content, it will be placed on that layer.

6. Select the **Next** button in the **Create AEC Content Wizard** dialog box.
7. In **Display Options,** press the **Browse** button.
8. At the **Save Content File** dialog box, locate the **Program Files\Autodesk ACD-A 2008\ Sample\Design Center** folder, name the file **CEILING FIXTURES,** and press the **Save** button to return to the **Create AEC Content Wizard** dialog box.
9. Type in a description for the masking block in the **Detailed Description** space, and press the **Finish** button (see Figure 22–9).

Note that the current viewport drawing is shown as an icon.

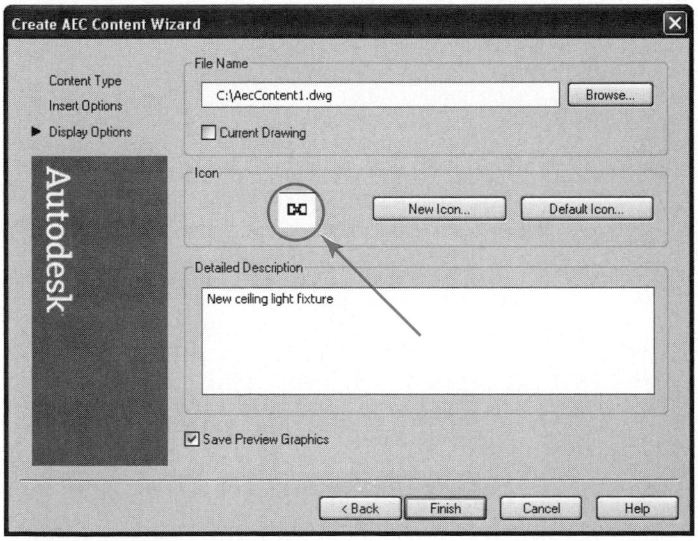

Figure 22–9

**Exercise 22-4:** Testing the New Light Fixture Mask Block from the DesignCenter

1. Erase everything in the previous drawing.
2. Select the **DesignCenter** icon from the **Main** toolbar or press **CTRL + 2** to bring up the **DesignCenter** palette.
3. Click on the CEILING FIXTURES drawing that you saved.
4. Select and drag the **NEW LIGHT FIXTURE** icon into a new drawing, and zoom extents (see Figure 22–10).

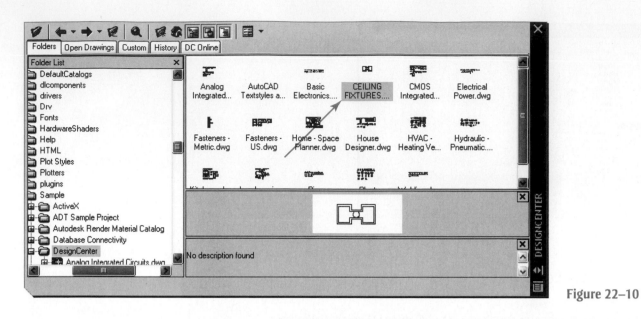

Figure 22–10

The **Create AEC Content Wizard** will place blocks, drawings, masking blocks, and custom command strings in the **DesignCenter.** The process is essentially the same for all these different forms of content.

# Multi-View Blocks

## 23

## Section
### Objectives

- Learn how to create the **Autodesk Website** icon.
- Learn how to get content from a website.
- Know how to create content from a 3D **Mesh.**
- Know how to create the **Multi-View Block.**
- Know how to test the **Multi-View Block.**

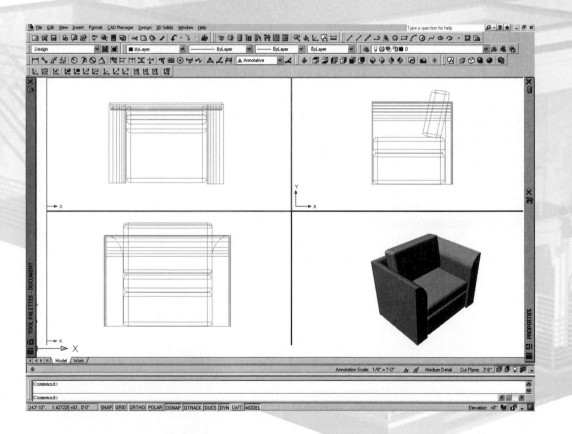

In combination with AutoCAD Architecture 2008's display system, the program uses a multi-view block system. This system allows you to place content in one view, and have the appropriate view appear in the other viewports. Although the program comes with a great deal of content, it includes controls that enable you to create your own custom content.

The following exercise illustrates the creation of a custom multi-view block.

## THE CHAIR

For this exercise you will need to use the Web to get content. You can go directly to the Web from inside AutoCAD Architecture 2008 by activating the **Autodesk Website** icon from the **Main** toolbar.

### Exercise 23-1: Creating the Autodesk Website Icon

If you do not have this icon on any toolbar, do the following:

1. **RMB** on any toolbar icon, and select **Customize** from the contextual menu that appears to bring up the **Customize User Interface** dialog box.
2. Change to the **Customize** tab.
3. Follow the directions in Figure 23–1, and drag the **Autodesk Website** icon to the **Standard** toolbar.
4. Press the **OK** button in the **Customize User Interface** dialog box to close it.

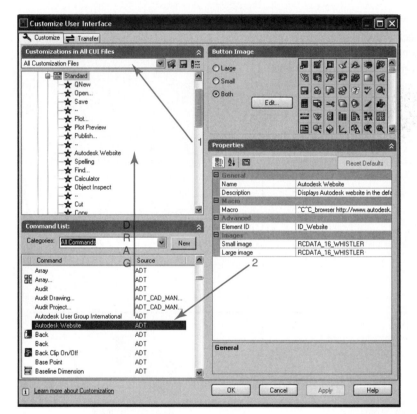

**Figure 23–1**

The **Autodesk Website** icon will now appear in the **Standard** toolbar above the Drawing Editor.

### Exercise 23-2: Going to the Chair at the 3D Cafe Website

1. Go to **http://www.max-realms.com.com/**
2. In the **Main Menu** on the left side, click the 3ds **Max Models** button to take you to the next page.
3. On the next page, click on **3ds Furniture** to go to the furniture page.
4. On the furniture page, go to page **(2).**
5. On page **(2),** at the bottom, download **3ds Chair, Stuffed** (see Figures 23–2 and 23–3).

**Note:**
Sometimes websites change addresses or just close down. At the time of publishing, the site for this exercise was active. If the site is now unavailable, you can search the Web for 3D content in 3DS (3D Studio, VIZ, or MAX content).

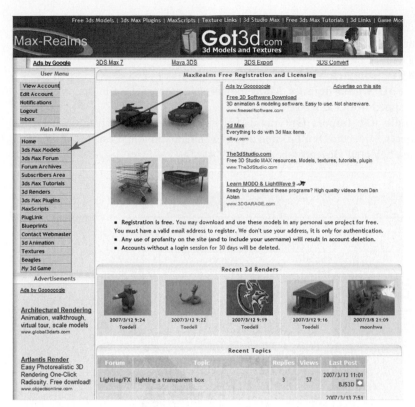

Figure 23–2

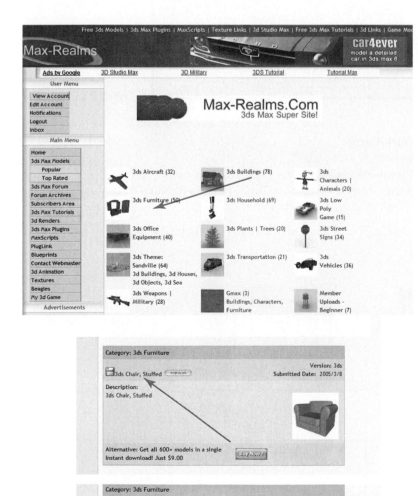

Figure 23–3

**Exercise 23-3:** Creating Content from a 3D Mesh

1. Start a new drawing using the AEC Model (Imperial Stb) template.
2. Change to the **Model Layout.**
3. Change to the **SW Isometric View.**
4. Select **Insert > 3D Studio** from the **Main** toolbar, and import the file that was downloaded and unzipped from the Web.
5. At the **3D Studio File Import Options** dialog box select the Sofa1b mesh from the **Available Objects,** select the **Don't Assign a Material** radio button, press the **Add** button, and add it to the **Selected Objects** (see Figure 23–4).

### 3D Studio File Import Options

**Available Objects**

| Object Name: | Type: |
|---|---|
| Global Settings | |
| Camera01 | Camera |
| Light01 | Light |
| Light02 | Light |

[Add All]  [Add]

**Selected Objects**

| Object Name: | Type: |
|---|---|
| Sofa1b | Mesh |

[Remove]  [Remove All]

**Save to Layers:**
- (•) By Object
- ( ) By Material
- ( ) By Object Color
- ( ) Single Layer

**Multiple Material Objects:**
- ( ) Always Prompt
- ( ) Split by Material
- ( ) Assign First Material
- (•) Don't Assign a Material

[OK]  [Cancel]  [Help]

Figure 23–4

6. Change to the **Work Layout.**
7. Erase all the viewports.
8. Select **View > Viewports > 4 Viewports** from the **Main** menu.
9. Change all the views in each viewport to **Top, Front, Left,** and **SW Isometric,** respectively, and zoom extents in all viewports.

You have now imported a 3D mesh model of a chair (see Figure 23–5).

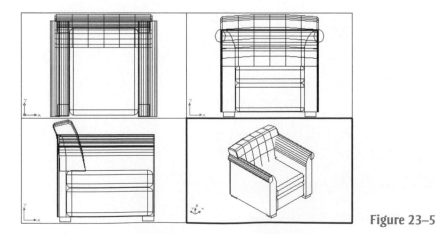

Figure 23–5

10. Select the **Content Browser** icon from the **Main** toolbar to open the Content Browser.
11. Select the **AutoCAD Architecture Stock Tool Catalog.**
12. Select the **Helper Tools** folder.
13. From the **Helper Tools** folder drag the **Hidden Line Projection** to the **Design** tool palette.
14. Select the **Hidden Line Projection** icon, select the chair, and press **Enter.**
15. Select any block insertion point, and type **Y** in the **Command line** to insert in **Plan View.**
16. Return to an **SW Isometric View** to see the chair and its new 2D hidden line projection.

You have now created a 2D hidden line projection of the left view of your model (see Figure 23–6).

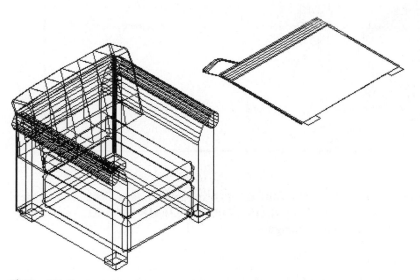

**Figure 23–6**

17. Repeat this process for the **Top** and **Front Views** (see Figure 23–7).
18. Select an empty place in the viewport, **RMB,** and select **Basic Modify Tools > 3D Operations > 3D Rotate** from the contextual menu that appears. Rotate the front and side views, and place them as shown in Figure 23–8. Create insertion points that align all the views and the model.

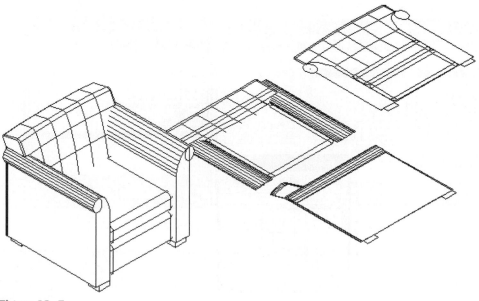

**Figure 23–7**

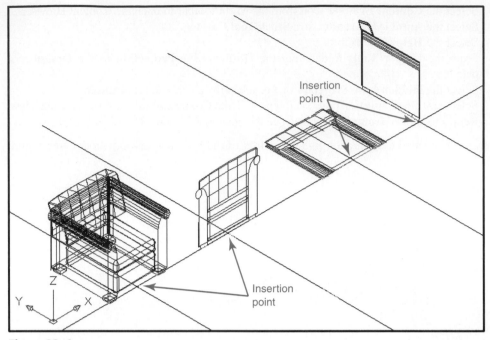

**Figure 23–8**

19. Select **Format > Blocks > Block Definition,** and save each view as a block, naming them **CHAIR FRONT, CHAIR SIDE, CHAIR TOP,** and **CHAIR MODEL,** respectively, using the insertion points shown in Figure 23–8.

**Exercise 23-4:** Creating a Multi-View Block

1. Select **Format > Multi-View Block > Multi-View Block Definitions** from the **Main** toolbar to bring up the **Style Manager** dialog box.
2. Select the **New Style** icon and create a new style; name it **CHAIR.**
3. Select **Chair Style, RMB,** and select **Edit** from the contextual menu that appears to bring up the **Multi-View Block Definition Properties** dialog box.
4. Select the **View Blocks** tab.
5. Select **General,** press the **Add** button, and select the **CHAIR FRONT** block.
6. After adding the **CHAIR FRONT** block, check the **Front** and **Back** check boxes under **View Directions** (see Figure 23–9).

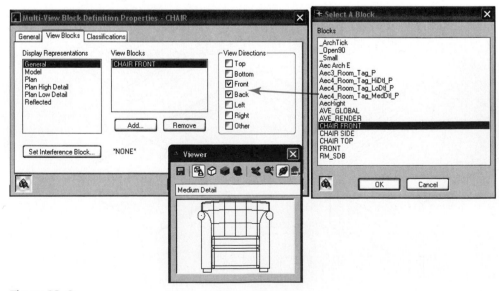

**Figure 23–9**

7. Repeat this process for the **CHAIR SIDE** and **CHAIR TOP** blocks, selecting the check boxes as shown (see Figures 23–10 and 23–11).

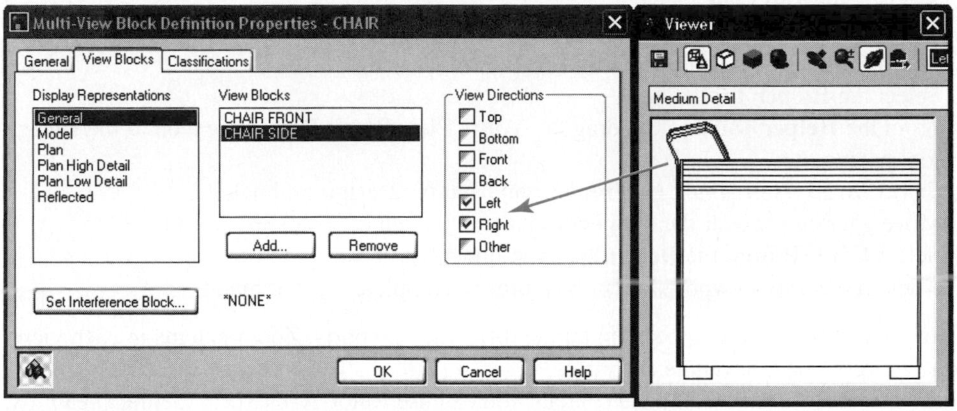

Figure 23–10

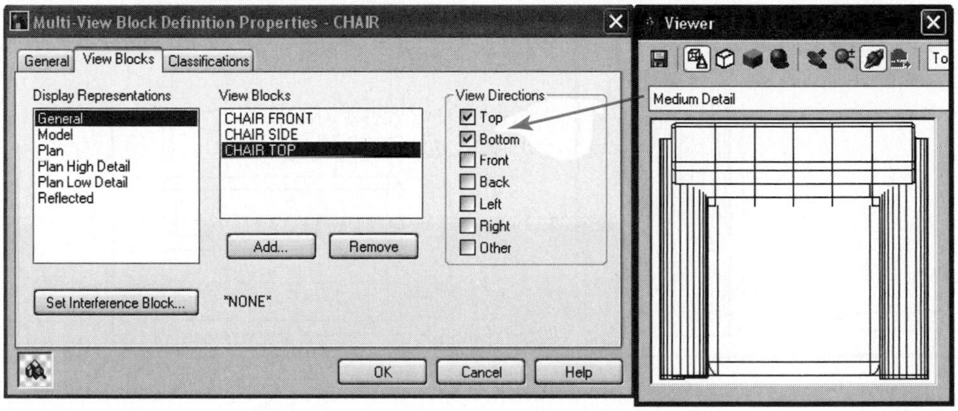

Figure 23–11

8. Select **Model** from the **Display Representations,** add the **Model** block, and check the **Other** check box (see Figure 23–12).

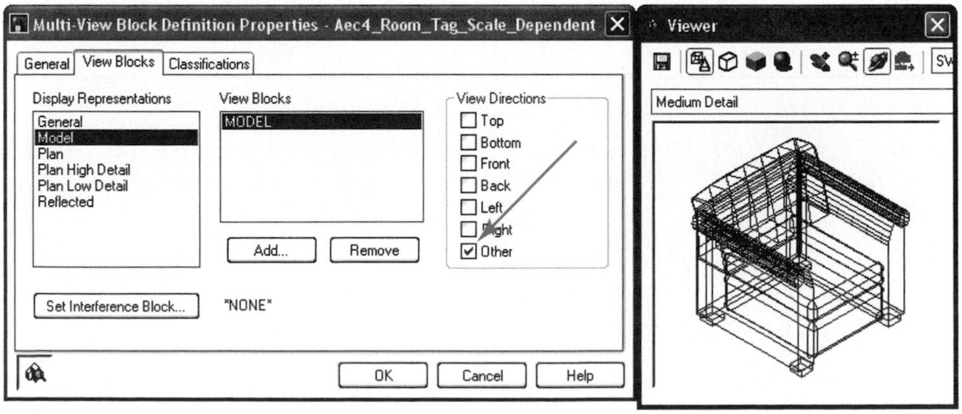

Figure 23–12

You have now created the multi-view block.

**Exercise 23-5:** Testing a Multi-View Block

1. Erase everything in the drawing.
2. Change to the **Work Layout.**
3. Activate the **Top View** viewport.
4. Select the **Content Browser** icon from the **Main** toolbar to open the Content Browser.
5. Select the **AutoCAD Architecture Stock Tool Catalog.**
6. Select the **Helper Tools** folder.
7. From the **Helper Tools** folder drag the **Multi-View Block Reference** icon to the **Design** tool palette.
8. Select **Multi-View Block Reference** icon from the **Design** tool palette.
9. Move your cursor over the **Properties** palette to open it.
10. Select **CHAIR** from the **Definition** drop-down list.
11. Click in the **Top** viewport, and press **Enter** to complete the command.

The correct view of the chair appears in all the different viewports. Zoom extents in each viewport (see Figure 23–13). Save this exercise.

There are many ways to make 3D content. You can use AutoCAD's 3D modeling capability, 3D Studio Viz, or search the Web for free content. With multi-view blocks, the sky is the limit.

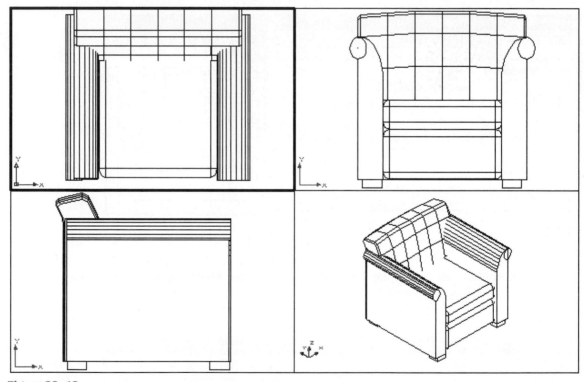

**Figure 23–13**

# The DesignCenter

## 24

## *Section* Objectives

- Use the **DesignCenter** to create a kitchen.
- Learn how to add appliances.
- Learn how to create the counter.
- Learn how to place the sink.
- Know how to generate a kitchen secton/elevation.

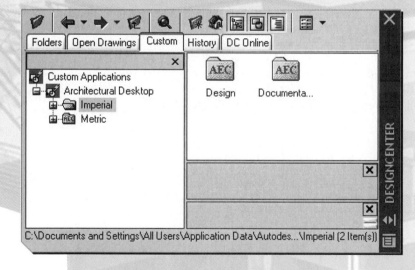

In order to understand architectural construction documents, designers include symbols of equipment such as bathroom fixtures, beds, chair, and kitchen cabinets. AutoCAD Architecture 2008 includes a comprehensive set of generic content symbols in both 2D and 3D. Much of the content is created utilizing AutoCAD Architectures multi-view block representation system. (See Exercise 22.3, "Using Create AEC Content to Place the New Light Fixture in the DesignCenter," page 442 in Section 22, and Section 23, "Multi-View Blocks"). Multi-view blocks allow the Display System to place the representation of the object in the appropriate view (e.g., 3D in Model View, plan representation in Plan View, etc.)

**Note:**
Everything shown in this section can also be gotten from the Content Browser Catalogs; the DesignCenter is another method.

## CONTENT

All the symbols as well as schedules, documentation symbols, and styles are contained in a folder called **AEC Content** in **C:\Documents and Settings\All Users\Application Data\Autodesk\ ACD-A 2008\enu\AEC Content\Imperial\ (C:\Documents and Settings\All Users\Application Data\Autodesk\ACD-A 2008\enu\AEC Content\Imperial\Design**—if you are using **Metric**). This content is placed in this location by default. Be sure you have sufficient space on your C drive regardless of whether you assign the AutoCAD Architecture 2008 program to a different drive than the C drive.

All content is held in standard AutoCAD drawings (DWG) and can be modified using standard AutoCAD commands.

**Exercise 24-1:** Using the DesignCenter to Create a Kitchen

### Creating the Kitchen

1. Start a new drawing using the AEC Model (Imperial Stb) template.
2. Change to the **Model Layout.**
3. Change to the **Top View.**
4. Place a 15'-0" × 10'-0" rectangle.
5. Select the **Walls** icon from the **Design** tool palette, **RMB,** and select **Apply Tool Properties to > Linework** from the contextual menu that appears.
6. Select the rectangle.
7. Type **Y** (Yes) in the **Command line** to erase the geometry (rectangle), and press **Enter** to create walls.
8. With the walls still selected, move your cursor over the **Properties** palette to open it.
9. Set the following parameters:
   a. Wall width = **4"**
   b. Base height = **8'-0"**
   c. Justify = **Right**
10. Modify the walls to create the enclosure shown in Figure 24–1.

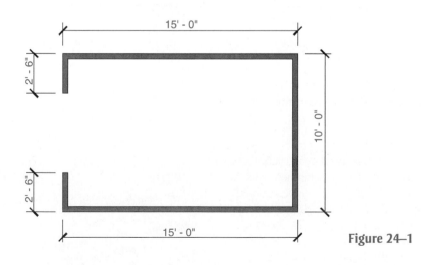

**Figure 24–1**

### Adding the Appliances

11. Select the **DesignCenter** icon from the **Main** toolbar (or press **Ctrl** + **2**) to bring up the DesignCenter.
12. Select the **AEC Content** tab.

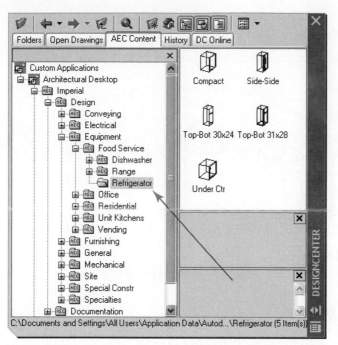

**Figure 24–2**

13. Select **Custom Applications > Architectural Desktop > Imperial > Design > Equipment > Food Service > Refrigerator** (Figure 24–2).
14. Double-click the **Refrigerator** folder to open it.
15. Select the **Side-Side** refrigerator, and drag it into the Drawing Editor.

The refrigerator will come into the drawing with the insertion point at its rear center.

16. Type **R** in the **Command line,** and press the **Enter** key on your keyboard.
17. Enter **270,** and press the **Enter** key on your keyboard.
18. Enter **B** (Base point) in the **Command line,** and press the space bar or **Enter** key on your keyboard.

This will allow you to relocate the insertion point of the refrigerator. Select the upper left corner of the refrigerator in the plan.

19. With the **End point** Object Snap set, place the refrigerator as shown in Figure 24–3.
20. Return to the **DesignCenter** and select **Architectural Desktop > Imperial > Design > Furnishing > Casework.**
21. Double-click the **Base with Drawers** folder to open it.

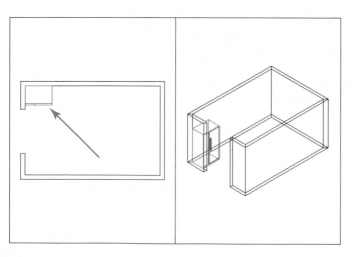

**Figure 24–3**

22. Continue to place base cabinets, a stove, and a tall cabinet until you create a kitchen lay-out similar to the one in Figure 24–4. Save this drawing as **Kitchen.**

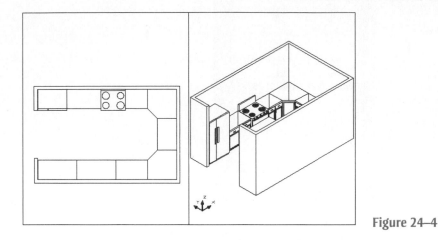

Figure 24–4

## The Counter: The Splash Edge Style

23. Use the previous drawing.
24. Select the **Rectangle** icon from the **Draw** toolbar, and create a **1″ × 4″**-high rectangle.
25. Select the rectangle, **RMB,** and select **Convert To > Profile Definition** from the contextual menu that appears.
26. Pick the lower right corner of the rectangle to bring up the **New Profile Definition** dialog box.
27. Enter **SPLASH PROFILE** in the **New Name** field, and press **OK** to create the profile.
28. Select **Format > Style Manager** to bring up the Style Manager.
29. Select **Architectural Objects > Slab Edge Styles.**
30. Select the **Slab Edge Styles** icon, **RMB,** and select **New** from the contextual menu that appears.
31. Rename the new slab edge style **SPLASH EDGE.**
32. Select **SPLASH EDGE, RMB,** and select **Edit** from the contextual menu to bring up the **Slab Edge Styles - SPLASH EDGE** dialog box.
33. Select the **Design Rules** tab.
34. Check the **Fascia** check box, and select **SPLASH PROFILE** from the drop-down list (see Figure 24–5).
35. Press **OK,** and close all the dialog boxes.

Figure 24–5

You have now created the splash edge style. You can keep this style for any future use.
    Now it's time to place the counter.

36. In the **Top View,** place polylines where you want counters (make sure the polylines are on
    the 0 layer, and that 0 is the active layer).
37. Using the **Layer Manager,** turn off visibility for everything but the 0 layer (see Figure
    24–6).

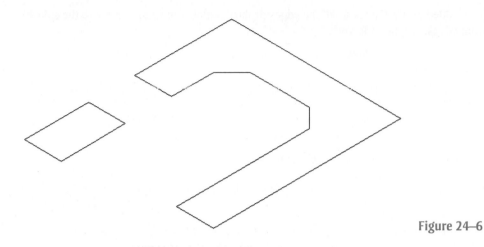

**Figure 24–6**

38. Select the **Slab** icon from the **Design** tool palette, **RMB,** and select **Apply Tool Proper-
    ties to > Linework and Walls** from the contextual menu that appears.
39. Select the two polylines you just created.
40. Enter **Y** (Yes) in the **Command line** and press **Enter.**
41. Enter **P** (Projected) in the **Command line** and press **Enter.**
42. Enter **36″** in the **Command line,** and press **Enter.**
43. Enter **T** (Top) in the **Command line** and press **Enter** to create the counter.
44. Turn the visibility of everything back on in the **Layer Manager,** and regenerate the drawing.

You have now created the counter over the base cabinets (see Figure 24–7).

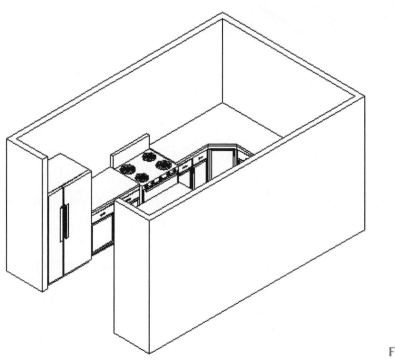

**Figure 24–7**

45. Select a counter you created, and move your cursor over the **Properties** palette to open it.
46. Set the **Thickness** to **2″**, and press the **Edges** icon to bring up the **Slab Edges** dialog box.
47. Select all the edges, and then select **SPLASH EDGE** from the **Edge Style** drop-down list, and then press **OK.**
48. Repeat Steps 11 and 12 for the other counter.

You have now added a splash edge to all the edges of the counter. You need to remove the splash from the front edges. Do the following:

a.    Select a counter, **RMB,** and select **Edit Slab Edges** from the contextual menu that appears.
b.    Select the slab edge you wish to remove, and press **Enter** to bring up the **Edit Slab Edges** dialog box.
c.    Select **Standard** from the **Edge Style** drop-down list and press **OK.**
d.    Repeat Steps b and c for the other counter.

You have now completed the counters (see Figure 24–8).

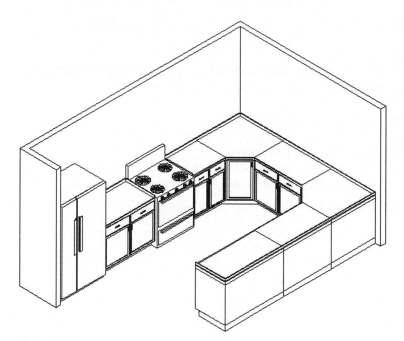

Figure 24–8

## Placing the Sink

49. Change the **UCS** (User Coordinate System) to a **Z height** equal to the top of the counter.

This will allow the sink to be brought in at counter height.

50. Select the **Architectural Desktop > Imperial > Design > Mechanical > Plumbing Fixtures > Sink** from the **DesignCenter.**
51. Double-click the **Sink** folder to open it.
52. Select the **Kitchen-Double B** sink, **RMB,** and drag it into your drawing.
53. Place the sink in the center of the counter.

Turning on **Gouraud** shading shows that the counter cuts through the sink (see Figure 24–9).

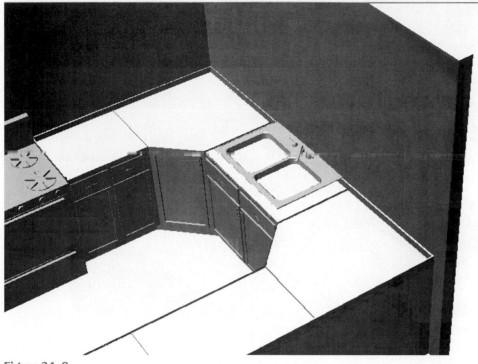

**Figure 24–9**

Real counters need cutouts for sinks.

54. Select the **Rectangle** icon from the **Draw** menu and place a rectangle as shown in Figure 24–10.

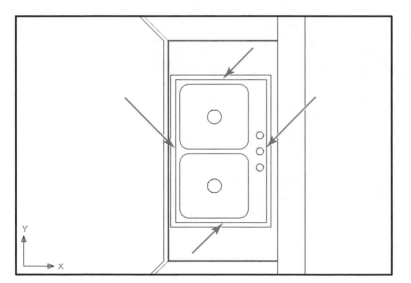

**Figure 24–10**

55. Select the **Slab, RMB,** and select the **Hole Add** icon from the contextual menu that appears.
56. Select the rectangle and press **Enter.**
57. Enter **Y** (Yes) in the **Command line** and press **Enter.**

The sink and counter are shaded correctly (see Figure 24–11).

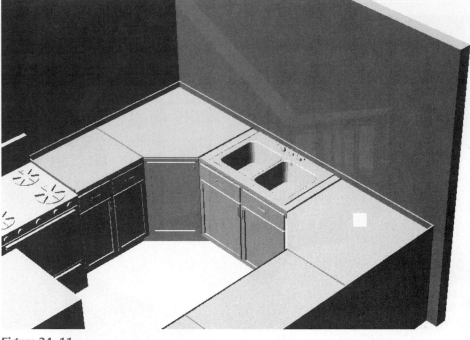

**Figure 24–11**

58. Place the upper cabinets and a window, and complete the kitchen (see Figure 24–12).

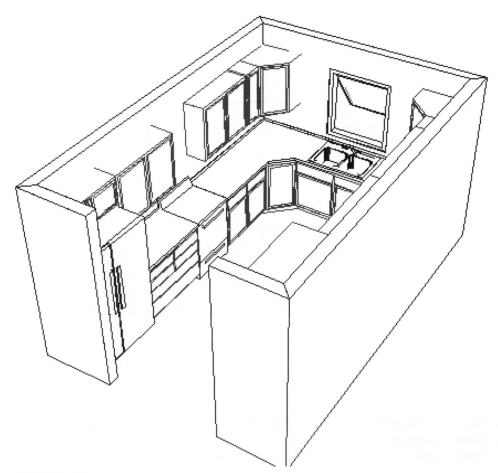

**Figure 24–12**

## Kitchen Section/Elevation

59.  Select the **Elevation Line** icon from the **Design** tool palette.
60.  Place an elevation line through the kitchen as shown in Figure 24–13.

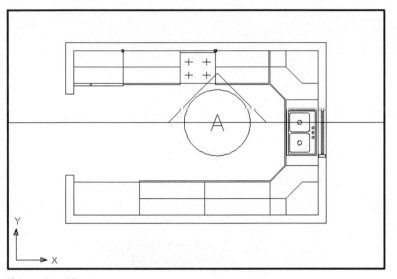

Figure 24–13

61.  Select the elevation line, **RMB,** select **Generate Elevation** from the contextual menu, and generate an elevation of your finished kitchen (see Figure 24–14).

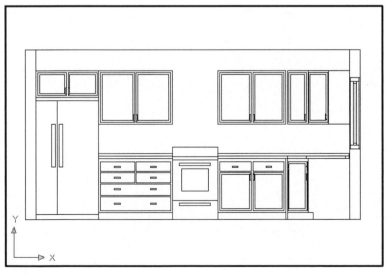

Figure 24–14

# AEC Project Standards

# 25

## Section
## Objectives

- Understand how to use the **AEC Project Standards.**
- Know how to create and locate the **Standards Drawing.**
- Load the **CAD Manager** and configure the **Standards Drawing.**
- Change a project drawing(s) by synchronizing the project with the **Standards Drawing.**
- Replace an AEC Object in a project drawing by synchronizing it with the **Standards Drawing.**

The Project Standards feature lets you establish, maintain, and synchronize standards across all drawings in a project. Project standards include standard styles, display settings, and AutoCAD standards that are used across all project drawings. AutoCAD blocks and the new Dynamic blocks are *not* managed by Project Standards. Standard styles and display settings are specified in one or more standards drawings associated with the project. Project drawings can then be synchronized with these standards throughout the project life cycle, either automatically or on demand. In addition, you can designate tool palettes and a Content Browser library that are associated with the project.

Project Standards is optional; however, the advantage of making changes across multiple files without opening them individually is very compelling.

## PROJECT STANDARDS TERMINOLOGY

*Project Drawing:* A drawing file belonging to an AutoCAD Architecture project. A drawing must be part of a project to access and be synchronized with project standards.

*Standards Drawing:* A file (DWG, DWT, DWS) that contains standard styles and display settings associated with the project. Standards drawings can be placed in a folder within the project folder, if they contain project-specific standards, or outside the project folder if they contain department-specific or companywide standards.

*Standard Style or Display Setting:* A style or display setting that has been defined as a standard for a certain project. To be defined as a standard style or display setting, *it needs to be contained in a standards drawing.* Standard style types and display settings include the following:

- Object styles (e.g., wall styles, door styles, etc.)
- Property set definitions
- Property data formats
- Schedule table styles
- Classification definitions
- Display theme styles
- Layer key styles
- Mask block definitions
- Material definitions
- Multi-view block definitions
- Profile definitions
- Display properties
- Display sets
- Display configurations

*Synchronization:* The process of checking a drawing or project against its associated standards to identify and remove version discrepancies between the standards and the project. Synchronization can run invisibly in the background, run automatically with user prompting, or be manually initiated by the user.

### Standards Drawing Location

When standards drawings, catalogs, and libraries are located within the project folder, they are treated as project-specific. For example, if the project is used as a template for a new project, all files from the standards folder are copied to the new project to enable changing and overwriting them in the new project. Standards files that are located outside the project folder are not copied when creating a new project; they are only referenced from their original location in both the existing and the new project. This would be appropriate for files containing company standards that should not be changed from project to project.

Specify AutoCAD Standards files containing dimension, layer, linetype, and text styles. Project drawings may be checked against these standards using the **CheckStandards** command or the **Batch Standards Checker.**

Project standards can be accessed from a variety of AutoCAD file formats. They can be saved in one or more drawing files (DWG), drawing templates (DWT), or AutoCAD standards drawings (DWS). Each of these file types can be associated with a project as standards drawings.

### Exercise 25-1: Creating and Locating the Standards Drawing

1. Before opening AutoCAD Architecture 2008, use the **Windows "My Computer"** to create a new directory called **TEST PROJECT STANDARDS DIRECTORY.**
2. From the standard Windows desktop, start AutoCAD Architecture 2008 or maximize it if it is already loaded.

3. In AutoCAD Architecture select **File > Project Browser** from the **Main** menu to open the **Project Browser** dialog box.

4. In the **Project Browser** dialog box, double-click on the **TEST PROJECT STAN-DARDS DIRECTORY** to make it the current directory (see Figure 25–1).

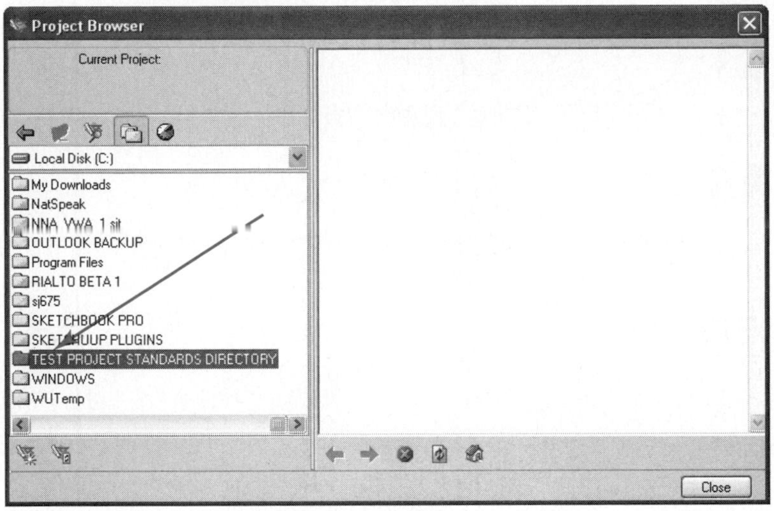

**Figure 25–1**

5. Click the **New Project** icon at the bottom left of the **Project Browser** dialog box to bring up the **Add Project** dialog box.

6. In the **Add Project** dialog box enter **001** as the **Project Number,** and **PROJECTS STANDARDS EXERCISE** as the **Project Name,** and press the **OK** button (see Figure 25–2).

7. Press the **Close** button at the bottom-right corner of the **Project Browser** to bring up the **Project Navigator.**

You have now automatically created all the project folders and subfiles that make the Project Navigator work for this new project. If you minimize AutoCAD Architecture and again use the **Windows "My Computer"** to go into the **TEST PROJECT STANDARDS DIRECTORY,** you will see the files and folders that have been created (see Figure 25–3).

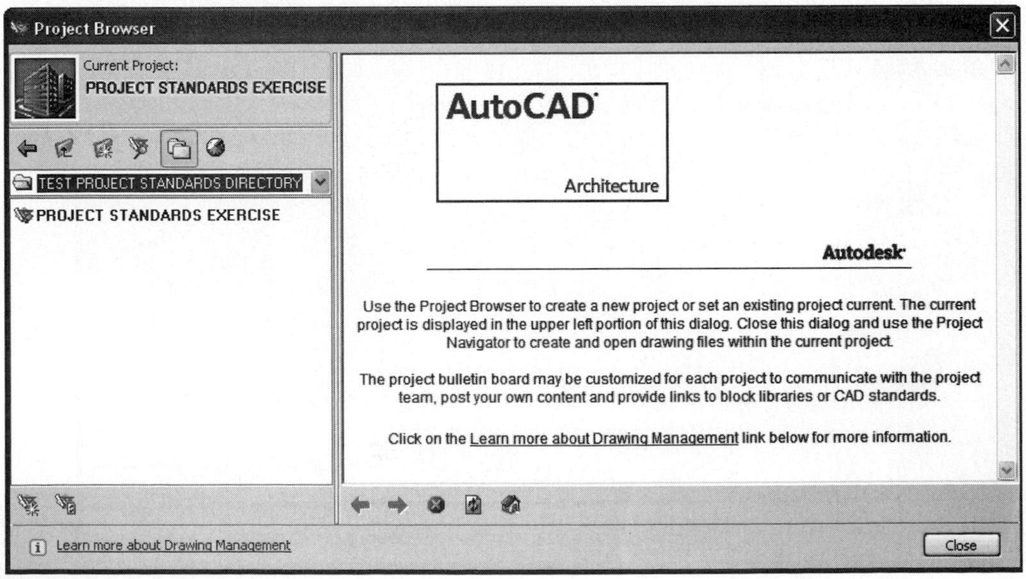

**Figure 25–2**

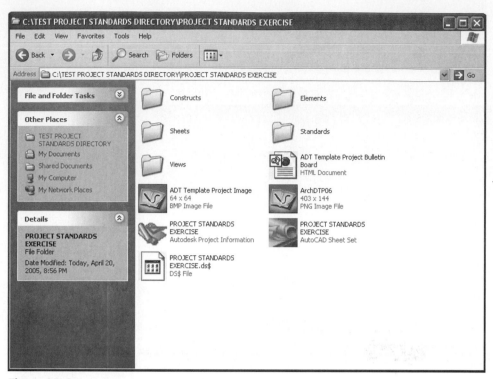

**Figure 25–3**

8. Maximize AutoCAD Architecture, and notice that you now have an empty Project Tools tool palette labeled **PROJECTS STANDARDS EXERCISE** and that the drawing in the Drawing Editor is labeled (Drawing1.dwg).
9. Select **File > Save As** from the **Main** menu, and save this drawing as **WINDOW and DOOR STANDARDS** in the **TEST PROJECT DIRECTORY > PROJECTS STANDARDS EXERCISE** folder (see Figure 25–4).

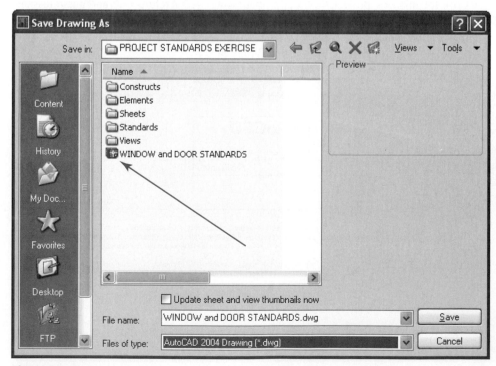

**Figure 25–4**

**Exercise 25-2:** Loading the CAD Manager and Configuring the Standards Drawing

1. Select **Window > Pulldowns > CAD Manager Pulldown** to load the **CAD Manager** into the **Main** menu (see Figure 25–5).

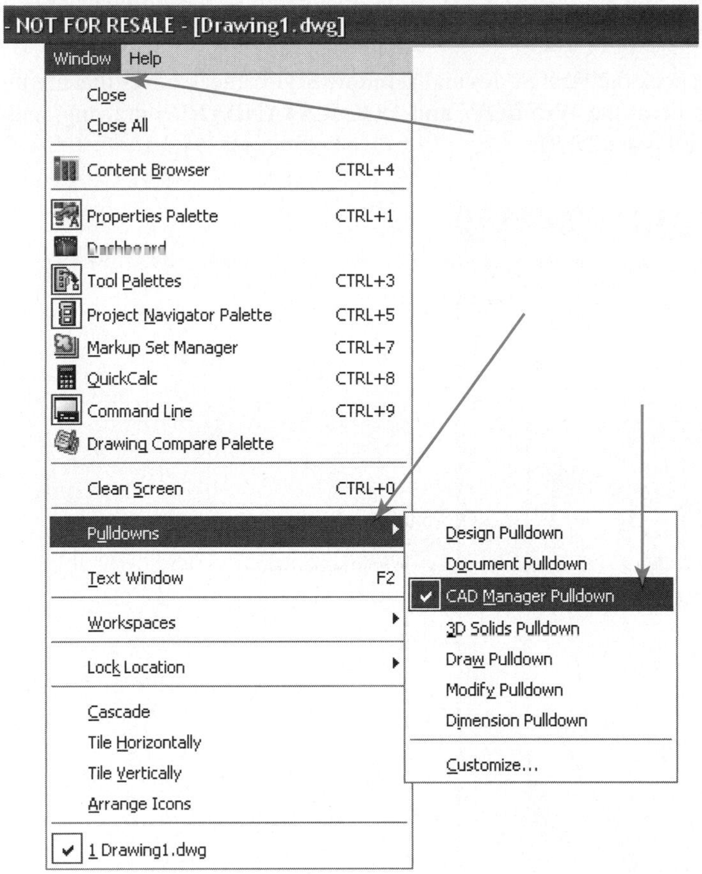

**Figure 25–5**

2. After the CAD Manager pulldown is loaded, select **CAD Manager > AEC Project Standards > Configure** from the **Main** menu to bring up the **Configure AEC Project Standards** dialog box (see Figure 25–6).

3. In the **Configure AEC Project Standards** dialog box, select the **Standard styles** tab, and make sure **All Objects** is showing in the object display drop-down list.

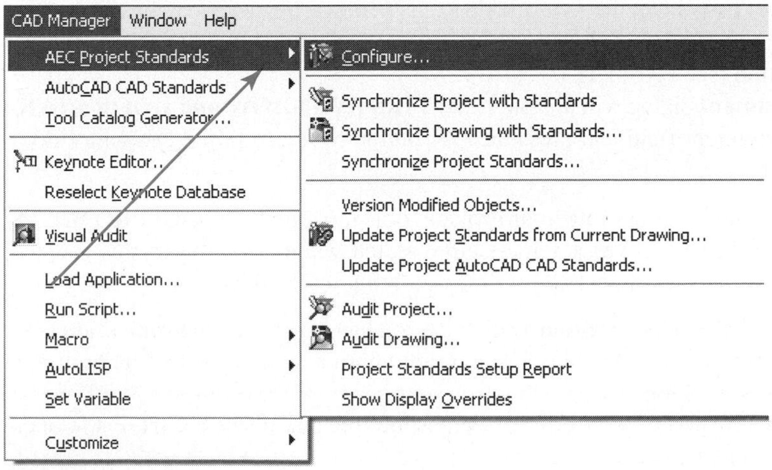

**Figure 25–6**

4. Press the **Add** icon to the right of the **Configure AEC Project Standards** dialog box, and select the **WINDOW and DOOR STANDARDS** drawing in the **TEST PROJECT DIRECTORY > PROJECTS STANDARDS EXERCISE** folder.

5. Press the **Open** button to return to the **Configure AEC Project Standards** dialog box.

You have now set the **WINDOW and DOOR STANDARDS** drawing to be a **Standards** drawing. Next you will tell the program which objects that drawing controls.

6. Under the **Objects** list, check the **Wall Styles** and **Window Styles** check boxes that are in line with the vertical name of the **WINDOW and DOOR STANDARDS** drawing, and press the **OK** button (see Figure 25–7).

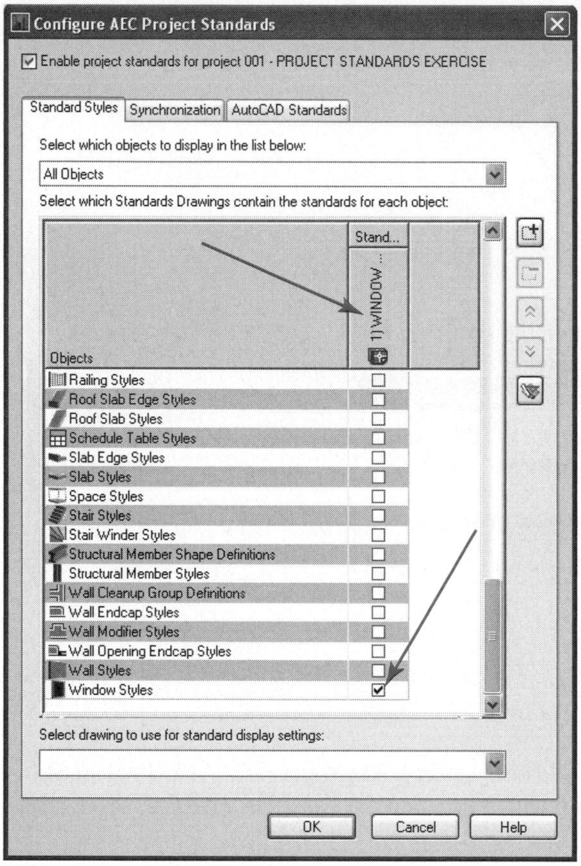

Figure 25–7

This purpose is to set the relationship between the **Standards** file and the objects to be managed.

7. Under the **Objects** list, check the **Door Styles** and **Window Styles** check boxes that are in line with the vertical name of the **WINDOW and DOOR STANDARDS** drawing, and press the **OK** button (see Figure 25–7).

8. The **Version Comment** dialog will appear. Enter **FIRST WINDOW and DOOR STANDARDS** in the comment field and press the **OK** button to return to the Drawing Editor (see Figure 25–8).

You will now place doors and windows into your Project Tools tool palette labeled **PROJECTS STANDARDS EXERCISE,** which was automatically created when you created this project. This tool palette will automatically appear every time you bring up this project.

9. In the **Configure AEC Project Standards** dialog box, change to the **Synchronization** tab.

10. In the **Synchronization** tab, select the **Manual** radio button, and press the **OK** button to return to the Drawing Editor.

11. Select the **Content Browser** icon from the **Navigation** tool bar or select **Ctrl + 4** to open the Autodesk **Content Browser.**

12. From the **Content Browser > Design Tool Catalog - Imperial,** drag the **Awning Halfround, Awning-Double, Awning-Double Octagon,** and **Bay** windows into the locked-open

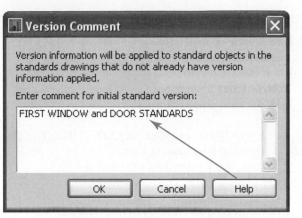

Figure 25-8

**PROJECTS STANDARDS EXERCISE** Project Tools tool palette.

13. Repeat this process dragging the **Hinged-Double-6 panel, Hinged-Double-6 Panel Half Lite, Hinged-Single-Arched Full Lite,** and **Hinged-Single-Halfround** doors into the **PROJECTS STANDARDS EXERCISE** Project Tools tool palette.

14. Finally, drag one of the doors into the **WINDOW and DOOR STANDARDS** drawing.

15. At the **Command line,** press **Enter,** and click the mouse button to place the door.

16. Press the **Enter** key twice to complete the command, and place the door.

17. Repeat for all the doors and windows.

18. Save the **WINDOW and DOOR STANDARDS** drawing again, and then close it (see Figure 25–9).

**Note:**
It would be a good idea to read in the **Synchronization** tab the explanation of the Manual standards synchronization behavior. If you select the other radio buttons, you can read their behavior.

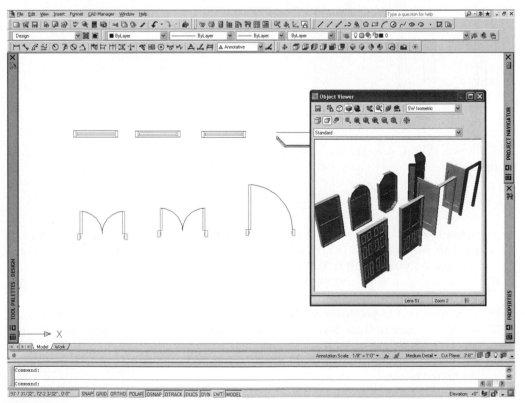

Figure 25–9

**Exercise 25-3:** Changing a Project Drawing by Synchronizing It with the Standards Drawing

1. In the **PROJECT STANDARDS EXERCISE,** open the **Project Navigator** and change to the **Constructs** tab.
2. In the **Constructs** tab click the **Add Construct** icon to bring up the **Add Construct** dialog box.

This is a good opportunity to check what you learned in Section 16, "Drawing Management."

3. In the **Add Construct** dialog box, enter **WINDOW and DOOR CONSTRUCT** in the name field, and press the **OK** button to return to the Drawing Editor.
4. Open the **Project Navigator** again, select the **Constructs** tab, and double-click on **WINDOW and DOOR CONSTRUCT** to bring it up in the Drawing Editor.
5. From the **Design** tool palette, select and place a **Standard** 6″ wide wall with a base height of 8′-0″ and 15′ long into the **WINDOW and DOOR CONSTRUCT** drawing.
6. From the **PROJECT STANDARDS EXERCISE > Project tools** tool palette place a **Hinged-Single-Halfround** door, an **Awning Double,** and an **Awning Halfround** window in the wall you previously placed.
7. Change to the **SW Isometric** view (see Figure 25–10).

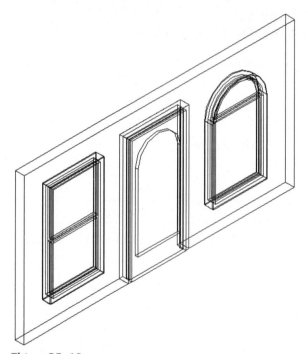

**Figure 25–10**

8. Select **Format > Style Manager** from the **Main** menu to bring up the **Style Manager.**
9. Click the + next to **001 PROJECT STANDARDS EXERCISE** at the top left pane to expose the **WINDOW and DOOR STANDARDS.dwg.**
10. Click the + next to **WINDOW and DOOR STANDARDS.dwg** to expose the **Architectural Objects** in that drawing.
11. Click the + next to **Architectural Objects** to expose the **Door Styles** and **Window Styles.**
12. Click the + next to **Door Styles** and **Window styles** to expose their different doors and windows (see Figure 25–11).
13. Click on the **Awning-Double** window style to bring up its properties in the right pane of the **Style Manager.**

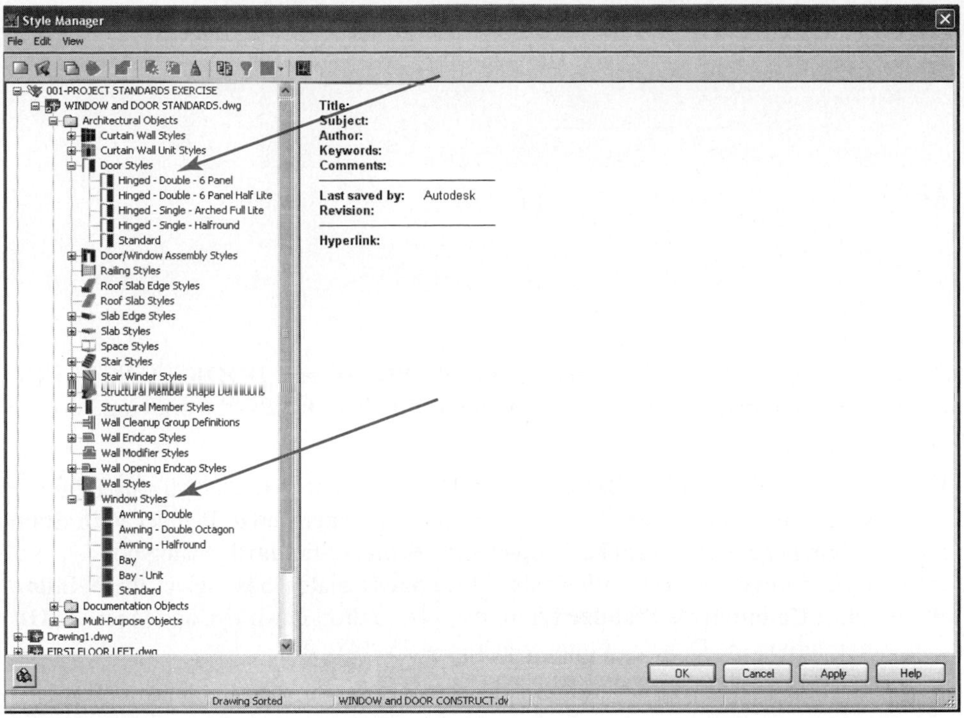

**Figure 25–11**

14. Change to the **Dimensions** tab.
15. In the **Dimensions** tab, change the **B-Depth** to **24″.**
16. Change to the **Version History** tab.
17. In the **Version History** tab, press the **Version** button to bring up the **Version Object** dialog box.
18. In the **Version Object** dialog box, enter **24″ B-Depth** (see Figure 25–12).

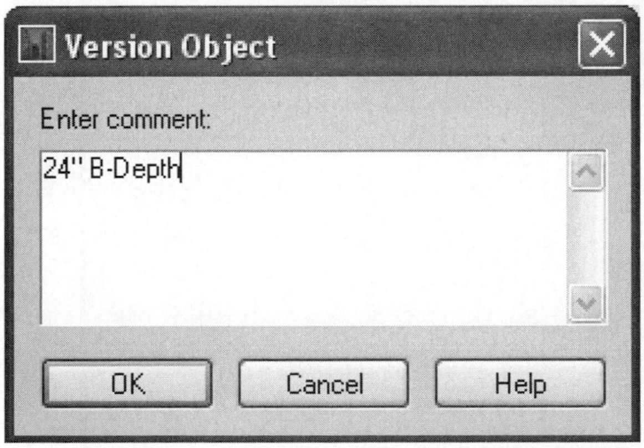

**Figure 25–12**

19. In the **Version Object** dialog box, press **OK** to return to the **Style Manager** dialog box, and press **OK** in the **Style Manager** dialog box to close it.

An **AutoCAD** information dialog box will now appear telling you that you have changed the **Standards** drawing, and asking if you wish to save the changes. Press the **Yes** button to save the changes and return to the Drawing Editor (see Figure 25–13).

**Figure 25–13**

To synchronize the Awning-Double window in the **WINDOW and DOOR CONSTRUCT** drawing with the changed Awning-Double window in the **Standards** drawing, do the following:

20. Be sure the **WINDOW and DOOR CONSTRUCT** drawing is in the Drawing Editor.
21. Select **CAD Manager > AEC Project Standards > Synchronize Project with Standards** to bring up the **Synchronize Project with Project Standards** dialog box.
22. In the **Synchronize Project with Project Standards** dialog box, select the **Window Style,** select **Update from Standard** from the **Action** drop-down list, and press the **OK** button to return to the Drawing Editor (see Figure 25–14).

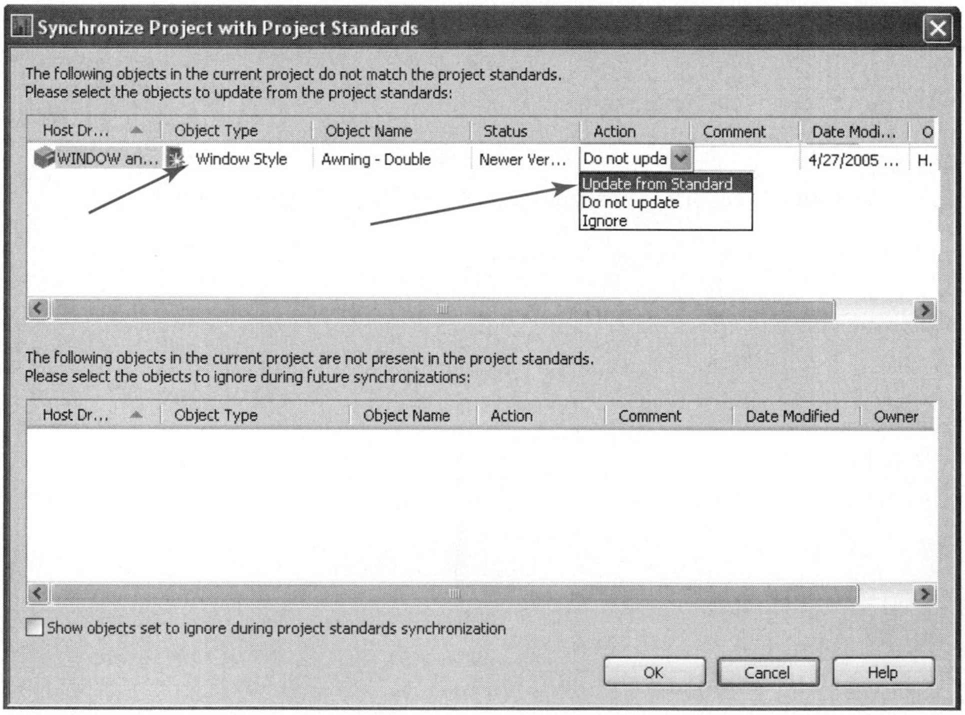

**Figure 25–14**

23. Select **Flat Shaded, Edges On** from the **Shading** tool bar, and notice that the **Awning** window in the **WINDOW and DOOR CONSTRUCT** drawing has changed (see Figure 25–15).

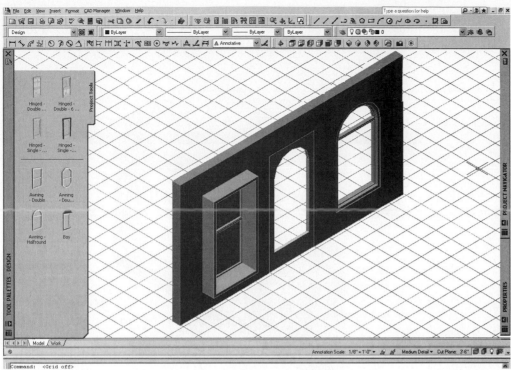

**Figure 25–15**

**Exercise 25-4:** Replacing an AEC Object in a Project Drawing by Synchronizing It with the Standards Drawing

1. Open the **WINDOW and DOOR STANDARDS** drawing from the **TEST PROJECT DIRECTORY > PROJECTS STANDARDS EXERCISE** folder.
2. In the **WINDOW and DOOR STANDARDS** drawing, delete the **Awning-Double** window, and save the file.
3. Select **Format > Style Manager** from the **Main** menu to bring up the **Style Manager.**
4. Click the + next to **001 PROJECT STANDARDS EXERCISE** at the top left pane to expose the **WINDOW and DOOR STANDARDS.dwg.**
5. Click the + next to **WINDOW and DOOR STANDARDS.dwg** to expose the **Architectural Objects** in that drawing.
6. Click the + next to **Architectural Objects** to expose the **Window styles.**
7. Click the + next to **Window styles** to expose its windows.
8. Select the **Awning-Double** window style, **RMB,** and select **Purge** to purge the **Awning-Double** window style from the **Style Manager.**
9. With the **Style Manager** still open, change the name of the **Awning-Double Octagon** style to **Awning-Double,** and press **OK.**
10. In the AutoCAD warning dialog box, press the **Yes** button to return to the Drawing Editor.

Since the left window in your **WINDOW and DOOR CONSTRUCT** drawing was originally named **Awning-Double,** the renamed **Awning-Double Octagon** window will replace it. Do the following:

11. Be sure the **WINDOW and DOOR CONSTRUCT** drawing is in the Drawing Editor.
12. Select **CAD Manager > AEC Project Standards > Synchronize Project with Standards** to bring up the **Synchronize Project with Project Standards** dialog box.
13. In the **Synchronize Project with Project Standards** dialog box, select the **Awning-Double** Window Style, select **Update from Standard** from the **Action** drop-down list, and press **OK** to return to the Drawing Editor.

14. Select **Flat Shaded, Edges On** from the **Shading** toolbar, and notice that the **Awning** window in the **WINDOW and DOOR CONSTRUCT** drawing has changed to the **Awning-Double Octagon** window (see Figure 25–16).

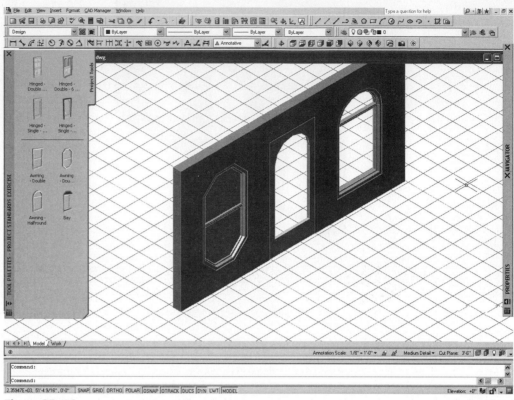

**Figure 25–16**

Experiment with changing different doors and windows until the operation becomes natural. Door widths and heights cannot be changed and synchronized unless you substitute different styles as shown in the above exercise.

The following points need to be taken into consideration to work efficiently with the Project Standards feature:

- Project standards can be used only with projects. A drawing must be part of a project to be synchronized with project standards. Project standards cannot be applied to stand-alone drawings. You can copy standard styles and display settings into stand-alone drawings, but they will not be synchronized when the standards change.

- Project standards can be distributed among multiple standards drawings, if desired. However, only one drawing can be designated for the display settings in a project.

- Project standards can be stored in DWG, DWT, and DWS files.

- AutoCAD standards for layers, text styles, linetypes, and AutoCAD dimension styles must be placed in DWS files.

- Demand loading needs to be enabled for working with project standards. The XLOADCTL system variable must be set to 2 (default value).

- There is no auto-updating between Project Standards and Project-based catalogs and Project-based tool palettes in the workspace.

# Display Themes

## 26

*Section*
## Objectives

- Set up an AEC Object for **Display Themes.**
- Coordinate an AEC Object with the **Display Themes Style.**
- Know how to place a **Display Theme Schedule** object.

## DISPLAY THEMES

Typically, manual properties of an object—such as a wall's fire rating or a door's manufacturer—are not visible in a drawing. Display themes let you incorporate such nongraphic data in your drawing by using certain colors, fills, or hatches to highlight objects that meet criteria (theme rules) you establish in a display theme style. For example, you might define a property named Function for room objects, and then set up a theme rule specifying that rooms with a Function value equal to "storage" will be displayed with a solid yellow fill.

Theme by
Space Size

Theme by
Fire Rating

Theme by
Space Typ...

Theme by
Space Typ...

Theme by
Space Typ...

Theme by
Space Typ...

DISPLAY THEMES

TOOL PALETTES - DISPLAY THEMES

**Exercise 26–1:** Creating a Test Floor

1. Using the **Wall** tool from the **Design** tool palette, create the floor and walls shown in Figure 26–1.

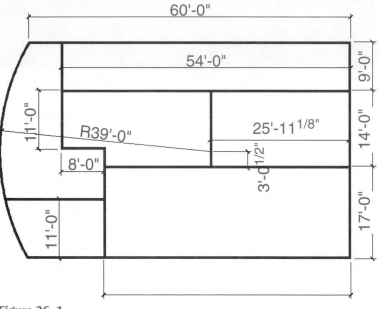

**Figure 26–1**

2. Select the **Space Auto Generate** tool from the **Design** tool palette, and place spaces (see Figure 26–2).

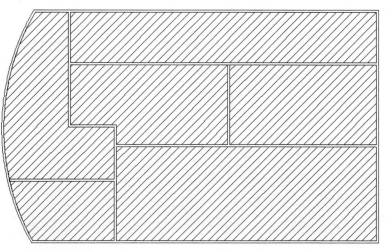

**Figure 26–2**

3. Select one of the spaces, **RMB,** and select **Edit Space Style** from the contextual menu that appears to bring up the **Space Style Properties** dialog box.
4. In the **Space Style Properties** dialog box, press the **Property Sets** button to open the **Edit Property Set Data** dialog box.
5. In the **Edit Property Set Data** dialog box, select the **Add Property Sets** icon to open the **Add Property Sets** dialog box.

6. In the **Add Property Sets** dialog box, make sure the **SpaceStyles** check box is checked, and press the **OK** buttons to return to the Drawing Editor (see Figure 26–3).

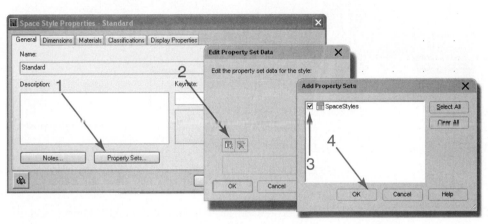

**Figure 26–3**

7. Select the **Theme by Space Size** tool from the **Schedules** tool palette.
8. Click in the **Drawing Editor,** and then press the **Enter** key to complete the command. The spaces now change color according to size as dictated in the **Display Theme** schedule (see Figure 26–4).

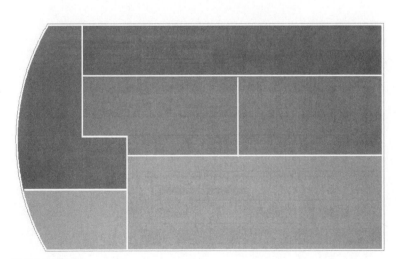
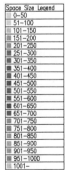

**Figure 26–4**

To understand what is happening, select the **Display Theme** schedule you just placed, **RMB,** and select **Edit Display Theme Style** from the contextual menu that appears to bring up the **Display Theme Style Properties** dialog box. In the **Theme Rules for selected Theme Setting** panel you will find the drop-down lists for the **Property Set Definitions, Property,** and **Condition** that connect AEC Objects to Theme Display schedules (see Figure 26–5).

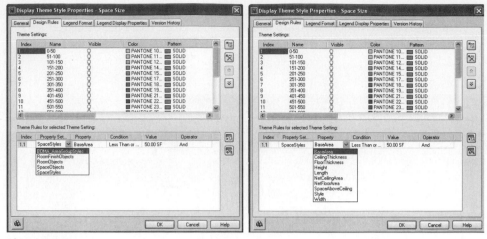

**Figure 26–5**

Try experimenting with different property set definitions for different AEC Objects and different configurations for Display Theme schedules. It is really quite easy.

# Rendering and Visualization

**27**

## *Section* Objectives

- Know how best to learn the Visualization process.
- Learn how to make a simple scene and use the **Materials** tool palette in **AutoCAD Architecture 2008.**
- Learn how to create shadows in **AutoCAD Architecture 2008.**
- Learn how to use the **Camera** tool in **AutoCAD Architecture 2008.**
- Know how to create and modify **Materials in AutoCAD Architecture 2008.**
- Know how to adjust **Materials in AutoCAD Architecture 2008.**
- Know how to use **Archvision RPC** content in **AutoCAD Architecture 2008.**
- Learn how to **Export to DWG for import into Autodesk 3DS MAX 9.**
- Learn how to visualize using **Autodesk 3DS MAX 9.**
- Create and place **Materials** in **Autodesk 3DS MAX 9.**
- Learn how to create **Grass** in **Autodesk 3DS MAX 9.**
- Know how to use **Archvision RPC** content in **3D Studio MAX 9.**

AutoCAD Architecture 2008 utilizes the built-in rendering system native to AutoCAD 2008. For all general purposes this is an excellent system utilizing the same rendering engine as Autodesk VIZ and Autodesk 3DS MAX. With this native system, you can add cameras, lights, and materials; control shadows; and do basic animations. Regardless, if you want top quality and control, nothing beats Autodesk VIZ and Autodesk 3DS MAX. Because these programs are also Autodesk products, their DWG import and export capabilities are flawless, allowing you to bring files from AutoCAD Architecture 2008 into them with no loss of data. In this series of tutorials, you will learn the basics of the native rendering system, and also the basics of Autodesk 3DS MAX 9. Do note that you can also use earlier versions of VIZ and 3DS MAX, and that a new integration plug-in will soon be available for export between AutoCAD Architecture 2008 and 3DS MAX 9.

## HOW BEST TO LEARN THE VISUALIZATION PROCESS

The best way to learn the Visualization techniques is to start out with a very simple structure. Once you have learned the methodology, you can easily apply it to more complex structures. You can get a "good" result in a relatively short amount of time, but getting an "excellent" result, in my opinion, increases the amount of time spent exponentially. There are many controls in the AutoCAD visualization system, but they pale in comparison to the number of controls in 3DS MAX. You pay for what you get; MAX can do anything, and do it subtly, but it is more difficult to learn. The tutorials in this section are only an introduction to this broad area. Keep your experimentation simple, make one change at a time, and observe the changes.

**Exercise 27-1:** Making a Simple Scene and Using the Materials Tool Palette

1. Start a new drawing using the AEC Model (Imperial Stb) template.
2. Change to the **Top View.**

3. Using Standard 6″ × 8′-high walls, create a 20′-long by 10′-wide enclosure.
4. Place a roof on the structure with the following parameters:
   a. Thickness = **10″**
   b. Edge cut = **Plumb**
   c. Overhang = **1′-0″**
   d. Plate height = **8′-0″**
   e. Slope = **45.00**
5. Select the roof to activate its grips, and pull the center end grips to create gable ends (see Figure 27–1).

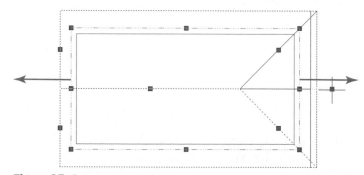

**Figure 27–1**

6. Enter **roofline** in the **Command line,** and press **Enter.**
7. Enter **A** (Auto project) in the **Command line,** and press **Enter.**
8. Select the two end walls, and press **Enter.**
9. Select the roof and press **Enter** twice to make the walls meet the roof peak, and finish the command (see Figure 27–2).

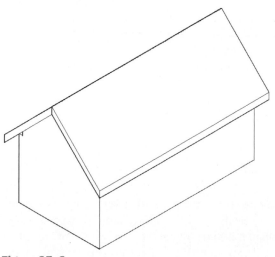

**Figure 27–2**

**Note:**
The base is considered an AutoCAD object because it was made using AutoCAD commands while the roof and walls are considered AutoCAD Architecture AEC objects.

10. Place a rectangle 40′-0″ × 40′-0″.
11. Enter **extrude** in the **Command line,** and press the **Enter** key on your keyboard.
12. Enter **-6′-0″** to create the base shown in Figure 27–3.

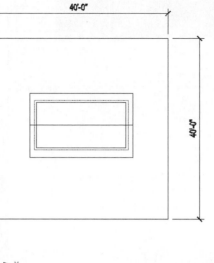

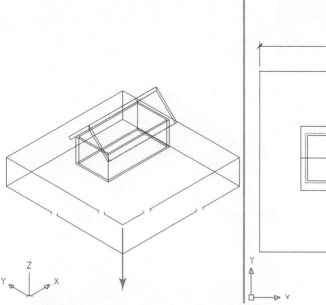

**Figure 27–3**

13. Select **View > Render > Materials** from the **Main** menu to bring up the **Materials** palette (see Figure 27–4).
14. In the **Materials** palette, notice that there are three colored spheres, two of which have the DWG symbol near their right corner.

**Note:**
The spheres represent Materials, and the DWG symbol means that this drawing contains these Materials.

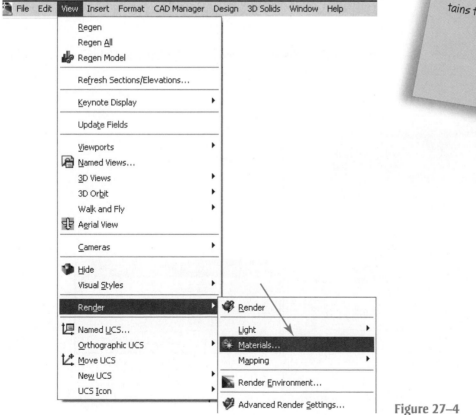

**Figure 27–4**

Notice also the name of the material (see Figure 27–5).

15. Press the **Create New Material** button to bring up the **Create New Material** dialog.
16. In the **Create New Material** dialog box, enter **GROUND GREEN**, and press the **OK** button to create a new **Material** sphere (see Figure 27–6).

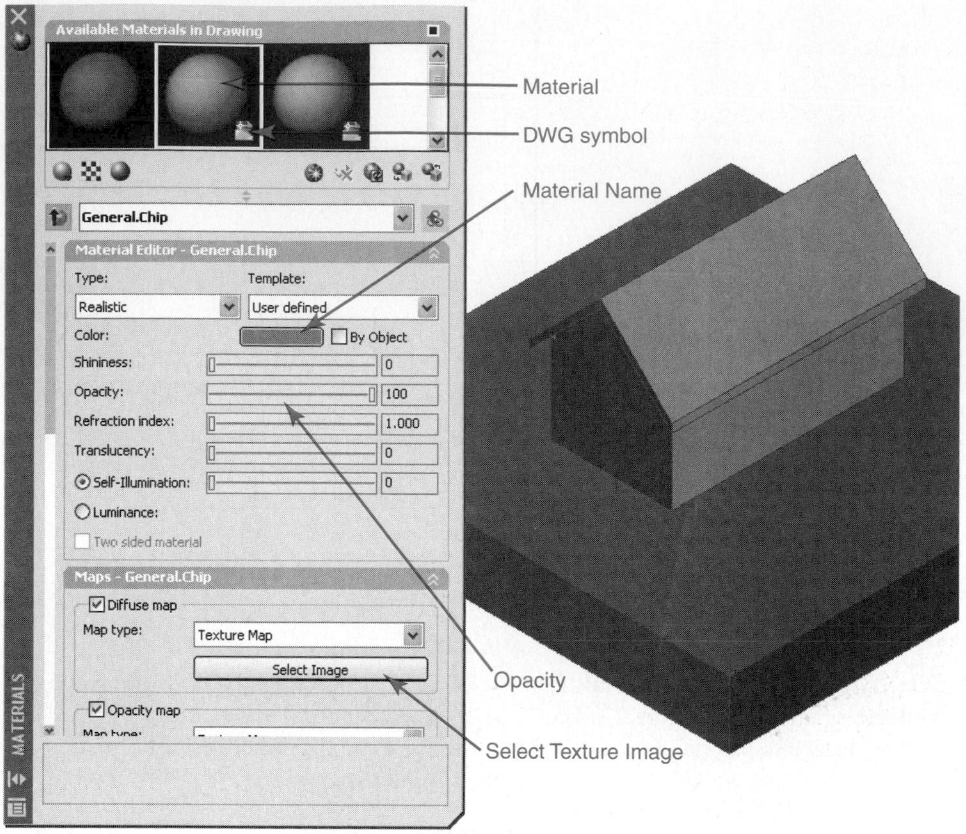

**Figure 27–5**

17. Select the new **GROUND GREEN** sphere, and press the **Diffuse Color** button to bring up the **Select Color** dialog box.

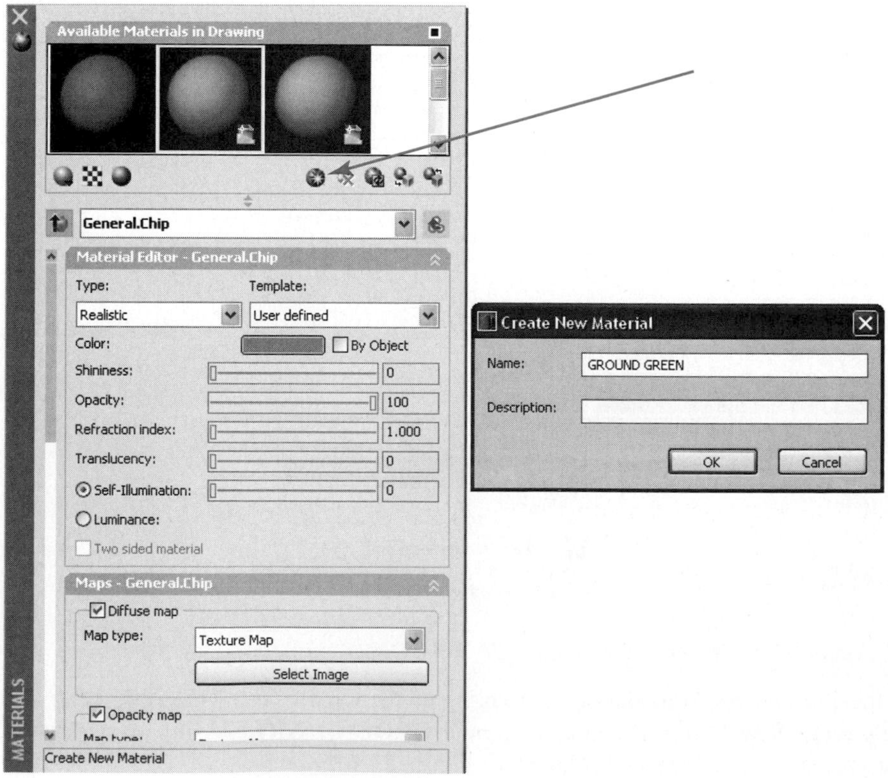

**Figure 27–6**

18. In the **Select Color** dialog box, select a green color (see Figure 27–7).
19. Select and drag the **GROUND GREEN** sphere onto the Base—the Base turns Green.
20. Select and drag the **GROUND GREEN** sphere onto the Roof—nothing happens.

**Note:**
Diffuse Color is the term used to indicate the color of an object.

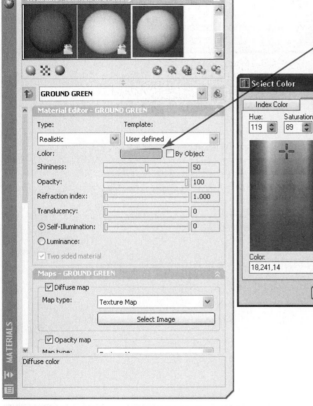

**Figure 27–7**

Materials that are created in the **Materials** palette can only be dragged to change AutoCAD objects, not AutoCAD Architecture objects such as the roof or walls.

**Note:**
Textures are nothing more than JPG pictures. You can place any texture on an object. You also can make your own textures.

21. Press the **Create New Material** Button to bring up the **Create New Material** dialog.
22. In the **Create New Material** dialog box, enter **WALL MATERIAL,** and press the **OK** button to create a new **Material** sphere.
23. Scroll down the **Materials** palette, check the **Diffuse map** check box, and select **Texture Map** from the **Map type** drop-down list.
24. Press the **Select Image** button to take you to the **AutoCAD Architect -Textures** folder.

25. In the **Textures** folder, pick the **Masonry.Unit.Masonry.Brick.Modular.Cored** texture (see Figure 27–8).

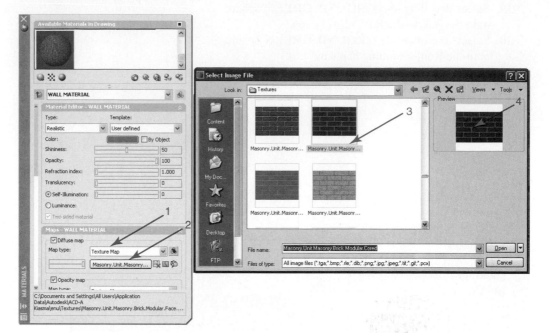

**Figure 27–8**

26. Scroll down the **Materials** palette, check the **Bump map** check box and select **Texture Map** from the **Map type** drop-down list.
27. Press the **Select Image** button to take you to the **AutoCAD Architect -Textures** folder.
28. In the **Textures** folder, pick the **Masonry.Unit.Masonry.Brick.Modular.Face.Grout** texture (see Figure 27–9).

You have now created materials using texture maps. For AutoCAD Architecture AEC Objects, you must assign **Material Definitions** in the **Style Manager.**

**Note:**
Bump maps are used to give the texture maps more 3D quality. They are typically gray versions of the same texture map used for the Diffuse map.

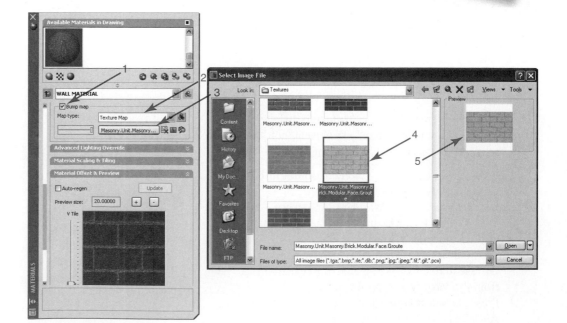

**Figure 27–9**

29. Select **Format > Material Definitions** from the **Main** menu to bring up the **Style Manager** dialog box for **Material Definitions**.
30. In the **Style Manager, RMB** and select **New** from the contextual menu that appears to create a **New Style.**
31. Change the name of the **New Style** to **WALLS.**
32. In the right pane of the **Style Manager,** change to the **Display Properties** tab.
33. In the **Display Properties** tab, select the **General Medium Detail** field, and press the **Edit Display Properties** icon to bring up the **Display Properties** dialog box.
34. In the **Display Properties** dialog box, select **WALL MATERIAL** from the **Render Material** drop-down list (see Figure 27–10).

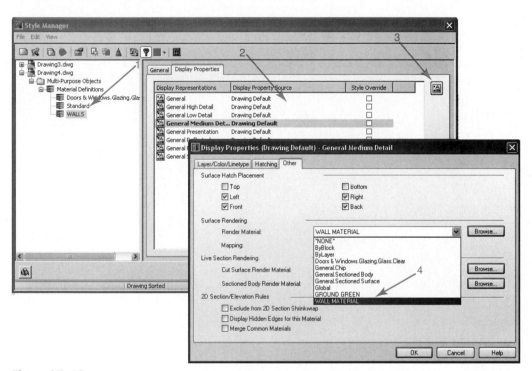

**Figure 27–10**

Now that you have made the Material Definition called **WALLS** from the **WALL MATERIAL,** you can place it in the walls on your building.

35. Select one of the walls of your building, **RMB,** and select **Edit Wall Style** from the contextual menu that appears to bring up the **Wall Style Properties** dialog box.
36. In the **Wall Style Properties** dialog box, select the **Materials** tab.
37. In the **Materials** tab, select **WALLS** from the **Material Definition** drop-down list, and press the **OK** button to apply the material.
38. Select the **Material** tool in the **Design** tool palette, and click on one of the walls of your building (see Figures 27–11 and 27–12).

Save the file.

## Creating Shadows in AutoCAD Architecture 2008

1. Type **dashboard** in the **Command line,** and press the **Enter** key on your keyboard.
2. In the **Dashboard,** expand the **Lights** panel.
3. In the **Lights** panel, click the **Sun Status** icon to turn the sun **On.**

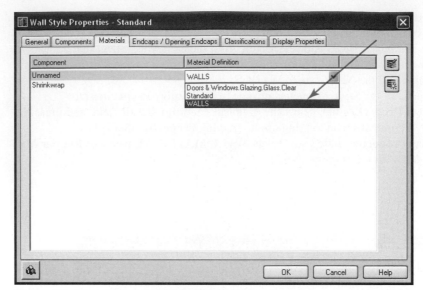

**Figure 27–11**

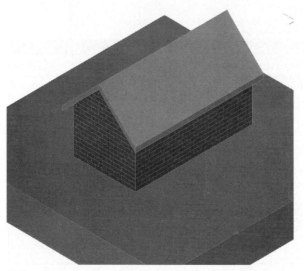

**Figure 27–12**

4. You will get a **Viewport Lighting Mode** warning, asking if you want to turn off the default lighting when you turn the sun on. Press the **Yes** button (see Figure 27–13).

**Figure 27–13**

5. Type **render** in the **Command line**, and press the **Enter** key on your keyboard to render the scene and see the shadows (see Figure 27–14).

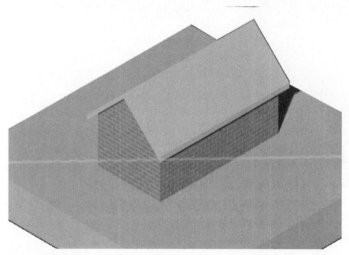

Figure 27–14

The shadows will probably not be where you want, and that is because of the direction of the sun and time of day. To change this, do the following.

6. In the lights panel, click on the **Geographic location** icon (Earth) to bring up the **Geographic Location** dialog box.
7. In the **Geographic Location** dialog box, enter **335** in the **North Direction Angle** box, choose the **Nearest City** from the drop-down list, or pick it on the map, and press the **OK** button (see Figure 27–15).

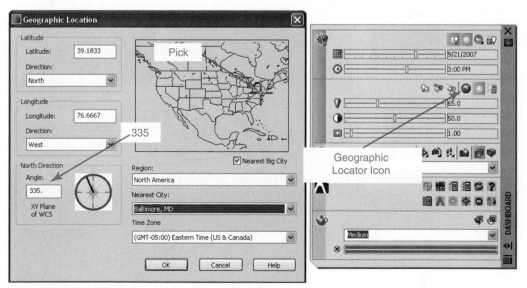

Figure 27–15

8. Type **render** in the **Command line** again, and press the **Enter** key on your keyboard to render the scene and see the change in the shadows (see Figure 27–16).
9. Experiment with changing the shadows, and then save the file.

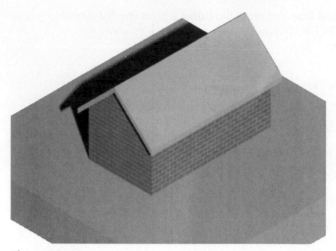

**Figure 27–16**

## Using the Camera Tool in AutoCAD Architecture 2008

1. Change to the **Top** view.
2. In the **Dashboard,** expand the **3D Navigate** panel.
3. In the **3D Navigate** panel, select the **Create Camera** icon.
4. Click the camera at the location from which you will be viewing, and then click again in the center of the building.
5. Press the **Enter** key on your keyboard to exit, and create the camera.
6. Click on the camera you placed to open the **Camera Preview** dialog box (see Figure 27–17).

**Note:** You can also create a camera by going to **View** > **Cameras** > **Add** in the **Main** menu.

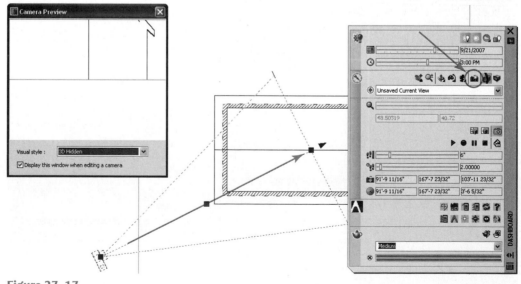

**Figure 27–17**

7. Change to the **Front** view.
8. Again click on the camera you placed to open the **Camera Preview** dialog box.

9. Select the **Camera** grip, and move the camera while watching the preview.
10. Select the **Camera target** grip and move it while watching the preview (see Figure 27–18).

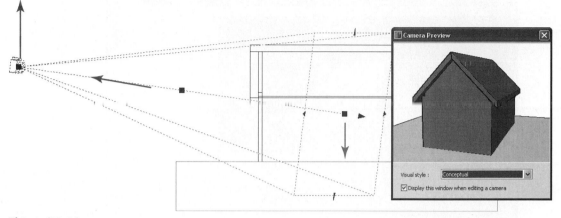

**Figure 27–18**

11. When you have the view you want in the **Camera Preview** dialog box (you may have to switch back to the **Top** view for further adjustments), **RMB**, and select **Set Camera View** from the contextual menu that appears.

If you now click on the camera in the view, you will get a dashed rectangle with arrow grips. The scene extents that you will render are inside the rectangle (see Figure 27–19).

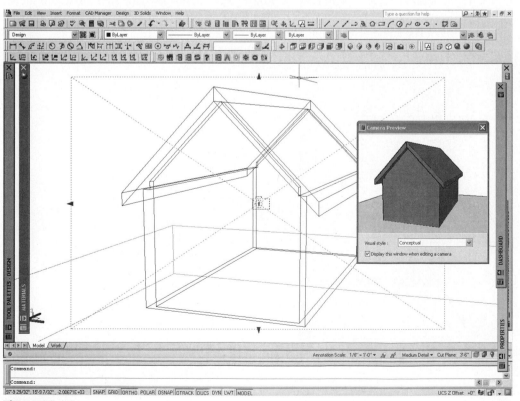

**Figure 27–19**

12. Type **render** in the **Command line**, and press the **Enter** key on your computer, or press the **Render** icon in the **Render** panel of the **Dashboard** to render the scene (see Figure 27–20).

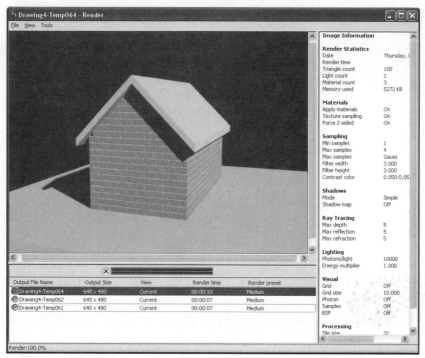

**Figure 27–20**

13. If you want to save the picture, select **File > Save** at the top of the **Render** screen shown in Figure 27–20. Save the picture in a location on your computer, and choose an image format. (The author prefers jpg or JPEG.)
14. If you want to change the rendering resolution or location to save, change these in the expanded **Render** panel (see Figure 27–21).

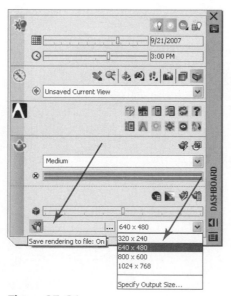

**Figure 27–21**

## Adjusting Materials in a Visualization Scene

1. Change to the **Top** view, and add a hinged –**Single Full lite** door from the **Door** tool palette and some **Casement** windows from the **Windows** tool palette.
2. Open the **Materials** tool palette. Notice that it now contains more material spheres.

When you add AEC Objects into a scene, the materials that are in the objects show up in the **Materials** tool palette.

3. **RMB** on the camera again, and select **Set Camera View** again.
4. Change to **Realistic** in the **Visual Styles** toolbar (see Figure 27–22).

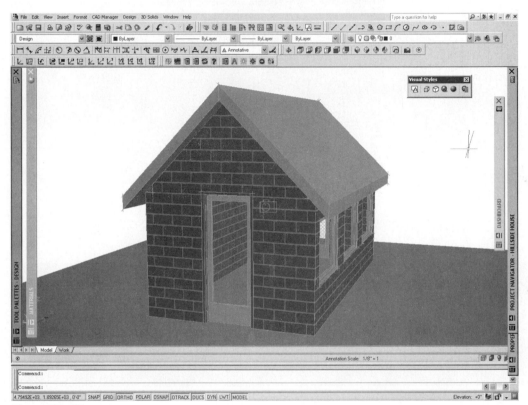

**Figure 27–22**

5. Open the **Materials** tool palette. Select the **WALL Material** sphere.
6. Scroll down to **Diffuse** map, and select the texture button containing the **Masonry.Unit. Masonry. Brick.Modular.Cored** texture.
7. Change the texture to **Masonry.Unit Masonry. CMU.Screen.Stacked** (see Figure 27–23).
8. Render the scene and save the file.

**Note:** Changing a material in the material editor that is assigned to an object changes the material of that object in the Drawing Editor or scene.

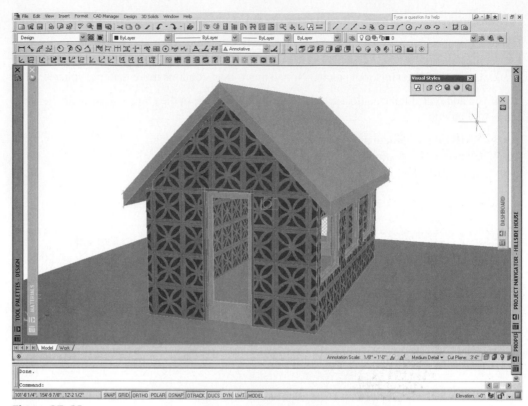

**Figure 27–23**

## Using Archvision RPC Content in AutoCAD Architecture 2008

RPC content is manufactured by Archvision **http://www.archvision.com.** It is the premier product that contains people, trees, cars, and so on for your scenes. All the top architectural and engineering firms in the world use RPC content.

A new free plug-in for RPC content is available for AutoCAD Architecture 2008, and there is free demo content. The free content is low-resolution, but high-quality content is available in a series of libraries, and all the content is available by subscription.

Note: At the time of writing this book, both AutoCAD Architecture 2008 and the new Archvision plug-in had not been released. Regardless, the new RPC plug-in will be available when AutoCAD Architecture 2008 is released. Previously Archvision RPC plug-ins were available in the Content and Plug-ins folder in the Content browser. If they are not there in this release, just go to the Archvision website and download them there.

The RPC content is very powerful, and there is not enough room in this book to show you all the capabilities of the content, or the installation system. If you are interested in using this content (and you should definitely use it), it is highly recommended that you go to the Archvision website, and look at its tutorials. If you have any problems, Archvision has an excellent support group that can help you get up to speed.

1. When you download and install the plug-in, it will install a **Content Manager** icon in the icon tray at the bottom of the **Windows** screen.
2. Double-click on the icon in the icon tray to bring up the **Content Manager** (see Figure 27–24).

**Figure 27–24**

The Content Manager is where you set the paths for the content, set the license, and set the download management.

3. When you download and install the **RPC** plug-in, it also installs a toolbar, and makes the toolbar available in the Dashboard. To bring the **RPC** toolbar into the **Dashboard, RMB** on an empty space in the **Dashboard,** and select **RPC** from the list that appears (see Figure 27–25).

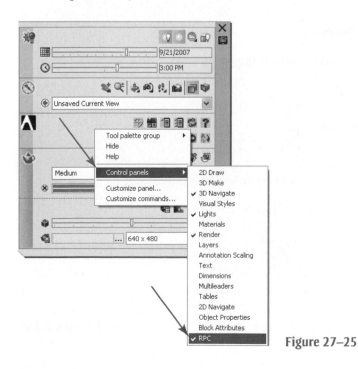

**Figure 27–25**

4. Click on the camera, and select **Set Camera View** again.
5. In order to place content, select the **RPC** place icon in the **RPC** toolbar to bring up the **RPC Selection** dialog box.
6. In the **RPC Selection** dialog box, select the content you wish to place, and press the **OK** button to return to the Drawing Editor.
7. Click in the Drawing Editor and then move and/or rotate the content, and click again to set it in place (see Figure 27–26).

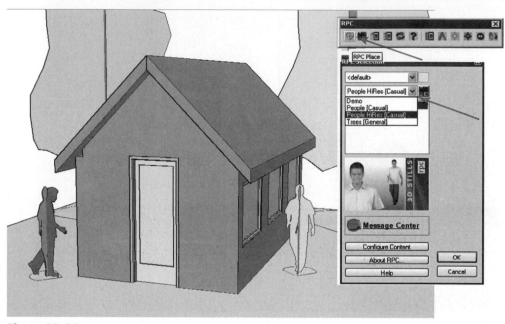

**Figure 27–26**

8. Select the **RPC Mass Edit** icon in the **RPC** toolbar to bring up the **RPC Mass Edit** dialog box.
9. In the **RPC Mass Edit** dialog box, click under the **3D** column to turn on the **S** (shadows), and press the **OK** button to return to the Drawing Editor (see Figure 27–27).

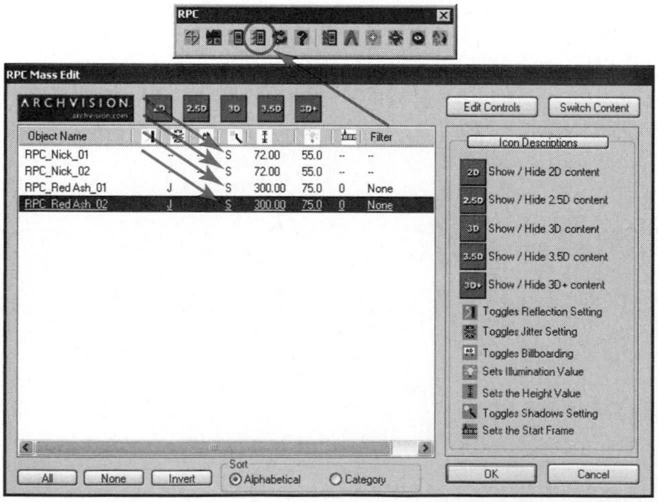

**Figure 27–27**

10. Expand the lights panel in the **Dashboard,** and select **Sky** background from the **Sky** drop-down list (see Figure 27–28).

**Figure 27–28**

11. Type **render** in the **Command line**, and press the **Enter** key on your computer, or press the **Render** icon in the **Render** panel of the **Dashboard** to render the scene (see Figure 27–29).

**Figure 27–29**

Save the file.

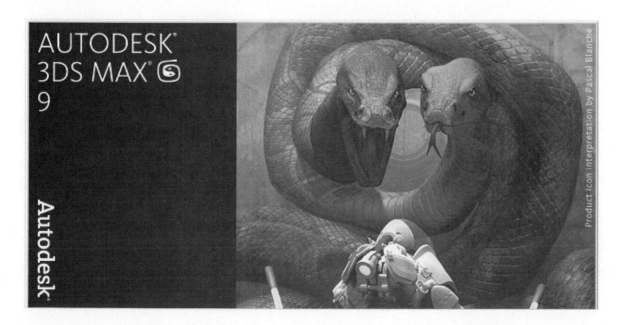

## Visualization with 3DS MAX

MAX can do any visualization task, and do it quickly, but MAX results are not interactive with AutoCAD Architecture. Any changes made in 3DS MAX (and VIZ) cannot be exported back to AutoCAD Architecture as intelligent objects. This series of tutorials is designed to give you an insight into the capabilities of 3DS MAX.

1. Using the previous file, change the wall materials to **Standard,** remove the **Base** object, the camera, and the **RPC** content.
2. Save the file as **MAX VISUALIZATION.dwg.**
3. Start **3DS MAX** (this tutorial uses 3DS MAX 9).
4. Select **File > Import** from the **Main** menu to bring up the **Select File to Import** dialog box.
5. In the **Select File to Import** dialog box, browse to the place where you saved **MAX VISUALIZATION.dwg,** and press the **Open** button.

You will get a **Proxy Objects Detected** dialog box telling you that there are custom objects in the drawing. Press the **Yes** button to import the file anyway.

6. Next you will get the **AutoCAD DWG/DXF Import Options** dialog box. Accept the defaults, and press the **OK** button to import the building (see Figure 27–30).

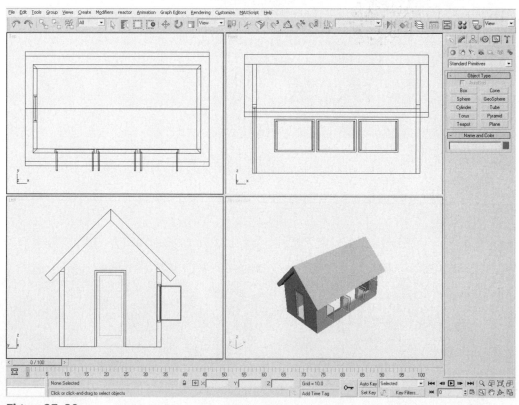

**Figure 27–30**

7. Select the **Zoom All** tool at the bottom right of the interface, and zoom all the viewports smaller (see Figure 27–31).
8. Using the **Create** tools add a **Camera – Target** tool, place a camera to the left of the building, and then drag and click its target at the center of the building.
9. After placing the camera, select the lower right viewport (Perspective), and press the **C** key on your keyboard to change it to the view through the camera (see Figure 27–32).

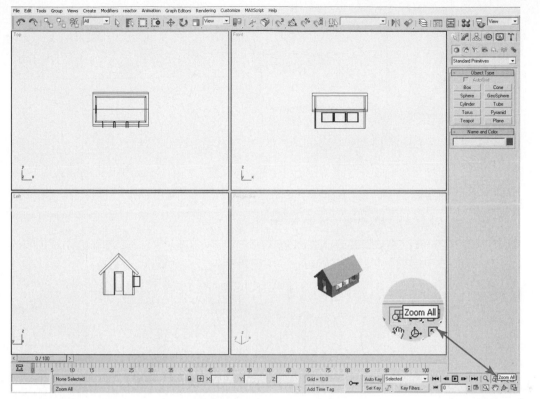

**Figure 27–31**

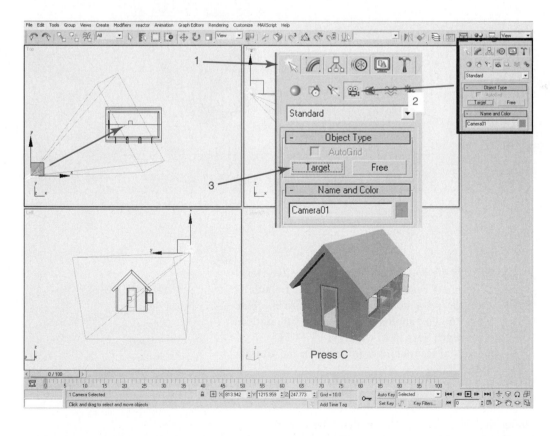

**Figure 27–32**

10. Select the **Camera** viewport, and using the **Navigation** tools (**Distance, Pan,** and **Rotate**) at the bottom right of the screen, adjust the view to the scene you wish (see Figure 27–33).

11. Using the **System** tools, add a **Sunlight** tool. Click and drag to set the **Compass**, and then drag your cursor upwards and click to set the height of the **Sunlight** (see Figure 27–34).

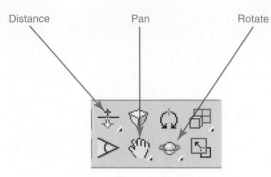

Distance    Pan    Rotate

**Figure 27–33**

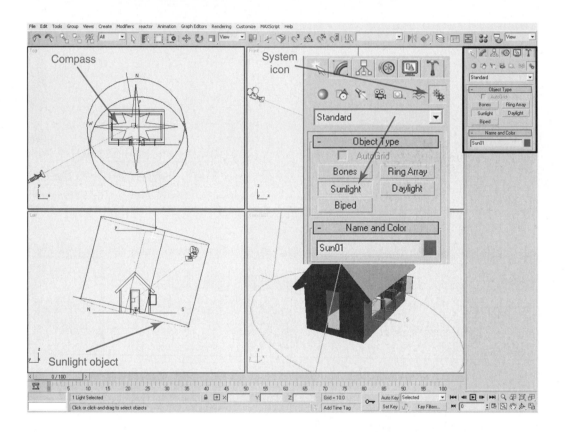

**Figure 27–34**

12. Click in the **Top** view to make it the active view.
13. Using the **Create** tools, add a **Plane.** Be sure to click the color box, and set it to a green color. Make the box approximately 50′ × 50′, and set the **Length Segs** to **1** (see Figure 27–35).
14. Select the **Render** icon to bring up the **Render Scene** dialog box.
15. In the **Render Scene** dialog box, press the **Render** button to render the scene.

Notice that the rendering is dark; that is because the sunlight is coming from the back (see Figure 27–36).

16. Select the **Sun** object, and then select the **Motion** icon in the upper right of the **MAX 9** interface to open the **Motion** parameters.

**Note:**

The **Render Scene** dialog box contains all the controls for size, Renderer, and so on. For these tutorials, just use the defaults.

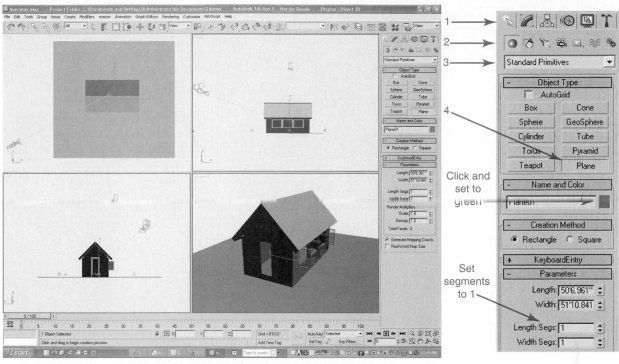

**Figure 27–35**

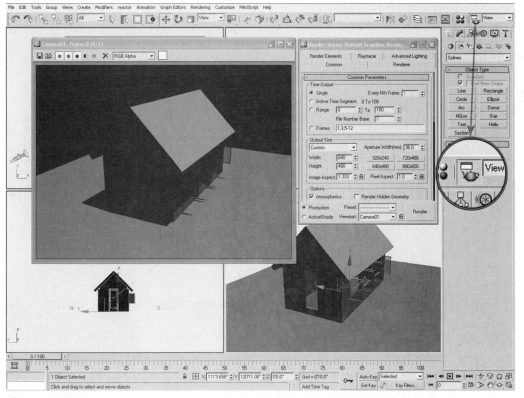

**Figure 27–36**

17. Adjust the **Latitude** and **Longitude** and watch how the light changes in the scene. This author set the **Latitude** to **75**, and the **Longitude** to **56** for the default location (see Figure 27–37).

18. Re-render the scene. It is better, but the shadows are too dark on the right side.

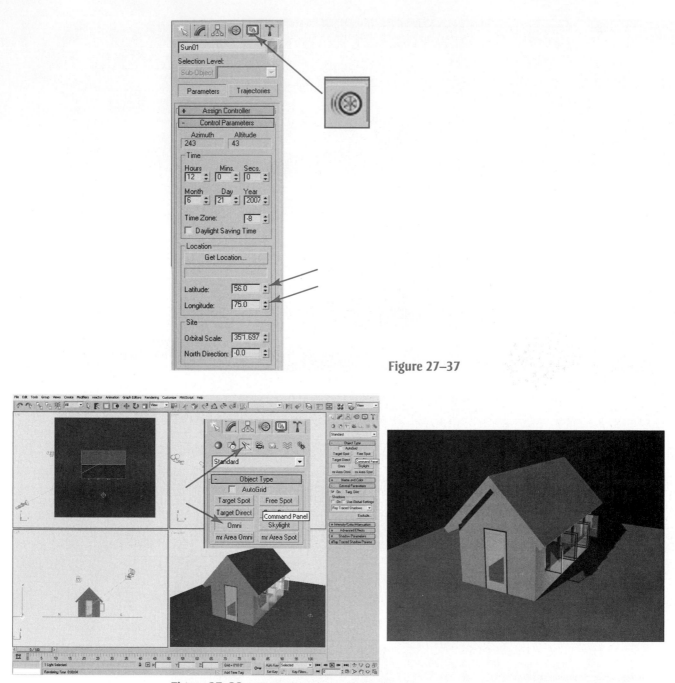

**Figure 27–37**

**Figure 27–38**

19. To fix this, select **Lights – Omni** from the **Create** panel, and place an omni light at the right side of the building.

20. Click in the **Camera** view, re-render, and save the file (see Figure 27–38).

## Creating and Placing Materials in Autodesk 3DS MAX 9

1. Select the **Material Editor** icon at the top right of the **MAX** interface to bring up the **Material Editor.**

2. In the **Material Editor,** enter **WALL MATERIAL** in the list shown in Figure 27–39.

3. Expand the **Material** display shapes, and pick the **Block** shape.

4. Double-click on the **Material** shape to expand it for better viewing (see Figure 27–40).

5. With the **WALL MATERIAL** shape selected, press the **Diffuse Color** button to open the **Material Map Browser** dialog box.

6. In the **Material Map Browser** dialog box, double-click on **Bitmap** to bring up the **Select Bitmap Image** dialog box.

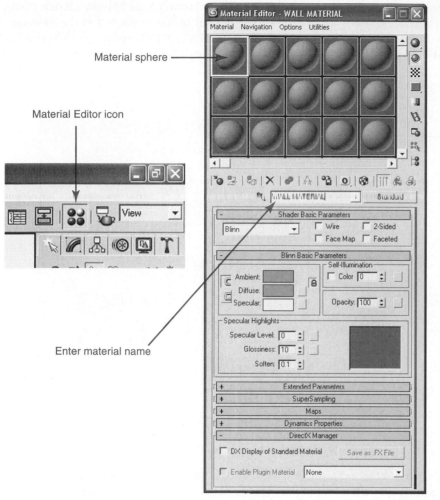

Material sphere

Material Editor icon

Enter material name

**Figure 27–39**

7. In the **Select Bitmap Image** dialog box, browse to the location where your bitmap pictures are stored. (They are in the same place as was shown in the **AutoCAD Architecture Materials** tutorial earlier in this section.)

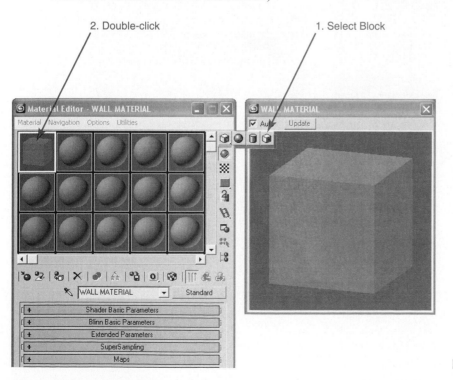

2. Double-click

1. Select Block

**Figure 27–40**

8. In the **Select Bitmap Image** dialog box, select the **Masonry.Unit Masonry.Brick.Modular.Flemish Diagonal** bitmap, and press the **Open** button to place it in the **Material Editor.** Repeat this process creating **ROOF MATERIAL** using the **Thermal - Moisture.Roof Tiles.Spanish.Red** bitmap (see Figure 27–41).

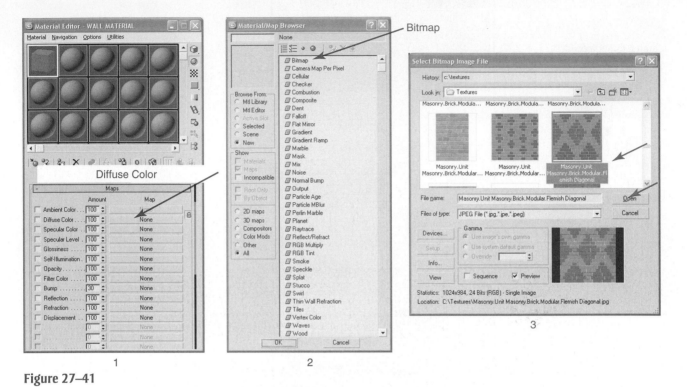

**Figure 27–41**

9. Select the **Show Map in Viewport** button, and drag **WALL MATERIAL** onto the walls. Repeat by dragging **ROOF MATERIAL** onto the roof (see Figure 27–42).

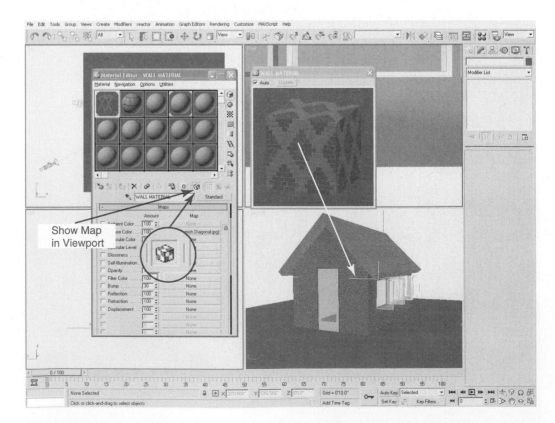

**Figure 27–42**

10. Select a wall, and then select the **Modify** icon from the **Create** panel to bring up the **Modifier** list.
11. In the **Modifier** list, select the **MapScaler.**
12. Select the other walls and roof, and repeat step 11 (see Figure 27–43).
13. Press the **Select by Name** icon at the top left of the **MAX** interface to bring up the **Select Objects** dialog box. (You can select all the objects in your scene here.)

**Note:** The **WALL MATERIAL** and **ROOF MATERIAL** do not look like the bitmaps you selected— they are too small. To correct this follow steps 10–12.

Modify

MapScaler

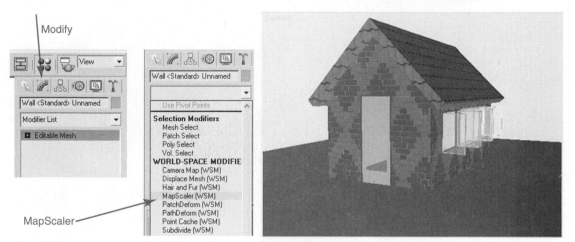

**Figure 27–43**

14. In the **Select Objects** dialog box, choose **Roof Body,** and then press the **Select** button (see Figure 27–44).

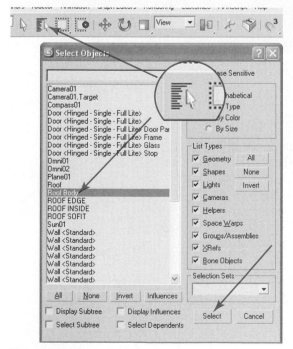

**Figure 27–44**

15. Select the **Modify** icon from the **Create** panel to bring up the **Modifier** list.
16. In the **Modifier** list, select and expand **Editable Mesh.**
17. In the expanded **Editable Mesh,** select **Polygon.**
18. Select the edge of the roof (it will turn red), and then press the **Detach** button to bring up the **Detach** dialog box.
19. In the **Detach** dialog box, enter **ROOF EDGE,** and press the **OK** button.
20. Repeat steps 13–19, and detach the other roof edges, and the inside of the roof. Give each detached object a unique name such as **SOFIT,** and so on (see Figure 27–45).

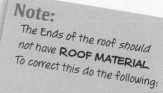

Note:
The Ends of the roof should not have **ROOF MATERIAL.** To correct this do the following:

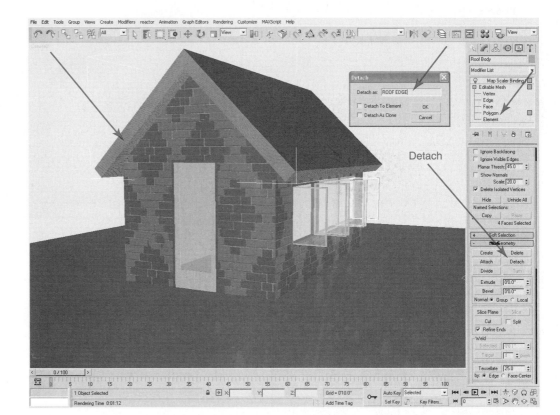

**Figure 27–45**

21. Open the **Material Editor,** and create a new material called **ROOF EDGE MATERIAL.**
22. Click on the **Ambient** button to open the **Ambient Color** selector, and choose a color (the author chose white) (see Figure 27–46).
23. Again, press the **Select by Name** icon at the top left of the **MAX** interface to bring up the **Select Objects** dialog box.
24. In the **Select Objects** dialog box, choose the new roof objects you created to select them.
25. With the new roof objects selected, press the **Assign Material to Selection** icon to apply the **ROOF EDGE MATERIAL** to them (see Figure 27–47).

Note:
You have now detached the **ROOF EDGE,** and it has become a separate object. You cannot do this in the built-in visualization system in AutoCAD Architecture 2008.

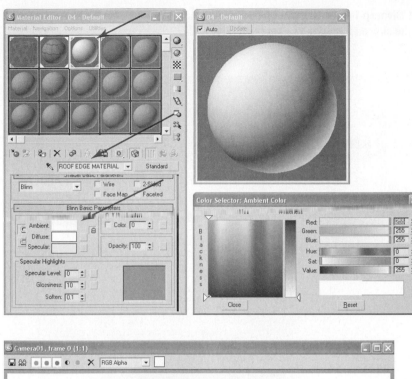

Figure 27–46

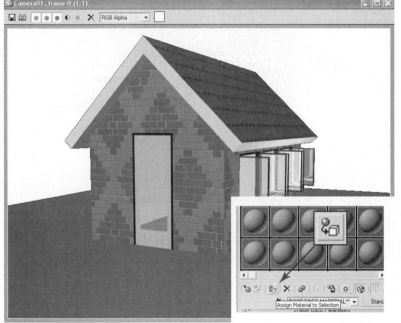

Figure 27–47

## Adding the SKY in Autodesk 3DS MAX

26. In the **Select Bitmap Image** dialog box, select the **Sky** picture you have created or found, and press the **Open** button to place it in the **Material Editor.**

27. Select **Rendering** > **Environment** from the **Main** menu to bring up the **Environment and Effects** dialog box.

28. In the **Environment and Effects** dialog box, select the **Use Map** check box, and then press the **Environment Map** button to bring up the **Select Bitmap Image File** dialog box.

**Note:**
The author took a picture of a cloudy sky with his digital camera and saved it in his textures folder. You can also search the Internet for pictures, or purchase texture maps (pictures).

29. In the **Select Bitmap Image File** dialog box, browse to the folder where you have placed a picture of the sky, and open the picture (see Figure 27–48).

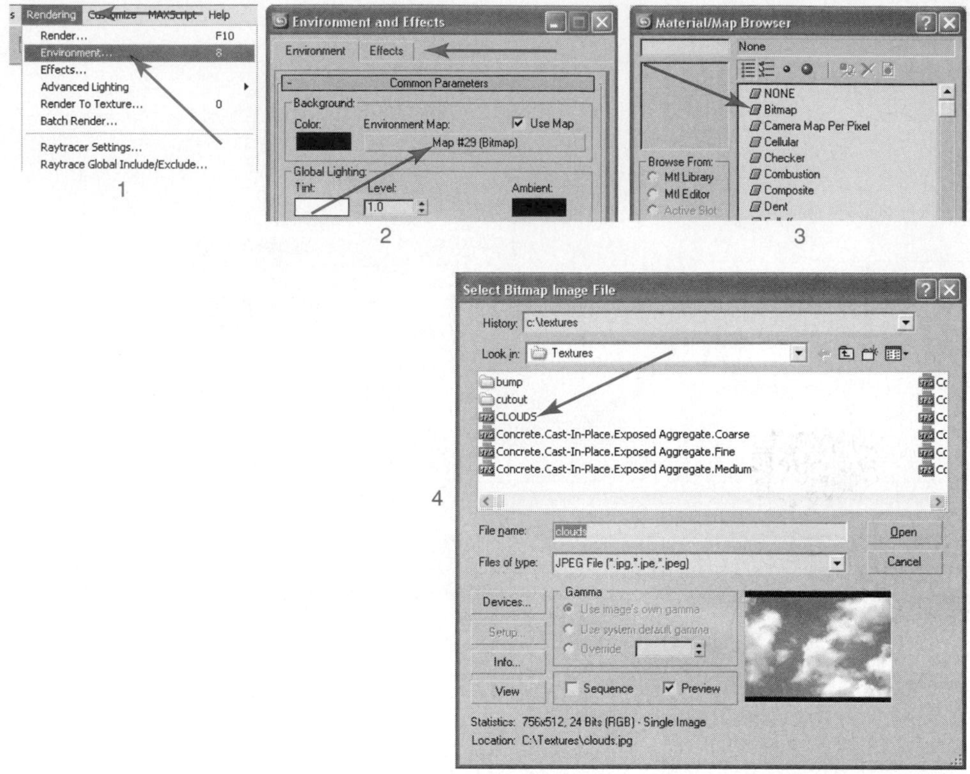

**Figure 27–48**

## Creating Grass in Autodesk 3DS MAX 9

3DS MAX 9 has a Modifier called *Hair and Fur.* It has this name because MAX is often used in the gaming industry, and it is used to apply hair and fur to people and animals. This is a very sophisticated modifier, and can be easily used to create realistic grass for architectural visualizations.

Hair and Fur only renders in the Camera view, so you will not see its effects in any other views. For architectural visualizations, this author suggests only attaching the Hair and Fur modifier to a Plane object.

Because this is a very sophisticated modifier, this tutorial has been simplified. Please check the help file for more in-depth information.

1. Select the **plane** that you created in step 13 of the "Visualization with 3DS MAX" tutorial.
2. Select **Modifiers > Hair** and **Fur > Hair and Fur (WSM)** from the **Main** menu to apply it to the selected **plane.**
3. Select the **Modifier** icon in the **Create** panel to expose the **Hair and Fur** controls.
4. In the **Hair and Fur** controls, set the following:

General Parameters

   a. Hair count = 30,000
   b. Scale = 2 (height of grass)
   c. Rand Scale = 40 (40% random sizes)
   d. Root Thick = .4 (thickness of grass root)
   e. Tip Thick = .4 (thickness of grass tip)

Material Parameters

   a.  Tip Color = make light green

   b.  Root Color = make dark green

Frizz Parameters

   a.  Make all the Frizz Parameters = 0 (makes the grass vertical)

Multi Strand Parameters

   a.  Count = 3

   b.  Root Splay = .82

   c.  Tip splay = 1.82

(See Figure 27–49.)

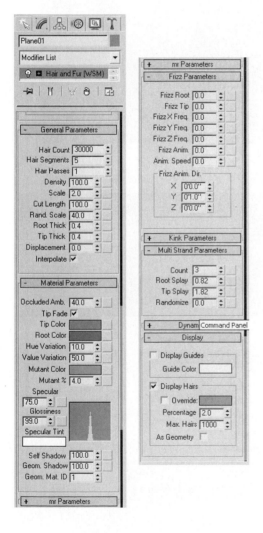

**Figure 27–49**

5. Render the picture (be patient, this render takes two passes), and save the file (see Figure 27–50).

**Figure 27–50**

### Using Archvision RPC Content in Autodesk 3DS MAX 9

If you downloaded and configured the Content Manager in the tutorial for RPC content in AutoCAD Architecture 2008, you will already have the content on your computer. You will have to download a separate plug-in for 3DS MAX 9, however, to enable you to place the content.

1. Using your Internet browser, go to **http://www. archvision.com.**
2. At the first screen, select **Software Updates** from the **Support** drop-down to take you to the **Software Updates** screen.
3. In the **Software Updates** screen, download and install the **RPC 3.11.8.0** plug-in **Release date 01.07**.
4. Once you have installed the plug-in, select the **Geometry** icon in the **Create** panel, and then select **RPC** from the drop-down list.
5. Once you have selected **RPC** from the drop-down list, the **RPC** parameters will appear.

**Note:**
All software companies are always updating software. This plug-in was the latest release as of the writing of this book (see Figure 27–51).

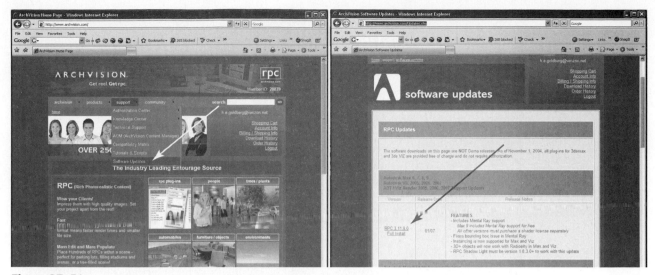

**Figure 27–51**

6. From the **RPC** parameters, select the **RPC** button, select content you want, and then place and rotate it in your scene (see Figures 27–52, 27–53, and 27–54).

Geometry icon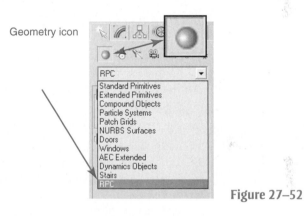

**Figure 27–52**

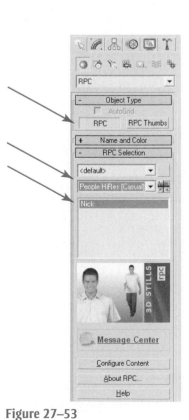

**Figure 27–53**

**Figure 27–54**

## Shadowing the RPC Content

7. Select one of the **RPC** content objects you placed, and select **Mass Edit** from the **RPC** parameters to bring up the **RPC Mass Edit** dialog box.
8. In the **RPC Mass Edit** dialog box, select all the content, and then click under the **3D** column. When an **S** appears opposite the content, the object is set to shadow (see Figure 27–55).

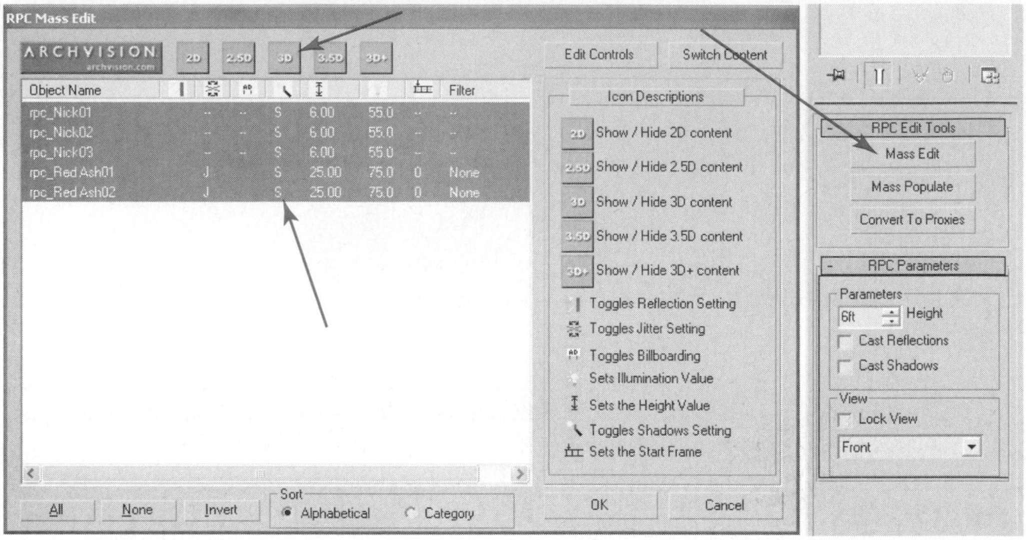

**Figure 27–55**

9. Press the **Select by Name** icon at the top left of the **MAX** interface to bring up the **Select Objects** dialog box. (You can select all the objects in your scene here.)
10. In the **Select Objects** dialog box, choose **Sun01**, and then press the **Select** button.

RPC content needs to be included in the **Sun** parameters to be seen. Sun01 is the default name that was given when you first placed the Sunlight object.

11. With the **Sun01** selected, press the **Modify** icon in the **Create** panel.
12. In the **General** parameters, check the **Shadows** check box, and then press the **Include** button to bring up the **Exclude/Include** dialog box.
13. In the **Exclude/Include** dialog box, make sure that the **Include** *radio* button is pressed, and that all the content in the scene is together on the Include side (see Figure 27–56).
14. Finally, select **Rendering > Environment** from the **Main** menu to bring up the **Environment and Effects** dialog box.

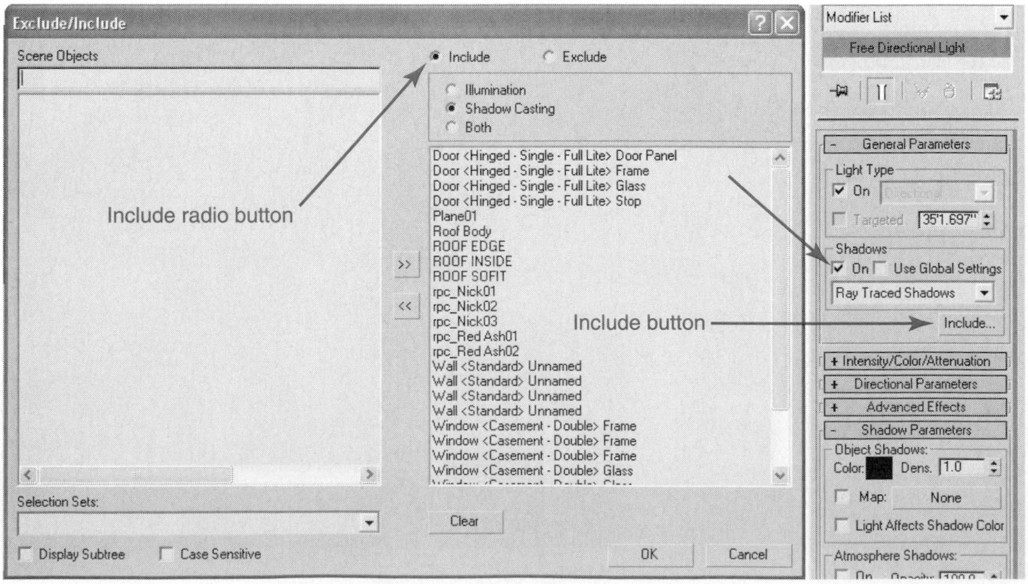

**Figure 27–56**

15. In the **Environment and Effects** dialog box, select the **Effects** tab (see Figure 27–57).

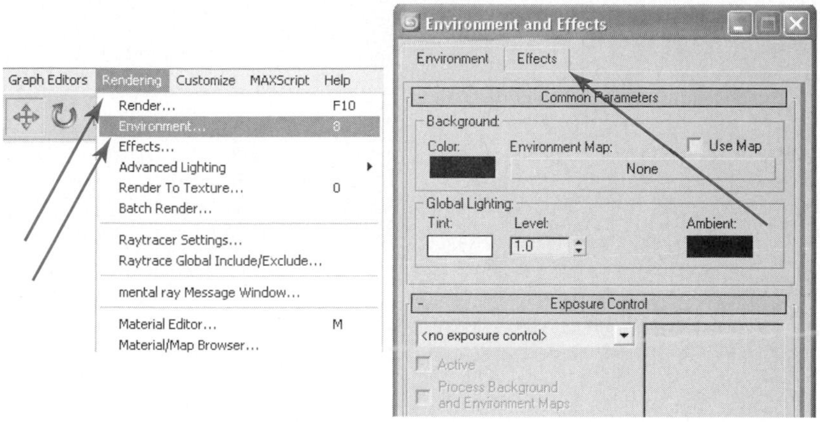

**Figure 27–57**

16. In the **Effects** tab, select **Hair and Fur** to bring up the **Hair and Fur** effects parameters.
17. In the **Hair and Fur** effects parameters, select the **GBuffer** radio button, and then press the **Custom** radio button under **Occlusion Objects.**
18. Render the scene (see Figure 27–58).
19. Render the scene and save the file (see Figure 27–59).

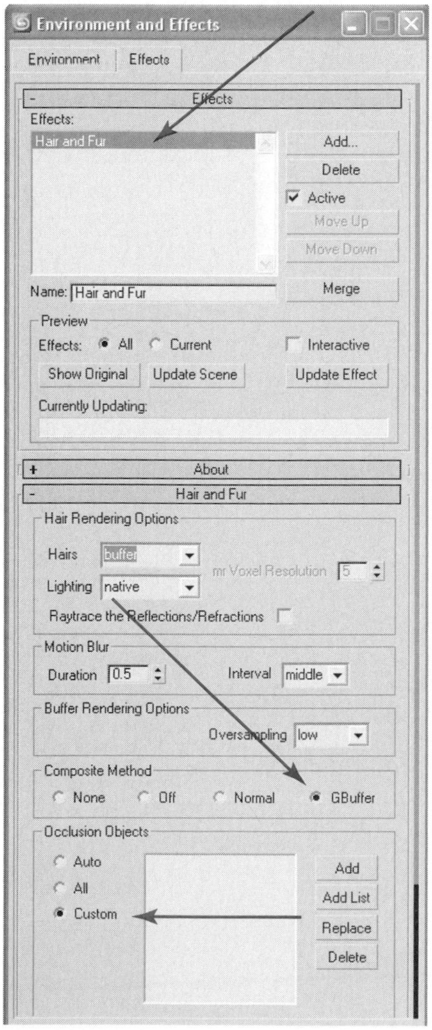

**Figure 27–58**                                            **Figure 27–59**

# Tutorial Project

## 28

For the tutorial project, this author has chosen a two-story hillside house. The project progresses through the design process to the construction documentation stage.

Before starting the project, it will be necessary to create a customized plotting sheet that includes the company logo. Using Adobe Illustrator, Adobe Photoshop, Corel Draw, Paint Shop Pro, Macromedia FreeHand, Canvas, or even Windows Paint, create a JPG of your logo. The logo the author created looks like Figure 28–1.

The author started with an Adobe Illustrator file and exported it as an RGB JPG.

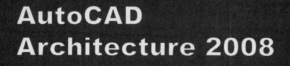

**Figure 28–1**

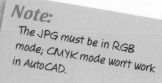

*Note:*
The JPG must be in RGB mode; CMYK mode won't work in AutoCAD.

**Exercise 28-1:** Placing the Logo in the Template File

1. Select **File > Open** from the **Main** menu to bring up the **Select File** dialog box.
2. In the **Look in** drop-down list, browse to the C drive.
3. Browse to **Documents and Settings > All Users > Application Data > Autodesk > ACD-A 2008 > Enu > Template.**
4. In the **File** dialog box, select **Drawing Template (*.dwt)** from the drop-down list.
5. Select the AEC Sheet (Imperial Stb) .dwt template.
6. Change to the preset **Arch D (24 × 36)** layout (see Figure 28–2).
7. Select **Insert > Raster Image Reference. . .** from the **Main** menu to bring up the **Select Image File** dialog box (see Figure 28–3).
8. Select the logo you created, and press **Open** to bring up the **Image** dialog box.
9. Check the **Insertion point** and **Scale Specify on-screen** check boxes, and press **OK** to return to the Drawing Editor (see Figure 28–4).

**Note:**
The default template files will appear. This author suggests that novice users modify a predefined template file; seasoned AutoCAD users should be able to create template files from scratch and add blocks with attributes. Template files are ordinary AutoCAD files with a .dwt file extension.

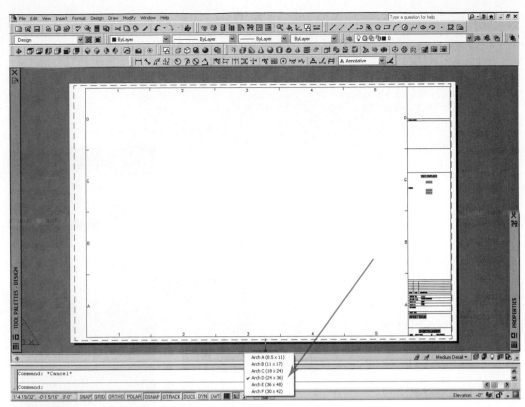

**Figure 28–2**

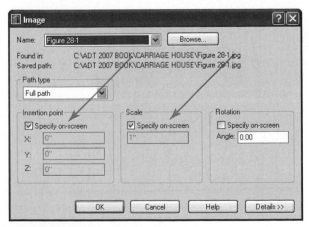

**Figure 28–3**

**Figure 28–4**

10. Place the logo JPG in the AEC Model (Imperial Stb) template (see Figure 28–5).
11. Save the template drawing as **HILLSIDE HOUSE,** and be sure the **Files of type** drop-down list is set to **AutoCAD drawing Template (\*.dwt).** Press the **Save** button.

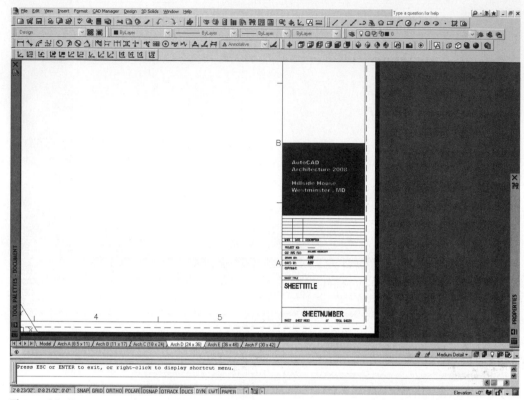

**Figure 28–5**

12. The **Template Options** dialog box will appear; enter a description of the template and press **OK** (see Figure 28–6).

You have now created a custom plotting sheet.

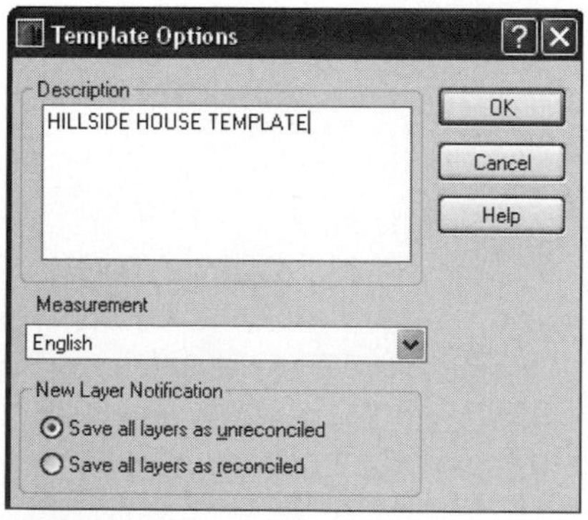

**Figure 28–6**

## Setting Up the Project

1. Select the **My Computer** icon on your desktop or from the **Start** menu, select **All Programs** > **Accessories** > **Windows Explorer** to bring up the **My Computer** or **My Documents** dialog box.
2. Create a new folder and name it **HILLSIDE HOUSE.**
3. Select **File** > **Project Browser** from the **Main** menu to bring up the **Project Browser** dialog box.
4. Locate the **HILLSIDE HOUSE** folder, and press the **New Project** icon to bring up the **Add Project** dialog box.
5. Enter the following:

   a.   Number = **2008**
   b.   Name = **HILLSIDE HOUSE**
   c.   Description = **HOUSE CREATED IN AUTOCAD ARCHITECTURE 2008**
   d.   *Uncheck* the **Create from template project** check box and press the **OK** button to return to the **Project Browser** (see Figure 28–7).

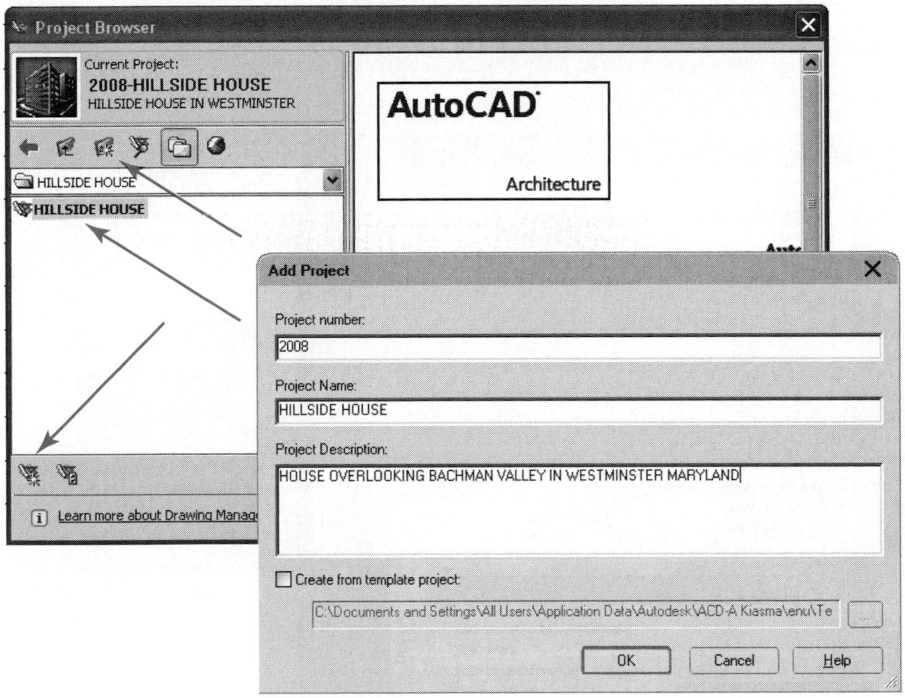

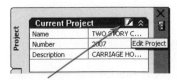

**Figure 28–7**

6. In the **Project Browser,** press the **Close** button to load the **Project Navigator,** and create the blank **CARRIAGE HOUSE** tool palette.
7. Open the **Project Navigator,** and select the **Project** tab.
8. In the **Project** tab, select the **Edit Project** icon (see Figure 28–8) to bring up the **Modify Project** dialog box.

**Figure 28–8**

9. In the **Modify Project** dialog box, select **Yes** from the **Prefix Filenames with Project Number** drop-down list.
10. Press the **Edit** button to bring up the **Project Details** dialog box.
11. In the **Project Details** dialog box, enter **WESTMINSTER MARYLAND** in the **Project DATA** fields. You can add any other information you wish in the remaining fields, or you can add fields. Press the **OK** buttons to return to the **Project Browser** (see Figure 28–9).

**Figure 28–9**

## Assigning the Custom Sheet Template

1. Open the **Project Navigator.**
2. Change to the **Sheets** tab.
3. **RMB** on **HILLSIDE HOUSE,** and select **Properties** to bring up the **Sheet Set Properties** dialog box.
4. Click on the **Sheet creation template** for the browser to bring up the **Select Layout as Sheet Template** dialog box.
5. Select the **Arch D (24 × 36)** layout from the **Select a layout to create new sheets** list, click the **Drawing template file name** browser, and select **HILLSIDE HOUSE.dwt,** the template you created in the previous exercise and press the **OPEN** button (see Figure 28–10).

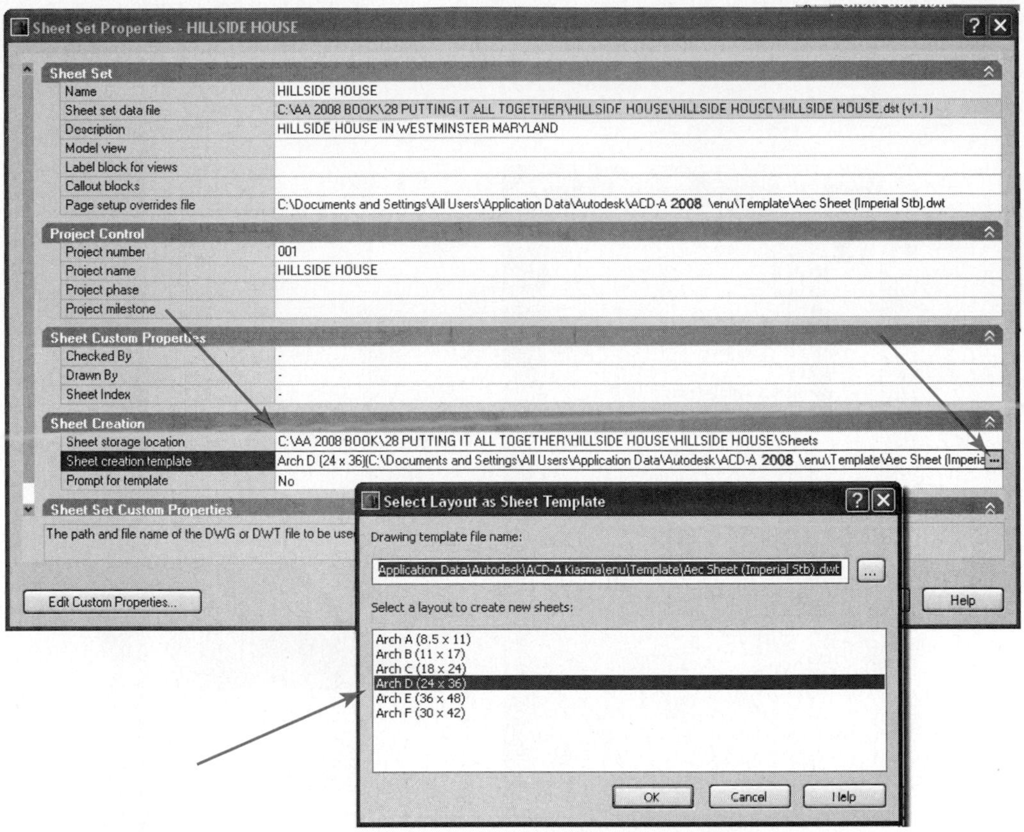

**Figure 28–10**

6. Press the **OK** buttons to close the dialog boxes and bring up the **Confirm Changes** dialog box (see Figure 28–11).
7. Press the **Yes** button to apply the changes you just made to all the nested subsets.

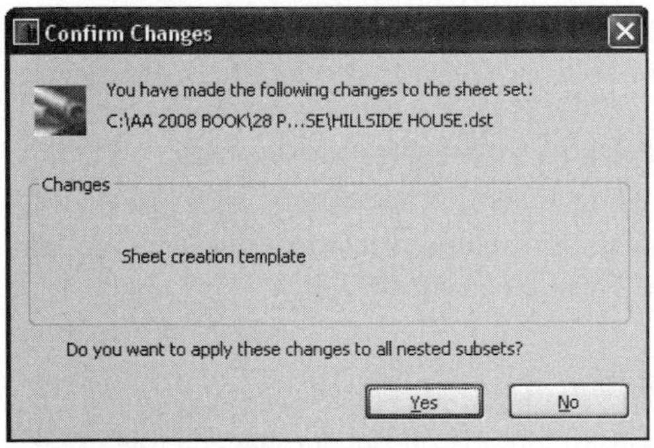

**Figure 28–11**

## Testing and Modifying the Custom Sheet

1. In the **Sheets** tab of the **Project Navigator,** select **Plans,** and select the **Add Sheet** icon to bring up the **New Sheet** dialog box (see Figure 28–12).
2. In the **New Sheet** dialog box, enter **A-101** in the **Number** field, **SHEET TEST** in the **Sheet title** field, and press **OK** to return to the Drawing Editor.
3. In the **Sheets** tab of **Project Navigator,** double-click on **A-101 SHEET TEST** to bring that drawing up in the Drawing Editor.

4. Zoom in to examine the drawing, and notice that the title block contains the custom logo, project name, owner's name and address, project number, CAD DWG file name, sheet title, and drawing number (see Figure 28–13).

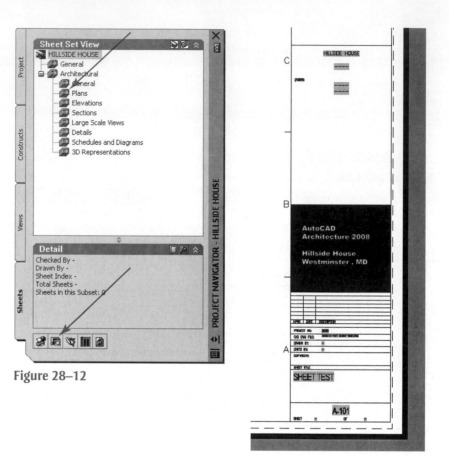

**Figure 28–12**

**Figure 28–13**

5. In the **Project Navigator, RMB** on **A-101 TEST SHEET** in the **Sheets** tab, and select **Properties** from the contextual menu that appears to bring up the **Sheet Properties** dialog box.
6. Put your initials in the **Checked By** and **Drawn By** fields and then press **OK.**
7. **RMB** on the topmost icon in the **Sheets** tab (the project name) and select **Resave All Sheets** from the contextual menu that appears to save the set. Close the drawing, and reopen it to see your initials in the **Checked By** and **Drawn By** fields.

## Making, Modifying, and Placing Sheet Lists

AutoCAD Architecture 2008 features a sheet list option. This creates an automated table of all your drawings that can be added to a cover page.

1. Using what you just learned in the previous exercises of this section, create several new plan drawings labeled **A-101** to **A-104.** Give each drawing a different name.
2. Select the **General** icon at the top of the **Sheets** tab, select the **Add Sheet** icon at the bottom of the tab, and name the sheet **TITLE SHEET.**
3. Double-click **TITLE SHEET** in the **Project Navigator** to bring it up in the Drawing Editor.
4. **RMB** on **HILLSIDE HOUSE** (under **Sheet Set View**) at the top of the **Sheets** tab, and select **Insert Sheet List** from the contextual menu that appears to bring up the **Insert Sheet List Table** dialog box.
5. In the **Insert Sheet List Table** dialog box, select the **Standard Table Style.**

6. Under **Column Settings,** select **Drawn By** from the third drop-down list, and press the **OK** button to return to the Drawing Editor (see Figure 28–14).
7. Place the sheet list in the **TITLE SHEET** (see Figure 28–15).

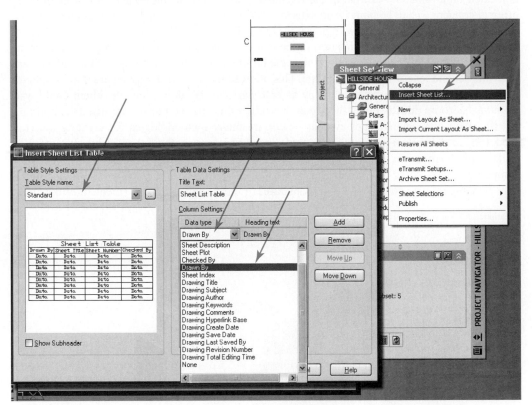

**Figure 28–14**

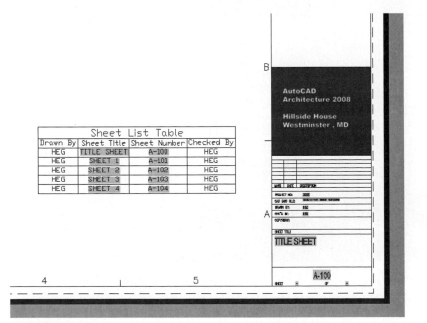

**Figure 28–15**

## THE TWO-STORY CARRIAGE HOUSE PROJECT

This project is patterned after a real project that I, along with Rick Donally, designed in 1978. It is located on a hillside overlooking the Bachman Valley, and sits on 60 acres of farmland. The original concept was to be built on an exterior exposed steel frame set on concrete piers, and the exterior walls were to be faced with plywood siding. The final building used a more conventional brick and block foundation with wood frame bearing walls and redwood siding. To take advantage of the site, Rick and I decided to place the building away from the ridge of the hillside, and enter the second level by way of a bridge. This allowed us to place the living areas at the treetop level, and access the lower bedrooms by an external stair. By doing this, the client could walk from his bedroom directly out to the ground level. For this project, I have simplified the building, but the main concepts still are evident. There are many methodologies for creating a virtual model in AutoCAD Architecture 2008; this project uses one method. As you become more familiar with the program, you will discover the methods and tools that best suit the way you work. I hope you enjoy doing this project, and enjoy experiencing both the design and methodology concepts. Figures 28–16 and 28–17 show pictures of the cardboard model I created for the client.

Figure 28–16

Figure 28–17

### Creating the TITLE SHEET

1. Make sure that you have the **HILLSIDE HOUSE** set as the current project in the **Project Browser.**
2. Close the **Project Browser** to bring up the **HILLSIDE HOUSE.**
3. In the **Sheets** tab of the **Project Navigator,** create a sheet named **TITLE SHEET.**
4. In the **TITLE SHEET,** insert a sheet list as explained in the previous exercise.
5. Save and close the **TITLE SHEET.**

## The Current Project Settings

1. Change to the **Project** tab.
2. Select the **Add Levels** icon to bring up the **Levels** dialog box.
3. Check the **Auto-Adjust Elevation** check box.
4. Make the settings shown in Figure 28–18 and press **OK.**

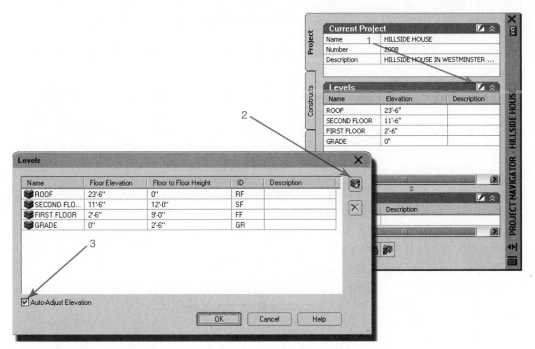

**Figure 28–18**

| Name | Floor Elevation | Floor-to-Floor Height | ID |
|------|----------------|----------------------|-----|
| PARAPET | 23'-6" | 0'-0" | |
| SECOND FLOOR | 11'-6" | 12'-0" | SF |
| FIRST FLOOR | 2'-6" | 9'-0" | FF |
| GRADE | 0'-0" | 2'-6" | GR |

## The TERRAIN Element: Creating the SITE

1. Change to the **Constructs** tab.
2. Press the **Add Element** icon to bring up the **Add Element** dialog box.
3. In the **Add Element** dialog box, enter **TERRAIN** in the **Name** field, and press the **OK** button (see Figure 28–19).
4. In the **Constructs** tab, double-click on **TERRAIN** to bring up the **TERRAIN** Element in the Drawing Editor.
5. Set the **Scale** to **1/4″ = 1'-0″.**
6. Change to the **Front** view.

**Note:**
Elements don't have levels; they can be moved in any vertical direction.

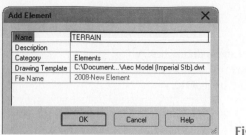

**Figure 28–19**

7. Using the **Polyline** tool from the **Draw** menu, create the line drawing shown in Figure 28–20.

**Figure 28–20**

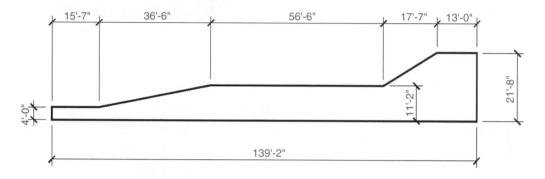

8. Change to the **SW Isometric** view.
9. Select **Window > Pulldowns** from the **Main** menu, and check the **3D Solids Pulldown** checkbox to load the **3D Solids** into the **Main** menu string.
10. When the **3D Solids** menu appears in the **Main** menu string, select it, and then select **Extrude** from the drop-down list.
11. Select the polyline you created in step 7, and drag and extrude the polyline **85′-0″** to form the site model (see Figure 28–21).
12. Save the file.

**Figure 28–21**

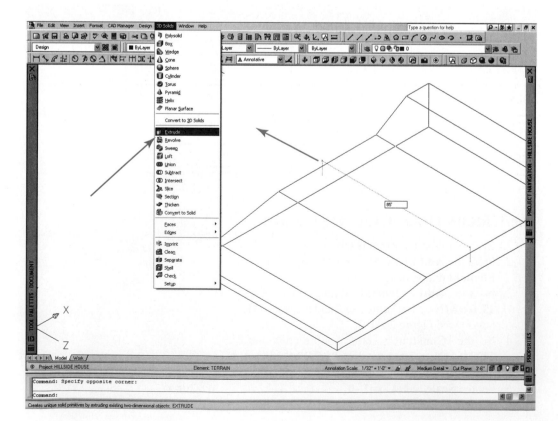

## The FOUNDATION Construct: Creating the Foundation Walls

1. Change to the **Constructs** tab.
2. Press the **Add Construct** icon to open the **Add Construct** dialog box, and create a new construct called **FOUNDATION WALL,** check the **GRADE Division** check box, and press **OK.**
3. In the **Constructs** tab, double-click on **FOUNDATION WALL** to bring up the **FOUNDATION WALL** construct in the Drawing Editor.
4. Set the **Scale** to **1/4″ = 1′-0″.**
5. Change to the **Top** view.
6. Select the **Concrete-8 Concrete 16 × 8- Footing** wall from the **Walls** palette, and place a **4′-0″** long wall in the Drawing Editor.
7. **RMB** the wall you just placed, and select **Copy Wall Style and Assign…** from the contextual menu that appears to bring up the **Wall Style Properties** dialog box.
8. In the **Wall Style Properties** dialog box, change to the **General** tab.
9. In the **General** tab, change the name from **Concrete-8 Concrete 16 × 8- Footing** to **FOUNDATION.**
10. Change to the **Components** tab. In the **Components** tab place the dimensions shown in Figure 28–22, and press the **OK** button to return to the Drawing Editor.

> **Note:**
> By placing a small portion of wall in the Drawing Editor, you can copy and modify its components, and then copy this new modified wall back to the **Walls** palette for future use.

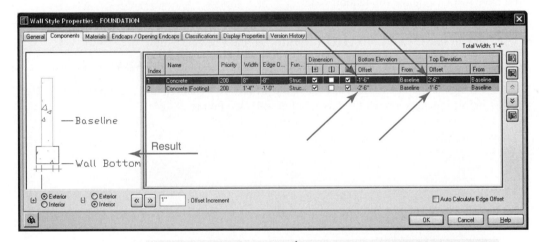

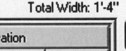

**Figure 28–22**

This will create a **Foundation** wall with a 12″ high footing.

11. Change to the **Front** view, and notice that the 4′-0″ length of wall doesn't show the footing.
12. Select the **4′-0″** length of wall, **RMB,** and select **Roof/Floor Line > Modify Floor Line** from the contextual menu that appears.

13. Enter **O** (Offset) in the **Command line,** and press the **Enter** key on your keyboard.
14. Enter – **2′-6″** in the **Command line,** and press the **Enter** key on your keyboard.
15. Change back to the **Top** view.
16. Select and drag the 4′-0″ length of wall into the **Walls** tool palette to create a new Wall tool (see Figure 28–23). Delete the 4′-0″ wall and save your file.

**Note:**
The Foundation wall now shows its footing.

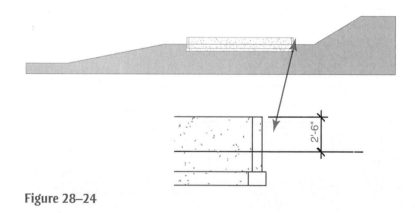

Figure 28–23

17. Select the **FOUNDATION** tool you just created in the **Walls** tool palette and place a **20′-0″ wide × 40′-0″ long** enclosure in the Drawing Editor.

You have just created the foundation walls.

18. Select the **TERRAIN** element from the **Constructs** tab in the **Project Navigator,** and drag it into the **FOUNDATION** construct in the Drawing Editor.

You now have the foundation walls and **TERRAIN** element in the **FOUNDATION** construct.

19. Change to the **Front** view, and move the **TERRAIN** element until its top surface is **2′-6″** below the top surface of the foundation wall (see Figure 28–24).

Figure 28–24

20. Change to the **TOP** view, and move the foundation walls until they are as shown in Figure 28–25.

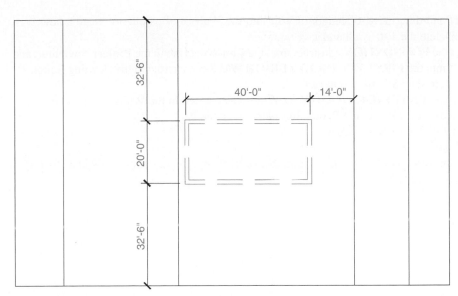

**Figure 28–25**

Save the **FOUNDATION** construct.

## Creating the FIRST FLOOR EXTERIOR WALLS

1. Change to the **Constructs** tab.
2. Press the **Add Construct** icon to bring up the **Add Construct** dialog box.
3. In the **Add Construct** dialog box, enter **FIRST FLOOR EXTERIOR WALLS** in the **Name** field, check the **FIRST FLOOR Division** check box, and press the **OK** button.
4. In the **Constructs** tab, double-click on **FIRST FLOOR EXTERIOR WALLS** to bring up the **FIRST FLOOR EXTERIOR WALLS** construct in the Drawing Editor.
5. Set the **Scale** to **1/4″ = 1′-0″.**
6. Select the **Stud-4** wall from the **Walls** palette, and place a **4′-0″** long wall in the Drawing Editor.
7. **RMB** the wall you just placed, and select **Copy Wall Style and Assign...** from the contextual menu that appears to bring up the **Wall Style Properties** dialog box.
8. In the **Wall Style Properties** dialog box, change to the **General** tab.
9. In the **General** tab, change the name from **Stud-4** wall to **EXTERIOR WOOD WALLS.**
10. Change to the **Components** tab. In the **Components** tab place the dimensions shown in Figure 28–26, and press the **OK** button to return to the Drawing Editor.

**Figure 28–26**

11. Select and drag the 4'-0" length of wall into the **Walls** tool palette to create a new Wall tool. Delete the 4'-0" wall and save your file.

12. Select the **FOUNDATION** construct from the **Constructs** tab in the **Project Navigator,** and drag it into the **FIRST FLOOR EXTERIOR WALLS** construct in the Drawing Editor.

13. Change to the **SW Isometric** view.

14. Select the **EXTERIOR WOOD WALL** tool you created in the **Walls** tool palette.

15. Move your cursor over the **Properties** palette to open it.

16. Enter **9'-0"** in the **Base height** field.

17. Set **Justify** to **Baseline.**

18. With the **Intersection Osnap** on, trace the outside of the foundation walls in a clockwise direction (see Figure 28–27).

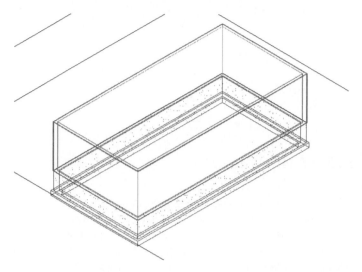

Figure 28–27

19. Select the **Manage Xrefs** icon at the bottom right of the Drawing Editor to bring up the **File References** dialog box.

20. In the **File References** dialog box, select the **FOUNDATION** and **TERRAIN** Xrefs, **RMB,** and select **Detach** from the contextual menu that appears (see Figure 28–28).

Save the **FIRST FLOOR EXTERIOR WALLS** construct.

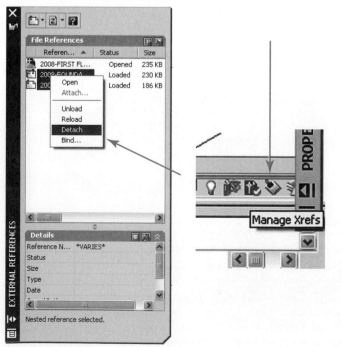

Figure 28–28

## Creating the FIRST FLOOR FLOOR

1. Change to the **Constructs** tab.
2. Press the **Add Construct** icon to bring up the **Add Construct** dialog box.
3. In the **Add Construct** dialog box, enter **FIRST FLOOR FLOOR** in the **Name** field, check the **FIRST FLOOR Division** check box, and press the **OK** button.
4. In the **Constructs** tab, double-click on **FIRST FLOOR FLOOR** to bring up the **FIRST FLOOR FLOOR** construct in the Drawing Editor.
5. Set the **Scale** to **1/4″ = 1′-0″.**
6. Select the **FIRST FLOOR EXTERIOR WALLS** construct from the **Constructs** tab in the **Project Navigator,** and drag it into the **FIRST FLOOR FLOOR** construct in the Drawing Editor.
7. Select the **Space Generate** tool from the **Design** tool palette, and click inside the **FIRST FLOOR EXTERIOR WALLS** to create a **Space** object.
8. **RMB** on the **SLAB** tool in the **Design** tool palette, and select **Apply Tool Properties to > Space** from the contextual menu that appears.
9. Select the **Space** object you just created, and press the **Enter** key on your keyboard to bring up the **Convert Space to Slab** dialog box.
10. In the **Convert Space to Slab** dialog box, check the **Convert Floor to Slab,** and **Erase Layout Geometry** check boxes, and then press the **OK** button to create the slab.
11. Select the slab you just created, and drag its grips to the outer edges of the wall studs (see Figure 28–29).

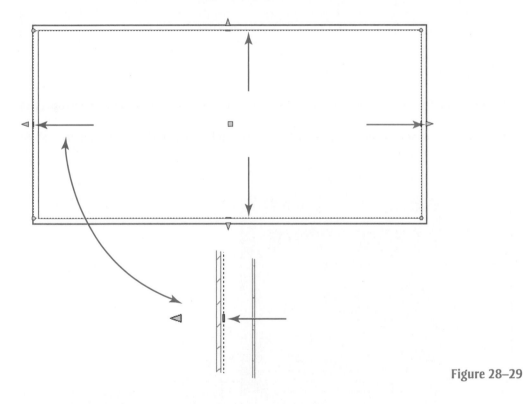

Figure 28–29

12. Change to the **Front** view.
13. Double-click the slab you created to bring up the **Properties** palette.
14. In the **Properties** palette, set the slab **Thickness** to **3/4″.**
15. Select **Format > Structural Members > Catalog** from the **Main** menu to bring up the **Structural Member Catalog** dialog box.
16. In the **Structural Member Catalog** dialog box, expand the **Imperial > Timber > Plywood Web Wood Joists** folders.
17. In the **Plywood Web Wood Joists** folder, double-click on the **12in Plywood Web Wood Joist** to bring up the **Structural Member Style** dialog box.

18. In the **Structural Member Style** dialog box, press the **OK** button to load the joists in the system, and close the catalog to return to the Drawing Editor (see Figure 28–30).

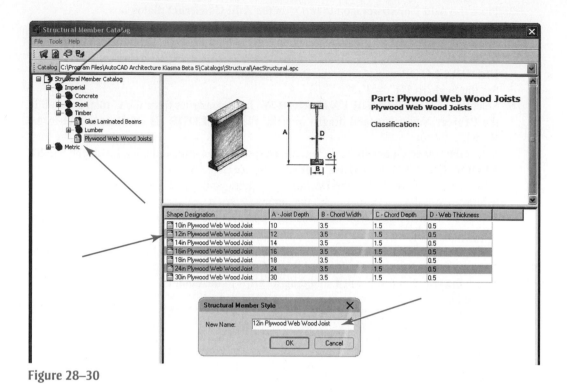

**Figure 28–30**

19. Select the **Beam** tool from the **Design** toolbar, and move your cursor over the **Properties** palette to open it.
20. In the **Properties** palette, make the settings shown in Figure 28–31, and click on the slab **8″** from the left edge.

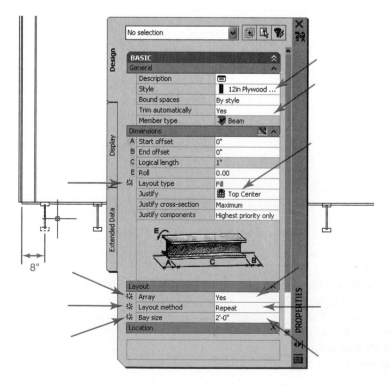

**Figure 28–31**

You have now placed all the floor joists with one click. But some adjustments need to be made. Notice that the joists are attached to the top of the 3/4″ floor slab, so select them all, and move them to the bottom of the slab. Next, you will need to trim the joists so that they will sit on the foundation.

21.  Using the **Xref Manager,** detach the **FIRST FLOOR EXTERIOR WALLS**.
22.  Change to the **Top** view.
23.  Select all the floor joists, **RMB,** and select **Trim Planes > Add Trim Plane** from the contextual menu that appears.
24.  Press the **Enter** key on your keyboard to specify trim line points, and pick two points – 4″ from the bottom edge of the 3/4″ floor slab, and then move your cursor to the side of the joists that you want removed, and click (see Figure 28–32).

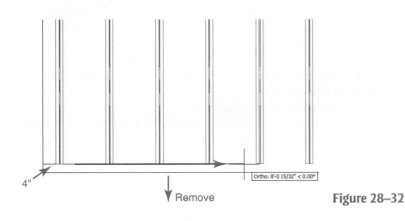

4″

Ortho: 8′-0 15/32″ < 0.00°

↓ Remove                    **Figure 28–32**

25.  Repeat the previous procedure for the other side, and save the file (see Figure 28–33).

Figure 28–33

## Creating the SECOND FLOOR EXTERIOR WALLS

1.  Change to the **Constructs** tab.
2.  Press the **Add Construct** icon to bring up the **Add Construct** dialog box.
3.  In the **Add Construct** dialog box, enter **SECOND FLOOR EXTERIOR WALLS** in the **Name** field, check the **SECOND FLOOR Division** check box, and press the **OK** button.
4.  In the **Constructs** tab, double-click on **SECOND FLOOR EXTERIOR WALLS** to bring up the **SECOND FLOOR EXTERIOR WALLS** construct in the Drawing Editor.
5.  Set the **Scale** to **1/4″ = 1′-0″.**
6.  Select the **FIRST FLOOR EXTERIOR WALLS** construct from the **Constructs** tab in the **Project Navigator,** and drag it into the **SECOND FLOOR EXTERIOR WALLS** construct in the Drawing Editor.

7. Set the **Endpoint** Osnap **On.**
8. Set the **Elevation relative to selected level to 0**, and turn on the **Replace Z value with current elevation** toggle (see Figure 28–34).

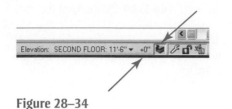

**Figure 28–34**

9. Select the **EXTERIOR WOOD WALLS** tool from the **Walls** tool palette that you created for the **FIRST FLOOR EXTERIOR WALLS**.
10. Move your cursor over the **Properties** palette to open it.
11. In the **Properties** palette, set **Justify** to **Left**, and trace the **FIRST FLOOR EXTERIOR WALLS** in the "Clockwise" direction (see Figure 28–35).

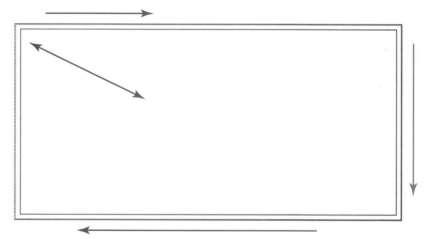

**Figure 28–35**

12. Select the **Manage Xrefs** icon at the bottom right of the Drawing Editor to bring up the **File References** dialog box.
13. In the **File References** dialog box, select the **FIRST FLOOR EXTERIOR WALLS** Xref. **RMB** and select **Detach** from the contextual menu that appears.
14. Select the top and bottom walls and drag them out 10'-0" to form "wing walls" as shown in Figure 28–36.
15. Turn the **Endpoint Osnap** on.

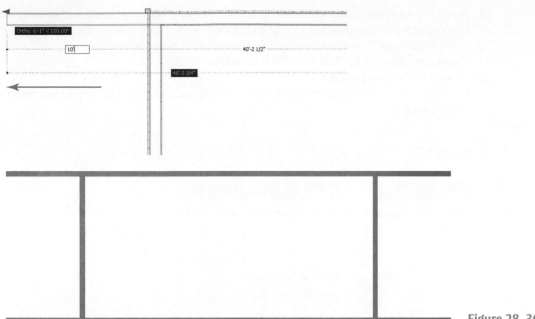

Figure 28–36

16. With nothing selected, **RMB** in an empty space in the Drawing Editor and select **Basic Modify Tools > Break** from the contextual menu that appears.
17. Select the top wall, and press the **Enter** key on your keyboard.
18. Pick the point outside the left wall, and click to break the wall (see Figure 28–37).

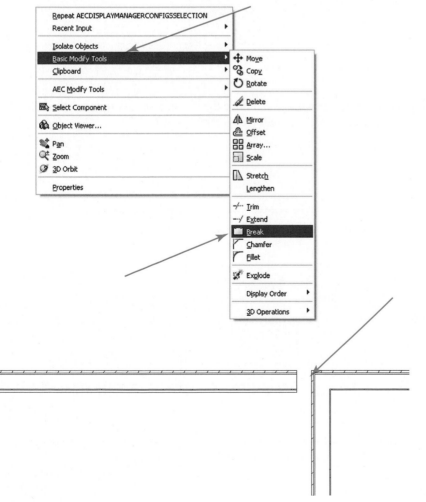

Figure 28–37

19. Select the separated "wing wall," **RMB,** and select **Copy Wall Style and Assign** from the contextual menu that appears to bring up the **Wall Style Properties** dialog box.

20. In the **Wall Style Properties** dialog box, change to the **General** tab.

21. Change the name to **EXTERIOR WOOD WING WALLS.**

22. Change to the **Components** tab.

23. Change the components as shown in Figure 28–38, and press the **OK** button to return to the Drawing Editor.

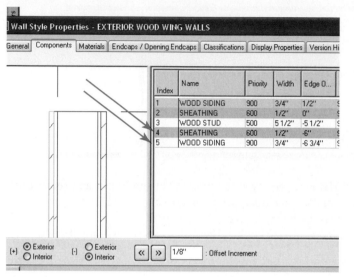

**Figure 28–38**

Zooming in close to the end of the wing wall, notice that the end is not capped with siding. This is corrected by using the **Endcaps** commands (see Figure 28–39).

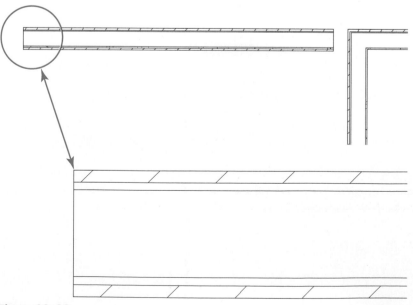

**Figure 28–39**

24. Set the **Elevation relative to selected level to 0,** and turn on the **Replace Z value with current elevation** toggle.

25. Place a line perpendicular across the wing wall, and using polylines, trace counterclockwise as shown in Figure 28–40.

**Note:**
In order to use this Endcap command, all the polyline start and end points must start and stop at the same point. This is why you place a perpendicular line.

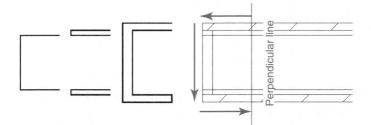

**Figure 28–40**

26. Select the wing wall, **RMB,** and then select **Endcaps > Calculate Automatically** from the contextual menu that appears.

27. Select all the polylines that are traced over the end of the wing wall, and press the **Enter** key on your computer.

28. Enter **Y** (Yes) in the **Command line** to erase the selected polylines, and then press the **Enter** key on your computer.

29. Enter **O** (Override) in the **Command line,** and then press the **Enter** key on your computer to bring up the **New Endcap Style** dialog box.

30. In the **New Endcap Style** dialog box, enter **WING WALL ENDCAP,** and press the **OK** button to return to the Drawing Editor (see Figure 28–41).

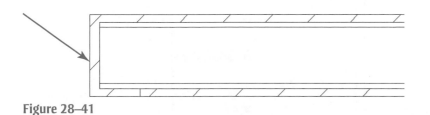

**Figure 28–41**

31. Select the other wing walls, and move your cursor over the **Properties** palette to open it.

32. In the **Properties** palette, select **EXTERIOR WING WALLS** from the **Style** drop-down list to change all of them to **EXTERIOR WOOD WING WALLS** (see Figure 28–42).

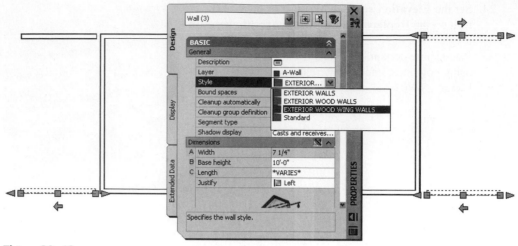

**Figure 28–42**

33. With nothing selected, **RMB** in an empty space in the Drawing Editor, and select **Basic Modify Tools > Extend** from the contextual menu that appears.

34. Press the **Enter** key on your keyboard to select all, and then click the end of the wing wall that you wish to join to the main building. Click all the other ends of the wing walls to make them also join the main building (see Figure 28–43).

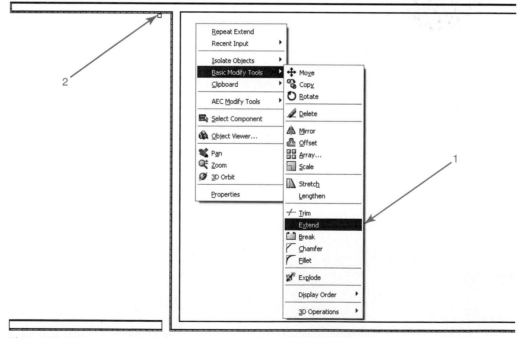

**Figure 28–43**

35. Select one of the wing walls, **RMB,** and select **Add Selected** from the contextual menu that appears.

36. Move your cursor over the **Properties** palette, and change **Justify** to **Right.**

37. Click on the sidewall, drag your cursor down, enter **10′-0″,** and continue to click and enter dimensions until you create the walls as shown in Figure 28–44. Press the **Enter** key to complete the command.

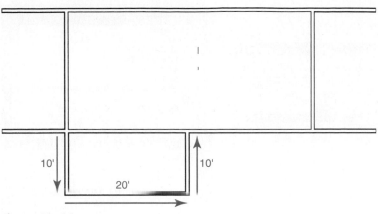

**Figure 28–44**

38. Select all the walls, move your cursor over the **Properties** palette, and set their base height to **12'-0"**.

You have now created the **SECOND FLOOR EXTERIOR WALLS**. Save the **SECOND FLOOR EXTERIOR WALLS** construct (see Figure 28–45).

**Figure 28–45**

## Creating the PARAPET WALLS

1. In the **Project Navigator,** change to the **Constructs** tab.
2. **RMB** on the **SECOND FLOOR EXTERIOR WALLS** construct, and select **Copy Construct to Levels** from the contextual menu to bring up the **Copy Constructs to Levels** dialog box.
3. In the **Copy Constructs to Levels** dialog box, check the **PARAPET** check box, and press the **OK** button to create the new construct.

> **Note:**
> The new construct will be named SECOND FLOOR EXTERIOR WALLS (PARAPET) (see Figure 28–46).

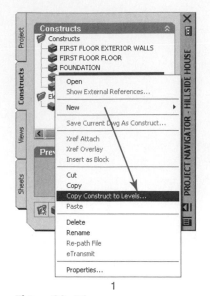
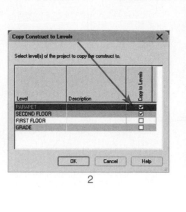
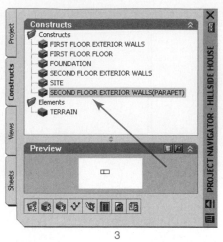

**Figure 28–46**

4. Change the name of the new construct you just created to **PARAPET.**
5. Double click the **PARAPET** construct to bring it into the Drawing Editor.
6. Select all the parapet walls, and move your cursor over the **Properties** palette to open it.
7. In the **Properties** palette, change the **Style** to **EXTERIOR WING WALLS**, and the **Base height** to **2′-0″** (see Figure 28–47).

Note:
The PARAPET is an exact copy of the SECOND FLOOR EXTERIOR WALLS, but it sits on top of the SECOND FLOOR EXTERIOR WALLS. You will have to change the **PARAPET** **Base height,** and make it the same wall style as the wing walls because it will have siding on both sides.

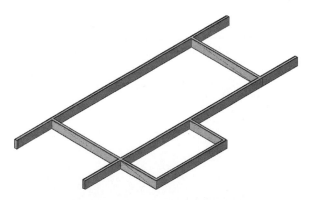

**Figure 28–47**

Next you need to create the atrium.

8. Change to the **Front** view, and using the polyline tool, trace over the top of the parapet walls to create the line shown in Figure 28–48.

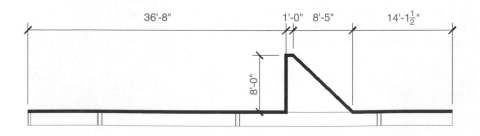

**Figure 28–48**

9. Change to the **SW Isometric** view.
10. Select one of the parapet walls, **RMB**, and select **Roof/Floor Line > Modify Roof line** from the contextual menu that appears.
11. Enter **P** (Project to polyline) in the **Command line,** and press the **Enter** key on your keyboard.
12. Select the polyline. The wall bottom changes. Repeat for the other side (see Figure 28–49).

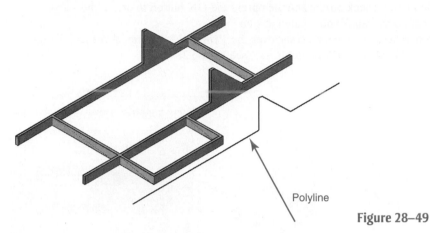

Polyline

**Figure 28–49**

You have now created the parapet walls. Save the **PARAPET** construct.

## Creating the SECOND FLOOR FLOORS

1. Change to the **Constructs** tab.
2. Press the **Add Construct** icon to bring up the **Add Construct** dialog box.
3. In the **Add Construct** dialog box, enter **SECOND FLOOR FLOOR** in the **Name** field, check the **SECOND FLOOR Division** check box, and press the **OK** button.
4. In the **Constructs** tab, double-click on **SECOND FLOOR FLOOR** to bring up the **SECOND FLOOR FLOOR** construct in the Drawing Editor.
5. Set the **Scale** to **1/4″ = 1′-0″.**
6. Select the **SECOND FLOOR EXTERIOR WALLS** construct from the **Constructs** tab in the **Project Navigator,** and drag it into the **SECOND FLOOR FLOOR** construct in the Drawing Editor.
7. Select a wing wall, **RMB,** and select **Add Selected** from the contextual menu that appears. Move your cursor over the **Properties** palette to open it, and set **Justify** so that you add a wall to the outside of the porches (see Figure 28–50).

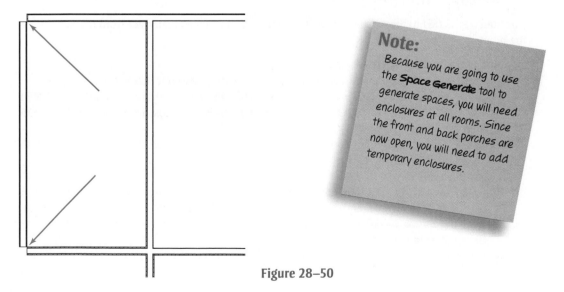

**Note:**
Because you are going to use the **Space Generate** tool to generate spaces, you will need enclosures at all rooms. Since the front and back porches are now open, you will need to add temporary enclosures.

**Figure 28–50**

8. Select the **Space Generate** tool from the **Design** tool palettes; enter **G** (Generate all) in the **Command line** to generate spaces in all the enclosures.
9. **RMB** on the **SLAB** tool in the **Design** tool palette, and select **Apply Tool Properties to > Space** from the contextual menu that appears.
10. Select the **Space** object you just created, and press the **Enter** key on your keyboard to bring up the **Convert Space to Slab** dialog box.
11. In the **Convert Space to Slab** dialog box, check the **Convert Floor to Slab** and **Erase Layout Geometry** check boxes, and then press the **OK** button to create the slabs.
12. Erase the temporary walls you created in step 7.
13. Select the porches, move your cursor over the **Properties** palette, and then change the **Thickness** to **1′-1/4″**, and **Elevation** to **-4″** (see Figure 28–51).

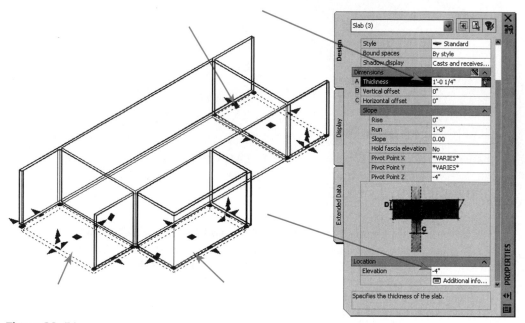

**Figure 28–51**

14. Change the main floor slab **Thickness** to **1′-1/4″,** and leave the **Elevation** at **0″.**

## Creating the STAIRWAY

The stairway is tied to the exterior of the building so that it doesn't subtract from the area inside the house.

1. Change to the **Constructs** tab.
2. Press the **Add Construct** icon to bring up the **Add Construct** dialog box.
3. In the **Add Construct** dialog box, enter **STAIRWAY** in the **Name** field, check the **FIRST FLOOR, SECOND FLOOR,** and **PARAPET Division** check boxes, and press the **OK** button.
4. In the **Constructs** tab, double-click on **STAIRWAY** to bring up the **STAIRWAY** construct in the Drawing Editor.
5. Set the **Scale** to **1/4″ = 1′-0″.**
6. Select the **FIRST FLOOR EXTERIOR WALLS** construct from the **Constructs** tab in the **Project Navigator,** and drag it into the **SECOND FLOOR FLOOR** construct in the Drawing Editor.
7. Select the **Stair** tool from the **Design** tool palette.
8. Move your cursor over the **Properties** palette to open it.
9. In the **Properties** palette, set the settings shown in Figure 28–52.

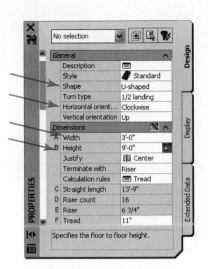

Figure 28–52

10. Place the stair 17'-0" from the right inside corner as shown in Figure 28–53.

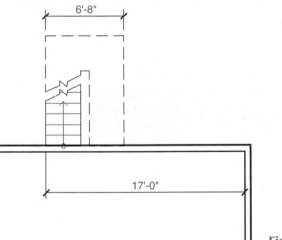

Figure 28–53

11. Select the **EXTERIOR WOOD WALLS** tool you created in the **Design** tool palette.
12. Move your cursor over the **Properties** palette to open it.
13. In the **Properties** palette change **Justify** to **Right.**
14. Starting on the left side of the stair, trace clockwise the stair you just placed (see Figure 28–54.

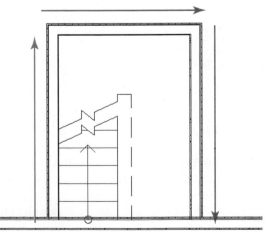

Figure 28–54

15. Change to the **Back** view, select the back wall of the stairway, and change its base height to **13′-6″**.
16. Change to the **Right** and **Left** views, and drag the walls as shown in Figure 28–55.

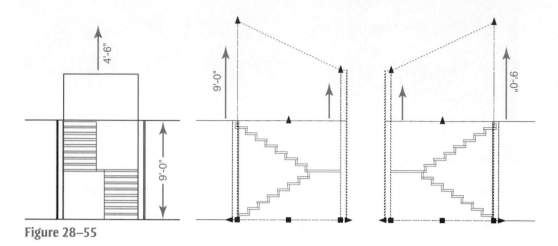

**Figure 28–55**

17. Detach the **FIRST FLOOR EXTERIOR WALLS** construct.
18. Change to the **Right** view and draw a polyline as shown in Figure 28–56.

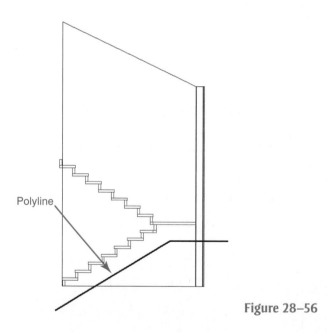

Polyline

**Figure 28–56**

19. Change to the **SW Isometric** view.
20. Select the wall, **RMB,** and select **Roof/Floor Line > Modify floor line** from the contextual menu that appears.
21. Enter **P** (Project to polyline) in the **Command line,** and press the **Enter** key on your keyboard.
22. Select the polyline. The wall bottom changes. Repeat for the other side.
23. Change to the **Back** view, place a polyline, and repeat steps 20–22 for the back wall of the stairway (see Figure 28–57).

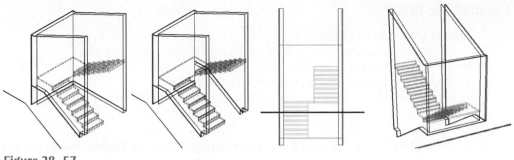

**Figure 28–57**

Next you will need to create the roof and floor of the stairway.

24. Change to the **Right** view.
25. Turn off all the OSNAPs except the **Endpoint** Osnap.
26. Using the **polyline** tool from the **Shapes** toolbar, trace the top and bottom of the stairway walls.
27. Offset the polylines **8″**, and then join them into one polyline for the roof and one for the floor.
28. Change to the **SW Isometric** view.
29. Enter **Extrude** in the **Command line,** and press the **Enter** key on your keyboard.
30. Select the two polylines you just created, and select the start and end points to create the extrusions (see Figure 28–58).

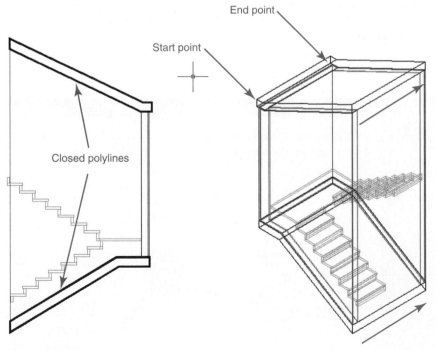

**Figure 28–58**

31. Select the roof extrusion, **RMB,** and select **Convert to Roof Slab** from the contextual menu that appears.
32. Enter **Y** (Yes) in the command line to erase the extruded object, and press the **Enter** key on your keyboard to bring up the **Roof Styles** dialog box.
33. In the **Roof Styles** dialog box, press the **OK** button to create the roof slab.
34. Repeat steps 3–33 converting the stair floor to a slab.
35. Add hand rails, and save the file.

## Creating the ROOF

1. Change to the **Constructs** tab.
2. Press the **Add Construct** icon to bring up the **Add Construct** dialog box.
3. In the **Add Construct** dialog box, enter **ROOF** in the **Name** field, check the **FIRST PARAPET Division** check box, and press the **OK** button.
4. In the **Constructs** tab, double-click on **ROOF** to bring up the **ROOF** construct in the Drawing Editor.
5. Set the **Scale** to **1/4″ = 1′-0″.**
6. Select the **PARAPET** construct from the **Constructs** tab in the **Project Navigator,** and drag it into the **ROOF** construct in the Drawing Editor.
7. Select the **Space Generate** tool from the **Design** tool palette, and click inside the **PARAPET walls** to create a **Space** object.
8. **RMB** on the **SLAB** tool in the **Design** tool palette, and select **Apply Tool Properties to > Space** from the contextual menu that appears.
9. Select the **Space** object you just created, and press the **Enter** key on your keyboard to bring up the **Convert Space to Slab** dialog box.
10. In the **Convert Space to Slab** dialog box, check the **Convert Floor to Slab** and **Erase Layout Geometry** check boxes, and then press the **OK** button to create the slab.
11. Select the slab you just created, and drag its grips to the inner edges of the walls.
12. Change to the **Front** view.
13. Double click the slab you created to bring up the **Properties** palette.
14. In the **Properties** palette, set the slab **Thickness** to **3/4″.**
15. Select the **Manage Xref** icon in the **File References, RMB,** and **Detach** the **PARAPET** Xref.
16. Press **Ctrl + 4** on your keyboard to bring up the **Content Browser.**
17. In the **Content Browser, Search** for **bar joists.**
18. When the **Bar joists** catalog appears open it, and drag the **Steel Joist 14** into the **Design** tool palette (see Figure 28–59).

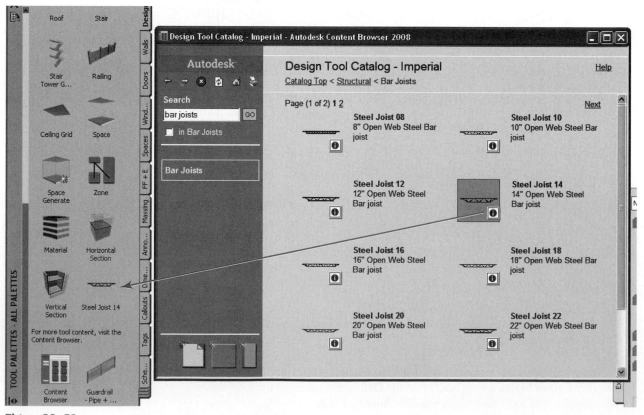

**Figure 28–59**

19. Select the **Steel Joist 14** tool from the **Design** toolbar, and move your cursor over the **Properties** palette to open it.
20. In the **Properties** palette, make the settings shown in Figure 28–60, and click on the right corner to place the bar joists.

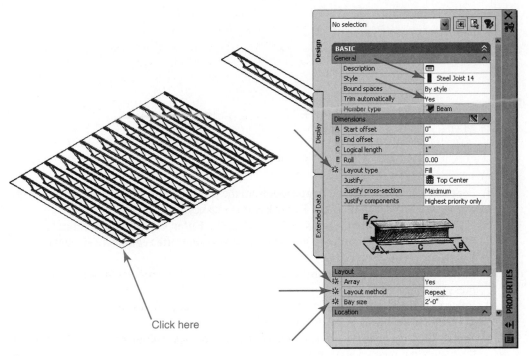

Click here

**Figure 28–60**

The Fill layout option for the joists omits the edge joists.

21. Again select the **Steel Joist 14** tool and in the **Properties** palette, change the **Layout type** to **Edge.**
22. Click at the location where joists are needed to place joists.

You have now placed all the roof bar joists. But some adjustments need to be made. Notice that the joists are attached to the top of the 3/4″ floor slab, so select them all, and move them to the bottom of the slab.

Next you will need to add sloped insulation to the top of the 3/4″ slab.

23. Select all the bar joists, press the **Isolate objects** icon at the lower right of the Drawing Editor, and then select **Hide objects** (see Figure 28–61).

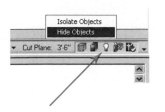

**Figure 28–61**

24. Using the **Line** command from the **Shapes** toolbar, make the shapes shown in Figure 28–62. Select the shapes, and drag them downward 5″.

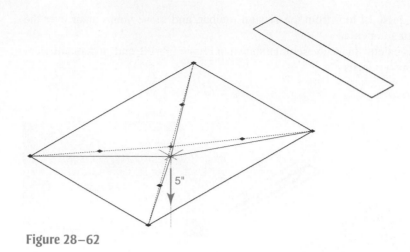

**Figure 28–62**

25. For the front roof, select the **Drape** tool from the massing tool palette, select the two poly-lines you created, and press the **Enter** key on your keyboard.
26. Enter **Y** (Yes) to **Erase** the polylines, and press the **Enter** key on your keyboard.
27. Enter **N** (No) in the **Command line** when asked to **Generate regular mesh,** and press the **Enter** key on your keyboard.
28. Enter **N** (No) in the **Command line** when asked to **Generate rectangular mesh,** and press the **Enter** key on your keyboard.
29. Enter **8″** in the **Command line** when asked to **Enter base thickness**, and press the **Enter** key on your keyboard to create the sloping **Mass Element.**
30. Select the mass element you just created, **RMB,** and select **Convert to Roof Slab** from the contextual menu that appears.
31. For the rear roof, use a **Freeform Mass object,** and slope its top face to the rear.
32. Again, select the mass element you just created, **RMB,** and select **Convert to Roof Slab** from the contextual menu that appears.
33. Press the **Isolate objects** icon at the lower right of the Drawing Editor, and then select **End Object Isolation** to show the insulation, roof slab, and bar joists (see Figure 28–63).
34. Save the file.

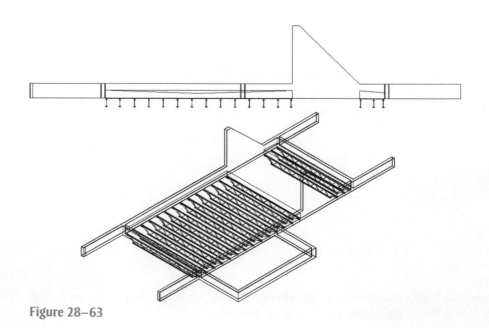

**Figure 28–63**

## Creating the BRIDGE

1. Change to the **Constructs** tab.
2. Press the **Add Construct** icon to bring up the **Add Construct** dialog box.
3. In the **Add Construct** dialog box, enter **BRIDGE** in the **Name** field, check the **SECOND FLOOR** level check box, and press the **OK** button.
4. In the **Constructs** tab, double-click on **BRIDGE** to bring up the **BRIDGE** construct in the Drawing Editor.
5. Set the **Scale** to **1/4″ = 1′-0″.**
6. Select the **FOUNDATION** and **SECOND FLOOR EXTERIOR WALLS** constructs from the **Constructs** tab in the **Project Navigator,** and drag them into the **BRIDGE** construct in the Drawing Editor.
7. Change to the **Top** view.
8. Select the **Rectangle** tool from the **Shapes** menu, and place a **22′-0″ × 4′-6″** rectangle as shown in Figure 28–64.

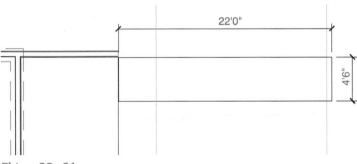

**Figure 28–64**

9. **RMB** the **Slab** tool from the **Design** tool palette, and select **Apply Tool Properties to > Linework and Walls** from the contextual menu that appears.
10. Select the rectangle you just placed, and press the **Enter** key on your computer.
11. Enter **Y** (Yes) in the **Command line** to erase the Layout geometry, and press the **Enter** key on your computer.
12. Enter **D** (Direct) in the **Command line,** and press the **Enter** key on your computer.
13. Enter **T** (Top) in the **Command line,** and press the **Enter** key on your computer.
14. Select any edge of the rectangle to create the slab.
15. Double click on the slab object you just created to open the **Properties** palette.
16. In the **Properties** palette change the **Thickness** to **12′-1/4″.**
17. Select the **Manage Xrefs** icon at the bottom right of the Drawing Editor to bring up the **External References** dialog box.
18. In the **External References** dialog box, **RMB** on the **FOUNDATION** and **SECOND FLOOR EXTERIOR WALL** constructs, and **Detach** them.
19. Press **Ctrl + 4** on your keyboard to bring up the **Content Browser**.
20. In the **Content Browser, Search** for **Railings.**
21. When the **Railings** catalog appears open it, and drag the **Guardrail − Pipe + Rod Balusters** tool into the **Design** tool palette.
22. Select the **Guardrail − Pipe + Rod Balusters** tool from the **Design** tool palette.
23. Enter **A** (Attach) in the **Command line,** and press the **Enter** key on your computer.
24. Enter **N** (None) in the **Command line,** and press the **Enter** key on your computer.
25. Select a point on the slab, drag to the other end of the slab, and click again, and then press the **Enter** key on your computer to place the railing.
26. Copy the railing to the opposite side of the slab.
27. Save the file (see Figure 28–65).

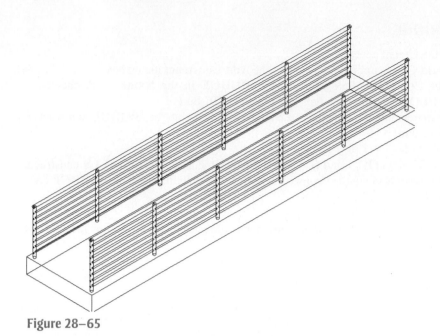

**Figure 28–65**

## Creating the TOTAL View

The TOTAL view is a view used for the purpose of making elevations and sections.

1. Change to the **Views** tab.
2. Press the **Add View** icon to bring up the **Add View** dialog box.
3. In the **Add View** dialog box, select the **General View** radio button, and press **OK** to bring up the first **Add General View** dialog box.
4. In the **Add General View** dialog box, enter **TOTAL VIEW** in the name field, and press the **Next** button.
5. In the next screen, check all the check boxes, and press the **Next** button.
6. In the final screen, check all the check boxes *except* **SITE,** and press the **Finish** button (see Figure 28–66).

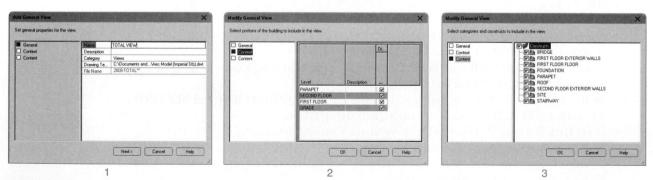

**Figure 28–66**

7. In the **Views** tab, double-click on **TOTAL VIEW** to bring up the **TOTAL** in the Drawing Editor.
8. Select the **SW Isometric** view, and select **Conceptual** from the **Visual Styles** toolbar to color the model (see Figure 28–67). Save the file.

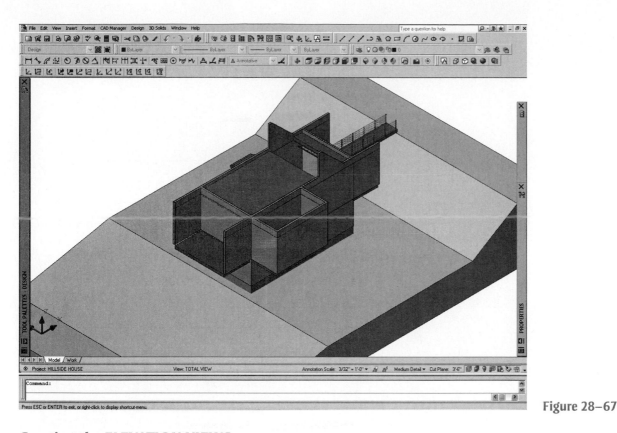

Figure 28–67

## Creating the ELEVATION VIEWS

1. In the **Views** tab, double-click the **TOTAL VIEW** to bring it up in the Drawing Editor.
2. Select **2D Wireframe** from the **Visual Styles** toolbar.
3. Change the scale to **3/32″ = 1′-0″.**
4. Select the **Properties** icons at the bottom left of the **Tool Palettes,** and choose **Document** to bring up the **Document Tool** palettes. Select the **Callouts** tab and then click and select **Exterior Elevation Mark A3** from the **Callouts** palette.
5. In the **TOTAL VIEW,** in the **Top** view, place a selection window around the building and grade, and click to bring up the **Place Callout** dialog box.
6. In the **Place Callout** dialog box, check the **Generate Section/Elevation** check box, select **3/32″** from the **Scale** drop-down list, and select the **Current Drawing** icon (see Figure 28–68).
7. Click to the right of the building to locate the first building elevation.

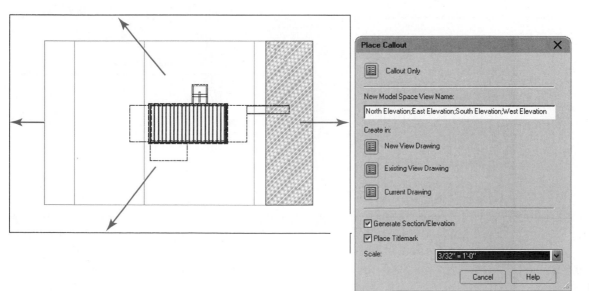

Figure 28–68

8. Move your cursor down 5′ vertically (this will dictate the distance between the four elevations) and click your mouse button. The **Generate Elevation progress** dialog screen will appear telling you when the elevations have been created in a new file (see Figure 28–69).
9. Press **Ctrl + S** on the keyboard to save this file.

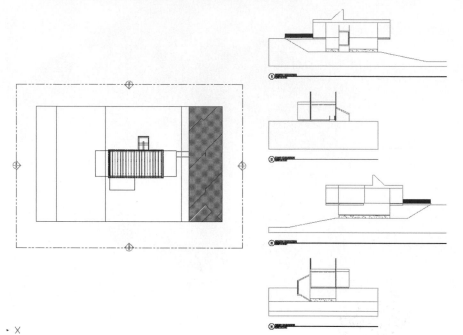

**Figure 28–69**

## Creating the SECTION VIEWS

1. Again in the **TOTAL PROJECT** view, be sure to be in the **Top** view, and set the **Scale** to **3/32″ = 1′-0″.**
2. Select **Section Mark A2T** from the **Callouts** tab.
3. In the **TOTAL VIEW** in the **Top** view, click to place the tail and then place the section mark through the building from top to bottom. Click again to place the head and press **Enter.**
4. In the **TOTAL PROJECT** view drag your cursor past the left-hand extents of the building, and click again to bring up the **Place Callout** dialog box.
5. In the **Place Callout** dialog box, enter **SECTION A-A** in the **New Model Space View Name** field, check the **Generate Section/Elevation** and **Place Titlemark** check boxes. Select **3/32″** from the **Scale** drop-down list, and select the **Current Drawing** icon (see Figure 28–70).

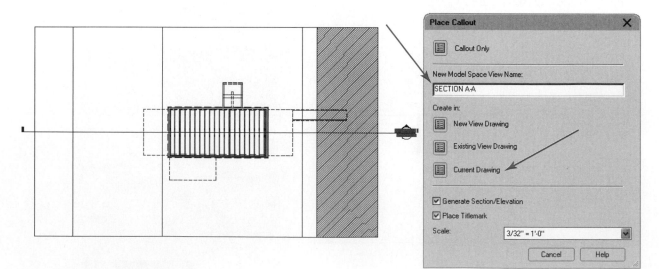

**Figure 28–70**

6. Click to the right side of the building to place the section.
7. Press **Ctrl + S** on the keyboard to save this drawing (see Figure 28–71).

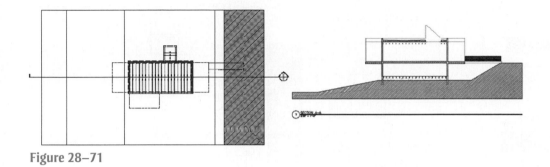

**Figure 28–71**

Repeat the process shown in the last seven steps to create a longitudinal section labeled **SECTION B-B** (see Figure 28–72).

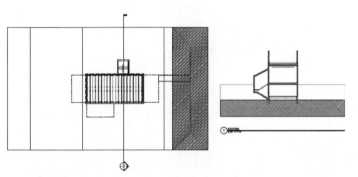

**Figure 28–72**

Once you create the elevations and sections, you can move them around.

Save the **Total** file (see Figure 28–73).

> **Note:**
> If you enter **V** (View) in the **Command line** and press **Enter**, you will get the **View** dialog box listing all the views you have created. When you create a section or elevation in AutoCAD Architecture, you are creating views.

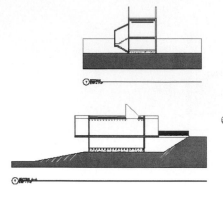

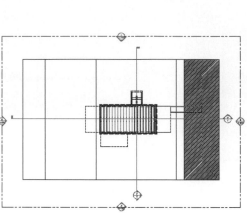

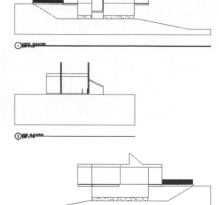

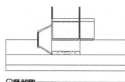

**Figure 28–73**

## Creating the FLOOR PLAN VIEWS

1. Change to the **Views** tab.
2. Press the **Add View** icon to bring up the **Add View** dialog box.
3. In the **Add View** dialog box, select the **General View** radio button, and press **OK** to bring up the first **Add General View** dialog box.
4. In the **Add General View** dialog box, enter **FIRST FLOOR PLAN VIEW** in the name field, and press the **Next** button.
5. In the next screen, check the **FIRST FLOOR Division** check box, and then press the **Next** button.
6. In the final screen, check the **FIRST FLOOR EXTERIOR WALLS** and **STAIRWAY** check boxes, and then press the **Finish** button to create the **FIRST FLOOR PLAN VIEW** drawing.

> **Note:**
> If your sections insert with the grade and walls filled in black, do the following:
> 1. Open the **TOTAL VIEW** drawing.
> 2. Select one of the sections, **RMB**, and select **Edit 2D Elevation/Section Style** from the contextual menu to bring up the **2D Section/Elevation Style Properties** dialog box.
> 3. In the **2D Section/Elevation Style Properties** dialog box, select the **Display Properties** tab.
> 4. In the **Display Properties** tab, click on the Edit **Display Properties** icon at the top right of the tab to open the **Display Properties** dialog box.
> 5. In the **Display Properties** dialog box, turn off the **Shrinkwrap Hatch** visibility, and press the **OK** button to close the dialog box.
> 6. Press **Ctrl + S** on the keyboard to save the file.

7. In the **Views** tab of the **Project Navigator,** double-click on the **FIRST FLOOR PLAN VIEW** to bring it up in the Drawing Editor. Change the scale to **1/4″ = 1′-0″.**
8. Repeat the process creating the **FOUNDATION PLAN VIEW** using the **FOUNDATION** construct, and the **SECOND FLOOR PLAN VIEW** using the **SECOND FLOOR EXTERIOR WALLS, STAIRWAY,** and **BRIDGE** constructs. Save both files.

## Creating the PLOT SHEETS

1. In the **Sheets** tab of the **Project Navigator,** create sheets called **A-100 TITLE SHEET, A-101 FLOOR PLANS, A-102 ELEVATIONS,** and **A-103 SECTIONS** under the **Plans, Elevations,** and **Sections** icons (see Figure 28–74).

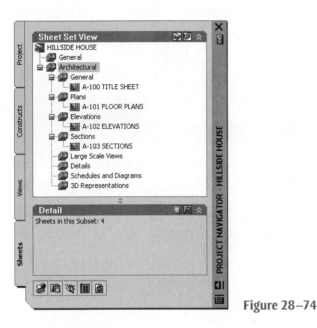

Figure 28–74

2. In the **Sheets** tab of the **Project Navigator,** double-click on **A-101 FLOOR PLANS** to bring it up in the Drawing Editor.
3. Change to the **Views** tab of the **Project Navigator.**
4. Drag the **FIRST FLOOR PLAN VIEW** from the **Views** tab into the **A-101 FLOOR PLANS** drawing in the Drawing Editor.
5. Repeat this process until the **FOUNDATION FIRST FLOOR** and **SECOND FLOOR** views have been placed in the **A-101 FLOOR PLANS** sheet. These are viewports, so you can move them around and expand them. Press **Ctrl + S** on the keyboard to save the sheet (see Figure 28–75).

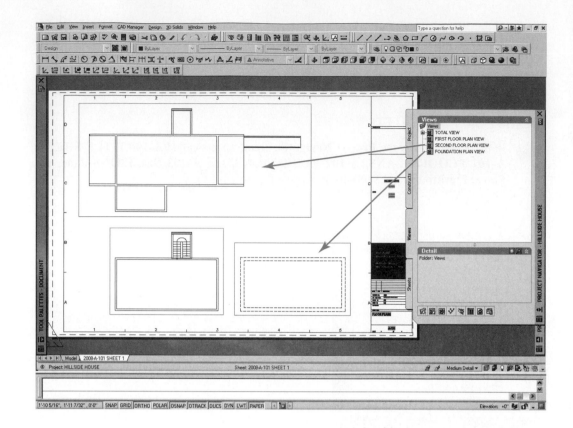

**Figure 28–75**

6. In the **Sheets** tab of the **Project Navigator** Palette, double-click on **A-102 ELEVA-TIONS** sheet to bring it up in the Drawing Editor.
7. Change to the **Views** tab, expand the **TOTAL VIEW,** and drag the **North Elevation, East Elevation, South Elevation,** and **West Elevation** into the **A-102 ELEVATIONS** sheet.
8. Press **Ctrl + S** to save the sheet (see Figure 28–76).

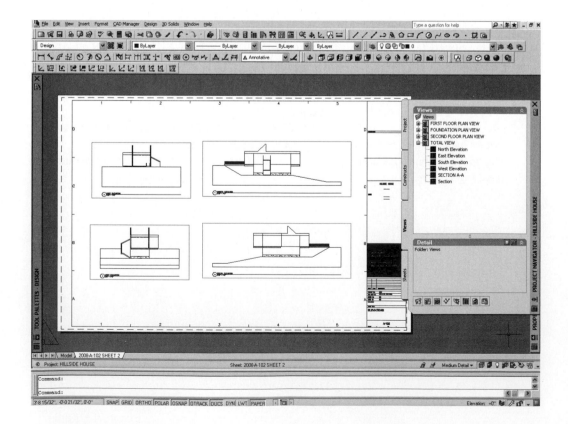

**Figure 28–76**

9. In the **Sheets** tab of the **Project Navigator** tab, double-click on the **A-103 SECTIONS** sheet to bring it up in the Drawing Editor.
10. Change to the **Views** tab, expand the **COMPOSITE VIEW,** and drag the **SECTION AA** and **SECTION BB** views into the **A-103 SECTIONS** sheet (see Figure 28–77).
11. Press **Ctrl + S** on the keyboard to save the sheet.

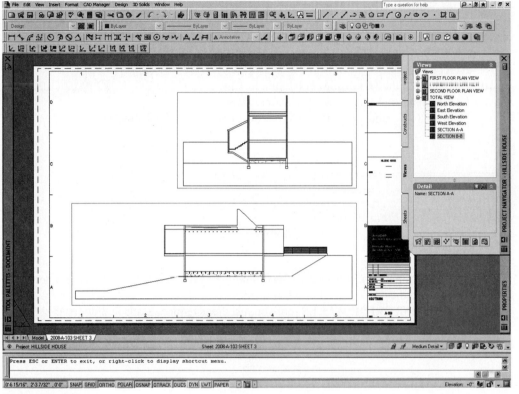

**Figure 28–77**

You have now created the basic Plot Sheets.

Now that you have created and saved the sheets, you can return to modifying the building model, and all your changes will be updated on the sheets.

## Creating the INTERIOR

1. Change to the **Constructs** tab.
2. Press the **Add Construct** icon to bring up the **Add Construct** dialog box.
3. In the **Add Construct** dialog box, enter **FIRST FLOOR INTERIOR** in the **Name** field, check the **FIRST FLOOR Division** check box, and press the **OK** button.
4. In the **Constructs** tab, double-click on **FIRST FLOOR INTERIOR** to bring up the **FIRST FLOOR INTERIOR** construct in the Drawing Editor.
5. Set the **Scale** to **1/4″ = 1′-0″.**
6. Select the **FIRST FLOOR EXTERIOR WALLS** and **STAIRWAY** constructs from the **Constructs** tab in the **Project Navigator,** and drag them into the **FIRST FLOOR IN-TERIOR** construct in the Drawing Editor.
7. Enter **Ctrl + 4** on your keyboard to bring up the **Content Browser.**
8. In the **Content Browser,** locate the **Design Tool Catalog – Imperial > Walls > Stud folder.**
9. Open the **Stud** folder, and go to page **2.**
10. In page **2,** locate the **Stud-3.5 GWB-0.625 Each Side** wall.
11. Drag this wall into your **Walls** tool palette.

12. Select the **Stud-3.5 GWB-0.625 Each Side** wall from the **Walls** palette, and place a **4′-0″** long wall in the **Drawing Editor.**

13. **RMB** the wall you just placed, and select **Copy Wall Style and Assign . . .** from the contextual menu that appears to bring up the **Wall Style Properties** dialog box.

14. In the **Wall Style Properties** dialog box, change to the **General** tab.

15. In the **General** tab, change the name from **Stud-3.5 GWB-0.625 Each Side** to **INTERIOR PARTITIONS.**

16. Change to the **Components** tab. In the **Components** tab place the dimensions shown in Figure 28–78, and press the **OK** button to return to the Drawing Editor.

**Note:**
By placing a small portion of wall in the Drawing Editor, you can copy and modify its components, and then copy this new modified wall back to the **Walls** palette for future use.

| Index | Name | Priority | Width | Edge Offset |
|---|---|---|---|---|
| 1 | GWB | 1200 | 1/2″ | 0″ |
| 2 | Stud | 500 | 3 1/2″ | -3 1/2″ |
| 3 . | GWB | 1200 | 1/2″ | -4″ |

**Figure 28–78**

17. Select and drag the **4′-0″** length of wall into the **Walls** tool palette to create a new Wall tool. Delete the **4′-0″** wall and save your file.

18. Using the **INTERIOR WALLS** tool you just created, place walls and doors as shown in Figure 28–79.

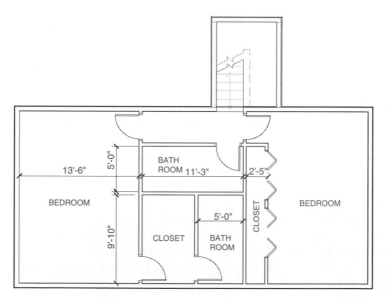

**Figure 28–79**

19. Select the **Manage Xrefs** icon at the bottom right of the Drawing Editor to bring up the **File References** dialog box.

20. In the **File References** dialog box, select the **FIRST FLOOR EXTERIOR WALLS** and **STAIRWAY** Xrefs, **RMB,** and select **Detach** from the contextual menu that appears.

21. Save the file.

22. Press the **Add Construct** icon again to bring up the **Add Construct** dialog box.

23. In the **Add Construct** dialog box, enter **SECOND FLOOR INTERIOR** in the **Name** field, check the **SECOND FLOOR Division** check box, and press the **OK** button.

24. In the **Constructs** tab, double-click on **SECOND FLOOR INTERIOR** to bring up the **SECOND FLOOR INTERIOR** construct in the Drawing Editor.
25. Set the **Scale** to **1/4″ = 1′-0″.**
26. Select the **FIRST FLOOR EXTERIOR WALLS** and **STAIRWAY** constructs from the **Constructs** tab in the **Project Navigator,** and drag them into the **FIRST FLOOR IN-TERIOR** construct in the Drawing Editor.
27. Using the **INTERIOR WALLS** tool you previously created in the **Design** tool palette, place walls and doors as shown in Figure 28–80.

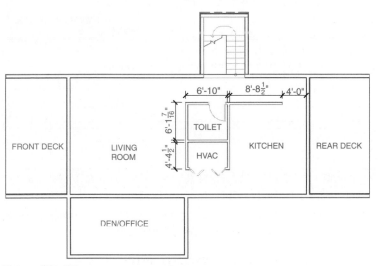

**Figure 28–80**

## Placing Exterior Doors and Windows

1. Change to the **Constructs** tab.
2. In the **Constructs** tab, double-click on **FIRST EXTERIOR WALLS** to bring up the **FIRST EXTERIOR WALLS** construct in the Drawing Editor.
3. Drag the **FIRST FLOOR INTERIOR** into the Drawing Editor.
4. Add exterior doors and windows to the **FIRST FLOOR EXTERIOR WALLS.**
5. **Detach** the **FIRST FLOOR INTERIOR,** and save the file.
6. Repeat steps 1–5 for the **SECOND FLOOR EXTERIOR WALLS.**

## Creating the Wall Detail

1. In the **Views** tab, expand the **TOTAL VIEW.**
2. Double-click on **SECTION A-A** to bring it up in the Drawing Editor.
3. Select the **Detail Boundary B:** callout from the **Callouts** palette, and place the callout around the exterior wall as shown in Figure 28–81 to bring up the **Place Callout** dialog box.

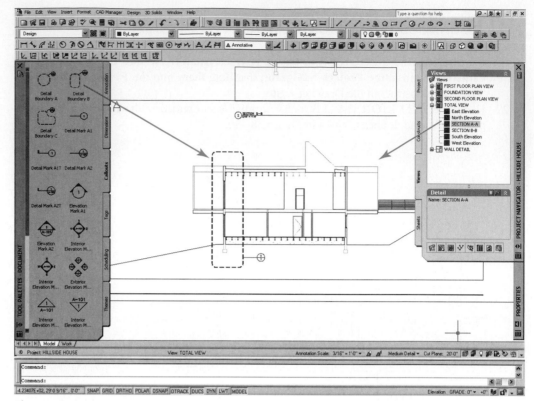

**Figure 28–81**

4. In the **Place Callout** dialog box, enter **Detail of SECTION A-A** in the **New Model Space View Name** field.
5. Select **1/2″ = 1′-0″** from the **Scale** drop-down list.
6. Press the **New View Drawing** icon, and click in a clear place in the current drawing (see Figure 28–82).

**Note:**
When placing **New View Drawing**, clicking in a place actually creates the new drawing—so you will see nothing in the present drawing.

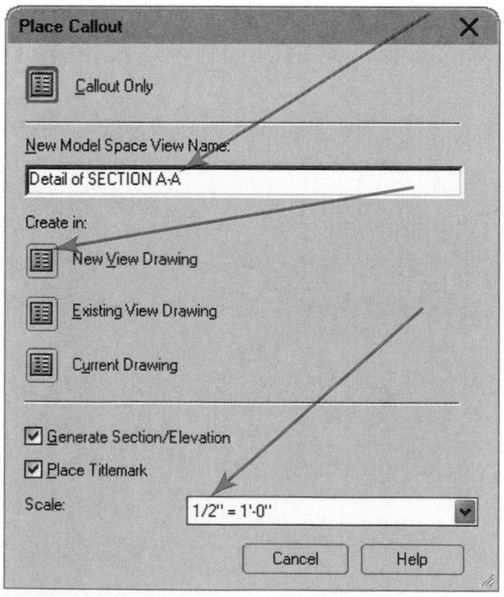

**Figure 28–82**

7. The **Add Detail View** dialog box will appear.

8. In the **Add Detail View** dialog box enter **WALL DETAIL** in the **Name** field.

9. Press the **Next** button at the bottom of the **Add Detail View** dialog box twice until you get to the **Finish** button, and press the **Finish** button to create the new **WALL DETAIL** drawing in the **Views** tab of the **Project Navigator.**

10. The new **WALL DETAIL** drawing will appear in the **Views** tab of the **Project Navigator.**

11. Double-click **WALL DETAIL** to bring it into the Drawing Editor.

12. Using Detail Components and Reference Keynotes as demonstrated in Section 18, detail the **WALL DETAIL** drawing.

13. After detailing the **WALL DETAIL** drawing, select **1-1/2″=1′-0″** from the **Annotation Scale** drop-down list.

14. Save the **WALL DETAIL** drawing.

15. Change to the **Sheets** tab in the **Project Navigator,** and create a new sheet labeled **A-104 WALL SECTION.**

16. Change to the **Views** tab in the **Project Navigator.**

17. Drag two copies of the **WALL SECTION** drawing from the **Views** tab into the **A-104 WALL SECTION** plot sheet.

18. Select the second copy of the **WALL SECTION** drawing you placed in the plot sheet, and unlock the **VP** scale.

19. Set the **VP** scale for this copy to **1-1/2″ =1′-0″** (see Figures 28–83 and 28–84).

**Note:**
Be sure that the "Automatically add scales to annotative objects when the annotation scale changes" toggle is on so that you can adjust the annotation scale in the Plot sheet.

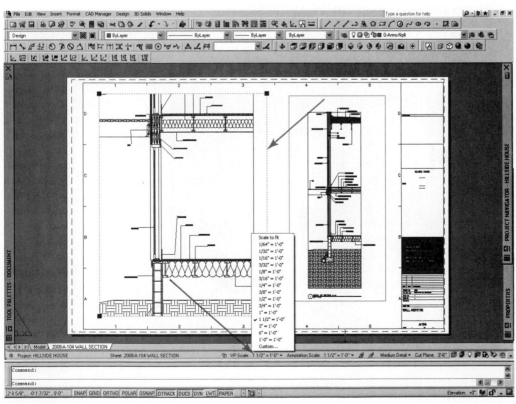

**Figure 28–83**

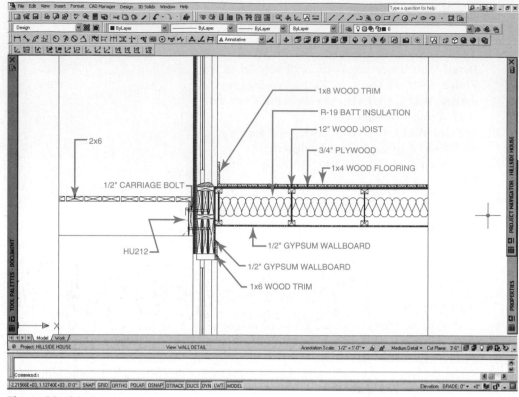

**Figure 28–84**

## Lowering the Bottom of the Wing Walls

Because the decks are 4″ lower than the main building, the bottoms of the wing walls need to be lowered (see Figure 28–85).

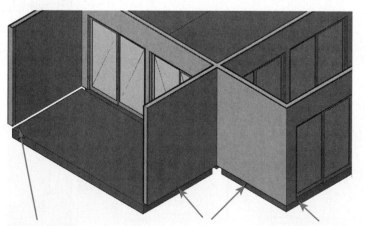

**Figure 28–85**

1. In the **Constructs** tab double-click on the **SECOND FLOOR EXTERIOR WALLS** construct to bring it up in the **Drawing Editor.**
2. Select all the wing walls plus the walls of the den, **RMB,** and select **Roof/Floor Line > Modify Floor Line.**
3. Enter **(O)** Offset in the **Command line,** and press the **Enter** key on your keyboard.
4. Enter **-1′-4″** (the 1′-0″ thickness of the decks, and 4″ lower elevation) and press the **Enter** key on your keyboard to lower the wall bottoms (see Figure 28–86).

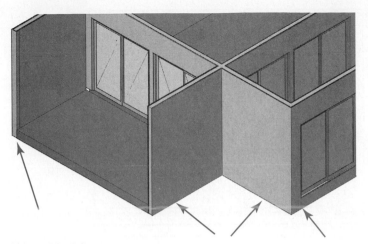

**Figure 28-86**

## Placing and Coordinating Room and Door Numbers plus Placing Window and Wall Tags

1. In the **Constructs** tab, double-click on the **FLOOR EXTERIOR WALLS** and **FIRST FLOOR INTERIOR** to bring them up in the **Drawing Editor.**
2. Press the **Manage Xrefs** icon at the lower right of the **Drawing Editor** to bring up the **File References** dialog box.
3. In the **File References** dialog box **RMB** the **FIRST FLOOR INTERIOR,** and select **Bind** to bring up the **Bind Xrefs** dialog box.
4. In the **Bind Xrefs** dialog box, select the **Insert** radio button, and press the **OK** button.

> **Note:**
> Binding an Xref breaks the electronic link and makes the Xref a permanent part of the host drawing (see Figure 28-87).

**Figure 28-87**

An AutoCAD warning dialog will appear; press the **OK** button.

5. Explode the bound Xref to correct all the walls.
6. Erase all the clutter.
7. Select the **Space** tool from the **Design** tool palette, enter **G** (Generate all) in the **Command line,** and press **Enter** to put spaces in all the rooms (see Figure 28-88).

> **Note:**
> The reason you have to bind the Interior walls when placing room and door numbers is because the door numbers do not coordinate to room spaces over Xrefs.

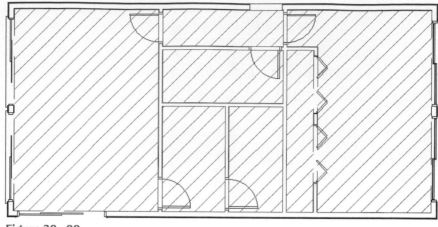

**Figure 28–88**

8.  Select all the space objects you just created, and move your cursor over the **Properties** palette to open it.
9.  In the **Properties** palette, change to the **Extended Data** tab.
10. In the **Extended Data** tab, select the **Add property sets** icon to bring up the **Add Property Sets** dialog box.
11. In the **Add Property Sets** dialog box, check the **SpaceObjects** check box, and press the **OK** button (see Figure 28–89).

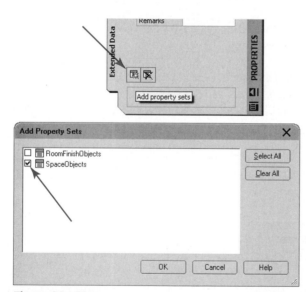

**Figure 28–89**

12. Double-click each space to bring up its **Properties** palette.
13. In the **Properties** palette, in the **Design** tab, enter the name of the space in the **Name** field. Repeat and name each space.
14. Change to the **Document** tool palette.
15. Change to the **Tags** tab.
16. In the **Tags** tab, select the **Room Tag – Project Based** tag.
17. Select the first space (a bed room), and click to open the **Edit Property Set Data** dialog box (you can add more room information here). Make sure the **Increment** for the first room is set to **01,** and press the **OK** button to place the room tag.
18. Enter **M** (multiple) in the **Command line,** and press the **Enter** key on your keyboard.

19. Select all the spaces, and press the **OK** button (when the warning appears, press the **No** button). Finally, press the **Edit Property Set Data** dialog box again to place the rest of the room numbers.

20. Notice that the room number includes an **FF.** That stands for **FIRST FLOOR,** and corresponds to the **ID** that you placed in the **Levels** dialog box at the beginning of this project (see Figure 28–90).

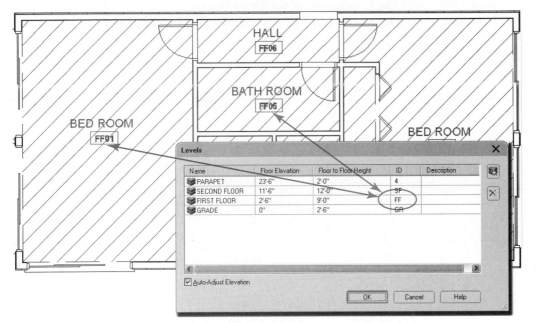

**Figure 28–90**

21. Select the **Door Tag – Project Based** tag, and tag all the doors.

22. In the **Layer Manager,** turn off the visibility of the **A-Area-Space** layer.

Notice that the door tags match their adjacent room tags (see Figure 28–91).

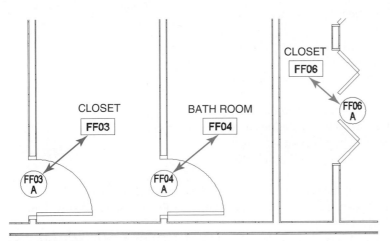

**Figure 28–91**

23. Tag the windows with the window tag.

24. Tag the walls, and notice that they contain two dashes in the tag field. This is because a type has not been set for those walls.

25. To set a type, select **Format** > **Style Manager** to bring up the **Style Manager.**

26. In the **Style Manager,** select **FLOOR FLOOR EXTERIOR WALLS construct.dwg** > **Architectural Objects** > **Wall Styles** > **EXTERIOR WOOD WALLS.**

27. In the **EXTERIOR WOOD WALLS** wall style, select the **General** tab.
28. In the **General** tab, press the **Property Sets** button to bring up the **Edit Property Set Data** dialog box.
29. In the **Edit Property Set Data** dialog box, enter **A** in the **Type** field, and press the **OK** buttons to return to the **Drawing Editor**.
30. Repeat the previous steps for the **INTERIOR PARTITIONS** wall style, enter **B** in the **Type** field, and press the **OK** buttons to return to the Drawing Editor.
31. Select the **Wall Tag (Leader)** and place the wall tags.
32. Press **Ctrl + S** on the keyboard to save the **FIRST FLOOR WALLS** construct (see Figure 28–92).

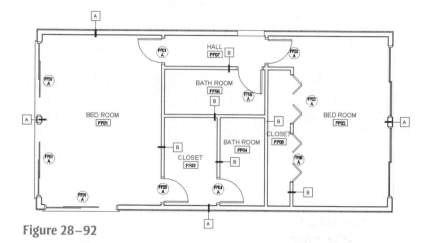

**Figure 28–92**

Repeat the numbering process for the **SECOND FLOOR EXTERIOR WALLS.**

## Creating the Door Schedules

1. In the **Sheets** tab, double-click on the **TITLE SHEET** sheet.
2. Change to the **Document** tool palettes, and select the **Scheduling** tab.
3. **RMB** on the **Door Schedule – Project Based** icon and select **Import 'Door Schedule Project Based' Schedule Table Style** from the contextual menu that appears.
4. **RMB** on the **Door Schedule – Project Based** icon again, and this time select **Schedule Table Styles** from the contextual menu that appears to bring up the **Style Manager** for the **Schedule Table Styles.**

*Note:*
This loads the **Door** schedule into the drawing database.

5. Expand the **Schedule Table Styles,** and select the **Door Schedule** style.
6. **RMB,** and copy and paste a copy of the **Door Schedule Project** style. This will create **Door Schedule Project (2).**
7. Select **Schedule Project Based (2),** and rename it **HILL HOUSE DOOR SCHEDULE.**
8. Click the **HILL HOUSE DOOR SCHEDULE** to open it for editing.
9. Change to the **Columns** tab.
10. Delete all the columns except those shown in Figure 28–93.

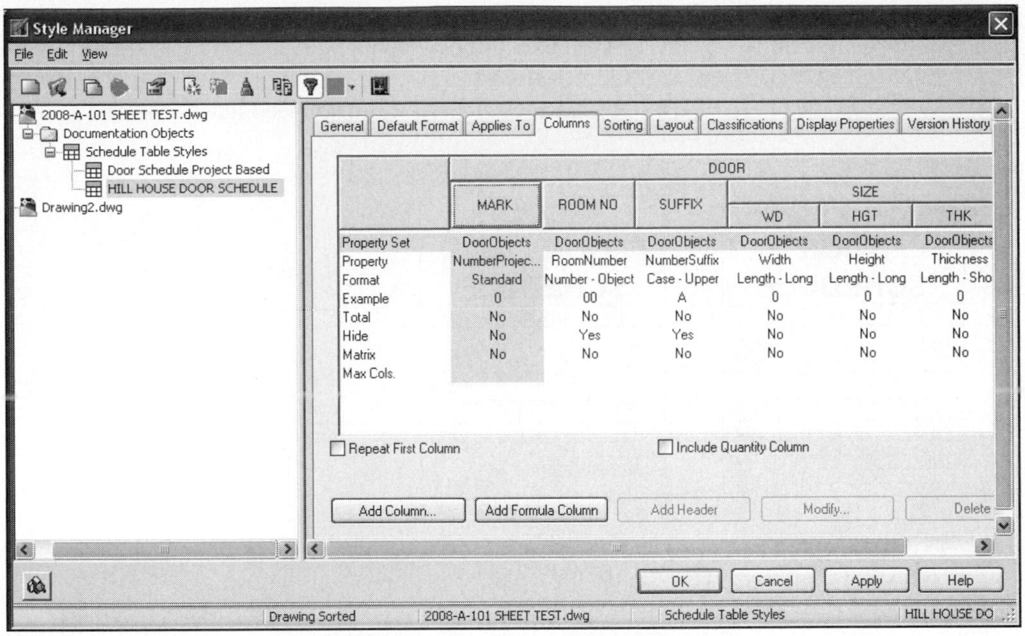

**Figure 28–93**

11. Press **OK** to return to the Drawing Editor.
12. Return to the **Document** tool palette. In the **Scheduling** tab, select the **Door Schedule** icon, and move your cursor over the **Properties** palette to open it.
13. In the **Properties** palette, select from the **Style** drop-down list.
14. Click in the **TITLE** sheet, and press **Enter** on your keyboard (to maintain the same scale as the drawing).
15. Double-click on the door schedule you just placed to open the **Properties** palette.
16. In the **Properties** palette, in the **Title** field, enter **FIRST FLOOR DOOR SCHEDULE.**
17. Again in the **Properties** palette, under **ADVANCED,** select **Yes** from the **Schedule external drawing** drop-down list, and browse for **FIRST FLOOR EXTERIOR WALLS.dwg** in the **External drawing** drop-down list (see Figure 28–94).

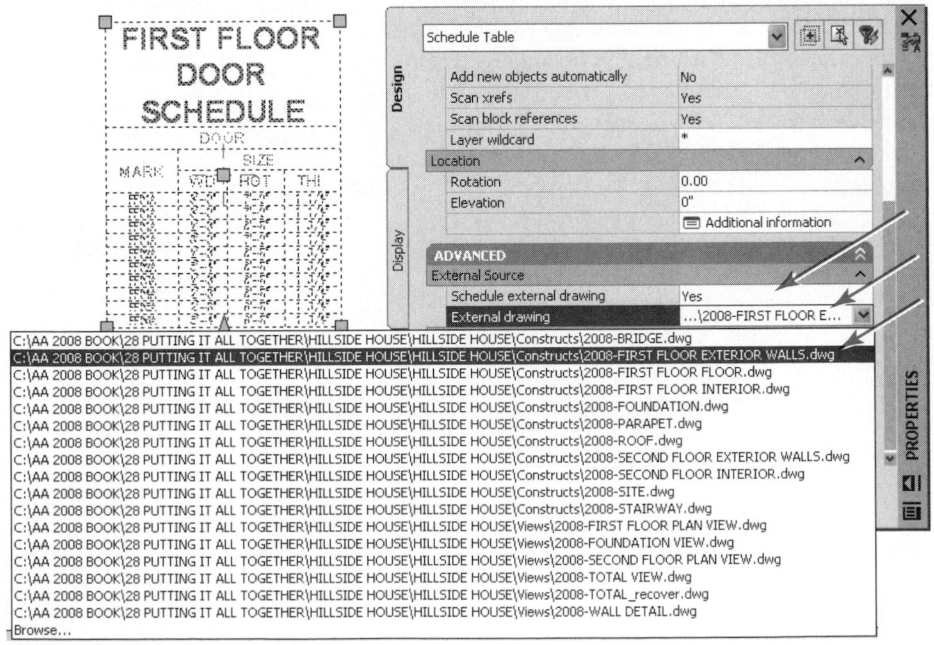

**Figure 28–94**

18. Select the door schedule you placed, **RMB,** and select **Update Schedule table** from the contextual menu that appears. The table will now contain the marks and sizes for all the doors on **FIRST FLOOR EXTERIOR WALLS.dwg.**

19. Repeat for **SECOND FLOOR EXTERIOR WALLS.dwg** (see Figure 28–95).

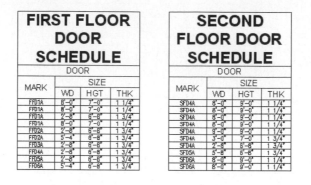

| Drawn By | Sheet Title | Sheet Number | Checked By |
|---|---|---|---|
| HEG | TITLE SHEET | A-100 | HEG |
| HEG | FLOOR PLANS | A-101 | HEG |
| HEG | ELEVATIONS | A-102 | HEG |
| HEG | SECTIONS | A-103 | HEG |
| HEG | WALL SECTION | A-104 | HEG |

**Figure 28–95**

## Creating the INTERIOR, KITCHEN, and BATH

Although AutoCAD Architecture 2008 has an excellent selection of content in its Content Browser, you can also make much use of Odin Cary's content. Odin's website is called ARCHIdigm, and its URL is **http://www.archidigm.com.** Besides Architectural Desktop and AutoCAD Architecture tutorials, Odin offers several reasonably priced eKITs on CD containing Kitchens, Bathrooms, Fences, and street fixtures. You use these eKITs by loading them into the Content Browser, and then dragging the content into your tool palette (see Figure 28–96).

**Note:**
You will have to have separate door schedules for the **FIRST FLOOR EXTERIOR WALLS** construct and **SECOND FLOOR EXTERIOR WALLS** construct, so be sure to change the title of the schedule to reflect the floor it is referencing.

Figure 28–96

## Placing Wall Materials

1. In the **Constructs** tab double-click on the **FLOOR EXTERIOR WALLS** construct to bring it up in the Drawing Editor.
2. Change to the **SW Isometric** view.
3. Select **Visualization** from the **Workspaces** drop-down list. Press the **Ctrl** key on your keyboard to bring up the tool palettes.
4. Select the **Content Browser** icon or press **Ctrl + 4** on the keyboard to bring up the **Content Browser.**
5. In the **Content Browser,** select the **Visualization** catalog.
6. In the **Visualization** catalog, select **Render Materials > Thermal and Moisture > Roofing & Siding Panels** and drag the **Panels.Wood. Horizontal.White** material into your **Design** tool palette.
7. In the **Design** tool palette, select the **Panels.Wood.horizontal.White** material you just placed, **RMB,** and select **Convert to AEC Material** from the contextual menu to bring up the **Create AEC Material** dialog box.
8. In the **Create AEC Material** dialog box, enter **WOOD SIDING PANELING** in the **New AEC Material Name** field, and press **OK.**
9. Select the **WOOD SIDING PANELING** icon, and pick one of the exterior walls to bring up the **Apply Material to Components** dialog box.
10. In the **Apply Material to Components** dialog box, select **Style** as shown in Figure 28–97, and press **OK** to return to the Drawing Editor.

Note:
You will now get an AutoCAD warning to save the drawing. Press **OK** to save it.

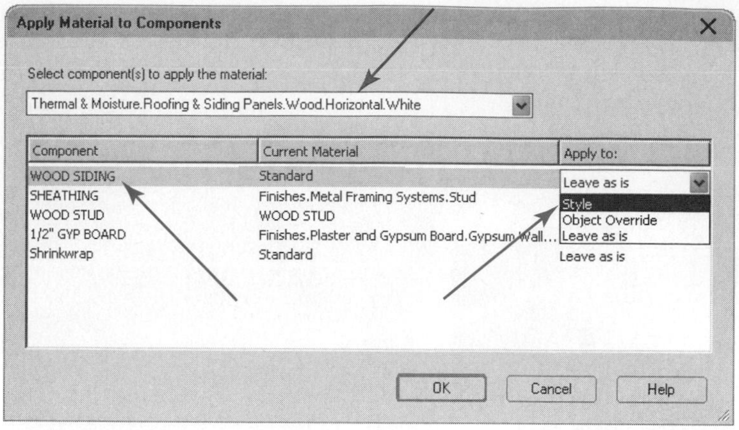

**Apply Material to Components** ✕

Select component(s) to apply the material:

Thermal & Moisture.Roofing & Siding Panels.Wood.Horizontal.White ▾

| Component | Current Material | Apply to: |
|---|---|---|
| WOOD SIDING | Standard | Leave as is ▾ |
| SHEATHING | Finishes.Metal Framing Systems.Stud | Style |
| WOOD STUD | WOOD STUD | Object Override |
| 1/2" GYP BOARD | Finishes.Plaster and Gypsum Board.Gypsum Wall... | Leave as is |
| Shrinkwrap | Standard | Leave as is |

[ OK ]    [ Cancel ]    [ Help ]

**Figure 28–97**

11. You have now applied horizontal wood siding paneling to the **SECOND FLOOR CON-STRUCT** exterior walls.

But the client wants vertical siding, so you must make adjustments.

12. Press the **Materials** icon in the **Dashboard** to bring up the **Materials** tool palette (see Figure 28–98).

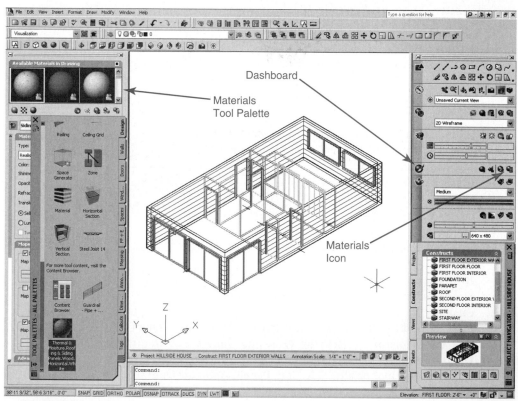

**Figure 28–98**

13. Press the **Render cropped region** icon in the **Dashboard,** and select an area of the **First Floor Exterior Walls** construct to **Render** that area (see Figure 28–99).

**Note:**
When you apply a material to an object or style, that material shows up in the **Materials** tool palette. You can adjust the way it renders in the **Materials** tool palette.

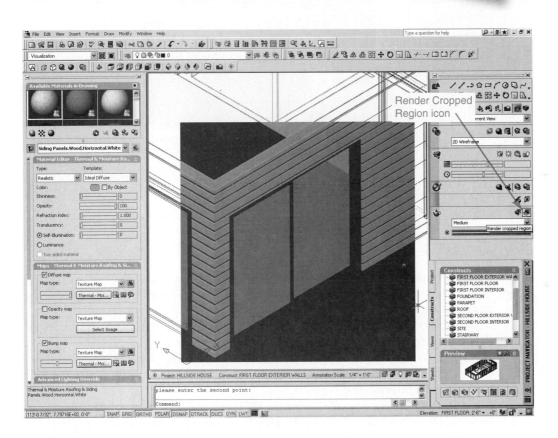

**Figure 28–99**

The siding is going horizontal.

14. Scroll down to the bottom of the **Materials** panel.
15. Change the **Rotation** to **90** degrees, and press the **Update** button.
16. Render a cropped region again and notice that the paneling renders vertically (see Figure 28–100).

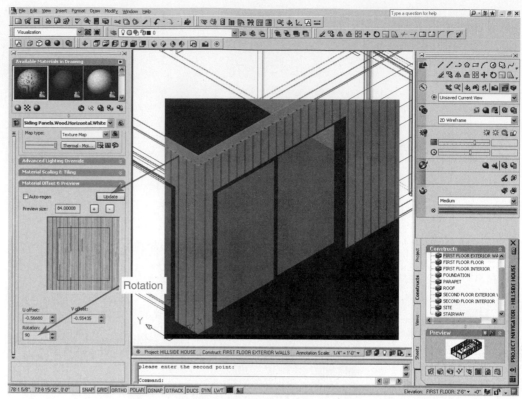

**Figure 28–100**

The wall renders vertically, but the surface hatch is still vertical.

17. Select **Format > Material Definitions** to bring up the **Style Manager.**
18. Select **Thermal and Moisture.Roofing & Siding Panels.Wood.Horizontal.White,** and change to the **Display Properties** tab.
19. In the **Display Properties** tab, double-click on the **General Medium Detail** field to open the **Display Properties** dialog box.
20. In the **Display Properties** dialog box, change to the **Hatching** tab.
21. In the **Hatching** tab, select the **user single Pattern** in the **Surface Hatch** field to bring up the **Hatch Pattern** dialog box.
22. In the **Hatch Pattern** dialog box, select the **ISO** type, and pick the **ANSI31** pattern type.
23. Press the **OK** buttons to return to the **Display Properties** dialog box, and set the **Scale** for the **Surface Hatch** to **35,** and the **Angle** to **45** (see Figure 28–101).

**Figure 28–101**

24. Repeat applying the **SIDING** material to all the exterior walls in the **FIRST FLOOR CONSTRUCT,** and then open the **SECOND FLOOR EXTERIOR WALLS, STAIRWAY,** and **PARAPET,** and apply the **WOOD SIDING PANELING** to them.
25. **SAVE** all the files (see Figure 28–102).

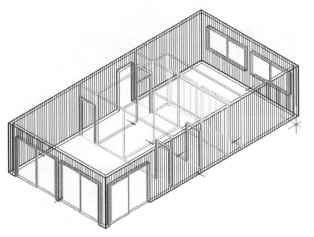

**Figure 28–102**

Once you have added materials to all the walls, you will want to update all the files.

Change to the **Views** tab in the **Project Navigator.**

26. Select **View > Refresh Sections/Elevations** from the **Main** menu to bring up the **Batch Refresh 2D Section/Elevations** dialog box.
27. In the **Batch Refresh 2D Section/Elevations** dialog box, select the **Current Project** radio button, and press the **Start** button.
28. When the processing is finished, press the **Close** button (see Figure 28–103).

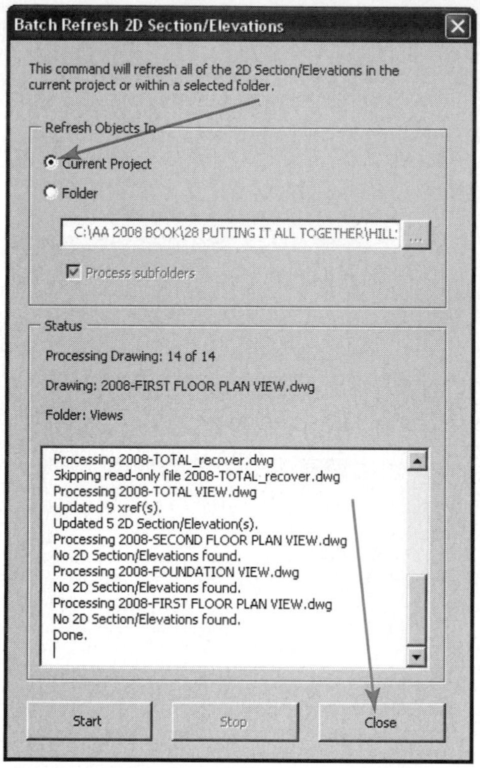

**Figure 28–103**

## Rendering the Model

AutoCAD Architecture 2008 has a built-in Renderer that will give you acceptable visualizations. For top-notch visualizations, this author prefers Autodesk VIZ or Autodesk 3DS MAX. In this tutorial both the AutoCAD Architecture 2008 Renderer and Autodesk 3DS MAX are used.

## Using AutoCAD Architecture 2008's Built-in Renderer

1. Change to the **Views** tab in the **Project Navigator.**
2. Double-click the **TOTAL** view to bring it up in the Drawing Editor.
3. Change to the **Top** view.
4. Change to the **Visualization Workspace.**
5. Enter **dashboard** in the **Command line,** and press the **Enter** key on your keyboard to bring up the **Dashboard.**
6. In the **Dashboard,** expand the **Light Control Panel.**
7. In the **Light Control Panel,** click the **Sun Status** icon to turn it **ON.**

**Note:**
It is a good idea to review the explanation of the Dashboard and its components at the beginning of this book.

8. In the **Light Control Panel,** click the **Geographic Location** icon, and choose your location.
9. In the **TOTAL** view, **Isolate > hide** all the sections and elevations, and all the section and elevation marks.
10. Select **View Cameras > Add** from the **Main** menu, and then click and drag the camera to the center of the house, click again, and press the **Enter** key on your keyboard to place the camera.
11. Click on the camera to open the **Camera Preview** screen.
12. Move your cursor over the **Properties** palette.

*Note:*
*If you want to adjust the shadows manually, adjust the **North Direction** control. All this is discussed in the "Getting Started" section of this book under "Shadows" (see Figure 28–104).*

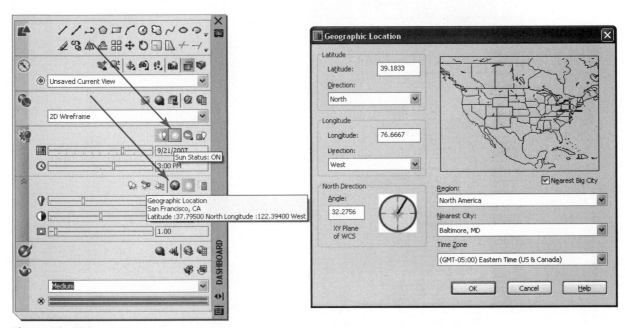

**Figure 28–104**

13. In the **Properties** palette, adjust the **Camera Z** to **25′.**
14. **RMB** on the camera, and select **Set Camera View** to enter the **Camera** view (see Figure 28–105).

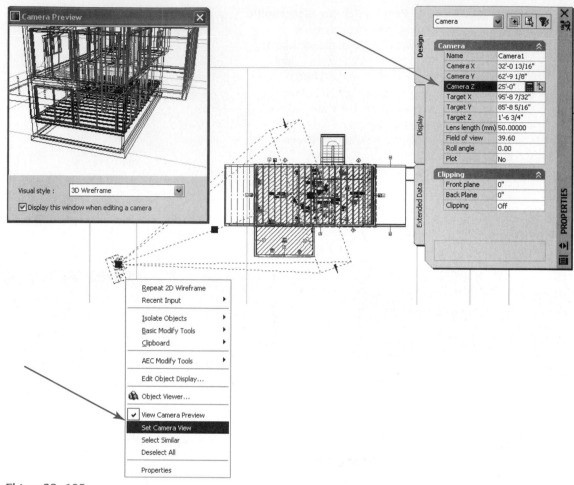

**Figure 28–105**

15. Using the **Free Orbit, Zoom,** and **Pan** controls in the **3D Navigate** panel of the **Dashboard,** adjust the view.
16. Press the **Render** icon in the **Render** panel of the **Dashboard** to render the view (see Figure 28–106).

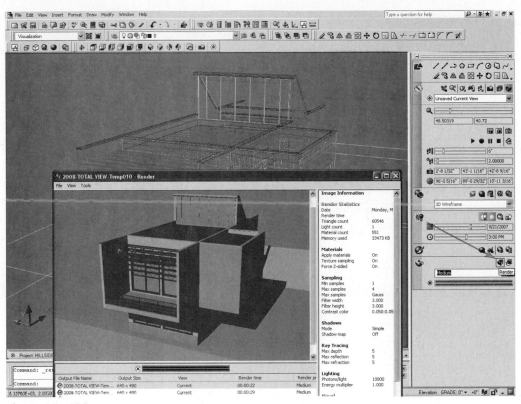

**Figure 28–106**

17. Select **File > Save Copy,** and save the rendering as a **JPG** on your computer.

Using AutoCAD 3D S MAX

1. Change to the **Views** tab in the **Project Navigator.**
2. Double-click the **TOTAL** view to bring it up in the Drawing Editor.
3. In the **TOTAL** view, **Isolate > hide** all the sections and elevations, and all the section and elevation marks.
4. Change to the **SW Isometric** view.
5. Select **File > Export to AutoCAD > 2008** format from the **Main** menu, and save the file on your computer.
6. Close **AutoCAD Architecture 2008.**
7. Start **Autodesk 3DS MAX.**
8. In **AutoCAD 3DS MAX** select **File > Import** from the **Main menu** to bring up the **Select File to Import** dialog box.
9. In the **Select File to Import** dialog box, select AutoCAD Drawing **(*.DWG, .DXF)** as the file type, locate the file you just exported from **AutoCAD Architecture 2008,** and press the **Open** button.

> **Note:**
> AutoCAD 3D S MAX 9 was used for this tutorial, but earlier versions of MAX and Autodesk VIZ work in the same manner.

> **Note:**
> You must be in a 3D view in AutoCAD Architecture when you export.

10. You may get a **Proxy Objects Detected** dialog box. Press the **Yes** button to bring up the **AutoCAD DWG/DXF Import Options** dialog box.
11. In the **AutoCAD DWG/DXF Import Options** dialog box, check the check boxes shown in Figure 28–107, and press the **OK** button to import the **AutoCAD Architecture 2008** file.

**Note:**
You can use earlier versions of Autodesk 3DS MAX or VIZ, but you may have to export to earlier formats.
As of the writing of this book, Autodesk was working on a newer export plug-in, but had not released it.

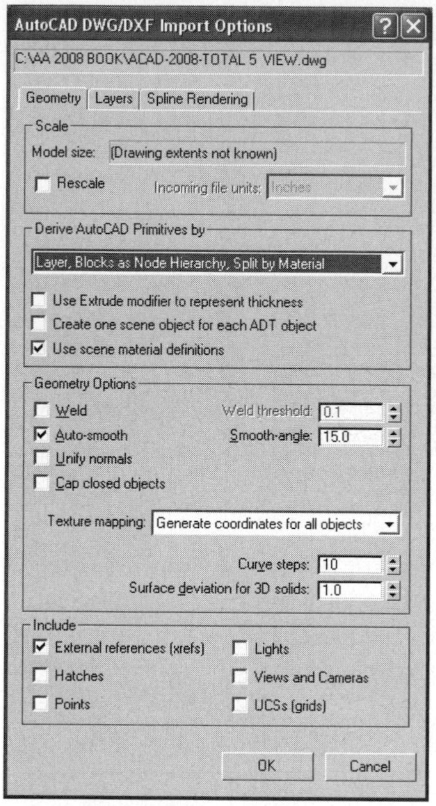

Figure 28–107

12. Select the **Camera > Target** icons, and drag and place a camera in the **Top** view (see Figure 28–108).

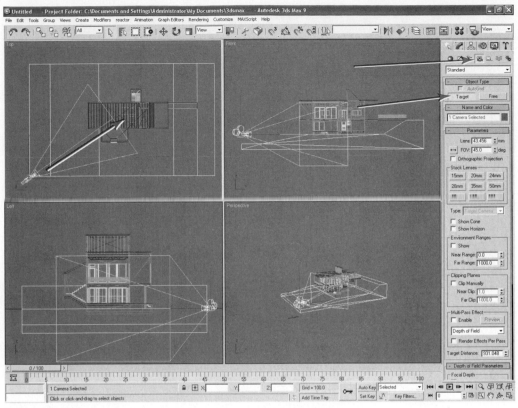

**Figure 28–108**

13. Click in the **Perspective** view, and press **C** on the keyboard to change the **Perspective** view to the **Camera** view—the view through the camera.
14. Using the **Orbit, Pan,** and **Distance** tools at the bottom right of the screen, adjust the **Camera** view (see Figure 28–109).

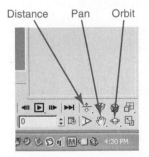

**Figure 28–109**

15. Select the **Systems > Sunlight** button, and in the **Top** view click and drag the compass centered on the building.
16. Release the mouse button, and move your cursor to over the **Front** view,
17. Move your cursor upwards to move the sun arrow in the air, and click again to set the sun (see Figure 28–110).

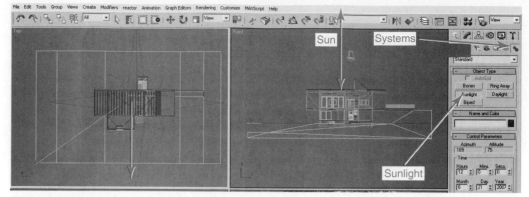

**Figure 28–110**

18. Place **Lights > Omni** to help light the scene.
19. Select **Ray Trace Shadows** if you want a "hard edge shadow," set the resolution to **800x600** for an average sized rendering, and press the **Render** button.

> **Note:**
> Adding some Omni lights below the scene will light through the ground and brighten up the underside of the overhang (see Figure 28–111).

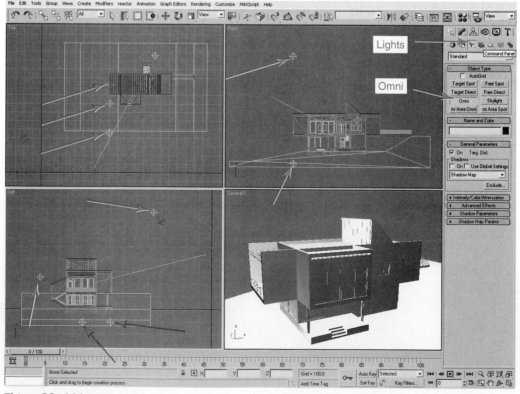

**Figure 28–111**

If you need large renderings, set the resolution higher. Remember, higher resolutions take more time to generate (see Figure 28–112).

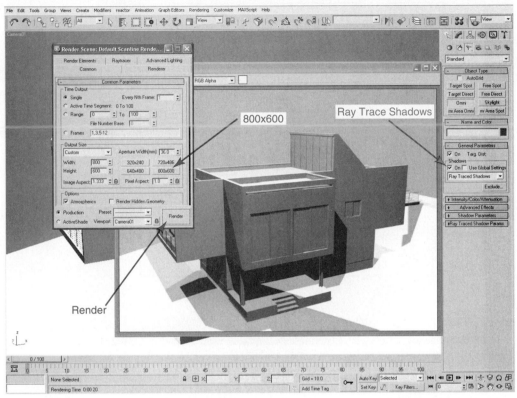

**Figure 28–112**

20. After the rendering has been generated, press the **Save Bitmap** button, and save the picture. (See Figure 28–113.) This author saves pictures as **JPG, TIF** or **TGA** formats. I added trees and materials that I found on the Internet. I also added furniture from the Content Browser (see Figure 28–114).

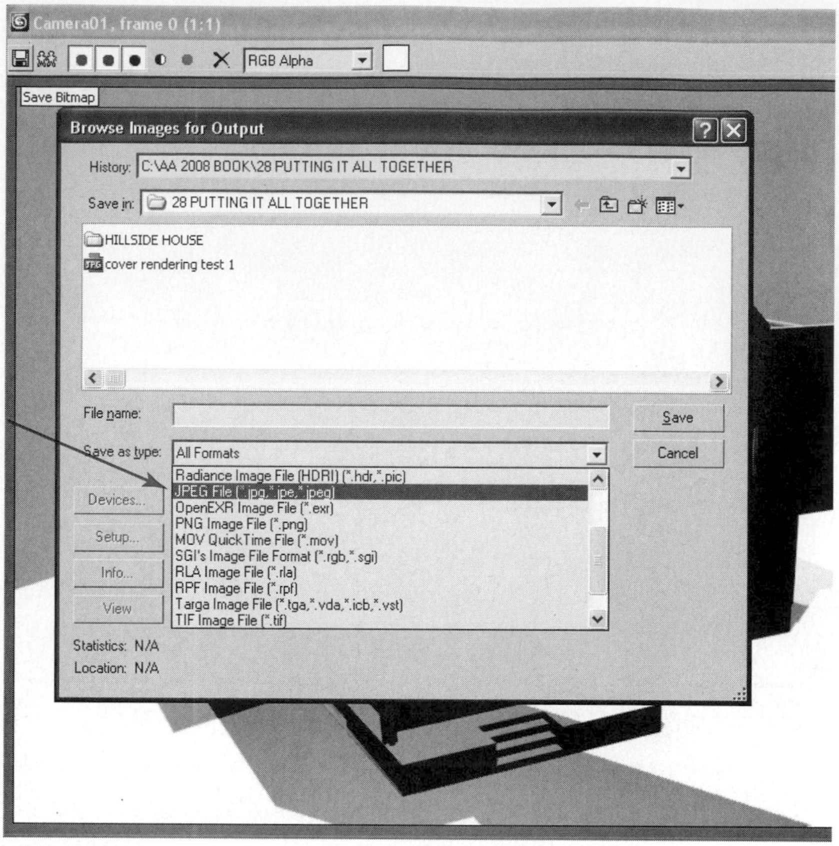

Figure 28–113

Figure 28–114

This is as far as we go; the rest is up to you. Remember to make new constructs, views, and sheets. Once you have the methodology down, the system is really quite straightforward (see Figures 28–115 through 28–123).

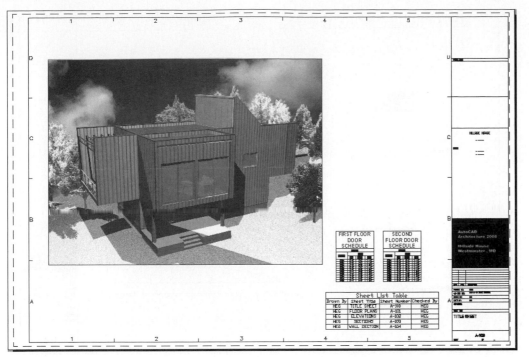

**Figure 28–115**

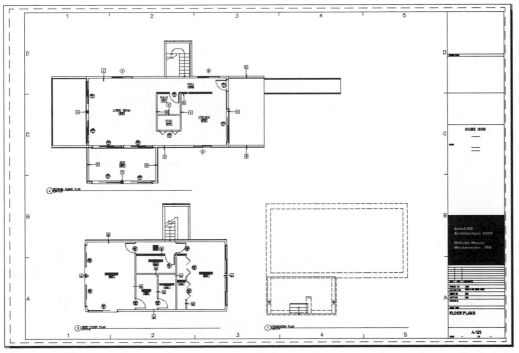

**Figure 28–116**

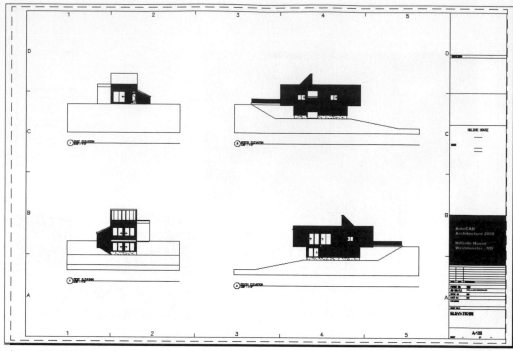

**Figure 28–117**

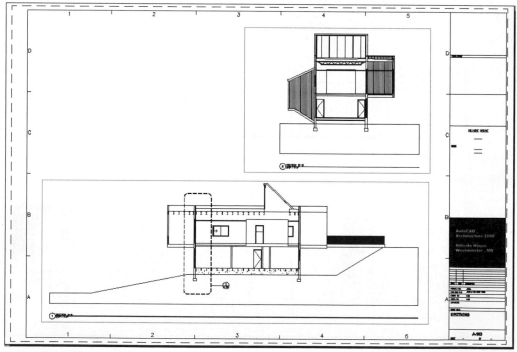

**Figure 28–118**

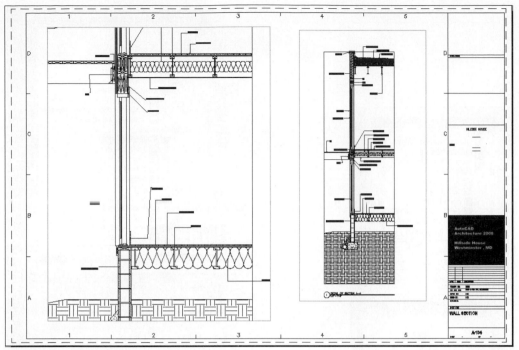

**Figure 28–119**

**Figure 28–120**

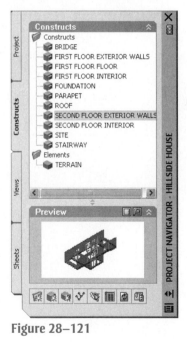

**Figure 28–121**

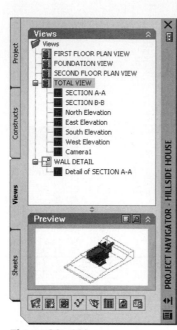

**Figure 28–122**

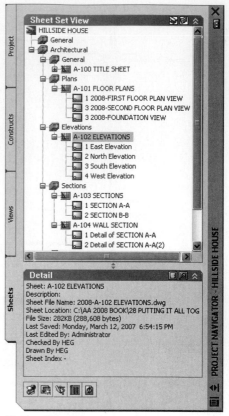

**Figure 28–123**

# Autodesk Drawing Compare

## DRAWING COMPARE FEATURE

Designing buildings has always been a collaborative venture, whether between engineer, contractor, client, or all three. In today's electronic world, with the ease of sending drawings electronically, lack of coordination between documents can break a project financially. Slight modifications such as the elimination of a wall or moving a window may seem small, but if the entire team isn't aware, these changes or modifications can be very costly. Whereas word processing software for a long time has had features that show what changes have been made between documents, no comparable feature exists for architectural software.

Autodesk's new Drawing Compare feature, available through the Autodesk Subscription program, has tools that take the guesswork out of interpreting drawing reviews. The module is only for AutoCAD Architecture and Autodesk Building Systems. With Drawing Compare, AutoCAD Architecture and Autodesk Building Systems have introduced another great collaboration tool for architects to improve communication and shorten review cycles when working with an extended design team.

Drawing Compare has automated tools that track what has been added, changed, modified, and even deleted in a project drawing. Architects and designers now have a more efficient alternative to the error-prone methods traditionally used in the past.

The following tutorial explains the Drawing Compare methodology.

1. Create a **REVIEW** folder in your project folder.
2. Drawing Compare, which can be downloaded at the Autodesk Subscription site (**www.autodesk/subscription**), is accessible from the standard AutoCAD Architecture menu bar (see Figure 29–1).

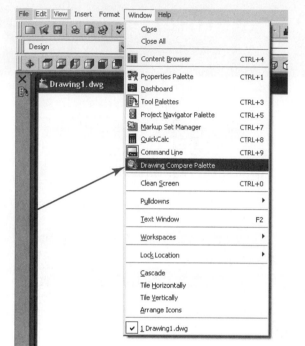

**Note:**
Only subscription customers have access to the "subscription portal" that contains the Drawing Compare module. Each AutoCAD Architecture subscriber has been given a unique username and password.

**Figure 29–1**

3. Bring up the **Drawing Compare** palette.
4. In the **Drawing Compare** palette select your project folder, and the **REVIEW** folder you previously created (see Figure 29–2).

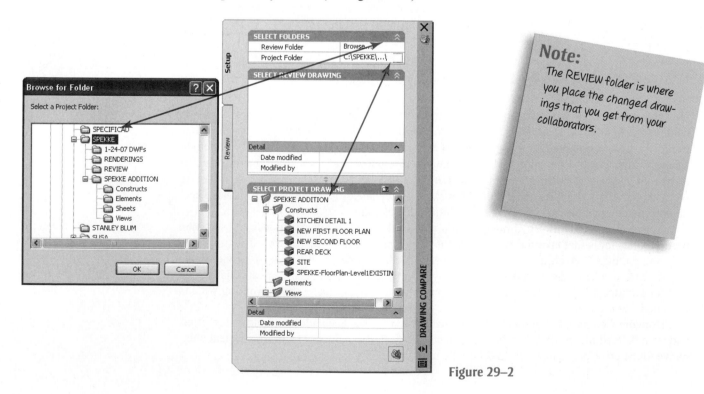

**Note:**
The REVIEW folder is where you place the changed drawings that you get from your collaborators.

**Figure 29–2**

Here is a project drawing (by the author) on the left (1), and the client's changes on the right (2). Can you find all the changes? (See Figure 29–3.)

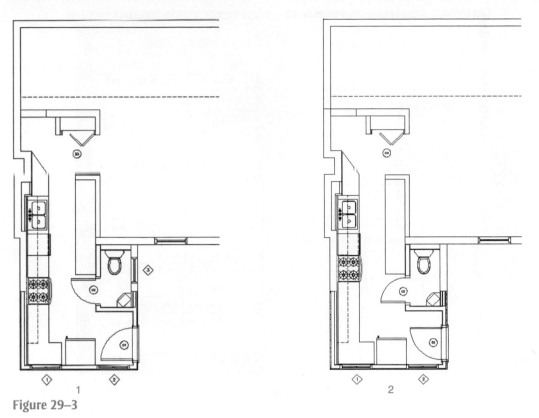

**Figure 29–3**

Let's see what **Drawing Compare** tells you.

5. With the review drawing (1) loaded, double-click the project drawing (2) you wish to be compared (see Figure 29–4).

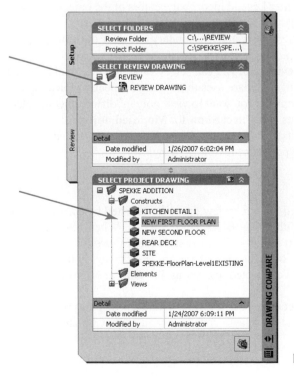

**Figure 29–4**

6. The **Review** tab and **Drawing Compare** toolbar appear (see Figure 29–5).

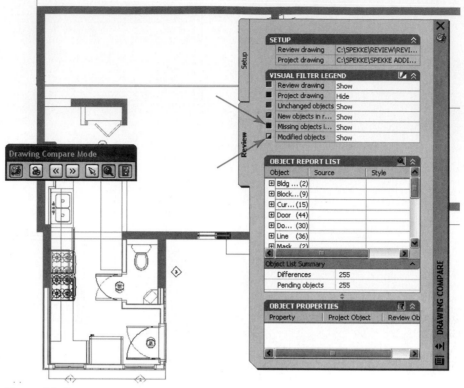

**Figure 29–5**

## Visual Filter Legend

This legend displays colors used in the Drawing Compare mode, and it specifies which review groups display in the drawing area. You can make changes to both settings.

The colors of the icons on the Visual Filter Legend identify the colors of the object groups in the review, such as gray for unchanged objects and yellow for modified objects. You can specify a primary color for an object that is pending review, and a secondary color for the object once it has been viewed. You can also specify the plot style of an object in the visual filter.

In the **Visual Filter Legend** on the **Review** tab, you can select **Show** or **Hide** to change the visibility of objects on your screen. Drawing Compare uses this setting to specify which objects are displayed in the drawing area. For example, if you want to view only modified objects, select **Hide** for all values except **Modified objects**, and select **Show** for **Modified objects.** If you hide all of the new, modified, and missing objects, the remaining objects are displayed with their original colors as they appeared in the original project or review drawing.

## Object Report List

Objects that are new, missing, and modified in your review drawing are listed by category in alphabetical order, such as Circle, Door, Multi-View Block, and Polyline. When the list is displayed, all of the information is in bold text initially. This text style identifies objects as not yet viewed. The text does not change until that object is viewed, then another object in the list is selected for review. A group of objects can be selected and set as **Pending** or **Viewed** from the context menu.

When you hold your cursor over objects in your drawing, a tool tip displays information about the object. New and modified objects display a lock icon and cannot be changed (see Figure 29–6).

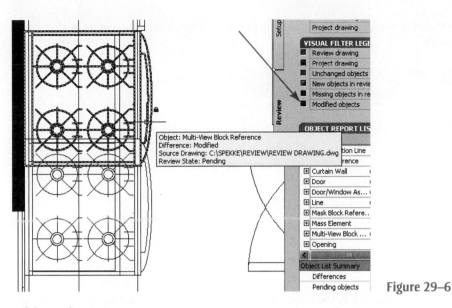

Figure 29–6

## Object List Summary

This summary displays the total number of objects changed and the total number of objects waiting for review. In the following example, a total of 209 objects changed in the review drawing in some way, and seven were reviewed, leaving 202 objects still pending review. When an object's status is pending, it means that Drawing Compare has identified a difference between the project and review object, but the object in question has not yet been selected in the Object Report List.

## Object Properties

This section lists properties that have changed for the object currently selected in the Object Report List, showing the current parameters for the property in the project drawing and the review drawing (see Figure 29–7).

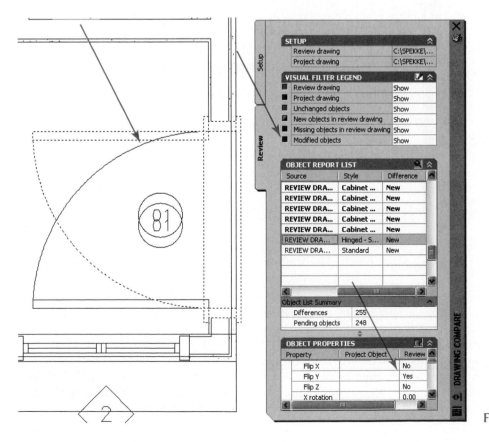

Figure 29–7

By using the Drawing Compare toolbar, a compared object automatically zooms to that object (see Figure 29–8).

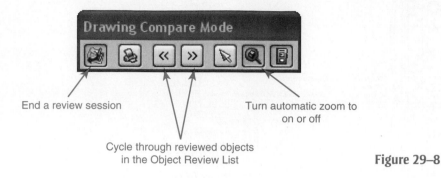

End a review session

Turn automatic zoom to on or off

Cycle through reviewed objects in the Object Review List

**Figure 29–8**

Did you find all the changes between the two drawings? Take a look at just a few of the changes that Drawing Compare found in the simple kitchen drawing. (The cabinet heights were also changed, which showed up in the Object properties area.) If these changes can happen in a simple kitchen, imagine how many hidden changes Drawing Compare can find in a multi-story project (see Figure 29–9).

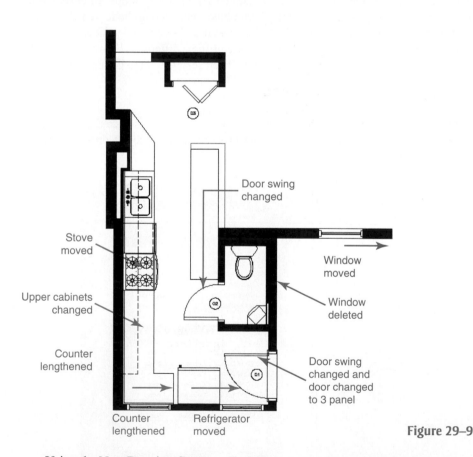

Door swing changed

Stove moved

Window moved

Window deleted

Upper cabinets changed

Counter lengthened

Door swing changed and door changed to 3 panel

Counter lengthened

Refrigerator moved

**Figure 29–9**

Using the New Drawing Compare Feature, you can now track what has changed graphically. You can also track changes to vital nongraphic information that could potentially affect documents, such as sections, elevations, and schedules.

Drawing Compare works with both AutoCAD Architecture objects and AutoCAD entities, giving you the flexibility to use this feature on any AutoCAD-based drawing. This is extremely helpful as you work with other professionals who are also using AutoCAD-based workflows across various disciplines. Where more clarity is needed, you can even plot the Drawing Compare session as a DWF, mark it up in design review, and circulate it back to the team.

# Index

Page numbers followed by f indicate figure.

# D